Challenge for Change

D1141725

Challenge for Change
Activist Documentary
at the
National Film Board of Canada

Edited by
THOMAS WAUGH | MICHAEL BRENDAN BAKER | EZRA WINTON

McGill-Queen's University Press · Montreal & Kingston · London · Ithaca

ISBN 978-0-7735-3662-3 (cloth)
ISBN 978-0-7735-3663-0 (paper)

Legal deposit first quarter 2010
Bibliothèque nationale du Québec

Printed in Canada on acid-free paper that is 100% ancient forest free
(100% post-consumer recycled), processed chlorine free.

This book has been published with the help of the Aid to Research Related Publication
Program of the Office of the Vice-President, Research and Graduate Studies, and of
the Faculty of Fine Arts, Concordia University, together with research funds of the
Faculty of Fine Arts and the Concordia Research Chair in Sexual Representation and
in Documentary.

It has also been published with the help of a grant from the Canadian Federation
for the Humanities and Social Sciences, through the Aid to Scholarly Publications
Programme, using funds provided by the Social Sciences and Humanities Research
Council of Canada.

McGill-Queen's University Press acknowledges the support of the Canada Council for
the Arts for our publishing program. We also acknowledge the financial support of the
Government of Canada through the Book Publishing Industry Development Program
(BPIDP) for our publishing activities.

Library and Archives Canada Cataloguing in Publication

Challenge for change/Activist Documentary at the National Film Board of Canada /
edited by Thomas Waugh, Michael Brendan Baker, Ezra Winton.

Includes bibliographical references and index.
ISBN 978-0-7735-3662-3 (bnd)
ISBN 978-0-7735-3663-0 (pbk)

1. Challenge for Change (Program)—History and criticism. 2. Documentary
films—Canada—History and criticism. 3. Canada—Social conditions—1945-.
4. National Film Board of Canada. I. Waugh, Thomas, 1948– II. Baker, Michael
Brendan III. Winton, Ezra

PN1995.9.D6C43 2010   070.1'8   C2009-906750-1

This book was designed and typeset by studio oneonone in Sabon 10/13

Contents

PART 4
DISCURSIVE SPACES: THEORIZING CHALLENGE FOR
CHANGE/SOCIÉTÉ NOUVELLE

Illustrations

All film production stills and frame enlargements are courtesy of and © National Film Board of Canada, except where otherwise noted.

Acknowledgments

A book of this ambitious breadth and depth would not have been possible without the many individuals and institutions, past and present, who provided essential material, moral, and political support.

We are grateful to the following authors, publishers, and associations for their kind authorization to reprint material in this collection: Deirdre Boyle and *Wide Angle* for "O, Canada! George Stoney's Challenge," in *Wide Angle* 21, no. 2 (1999): 48–59; Ron Burnett and University of Minnesota Press for "Video: The Politics of Culture and Community," in Michael Renov and Erika Suderburg, eds, *Resolutions: Contemporary Video Practices* (Minneapolis: University of Minnesota Press, 1996), 283–303; Colin Low and ECW Press for "Grierson and 'Challenge for Change,'" in *The John Grierson Project, John Grierson and the NFB* (Toronto: ECW Press, 1984), 111–17; Scott MacKenzie and the *Canadian Journal of Film Studies* for "Société nouvelle: The Challenge for Change in the Alternative Public Sphere," *Canadian Journal of Film Studies* 5, no. 2 (Fall 1996): 67–83; Janine Marchessault and YYZ Books for "Reflections on the Dispossessed: Video and the Challenge for Change Experiment," *Screen* 36, no. 2 (Summer 1995): 131–46; Alan Rosenthal together with George Stoney and University of California Press for "*You Are on Indian Land*," in Alan Rosenthal, ed., *The Documentary Conscience: A Casebook in Filmmaking* (Berkeley: University of California Press, 1980), 346–58; and the Association for Canadian Studies in the United States for Peter K. Wiesner, "Media for the People: The Canadian Experiments with Film and Video in Community Development," *American Review of Canadian Studies*, Spring 1992, 65–99.

Likewise, the following articles originally appeared in the CFC/SN newsletter (formally named *Access/Médium-Média • Challenge for Change/Société nouvelle* beginning Spring 1972): Fernand Dansereau, "Saint-Jérôme: The Experience of a Filmmaker as Social Animator," no. 2 (Fall 1968): 10; Dan Driscoll, "Can We Evaluate Challenge for Change?" no. 10 (Autumn 1972): 22–3; Léonard Forest, "Fiction Film as Social Animator," no. 7 (Winter 1971–72): 18–22; John Grierson, "Memo to Michelle about Decentralizing the Means of Production," no. 8 (Spring 1972): 4–5; Dorothy Todd Hénaut and Bonnie Sherr Klein, "In the Hands of Citizens: A Video Report," no. 4 (Spring-Summer 1969): 2–5; Kathleen Shannon, Elizabeth Prinn, Doris Mae Oulton, and Irene Angelico, "Working with Film: Experiences with a Group of Films about Working Mothers," no. 14 (Spring 1975): 2–12; and Noel Starblanket, "A Voice for Canadian Indians: An Indian Film Crew," no. 2 (Fall 1968): 11.

More abstractly perhaps, we owe a tremendous debt to the thousands of citizens who participated in the CFC/SN films and videos, as well as in the many screenings and discussions that followed – their names are largely unknown to us, but their faces, words, and actions continue to inspire us forty years later. We are equally indebted to the filmmakers, video-makers, and countless community activists, policy wonks, bureaucrats, sponsors, and muckrakers who collectively embodied the CFC/SN moment in Canada's – and the world's – history of community media, culture, and politics. Far from unknown are CFC/SN pioneers Tanya Ballantyne Tree, Clay Borris, Maurice Bulbulian, Martin Duckworth, Léonard Forest, Dorothy Todd Hénaut, Bonnie Sherr Klein, Pierre Lasry, Colin Low, Mike Mitchell, Anne Claire Poirier, Michel Régnier, Boyce Richardson, George Stoney, and Adam Symansky, who, whether somewhere along our eight-year path or throughout, directly or indirectly, contributed to this book, to the process that led up to it, or to individual chapters, and have honoured us beyond measure with their legacy and trust.

We express our indebtedness also to their heirs, individuals working today in the tough business of independent and political documentary: Cecilia Araneda, Katerina Cizek, Dan Cross, Magnus Isacsson, Kier-La Janisse, P.V. Satheesh and the Community Media Trust, Michelle Smith, Martha Stiegman, and many others too numerous to mention, who are reinventing their CFC/SN ancestors' practice in today's arguably harsher, more cynical climate.

Connected to this community are the very helpful and tolerant folks at today's National Film Board of Canada/Office national du film (NFB/ONF) who dug up dusty documents and production stills and kept the Board in step with the project: André D'Ulisse, Claude Lord, Bernard Lutz, James Roberts, Michelle Van Beusekom, and our special liaison and friend Adam Symansky.

This collection was first imagined in a different form by Concordia MA students Isabelle Lavoie and Diane Cantin way back in 2002. It would not have materialized without their support and that of the other engaged students who made the Film Studies 655 seminar at Concordia University that year an intellectual and political adventure: Isabel Arredondo, Christa Chen, Farbod Honarpisheh, Corey Kohn, Chris Meir, Emren Meroglu, François Pelchat, Anna Phelan-Cox, Gary Porter, Charlotte Selb, Michael Vesia, and Jason Woloski. The camaraderie and encouragement of our peers in the academic community have also been vital to a process such as this, and so we thank Charles Acland, Martin Allor, Daniel Cross, Liz Miller, and

Leslie Shade, as well as the participants and attendees of the CFC/SN panel at the Film Studies Association of Canada Conference in Saskatoon in 2007.

Our appreciation to the pioneers of CFC/SN scholarship and criticism who blazed a trail for us – Elizabeth Anderson, Bruno Cornellier, Gary Evans, Michael Burns, Seth Feldman, D.B. Jones, Marie Kurchak, Ron Moore, Joyce Nelson, Christina Pochmursky, and Patrick Watson, as well as our contributors Ron Burnett, Scott MacKenzie, Janine Marchessault, and Peter K. Wiesner – and of course to the dozens of contributors to the influential CFC/SN newsletter over the decade of its active life.

At Concordia University, heartfelt *remerciements* are extended to the Mel Hoppenheim School of Cinema faculty and staff; to Dean Catherine Wild, Associate Dean Lynn Hughes, and Research Facilitator Lyse Larose of the Faculty of Fine Arts, and to Dr Louise Dandurand, vice-president research and graduate studies, for their indispensable financial and academic encouragement; and to Oksana Dykyj, Luis Nasim, and their helpful staff at Visual Media Resources for technical and media support.

This book would also not have been possible without the generous funding of the Social Sciences and Humanities Research Council of Canada for our "Documentary in Canada" research project and the Concordia Documentary Centre since 2005, without the Aids to Scholarly Publications Programme, and without the ever-threatened principle of public funding of humanities research, creative expression, and the arts in Canada.

The editors would like to extend a huge thank you to McGill-Queen's University Press, especially our editor, rugby player Jonathan Crago, who grabbed this book in Saskatoon and ran with it. We appreciate as well the other imaginative and calm production, design, and editorial staff, notably coordinating editor Joan McGilvray and sharp-eyed copy-editor Judith Turnbull.

This book would not have been possible without the tireless, resourceful, and good-humoured contribution of student research assistants Alain Chouinard and, above all, Robert Vitulano.

Lastly, and on a personal note, Thomas Waugh, Michael Baker, and Ezra Winton would like to thank their partners, respectively Francie Brady, Laurel Wypkema, and Svetla Turnin. Without the continuous generosity, humour, and sacrifice of all three, we ourselves could not have risen to the challenge of change.

Foreword

Putting Ideas into the World: A Conversation with Naomi Klein about Starting Conversations with Film

■

EZRA WINTON AND NAOMI KLEIN

In the fall of 2008 we discussed Challenge for Change/Société nouvelle (CFC/SN) with the daughter of one of the program's famous and still actively engaged filmmakers. Naomi Klein was knee-high to a grasshopper when her mother, Bonnie Sherr Klein, was making controversial films like *Not a Love Story* (1981), but the formative experiences of growing up with a political filmmaker parent and being dragged to emotionally and politically charged community screenings helped shape this activist, writer, journalist, and film-maker who is arguably one of Canada's most celebrated and controversial personalities.

Klein is known around the world for her international best-seller *No Logo: Taking Aim at the Brand Bullies*, first published by Knopf in 2000. The book quickly became the bible for a nascent anti-globalization movement born out of the World Trade Organization (WTO) Seattle protests of 1999. Well researched and accessible, *No Logo* has influenced generations of activists and teachers, the latter incorporating its critique of corporate culture into their classrooms. And if there was ever any doubt about the work's pop-culture influence, one need only defer to Radiohead, who proudly claim that their 2000 album *Kid A* was inspired by Klein's treatise. After this monumental launch of an inspired career, Klein continued writing and producing books, her most recent climbing the international best-seller lists once again. As an exposé of capitalism's love affair with calamity, *The Shock Doctrine: The Rise of Disaster Capitalism* (2007) has brought Klein back to the forefront among those seeking to expose and resist neoliberalism in all its dressings.

But between these literary successes Klein produced a media work that more directly connects her to her mother's legacy as a political/activist docu-mentarist. In 2004 she and her partner, Avi Lewis, made *The Take*, a documen-tary that follows the takeover of Argentine factories by worker collectives responding to a massive economic meltdown in the country. A tribute to the workers, this visually rewarding film offers an impassioned account of a sig-nificant historic moment in the global struggle against neoliberal economic policy. While it may not have employed the collaborative production process

Director Bonnie Sherr Klein released her CFC documentary *The Point: Community Legal Clinic* in 1972, when her daughter Naomi was two. Frame enlargement.

that marked many of the CFC/SN projects, it is nonetheless recognized as a committed and political film, one that has been circulated both through grassroots activist channels throughout the Americas as well as in commercial cinemas in the United States and Canada. In the end, the film falls short of the kind of political-economic analysis found in Klein's literary works, but it has helped build cultural understanding and has fortified solidarity among activists in North America and Latin America. This bridging of community through film makes Klein not only an offspring of the CFC/SN generation, but an engaged and practised political descendent who continues to uphold some of the central tenets of the CFC/SN program. And so we offer this lively conversation, rather than the standard celebrity foreword, as an introit to this collection.

EZRA WINTON: Your mom, Bonnie Sherr Klein, was one of the original Challenge for Change filmmakers, and her films *Building an Organization* and *Citizen's Medicine*, which were done in 1968 and 1970, are considered early launching points and markers of the program and, in some way, they help set the course for the NFB [National Film Board] project. I know you've said your memory is spotty from this period, but could you speak of any early impressions?

NAOMI KLEIN: It's mainly because I wasn't born yet [laughter] – I was born in '70 [CFC/SN began in 1967].

EW: Basically, what I'm wondering is if you have any memories growing up around your mom's activist documentary filmmaking from the '70s and '80s.

NK: Yeah, I have very vivid memories of Studio D [the NFB studio created in 1974 for films to be produced for, by, and about women; it was the victim of budget cuts and shut down in 1996]. My mom would take me to work whenever I had a day off from school and I think my most vivid memory is the spirit in which they were working.

The discussions that would follow [the screenings] were most interesting. I would often not watch the films but go to the discussions. The spirit of that era of filmmaking was the idea that you make a film to start a discussion or conversation and that watching the film is a collective experience, a communal experience. You're gathering people in a room but afterwards you don't want to lose that moment, you don't want it to dissipate. The film is just the conversation starter and the goal is to keep people in the room and to keep them talking.

So, I have a lot of memories of very emotional discussions in theatres following films about disabilities, films about domestic violence, the *Not a Love Story* screenings. People would just cry and scream and fight. The films opened floodgates, emotional floodgates. Studio D was amazing at that. That was what I thought media was. I get called an activist journalist but I guess I just took it for granted because I grew up with this really powerful example in my home and my community, the idea that the documentary film was part of a movement, a movement for peace, a movement for civil rights, for women's rights. And the idea that you would somehow have to choose between being a media-maker and being an activist was never a delineation that meant anything to me growing up. And it still doesn't, frankly.

When I look back on CFC/SN, I have scenes of the films playing in my head; what I find wonderful are the similarities between what they were trying to do in that moment and the video revolution that was taking place with the democratization of the film movement and how much cheaper and mobile it has become. They were trying to be videographers, you know, and giving cameras to the people at a time when the technology really hadn't caught up to their dreams. They had a vision of really radical filmmaking but the cameras were still really bulky and also required a higher skill level.

But it still excited me that they were trying to do it. And now we are at this moment where the technology has matched that dream and so it has become a reality.

EW: You mentioned the emotional aspect of the political films that you grew up seeing as well as being around your mom in those times, but you also mentioned certain dialogue as starters of discussion. I'm wondering how you think those two things come together – emotion and dialogue – in cinemas as opposed to other media, because definitely the ethos of the CFC/SN project was dialogue.

NK: I think it has to do with the collective experience of watching film and the idea of the screening being a community meeting in a way – the idea that it is the *beginning* of a community meeting. It is such a different experience than reading a book alone, watching the television alone or with a couple of people, because even if what you see or read is incredibly moving, enraging, you're still alone. Your rage can be isolating. If you're in a room with people, you can immediately turn and say "what can we do about it" and that's the question. That was almost always the first question at the microphone after a CFC/SN film was shown. Okay, so what now? What do we do? And the people who might actually answer that are around you.

I think that is what is really unique about documentary. Also, documentaries are [often] made by a public institution like the NFB that sees the community role. The community-mobilizing role is part of its mandate because it's not necessarily the most profitable way to distribute film but it is the most transformative way.

EW: Before I move to the second question, I'm wondering if your mom's participation in the program had any influence on you in any way, especially considering the intersection between politics and media that have informed you and, I guess to larger extent, your professional career.

NK: Absolutely. I think the reason why I've been able to believe in this idea that I can be a writer and a filmmaker and an activist at the same time – that my work can be part of a movement for social change – is because that was my dominant role model of media-making as a kid. Even when I got my summer internship at the *Globe and Mail*, I was made to feel as if something was wrong with me because I cared passionately (and politically) about the stories that I was writing. And that wasn't the objective. I had this other more powerful example in my own life that told me that there was nothing wrong with that. That, in fact, it is something to celebrate – that political passion. That of course you write and make films about things that you care about passionately. I mean, why else would you do it?

There's this famous Kathleen Shannon (the founding head of Studio D) quote where she says that what objectivity means is "that I object to your activity." So when I started to get indoctrinated into neutrality and objectivity, I'd often think of that [statement]. It's been the most powerful influence on the choices I've made.

There's one other thing I think is interesting with CFC/SN and then Studio D – the idea that public institutions can have these radical pockets. They don't have to be monolithic. I think that's something that we really lost in the sort of streamlining, restructuring, and management consulting of all of our public institutions. It's that there are weird little pockets that have tended to disappear. But they [CFC/SN and Studio D] showed that it is possible for our public institutions to be more diverse, more democratic, more decentralized.

You know, my mother and her friends, they worked for the NFB but they were at war with the NFB at the same time. Their main discussions, when they weren't talking about the films themselves, were about the fight they were having with the programming board to get their films made. They very much saw themselves as dissonant within this big state institution. But they didn't turn on the institution. They just weren't swallowed by it – there was a real tension there. And it was a tension that people had respect for and that has sort of been lost, the idea that you can have those battles and everyone is enriched by them.

EW: What role do you feel the state can and should play, if at all? Obviously you feel it should play some role, in facilitating social solutions, facilitating social change – and progressive social change – to confront various problems, such as the ones that CFC/SN tackled and which continue to exist. Things like inequality, injustice, oppression, and many other social problems.

NK: For me, this is what is unique about Canadian funding for the arts. We have institutions that see social justice and political transformation as part of their mandate. And the measure of success for these projects, what they have really contributed to the advancements of those debates, is difficult to measure. The irony is that they've also achieved commercial success. *If You Love This Planet* (Terre Nash, 1982) enjoyed commercial success and won an Academy Award but they [the NFB] didn't set out to do that. They made a lot of films that didn't make money.

But success in the market was not the only measure and I feel that [that other kind of success] is certainly an idea that is fast disappearing – the measure back then was [along the lines of] how did this enrich us? How did this improve us? This is very hard to reconcile with market models and frankly it is possible to have a public institution that is public in name but is entirely governed by principles of market success – as opposed to these principles of social justice and transformation.

EW: You mentioned measuring success, and that leads nicely into my next discussion point. CFC/SN is predicated on the difficult-to-measure hypothesis that media can affect positive social change. Your book *No Logo* has been likened to the "bible" for the anti-globalization movement that began in the 1990s. Whether it is a film or book, media activists continue to invest great faith in the power of media to move people to action. Yet concrete results have remained elusive in this equation, and I run into this all the time as a social scientist researcher. Could you speak to this tension of expectation and measured effects?

NK: You know, all film can do, all books can do, is start a discussion. And you can't measure, nor should you. You put an idea out into the world and you can't control what's going to happen. You just have to believe in the value of the production of ideas. [You have to believe in] taking ideas seriously, taking stories seriously. And I think it is dangerous to think that you can control the effects afterwards, much less measure them.

But the film itself isn't the movement; the book isn't the movement. It's a conversation starter, a tool, an icebreaker. You can't control how people use that tool. Within my own family, my brother, Seth, was really concerned, as were a lot of young people in the '80s, about the nuclear movement. And he started a peace group called SAGE – Students against Global Extermination, which is a pretty heavy name but they kept it because it worked both in French and English. In French it was Solidarité anti guerre étudiants, which is actually better.

SAGE's primary organizational tool was *If You Love This Planet*. They would organize screenings. It was a terrifying film for young people. You had political speeches that were extremely alarmist in the old Ronald Reagan footage. Young people got traumatized by watching it, including high school students. But the point was to take that fear and turn it into an organizing tool. They did that starting in Montreal and then they did it across the country, and eventually internationally. They started hundreds of SAGE groups and really had a student-based anti-nuclear movement.

That to me is the best example [of what a film can do]. And then to be completely postmodern, my mother made a film about the SAGE tour for Studio D. But that was the best example for all of us of what true activist filmmaking can do. Terre Nash, when she made *If You Love This Planet*, didn't know that was going to happen. It wasn't her idea [what ensued]. Someone picked it up and ran with it.

EW: I think it's an important point because some – the marketers and social scientists in particular – are still trying to measure and show concrete examples of traceable ligaments between people's actions and what they watch or consume. And often these actions can be very nuanced and life changing and aren't always easily measurable. People are looking back at CFC/SN and are trying to measure whether it was effective or not. The anecdote that you just gave is really important in that discussion and shows the multiple and unpredictable ways political media can be harnessed and the ways it can live and grow through space and time.

Your film *The Take* is one such example. An NFB production that documents a workers' collective in Argentina, *The Take* was distributed and screened in both commercial cinema markets and grassroots activist spaces. CFC/SN films relied heavily on the latter in order to be disseminated to Canadian audiences. I'm wondering if you could speak to this tension between commercial and non-commercial cinema distribution and exhibition in Canada, especially given the context of our [commercial] theatre system and the mainly American fiction content that they show, and offer insight into the role of the grassroots for political documentaries such as *The Take*.

NK: Well, you know the commercial side of it is such a fad, right? We were lucky to get commercial distribution for *The Take*. It was a year and a half after *Fahrenheit 911* and there had been a couple of huge surprise documentary hits. Suddenly, commercial distributors thought there was money in documentary. But if you go out now and try to get a commercial distribution deal for a documentary film, you will be told people aren't interested in serious films right now because the last wave has failed. Not just documentary but also a lot of the films that involve Iraq.

We happened to get lucky. There was this moment where there seemed to be a trend. A few years later, people only wanted romantic comedy and teen flicks, right? It [the airing of serious issues] is too important to rely on the market. It's not that there can't be a market success. I've had market success for books about bashing corporations – it is possible. But just because it's possible doesn't mean that telling a story – the crucial stories of our culture and of our country – can be left entirely to the market and the forces of profit because they can be fickle.

EW: And the role of the grassroots, or the activist, off-the grid, non-mainstream film initiatives versus commercial distribution and exhibition?

NK: We don't make a distinction really. Every screening is the same. We made sure when we got a commercial deal to distribute *The Take* that we were able to have activist representation at the theatres, to have discussions at the theatres, tables with information, groups of people to get involved with. And we found that the theatres were very cooperative with that process.

EW: So regardless of the location, you created a political space.

NK: But the same kind of people come. Whether it is a community hall or a commercial theatre, people are coming for the subject matter. They're coming because they maybe heard about it on a listserv or on a website. I don't think that we are reaching a general audience because we're in a commercial theatre. I think we're still getting the same people who would come out regardless. They are not all that concerned about the venue. Anyone who goes to see a political documentary or comes to see a political author speak on some level wants to be engaged. They're leaving their house saying, "I care about this. I want to see a film about torture."

That's not a neutral act. I just feel it's a crime to not engage and inspire, and I feel the same about my book speeches as well, that I don't want people who just made this decision that's very serious to just go home afterwards and that's it. I make sure at my book events that there are activist groups that say, "Okay, if you want to get involved this is what is going on in our community. You can find out information here; there's a protest next week." I feel that when people gather in a room like that, there's a responsibility to try to keep the discussion going so that it isn't just a one-off screening or a one-off lecture. Because actually what people are doing in that moment is reaching out and wanting to be part of that community, and often that is wasted.

EW: I guess this discussion of *The Take* is somewhat of an exception to the rule that says much of the attention (including the written variety) that's directed at documentary cinema (including CFC/SN films) tends to be focused on aspects of production and the content of the films. It's important to look at how the film is screened and distributed because [even though] the films can be made, obviously if no one sees them, there's not much point in making them. This continues to be a challenge and a problem in Canada for activist and political filmmakers.

NK: Yes, it's true that a lot of great films are being made and no one is seeing them.

EW: So, if you were to resurrect CFC/SN today, what issues would top the program's list? Would the project still be run by the NFB and funded by the taxpayers? What would be the first film that you would like to see made under its auspices?

NK: I would document the community leading up to the 2010 Olympics in Vancouver. I think there are some really interesting coalitions being built that bring together environmental issues and civil society issues. There is a lot of surveillance going on with activists. It would be great to get lots of cameras in people's hands to document the way they are being treated by the police. And you could have screenings during the Olympics. Yeah, that's what I'd do.

EW: And if you could resurrect it, would it still be an NFB project?

NK: Yeah, it would be an NFB project but there would be autonomy. It would have its own organizing structure. So it would be under the umbrella but not controlled. There would have to be a great deal of autonomy.

EW: I have one last question. Your newest bestseller, *The Shock Doctrine*, has an accompanying short film directed by Alfonso Cuarón that has been distributed via the web. When CFC/SN was started, it was fuelled, in part, by the Portapak "revolution" in cheaper mobile video recorders. Progressive political media-makers, such as yourself, are now tapping their projects into a multi-channel, multi-platform universe that has less geographic and social restrictions than in the CFC/SN days. Why is a book not enough or a film not enough? Can you speak to why it is important to have the literature, the website, the film, the photo essay – all the media – all together?

NK: I think it just takes that. There is so much media, it takes so much to break through. For me personally, I wanted a film to go with the book because it's such visually rich material and, to me, they complemented each other really well. I don't think films are capable of building an argument as carefully as a non-fiction book. But film is so much better at emotion. I originally thought that I would just use the film at the start of my presentations and I found that went really badly because I couldn't follow the emotional impact of the short [film] because people were stunned by it.

And then just listening to someone talk was kind of anticlimactic. What I started to do was give my lecture, then have the film, then have the discussion. I've been playing with the different ways, trying to use each medium for its strengths so that you're not just repeating yourself in different mediums. You're looking at what this medium is better at. What can books do that films can't and what can films do that books can't? What can websites do that books can't? On the website, we have the research documents. That's original source material, which we could never do elsewhere. I mean, you have an endnote but what if you want to read the whole report? Then you'd have to find it yourself. We've made interactive endnotes so that you can go and read the document itself. I've tried to think about it not as bombarding through different platforms but [as] using different tools to strengthen the whole.

EW: On that note, of strengthening wholes, is there anything that you want to add about CFC/SN? This is going to be the beginning conversation to this book, this discussion between you and me. Is there anything you would like to add before we finish?

NK: I just feel that there was a moment of looseness with creativity within the public sector [at the time]. That [CFC/SN] is another way of thinking about the public sphere, which is so much more managed and regimented today. Not just in the culture industries but across the board. I think there was such of sense of play in that moment and it fits that you didn't have to choose between independent versus the state public. There was just much more fluidity. I think it is a really important model and hugely ahead of its time.

EW: I think it still continues in spirit in other films but it is fragmented and disjointed because it isn't under one organization like the National Film Board anymore.

NK: But it has created a community for filmmakers and I think filmmakers today feel much more isolated.

EW: Yes, that's a good point. I realize that you were a kid when your mom was in the program and that you're a little disconnected from it, but still the tendons are there between you and that past context. As a last comment, do you remember any specific moments or screenings that you were at during the formative years of the '70s or early '80s that you mentioned your mom took you to? Any specific screenings, or is it all a blur?

NK: I remember the *Not a Love Story* screening. It was consciousness raising. It was so emotional. Men would feel completely under attack. There were a lot of tears. It was group therapy essentially. I didn't think it was anything special – I thought it was the normal way to respond to film.

EW: So when you went to your first commercial film screening, was it strange because everyone was sitting in the dark, all still and quiet, and there wasn't any heated discussion or impassioned debate afterwards, such as what characterized so many CFC/SN screenings?

NK: Yes, definitely.

Challenge for Change

Introduction: Forty Years Later ... a Space for Challenge for Change/Société nouvelle

I

■

MICHAEL BRENDAN BAKER

THOMAS WAUGH

AND EZRA WINTON

This book was assembled as Canada hurtled through yet another crisis of late capitalism. Even though the full extent of the global economic down-turn was still on the horizon, the October 2008 federal election ominously brought out some of its most disturbing signs – at least in terms of Canadian social and cultural programs. In the wake of vengeful and petty arts funding cuts by the incumbent Tories, rumours had swirled that the first post-election act of a Tory majority would be the axing of the National Film Board of Canada (NFB), and for the first time in Canadian history, arts funding actually became a campaign issue. In fact, the morning-after pundits offered the consensus that Canadians had denied Prime Minister Stephen Harper, the snake-eyed Calgarian, his wished-for majority specifically because of arts-funding cuts, particularly in Quebec. It is reassuring that Canadians, as they participated in one of the fundamental exercises of democracy, were asking themselves whether the arts mattered, whether artists deserved public spon-sorship, and whether cultural heritage is worth preserving.

After the parliamentary dust had settled following a crisis of confidence in December 2008 and the proroguing of Parliament at the urging of a desperate and out-of-options Conservative minority government, the ruling Conservatives came back to power, tweaked the federal budget, and set about to systematically dismantle the arts anew. Fresh rumours based on phantom white papers circulated – the NFB wouldn't be axed, it would become a significantly pared down federal institution exclusively concerned with research – and other frightening tales took shape in reality. Under the shroud of a worldwide economic downturn, the government (true to Harper's utterance that "ordinary Canadians aren't interested in the arts") began its cuts, nips, and tucks to funding for culture – cutbacks that were part of a larger axing program that saw pay equity, adult literacy programs, women's shelters (and the status of women portfolio), accessible post-secondary education, national daycare, and other social services gutted. Whether as a result of the cancelling of the proposed National Portrait Gallery, the elimination of funding for travelling artists, or the massive cuts to the CBC (Canadian Broadcasting Corporation) in the spring of 2009,[1] the Canadian arts are now on the defensive in ways not seen since the 1980s axe-wielding prime minister Brian Mulroney.

The timing couldn't be better, then, for the reinvigoration of the memory of a media arts program infused with the ethos of critiquing government and emboldening the arts and democracy through the public purse. With current dominant narratives etching out economy *sans* arts, a book that marks out a formidable historical counter-narrative to twenty-first-century turbo-capitalism and its cheerleaders is sorely needed. Challenge for Change/Société nouvelle [New Society], the NFB's social activist documentary initiative dating from 1967 to 1980, is a glittering chunk of the heritage of both Canadian arts and Canadian democracy, with its bold artistic experimentation and its political dreams of transformation. This book is both a tribute to it and a most timely case study reflecting on the link between culture and democracy.

Challenge for Change/Société nouvelle (CFC/SN) was an ambitious initiative that brought together the unlikely partners of government bureaucrats, documentary filmmakers, community activists, and "ordinary" citizens. The program was launched in 1967 by the NFB and several other government agencies with the primary goal of addressing poverty in Canada through the production and dissemination of documentary cinema. The objective was to engender social change through media, and aspiring filmmakers of the New Left rose to the challenge. Over the fourteen years of the CFC/SN project, filmmakers working with citizens would take on many issues, from women's rights to housing to First Nations struggles to agriculture. The project – which saw filmmakers going into communities and collaborating with subjects instead of merely documenting them – garnered international attention and produced what many consider to be the most innovative and politically resonant films in the NFB catalogue. Many of the films have an enduring and exemplary aesthetic quality, as well as a political affect/effect, that surpasses their value as historical documents reflecting the political and artistic processes, achievements, and shortcomings of the programs.

Forty years after this landmark Canadian experiment entered the collective conscience of the country, *Challenge for Change: Activist Documentary*

---

[1] As of our final revisions, the National Film Board, grappling with the slashes, was in the process of eliminating an innovative interactive program expressly conceived of as the digital offspring of CFC/SN. By January 2010, we are told, the online grassroots forum Citizen*Shift* will no longer be in place.

The Challenge for Change logo. Frame enlargement.

at the National Film Board of Canada is the first volume dedicated to the films, filmmakers, and themes of that cultural moment. It brings together an international and interdisciplinary group of talented writers, historians, and film scholars offering diverse interpretations of CFC/SN. Readers and researchers may be hard-pressed to find CFC/SN's mention absent from any work of scholarship that discusses Canadian cultural policy, cultural industries, cinema, and especially documentary (but if one really tries, one can find such lacunae).[2] Indeed, the program is the subject of articles, book chapters, cultural critiques, missives, and musings both inside Canada and around the world. However, a comprehensive, critical collection on CFC/SN has never been published. Just as the CFC/SN initiative was inspiring, controversial, and boundary pushing, this collection aspires to similar qualities. As a volume that brings together cultural theory, political economy, historiography, and close readings of film texts, it provides a creatively coalesced space for students, scholars, documentary enthusiasts, Canadianists, and filmmakers interested in both the CFC/SN project and the larger context(s) that surround it.

Challenge for Change/Société nouvelle produced a particular and very special New Left corpus that Waugh has been teaching off and on since the mid-seventies and Baker and Winton have been discovering over the last

2 For example, Malek Khouri and Darrell Varga's *Working on Screen: Representations of the Working Class in Canadian Cinema* (Toronto: University of Toronto Press, 2006) astonishingly skips over this most pertinent corpus in its entirety, while Jim Leach and Jeannette Sloniowski's *Candid Eyes: Essays on Canadian Documentaries* (Toronto: University of Toronto Press, 2003), perhaps less egregiously considering that the volume covers canonical films and aims at the textbook market, does the same.

decade; it is a treasure-hoard of over two hundred films and videos produced between 1967 and 1980 by the NFB. This state-financed initiative in film/video community intervention is unique within Canadian – and indeed world – film history. Nowhere else did such a relatively well-financed program test in such a consistent and focused way many of the tenets of the international New Left and its cinematic cohort, the idealistic armies of shaggy baby boomers wielding 16mm cameras and Sony Portapak videos throughout the industrialized democracies and in much of what we then called the "Third World," most notably Latin America and India.

Of the approximately 145 films and videos produced in English and the over 60 produced in French for the CFC/SN program, the majority of the works that survived as "films" were made in 16mm but an important minority saw the light of day on Portapak Sony video (most of which are now seen as VHS or DVD copies of 16mm prints of the original video documents – a fascinatingly symptomatic technological peregrination to say the least). These four sub-corpuses – English film, English video, French film, French video – are all distinct, not surprisingly, given the sharply different cinematic cultures that artists like Colin Low, Peter Pearson, Bonnie Klein, George Stoney, Anne Claire Poirier, and Maurice Bulbulian all brought to the project. They are distinct as well in the institutional subcultures (and budgets) that characterized the anglophone and francophone branches – of which the average running times are only the most obvious index, twenty-four minutes on the English side and fifty-five minutes with Société nouvelle! All four sub-corpuses, however, are united by the common aim of community empowerment through media, which together test a wide variety of technological and aesthetic approaches to activism. At one end of the spectrum were projects aimed at producing film or video texts in the traditional aesthetic sense, and at the other were those aimed more at reflecting the processes of empowerment and enfranchisement than at delivering a conventionally finished media object. The collection of films and videos is also marked by the regional roots that the program officially encouraged, as well as by several fundamental binaries intrinsic to Canadian culture of the sixties and seventies – urban/rural, English/French, settler/indigenous, colonizer/colonized – and thus demonstrates the ways media activism is inflected by specific cultural environments. The period corresponds roughly to the Trudeau era of Canadian history and the triumph of liberalism – in both the higher-case and lower-case sense of the word. Marked by the traumas of peacetime (first by the "apprehended insurrection" of October 1970 (Marchessault 1995b, 159) and somewhat later in the 1970s by the epochal recession of that decade), this period is dramatically different from the same period in American left history, dominated in many ways as it was by the anti-war movement.

The films from CFC/SN have always been more or less available – even in Canadian diplomatic outposts abroad – except during the period of Mulroney cutbacks in the late 1980s. Indeed, it could even be argued that the corpus is not in need of our resuscitation. For several years nearly half of the English-language productions have been available for sale on the studio's website, while three-quarters of the French films have been available.[3] While the French studio has been more proactive in maintaining its films on the marketplace and bringing them to DVD format, there has existed a bountiful corpus of over 130 works in total available in either VHS or DVD format, certainly luxurious in comparison to any other corpus of New Left material anywhere in the world. While the tapes and discs are not cheap, especially for institutional customers (US customers pay $225 for a long film, $89 for a short, and prices for individual "home" consumers are much less), they are still good value in the context of the larger audio-visual marketplace. The situation could clearly be much worse, and one suspects that the materials were kept in circulation mostly owing to the inertia of that peculiar genus, the Canadian civil service. (But here is not the place to burden our international readership with a very Canadian rant about the bizarrely unaccountable bureaucracy of the institution with which Canadian cinematic stakeholders have had a love-hate relationship for seventy years.)

Bureaucracy, inertia, and love-hate may now be things of the past, for we are proud to say that an accessible and innovative selection of all-time CFC/SN hits has been launched alongside this book project, to be found on our online "playlists" (http://nfb.ca/playlist/challenge-for-change). We hope this collaborative relationship between academics and distributors will be the wave of the future. The restoration and distribution of films and videos such as these are crucial acts of not only remembering past political and artistic initiatives, but also of undertaking the pragmatic exercise of bringing these works out of the NFB vaults and into the public light where they can be accessed and deployed as new raw materials for contemporary audiences and activists. As tools for teachers interested in critical engagement with social issues by way of powerful media in the classroom, these titles are invaluable. Teachers practising critical pedagogy will find our collection – both the book

3 As of February 2008, a total of 63 French-language films and 145 English-language films are listed in the NFB catalogue; however, this figure includes several English-version French films and French-version English films. Given the social life of these films and the CFC/SN program as a whole, the question of whether these versions represent redundancies or unique entries is a difficult one to answer. Currently, 30 English titles are available on DVD and 54 on VHS, while 33 French titles are available on DVD and 18 on VHS.

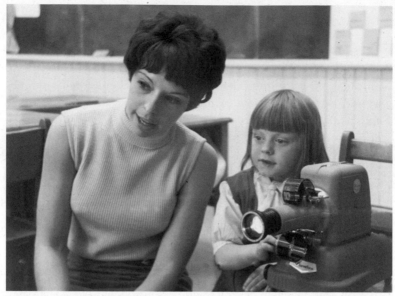

Critical pedagogy: the next generation in *Challenge for Change* (1968).
Production still.

and the playlists – especially useful as media that foreground empowered representation, creative collectivism, dialogic processes, and exposure of and resistance to power and oppression.

Now, almost thirty years after the demise of CFC/SN, there has been a renewal of interest in activist, community-based documentary, currents that merge under the banner "media democracy" – a term used by the NFB itself. The new viability of dissident theatrical documentary and the post-9/11 ratcheting up of geopolitical problematics for young activists (focused not only on the "global war on terror" but also on the entire gamut of globalization and environmental challenges) require us to reopen the epic chapter of the New Left activist documentary in general and of CFC/SN in particular.

There is also the expanding audience of documentary in general, with a continuing string of non-fiction box office hits and an explosion in the number of documentary programs and film festivals the world over. From San Francisco's Anti-Corporate Fest to Edmonton's Reel Waste to England's BEYONDTV, activist and political documentary festivals are ubiquitously dotting the ground of an interconnected world. Increasingly, curators, organizers, and filmmakers are conspicuously using the transformative power of political film to move citizens, to inspire action, to educate, inform and even entertain. Online, the picture is a diverse, mutating, and expansive mediascape of activist and political documentary "moments" that are flourishing virtually as they are materially. Sites and projects like Snag Films, Media Education Foundation, Media That Matters, and the multitude of documentary channels on video-feed aggregators all point to a growing online wilderness of important documentary media. This growing resource base requires accessible pathways, and among the most important are the paths that extend into the past and contextualize present moments and iterations. Contemporary activist documentary culture, in Canada as elsewhere, is all too intent on reinventing the wheel, too often uninformed of the rich heritage that can lie untapped and dormant, specifically the CFC/SN precedent and the impressive resource that the project offers in perpetuity. Among other things, this history we have sought to reinvigorate valorizes political documentary, community-based filmmaking, and studio collectives as producers, and provides a useful template for creative, media-making communities to access. Fleshing out CFC/SN in the complicated, proliferating undergrowth of documentary festivals, organizations, projects, businesses, and literature should provide a clearer perspective on the world of political shifts and material potentialities. We hope this book will carry out this task.

THE COLLECTION: ORIGINS

As three co-editors of varying experiences but equal enthusiasm, we can say that *Challenge for Change: Activist Documentary at the National Film Board of Canada* is the natural extension of our academic interests and personal stakes in the achievements of the program and its individual films.

Born in 1948, the year the NFB was releasing everything from *Why Won't Tommy Eat?* to *Feelings of Hostility* to mark its first decade of intense productivity, Waugh came of age during the late-sixties' first burst of the CFC/SN program. As an undergraduate aspiring to a New Left affiliation, he showed NFB short films to grassroots audiences in basement coffee houses in the summers of 1968 and 1969 in Halifax and Victoria respectively – though unfortunately the only films he actually remembers are the teenage pregnancy classic *Phoebe* and CFC/SN's best-seller *The Ballad of Crowfoot*. In the seventies, when he did graduate work in New York City, there was little encouragement to pay attention to Canadian film, but this did not prevent him from doing an MA thesis on another luminous beast within the NFB documentary stable, Pierre Perrault, maker of direct-cinema nationalist epics. Waugh's political convictions and passion for documentary led him to a predictable choice as a PhD topic, the internationalist Old Left documentarist Joris Ivens rather than the less glamorous and perhaps too current New Left Canadian corpus on his back porch. In the early eighties, when it came to developing *Show Us Life: Toward a History and Aesthetics of the Committed Documentary* (his anthology on political filmmaking), his Canadian-content quota was fully taken up by direct-cinema Quebec initiatives, the issue of independent distribution within English Canada, and a feminist independent documentarist – three out of twenty-four chapters was not bad for an American publication, though there is also the consideration that state-sponsored documentary, however salutary, did not make the cut. Waugh persistently taught CFC/SN films throughout the 1980s and 1990s in his documentary and Canadian courses at Concordia University, but it was only with a master's seminar on CFC/SN in 2000 that things coalesced – and that seminar was perhaps the most successful graduate course he has ever taught.

Born in 1972, the heyday of CFC/SN and a year whose bumper crop ranged from *Memo from Fogo* to *The Point: Community Legal Clinic*, Winton was converted to the dark side of documentary after attending a World Community Film Festival in Courtenay, British Columbia, in the 1980s, and some years later launched a bumpy career in community activism and committed documentary at Vancouver's Langara College. As a gung-ho undergraduate at Concordia in 2003, he founded Cinema Politica, an international documentary distribution/exhibition project he is still involved with today. He first stumbled on Challenge for Change in a dusty library looking for programming ideas. Throughout his MA and into his doctoral studies at Carleton after 2007, he continued to discover classics from the salad days of CFC/SN. A 2006 viewing of *You Are on Indian Land* hooked him for good, and he sought out more powerful works from the catalogue, incorporating these often overlooked works into a chapter on the program in his MA thesis (see chapter 37 of this volume). As an activist, academic, and programmer of political documentary, Winton continues to proselytize poor, unsuspecting undergraduate students and colleagues alike on the virtues of the CFC/SN oeuvre. Should he ever complete his PhD, this important work will be part of this ongoing self-pedagogical process, which has seen him not only curate and theorize political documentaries, but make them (*Alcant in India*, 2004) and star in them (*Wal-Town the Film*, dir. Sergeo Kirby, 2006).

Born in 1977, the year that CFC/SN, on its last legs, released the censored *Cree Way* and the anomalous *Rose's House*, Baker was first introduced to the films of CFC/SN while taking his undergraduate film degree in Toronto, and he returned his attention to the corpus as a participant in Waugh's MA seminar in 2002. The seminar was responsible for introducing fifteen grad students to the contradictions and passions of Challenge for Change/Société nouvelle. Forced to watch such gems as *Prince Edward Island Development Plan* (1969) and Michel Régnier's not-at-all-pedestrian *City Centre and Pedestrians* (1974), the group gained insights into a program available only to those brave souls with courage (and patience) enough to engage with the corpus as a whole. They were also required to go and meet a network of surprised veteran filmmakers (in their sixties, seventies, and eighties – even nineties) who no doubt thought themselves forgotten. The hundreds of pages of interview transcripts produced from the encounters with these charming and provoca-

The Ballad of Crowfoot (1968): CFC's all-time bestseller and a staple of 1960s basement coffee houses. Production still.

tive prophets-artists, compiled in part by colleagues Diane Cantin and Isabelle Lavoie, serve as valuable background material informing many of the new essays collected here. Baker, who teaches Concordia undergraduates survey courses on post-WWII documentary film that include modules on CFC/SN, went on to conduct a series of fruitful research projects at the NFB Archives on a range of subjects. His doctoral research on the intersections of non-fiction film and popular music (perhaps surprisingly) keeps him invested in many of the issues and thematics central to this collection.

THE COLLECTION: CONTENTS

The book you now hold is an ambitious initiative that aspires to the inter-disciplinarity, comprehensiveness, and eclecticism that the CFC/SN collection of documentary films and videos demands. This resource tome includes original essays by twenty-six authors from several different fields, ranging from investigative journalism to performance studies and, of course, film studies and communications. This core is supplemented by reprints of key articles on the subject of CFC/SN released during the life of the program, mostly by makers and other insiders, and several more that appeared within the two decades following its demise, generally by sympathetic but unsentimental observers and analysts. The contributors are from several different generations, with birthdates spanning from 1916 to 1977. They are mostly Canadian, but a few are from Europe and there is a solid contingent of

Americans whose presence hints that the behemoth may be awakening to the presence of a resilient film heritage north of the border (and let's not forget to mention the bountiful sprinkling of expatriate Americans whose discovery of Canada has been inseparable from their discovery of Canadian film). Throughout the book, we have aimed for the kind of jargon-free and accessible but nonetheless penetrating and inclusive discussion that was characteristic of the Challengers themselves, hoping that everyone from film fans to community activists and local historians will read this book alongside our primary audience of students and teachers. We think we have, for the most part, succeeded.

The thirty-eight chapters of this anthology are divided into five sections, each carrying out a distinctive task. Part 1, "Historical Spaces: In the Heat of the Action," introduces the reader to the overarching conceptual, thematic, and political goals of CFC/SN through the presentation of material published during the lifetime of the program. Some of these noteworthy essays and memos were published by participating filmmakers in the *Access/ Médium-Média* newsletter, an NFB in-house publication that accompanied the film productions of the program through 1973 and had a small subscription base of citizens and practitioners. Serving as a foil to these often utopian tracts is an evaluation of the CFC/SN's successes and failures from the vehement, opinionated, and brilliantly insightful NFB founder John Grierson (whose piece was among those published in the *Access* newsletter).

Part 2, "Community Spaces: Filming at the Margins," offers five longer articles focused on the pragmatics and principles of grassroots politics as embodied by CFC/SN films and filmmakers. These selections include several takes on the original anti-poverty impetus of the program as well as on the lasting legacy of video activism, most evident in Quebec, and on the growing focus on gender inequity that re-energized both the English and French programs in the 1970s.

Part 3, "Screen Spaces: Spotlight on the Films and Filmmakers," follows, featuring sixteen essays focusing on specific CFC/SN films or groups of films, as well as on specific filmmakers within CFC/SN. These essays offer readers a representative window into the extensive CFC/SN catalogue of films, with methodologies ranging from contextual to textual analysis, often incorporating theoretical and ideological inquiry as well as new archival research or oral histories. Forgotten gems such as *Wilf* (1968), *Mrs. Case* (1969), and *Rose's House* (1977) are finally given their due, while new perspectives on established classics such as *Cree Hunters of Mistassini* (1974) and the Fogo Island films (1967) are presented alongside a fresh look at the pioneering "Working Mothers" films by the former Studio D executive producer Rina Fraticelli. New work is presented on the films of Michel Régnier, Léonard Forest, and Maurice Bulbulian – major figures from Société nouvelle who until now have received scant attention from English-language film scholars – while previously published material by and about George Stoney (founding executive producer of the program) bookends the section.

Part 4, "Discursive Spaces: Theorizing Challenge for Change/Société nouvelle," engages the corpus at a reflective distance. While Parts 2 and 3 revels in grassroots nitty-gritty, Part 4 offers three key 1990s reprints and three original articles that provide theoretical appraisals of the CFC/SN project in its historical and discursive context. With the benefit of one or two generations of hindsight, how does this monumental project (and the first wave of serious academic study on the subject) stack up next to evolving ideas about the public sphere, documentary ethics, and the ever-forgotten but crucial operation of media dissemination and democracy?

Finally, in Part 5, "Conclusion: Contemporary Reincarnations," we offer two parting shots from the voices of two luminous women film activists, current National Film Board Filmmaker-in-Residence Katerina Cizek (born in 1969) and Indian documentary pioneer Vijaya Mulay (born in 1921). Cizek is interviewed by another activist documentarist of her generation, Liz Miller, and discusses how her activities on the public health political front in inner-city Toronto revive and reinvent some of the original key tenets of CFC/SN. Meanwhile, Mulay casts the spotlight on a program of rural women's video activism in the Indian southern state of Andhra Pradesh, the Community Media Trust (CMT) program of the Deccan Development Society (DDS). Started in 1996, the CMT is an exemplary case of contemporary video-based community activism, and Mulay reveals how, among other things, it has avoided some of the fundamental mistakes of CFC/SN.

That's not all. The book is set in motion by what is hopefully our only indulgence in publishing industry cliché – a celebrity foreword. In typical CFC/SN style, this is in a dialogic format rather than a univocal overture. We are proud to have ex-Montrealer Naomi Klein on board (in conversation with co-editor Winton), not only because of her international stature as a committed documentarist and critic of neoliberal globalization but also because she, as the daughter of CFC/SN pioneer Bonnie Sherr Klein, epitomizes our mission to enact a generational extension of the CFC/SN project. Naomi was born in 1970, the year her mother made *Citizen's Medicine* (her mother's voice from that era is part of chapter 7 and her work the subject of chapter 18), and we think her visionary practicality is a fitting legacy of her mother's activism.

At the end of the anthology are two resource sections (the parts that we hope will become most dog-eared during this sturdy volume's shelf life in your library): an annotated filmography, in the form of a comprehensive and detailed inventory of the CFC/SN catalogue, and a bibliography featuring the majority of previously published work on the subject of CFC/SN.

The comprehensive nature of the annotated filmography is not, however, reflected in the anthology as a whole. We regret that we could not cover every aspect of this complex, multilingual, multi-regional, multicultural, and ideologically diverse concatenation of image-making. Inevitably, it was difficult to address the true diversity of the program within the limitations of this book project. As a result, there are filmmakers, topic areas, and entire series that remain unattended. We are aware that some readers' favourites are conspicuously absent from this pedagogical package, and we welcome any flak coming our way, since flak indexes passion. But the reality is that, as a result of poor film sources or issues beyond our control, even some of our own favourite films did not make the cut. We are even more contrite that significant swaths of the CFC/SN corpus had to be omitted either because we found no takers for these subjects or because there was no room in the table of contents. Noteworthy absences include the fertile but less than glamorous series on workplace safety and ecology – for example, *Anthony Mazzocchi Talks about Chemicals and the Workers* (Boyce Richardson, 1978), which in retrospect constitutes a poignantly prophetic harbinger of today's number one activist topic: the politics of the environment. And we apologize to Québécois and Acadian constituencies as well, since, despite our best efforts, the French-language output of Société nouvelle receives short shrift in this English-language project (just as it did during the life of the program with English-language audiences). We hope this collection serves as both a resource and inspiration for additional studies of these films and filmmakers, indeed the program as a whole. Ultimately, we hope that our selection of thirty-eight chapters on films, filmmakers, political issues, contextual factors, and CFC/SN descendants will provoke readers to go out and fill in the gaps in historical, theoretical, and ideological research, as well as in artistic and political practice. Perhaps it will inspire both.

PART 1

Historical Spaces: In the Heat of the Action

■

PREFACE

This section situates Challenge for Change/Société nouvelle in a historical context with a collection of eight essays and articles published during the existence of the program. Special emphasis is placed upon work published in *Access/Médium-Média*, the program's official newsletter, published by NFB/ONF staff and filmmakers from 1968 to 1975. With over seventy articles spanning fourteen issues, the newsletter featured the work of filmmakers and volunteers in both official languages and enjoyed a committed following of subscribers from across Canada and the world. The articles we have selected capture the zeitgeist of shifting cultural policy and emerging counter-publics in Canadian society, as well as debates about frontline media strategy. Together, the pieces in this section set the historical stage for a successful understanding of the CFC/SN project and its many cultural and historical readings, such as those provided by our contributors in Parts 2, 3, 4, and 5.

2   Grierson and Challenge for Change (1984)

■

COLIN LOW

Part 1 opens with this 1984 memoir by NFB pioneer Colin Low, whose storied career at the institution stretched from the final moments of founding-commissioner John Grierson's tenure through the rise and fall of CFC/SN. In the only piece in this section not originally published in the CFC/SN newsletter, Low (the executive producer of the program for about a year following George Stoney's departure in 1970) reflects on the lessons he learned from a titan of documentary cinema and responds to the view of the program held by Grierson (see chapter 8). Having effectively launched CFC/SN with the groundbreaking multi-part Fogo Island film experiment, Low here offers valuable in(hind)sight into the mandate of the program and its ability to effect change. This paper was delivered at a 1981 conference sponsored by McGill University's "John Grierson Project" (one of two Grierson archives in the world) and published three years later in the collection *The John Grierson Project: John Grierson and the NFB* (Toronto: ECW Press, 1984).

Dr Grierson had a love-hate relationship with the Challenge for Change program. One got the feeling that he sincerely hoped it would succeed but was sure that it would fail.

He had always talked about the "teacher/filmmaker" the "educator/filmmaker." He conceded that these people should also be blessed with artistry and wisdom. He tried to preach these people into existence.

Here, in the late sixties, in this Film Board program, were a few energetic, naïve enthusiasts who, for a short time, believed again that it was possible to change the world with the camera.

That excited Grierson. They were teachers, social workers, filmmakers, and they were not only prepared to teach with film, they were also prepared

Originally published in *The John Grierson Project: John Grierson and the NFB* (Toronto: ECW Press, 1984), 111–17.

CFC founder Colin Low in the editing room during the Fogo Island project.
Production still.

to help ordinary people to make their own films. That bothered Grierson.
That was carrying things too far.

In late 1971 I had three encounters with Dr Grierson that were illumi-
nated by his exasperation with the program.

I was just emerging from five years of "Challenge for Change." The Fogo
Island project, which became a cornerstone of that program, was like one of
those events in science where conditions come together and seem to prove
something fundamental. But then, try and duplicate the results in another
laboratory! I was still defending the Fogo approach as not only practical,
but essential.

For those people now who have never heard of the Fogo Island project –
and there will be many who have not – I will put it in a nutshell. I used to
take much longer to describe it. It was a community development program
in Newfoundland, well planned and well funded, that used film as a catalyst
to generate local debate – to give local people a voice and even editorial control – and to provide those people with access to people in power, via film.
Not one film but a whole series of mini-films. It was meant to be a step in incorporating media into the democratic process. The creation of a communication loop, as we called it. All of these are things one can imagine Dr
Grierson applauding. It seemed to work. It seemed to foster positive, creative social change. But there has never been any way of proving that film

caused the change. Later projects substantiated the approach. Few were quite as dramatic.

Fourteen years later, Fogo Island is one of the healthier communities in Newfoundland, and we can't say for sure why it is that way.

Grierson referred to his McGill class at that time as a "very promising group" of young teachers. He had weeded them out of a much larger group because he was fed up with film groupies and dilettantes, he said.

They were the *crème de la crème* and he wanted me to talk to them about "community," and would I bring some film to run?

I thought I could do this with my eyes shut. I had done it a dozen times before. I picked three films with not much thought. Oddly enough, apart from social gatherings, where I had felt very comfortable in his presence, this was the first time I saw Grierson on his professional ground as a teacher.

He looked small and fragile when he arrived, but his looks were deceiving. He first of all berated one of the very large, bearded, long-haired students for putting his foot on a seat in Theatre Six at the Film Board. It was a seat that many feet had been applied to, in the course of fifteen years, but I gathered that Dr Grierson did not appreciate such a lack of formality in his class. By the time he had finished, he had everyone's attention, including mine. I must say, at this point I started to worry.

He then launched into a recapitulation of the previous lecture, which had to do with his experience working as a reporter for the Hearst Press in Chicago – and his interest in yellow journalism for its active and dramatic method of arresting popular attention. The expression "something does something to something" was used to illustrate the idea of the kind of storytelling in such dramatic journalism. Such headlines as AIRPLANE HITS HILL illustrated the device. Not AIRPLANE CRASHES ON HILL.

From there he went on to indicate that he had tried to apply some of these ideas to documentary film, to galvanize interest in large political, social, economic issues, in the conviction that the man in the street could be interested, and involved, and participate in shaping the world.

He also sketched the growth of fascist propaganda-film and pointed out some of the differences between democratic media and fascist media, as expressed in wartime and peacetime situations, but always emphasizing the dramatic.

I had been much impressed by reading Dr Grierson's ideas on the general sanction of Parliament as applied to the National Film Board: the idea that, as a filmmaker, one had to respect the constraints as well as the possibilities of this sanction. I had used the paragraph to influence filmmakers in Challenge for Change who had resorted to very subjective and emotional positions in the expression of situations in films.

At this point Dr Grierson began to emphasize the importance of expression, personal style, passion, poetry, as important elements in the documentary. He then introduced me and made some very positive remarks about the style and expression of some of my films. Unfortunately, they were not the films I was about to show. I showed a film called *The Hutterites*, done long before the Challenge for Change program, my first experience of trying to bridge the gap between a remote and unusual community and the outside world.

Dr Grierson hated it. He saw *The Hutterites* as essentially antisocial and the style of the film as pedestrian. His critique was devastating.

My colleagues at the NFB had been critical of the film when it was completed because it did not highlight the serious conflict between the Hutterites and their western materialist neighbours. They said it was too pals-y with the Hutterites. It was not dramatic enough for television.

I had argued with them that there would never be a decent discussion between the Hutterites and their neighbours until there was some common base of goodwill and mutual respect, and part of that was being able to show the minority group as unique, but admirable, folks. Highlighting the tensions on TV was not going to contribute to community peace.

But I didn't know what to say to Dr Grierson. Here was a man who had told us in the forties that our task was to make peace more exciting than war. I had brought him my film to praise for its sincere effort, and he had ripped it to shreds. "In a film you must tell a story," he said, "otherwise you are boring, you will not have an audience. Something *does* something *to* something. You must reveal the secret inside of that interaction, whether it is a psychological story, a political story, or a story about tying shoelaces."

I sulked at the side of the theatre. "But, but," I protested silently in my own head. "In a community the best story is the peaceful and collaborative solution of problems. That is not theatre. The best community development is evolutionary, not revolutionary. Why is that not an exciting story? Do people have to hang on the edge of survival in order to be interesting? Is accommodation more ignoble than a western shootout? Haven't we had enough of that media crap?"

"We'll now look at the next film," said Dr Grierson. I wished I was in another city. I ran the film *Billy Crane [Moves Away]*, a Fogo Island fisherman who, that day, was pulling up his nets to leave and go to Toronto to work in a factory. It is a monologue – a quiet, bitter, unstructured verbal ramble.

Dr Grierson liked Billy Crane. He didn't think much of the film but he pointed out Billy Crane's verbal skill and dramatic flair in storytelling – his superb timing and phrasing, the pauses, the punctuation of his thinking with little actions. He suggested that many local people have a great oral tradition, an untutored but superb command of language in its essence.

I started to relax. I wanted to say that the film had been most important for our work and had been received initially with shock and then with enthusiasm. The provincial government had a hard time answering Billy Crane. But they did answer him. I wanted to say that this *"giving a voice* to people" was what it was all about, but I was too late.

"What," Dr Grierson wanted to know, "was the value of the film off Fogo Island? Was it good for television? Mass media? What did it say to Canada?" I was deflated. "What did it say to the world?"

I had to admit the film wasn't worth much outside the context of the situation – outside the mainland of Newfoundland. Billy Crane's accent was hard to understand. It had some specialized value in Ottawa, but it did not say much to farmers in Alberta, except that centralization and central decisions of government are not necessarily always right.

"How can you afford to make expensive films for such a limited clientele? Why would the Canadian taxpayer allow such an indulgence?" Dr Grierson asked.

I pointed out that we recognized the cost but that it was experimental, and the whole project – twenty-seven films for local use – cost less than one CBC television hour at current costs. Now I was fighting back. "Besides," I said, "welfare in any depressed area was expensive, but if development was accomplished – "

"Twenty-seven films for local, limited consumption!" Dr Grierson interrupted. "Did any of these films define the problems, and recommend solutions to the problems of the island?" Grierson wanted to know.

"Well, no," I said. "The films were an effort to help the community define its own solutions, by playing back their tentative efforts of formulation. Video equipment and tape were also useful, and cheaper than film."

"So the filmmaker is nothing but a tool, a camera operator or projectionist in the formulation of these problems and solutions. What about the intelligence, world experience, expensive education that could be brought to these people? If you have no opinions, no ideas, no commitments, nothing to say, why further burden these poor folks, whose lives are difficult enough, with manipulative nonsense? They need all their working energy and time to simply get by."

At this point I caved in temporarily. I said I often had the same questions in my head on Fogo Island but that honestly I could not recommend anything to these people. Their situation, which seemed to me initially simple, became more and more complex as I learned more and more about them. We were working with a community-development man from Memorial University on Fogo. The university supplied the hard information on many subjects; I supplied the film know-how. I think I blurted out that a lot of documentary films are simply massive oversimplifications of reality.

Dr Grierson looked profoundly skeptical. I felt barely conscious as I walked out the door. "We haven't finished," said Dr Grierson. "Come back next week. I think you've got another film. Oh! Better book the theatre."

Next week Dr Grierson asked me to tell the class about the film we were going to see. My remarks were succinct. This is what I said: "At the height of Kennedy's famous war on poverty, a one-and-a-half-billion-dollars-a-year agency called the Office of Economic Opportunity in Washington heard about the Fogo Island experiment. Subsequently, a number of similar experiments were conducted in the United States: the Farmersville project in California; the Hartford project in Connecticut; the Skyriver project in Alaska; the White House report on hunger. All modelled after Fogo. Altogether, several million dollars of effort.

"*Hector and Reuben* is an interview with two young Spanish American war veterans. The war was Vietnam; they had just returned. Their father and mother were illegally entered Spanish American agricultural workers, orange pickers, in a town called Farmersville, California. The town was a tinderbox of racial resentment. The film did a great deal to start the two sides talking. Washington was impressed." We ran the film for Dr Grierson's class …

After the screening, Dr Grierson asked the class what they thought about the film. Some of the class were American conscientious objectors, including the big guy with long hair whom Dr Grierson had mauled a week before in the foot-on-the-seat incident. The opinions of the class were mixed. Some thought Hector and Reuben were telling the interviewer what he wanted to hear. Some saw in the cautious discussion only embarrassment. Some saw in it subservience.

"Brown Uncle Tom-ism" was the phrase. One student thought that anyone who fired a gun in Vietnam was a criminal.

Other students objected to this interpretation. They thought the boys had guts. The discussion became very heated.

"The film was a catalyst," I protested. "Only these two boys, who had served in the army, in a town dominated by American war veterans of three wars, could possibly broach the subject of racism." I felt that in a polarized situation teetering on the edge of violence, someone had to make the gesture, but it could not have the implication of threat.

"One must try to generate a base of goodwill," I said, "before any discussions can begin. This kind of medium is totally different from mass media, and this is what is driving me crazy about Dr Grierson's interpretation."

Dr Grierson objected, "Not all human situations can be solved without conflict. Goodwill is not enough. Do not get confused with sentimentality. Intelligence and strategy are at the heart of diplomacy. You cannot achieve peace out of love and wishful thinking alone.

"Furthermore, the film is ambiguous. It is not an affirmation of love or

Christianity. It is not a real service to the subject of the film. It uses them but does it support them with evidence? Evidence, proof: *that* is what you must bring to the situation if you are to be these people's advocate." At this point I stopped being resentful and defensive, and tried to listen. But it was the end of the class.

In the last of the three classes the following week, Dr Grierson recapitulated. I realized, at that point, that he had tricked me. He knew the answers to all the questions he had asked me. I thought his hostility was genuine – it was his brand of theatre. "Something does something to something" – or to someone. If his students have forgotten the lesson, which I doubt, I have not.

After his death three months later, Challenge for Change published in its newsletter his "Memo to Michelle" [see Grierson, chapter 8, this volume]. It expressed his hopes and doubts and faith concerning the decentralization of the means of production. Indeed he hoped it was practical. It was a question of method.

What has happened to Challenge for Change? you might ask. As Dr Grierson predicted, some of our methods were impractical. Somewhere in the mid-seventies the program slowly expired – after several attempts to revitalize it – for those reasons Dr Grierson so deftly fingered in his criticism of the program.

"Evidence." That's what you must bring to these situations – and what you must carry away from the situation.

Government wants evidence. Evidence of change. Cost-benefit analysis. As money became tighter – as the idealistic citizen-participation rhetoric of the sixties did a cross-mix to the rhetoric of energy economics – we saw the emergence of another approach. "Something does something to something," in no uncertain terms. Referendums are won by the merchants of hard sell. The advertising companies *do* their homework, with statistical evidence. For X dollars you reach Y people with Z impact. They are hard to refute. They have fifty years of advertising theory and practice behind them and a conditioned populace which, if it does not totally believe the message, at least tolerates it. Repetition does wonders in blurring skepticism. But does that approach to social change alter anything for long?

I could not have acted differently if I had fully understood the implications of Dr Grierson's message ten years ago. I have faith that the opportunities will return again – and that the methods will be refined by another generation with energy and wisdom.

I cannot forget the actual experience of that program. I am compelled to remember it. Some of our evidence was good, but not always complete.

Those moments when rancour and hostility and anger are transformed by reason and become cooperation and accommodation: I have seen them triggered by an appropriate film. This attitudinal change is hard to get on film, but it is the very root of community. Those moments are hard to record. There are cultures that understand that, in negotiations, people must not be allowed to lose face; they must be able to maintain dignity for the good of the entire community. In Japan this is not theory, this is everyday practice, and there is much to learn in that tradition.

When we ran *Hector and Reuben* for a large Farmersville audience, the Veterans' Hall was packed. The Anglos (white folks) sat on one side of the hall, the Chicanos (brown folks) sat on the other side. When the film was over, an old gentleman with a Midwest Oklahoma accent, a former white migrant labourer from the days of *The Grapes of Wrath*, stood up.

"Well," he said, "I appreciated seeing that film and listening to those young men, and I learned something from them. I've got a good Spanish-speaking friend in this town. I've known him for twenty years but I honestly have to admit we don't talk about much except the weather."

His friend across the hall hesitantly stood up and said, "Yes, that's true. We don't talk about much except the weather, and maybe we're both too old to be interested in other things, but why is it not possible for our children to talk about other things?"

It was one of those moments. I might have turned the camera on, I might have got the ensuing discussion, which went on quietly for an hour. But I don't think it would have happened. Is it possible there is some evidence outside the witness of the camera?

No, I don't think the experience and ideas of Challenge for Change were impractical. Our world is impractical. This is a watershed of history. Violence as a method of social problem solving is now impractical.

At one time a tribal skirmish might have been ugly and brutal, or heroic and exhilarating, necessary or unnecessary depending on what side you were on. It only affected those two tribes.

Violence is impractical because geography, space, and nature no longer contain small violence. Now, what is one day a remote tribal skirmish is the next day the *cause célèbre* for a superpower or the invasion of a larger vested interest. Instantaneous media do not seem to calm the nervous trigger fingers, they exacerbate alarm. But we know that it is either a question of cooperation and accommodation or annihilation on a global scale.

No, the ideas of that program were not impractical, Dr Grierson. Too early, too late, or too little, perhaps.

If we cannot improve our local, regional, and national communication – if we cannot improve the quality of our own community dialogue – how can we walk with any authority upon a world stage and change the nature of that desperate argument?

3   In the Hands of Citizens: A Video Report (1969)

■

DOROTHY TODD HÉNAUT

BONNIE SHERR KLEIN

"In the Hands of Citizens: A Video Report," from Dorothy Todd
Hénaut and Bonnie Sherr Klein, is perhaps the most widely read
and (in its time) the most influential article to appear in *Access*,
the CFC/SN newsletter (issue no. 4, Spring-Summer 1969). Hénaut
(the founding editor of the newsletter) and Klein (who marked
her arrival at the NFB from the United States with a number of key
contributions to the program) situate their work with video and
the St-Jacques Citizens Committee in opposition to mass media.
Embraced and challenged in equal measure, their thoughts on the
value and impact of video technology in small communities resonate throughout this collection (see Charbonneau, chapter 21, this
volume). Both Hénaut and Klein are still lively media activists.

PREFACE

Challenge for Change attempts to implicate the communications media in
the process of social change. Very few people have access to the media of
communication in our society. This fact is particularly obvious, or at least its
consequences are particularly dramatic, in relation to poor people.

The Fogo Island project used film to catalyze community development
by opening channels of communication where few existed. Through film,
people talked to each other and talked to their government representatives.
In Newfoundland, the cameras have passed from NFB [National Film Board]
hands to the NFB-trained hands of community-development workers at
Memorial University of Newfoundland, a first step in the process of decentralizing the communications media. The training of an Indian Film Crew,
Company of Young Canadians volunteers, is based on the belief that people
should speak for themselves instead of being spoken for.

The videotape recording (VTR) project in St-Jacques is an attempt to
extend to its logical conclusion the conviction that people should partici-

pate in shaping their own lives, which means among other things directing and manipulating the tools of modern communication necessary to gaining and exercising that participation.

COMITÉ DES CITOYENS DE ST-JACQUES

The Comité des citoyens de St-Jacques, a dynamic citizens organization in one of downtown Montreal's many poor areas, was founded in March 1968 at a public meeting called by a handful of concerned citizens with the help of a community organizer from the Urban Social Redevelopment Project. At the meeting the citizens agreed that bad health was their most immediate problem. On receiving no help from provincial and civic authorities, the citizens decided they would take the affair into their own hands. They rented an apartment in the area, renovated it themselves, and recruited medical and dental workers who were interested in the idea of a citizen-run community clinic. By October, they had opened their clinic five nights a week.

NFB INVOLVEMENT

There seemed to be a convergence between the needs and ideas of the Citizens Committee and those of Challenge for Change, and we approached the committee with the idea of a project that would explore the use of videotape recording equipment in community organizing. The committee recognized the potential effectiveness of VTR as an organizing tool and formed a VTR-film group. This group has eight members, of whom six are from the neighbourhood and two from the NFB (the authors of this article), so the term "we" is used here to refer to the VTR-film group. This group has carried out all the activities with the video equipment; it has also guided an NFB film crew in the shooting of 16mm film, has organized the screening of rushes for the Citizens Committee, and is now working closely on the editing process. We hope to present three films – on the VTR project, the clinic, and the Citizens Committee – each in both French and English versions. The group brings all important questions of policy to the Citizens Committee as a whole for a decision.

CONSENSUS ON THE AIMS

We held our first meeting in November 1968 and discussed the various possibilities for using the VTR equipment. The most important thing that came out of this discussion was the firm consensus that the VTR equipment should be used to serve the aims of the Citizens Committee and should riot distract the members from those aims. The broad objectives of the Comité

The Portapak in *VTR St-Jacques* (1969): citizens manipulate the tools of modern communication in order to participate in shaping their own lives. Production still.

des citoyens de St-Jacques are to work as citizens to gain as much control as possible over their own lives. The main job of the information team to which the VTR group is attached is to sensitize the inhabitants of the area to their common problems and to convey to the committee the hope that together they can act to change the situation.

FAMILIARIZING OURSELVES WITH THE EQUIPMENT

In the following weeks we discovered that even though the equipment was left in the offices, nobody used it. But once various members of the VTR group started taking it home to video their children, we got over our diffidence about using the equipment, as we learned how easy it was to use. Or, to translate the citizens' description, we "tamed" or "domesticated" our VTR.

We usually formed two-man teams, with one person on camera, the other interviewing with the microphone. We all made errors, mostly at the beginning, and each of us at one time or another has brought back an underexposed tape or a tape with no sound because the microphone was not plugged in properly or nothing at all because the tape was inside out. We rarely made the same error twice, and there are not very many you can make with a VTR.

AN EARLY USE

Students sought to ally themselves with the Citizens Committee. With mixed feelings of suspicion and need, the committee organized a teach-in and fund-raising blitz in all the community colleges and technical schools in the area. We used the VTR equipment, both camera and playback, which we set up in the cafeteria of the school. We played tapes of citizens meetings and then taped the students while we explained to them the activities and aims of the Comité des citoyens and requested their support and donations. These tapes were then played back on the monitor.

The most-interested students took camera and mike in hand and went from classroom to classroom eliciting funds from students and teachers alike. The whole operation was infused with the aura of glamour and gadgetry associated with this new technology. It was fun.

OPÉRATION BOULE DE NEIGE

We were still floundering around, testing possible uses of the equipment, when the information team proposed a week-long information and organizing campaign for the end of January. The aims of the campaign would be to inform the residents of the community of the existence of the Citizens Committee, to stimulate debate on their collective problems, to gain new and active members, and subsequently to decide on new projects. The format of Operation Snowball (thus named because it starts small but can turn into an avalanche) was to include a press conference on Monday, a series of five public meetings in various areas of St-Jacques from Monday to Friday, and then a big *fête populaire* on the Saturday night.

A PROGRAM TO PREPARE

This was exactly what the VTR group needed to give it some direction. We proposed that we prepare a half-hour program on the problems of the people in the area that would be shown at the opening of each meeting. Building on the existence of the clinic, the theme of the campaign was "Why are we sick?" This led to an exploration of the causes of ill health: bad housing, unemployment, insufficient welfare, few recreational facilities, inadequate education, and poor medical care. We did some practice shooting. This was in December and January, and the bitter cold required special techniques,

such as covering the equipment with blankets to keep it warm if we wanted
to interview people on the street.

In early January we drew up a tight schedule and divided ourselves into
two- or three- man teams to cover the various problems.

A REACTION OF THOSE IN AUTHORITY

For the section of the program dealing with medical care, two of the members of the VTR group went to the out-patient clinic of one of the large
municipal hospitals to talk to the people in the waiting room. Within ten
minutes the director of the hospital hauled them into his office, confiscated
the tape, and demanded that they come back and erase it. After a discussion
with the other committee members, it was decided they should comply with
the hospital's wishes, since the committee had chosen neither this subject nor
this terrain for a confrontation. But we took full measure of the effect this
simple recording device could have on an authority that did not value free
access to information.

SHOOTING SITUATIONS

Having learned this lesson, we decided not to shoot inside the Welfare or
Manpower Offices and thereby waste time on confrontation, but instead to
interview the people coming out of these offices. Our strategy was amply
rewarded with some frank, stark statements from welfare recipients and job
applicants.

For the housing segment, we began by shooting exteriors, but the cold
rapidly sent us into the corner restaurant. This proved a good tactic, for we
started a discussion with the owner and one of his customers, learned a great
deal about the neighbourhood, and were introduced to a woman who lived
in one of the worst slum buildings in Montreal. She invited us into her home
to show us where part of her ceiling had fallen down last July.

EDITING

The material was edited down from about four hours to forty minutes. At
first, committee members came to the Film Board to do the editing – by electronic transfer – with the NFB technicians. The travelling, together with the
necessity to do this during working hours, proved difficult, so subsequently
we brought the tapes to the NFB with notes from the group on exact
footages for editing. Neither this system nor the visual results of the trans-
ferring were very satisfactory, and we are just now going to try to edit by

physically cutting the tapes, which the citizens can do themselves and which is visually less irritating.

THE PUBLIC MEETINGS

The VTR group did some interviewing in the streets on the day of the meetings, inviting people to come and see themselves on TV. These tapes were run, unedited, a half-hour before the start of the meetings, as people were coming in.

The public meetings were held in school halls or church basements. We placed six 23-inch monitors around the room, with about twenty chairs in a half-circle in front of each. The active members made a point of spreading themselves among each group.

When the thirty-minute video presentation was over, each group moved its chairs into a circle and plunged into a discussion. Having seen people like themselves on the familiar TV screen, discussing their problems with utter frankness, they lost much of the reticence and timidity people generally have in a group of strangers. They simply said, "I guess this is the place where I can talk freely," and they then talked at length of shared problems and possible collective solutions.

PARTICIPATION

The Citizens Committee had refused to propose some special project at the public meetings because it felt strongly that new members, who would be participating in any new action, should also participate in deciding what that new action should be. The consensus at the end of the week's discussion was that immediate action should be taken on housing, a food cooperative, recreation, welfare, and baby-sitting services. At the next regular meeting of the committee, new work groups, comprising many new members from Operation Snowball, were set up to organize these actions.

VTR AS RECORD

We recorded on tape a number of meetings of various types, but we found that people rarely had the time to view the tapes afterwards. The few members who have taken the time to view old tapes have gained a good deal in self-awareness and in understanding others, as well as in their overall perspective on their own progress.

When the welfare team organized a large demonstration, the action was taped and shown that night at an evaluation session. The participants were excited and thrilled to see their demonstration on the screen, and they made use of the opportunity to view the action in a different perspective and to evaluate it. A few attitudes began to change, especially towards the police, who are held in some fear but who behaved quietly and without menace during the demonstration.

DEMOCRATIZING

One of the things that has disturbed the VTR group is that we have been too privileged in being the ones to use the equipment. It is now being further democratized. For example, members of the VTR group have joined the various other work teams to help them use the VTR in their actions. As well, anyone who expresses interest in joining the VTR group has always been welcomed.

FUTURE PROJECTS

The committee has just obtained a meeting place, the Maison des citoyens, and we intend to run tapes there so that many more of the members can view them and new members will be able to catch up with the others.

Future plans include using video to improve communications between the various working committees, placing the viewer in local shops and taping discussions with people in the neighbourhood, and recording future actions. There is also the possibility of taping reports and research on various institutions in the city, as well as the hope of preparing programs that might be broadcast on public television. Videos will also be used to help young people in the neighbourhood make 8mm films. Courses in history or civil liberties will be dramatized for video presentation.

EVALUATION

In March we taped a meeting of the film-VTR subcommittee in which the use of the video equipment was evaluated. The following quotations, gathered under subjects, are from that discussion:

> ■ Effects on the individual
> "We were not very interested in ourselves when we started."
> "But it helped me a lot to know myself. You see how you function."
> "It helped me gain more confidence in myself. It's important to know who you are."
> "It develops your critical senses. You become two people – he who acts and he who watches himself act."
> "The people we interviewed on the street – I really felt they wanted to

get a message across. They wanted other people to hear about their problems, to share them. People feel pretty isolated."

"I think the people hoped their message would reach the powers-that-be. They had never had the chance before."

"When we watch the tapes, we don't just learn to know ourselves better: we also come to understand others better. After that, it's much more fun to work together."

▪ An organizing tool

"Could we have stopped people in the street and questioned them, the same way if we had not had the camera and microphone? I don't think so. It's a good pretext for talking to them."

"When people were interviewed, they became interested in the committee. Then they came to the public meetings and became involved and eventually joined the team."

"During the public meetings, with the video program, I had the impression that people really recognized the face of the neighbourhood. And they had felt very isolated from one another."

"People are suspicious at first. They don't know if they are free to talk. The video program showed people talking freely, so they saw how far they could go themselves."

▪ Objectivity

"We didn't pretend to be objective, like journalists do."

"Yes, sometimes when we asked questions, we also gave the answers, and when someone didn't know what we were talking about, we gave him the information."

"If someone didn't know how to express himself, we sometimes helped him with the words."

"People could tell it was another citizen like themselves doing the interview, and they had more confidence in us than they would in someone from the CBC or the NFB, or other media. Often the press deforms what is said: they don't transmit exactly what we have to say."

"On the other hand, the people knew they couldn't pull the wool over our eyes. They couldn't try any affectations. With ordinary citizens doing the interviewing, they knew we knew who they were. They couldn't get away with any tall stories."

MASS MEDIA STILL CLOSED TO CITIZENS

Their experience with video – conceiving, shooting, editing, and presenting their own programs – made the citizens particularly aware of the myth of objectivity in mass-media reporting and sensitive to conscious and unconscious manipulation. They have become a less gullible public.

Ordinary citizens have a good deal of difficulty in getting their opinions expressed in the information media. Articles or programs about the committee that have appeared in the local media have almost invariably been distorted pictures. The press seems incapable or unwilling to comprehend the nature or aims of the committee.

On one occasion, the citizens discovered that journalists, who talk loudly of freedom of the press, consider themselves immune from interviews or cameras; they became angry when they became subjects for the citizens' cameras during the press conference for Operation Snowball. They were unwilling to be recorded as individuals and became even more hostile to the citizens.

Hopefully, by using the ½" video equipment enough, a citizens group could eventually propose to their local TV outlet that they make their own programs about themselves to inform the population-at-large about their lives and aims and to help bring about needed changes. Unfortunately, ½" video cannot be transferred to the 2" broadcast video with any degree of technical satisfaction, for the moment. Perhaps technological advances will overcome this obstacle in the near future.

WARNING

We hope that video does not become a mystique. "Communications," with all its glamour and mystification, can become an end in itself rather than a means towards better human lives. Some may want to use it to divert people from their social goals. It could become one more way of avoiding real social change.

It should be clear that community self-awareness and intercommunications are powerful leavening agents and can set off an unpredictable chain of reaction. There must be a real sense of continuity – and a commitment to continuity – if film and video are to be used for real social gain rather than social disaster. Communities cannot be used as guinea pigs for technology.

TECHNOLOGY MUST SERVE THE COMMUNITIES

In St-Jacques, a strongly organized Citizens Committee guaranteed responsibility and continuity. These same video techniques should be used in the early stages of organizing by a community organizer who is committed to staying in the community a certain length of time. Social continuity is essential.

Video should not be used in a vacuum, and it should not be used to divert citizens from their social aims.

CONCLUSIONS

Video does not create dynamism where none is latent. It does not create action or ideas; rather these depend on the people who use video. Used responsibly and creatively, video can accelerate perception and understanding, and therefore accelerate action.

The Comité des citoyens de St-Jacques could have accomplished any of its actions without using video equipment. We cannot say that at any one time video made the difference between success and failure. But it made good things better and helped people to grow, and so we can say it is a useful tool.

Saint-Jérôme: The Experience of a Filmmaker
4 as Social Animator (1968)

■

FERNAND DANSEREAU

Fernand Dansereau, a pioneer of socially engaged filmmaking at the NFB/ONF and a key contributor to SN with his docu-fiction experiment *Tout le temps, tout le temps, tout le temps ... ?* (1969), echoes Hénaut and Klein's comments on the role and responsibilities of filmmakers working within communities. In *"Saint-Jérôme*: The Experience of a Filmmaker as Social Animator" (CFC/SC newsletter, issue no. 2, Fall 1968), Dansereau shares his thoughts on the power of film as an instrument of communication while discussing *Saint-Jérôme* (1968). *Saint-Jérôme*, a collaborative documentary on a small Laurentian city, was the product of Dansereau's Groupe de recherches sociales (Social Research Group), the precursor of Société nouvelle. It provided a model for much subsequent work on issues of class, social welfare, and modernization, as well as a training ground for several SN key players.

A few years ago we shot a film that was intended to be a study of a poor neighbourhood in Montreal – *À Saint-Henri le cinq septembre* (Hubert Aquin, 1962). When the film went into distribution and was televised, it provoked an astonishingly violent negative reaction from the people who had been filmed. They felt debased by our *outsiders'* observations of them. Worse yet, certain people who played a role in the film felt deeply and personally hurt. One of the families that had been filmed, for example, was overcome with a sort of shame so great they decided to remove their children from the local school. Because of the severity of these repercussions, a feeling of deep remorse has remained with me, in spite of our undeniable goodwill.

   In December 1966, the National Film Board again proposed a subject of this kind: a study, in a small town in Quebec, of the way individuals and institutions behave in periods of rapid change. Saint-Jérôme, a town of 35,000 inhabitants, thirty miles from Montreal, was to be our centre of operations.

   To avoid a repetition of what happened in Saint-Henri, I adopted a special principle: I pledged to all the people whom I met (except the politicians) and who could possibly participate in the filming that they would have the right to censor the material that I would shoot with them. That is, at the stage of final editing each of these people would have the privilege of cutting out of his own interviews anything that he no longer liked. I was abandoning myself to their goodwill. I told myself that it was placing the same confidence in them that I was asking them to place in me. We did not start shooting until this confidence was sufficiently established. I then found that I had embarked on a very special type of filming. Because of this initial pledge and because of the human relations that were developing between the filmmakers and the residents of the locality, the major part of the shooting was taking the form of interviews. Any efforts at staging or even creating situations that I tried at the beginning proved false and frustrating, whereas when I simply listened to people without trying to change them or trap them, the quality of the things being said and being lived before the camera attained a rare significance for me.

I sometimes worried about this strange film that was slowly taking shape. It looked a bit like television, which didn't make me particularly happy. But then I simply had to continue. My hope was rooted in the fact that I was to keep on filming for nine months in Saint-Jérôme and that I would surely find a way out of my problems. But in the end the filming retained this characteristic. When, a little later, I attempted to intervene as director, I always had the same feeling of being disrespectful, of unjustified manipulation on my part. The final footage was composed entirely of interviews and events that had authentically happened quite outside my control.

I found myself in the cutting room with 65,000 feet of film and the job of making something out of it. After a good deal of sweat and anguish it became evident to the editor and myself that only one possibility was open to us: to attempt to bring out, through the editing, a perception that would be our own, that could *not* be presented as an objective documentary about the reality of these people. We would attempt to communicate what we felt about them. The film, finally, is two hours long and has indeed taken a very personal view.

During these months of editing, the thing that impressed me most was how much the people, plus all the research we had done, had taught me about myself. I was forced to clarify my ideas on objective problems – economic, sociological, and psychological, of course – but I was also forced, as a total person, to situate myself in the world of today.

We gradually came to feel a strong identification with the people of Saint-Jérôme, in the sense that we shared with them the same confusion over the rapid changes we are living through and the same concern about the need to protect our own fundamental human values without refusing progress.

When I had finished the editing, my position as a Québécois was more important to me than my position as a filmmaker.

On the other hand, with hindsight we realized that our presence in Saint-Jérôme had had an influence in itself, outside that of the film being produced. As an example: we wandered from group to group, asking approximately the same questions, presenting the same interrogation. It seemed to me that this created a new sort of communication between the people and pushed a number of them to analyse their own situations further.

At different stages of filming we invited our principal participants to screen rushes with us. We continued to do so at different stages of editing. This, of course, taught us a great deal and changed us considerably. But it also changed the people. After having seen themselves in the footage as in a sort of mirror, yet one that had all the security that surrounds an event that has been lived, is known, and is past, they were free to criticize themselves and to decide to change themselves if they felt the need. I am speaking, of course, not from a filmmaker's point of view, but from the point of view of the very being of these people. In other words, the screenings could, in certain cases, exercise an effect of collective therapy.

I must add right away, however, that we had never planned to go in this direction. It occurred, when it did occur, as a sort of accident.

Finally, our effort in editing to structure the material, our search for a meaning and rationality in all this footage, may also have played a certain role. Our friends, who were obviously not lacking in structures themselves, found themselves obliged to question their theories and their hypotheses simply because of our approach, and they were obliged to do this in relatively heterogeneous groups. As a consequence, many ideas and emotions were stirred up. This may also explain why the filmmakers at no time received the veto of their close collaborators. The two approaches coincided and grew together, and the film was accepted without difficulty.

We have no proof that the filming exercised a certain influence on the participants. A team of sociologists would have had to accompany us and measure what was happening if we had wanted to have such proof. But we were not looking for any. Let us say that I have always had this very strong impression.

The film is now in distribution. It is long. Most of the time all you can see is people talking. At first we wondered if such a product would have any significance for people other than the citizens of Saint-Jérôme. Our experience in distributing the film seems to indicate that it awakens echoes in all kinds of other Quebec communities. People seem to recognize themselves in it. I am not sure if it would be the same outside of Quebec, but here the sort of liberation in language and reflection that the film provokes seems to have come at the right moment.

As a matter of fact, we have had to invent new distribution methods. Since the film communicates our perception and that of our principal collaborators of the reality we have lived, it seems interesting to reconstitute all the footage as closely as possible to its original state and to offer to viewers a series of satellite films. In this way, the viewers can contest our interpretations and, going back to the beginning, interpret the footage in their own way and do their own editing. During the discussion following the screening of the main film, for instance, the animator, according to the questions that are asked, can refer to one of the satellite films and in this way complement the first perception of reality that the main film had offered.

Of course, this way of using film can rarely be done in commercial theatres, but groups of students, workers, or citizens who wish to reflect on their own situation can find within these films a starting point for their work. This is a young, active, impassioned audience, an audience that is *moving* in society, a choice participant, a real public.

Without particularly trying to, we found ourselves making a film tool. Yet, all added up, the experience was certainly not disagreeable, on the contrary. The filmmaker, in any case, was certainly never bored. The people of Saint-Jérôme brought him, through their actions and sometimes even their words, a certain confirmation – that the filmmaker was a useful person, a person who had a particular aptitude for seeing people and objects and for transmitting, as a reflection, the image of these beings and these things. The image, of course, was coloured by the personality of the filmmaker, but it was that, really, that seemed to be appreciated. At the same time, this experience has offered me confirmation of the aesthetic value and usefulness of the roles of my trade. And I can feel within me the recognition of the people with whom we lived, a recognition infinitely stronger and more durable than that from either critics or an anonymous public. It is they, finally, who assure me of my function as an artist.

A final, technical note: we worked with light equipment, an Éclair camera, Nagra recorder, virtually no lighting. There were three of us. I was able to observe that the cameraman and the sound man were obliged to have a sort of sixth sense, a talent for divination, to work in these conditions. Sometimes I had the impression, when I saw them brusquely turn towards someone just before something happened, that they really had eyes in the back of their heads.

I think it was the quality of the relationships the filmmakers developed with the people that was the essential element. And, in the final analysis, this is the source of beauty in this kind of film. Film is no longer a study in form, but a sudden coinciding of the truths of a moment – an event, a communication – of everything that is cinema and everything that is the reality of people.

A Voice for Canadian Indians: An Indian Film Crew (1968)

5

■

NOEL STARBLANKET

In "A Voice for Canadian Indians: An Indian Film Crew" (CFC/SN newsletter, issue no. 2, Fall 1968), Noel Starblanket, an original member of the first NFB/ONF film crew composed entirely of First Nations youth, speaks candidly about the Board's efforts to develop an "Indian point of view" within CFC/SN (see Stewart, chapter 16, this volume). Starblanket explains his disappointment with the Indian Film Crew, organized in cooperation with the Company of Young Canadians (a government-sponsored youth program, not unlike the U.S. Peace Corps, which operated from 1966 to 1977), and offers both a blunt assessment of the endeavour and his estimation of the future for First Nations filmmakers at the Board.

Eighteen films have been produced about Indians by the National Film Board [NFB], and all of them have been made by *outsiders* looking in on the situation.

Last year the Challenge for Change program included three more films about Indians. These three were not sponsored by any particular government department with a specific message. They were closer to depicting a truer perspective of the "Indian problem." However, these films still lacked a real Indian point of view.

A number of people felt that the next logical step would be to involve Indians as filmmakers. With this in mind, Jerry Gambill (then associate director of the Company of Young Canadians) was asked to seek and recommend young Indian volunteers from across Canada.

In the spring of 1968, the NFB started training a number of people from the Extension Department of Memorial University, St John's, Newfoundland. In order to expedite administration and avoid further tie-ups of professional personnel, the NFB proposed that the Indian crew be sent to Montreal to undertake the training simultaneously. The original plan was a crash course of six weeks, during which time the potential capability and aptitude of the crew could be felt out.

The NFB has anticipated selecting three or four people out of the original seven, but after the initial six weeks it was felt that all the crew merited further training. At the same time, the crew felt that this was the first time the knowledge, opinions, and feelings of Indians were being sought, encouraged, and appreciated by any kind of government agency.

As one phase of their training, the crew shot a film at St Regis Mohawk Reserve, Cornwall, each member of the crew serving in turn as cameraman, director, and interviewer. There was no script for the film, and each member of the crew expressed his own feelings as the work progressed, so that the end result was a collaborative effort in terms of the choice of subjects and how each was handled.

As a result of the individual interest and performance on this location, the members of the crew progressed to more specialized training in each field: Barbara Wilson and Tom O'Connor (camera), Noel Starblanket and Roy Daniels (sound and editing), Willie Dunn and Mike Mitchell (direction and production).

During the next phase, Barbara and Tom accompanied regular NFB location crews as assistant cameramen, Noel and Roy each edited a version of the St Regis footage, and Willie selected and shot footage on archival photographs depicting an Indian history of the West.

The interesting part about the final-cut copies of these two films was that, of all the St Regis film that was exposed, the dominant message projected was that of the laws of the Six Nations Iroquois Confederacy and the Longhouse concepts of peace and brotherhood.

Simultaneously, Willie was cutting his picture material to a song he composed and recorded about Crowfoot, a Blackfoot chief of the 1880s.

While the crew is operating in two groups doing practice shooting, we are also screening the two versions of the St Regis film in various Indian communities and filming the reactions and discussion among audiences. This latter practice will act as a prelude to future projects.

The crew has gone on and is presently developing the following project: Company of Young Canadians involvement in the Lesser and Great Slave Lakes area has volunteers seeking to develop communication between government and people.

A representative organization has been set up to discuss the needs of that area – that is, human resource development. But the machinery of democracy has creaked to a halt – communication broke down, action was deferred, and people were left with their definition of participatory democracy. Social protest marches and demonstrations are the only alternatives left to these people. The Indian Film Crew feels it would be valuable if we could become involved in this struggle. Our purpose? To facilitate communication between the people and the government – to help this Indian community.

Originally the Indian Film Crew project was a joint undertaking between the National Film Board and the Company of Young Canadians, the NFB providing training, production material, and facilities, and the CYC providing minimal living expenses, both in Montreal and on location. However, since the cutback in the CYC's budget, they are now only supporting the crew in Montreal. The lack of funds for travelling has severely limited the crew's activities.

Probably the most discouraging limitation has to do with our dissatisfaction with the present set-up – the CYC-NFB arrangement. There is discontent with lack of funds for location expenses; even though we are becoming semi-professional filmmakers, we exist on the barest of living expenses. We are deeply interested in this communications medium and have discovered that we are dealing with a powerful outlet for emotion and a power that even administrations recognize. Because of our strong feelings about social change, governmental bureaucracy, Indians, etc., because we are a diverse group, because we are individualistic, there is difficulty in preventing the crew from splintering. But a greater danger is not that the group will splinter but that we may not be able to carry on our work with full independence. Our future is not assured. Is a strong, independent voice for the Indians worth supporting?

Vive les sauvages libres!

Fraternally,
#115, Starblanket, Noel

6   Fiction Film as Social Animator (1971–72)

■

INTERVIEW WITH LÉONARD FOREST
BY DOROTHY TODD HÉNAUT

"Fiction Film as Social Animator" (CFC/SN newsletter, issue no. 7, Winter 1971–72) offers a discussion between Dorothy Todd Hénaut and Acadian director, editor, producer, scriptwriter and poet Léonard Forest on the role of film as an organizational tool. In an economically depressed French-speaking area of coastal New Brunswick, politically and linguistically marginalized from the rest of the Maritimes and Canada at large, Forest sought out community leaders and began investigating the benefits of using film as way of organizing the political voices of neighbouring (yet disparate) villages to command the attention of local and provincial governments. The community-scripted feature-length film that resulted, *La noce est pas finie* (1971), was boldly experimental in its hybridization of fiction and documentary, and is unique to this day in the NFB catalogue. In it, the voices of these disenfranchised rural Acadians deal openly with their fears of "development," and their honest hopes for a bright future (see Deslandes, chapter 23, this volume).

DOROTHY TODD HÉNAUT: I'd like to go back to the very beginning. How did you get the idea for doing a fiction film in New Brunswick and where did you get the people? It seems to me that must be really hard.

LÉONARD FOREST: Somebody in New York once described it as a "very sophisticated idea" and I was surprised. I never thought of it that way. It was actually an idea that had been labouring in my mind for a long time in very diverse forms. I thought for some time about making a film on a story being played by actors who would stop now and then to discuss what they were doing and why they were doing it, and did it feel right – did what they were doing correspond in any way to their own real feelings? It was an idea that I could have used with professional actors and we could have tried it out.

But, then, it happened that I was also concerned with my home, New Brunswick, and the Acadians there. Knowing that region somewhat, I was already aware of the political, social, and economic problems. I had quite a bit of information even by that time, enough elements to know that the film I wanted to make was possible there. So, with this film idea in mind, I went down there one spring, to northeastern New Brunswick, and renewed contact with the people (I had shot sequences there for my previous film).

So I met with some of these people and met quite a few others, including what we call a social animator who had been working there for two or three years on a kind of very open-ended social animation. At that time, the government had animators all over the place, getting people to talk and getting people together. They didn't know what the hell was going to happen. Well, especially in this area where I later shot my film, it really worked: this guy (the animator) came down and very modestly, very quietly had people talk about their problems. He never programmed them to be ready to accept government plans. He really wanted to find out what *they* wanted – and they took it seriously.

Northeastern New Brunswick is economically a very depressed area of the Maritimes – and that's saying a lot because the whole of the Maritimes is depressed! This is a solid Acadian population and they are outside the main line of economic development; they just don't exist for the rest of the province, except at election time. These people were ready, I felt, to participate in this kind of film I was hoping to make. I felt they were ready because they had the habit, by then, of getting together and talking about their problems, using words expressing a lot of things – their fears, their hopes, their aspirations – all sorts of things. They had at least a basic habit of doing this exercise of learning to express themselves.

The idea of the film was still a difficult proposition. But the thing that really set it off for me was an event that happened at Tracadie, a small town up there, on a Sunday afternoon. All the local committees of the whole county – the citizens committees that had been formed by the underprivileged of the area – got together at a general meeting. They called it "le congrès des pauvres," meaning "don't tell us any more lies – we're poor and this is our congress."

So I attended this meeting and I sat there with the social animator as kind of a mysterious guest from the film world. These people were way beyond being impressed by a filmmaker. They didn't care. They had invited all the local members of Parliament too, and not one came, and [all] the priests, and not one came.

But they held their meeting. They split up into a number of subcommittees, one of which I attended. I was absolutely fascinated by this new thing – that they could talk. This committee was presided over by an elderly man who has his Grade 3 but is the most real radical I have met in Canada, a quiet radical, a thinking radical. He says one word every three hours but that word counts. In presiding over the meeting he would say, "That's your opinion and now you must give this other person a chance to express his opinion" – and it was beautiful democracy at work.

But the real thing was when all the committees came together in the big hall. There had been student volunteers to take minutes of each discussion. They came up one by one to read their notes, and suddenly the minutes started coinciding – and you knew that there had been no lying. There were the same facts, the same grievances, the same explanations of injustices they had had from social assistance, from MPs ... and suddenly it was [there] for everybody, the proof that they were right.

That was the day I said to myself: You've got to make this film, even if it's a flop in film terms, in aesthetic terms. You've got to make it. It's the only thing you can do to help these people, to show that you really care. And that is the spirit in which I started the whole damn thing: that it could be a complete flop but it was better to make a flop with these people than to make a success with other things, and they deserved it; they were real people.

DH: Did you present the idea of the film at that meeting?

LF: No, it wasn't important at that moment. What they were doing was more important.

DH: Well, how did you go about proposing the film?

LF: I don't remember, quite. I just kind of came back to the area, quietly, with a little help from my friends, and started the ball rolling very quietly and asked people whether they were interested. First, it was two or three people I had been introduced to by this social animator – a few people I knew beforehand. We started talking about it over the counter of a store ... a woman who played in the film was the storekeeper ... her husband was the stationmaster ... and another person. They said yeah, it could be fun, it might be interesting. And then a group formed; I can't even describe how it formed. At our first meeting there were a few people. Then others came who were interested.

The project had up to that time been very abstract for me: just that I would go and work with a group of what you'd call ordinary citizens to make a feature-length film, a story film; that it would be conceived and written with them, based on their own preoccupations, ideals, dreams – whatever came out. Now, I didn't know what would come out. There was also the idea that as we made the fiction, we could reflect on the fiction, that we would stop the process periodically and say, "What are we doing? Why are we doing it? Is the fiction going as far as reality goes, or not as far?" And that would be part of the film, too. So there would be two parallel things: the fiction and reflection.

DH: So you began with a group that had a social animator. Was the animator still with the group?

LF: He was with the group until the moment the film started. That was a very interesting thing. By himself, he decided to disappear after I came. When the first meeting jelled, he said, "Well, I have to go on vacation," and I asked why, as I thought he would be part of the thing. He only explained it when he came back after the last night of shooting. We had invited him to come and share in the excitement of the end of production, and the people were very happy to see him back, too. Afterwards, he told me, "I disappeared because you had become the social animator and there should not be two working at the same time."

When the crew and I left, he came back; the people were not left alone. He is a terrific guy, unpretentious, unintellectual. He has travelled and had many experiences and he's just *with* the people completely. For the Establishment, he's dynamite. They've tried all kinds of ways to get rid of him – including violence. The violence that you see in the film, they tried on him after the film.

What helped me a lot was my role as filmmaker. The Establishment [in Tracadie] is very small, a few people, and they just didn't take us seriously, you know. "What's this guy doing with these poor crummy people?" they said. "It just won't work." At our meetings, we weren't exclusive. At the first meeting, there was a lawyer – we had invited him. A doctor came – he came to one meeting. He was bored with all the discussions, all this crap about democracy. "All that talk will get you nowhere." He didn't come to any other meetings. He wasn't excluded; he excluded himself. Right up until the last minute, people said, "What's this crazy bunch of poor people doing pretending they're making a film?

When I told the group at the end, as a filmmaker, that it was "in the can," that we had made our film, they were so damned proud. You see, in the beginning I had told them, "This is a project. You can have a project to build a school or make a bridge or make a feature-length film." And they were so happy that they had completed it. It was true; it was shot. Even at that point then, before the film was even edited, we had accomplished something important.

But I am trying to tell you too many things at the same time. Maybe, I should tell you exactly how I proceeded. Take into account that I must have been a little bit crazy! I had renewed contact with the region in spring or early summer. I had decided the film was possible and I wanted to do it because they deserved it.

So I came back to Montreal and submitted the idea to the program committee. All I could do was describe the idea. I finally ended up with an okay and a budget. The budget was extremely precise; it gave me a total of six weeks preparation! Six weeks to work with the group, arrive at a script, and organize the shooting. On the first day of the seventh week we had to start shooting: the crew would be arriving and we would have exactly four-and-a-half weeks to shoot by union standards (i.e., an eight-hour day, five days a week).

So then I went out all by myself to find people from two citizens committees in Lamèque and Shippagan, which are separated by a bit of water and two centuries of quarrelling. They had never had a common project together. Plus a few students, some of whom I had known before from neighbouring villages, Tracadie and Caraquet.

So I had my six weeks to get a group together, get a script together, and organize to shoot a feature-length story film. So I got my groups together and we talked – that's all we did, we talked. One of the local girls, who acted as script girl and secretary and everything, took notes. I didn't know what would come out of it. I didn't know what the story would be. I knew what my idea of their basic concerns was but I didn't know what *they* would decide were their basic concerns. I would say. "Is it going to be the conflict between generations? Is it going to be the Pill? Is it going to be Love?" So I just sat and talked and asked questions and directed the conversations in some ways, always trying to find out what their concerns were. After a while I discovered that it always came back to the same basic themes: the feeling of being impotent because of political powers; the feeling that they could never take any initiative because if they had, it was blocked. They were humiliated by welfare assistance; they knew that even welfare assistance was politicized. It always came back to those things.

Sometimes I tried to get them onto themes that interested me, like: Why the hell do you want to live *here* in all this misery? – because I could sense their basic love for the sea and all kinds of things. They would say a few words but then they would go back to their own stories. So, after a few weeks of reading these notes every night, it was quite obvious to me that they really had built a story without knowing it, by telling me very precise incidents. For example, in the film, a tent is burned at one point. Well, they had schools, other government buildings, and private property that were burned.

I'm not a specialist at psychodrama or anything, but we tried a few little situations of putting two or three people together and saying, "Let's pretend that you are this or that." And some things just clicked. They immediately

entered into the characters, and it was good. The dialogue that they improvised was great.

At the beginning, I had told them, "I'm not going to pretend to be one of
you. I'm not going to hide behind the woodwork. I'm a filmmaker and a
writer, and I'm going to work with you to make a film." One day, I said, "Well,
here's what you've been telling me." I had put it down on paper, three or
four pages. I remember that morning – I don't normally eat much in the
morning, and that morning I didn't eat at all! I walked along the bay and I
almost vomited what I hadn't eaten. You know, it would either work or it
wouldn't work – and *they* were deciding. If they didn't like it, there would
be nothing for me to do but pack my bags and come back to Montreal. So
we sat down and I told them the story.

There was a long, long silence. And then, women being braver always, it
was a woman who put her hand up and said, "Monsieur Forest, c'est nous,
ça." That's us. And from that moment on, it was work. Then we started saying, "Well, this sequence, it wouldn't happen quite like that."

DH: What is the story? The only thing I know about it is that it is the effect
of a stranger on the population.

LF: I can't tell the story because it developed so organically that I don't think
of it as a story any more. It developed out of one of those little psychodra-
mas we were talking about. It had come out of the blue, or out of conversation, and we said, "Let's try it." Something about a new teacher who is a
non-conformist, in a situation of conflict with his principal, and the chairman
of the school board being referee. They got right into it; it was fantastic.

But the story as it finally developed involves this guy who comes myste-
riously to fill a teaching position. Nobody knows exactly why he was hired
ahead of others who had more qualifications. Actually, it was only when we
were shooting the film that we filled in why this happened. We talked about
it, and people improvised things. It happens finally that he has been hired as
a political favour to his father. He's not an activist in any way; he's an easy-
going, long-haired, guitar-playing, song-making guy who just walks into the
village and plays himself. And, without his wanting to do anything, things
start happening just because he's too real, too honest. And then it explodes
into all kinds of things, politics intervening, social assistance. Suddenly, the
politicians find themselves caught in this position: that they've hired him,
they have to protect him, and they're caught in their own game.

EP: And the next stage for you was ...

LF: Well, the next stage was: now we've got a story, so we've got to do it. I'm
going to play the role of director and set it up. Then I said, "I'm going to sit

Citizen scriptwriters/performers in Léonard Forest's *La noce est pas finie* (1972): "... it was beautiful democracy at work." Frame enlargement.

down for three days and I don't want to see you. I'm going to make a production calendar and choose locations." I chose the actors in front of the people. I'd say, "I think so-and-so should play such a role." As it's strange, there were no conflicts, nothing. The only people who felt sad were those who didn't get a role the first day – but they all knew that they would get a role eventually. So that was fun.

And then we set it up: Monday morning, we'll shoot here, and Tuesday, outdoors. And if it rains, we'll shoot inside, there. Like a conventional feature film. The only difference was that these people were going to play roles; there was no written script, just a synopsis. They made up the dialogue as we shot each scene and they brought to it everything that they know of their own milieu. They were the experts on the milieu. We reshot only a few scenes with the sophisticated parts; we might do a sequence a second time after a rest. The camera would be almost a newsreel camera covering the thing that happened.

I was constantly surprised at the way people got into the roles: not one of them failed me as an actor.

One of my basic hypotheses had been as people played out these roles they would discover things about themselves – in telling the story they would discover meanings they didn't know were there. Nonetheless, I was continually surprised at the way the most unexpected people would begin to improvise, identifying with the roles. In one of our few retakes, I had one little girl who cried twice.

DH: There were changes in people during shooting, then, in terms of strengthening and articulating. But what effect did the finished film have on them and on other people in the area?

LF: All I know so far is what happened at the *avant-première*. The film was screened at Bathurst, which is the biggest place in the area. This had all been discussed ahead of time. Two representatives had come to Montreal to see the cutting copy and attend the editing for a week. They went back and told the group what happens in the editing process. Then we set up a screening in Bathurst and we invited all the people, including many of the poor. They filled the place twice in one night and still many could not get in. Which meant about sixteen to eighteen hundred saw the film in one night, and they were very enthusiastic. And the Establishment, not being that numerous (even though it's very strong), was drowned. If they wanted to criticize the film, they had to identify with the bad guys. The only way they found to put down the film later was to say, "This was only made by these poor trash!" They never discussed it head-on.

Beyond that, a [woman named] Hortense Roy from Société nouvelle came down, and one thing she noticed was that at the reception afterwards (everyone was invited) people would come up to me, and instead of saying, "Congratulations," they would say, "Thank you."

It was broadcast three weeks later on the French [CBC] network at 11:30 at night – that's 12:30 in New Brunswick. That's the only time.

DH: The first two NFB films cut by commercials on CBC were Société nouvelle films – this one and another one.

LF: It seemed so immoral to see real film about people in poverty intercut by commercials for finance companies, or a new fridge or a new car. It would be interesting to ask the people how they felt about it!

One thing Société nouvelle has organized – the film is being shown seventeen or twenty nights in a row in different centres of that region. Two of the participants are present at every screening, as well as a college-trained man who acts as projectionist and recording feedback. This way the process can continue. Whether it's liked or not liked, the film has to be shown.

An interviewer from the CBC in Moncton went around after the premiere talking to people. She felt the film had hit something.

DH: What kind of concrete changes is the film experience going to make there?

LF: A friend of mine, a sociologist, who has been working for the Department of Regional Economic Expansion during the past month, calls it "consciousness raising." I think it's the only thing you achieve, and once that is done, people go on to something else. Or they don't. If they don't, then it's their responsibility. You just help them to bring these things out in the open, to express them. I feel that to have playacted their fears was a great experience, because they saw them in sharper focus.

Everything became so real. The characters … George, the teacher, was so real that at the end of the film it was like a wake among the group. His tent had been burned and his car had left in a hurry. Was he going down to the village to break somebody's nose? Was he going back to Montreal? And that was the question I put to them for the last bit of shooting: What's George going to do? Is he going to stay? Has he left? And somebody said, "Well, I think he's probably left because it is understood that if he continues, worse things are going to happen." And someone else said, "He can't leave because, if he leaves, once again he'll be proven wrong by leaving." And Mme Basque said – and she has the last word in the film – "I have lived all my life in fear, but I am growing old and I don't want to do that anymore. We can't go back along the old paths. We must find new solutions."

EP: Have you heard any echoes since the showing? Have you been back?

LF: It would take a multiple Gallup poll to figure out a region like that right now. But a few years will tell more.

It was agreed when we decided on the multiple [screenings] I mentioned earlier that I should not be there, I should not influence the process. People should be free to say, "This is a stinking film. We don't like it."

One thing which happened, by coincidence really, was that the day after the screening in Bathurst there was a meeting of all the citizens committees of that region. And somebody who was there said that there had been tremendous change. The people came and said, "Well, now we've said it. We've blamed all the injustices. And now we're going ahead to find positive solutions." I was very happy that this was possible for them.

EP: How about the time lapse between shooting and screening? Did this affect the people in any way?

LF: The people from the main group, the people who had really gone into the film project fully, with confidence, were not worried. I maintained contact with them – not in any Boy Scout way – I didn't send a letter every week. The girls came up to see the editing at my suggestion, and I went down to see them once to say that I was working at it. But the other people around, of course, started rumours: that it would never come out, that it was being censored. They were confirming the things that the people were saying in the film!

Some people who were important in the film continued their own action. I think Mme Basque may have been in some ways encouraged. She was invited to Ottawa representing the poor of New Brunswick, and she spoke to the Senate Committee on Poverty with great courage and frankness. She went to other meetings and became a spokesman for her region. Now, whether the film had anything to do with that or whether I'm just lucky to have her in the film, I don't know.

When the film came back, it came back as an event – an event that they were shareholders in. They were proud to see that it had succeeded. They had proven something to the Establishment people who had said it would not succeed, that it was going to be censored, that it would not be worth showing.

EP: What about yourself? Do you think the experience changed you?

LF: I think it did but I couldn't say how. Perhaps it relaxed me toward people. I realize that people are so capable of doing things that they don't even realize themselves. The greatest lesson I learned there was that these people were able to become actors, which I think is a great accomplishment. For a person to play a role requires a great degree of control over emotions and self – and a great generosity, too. These people all played the game and I think they were only able to do that out of some basic feeling for "play" in its best sense. They were able to play, and liked it. Now, what they are going to play afterward is their real roles in life.

EP : What has happened to your own approach to film? Anything?

LF: The only thing I *can't* do right now is to make a sequel to that film; there is no point in making another film on the same level. What I hope is that these people will be ready soon – and I think the young people are going to join with them – to invent their own future. I think they'll find that they don't have to care anymore about the politicians and the bureaucrats and the people who are planning their future out of strange capitals. I think once they reach that stage they can invent their own society: maybe they don't need industry the way people think they need it. Maybe they just need to create a new society.

DH: It seems to me that one of the key things about the project, aside from the effect of the "stranger" that you had, was the really delicate balance between *your* drive and your expertise and *their* drives and their expertise.

LF: Yeah, I like that.

I showed the film at a recent conference in New York. The film being in French, I gave a running commentary – and between the reels – which from an aesthetic standpoint would, I thought, destroy the film. But people stayed to the end and asked questions. The next day I heard a sociologist from Chicago explaining the film to people in a workshop. He said, "I didn't understand the dialogue but it spoke to me as a film. I understood the process." These were new concepts for him.

DH: I was interested in getting at things a little outside the film. When are the people going to be able to get into action and what kinds of action are feasible?

LF: We must respect their liberty to the extent that we don't worry about that. I used to worry about that. I don't even know what my motives were, my deep-down motives. I only know the motives I can talk about. But some of them seem good, and some I don't know. But I had to take this risk: that the people would tell their story. And if they didn't want to tell it, there would be no film. And in the same way, now, their story is going to continue – and it's none of my business. It's going to be *their* story. All I can hope is that this film is going to be just one little element that will help them to flush out complexes or obstacles to their further development.

EP: Would you consider a request from animators in another area to do the same thing with them?

LF: I would certainly not do it before I met the people. I would entertain the idea inasmuch as I met people who were ready to enter into that process – and I think that these people were just ready by some chance. By some coincidence of my film project and their interest, the film was possible. They were just at the right level to get into this adventure. They were willing to take a certain risk at that point in order to achieve something further. It was shared risk. I was risking almost my career as a filmmaker, in a way. They were risking a ton of things too. They were risking reprisals; they were risking being catalogued as subversives and radicals.

EP: They also risked being made to look ridiculous.

LF: Yeah, it's the *first* risk one has to take.

7
Working with Film: Experiences with a Group
of Films about Working Mothers (1975)

■

KATHLEEN SHANNON

ELIZABETH PRINN

DORIS MAE OULTON

IRENE ANGELICO

"Working with Film: Experiences with a Group of Films about
Working Mothers" (CFC/SN newsletter, issue no. 14, Spring 1975)
offers a conversation between Kathleen Shannon, Elizabeth Prinn,
Doris Mae Oulton, and Irene Angelico – key figures involved with
the Working Mothers series, itself a forerunner of the NFB's Studio
D (the first permanent, state-funded women's film unit in the world).
Shannon, producer of the series and its guiding light, leads a discussion on a range of subjects, including the importance of carving
out a space for women on-screen and establishing an alternative
space for audiences to discuss the issues raised by films that examine
the lives of everyday Canadian women (see Fraticelli, chapter 29,
this volume).

PREFACE

Doris Mae Oulton, Kathleen Shannon, Elizabeth Prinn, and Irene Angelico
met together in January to explore the meaning of the Working Mothers
workshops. By this time, Kathleen had conducted a number of workshops
herself and participated in others. So had Elizabeth, who also had had many
years' experience with media and workshop design before joining the Challenge for Change program three years ago. Irene had been conducting seminars – entitled "Women's Place, Man's Place" – at Sir George Williams
University, and at the time this tape was made, she was co-directing and co-
editing a Working Mothers film, "... *and They Lived Happily Ever After*"
(1975). Doris Mae, who had coordinated Phase I of the distribution of Working Mothers films, was by this time coordinator of the community development program at Algonquin College in Ottawa.

THE DISCUSSION

KATHLEEN SHANNON: I'd like to give you an example of how people filter everything through their own perception and their own experience. I've had four different comments about *They Appreciate You More* (1974). One person said, "You can really tell that Aliette is the strong one and that she dominates him, because when he says something, he looks at her to check it out." Another said, "The roles haven't changed at all; he's still the boss, and she checks out everything she says with him." Someone else said, "The camera must have made them really nervous because they keep looking at each other all the time." And another said, "What I like best about that film is that you can see how much they love each other because they keep gazing into each other's eyes."

ELIZABETH PRINN: That may be a good way to introduce an animators' workshop ...

KS: ... you use whatever people have said ...

DORIS MAE OULTON: ... and help them take it a little further.

EP: The reason I asked you to meet me today is this: we have a great deal of information about the *kinds* of things that can occur when the films are used successfully. But we haven't said what is *happening*. What is the difference between a workshop and a screening? What are the qualities of a good animator? I'm hoping this issue of [the CFC/SN newsletter] will help animators be a little bit better, whatever stage they're at.

KS: What about the idea that everybody is on a path but it has bends in it, so you can't see around the next bend. And you can easily forget who you were behind that last bend ...

EP: ... or that the paths diverge sometimes and people go off in what seem to be different directions and come back to join again with people they had perceived as being further ahead or further behind.

DMO: It seems that the most valid way we approached the workshops goes back to that [mathematical] nine-dot exercise. If their only input is a film, you come, you see, you go away. But if there is some way of getting people outside the box they have built for themselves, or that other people have built for them, you can expand your perceptions of yourself, your perceptions of other people. You become more open to the people around you and to what the film is saying.

EP: And the role of the animator is not to stand there with the pen and say, "Do you want me to show you how to do it?" but to provide people with the pen and help them discover it themselves.

KS: There's another thing. The animator has to Listen with a capital L. Something has happened to me a number of times that I'd like to mention. Here's an example: I saw *They Appreciate You More* with a particular group. It was the two thousand and first time I'd seen it, maybe. At one point in the discussion I thought, That isn't what she means. What she is really saying is ... I heard a different way than I'd ever heard before. But I didn't say anything. The two other people in the group said, "You know, what she really was saying was ..." What came to me from some part of my unconscious had occurred to two other people in the group. There are dynamics at work that we really haven't pinned down, that you can't deliberately set in motion. But the currents are there if you can pick them up.

EP: Yes, I've done exercises in another context, exercises in meditation and imagery ... And four people would come up with the same turtle, or some other archetypical image. The collective unconscious at work?

KS: Yes.

EP: A common problem I find for some people is – as one person said to me – "I feel I have to choose between laying my trip on other people or putting a padlock on my mouth." They don't perceive the possibility of Listening with the capital L and responding to what they hear, to help it go further when it starts to stumble.

IRENE ANGELICO: I've learned that my opinion isn't the important thing and that each particular comment is not the important thing. I don't have to react with some statement that will "put this person in the right place." The importance is bringing out the individual, to be somewhat "impersonal" so that she/he can be personal. I make myself a "focus" for the people. Perhaps that isn't the right term. Perhaps what I'm trying to get across is this: the animator needs to be a "sounding board." When two people are talking together about something that's very personal, it's hard for them to hear what they're saying *themselves*. If there's someone in a more neutral position, like an animator, I think you can hear yourself better by directing a statement to *that* person. Otherwise, you're inclined to be busy trying to convince a listener of your opinion. People can hear themselves better, learn about their changing ideas, if they're not worried about someone coming back at them and saying, "No, you're wrong."

KS: I stand up, for example, so people can have someone to speak to. When I was sitting down "democratically," then it degenerated to people talking to each other in little groups – the larger group disappeared so to speak.

IA: I remove myself a little bit so that I can have an overview. And it's very important to have one so that when a particular point of view is being over-played and another one neglected, I can say, "Why don't we talk about this?" Even if it's a point of view I'm not particularly interested in but which could be important to the discussion.

KS: And from that position you can know that if you bring it up at a certain moment, it's going to fire off a lot of other things.

IA: In the beginning, when I was doing the seminar, I really shied away from asking direct questions of people who weren't participating, because I didn't want to manipulate them. I really didn't want to impose myself. I, too, had been very shy at one time. But now, I really think it's important to draw peo-ple out, even if it's scary for them for the first few moments. You're saying to them, "I'm interested in your opinions." When I do that, I find by the end of the period that everyone is participating.

KS: One of the things I think you have to establish at the beginning, some-how, is that there isn't one right answer. That's what's so scary: you're asked what you think and you don't know what is "right" to think this time!

DMO: One way to do that is to refrain from feeling that there *are* right answers which you know ahead of time ...

EP: ... you have to really mean it ... (laughter)

DMO: That really projects. If what you're doing is trying to get a group to come up with an answer you've already perceived, that will colour what hap-pens with the group.

KS: This is really important to emphasize. You've got to be willing to have the end result [be] something quite different from what you've anticipated. In just the same way as the films don't tell you what to think, the animator can't tell you what to think either.

EP: One animator said to me that two or three of the films "don't work." I said, "Well, I have to tell you that all of them *have* worked." (Of course, they don't work every time, even for the best of us.) (laughter)

DMO: In a training program I've been working in, training animators, we've made one thing very clear: it's not just a matter of understanding techniques, like the nine-dot exercise. That's part of it – you've got to have the tools to work with. The point is that you've got to know how to work with them. You've got to be flexible. You've got to take that exercise and that particular arrangement of people and really adapt to the situation, adapt to the answers that are coming out.

KS: You have to be willing to change every moment.

EP: The analogy that comes to my mind is a gardening analogy. You simply have to take a look at what needs to be done in the garden before you decide what tool you're going to use. The garden tells you; the plants tell you. You have to listen. You can't walk out of the house in the morning with a hoe in your hand and, when you discover pruning is what's needed, start pruning with a hoe. You change your tool. So, in animation, you take a whole kit of tools and see what's needed as you go along. The more tools you have, the more flexible you can be.

DMO: You can come up with the best, most expertly designed workshop in the world and it may not work with a particular group, because every group is different. You've got to learn to adapt to what's happening within that context.

EP: One thing, then, that someone has to learn when she's beginning animation of groups is to take risks.

DMO: Sure, you try to see what works.

KS: And if something doesn't work, it's no great loss. It isn't school; you won't be punished with a bad mark. And I haven't seen a situation where someone's life was going to be destroyed because a workshop didn't work.

DMO: But that brings me to another point I want to talk about and that's accountability. If you stir up people's emotions, where are they to go next?

IA: Yeah, I had some experiences that made me sit back and say to myself, "Look. Know what you're doing because you're really having an impact." Of course, you're not *totally* responsible.

KS: The time when someone points it out to me, I was grateful. There were people whose minds had jumped several levels that night. He said, "You know you can't just walk away with the films and leave no continuity." So we said, "Why don't you go on and meet again with some of the other films, use them as an occasion to meet."

EP: I've noticed in a number of situations that people within the group may respond to the needs of someone – the leader, if it's an ongoing group, or other members.

DMO: I think we should speak of one of the things we emphasized when we were first planning workshops: we were not trying to do a sensitivity group process in any way. I think that has proved valid. When there starts to be a group judgment of right and wrong or group attack on one individual, you're getting onto dangerous ground. We're not trained for it; we shouldn't be getting into it. So it's important to emphasize responsibility to see that this is *not* happening. If people are going to be prepared to take risks in that group, they have to be sure they will have the support that is necessary. They have to be able to take risks without having to defend what they just said.

KS: It's a supportive atmosphere we're trying to encourage.

DMO: That's a result of being able to Listen and to adapt, the qualities we talked about before.

KS: Part of what we're all about in these groups is to try to open ourselves to understand how other people feel and where they're at …

DMO: … not necessarily force them to change …

KS: Agreed. It's their business where they are. They're sharing it. And we have no right to tell them where they should be.

EP: It seems to be if the animator relates to the films in judgmental terms, it sets the scene for relating to each *other* in judgmental terms.

KS: Maybe we should say something to the effect that people who feel they know what's right for the world and how to change it should disqualify themselves as animators.

IA: If you think you're like that, get someone else to do the animation. You can run the projector.

EP: What about the whole question of imposing structure? Some people hesitate to do that. Yet the minute you arrange a workshop in a theatre, structure is in those rows of seats, with everyone facing away from everyone else, or facing people's backs. If you're accepting leadership in a situation, I think it's valid to accept with it the right to *change* the structure.

KS: You can provide new structures. The triads for example: they provide the kind of structure that's sometimes needed for discussion to start.

DMO: If people are locked into a structure that is unproductive, you can use another structure to "get outside the box."

IA: Every room has a structure that can affect what's going to happen, and if you're going to be an animator, you may have to juggle things so that things happen *between* people. My seminar was set up in a semicircle. Recently, I saw someone lecturing in a huge hall at the university, the worst possible place for conversation, with a stage in front. First she brought everybody down to the front – "Everybody, come down so we can talk to each other" – and then she came down from the stage to talk *to* the audience, not *at* them. So even though the physical setting was very, very bad for discussion, she changed things. She talked leaning forward toward the audience, bringing them together with her gestures.

DMO: The thing I want to see us make clear is [that] structure exists. It's part of nature. So the animator shouldn't hesitate to read the structure that's implicit in all kinds of things – the physical setting, the arrangement of furniture, how long you've got, how well you know each other. When she comes in, she must read that hidden structure in order to see when she might want to intrude another structure. You need to learn something about body politics. You spoke of someone who was leaning into the audience, using gestures, really good gestures, gestures of welcoming. If you want to encourage people to speak you have to appear open; you don't sit with your arms folded and legs crossed and a frown on your face. It almost goes without saying – but it's important to say it. If someone has difficulty speaking, just leaning toward them can be a supportive gesture. If you have a group that is scattered around, moving them together is almost mandatory if you want them to communicate. Appearing physically relaxed is also really important. We need to know that, but of course it isn't likely to happen unless you really are relaxed.

EP: And that can be helped by not having a stake in a *particular* outcome.

IA: Maybe it's wanting not to impose your views but rather to open the people up, or to help them open themselves up.

EP: You can't school yourself to appear open. People "hear" you. So maybe with these films we can create a situation which is in a good place, in between a propaganda situation and a "sensitivity" situation.

KS: I think a feeling to try to transmit to people is that we all have things to learn from each other.

EP: Even the people who think they have a firm grip on their lives are probably changing. (laughter)

KS: Life is not static and rigid. So even when you think you know what is best for everybody, remember that each person is different from minute to minute.

DMO: The only thing we *know* is best for everybody is that they should not be static and rigid.

KS: Ever! (much laughter)

EP: We did an exercise in Hamilton that I liked very much. We moved from the theatre structure – me alone with that woman on the screen – to exercises where we just talked to one or two people. Talking in triads about what were the most important issues that had been raised for us by the film.

KS: And the introductions! I found them just incredible! There was one occasion, in Hamilton, where I slipped back into the old way, you know: fifty minutes have gone by and we haven't looked at a film yet! But then I remembered, No, this is what we're trying to do. People need to know who else is there in order to be able to talk. Yet if people introduce *themselves*, they tend to give, you know, name, rank, and serial number. For some it's excruciatingly painful to say, I'm so and so. Instead we had people talk to each other in pairs and then introduce their partner to the others. What happens is just extraordinary. Because people will say, "What I was really interested to hear from so-and-so was ..." You get a picture of who that person is, or one part of them anyway.

IA: I've tried, "Introduce the person you're talking to by saying why they're here." Or, "Tell us five personal things about them." I use that approach with the class I have now.

KS: Well, you can use it in an even deeper way if people have been together before. I used to begin the "easy" way by introducing the Film Board person who was there. I found I didn't always know much about them either, really.

EP: Do you know what happened to me at one workshop? The women I spoke with was so flabbergasted that I was interested in *her*, she forgot to find out much about me! She said, "I never had anyone ask me about myself before."

KS: This is true for a lot of women, I think, when they're not going to be able to say whose wife they are or whose mother they are. And in Hamilton, the fifty minutes was no waste. People introduced each other in such a way that it said, I really value this person. And that set the tone for the whole workshop. It was a beautiful atmosphere in there.

EP: What happened to me by the end of that fifty minutes was a feeling that there is so much good energy in women and it is so close to the surface.

DMO: What we haven't mentioned, and I think we should, is that our input to the workshop is a temporary kind of thing – what has to happen is the identification of resources internal to that group.

KS: If it is a group. And if it isn't a group, and the situation is supportive enough, people can begin to identify other people who have resources that they need, people they can follow up.

8

Memo to Michelle about Decentralizing the Means of Production (1972)

■

Balancing the unrestrained optimism of the insider accounts offered elsewhere in this section is insightful commentary offered by NFB founder Grierson himself. "Memo to Michelle about Decentralizing the Means of Production" (CFC/SN newsletter, issue no. 8, Spring 1972) finds Grierson speaking on a range of topics, including technology (particularly the 8mm film format), documentary ethics, and the place of CFC/SN within the NFB's broader mandate as an information service. The piece serves as an interesting parallel (and in some ways an important corrective) to Low's remembrances of Grierson's point of view introduced in chapter 2 and foreshadows the study of the Indian NGO Deccan Development Society presented in the final chapter of this collection (Mulay, chapter 38). It was written at a time when the retired Grierson had returned to Canada to serve as a lecturer at McGill University in Montreal and was actively re-familiarizing himself with the output of the Board.

You will remember (*Benedictus benedicat*) Zavattini's idea of arming the Italian villages with cameras so they could send film letters to each other. This means, in or out of Italy, handing down the means of larger public expression to the people at the grassroots.

With cameras becoming smaller and lighter and easier to work and cheaper to buy, the decentralizing of filmmaking becomes an ever more practical possibility. We see it happening with home movies, with moviemaking in research departments, with teaching organizations who make their own films without benefit of clergy.

I have been watching it even more widely manifest in the undergraduate circles of the American universities, where the young people have declared for an "8mm revolution."

Much is claimed – and rightly – for the technical range of "Super 8." But I am skeptical. It troubles me to see people loosely waving a camera around. It is like loosely waving a baby around; for the camera, like the baby, has its rights. I shudder at all catch-as-catch-can film approaches, even when they claim to be catching a falling star. I find it odd that university teachers should spread the doctrine that shooting film any-old-how absolves the student from all need to read and write.

I am told that with the 8mm revolution we have a therapeutic tool of importance: that the youth will not only learn automatically to observe but – o fabulous joy – will also find the magical secret of "play" and "loving contact" with their neighbours.

There is something in this, but there are cheaper and more obvious ways of teaching or inducing observation and collaboration.

There was never a miracle road to observation, whatever passing priests like Mr McLuhan may say. "Look you, François," said de Maupassant to his servant. "To see well and distinguish well, one's eyes must be trained, and to get to that point one must notice everything when one is looking. Never be satisfied with 'almost everything,' give one's eyes all the time necessary to see everything that has to be noted, to define things well, to rout out the things one does not see very well; and it is only by long and patient exercise that one arrives at the point of being able to get from one's eyes all that they are capable of. Even the best artists must take great pains to form their eyes so that they will be really good and serviceable."

Whatever accounts of observation (and of form) you heed, you will soon have left most of our 8mm revolutionaries far behind. And you needn't depend on classical accounts that are identical in de Maupassant and Plato.

There is equally excellent, and again identical, guidance to be got from Paul Klee.

What I hear most about in North America is that the 8mm revolution will provide a magical path to what is all too loosely called self-expression. There are philosophical uses of the term which mean a great deal; but the way I hear it, it is more often a refuge from the normal disciplines of work (yes, and observation and collaboration). There are times again when self-expression means self-indulgence and this often at the expense of others. This matters, very much matters, where self-indulgence means public hurt. Perhaps it doesn't much matter in the midst of North American affluence but the anxiety for self-expression may weaken the political fibre of the next generation. In poorer countries, self-indulgence, involving the selfish use of a valuable means of public instruction and public expression, presents a simple and nauseous example of bad taste.

As you see, I am in a dilemma as I look on the potential of the 8mm revolution and see what, in some quarters, they are doing about it. I am all for easier cameras, lenses et al. I am all for the 8mm revolution, so long as the 8mm mind doesn't go with it. I came across a new word the other day: neaniolatry, meaning, they tell me, "infatuation with the immature." It seems to me that we have got the 8mm revolution all mixed up with this "neaniolatry" at the North American universities.

Having noted this, let us not be put off by it. There are other more vital paths for the 8mm revolution.

The National Film Board of Canada, for one example, is engaged in a more considered effort at decentralizing the production process. They have a continuing program they call Challenge for Change which is concerned with social problems at the local level. What makes it special is that it represents a genuine effort by the NFB to keep in contact with people at the grassroots. Challenge for Change makes much of cinéma-vérité but has cured itself of one cinéma-vérité deviation which has always been peculiarly attractive to the provincial mind: the secret camera's talent as a Peeping Tom and its ingenuity in catching the embarrassed reaction to the embarrassing question.

Like all harlots, the cinéaste of easy virtue is apt to run into power without responsibility, and it can go to his head.

The basic tendency of the Challenge for Change program is to follow decently in the original cinéma-vérité tradition which the English documentary people associate with *Housing Problems* (Edgar Anstey and Basil Wright, U.K., 1936). With that film there was talk of "breaking the goldfish bowl" and of making films "not about people but with them."

But not yet is there a real decentralizing of production. The cinéastes may make their films with the people and in the villages, but they are soon off and away from the people and the villages to their normal metropolitan milieu. The old unsatisfactory note of faraway liberal concern for humanity-in-general creeps in, in spite of these real excursions into the local realities.

What we have is presentation of local concerns without a real representation of local concerns. Presentation does not necessarily mean representation, much less participatory democracy.

Nevertheless, count the NFB as having contributed uniquely to the decentralizing process. You have only to compare its Challenge for Change program with, say, England's BBC-TV (except at Bristol) to realize that it has added – and in intimate terms – to local reporting. Its local portraits are better than any I know, and its use of the film to ease and give order to local discussion is important.

Two examples will illustrate the dangers attending the untutored or naïve cinéaste in troubled local waters. There was one otherwise excellent film of a long-unemployed man whose tale was sad to tell. Significant of the danger of naïveté was the fact that the director was a woman; and the truth about that unemployed character was what only a man who had been around would have spotted. He was not so much unemployed as unemployable. On a bet, no seaman would have gone to sea with him twice; no docker would have trusted him within fifty yards of a working crane.

The French phrase "s'écouter parler" has of course its horrible equivalent in cinema, and not least in cinéma-vérité. The NFB has one ugly example where the local subject gets so starry-eyed and grandiose in his new-found film personality that he destroys himself (or is destroyed) for all further reality.

Yes, naïveté can go with it, however honest the intention of the cinematic stranger from without. Where it matters is when the too local news is taken all too seriously and out of normal objective context.

The National Film Board has an example of good reportage from a ghost town in the West of Canada: a ghost town left on its uppers after the coal deposit has been worked out. The Challenge for Change program gives the abandoned townspeople, now mostly old people, the chance to discuss and record their complaints. They have no proper water supply, no gas supply, etc., etc. The Challenge for Change program gives the people the opportunity to view themselves, discover their strengths, and bring their ideas to better order. So it does help the townspeople to make their case and (because of the noise and the publicity, no doubt) be heard by politicians. Something indeed gets done.

News-in-depth? Why, in Canada, with its great distances and wild lands between, do most mining strikes have their own in-built time patterns. They last so long and no more. I was there when they made the big nickel strike at Moke Lake. They said, with excitement, it would mean not a fifty-year city but a hundred-year city.

In the wide and difficult land spaces, strike towns are like some island habitations in the wide and difficult sea spaces. The ghost towns are not always nor often worth keeping. The priorities are almost certain to be in a million and one distress centres elsewhere.

Many of these points are of course arguable. What is more certain is that the NFB and its Challenge for Change program will have a new and different opportunity of becoming both objective about and representational of local citizens and local affairs with the arrival of local TV by cable or otherwise. It is probable that government permits to operate these services will be dependent on the community being represented in the production management by a community league or something of the kind. This, as I see it, must mean that municipal authorities, schools, universities, trade unions, industries, chambers of commerce, and other associations will all have to look to their images and give an account of their stewardship; and, no doubt, all good radicals and true will see to it.

I can't for the life of me see that communities in the future will have the same sort of need for these faraway cinéastes. I start on the ground that a good teacher is, by the fact itself, a good exponent and a ready talent for exposition by film. So [it is] for all other professional exponents of cases and causes. The substandard film and the videotape are best seen now as relatively simple tools, to be locally owned and operated within the context of local reporting, local education, and democratic representation at the community level. The cost of equipment now puts the 8mm revolution within the reach of most groups and associations – at least in North America. The professional standards need not be lower than the standards associated with local newspapers when they were making their vital contribution to community building in, say, the twenties. These standards were very high indeed, as the memory of William Allen White and the *Emporia Gazette* testifies. Insofar as many associations have their counterparts in other communities, and some have their national fronts, Zavattini may even expect many of his local film letters to have their further circulation.

I leave it to others to say how it will operate in other countries, but I have been looking into decentralizing possibilities in India and think I see one possible great development there. In India there is a special imperative for decentralizing the filmmaking process. All the mass media together reach to only a hundred millions of the population, leaving four hundred and fifty millions to word-of-mouth, local educators, and the itinerant entertainments of native origin. Obviously the biggest role in economic and social progress of all kinds will be with the local educators, making it necessary to add, in every way possible, to their local powers of persuasion. Here, with the local educators, I associate all developments involving the community welfare. The local activist front is complex.

In India, too, there are many languages to contend with and areas distinctive in ethnic and cultural background. Filmmaking at the district level is, I would think, a logical development and one to which the various foreign aid programs should soon be giving their attention.

This means, among other peripatetic entertainments, the appearance of peripatetic teachers of filmmaking, moving modestly from district to district, teaching the doctor-teachers and other local educationists how to hold their cameras steady and shoot simply, as their own native powers of exposition direct them. That would be a real 8mm revolution anchored in necessity.

I submit this to the attention of any aging documentary types who may be on their way to Benares.

9   Can We Evaluate Challenge for Change? (1972)

■

DAN DRISCOLL

The first section closes with an evaluation of the CFC/SN's successes
and failures written at the time of the program's fifth anniversary.
"Can We Evaluate Challenge for Change?" (CFC/SN newsletter, issue
no. 10, Autumn 1972) was written by Dan Driscoll, an employee
of the NFB's Toronto branch and an enthusiastic supporter of the
program's social scientific approach to project execution. Yet he
struggles to find the proper criteria with which CFC/SN's various
endeavours should be judged. His call for "more intensive evaluation of individual projects" is precisely what the collection you
presently hold in your hands, especially Part 3, seeks to provide.

Recently, I wrote a three-page attempt at ironic fantasy entitled "Confes-
sions of a Media Button Freak," all about a character who made and wore
buttons like "Challenge Me, You Have Nothing to Lose but Your Change."
It lay on my desk over the long Easter weekend and was quite stale when I
looked it over on Tuesday. It might be helpful though if I tell you what the
main point of the button freak article was. I think I was trying to get at something which is so intangible that it's damned hard to get a mental hook onto
it. It relates to our tendency for becoming dependent on the aphorism, the
groovy phrase, even the cliché, in a kind of ritualized confrontation with our
shared anxieties. The subject is pretty close to home because, when we think
about it, we must admit that Challenge for Change is a phrase which could
have been dreamed up on Madison Avenue. It has all the qualities of an emotionally loaded symbol that commands attention and sympathy from a public
very much in need of both challenge and change.

RESISTING A NEW MYTH

In my own experience as an observer and to some extent a participant in the
program ever since its inception, I'm led to the conclusion that one of our
greatest challenges is to be found in resisting the creation of a new myth – in

avoiding the temptation to fall back on that beautiful, rhythmetic [*sic*], almost mantramistic [*sic*] slogan that some of us are already abbreviating as "C for C."

The value of a good publicity phrase can't be overestimated. It creates an atmosphere of openness and acceptance, invites a large measure of tolerance, and, in general, gets an organized process off on the right foot. Its danger is in the potential it has for warding off criticism. Like motherhood or patriotism, it can easily partake of elements that add up to "opiate of the people." The antidote, I feel, is a kind of dispassionate self-criticism that can ignore petty details of self-interest, management status, etc.

HOW TO EVALUATE OURSELVES

The models are to be found in places where social altruists are not inclined to look, namely in those areas where progress is sought through achievements of complex technology. We are inclined to think of the automotive industry, space projects, etc., as part of the problem, and indeed we are right in so thinking. But one of the reasons why the brain trusts of technology have become too successful can be seen in their highly developed capacity for self-correction, coupled with the fact that such a faculty has not been refined in the minds of social planners. When the spacecraft blows up on the ground, people gather around the table to find out what went wrong. The facts are clear – the thing was supposed to go up and it didn't. Why? There may be nervous blushes and hurt pride, but nursing these emotional ties to a dead duck doesn't move things ahead.

SOCIAL CHANGE EXEMPT?

In our business, that of social animation, community process, call it what you will, the failures are not so dramatic as an exploding nose cone. The detection of course-error and procedure for correction becomes a problem so complex that one's first reactions are to evade the issue. Many even deny the facts of historical progress, so dramatically evident in the sciences and in technology, and suggest that improvements in the quality of life are in some way exempt from nature's imperative of progressive change. While they view the advance of technology as an onrushing current threatening everything in its path, political and social process is given the appearance of an oil slick slowly spreading from its centre. Naturally, there are a lot of people on the sidelines wringing their hands.

Are we then able to borrow the best from technological process – its self-corrective and task-oriented features – while at the same time discarding its unfortunate limitation whereby progress in one field is achieved at the expense of total environment? I should like to think that this is possible, and I suggest that our own program is an excellent place for testing the theory.

MODEL OF CHALLENGE FOR CHANGE

The Challenge for Change program, looked at simply as a working model, is an instrument designed by political and social professionals for certain defined tasks. Very few people, so far as I know, can say who the designers were. The tasks and goals of the program are better known, a fact which reflects well upon [the CFC/SN newsletter]. My own understanding of the major goal gives me for definition, "to experiment with innovative designs for community integration and dialogue through use of communications media." Following through with the working model analogue, we can visualize the program both as system and as process. The system has static elements – a management structure, an inventory of equipment, people to carry out the projects. The process is socio-political, emerging from active elements existing in the community and triggered by the presence of a new element which, like a catalyst in the chemical process, makes a reaction possible instead of causing it or actively combining with the active energies peculiar to the community in question.

The emphasis on experiment and innovation suggests that projects should not take on characteristics of permanency, that they be visualized as having an endpoint where they can be evaluated, changed, terminated, or recycled to get clearer indications. In order to guarantee sustained emphasis on innovation, no one project should be so large as to drain off resources supporting other experiments.

HOW ARE OUR EXPERIMENTS WORKING?

At the risk of sounding more pragmatic than I should like to, it must be stated that the most important news to be communicated from the program to the widest possible audience has to do with whether or not an experiment is working towards desirable social end-products. This is tricky, because in a pluralist and democratic society a desirable end for one person or faction may not be so for another. The best one can hope for is carefully documented and objective reporting which can be evaluated by the public. An obstacle to this is our tendency to link our personal feelings of well-being and achievement with the interpretations we give to results obtained. Like enthusiastic schoolboys, we evaluate programs in terms of our own participation in them instead of [an] objective tabulation of results obtained. Here is where the catchphrase "psychology" can be reflected upon finally, by way of conclusion. If we feel ourselves to be persons who measure up to challenges, wholly aware of our participation in dynamic change, then we tend to evaluate the results of our activity in a very positive light. This, I submit, has been the Achilles heel of technical progress because it created a blind spot for those who had become expert in making things work.

To apply these criteria to the different project areas in the Challenge for Change program, to the low-budget documentary film program, the VTR community projects, [the newsletter] itself, would make this contribution overlong. The need for careful project definition, self-criticism, corrective procedures, balance between system design and process integration, all tending towards innovative social research, constitutes one of our most exciting challenges. A more intensive evaluation of individual projects must be the work of persons better qualified than I. The results would make for interesting reading in a future issue of [the CFC/SN newsletter].

PART 2

Community Spaces: Filming at the Margins

■

PREFACE

In this second section, five full-length chapters build on the general
political problematics that surrounded both the anglophone Challenge for Change program and its francophone counterpart, Société
nouvelle. Reconstructing the energy and radical optimism of the late
1960s (as well as the retrenchments of the 1970s), the five authors
relate the original anti-poverty and "development" impetus of the
programs to their cinematic output. In so doing, they assess two of
legacies of CFC/SN that are most important in terms of Canadian
cinema and world documentary. The first is the innovation of community-based video, whose legacy is perhaps most alive in Quebec;
the second is the emergence of a feminist documentary that dyna-
mized both CFC and SN in the 1970s and left a permanent imprint
on their institutional offshoots – Studio D and "Regards de femmes"
– and on the personal careers of many distinguished Canadian documentarists, from Anne Claire Poirier to Kathleen Shannon.

   In chapter 10, "Media for the People: The Canadian Experiments with Film and Video in Community Development," American
media educator Peter K. Wiesner succinctly sums up, from a 1992
outsider vantage point, CFC's philosophy, methods, achievements,
and problems, focusing principally on the program's flagship project
on Newfoundland and Labrador's Fogo Island. He concludes with
a wry and wistful comparative look at U.S. efforts inspired by the
CFC method. In chapter 11, "Cities for Change: The Housing
Challenge," Toronto-based experimental filmmaker, curator, and
professor Gerda Cammaer traces CFC's roots in anti-poverty politics,
spotlighting two early CFC films on housing in Halifax and Toronto
and detailing their production and exhibition context. In chapter 12,
"The En tant que femmes Series, the Film *Souris, tu m'inquiètes,*
and the Imaging of Women's Consciousness in 1970s Quebec,"

Montreal-based documentary scholar Marie-Ève Fortin chronicles
the roots of the groundbreaking feminist SN series in women's movement politics and aesthetic explorations; she zeroes in on a particular film in the influential series of six feature-length documentary
hybrids, Aimée Danis's *Souris, tu m'inquiètes* (1973). In chapter 13,
"Le mouton noir: Vidéographe and the Legacy of Société nouvelle,"
Toronto-based professor and Quebec film expert Scott MacKenzie
also concentrates on the under-examined francophone wing of the
program, focusing this time on its innovative video program, Vidéographe, its origins, its early highlights, and its enduring legacy.
Finally, in chapter 14, York University film studies professor and
prizewinning documentarist Brenda Longfellow revisits one of
CFC's core myths, the problematization of documentary ethics
by the anti-poverty exposé *The Things I Cannot Change* (1967);
Longfellow fleshes out the historical context of its production,
exhibition, and subsequent discursive framing, and relates them
to theories of the state and social change.

Media for the People: The Canadian Experiments with

10 Film and Video in Community Development (1992)

■

PETER K. WIESNER

> There was a more welfare-conscious government in power in Canada.
> It was in fashion to listen to "recipients of service."
> ■ George Stoney, 1988

Organized in 1967 as a consortium of several government agencies, including the National Film Board of Canada (NFB), the Challenge for Change (CFC) program linked film production with film utilization in the hope of using film not only to arouse public concern for the poor and the disenfranchised but also to stimulate positive social change at the grassroots level. Disbanded in 1975 [the program's last film was released in 1980. – Eds], CFC was "an experimental program to accelerate the understanding and acceptance of the need for constructive change in contemporary society" (Taylor and Taylor 1973). It was part of the Canadian government's anti-poverty effort, as exemplified by the Company of Young Canadians, which enlisted young people in community action programs.

One of the first and perhaps best-known experiments of CFC took place on Fogo Island, where NFB's Colin Low produced and exhibited film for the sole purpose of facilitating economic development in the fishing villages on this island off the coast of Newfoundland. In all, twenty-nine films were produced and utilized on Fogo (Watson 1977). Three of the original films, *Memo from Fogo, The Children of Fogo Island,* and *The Winds of Fogo,* are still being distributed by the NFB [in 1992] because they were produced with a wider audience in mind. Many of the other films featured interviews with fishermen and their families as well as recordings of meetings that were not intended for use outside of Newfoundland. These short films were widely acclaimed because they pioneered the use of the documentary for community development. For many years, CFC touted Fogo "as the success story which shows what the program can, in its finest, really accomplish" (Cohen 1977).

CFC sought to replicate the success of the Fogo project in other English- and French-speaking communities both within and outside of Canada. In the early 1970s, film and video community development projects were started at

Drumheller Valley (Alberta), Moose Jaw, Schreiber (northern Ontario), Prince Edward Island, northeastern New Brunswick, Halifax, Thunder Bay, Normandin (northern Quebec), St Jérôme, and Winnipeg, as well as in low-income areas in Toronto and Montreal. The "Fogo process," as it came to be called, was also attempted in the United States: in California, Connecticut, and Alaska.

The Fogo films and other CFC experiments attracted international attention and were replicated overseas. Berrigan (1979) attributed the use of media in "Third World" community development during the 1970s to CFC, and so did Litwin (1977) in his overview of community and video projects in both developing and developed countries. Kennedy (1984), in his unpublished dissertation, based his description of the role of the social animator on his work replicating the Fogo process in Alaska. Williamson (1988b), currently [1992] director of the Don Snowden Centre at Memorial University in Newfoundland, which played a major part in the Fogo project, wrote about recent uses of media in Third World community development.

DOCUMENTARIES UNDER CHALLENGE FOR CHANGE/
SOCIÉTÉ NOUVELLE

The CFC/SN program lasted for nearly a decade, and its legacy includes numerous documentaries for mass consumption that not only focused on local social concerns but also involved communities in the filmmaking process. Several of these films were about First Nations rights and life styles, including *Cree Hunters of Mistassini* (1974) and *Our Land Is Our Life* (1974), which attained wide circulation and influenced later film projects, such as *Incident at Restigouche* (Alanis Obomsawin, 1984), long after CFC was dissolved.

Progressive films about women's issues, environmental problems, and poverty continued to be made in the l970s and 1980s by filmmakers who had worked for CFC and advocated the use and control of media at the community level. By the time CFC ceased to be, the Film Board's decentralization effort had stimulated significant local production and distribution activity by regional filmmakers as well as amateurs. The experiments with locally controlled and produced media were over, although filmmakers continued to influence social change.

Since CFC emphasized social change rather than production values in the Fogo films, it is hardly surprising that most are rarely seen today. Documents relating to the project in the print archives provide both an overview of its intentions and impressions of what was actually accomplished. Why, then, focus attention on the Fogo Island project after more than twenty years? The answer is that Fogo was the first comprehensive effort to use media as a catalyst in community development. More than just a one-shot effort to inform and educate, the Fogo process entailed the interactive use of media over a period of time in order to develop local political skills for economic improvement.

This assessment of the CFC achievement is based on a review of its output – films, published articles, archival materials – as well as on recent interviews with Colin Low, George Stoney, Dorothy Hénaut, and others at the Film Board.

The Mission of Challenge for Change

The Fogo project, one of the first projects of CFC, was created by a consortium of seven departments of the Canadian government under the auspices of the Secretary of State. Société nouvelle, the French-speaking counterpart of CFC, was added later. At that time the Canadian government, under Pierre Trudeau, was open to innovative programs that sought to eradicate poverty and bring disenfranchised groups into the mainstream. Many felt that government could do more to be responsive to the needs of the poor. According to Hénaut (1975), the idealistic "bureaucratic renegades" of that time approached government "with the aim of influencing change in order to have a more just society." These are the kind of people who set the following objectives for CFC/SN:

1 To improve communication between individuals and groups in all segments of society who are concerned with or affected by poverty and social change.
2 To create a greater understanding and awareness among people of the causes of poverty and what it means to be poor.
3 To explore and promote new ideas and new approaches which are being used or which could be used to combat poverty and to evaluate the effectiveness of traditional approaches.
4 To provoke social change by changing attitudes which hinder the development of equal opportunities for everyone and inhibit their meaningful participation in society.
(Fortier, Petry, and Ford 1969)

According to Jones (1977), CFC "achieved almost instant fame" as the National Film Board's response to the government's "commitment to the principles of cultural democratization and cultural regionalization." The CFC/SN newsletter, edited by Hénaut, chronicled and promoted the experiments with film and video in community development from 1968 to 1975. CFC/SN resulted in some forty-five films [for an updated tally of CFC/SN productions, see chapter 1, this volume, p. 6] intended to raise public consciousness about the rights and needs of disenfranchised and disadvantaged groups. *Our Land Is Our Life* (1974) and *Cree Hunters of Mistassini* (1974) raised public consciousness about the ancestral hunting rights of First Nations, and *The Ballad of Crowfoot* (1968), filmed entirely by a First Nations crew, not only asserted Aboriginal rights but also placed the media in the targeted community's hands.

The Filmmaker's Role

According to Jones (1977), the CFC films represented a departure from an attitude glorifying the filmmaker "as culture hero or political revolutionary" (274) because these were not merely *about* the groups they portrayed but *on behalf* of them. To appreciate this shift in attitude by some at the Film Board in the 1960s, one must recall Grierson's ambiguous view of the filmmaker's role and mission: "Documentary was from the beginning – when we first separated our public purpose theories from those of Flaherty – an 'anti-aesthetic' movement. We have all, I suppose, sacrificed some personal capacity in 'art' and the pleasant vanity that goes with it. What confuses the history is that we had always the good sense to use the aesthetes" (Hardy 1971, 249).

Under Grierson's leadership, the NFB documentary filmmaker had played a starring role in producing the socially committed and aesthetically polished propaganda and information films that forged Canada's modern economic, political, and cultural development. Although in keeping with Grierson's vision of socially committed film, CFC was a departure because it encouraged some projects that minimized the creative role of the filmmaker in an effort to use film as a tool for progressive social change. It is for that reason that Grierson allegedly dismissed the amateurism that CFC encouraged as 8mm films for 8mm minds (see Grierson, chapter 8, this volume).

So CFC was not only about producing progressive films on social issues but also about the process of producing social change, using film production and distribution as a means of empowering politically and socially disenfranchised people. To accomplish this, CFC/SN established regional distribution centres that not only disseminated Film Board documentaries but utilized these for the express purpose of bringing about social change.

Many CFC films were influenced by cinéma-vérité techniques that favoured the use of synchronous sound segments without narration that had the effect of allowing situations to reveal themselves on the screen. This approach differed from the compilation approach used by Grierson and his followers in which the filmmaker imposed a point of view through on-camera and/or voice-over narration and the manipulation of images. Among the earliest examples of NFB cinéma-vérité films were the Candid Eye series (1958–61) and *Lonely Boy* (1962), which, according to Jones, still satisfied Grierson's concept of the documentary as the "creative treatment of actuality" (Jones 1977, 122).

Cinéma-vérité, made possible by portable synchronous sound film equipment in the early 1960s, was exemplified internationally in documentaries such as *Chronique d'un été* (*Chronicle of a Summer*, 1961) by Jean Rouch. CFC film and video projects, steeped in the radicalism of the sixties, found in cinéma-vérité an aesthetic that encouraged the portrayal of the everyday life of ordinary people. Cinéma-vérité eschewed those techniques that in themselves imposed interpretation.

Certainly, compilation documentary techniques could have been effectively used to promote the CFC political agenda in films focusing on social concerns such as poverty, social injustice, and environmental destruction. However, cinema-vérité techniques also subjected the very process of filmmaking to populist political standards. Keenly aware of Marshall McLuhan's dictum "the medium is the message," radicalized filmmakers questioned the relevance of the filmmaker as "auteur" even in the service of progressive causes. According to Hénaut (interview with the author, 3 July 1988), CFC produced "films about issues useful for people all over Canada, some very well made." On the other hand, many of the Fogo films, although not artistically excellent, were also important because they led to community video. They were forerunners of "a community process, media by the community."

Hénaut (1969b) wrote that poverty is not only physical deprivation but also the lack of opportunity for self-expression. She believed that the film medium itself could help to redress inequities. Film could perhaps reflect that physical deprivation and resultant way of life by opening up the communications links and letting people speak for themselves. Eventually, through film and/or direct action, people would be able to demand participation in decisions affecting their lives and they could be in a position to speak to those involved in the larger decision-making processes of government (44).

Hénaut wrote about a new kind of film, one in which the filmmaker serves as a midwife for community expression. Instead of using the community as material for "his [sic]" vision, the filmmaker must allow his skills to be in the service of collective expression: "[I]n 1966, within the Film Board, a small group of filmmakers was concerned with the *power* of the professional filmmaker, the power he has over the lives of the people he is filming. Usually, a filmmaker gets permission to film people, but he rarely shows them the finished product, and they never have anything to say about how their image is used. The filmmaker is not *accountable* to his subjects. This group of filmmakers, led by Colin Low, decided to change the *ethics* of the filmmaker, by making him responsible to the people he is filming, and by engaging the people on the screen as partners in the filmmaking process" (Hénaut 1975, 1).

This ethical stance emerged as filmmakers employed cinéma-vérité techniques that called upon ordinary individuals to function as actors on the screen. These techniques, even when motivated by the social consciousness of the filmmaker, sometimes resulted in films that unwittingly exploited those who were portrayed in them. For instance, *The Things I Cannot Change* (1967) showed everyday scenes from the lives of a poor family in Montreal that underscored the hopelessness of their situation. Its airing on local television invited ridicule from this family's neighbours, and so filmmakers began to question the ethics of filming for public consumption the private lives of vulnerable individuals (Jones 1977, 160). [For an updated view on this film, see Longfellow, chapter 14, this volume.]

Involving the Grassroots

The lesson learned from *The Things I Cannot Change* that some cinéma-vérité filmmakers, such as Richard Leacock, had already learned years earlier (Blue 1965) was put to good use in CFC documentaries. In an effort to avoid exploiting their subjects, CFC filmmakers brought participants into the filmmaking process. They would show rough edited versions using a dual 16mm film projection system, thereby gaining acceptance and credibility for the final edited version. In some cases, filmmakers would also show uncut "rushes" to insiders and use their comments to guide the editing and the use of the final program.

A respect and concern for those who were portrayed did not preclude artistry. *Cree Hunters of Mistassini* (1974) is still widely considered among the best examples of CFC cinéma-vérité films because of its sensitive and skilful portrayal of the lifestyle of First Nations families who lived and hunted in the Canadian wilderness. This film succeeded in creating a public awareness about wider environmental issues by conveying the Cree people's reverence for nature and understanding of environmental management. In addition, the film's use among the Cree prompted a renewed interest in hunting as a traditional pursuit. In another cinéma-vérité documentary, *You Are on Indian Land* (1969), Indians confronted white authorities over their treaty rights to land on the U.S.-Canadian border. This film publicized the Indians' side of the controversy and also empowered them to negotiate with Canadian officials in resolving it. In both films, cinéma-vérité techniques conveyed stories that could be revealed visually and whose essence was in the action itself and not in the interpretative voice-over narration. And since both films were first shown to the community before being released to the general public, the filmmakers were assured of community approval.

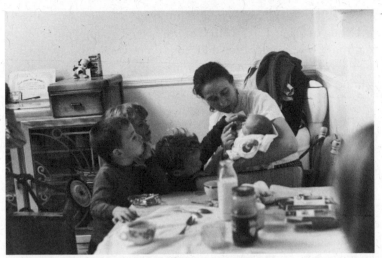

The Things I Cannot Change (1967): an experience the NFB learned from. Production still.

Yet, the involvement of the community in the filmmaking process invited criticism. Jones (1977) cautioned against the "abdication" of filmmakers who were unwilling to assert artistic freedom when confronted with the political agenda of the community being portrayed. He felt that such an abdication was no different from abdication in the face of corporate or government influence; in either case, artistic responsibility was a secondary consideration.

Ironically, the self-expression that Grierson had abhorred and had noticed in some of the Board's work when he visited Montreal in 1964– and which CFC had meant to counteract – was re-emerging. Only it wasn't the filmmakers who were expressing themselves, it was "the people." CFC, which had sprung up in part as a recoil from the aesthetics of self-expression, got rid of the aesthetics but not the self-expression (Jones 1977, 168).

The process of gaining community approval often meant letting people talk and restraining the filmmaker from manipulating the material. According to Jones, aesthetics suffer when filmmakers loosen their control over the medium, as did Fernand Dansereau in his film *St-Jérôme* (1969) in order to avoid the problem encountered in the making of *À Saint-Henri le cinq septembre* (1962), a film that unwittingly exploited community participants. Dansereau justified giving up artistic control: "I pledged to all the people ... (except politicians) ... that they would have the right to censor the material that I would shoot with them ... Because of this initial pledge ... the major part of the shooting was taking the form of interviews ... I simply listened to people ... When, a little later, I attempted to intervene as a director, I always had the same feeling of being disrespectful, of unjustified manipulation on my part. The final footage was composed entirely of interviews and events that had authentically happened quite outside of my control" (Dansereau, chapter 4, this volume, p. 35).

Giving Up the Art

The most problematic aspect of CFC, according to Jones (1977), was "the movement to democratize the media." In Montreal this movement led to projects such as Vidéographe, which sought to place the tools of motion picture production in the hands of the people. "Now, filmmakers were abdicating the authority, turning over the role of filmmaker to 'the people.' Filmmakers – it could be argued, were 'copping out'" (166).

What Jones called the near "abdication" by filmmakers amounted to the filmmakers' reluctance to set the agenda, to impose their view as a gatekeeper in the selection and treatment of topics for the documentary. However, this abdication was seen to be essential when the intent on part of CFC was *not* to produce documentary for public consumption, but rather to use media technology strictly to benefit certain practical goals, such as community and economic development.

Certainly, the difficulty of reconciling aesthetic and social responsibilities was recognized by the filmmakers who founded CFC after experimenting with the social applications of film on Fogo Island. They saw no reason to judge the "talking head" filmed interviews of Fogo Islanders by the same artistic standards used to evaluate films for mass consumption. According to Hénaut (1975), Fogo and other projects like it called upon filmmakers to be "technicians" willing to forgo their craft in order to further social goals. And she noted: "At the beginning the filmmaker had become a partner with the people he was filming. But he was still there, with his professional film crew and his cumbersome 16mm equipment. He was still the middleman, between citizen and their message" (3). Filmmakers were middlemen in more ways than one. Besides exercising control over technology, they also played a central role in deciding which community project to undertake and how to go about it. But with the advent of video technology, communities were able to assume technical control, as was demonstrated in numerous community video projects.

The shift from film to video made it possible to eliminate the technical services of the filmmaker-cum-artist by equipping and training communities to produce their own videos. So when Hénaut and others at the Film Board introduced video to communities, the overriding goal was to empower them. Hénaut (1988) noted: "When people gain their self-confidence, they see themselves on the screen and they see that they are good. People are brought up in our society to think so poorly of themselves. I have never seen people who are not lifted by seeing themselves in action on a video screen. They say, 'Hey, I am better than I thought I was.' And that enhancement of self-confidence is one reason why they are able to continue organizing. And video in the hands of a community organizer can enhance the confidence of the people they are working with."

Individual and group expression, expressed by being in front of the camera rather than behind it, was an important feature of the films produced for communities like those on Fogo and in Drumheller. The essence of these films was the process of making and showing them for a social purpose. They celebrated the expression of individual and community will. George Stoney, an American who headed CFC/SN for two years, noted (interview with the author, 20 September 1988): "Both film and video were crafted to make things happen, not the event itself." Hénaut (1975) agrees that neither the event nor personal expression should be subservient to the recording medium: "The important thing to remember is that the media are tools in the social process. They are not the social process itself. We have to keep the media in perspective, to keep them in their place" (4).

Instead of the filmmaker exercising artistic control, a "social animator" was to guide the communication process on behalf of community-development aims. In this way, self-expression was extricated from the events both on and off the screen. Although technical and artistic proficiency were to be respected, artistic value as an end in itself was irrelevant, although Marcorelles (1970) noted with some irony, "Sociological experience obviously takes on a poetic or political slant" (84). When it came right down to it, the media producer's goals were seen to be in potential conflict with the real needs of the community. Hénaut (1988) observed: "The problem is that this person [the producer] may not understand the real needs of the community. They can be distracted from knowing their own needs and get really involved in media, a sideline. You really need to talk to people, what it is you really need. Some have asked me to do a tape. After a lot of discussion, they ended up doing a newsletter because they needed it much more than a videotape."

Separating artistic ambition from community-development goals was always problematic. Few filmmakers at the Board understood the goals of the CFC, according to Stoney, (1988). Even when filmmakers became involved in projects involving social change, they found that "there was not enough ego gratification" in producing media solely for community use. Even the best of intentions to subordinate filmmaking to community development goals could never make it easy to upstage media. Hénaut (1975) wrote this epitaph: "One of the sad things I have seen in Canada, as video became more and more common across the country, was people trying to gain changes *only* through using video. Video or cable became their main aim, and they failed miserably at both video and social action ... No amount of video can replace a good community organizer, no amount of video can make fuzzy thinking turn into clear social and political analysis" (5).

CFC brought out the gulf between film artistry and community organizing. It is extraordinary that the NFB took on Fogo and other community development projects at all, given that its agenda, to no one's surprise, was determined by artists interested in film as product rather than process. CFC, conceived as an experiment, lasted seven years, much longer than expected. The Fogo project and others like it established the idea that film and video could be placed at the service of community development. For that reason, Fogo deserves another look.

THE FOGO ISLAND PROJECT

> In film I'd never been much of an action man, I'd always been more interested in using it for poetic document. But in Newfoundland, I discovered something very different.
> ▪ Colin Low (Gwyn 1972, 5)

Project Organization

By the time Colin Low visited Fogo Island in 1967, he had already established himself as one of the most artistically accomplished filmmakers at the Film Board as the producer of *Circle of the Sun* (1960). Yet, he was able to recognize that if films were to be used to further community development, the filmmaker would have to play not a starring but a supporting role.

With the Fogo Island project, the process of recording and showing films to a community clearly took precedence over the realization of artistically valid film projects. Low did not want to use the Fogo Islanders to make an artistic statement as Flaherty had used the Aran Islanders in his documentary *Man of Aran* (1934). Even years later, in response to the urging of Hénaut and others at the Film Board, he expressed ambiguous feelings about producing an overall artistic statement about Fogo with *The Winds of Fogo* and *The Children of Fogo,* the most artistically polished films among those made on Fogo Island – films that indicate what a single compiled portrait of the island might have been. The fact that Low had produced artistically polished films in the past suggests that the lack of artistry in many of the Fogo films was an intentional choice to give aesthetics a back seat.

What was all important to Low was that films meet certain overall political and economic objectives. On Fogo their purpose was to help Fogo Islanders overcome traditional animosities within the community by working together cooperatively to revitalize fishing and to deal effectively with

The Children of Fogo Island (1967): among the most artistically polished of the Newfoundland Project films. Production still.

regional public officials. Film was to provide a mirror for the islanders as they grappled with the difficult social and economic issues confronting them.

Fogo was a three-year project undertaken by the National Film Board and the Memorial University Extension Service at St John's, Newfoundland. Low is generally credited with introducing the idea of using film in community development, and according to Williamson (1988a), he was teamed up with Don Snowden, then director of the Extension Service at Memorial, who was said to have been angered by a report by the Economic Council of Canada that "described poverty from the point of view of an urban central Canadian, and which did not take any cognisance of the life-style and perceptions of rural Canadians. It was his [Snowden's] idea to make a series of films in Newfoundland through the Extension Service, to explore this bias and to show Canadians that the real poverty in places like rural Newfoundland was the poverty of information, of isolation from decision-making, and of lack of organization" (1).

The Problems of Fogo Island
Low's basic mandate had been to produce a documentary on rural poverty in Newfoundland, focusing on resettlement as well as industrialization, urbanization, education, and their relationship to joblessness. One of several

possible locations for filming, Fogo Island was situated ten miles off the northeast coast of Newfoundland, its population of about five thousand scattered in communities with names such as Joe Batt's Arm, Seldom Come By, Stag Harbour, and Tilting. Not only isolated from the mainland, these communities were isolated from each other.

In these little outposts, authority was vested in the local merchants and clergy who acted as brokers in purveying information to and from the decision-making centre of St John's, the capital of Newfoundland. The paternalism of church, state, and commerce helped convince unschooled people that what knowledge they had was of little value (Williamson 1988a, 3).

Settlements dating back three hundred years that had once been prosperous were reduced to poverty with the decline of the fisheries by the 1960s. Sixty per cent of the Fogo inhabitants were on public assistance. Divided by differences in religion and tradition, the islanders lacked any central organization to unite them. Fogo Island's roads were poor, and only one of the ten communities had local government, although each outpost had its own one-room schoolhouse and church. In the 1960s, many homes lacked electricity, telephones, and even reliable radio reception. There were no unions or cooperatives. As many as 50 per cent of the islanders were functionally illiterate. "A single future remained for them; resettlement at the government's discretion" (Gwyn 1972, 5).

What Low found was that the relocation scheme ran against the local wishes of the Fogo Island inhabitants, who wanted instead to revive fishing, their traditional livelihood. Low said that he selected Fogo Island for the film project because "(1) it had many social, economic, and educational problems; (2) the policy of the government towards this area was being formulated, in effect, its future was uncertain." Low also noted that Fogo Island was "large enough to offer problems in inter-community communication. There are ten villages on Fogo. Yet it was a geographical entity – in microcosm not unlike the Newfoundland situation" (Low 1968–69, 1).

The purpose of the project was to see how films could aid the islanders. Low realized, however, that conventional film techniques, focusing on issues, would only exacerbate the powerlessness of the Fogo Islanders. He recalled: "When I went to Fogo, I thought that I would make one, or perhaps two or three films. But as the project developed, I found that people were much freer when I made short vertical films: each one the record of a single interview, or a single occasion. In the end I did not do any inter-cutting at all, because if you inter-cut people on the basis of issues, what usually happens is that you get one person who is all wrong, one person who is partly right, and a third person who is right. He becomes the smart guy, who puts the others down. This putting down can harm people within a community" (Gwyn 1972, 5).

Low did extensive groundwork on Fogo Island and obtained a first-hand knowledge of the physical and social conditions before returning with a film crew. He was introduced to the islanders by Fred Earle, a native of Fogo as well as a Memorial University extension worker who had been engaged in community development and adult education on Fogo Island for some time. Fogo looked like a perfect choice for the project, and Low came back to the island for the summer, recruited some local students to apprentice with his film crew, and, with the help of Earle, started interviewing and filming Fogo Islanders (Williamson 1988a, 2).

Low came into contact with the island's Development Committee, which had been formed to explore economic development as an alternative to relocation. In conversation with local fishermen, Low became aware of their social and economic problems, which were later documented on film. The local fisheries were dying because fish were being caught far off the Newfoundland coast by huge factory ships. In order to compete, the islanders were faced with the necessity of acquiring modern "long liner" boats, capable of fishing in deeper waters, and of finding an economically sound way of shipping, storing, and processing fish caught during the short fishing season.

Although traditional fishing and processing methods were no longer viable, many Fogo Islanders still clung to traditional ways. They lacked not only the resources to modernize but also the political and organizational experience to deal with government and outside business interests. Both its lack of a communication infrastructure and its isolation from the mainland made Fogo Island an attractive site for the experimental use of film in community development.

The Fogo Films
In all, Low produced twenty-seven short "vertical" films, not including *Winds of Fogo* and *Memo from Fogo,* which were produced with outside audiences in mind. Many of the short films depicted islanders talking about local issues and concerns, such as appropriate fishing methods, producer cooperatives, ship building, education, resettlement, and the role of local government and merchants in their lives. Altogether, about six hours of edited film footage, reflecting a panorama of opinion and expression, were shown to the islanders in schools, churches, and other community meeting places.

Fishermen's Meeting (15 min.), *The McGraths at Home and Fishing* (10 min.), and *Dan Roberts on Fishing* (20 min.) are about fishing methods, including the controversial use of long liner boats. *Thoughts on Fogo and Norway* (12 min.) compares fishing methods, marketing, and welfare programs at Fogo with those in Norway. The desirability of forming a cooperative for processing and storage is discussed in *Andrew Britt at Shoal Bay* (20 min.),

The Founding of the Cooperative (20 min.), *The Merchant and the Teacher* (12 min.), *Tom Best on Cooperatives* (10 min.), and *Citizen Discussions* (14 min.). In *The Story of the Up Top* (10 min.) and *Jim Decker Builds a Long Liner* (20 min.), Fogo Islanders talk about how they managed to build boats without government help.

Several films deal with the Improvement Committee's attempt to enlist the help of the provincial government to spur economic development. In *Fogo Island Improvement Committee* (15 min.), members are seen preparing for the anticipated visit of the Newfoundland premier. In *Two Cabinet Ministers* (15 min.), the Newfoundland minister of municipal affairs and the Fogo member of the provincial legislature discuss the feasibility of one governmental entity on Fogo Island. *The Improvement Committee and the Cabinet Minister* (15 min.) shows the interaction between the Fogo Island Improvement Committee and Charles Granter, the federal member of Parliament for Fogo.

Other films deal with a wide range of social problems, such as fishermen's unions, the fish plant, welfare, and education. *Some Problems of Fogo* (20 min.) touches on several issues. *Brian Earle on Merchants and Welfare* (10 min.) and *Discussion of Welfare* (7 min.) are about the demoralizing effects of welfare. *A Woman's Place* (15 min.) concerns education and problems faced by women. The future of young people on Fogo are topics in *Joe Kinsella on Education* (10 min.) and *The Mercer Family* (10 min.); and the future of Fogo as seen by those who have stayed and those who have left is discussed in *William Wells Talks about the Island* (20 min.), *Fogo Expatriates* (15 min.), and *Billy Crane Leaves the Island* (20 min.). Films celebrating the culture and everyday life on Fogo include *The Songs of Chris Cobb* (10 min.), *Wedding and Party* (10 min.), *Jim Decker's Party* (5 min.), and *The Children of Fogo* (28 min.).

What made these films unique was that their production and utilization were intertwined. Recorded and edited statements by some islanders in one town were shown to people in other towns. Reactions to screenings were again filmed, edited, and shown to groups in both towns. This concatenation involved not only islanders but also officials outside the island, who thus became part of a community that was based on mediated discourse, a community that might not have come into existence in face-to-face situations.

THE FOGO PROCESS

If you take fishermen to the cabinet, they won't talk about the problems of their lives the way they will among other fishermen. But if you let government people look at films of fishermen talking together, the message comes through.
▪ National Film Board official (Gwyn 1972)

The "Fogo process," as it came to be known, was based on the following elements: the collaboration between filmmaker and permanent community-development officer; the selection of an isolated community that lacked community organizations to deal with its economic problems; the state having the goals of stimulating grassroots problem-solving and improving government-community communications; filming techniques based on rapport between filmmaker and subjects; a certain involvement of the community in editing decisions; and much emphasis on the playback of materials as a stimulus to discussion and problem solving (Taylor and Taylor 1973, 68).

George Stoney (1988) pointed out that there had to be three preconditions for the successful implementation of the Fogo process: (1) the willingness by individuals and groups to try mediation rather than confrontation in resolving conflicts; (2) the willingness of institutions with power to listen and respond to community expression of needs and concerns; and (3) the involvement of an intermediary, such as the National Film Board, trusted by both sides. As described by Taylor and Taylor (1973), the process called for the use of a "delicate rein" by the filmmaker and community development officer or "animator" to "encourage each subject to follow his own path, while the interviewer played the role of responsive, sympathetic and patient listener, [who led the subject] ... very gradually into areas of highly loaded emotional material" (68).

Vertical Editing

Instead of producing a conventional documentary, using editing techniques to condense the Fogo Island experience to a single story line, Low, with his vertical editing approach, produced films about individual subjects that encouraged Fogo Islanders to make inferences on their own. The Fogo process of producing and showing films was slow and deliberate, giving islanders time to sort out the issues. The films helped them to recognize common problems and differences by showing them removed from everyday interaction. The playback of these expressions in the community could reveal the contradictions in individual and also in group attitudes. It could be a beginning in the modifying of attitudes, achieved not through dissemination of information or propaganda but through a real participation that had the potential of creativity (NFB 1968a, 2).

Drawing from his own background growing up in a small farming community in southern Alberta, Low (1968–69) realized that film allowed viewers to consider issues that could not be discussed directly: "Individuals in small communities often avoid exchange because they are unwilling to generate negative emotional situations that they know from experience are the inevitable outcome of certain confrontations. Film sensitivity allows divergent news in proxy before the judgment of the community" (3).

Ethics and Filmmaking

Low (1968–69) expressed great concern about filmmakers' ethical obligation to avoid damaging the reputation of their subjects: "A person holding a certain job could be in danger of losing that job if he brought up questions connected with the unethical practices, for instance, of the firm he is employed in ... Sometimes it is hard to avoid such testimony if it is a vital question in the community. *I* think it is vital that the interests of the individual be protected and if it is necessary to bring out the *idea* that the welfare of the community is being jeopardized by unethical business practices it should be done by people who will not be damaged by the revelation" (5).

Low believed that filmmakers should not take advantage of people with physical and mental health problems and that they should be sensitive and open-minded in religious matters. Filming was never to take place without prior permission, and hidden camera techniques were to be avoided. To assure that filmmaking at Fogo proceeded with sensitivity and caution, many of the crew members were drawn from the island, setting a precedent for later CFC projects in which individuals from local communities were trained to produce and use media.

According to Low (1973), the following rules were formulated during the Fogo project. Rule 1 guaranteed the subject's editorial rights; this rule gave individuals the power to censor any part of their appearances. Rule 2 governed the exchange of information between individuals, groups, and communities and between a region and government; it specified that every effort should be made to arrange a prior guarantee of a response, such as from government officials upon their viewing community-made tapes or films requesting governmental action. Both rules were intended to prevent subjects from being used and to assure that the filming process was for their benefit (16).

The Fogo process, as carried out in Newfoundland, caught on and was melded with the CFC filmmaking agenda. Although the process was conceived for facilitating community development in rural areas, additional applications of the process quickly followed. The Fogo process was applied not only in rural and semi-rural areas, but also in cities, in community cable programming, and among Native peoples. In some projects, it was used as a form of therapy as well (Gwyn 1972, 3).

No matter how it was used, the Fogo process legitimized the use of film and media for the sole purpose of advocating social change for disadvantaged individuals and groups. It was thought that the process, if properly handled, would unfreeze individuals to become effective leaders and participants in social change.

IMPACT OF THE FOGO PROCESS

> Time is the best measurement of anything. Evaluation has never been practical
> because there has never been an adequate commitment to a time base that
> would mean something in relationship to social change.
> ▪ Colin Low (Jones 1977, 287)

Impact on Fogo Island

There were no formal studies that included quantitative measures of impact
of the Fogo project; however, the reports by Gwyn (1972), Taylor and Taylor
(1973), and Cohen (1977) provide a review of the NFB projects that sought
to enlist film and video to facilitate social change. The Fogo project itself was
not evaluated, although comments regarding its effectiveness were collected
from Fogo Islanders and others directly involved. Fred Earle, the community organizer from Memorial University, observed: "In 1967 there was a lot
of suspicion. But over the years, we made good use of the films. There used
to be no tradition of debate in our communities; people would avoid it. But
now, as the new films show, many more people are prepared to stand up and
express their opinions" (Gwyn 1972, 7).

Following the completion of the films, a fishing cooperative and a central
school committee were established on the island. Jim Decker, who appeared
in one of the films and subsequently became a community leader, attributed
progress on Fogo to the films: "It's anyone's guess what would have happened without the films. I think probably our situation here now would have
been quite different. Certainly, I don't think we would have had a shipyard
or even a cooperative formed. I'd say what could have happened – we might
have been all gone" (Gwyn 1972, 6).

Not everyone agreed. According to Cohen (1977): "Many of the people
interviewed felt that the novelty of the project and the enormous publicity
it had received had put a spotlight on Fogo Island. These people see the
government's positive response as a politically expedient solution to a
publicly embarrassing situation" (72). And Jones (1977) suggested that the
Fogo films may have retarded progress on Fogo by elevating a leadership
incapable of following through with economic-development efforts: "Four
years later, according to the program's own follow-up film, *A Memo from
Fogo* (1972), neither the co-op nor the marketing board [was] doing well.
The community leaders had been 'put on a pedestal through the films.' The
films had not exploited their subjects; they had glorified them. The new
leadership, however, lacked leadership qualities. A fisheries expert and community organizer had to be sent in to help sort out the resulting difficulties. But, the film suggests, the problems in the islands were now problems
of growth, not decline" (286).

Still, Hénaut and Low were convinced that film was a catalyst in community development on Fogo, yet both stressed that media, at best, supplemented regular community-development efforts. Low commented, "We did not create processes, we intensified them. When we arrived[,] Fogo was on the verge of action in a number of areas ... By communicating the action trends and by exposing the problems, the consensus was enlarged and intensified" (Taylor and Taylor 1973, 68). Low acknowledged the importance of the long-term commitment of Fred Earle. Yet the extent to which film was a crucial factor in stimulating community development was open to interpretation. Not surprisingly, the account offered by Tony Williamson of Memorial University, although in substantial agreement with Hénaut's and Low's, differed in tone and emphasis: "It is tempting to say that the films, in themselves, fostered all of these things and to draw linear relationships between the films and subsequent action and development; but it would be incorrect to do so. The Fogo Process ... was critically linked to a sustained program of community development efforts of the university and government. Although the attention Fogo Island received (the 'Hawthorne Effect') from the filming and screening undoubtedly helped to accelerate developments on the Island, a passive viewing of the films in isolation from any constructive discussions and follow-up planning meetings would have created no more than a passing moment of excitement and interest at best" (1988a, 7).

The Fogo project, an expensive undertaking, benefited greatly from federal government funding as well as from the pooled resources of the Film Board and Memorial University. Jones (1977) questioned its cost-effectiveness and noted that even with the introduction of videotape "the size, scope, and cost of the project ... could not be emulated" (288). There were attempts to introduce the Fogo process elsewhere in Canada through CFC. However, unlike at Fogo, where media became the tool of university extension service agents, many of the spinoffs focused more on community organizing against the local power structure than on community development in collaboration with local authorities. This occurred more frequently in urban areas in which social problems had become highly politicized. One community worker from Halifax's Tele-Video Services commented: "There is a difference between dealing with people who want to look at their surroundings and build a dialogue, and people who feel oppressed and trapped. We've got to do more than hand these people a Portapak and say, 'Go have fun.' We've got to take that weapon and use it" (Gwyn 1972, 16).

Although confrontation was not the only goal of urban media projects, nor consensus building the only aim in rural areas, media was more likely to be used to confront the power structure in urban areas. For instance, video was used as an organizing tool by the St-Jacques Citizens Committee, a militant community group in a low-income Montreal neighbourhood (Newsletter, Summer, 1969); the Parallel Institute in Montreal's Point St Charles area used video to confront welfare and government officials; and in Halifax, jobs were found for many unemployed youths after a screening of the film *Encounter at Kwacha House – Halifax,* which focused on discrimination against blacks (Fortier, Petry, and Ford 1969, 1).

Drumheller Valley

The Fogo process, designed for economic development in Newfoundland, was thought to have been more suitable for rural and semi-rural than for urban areas (Williamson 1988b). According to Taylor and Taylor (1973), the Drumheller Valley project, in which video was used instead of film, came closest among the CFC projects to replicating the Fogo process to the fullest. As on Fogo Island, the relocation of poor people was part of the redevelopment scheme in the Drumheller Valley in rural Alberta (see Rusted, chapter 20, this volume). Only this time relocation was not an option but rather a solution to the social and economic problems faced by the several thousand inhabitants of the declining mining communities in the valley. The Fogo process, on the other hand, had provided a voice for the disadvantaged, many of them elderly, in shaping how the relocation to public housing would take place.

A local community-development officer, Anton Karch, was hired by the School of Social Welfare and the Division of Continuing Education at the University of Calgary. According to Stoney (1988), Karch possessed qualities and skills similar to those of Fred Earle, the social animator at Fogo. Trained by CFC to record video to be edited at the Film Board, Karch became one of the first social animators to implement the Fogo process without the involvement of professional video-production specialists. He produced a videotape on youth and nine tapes on East Coulee, an outlying mining town on the decline.

Initially, the project did not jell because "the community had no formal organization of any kind – and it appeared that most people had accepted this condition and the fate of their community. The VTR [videotape recorder] had brought the community together but the community failed to respond to the challenge of taking some action to bring about change" (Karch 1971–72). Karch found fertile ground for the Fogo process in a neighbouring town, Rosedale, which like Fogo was sufficiently organized to foster change and development. The Rosedale Citizens' Action Committee responded positively to the idea of using video to assess community needs. One man noted: "I have been playing cards with these guys for years and we didn't know what the other guy was really thinking about the place until we had to speak out for the camera" (Hénaut 1971–72).

As on Fogo, the process of recording and playing back statements about important issues and needs led to action through subcommittees of the citizens committee. Home improvements and community cleanups took place.

Volunteers improved community recreation areas. Community pressure led to the installation of water and gas lines by the provincial government. Even industrial development, such as the installation of a small factory in a former schoolhouse, took place as the direct result of community action.

Community Television Spinoffs

The success of the projects at Fogo and Drumheller in large part hinged on the skills of the social animators. In other projects, primarily concerned with local video production, success was ultimately defined by the quality of the programs produced. Cable television changed the way video was used in places such as Thunder Bay, Vancouver, Roosevelt Park [Vancouver], and Winnipeg where CFC provided equipment and training to local community groups for cable television programming as well as community playback (Taylor and Taylor 1973, 87). As a means of reaching anonymous viewers, cable television was a significant departure from the Fogo process, the latter requiring the showing of video in face-to-face situations to bring about social change. The anonymity of the cable audience marginalized the role of the social animator. Taylor and Taylor (1973) noted: "The emerging pattern, if one examines the generation of projects over a period beginning with Fogo, is that of gradual withdrawal from active social intervention in specific communities to a policy of provision of service and information" (68).

Memorial University Projects

Many community video projects came to emphasize media as a product rather than a process. Instead of focusing on social change, many groups, particularly those with access to cable television, became concerned with upgrading production standards and fulfilling programming obligations (Stoney, 1988). However, the Fogo process continued to drive projects undertaken by Memorial University at Port au Choix on the northern peninsula of Newfoundland. Here, an extension agent worked with the newly funded Northern Regional Development Association to produce film modules on resettlement, economic development, and the needs and aspirations of youth. As on Fogo Island, the film subjects were given editorial rights over the materials.

Extension agents also used the Fogo process in Labrador in peer teaching about such topics as unscrupulous merchants who insisted on non-cash transactions. Films and later videos enabled communities to deal with issues that otherwise, because of the threat of interpersonal confrontation, were generally set aside. Williamson (1988a) noted: "Somehow, the film or video identified the speaker, removed the inherent threat of confrontation, and enabled a dialogue which might otherwise never have taken place. Hence, the Fogo Process also opened up new lines of communication and contributed significantly to conflict resolution" (12).

Memorial University used the Fogo process in major projects involving conflict resolution, including one designed by Don Snowden and Paul MacLeod in which video was used to bridge differences regarding the management of the Kaminuriak caribou herd between Inuit hunters of the Keewatin and biologists and government officials. Thirty-three tapes were produced, with sound tracks in two languages, demonstrating that "both sides of the dispute had much to learn from each other and that there were not inflexible nor rigidly held views about the subject" (Williamson 1988a, 19).

By 1970, fieldworkers from the Memorial University Extension Service routinely used video to facilitate community development. For some, video provided information to communities on topics such as the process of running elections; for others, film and video brought information to remote villages on things like the impact of oil drilling on fishing in the North Sea.

Institutional Use of the Fogo Process

Elsewhere in Canada, the Fogo process was used in institutional settings – mostly prisons and hospitals – which, like isolated rural communities, provided a closed social system in which there was little public discourse that would have facilitated identifying problems, resolving conflicts, and building a consensus for problem solving. The process was used successfully to mediate between prisoners and guards where communication between these groups was minimal. At Collins Bay Penitentiary, however, there were problems in using video to facilitate communication between prisoners and guards largely because the social animator showed a distinct bias in favour of the prisoners (Gwyn 1972, 35).

The process was also used in therapeutic situations. In a hospital for retarded children in Orillia, Ontario, for example, children recorded their own presentations that were then used in staff-development sessions, and at Thunder Bay Hospital, three emotionally disturbed teenagers made a film to express their views to the hospital community. Unfortunately, there are few published materials available about these institutional projects.

THE FOGO PROCESS IN THE UNITED STATES

> The Challenge for Change approach works only when you have people who are willing to try mediation before confrontation. That is almost considered cowardly in the United States.
> ▪ George Stoney (1988)

The success of the Fogo project led to its dissemination in the United States by representatives of the National Film Board and Memorial University, two institutions that had worked together on Fogo. In the waning years of President Lyndon Johnson's War on Poverty, Ann Michaels, an official of the now-defunct U.S. Office of Economic Opportunity (OEO), was among those who learned about the Fogo project at a conference organized at Memorial University. Her contacts with the Film Board led to Colin Low, Julian Biggs, and Don Snowden being invited to set up film projects similar to Fogo in Farmersville, California; Hartford, Connecticut; and Skyriver, Alaska.

OEO *Projects*

Ann Michaels (telephone interview with the author, September 1988) recalled that the "crazy idealistic Canadians" were new to the confrontational style of American politics and failed to comprehend the extent of the distrust of government at the grassroots level, a distrust that prevented the replication of the Fogo process at Farmersville and Hartford. Although these short-lived efforts may have yielded short-term benefits for the individual participants, there was no chance that the projects would have a lasting impact on these communities without a skilled and committed social animator to sustain community development over the long haul. Low (1968–69) recognized this limitation in Farmersville: "One real handicap was the lack of a community development person to serve as a liaison and to continue the work after our departure" (9). He nevertheless maintained that the films made in Farmersville did succeed in allowing various segments of the community, such as Chicano farm workers and Anglo supervisors, to see beyond stereotypes. But in the absence of any kind of sustaining political framework, the process could not take hold.

A subsequent project in Hartford in 1969 failed unequivocally in large part owing to the confrontational nature of race relations at that time. A third project involving Eskimos in Skyriver succeeded because the community development problems and approaches were similar to those on Fogo Island. Williamson (1988a) noted: "Lessons learned in the U.S. confirmed the process works best in pockets of isolation, where people have little access to information and where they have not been inundated by mass media" (21). There were few successful attempts to replicate the Fogo project in the United States despite the widespread interest in community media and local-access television. Stoney, who had left the National Film Board to become head of the Alternate Media Center at New York University, found it impossible to replicate the Fogo process in the United States. He recalled collaborating on a project with Low that involved documenting hunger throughout the United States for the White House Conference on Hunger. In all, the six hundred hours of footage that were recorded and edited down to six were found to be "too depressing by the White House people" and therefore were never shown.

Stoney also received a commission from the U.S. Department of Education, Office of Vocational Training, to use video to help mid-level managers see the impact of welfare programs. Video was to "put faces" on the statistical representations of clients that normally inform bureaucrats. In carrying out this project, he found that not a single regional office in the South would give him the time of day. He was finally sent to Pittsburgh and Detroit, and these missions resulted in "useful tapes which the agency head used in public presentations" (Stoney, 1988).

Stoney said that cultural factors make it difficult to implement the Fogo process in the United States. Civil servants, for example, regard criticism in confrontational terms. According to Stoney, the quality of the civil service is much higher in Canada: officials "really mean it when they say they want to hear from the poor ... and don't take criticism of their programs personally. I have never found an American who can adopt that attitude" (1988). This was confirmed by Watson (1970), who recalled the reaction of U.S. officials upon seeing *Up against the System,* a film critical of welfare programs in Canada. One U.S. official, surprised that the Canadian government not only tolerated but also fostered criticism of its policies, asked the Canadians, "How long do you think you can get away with it?" (20)

Skyriver, Alaska
The attitudinal barriers identified by Stoney are discussed in Tim Kennedy's doctoral dissertation, *Beyond Advocacy* (1984). He recounted the replication of the Fogo process in an Eskimo community at Skyriver from 1969 to 1972, a project that was funded by the U.S. Office of Economic Opportunity VISTA program. Kennedy subsequently worked as a program producer at CFC and was influenced by Don Snowden, then extension director of Memorial University who visited Skyriver in 1969. Kennedy (1984) recalled:

> I could see several similarities between Fogo Island and rural Alaska, particularly in regard to the problems resulting from geographic isolation from the centers of power, subsistence life styles, and the general feeling of helplessness among the residents. What impressed me most was that the fishermen were actively involved in a process of change that persisted long after the specific issue of relocation had been resolved. Although I had some concerns about the degree of control exercised by the Fogo organizers and their unwillingness to allow direct interaction between government officials and islanders, on the whole, I saw it as a significant improvement over traditional participatory strategies. (22)

Kennedy's experiences at Skyriver and later at the Film Board convinced him that film could be used to encourage communities to voice and act upon their concerns. The Skyriver project, Kennedy pointed out, differed from the typical VISTA project in which advocacy on behalf of the disadvantaged, no matter how well motivated, tended to discourage the development of local leadership. For all the rhetoric about encouraging "maximum feasible participation" by the poor in government projects, the advocates from OEO, according to Kennedy (1984), "avoided dealing with the major frustrations of poor people, namely their lack of control over decisions affecting their lives" (13). For that reason, Kennedy stressed the importance of attitude in approaching community development. He believed that social animators should exhibit empathy rather than sympathy or pity if individual and community independence and self-sufficiency are to be realized. Social animators, by definition, form relationships with communities based on mutual respect.

The concerns at Skyriver were similar to those at Fogo: to start a cooperative, to obtain government funding, and to improve educational services. According to Kennedy, films and videos played an important part in the community's efforts to start a cooperative for marketing salmon and to obtain government loans for housing. The films also highlighted, both for the community and for outsiders, the lack of local educational facilities; this was a hardship for the parents, who were forced to send their children away to boarding schools.

At Skyriver, as at Fogo, the films were first used to collect statements by members of the community, often in response to prior recorded statements. Through a public screening process, the community reached a consensus about the statements that would represent their general views of problems and potential solutions. All those who participated in the screening process had censorship rights over their own statements and could control how and where the recorded statements could be shown. Kennedy (1984) listed the functions served by the community screening of recorded statements:

1 It provided a candid exchange among community factions that led to consensus on community-wide needs and problems.
2 Opinion leaders were identified and were allowed to emerge, without threatening the formal leaders.
3 A mechanism was provided for opinion leaders to act out their leadership in a highly visible manner.
4 The opinion leaders provided a more focused and articulate expression of the community position.
5 It enhanced the community's sense of collective power by giving them the opportunity to exercise control over the technology and professional film crew.
6 It allowed for a more focused and articulate expression of the community position.

7 It defined a process of accountability between the opinion leaders and the general community.

8 By offering a solution as well as stating a problem or need, the opinion leaders provided reasoned and mature information for the community and government officials to respond to. (31)

As in the Fogo project, the Skyriver community had the right not only to be heard but also to hear from outside authorities. However, at Skyriver, videotape was used as a less costly film supplement to record and play back the statements that government officials made to the community. Here, too, the officials maintained editorial control over their statements. Kennedy's role as the social animator was to serve as a resource person and to develop leadership and independence in the community. Later, community members selected a local animator from their ranks.

The media production process at Skyriver, as on Fogo Island, was secondary to community-development aims. Kennedy (1984) stated that the traditional documentary, with all its artistry, was simply "another manifestation of social advocacy" (92) because of its dependence on artistic conceits rooted in the approval of external audiences. The Fogo and Skyriver process called upon the filmmakers' technical rather than interpretive skills. It discouraged filmmakers from "using" the community to express themselves. Ironically, the professional trappings of filmmaking and the status of film as a mass medium defined essential elements of the process. Not only did the presence of a professional crew and the attention of outsiders add to the sense of importance of the communications, but so did the drawn-out filmmaking process, the time needed to process and edit film. The lag time, according to Kennedy, fuelled anticipation and gave people time to think. It gave time for the Fogo process to take place – that is, the process of editing and self-censorship forced individuals to consider their statements in light of an emerging consensus.

Film and Video in Community Development
Although the film medium was initially used as a catalyst in community development on Fogo Island, other print and audio-visual media have served the same purpose. Film and video have been particularly effective in bringing about community participation not only because of their power to model effective political behaviour but also because these media invited the participation of politically talented individuals whose lack of formal education might otherwise have excluded them.

Community workers did find some significant differences between film and video. Kennedy (1984), for example, highlighted the status of film in comparison to its less costly alternative, video: "When immediacy, portability, and unintimidating presence are desired, video is the medium of choice. If one's goal is to increase the power and esteem of those on camera and/or bring a heightened sense of drama and excitement to a situation, film is preferable" (109). Despite the power of film, video has become the medium of choice because its lower cost permits local communities to produce their own programs. Editing video is a time-consuming if not expensive process, and thus video is particularly useful in situations where little editing is required. For instance, Stoney (1988) recalled that video was used to call attention to poor housing conditions by a housing group in Long Island that did not have sufficient time to edit footage to be presented to the authorities. Instead of editing their material, the group indexed it carefully and learned to "perform" segments during meetings to stimulate discussion. The real advantage here, according to Stoney, was that media was used to stimulate action and did not define or overwhelm the event.

Stoney's vision of community-based media can be regarded as the most radical version of CFC. By removing not only aesthetics but also the artist from media production, community media is no longer in the documentary tradition envisioned by Grierson.

CONCLUSIONS

> In 1967, Challenge for Change was viewed as an expert merit, it still considers itself an experiment ...
> ■ Virginia Stikeman, 1970

An Incomplete Experiment

CFC opened up the media to the people, at times sacrificing aesthetics to attain desirable social ends. According to Low and others associated with CFC, the Fogo process raised individual and group morale and at the same time served as a catalyst in producing social change. Yet, in indicating how this was done, the CFC experiments left much to the imagination. Although much has been written about the problems of socially relevant filmmaking, there was all too little analysis of media as a catalyst in social change and too little attention paid to the Fogo process itself. The lack of good field notes makes it difficult to reconstruct what transpired when the "experiments" took place. As a consequence, there is little to guide further replication.

Memorial University's continuing experiments with the Fogo process in India and Nepal, summarized by Williamson (1988b), may in the future yield the kind of data needed to evaluate the use of media as a catalyst in community development. One hopes that future research will take into account the use of mass media, particularly radio, in developing rural areas of Asia, Africa, and South America. Thus far, few writers have discussed the Fogo process in terms of mass media research – that is, in terms of the significance of local listening groups and opinion leaders in the acceptance of ideas transmitted via mass media.

Certainly, the ideological basis of the Fogo process cannot be ignored. The process worked in Canada because government was willing, at least to some extent, to risk social and political instability and unrest to bring about social change. However, given the political instability of many developing countries, one may wonder whether the Fogo process is a uniquely Canadian solution inappropriate for Third World community development problems.

The applicability of the Fogo process in urban areas is also uncertain. CFC undertook numerous urban media projects that focused public attention on specific problems and issues, such as housing, health care, welfare policies, employment opportunities, and recreation. While much has been written about the empowerment of local communities through media, little is known about the effectiveness of locally produced film and video in promoting social change in urban areas. In all likelihood, other less-expensive and easier-to-produce media – particularly newsletters – have played a much larger role in community development than either film or video.

The question is whether projects like Fogo could work in urban areas if properly designed, and if so, to what end. Under CFC, the goal of many urban media projects was community empowerment through advocacy – for example, through applying political pressure in areas such as minority rights, perceived to be inadequately handled in the mass media. The idea of using media in urban community development for purposes apart from advocacy was never attempted, in large part because of the political complexity of urban areas, in which "communities" are not as easily defined by ongoing interpersonal relationships as they are in rural and semi-rural areas. If full implementation of the Fogo process in urban community development is impractical, the question becomes whether this process might still have some limited application in urban problem solving. In the urban areas where the Fogo process was considered, it is difficult to tell whether the concept failed or whether would-be social animators failed to adapt the process to urban problems in a pertinent way.

Careful documentation of future efforts might help identify which avenues to explore in urban settings and which to discard. For instance, conflict resolution might be facilitated by the use of media within small urban interest groups to help them develop a strong agenda for dealing with the larger and very complex political fray. The gradual introduction of additional media-supported conflict-resolution techniques might be required before attempting to involve several groups in an urban area.

The cheap, accessible video technology of today certainly lends itself to further attempts to create urban "Fogos." Small-format video is already widely used by educators and other professionals in staff training and community education. In addition to the widespread use of prerecorded video programs in communities, video is also widely used to facilitate role-playing. The question is whether the video recording and playback used in conflict resolution and consensus building have any place in urban areas. Certainly, there are numerous social problems – drugs, AIDS, crime, teen pregnancy, housing, and police-community relations – that might be amenable to media-assisted problem solving.

Potential Applications

Stoney (1988) suggested that the Fogo process could be helpful in staff development in bridging the gap between the providers and recipients of service. For example, social workers, police officers, and health professionals could learn a great deal about their clients through videotape. Conversely, community residents could also learn about the problems faced by the agencies that serve them. Once clients feel that their views are being heard by policy-makers, they too might be willing to listen and even respond positively to the initiatives developed by professionals.

The problem with disadvantaged groups, however, is that they are un-likely to have the skills and motivation to take an active role in shaping the policies that affect them. There is always, as Kennedy (1984) pointed out, the danger that outsiders serving as advocates rather than as facilitators will impose solutions. For that reason the experiments on Fogo Island, in the Drumheller Valley, and at Skyriver are particularly useful, as they demon-strated the complex role of the social animator in making the Fogo process work. A social animator might be a social worker, a public health official, a literacy worker, or, better yet, a community leader able to win the confidence of people who have come to distrust authorities.

The Fogo process could be useful in resolving racial, religious, and eth-nic conflicts through the exchange of tapes that show the shared concerns and values of different groups. It could also be applied experimentally to resolving environmental issues. For example, communities facing complex issues such as the siting in their neighbourhood of hazardous manufacturing plants and waste disposal facilities may need more than public hearings and mass-media coverage to resolve differences. Video statements could be exchanged among the various disputants – government, industry, environ-mental groups, and individuals from an affected area. A neutral facilitator, skilled in mediation and conflict resolution, might use video statements in meetings and discussions in an effort to identify common ground as well as differences. Video used in this way can facilitate focused public discourse and thereby gain broad support for programs, such as waste recycling, that require substantial personal commitment for successful implementation. Rather than relying on mass-media propaganda techniques, the Fogo process assumes that a medium, by facilitating interpersonal communication, can have a strong influence on attitude and behaviour.

CFC undertook only limited experiments in urban video, using it locally in institutions, mostly hospitals and prisons, without conclusive results. One might wonder how purely local video would differ from a mass-media documentary, such as Frederick Wiseman's *High School* (1968), a controversial cinéma-vérité documentary that attracted much attention by highlighting some of the absurdities of everyday institutional behaviour. Wiseman's intentions were, after all, that of a *cinéaste* intent on exposing his subject to a broad audience. If the Fogo process had been applied in *High School* by a social animator, the resulting vertical films would have been less interesting from an artistic or journalistic standpoint but perhaps more useful for organizational development.

Future Research

In addition to the various written and verbal accounts available through the National Film Board, Kennedy's dissertation (1984), which contains more polemics than analysis, is nonetheless a good starting point for the practitioner interested in further demonstrations of the Fogo process in community development. There are a number of interesting questions that researchers might address. In particular, it would be useful to know how media can enhance community conflict resolution and problem solving. Researchers, for example, might test Low's hypothesis that film and video, if skilfully used, can provide a "mirror" to improve community discourse, helping participating individuals identify salient issues in the flow of interpersonal interactions. They might determine whether the playback of meetings and discussions can facilitate consensus by turning participants into observers.

Low's observations were based on Fogo Island, where media served as a catalyst in tightly woven interpersonal networks, breaking down the dysfunctional communication patterns that were preventing groups from engaging in constructive public discourse. The practitioner might ask to what extent the Fogo-style use of media in community education can be successfully applied to other groups and circumstances. How useful is it for people to scrutinize themselves and their peers through video? What major socio-economic factors might influence how the Fogo process affects individuals and groups? In what ways do urbanization and the influence of the mass media determine the feasibility of the Fogo process in community development?

Forging Ahead

According to Stoney (1988), professional social animators – including social workers, teachers, librarians, health workers, and other human-service professionals – should be trained to be skilled not only in the technical aspects of small-format video production, but also in the theoretical aspects of using media in community development. A theoretical grounding should be part of any program that trains professional social animators to produce and utilize media appropriate for community development or to train others in these skills. Social animators should understand the role of media in group processes in light of the research that has been conducted in the fields of communication, adult education, anthropology, and rural sociology. Their training should focus on the use of video as an adjunct to face-to-face communication and not become bogged down in the video production craft. However, they should also understand that the use of community-produced media does not preclude professional materials produced for a general audience. There are times when production values and artistry are essential.

Moreover, it is important to remember that video, far from a panacea, is simply another tool, usually no better than the social animators who use it. If the Fogo process is to work at all, those in power must be willing to solicit the views of the powerless and to use mediation, whenever possible, rather than confrontation in seeking solutions and making decisions. Certainly, if media are used in situations in which participation is restricted to those in power, they are merely public relations tools. Still, the experiments at Fogo showed that media in the hands of dedicated professionals can serve a progressive social agenda if there is a strong commitment to community involvement.

The contribution of CFC is that it legitimized the utilitarian use of documentary media. The Fogo project in particular fostered an aesthetic experience in the viewer thanks to the spirit of the project. It was not the perfect craftsmanship and artistic control that moved the audience; rather it was the excitement of the social experiment, the opening up of the medium of video to the people. This can be substantiated by the kind of loyalty accorded to CFC by people who are emotionally and aesthetically moved by the kind of message that documentaries foster, the kind that has been supported by the NFB all along.

In the end what you get are two different film/video forms, each with its own integrity – the auteur documentary for mass audiences and community media for local use. They can coexist as long as they are set forth as what they are and are executed honestly.

11   Cities for Change: The Housing Challenge

GERDA JOHANNA CAMMAER

The Challenge for Change (CFC) program officially started in February 1967, its main purpose to address poverty in Canada. It was also intended that by going to the people, the program would help the poor communicate with the government and vice versa. The idea behind this principle was to use participatory documentary as a means of enhancing participatory democracy. Many early CFC films – for example, *Up against the System* (Terence Macartney-Filgate, 1967) – expose some of the attitudes towards the poor that are engrained in a social system that helps to keep them poor and does not allow them freedom of speech. These films show how social aid projects make the underprivileged feel like second-class citizens, caught in a cycle of poverty while the middle class seems unconcerned. As the voice-over states in the introduction to *Halifax Neighbourhood Center Project* (Rex Tasker, 1967; hereafter referred to as HNCP), that is why "the poor are still with us, despite years of governmental aid, charitable help, social work, and all the best intentions in the world, they are still with us. We have been saying for a long time that we want to abolish poverty, but we haven't, and it is growing" (HNCP).

With the growing problem of poverty comes a growing problem of affordable housing for low-income families. However, "housing is not just another optional commodity. It is a fundamental necessity for health and wellbeing, and therefore a problem that is relevant to public policy. Adequate housing, like adequate health care, is a recognized human rights obligation" (Hulchanski 2005, 2). The failure of various levels of government to provide adequate housing for the poor and their denigration of the poor as tenants are at the core of the two CFC films discussed below, *Halifax Neighbourhood Center Project* (1967) and *I Don't Think It's Meant for Us* (Kathleen Shannon, 1971). True to the program's original mission, these films give the poor a chance to speak their minds about the issues at stake, and their voices grow stronger from the first film to the second. While the poor are spoken for in HNCP, they are the main – and strongest – characters in *I Don't Think It's Meant for Us*. The question remains whether their voices are heard beyond and after these films.

HALIFAX NEIGHBOURHOOD CENTER PROJECT

Halifax Neighbourhood Center Project was directed by Rex Tasker, an Atlantic film pioneer who in 1973 became the first director of the National Film Board's (NFB's) Halifax Production Centre.[1] In an undated working document related to preproduction work for the film *Poverty – Attitudes*, Tasker made this proposal:

> I think a valuable film could be made – concentrating not so much on problems and their solutions as on attitudes to and by the poor. This seems to be the crux of the problem. Solutions can be found if attitudes are right. A film such as this could be of great use to potential workers to show the human problems to be faced in going into a hostile environment – the necessity for abandoning preconceptions: the dangers of imposing middle class values: the limitations of the statistical and textbook approach. Therefore the film would be as much about the social worker's problems as about those of the poor. How to enter the situation – communicate with sympathy – help people to help themselves and avoid imposing values on them. (Tasker 1967b)

Tasker wrote this proposal with a film in mind about the impoverished black communities surrounding Halifax,[2] but to my knowledge that film was never made. In another working document, entitled "Halifax Projects" and dated 16 May 1967, Tasker reports to the NFB his findings after a ten-day stay in Halifax during which he investigated a number of "situations and possible film ideas." He concluded that a film based on the Halifax Neighbourhood Center Project "had the most potential to convey many aspects of poverty in

---

1 A prolific filmmaker, producer, and editor, his achievements are still honoured each year with the Rex Tasker Award for Best Atlantic Documentary at the Atlantic Film Festival.

2 This proposal was for a film about "a ring of small negro [sic] slum communities" around Halifax. I quote: "This is rural poverty. Usually these villages are strung along a dirt road off the main highway. Now that Africville is almost gone, attention is turning towards them. Most people don't know they even exist. Those that do, talk of the danger of going into them ... It's ugly" (Tasker 1967b, 1). It is worth noting that Tasker mentions Africville. Africville was a small un-incorporated community in Halifax, populated mostly by black families from a wide variety of origins who have settled there since the 1840s. The community and its dwellings were destroyed and the residents evicted during the late 1960s in advance of the opening of the nearby A. Murray MacKay suspension bridge. However, in the end the port development did

Citizen discussion in *Halifax Neighbourhood Center Project* (1967): well-meant initiatives to help the poor or degrading exercise? Production still.

the city" (Tasker 1967a, 1) … The most worthwhile film would be one in which we take the well-defined ghetto of poverty in Halifax and look at it as a Neighbourhood. By showing it from many viewpoints we would get some idea of the forces at work pro and contra, the hopes and despairs of the people themselves, and the possibilities for change which in many cases exist but are not being utilized" (4).

The ghetto in question is a neighbourhood in the centre of Halifax, to this day an area that has a questionable reputation. As Tasker states, "there are smaller pockets of poverty in Halifax, but this is the main one where

not extend as far east as Africville, and many questioned whether the forced evictions were not inspired by other motives. In light of the controversy surrounding the community, in 1980 the City of Halifax created Seaview Memorial Park on the site, preserving it from development. More recently, following continuous protests of former residents, the Africville site has also been declared a national historic site. Despite these actions, the City of Halifax has never taken full responsibility for what happened to Africville, and former residents are still seeking compensation from the city. The Halifax Neighbourhood Center Project, the subject of the film discussed here, is located in the neighbourhood just north of where Africville used to be. For more information on the history of Africville, see the NFB documentary *Remember Africville* (Shelagh Mackenzie, 1991) and the following CBC excerpts on the issue: http://archives.cbc.ca/society/racism/topics/96/ and http://www.collectionscanada. gc.ca/northern-star/002036-2600-e.html.

most of the 'less-privileged' members of the city live. The area is dirty, run down and *looks* poor" (his emphasis). With an opening statement like that, one wonders to what extend aesthetic concerns about the setting for the film influenced his choice of subject.

The main topic of the final film is – as the title suggests – the Halifax Neighbourhood Center Project, a three-year test project financed by federal welfare grants and the Laidlaw Foundation. Its aim was to help residents help themselves by making them aware of existing agencies, to pressure those agencies to improve or extend their services, and to make the poor aware of their own power as a pressure group. The project was run by four full-time staff (two white skilled social workers and two black residents without specific education, all men) and three part-time workers (all women). In the film we see them all at work, but Marvin Burke, who functions as spokesperson, is the one most seen on the job. He is also the voice for the film.

In his pitch Tasker promises that the film "will be a fast-moving kaleidoscope of impressions (30 min. b/w) with a strong voice-over track (this to be mainly supplied by the four Halifax Neighbourhood Center Project personalities)" (Tasker 1967a, 5). After listing twenty-two possible sequences for the film, he modestly ends this document by stating, "[A]ny conclusion to the film will have to come out of the footage and tracks obtained – I certainly don't intend to propose any solutions to poverty" (9).

The film opens with images of shabbily clothed men, many of them elderly, walking into a shelter and gathering around a table for a simple meal. They are all having coffee and a slice of bread. A note on the wall reminds them that "if you can't eat a sandwich we don't give just coffee." It is unclear what inspired this unusual rule and how it could be helpful to the poor. After this brief introduction and the title of the film, the neighbourhood in question is presented as "a ghetto in the centre of the city. Around seven thousand people live here, one in five is Negro [sic]. All the usual conditions of poverty apply: lower income, more welfare payments, less employment, slum housing. And there are over one hundred agencies doing their individual best to help" (HNCP voice-over). We are immediately introduced to the abundance of help offered to the poor with the best intentions but through agencies that have become so specialized that the poor don't get what they need. One man tells how he was refused clothes for his children by a Catholic charity because he is a Protestant. He was sent away with the message to go spend his welfare voucher at the United Church's charity. Much like the discourses in *Up against the System*, the film states that the concept of charity has gone, or should go, since these services to the poor make them more dependent and force them to express gratitude in strange ways. The film shows a woman at a "goodwill centre" telling the volunteer at the checkout counter the articles she has picked out. Rummaging though her large paper bag, she shyly mentions "some pieces of underwear" and then she cheerfully pulls out a small white purse. The volunteer gives her a sneer: "I hope that you have something to put in it." The poor woman whispers back, "Maybe some day." Strangely, the volunteer then prompts her to donate some money to the charity.

The above sequence clearly shows how middle- and upper-class initiatives to help the poor, although well meant, are degrading for the recipients. But it is not just these charities that treat the poor with disdain. The welfare department itself (see the social worker's comments in *Up against the System*, below) as well as landlords and civil servants in housing departments all do as well. The Halifax Neighbourhood Center Project was initiated in reaction to this and as an attempt to help the poor set up their own projects to help themselves and in the long run "exert pressure on apathetic, negligent and discriminatory institutions" (*HNCP* voice-over). Bill Privault, a volunteer with the centre, explains that a major difference in the approach of the centre's staff is that they visit the people; they go to see the conditions in which the poor live. His comment "It does something to you" is then illustrated with a filmed visit to a family of eight: their house looks shabby, and the children are dirty and don't play or smile.

The next sequence in the film deals with one of the centre's small successes, namely to have the Ministry of Labour open an office in the neighbourhood (close to where its main clients are). Civil servants are sent out to get to know the unemployed (their education levels and skills) and then look for jobs for them. They prove with ample success that it is untrue that the poor do not want to work and prefer to stay on welfare. When offered a job that suits their qualifications and preferences, they all take it. No less than 350 people from the neighbourhood find a job thanks to this intervention of the centre.

Another major task of the centre is to gather complaints about housing problems from those who are not afraid to talk and risk eviction. A man tells a worker from the centre how he has to live with two or three leaks in the roof, electrical fixtures that hang from open holes in the damp ceiling, a lack of security, and the landlord's overall lack of care for the house. When Marvin Burke calls the landlord, who happens to be a clergyman, and asks him about these problems, the latter blames the tenant's drinking habits for the humidity in the house and his throwing up while drunk for the holes in the ceiling. Burke doesn't seem too puzzled by this most surreal conversation; it's as if he has heard this before or at least understands the logic behind this nonsense. Indeed, when he asks the landlord whether the city may have an interest in purchasing these homes, the answer is positive, which explains why the landlord sees no need to fix anything. He will get a good price for these slum houses when the city goes ahead with its new developments. It is shocking, though, that a minister of a church does not care whatsoever for his already unfortunate tenants and that he has such ridiculously negative ideas about how they live.

But it gets worse. A woman recounts how she stopped paying rent when her roof began to leak. She just asked that it be fixed and then she would pay rent again. It was never fixed and thus she will be evicted for not paying her rent. Her house is owned by the City of Halifax itself. Same story, same idea: the city had bought the house for some major developments and in the mean-time rented it out cheaply – hence to poor people – without any further care for the property. In the long run, all these slum houses will be taken down and replaced by public housing projects. If this initially sounds promising as a possible solution, the film quickly makes you think again. On a visit to one of the new apartments, Burke learns from a man who has lived there with his family for only three months that it is already all falling apart: the tiles come off, the floors are warped, and, as his young daughter swiftly illustrates, the front door doesn't open easily, since it is mounted on crooked walls. They have heat in the summer but not in the winter, and they have rats, which are dangerous for their newborn baby.

Now that the centre has gathered the main facts and has become com-pletely fed up with runarounds and non-committal answers like "We will think about it," it has decided that it is time to take action – specifically, to form a tenants association to fight the city. As Burke explains to the filmmaker, there is safety in large numbers and power in group petitions and letters, since the city council is very afraid of negative publicity. Burke thus also organizes a tour of the slum housing in the neighbourhood for the entire Haligonian press. This particular action prompts Frank Fillmore, a freelance reporter who was asked to add commentary to the film, change his mind about the Halifax Neighbourhood Center Project, and he encourages all of the poor and their organizations to make much more use of the media as a means to put pressure on governments. He actually forgets that this NFB film is already giving the centre a voice in the media. Could this be because this is a film made by a gov-ernment institution itself? He seems to assume that "government-sponsored subversion," a term used by George Stoney to explain CFC to the Americans (Evans 1991, 167), is less effective in achieving social change. He might be right. Just how much this film effectively helped to change the housing situa-tion for the poor in Halifax remains an open question.

In all fairness, though, according to the original mission of Challenge for Change, this film was made because it treats a subject that a specific group can use (there is an educational purpose). However, as it reads in the film's project file, it "is primarily aimed at specialists working in the field" (NFB, Notice of Test Print Approval, February 1968) – and indeed, it seems to have made waves there. Contrary to other CFC films, there is no record available of the test screenings of this film, but from letters and notes, we know that the film was up for "drastic revisions" after it had already been approved for release (NFB letter from Barrie Howells, 13 June 1968). One of the specialists in the field is F.R. MacKinnon, deputy minister of public welfare in Nova Scotia. He saw the film with its sister film, *Encounter at Kwacha House* (Rex Tasker, 1967),[3] at a conference of deputy ministers in Ottawa. In a letter to John Kennedy, producer of the film, he goes on a tirade against the "Kwacha film" and concludes that "*Halifax Neighbourhood Center Project*, which I understand has now been withdrawn, suffered by association with the Kwacha film. Why the Neighbourhood Center, which has a highly responsible and thoughtful approach to meeting some of the problems that we have in this community, should be mixed up with or portrayed in the same film with Kwacha is beyond my understanding. I am grateful indeed that this film has been withdrawn from circulation" (letter from MacKinnon to Kennedy, 9 May 1968).

In his reply, Kennedy explains how, after filming was done for *Halifax Neighbourhood Center Project* and the resulting footage was shown, "the material on the project that dealt with Kwacha House was felt to constitute an important enough segment to be made into a separate film" (letter from Kennedy to MacKinnon, 28 May 1968). He goes on to say that both films could serve a useful purpose and that this has been proved by the reactions to the screenings of both films: "As is the normal procedure for all films produced under the Challenge for Change program, both were screened to members of the Interdepartmental Committee before being released. The Mayor of Halifax, Mr. Allan O'Brien, has also shown the films on a number

---

3 The film *Halifax Neighbourhood Center Project* has a third part that focuses on the problems of (mostly black) youth in Halifax. Since this part is not relevant to the housing issues discussed here, I left it out of my analysis. In this part of HNCP, young people meet at Kwacha House, an interracial club, and freely discuss how racial discrimination reigns in Halifax. Their discussions are intercut with scenes showing rather lethargic clergymen discussing what they see as the threat of black power in Halifax and the possibility of violent outbreaks. The clergy do not show much understanding or initiative. The film goes on to show how the black community itself started a recreation program to keep youngsters off the streets, contrasting this initiative with more scenes of the clergy just talking. The film ends with the rather vague and almost desperate statement that it will be up to the young to fix problems in the future. The interesting thing is that the discussions at the interracial club became the subject of another film, *Encounter at Kwacha House – Halifax* (Rex Tasker, 1967; see Banning, chapter 17, this volume). In this latter film the discussions are not intercut and the editing is not as heavy. Segments of this film (17 min., 55 sec.) are available for viewing online as part of the Documentary Lens Project and Citizen*Shift*: http://www.nfb.ca/objectifdocumentaire; http://citizen.nfb.ca/encounter-kwacha-house.

of occasions. These screenings met with positive reactions." He also corrects the deputy minister, pointing out that the HNCP was not withdrawn from distribution: "It has been circulated for testing and is undergoing some revisions to correct and amplify certain aspects. This is a normal course of procedure in the production of films in the Challenge for Change program."

These revisions took some time. Based on correspondence between George Stoney, executive producer of the CFC program at the time, and Jack O'Neill, a local NFB worker involved in the reshooting and re-editing of HNCP, it looks as though the project dragged on until the fall of 1969. Reasons for this delay include CFC's struggles with the NFB administration over the film's growing budget and the budget cuts and layoffs (O'Neill being one of them) that followed.[4] It is impossible to track which and how many sequences were changed, but one obvious re-editing strategy was to include freelance journalist Frank Fillmore in the film. He is first introduced with an over-the-shoulder shot of him watching the HNCP film and a voice-over telling the viewer that "you will be hearing his criticism on our approach to poverty in addition to the film's commentary." The actual film begins after a zoom shot, with images of poor people entering a Halifax shelter (described above). During the film, Fillmore appears at key moments to give his comments, first following a circular pan from the film on the screen to him in the theatre, reading his notes; later he is captured with inventive cuts from an image over his shoulder, his head in the film image, to simple cuts from the film directly to him, again reading his notes. For example, when the Neighbourhood Center's first task is identified as to gather data, he expresses mistrust, saying the centre "appears to be one more study group ... Enough study has already been done, it is time for action" (HNCP). Later in the film, when the media are given a tour of the slum houses, he applauds the initiative as positive. From the way he is introduced in the film, I assume that he spoke his mind at one of the test screenings. As it is in the spirit of Challenge for Change to encourage dialogue, the filmmakers must have thought that this was a creative way to integrate critical feedback on their own work into the film itself – that it reflected the CFC ideal of participatory democracy. But are not participatory documentaries are films in which the people whose social problem is exposed talk for themselves rather than have others speak for them. Moreover, Fillmore adds an unnecessary voice of authority to the film; he reads the picture for us and thus compromises our freedom to form our own opinions on what is said in the film. Somehow, in its second cut, this CFC film has returned to the voice-of-god-commentary documentary style, with an outsider as god.

4 George Stoney's letters to Jack O'Neill of 23 May and 2 September 1969 (NFB Archives) and an NFB memorandum of 14 July 1969.

Nevertheless the film succeeds in exposing some of the middle-class biases towards poor people and their housing problems, as well as the outrageous treatment of poor tenants by the establishment (the clergy, public housing authorities, and the City of Halifax itself). However, where the film lets the people speak for themselves, it does so only in their conversations with the Halifax Neighbourhood Center Project staff, and it is these workers, particularly Marvin Burke, who voice the main concerns. A different approach is taken in the next CFC film that deals with the housing problems of Canada's poor.

I DON'T THINK IT'S MEANT FOR US

Two years later, still with Stoney as producer, Kathleen Shannon made a film that took up the subject of housing problems where the Halifax Neighbourhood Center Project had left off, notably the topic of public housing. *I Don't Think It's Meant for Us* (1971; hereafter *IDTIMFU*) is a film entirely about "living in a project" (this was actually one of the working titles for the film), "a film made in cooperation with tenants of public housing, to present some of their concerns and their perceptions of the public housing positions of federal, provincial and municipal levels of government" (NFB, Cumulative Information Form for the film). The film starts with the facts (at the time) that "some 40,000 Canadian families live in public housing and 20,000 to 30,000 additional units are or will be under construction in the years 1970–1972. They are then a fact of Canadian life, perhaps if never so good as their proponents hoped, also seldom as bad as their critics would have us believe" (NFB, another Cumulative Information Form for the film).

The key figure in this film is Dorothy O'Connell, a tenant in the Rochester public housing complex in the Ottawa Region. Most of the voice-over is by her, as well as the interviews; she is also filmed having discussions with a municipal housing authority staff member, provincial authorities, and even the federal minister responsible for housing. At the beginning of the film, she efficiently paints a picture of the bleak living conditions of people in public housing: the lack of recreation spaces, no basements or storage space, too little room for families, unsafe courtyards, and the unpleasant sameness of all the units. She concludes in a voice-over: "Nobody chooses to live here … This is as far down as you can go, except slums." After talking with the local housing authority about giving tenants a chance to read their leases before they sign, she describes some of the problematic clauses in the lease, clauses that contain obvious assumptions about tenants' low morals and expose the prejudices towards poor people of the bureaucrats who designed the leases: "There's one that says we're not allowed to operate a business, profession, commercial enterprise, or do anything illegal or immoral in the houses. And we questioned the 'immoral' and they said that's prostitution. And we said no, that's *illegal* [her emphasis]. You mean something *besides* 'illegal.' Just what do you mean?" The image cuts to a larger frame. We see O'Connell again, sitting at the table in her kitchen with a friend, in conversation with the filmmaker. She continues: "Something that struck us as really hilarious at the time and that we publicized as much as possible was that right after the clause about not being immoral in the houses there was a clause about not using the fixtures for anything other than what they were designed for. It presented just a beautiful picture ... you know ... just what could we possibly be doing with the fixtures!" The two women laugh. O'Connell quickly regains her composure and explains: "The immoral clause was one that bothered us because it was sort of a slap in the face – 'You never know what these people are up to.' And another one that bothered us said that they could come in at any time and search our personal possessions for bugs ... That was humiliating."

The film in its entirety is very much about the ridiculous rules in public housing projects that make it impossible for tenants to live peacefully and save up enough money to go live elsewhere. O'Connell is the spokesperson for the Rochester complex and is recognized as such by the respective housing authorities, although it is unclear to what extent the presence of the camera and an NFB person contributed to this. On the other hand, true to the CFC mission, the film does help poor people and the government to communicate. Moreover, it also serves as a communication facilitator for the representatives of public housing tenants from all over Canada. O'Connell testifies to this in the film: "I realized we weren't alone when I saw this film of a meeting of public housing tenants from all across the country, who were planning a national conference. The differences in our concerns are ... really just details. The substance of our concerns is the same."

And the main problems stem from the respective authorities' attitudes towards tenants and the way these attitudes are reflected in the rules they issue for public housing projects. An anonymous tenant from Winnipeg came up with the idea that to avoid misunderstandings, the projects should have mixed populations, not just low-income or welfare people: "I feel that the rich can benefit from living beside the poor and the poor can benefit from living beside the rich." Later in the film, when the interviewer asks a meeting of tenants if there are questions they would like to ask the officials of a provincial housing corporation, an unnamed tenant from Toronto suggests asking "why they've taken what was originally a good concept of public housing – something honourable – and manipulated it and destroyed the whole damn thing, so that even the tenants themselves feel that they're second-class citizens in there now."

In the film O'Connell presents interesting proof that the authorities do indeed perceive the tenants as second-class citizens and as both immoral and unintelligent. She pulls out a book entitled *Ontario Housing* while commenting that she doesn't think that it is meant for tenants (hence the title of the film): "It's definitely not put out for us. It's got a paragraph in here that just makes my teeth grate together, you know. It's where they're talking about verifying your income and so on. [She reads the paragraph.] And that [paragraph] is loaded against us, so it's obviously not for us." She also tells the interviewer about a much more "hush-hush book," namely a manual that is given to the housing authorities: "You know, a handy little booklet about what to do if the tenant does such and such ... That's where I found out about the 'penalty rent.' If your income exceeds the level which they think your income should be at for a poor person, then ... they take a percentage of what you're earning above it. And it's called a penalty rent ... you know, right in the book it says 'penalty rent,' which means that it is a sin to be earning more than you're supposed to."

Earlier in the film the federal minister responsible for housing tries to address the "sensitivity" of authorities towards public housing, which he calls "an intangible thing" and "probably the area where the greatest improvements can be made." He comments: "I think that there are immediate improvements that can be made in the sensitivity with which the institutions responsible for the administration of public housing projects is effected. Public housing in Canada has not been a big quantitative thing, it is becoming so now, and most people that are given responsibility to, quote, 'manage' public housing, and 'manage' the people in the public housing – have not been professionals in this field. I think we need more of the sociologist, social worker, community worker type of approach to that kind of thing than just a rent collector." Which prompts O'Connell to ask why he should specify sociologists and social workers – why not get tenants involved?

The remainder of *IDTIMFU* considers some of the ways public housing tenants could be given a bigger say in the administration and management of the projects they live in. The film cuts back and forth between tenants at the national meeting, O'Connell, the interviewer, and authorities at the municipal, provincial, and national levels. While the issue of authorities passing the buck is tackled in some questions, it is clear that they can also do this in front of the camera without blinking. In a longer interview the federal minister recognizes the complexity and lack of efficiency in having ten different systems handle housing problems: "You get into constitutional issues here, jurisdictional issues, which is increasingly frustrating to a lot of people who are the recipients of what seems to be a confusing picture." Somewhat later in the film he has another epiphany:

There is a bureaucratic tendency, I'm afraid, and this is historic, it's gone on for centuries, for the bureaucrat or the official or the power, the authority to impose conditions. I think that the sensitivity that I'm referring to really requires you to recognize that a very light hand is required – the less choice the people you're dealing with really can exercise themselves, government or powerful institutions have to back off that ... I would rather do everything possible to have those kind of behavioural "rules" if that is what you call them, evolved and administered by the tenants themselves, have them run those kind of things, run everything themselves that they possibly ... that's feasible for them to run.

But this kind of democracy was obviously only in the stages of wishful thinking at the time of the making of *IDTIMFU*. Maybe we should also understand the title in this sense, even if it was obviously inspired by the title of a book of guidelines for housing authorities that O'Connell was able to get her hands on. The film ends with her laughing uncontrollably: "This is one of the reasons that we're inclined to be ... skeptical about 'them' when they say that, you know, ... we need guidance ... I think that's what they mean when they say that we're not terribly intelligent and we need guidance ... I don't really know who they write it for but ... they need guidance!"

IDTIMFU, as well as *HNCP*, exposes how there is something structurally wrong with the housing system in Canada. As Hulchanski describes it, "it should work for all households, but it does not" (2005, 3). He argues that in Canada the market demand for housing is addressed, but the social need for housing is not: "Canada stands out as one of the few Western nations that rely almost completely on the market mechanism to supply, allocate, and maintain its housing stock ... [But] households living in extreme poverty with an inadequate safety net do not contribute to market demand for housing. Markets respond to market demand. If households have too little income or wealth to stimulate market demand for a particular good, the market will ignore them" (1–2).

For Hulchanski, Canada's housing problems are an unintended consequence of its established laws, institutions, and social practices (2005, 3). But "[a] just society seeks to ensure that the benefits and costs of our institutions are shared. It seeks to improve the functioning of its institutions over time – especially as more resources (overall social wealth) become available. Its professionals and experts, whether civil servants, academics, or consultants, have a duty to speak up when institutions cause harm rather than offer benefits" (4). If it is obvious from Hulchanski's study that the system has not changed much since the making of these two films (his article was published thirty years later), Tasker and Shannon must at least get credit for speaking up about issues related to poverty and housing in Canada and making films that provoked discussion at a time when this was not common. Indeed, in an

NFB report on the test screenings of *IDTIMFU*, the film is hailed as a great discussion starter. A longer report on the screening of the film at the 20th Housing Conference on Housing in Windsor opens with this statement: "[Y]ou will be amused at the success of this screening after the trepidation with which this film's distribution was anticipated. In brief, we have a sensitive film here which seems to present no threat and which definitely clears the decks for a stimulating in-house discussion of issues" (NFB memorandum, 20 October 1972).

There are extensive reports on the cross-country test screenings of *ID-TIMFU*.[5] For our purposes here it is worth taking a closer look at the reactions in Halifax, where the film was screened on 19 September 1972. The test audience counted twenty people, and a third of them stated that they would make use of the film. Interestingly, "some felt that the film would not provoke much discussion but a heated discussion actually took place during the evaluation of the film between housing officials and those representing tenants' groups" (NFB memorandum, 21 September 1972). It is also worth noting that there were indeed representatives of tenants' groups at this point, which shows progress since the time *HNCP* was made. But the comments vary and suggest that otherwise little progress was made. Some remark on the film itself: "negative film, showed many reasons for problems but no solutions" or "editing biased film in favour of tenants" or "I don't see what the filmmakers are trying to say." Others comment on the participants: "not true picture of tenants, those in the film are too jocular, not serious enough." Still others reject the idea that their housing problems have any similarity with those in Halifax: "[T]he problems in Ontario faced by O.H.C. [Ontario Housing Corporation] were much more serious than those in Nova Scotia" and "it does not reflect local conditions" (survey respondent quoted in ibid.). Obviously, we know differently, having seen Tasker's film and having become familiar with the issues the Halifax Neighbourhood Center Project was trying to tackle.

From just a look at the list of subsequent CFC films, it is clear that the attention later shifted to projects that allowed for more tenant participation (this might even have been inspired by some of the reactions to this film) and to films that gave the tenants more of a voice. In 1975 for example, Shannon produced two films on co-op housing directed by Laura Sky: *Co-op Housing: Getting It Together*, a film about the setting up and functioning of a housing co-op, as told by the people who live in one, and *Co-op Housing: The Best Move We Ever Made*, a film that tries to define co-op housing and the

5 These test screenings are summarized in a substantial report by Leila Sujir entitled "Report to Challenge for Change on the Promotion of *I Don't Think It's Meant for Us*," January 1974.

examines the potential of these projects, also mainly described by the people who live in them. With respect to the two films discussed earlier in this article, it seems that for the participants the process did not go beyond provoking discussion. It remains uncertain whether IDTIMFU led to the tenants getting more involved in the management of the housing projects or whether HNCP succeeded in getting the poor people's voices heard by those who provided them with bad housing. A valuable critique was made at the test screenings of IDTIMFU: "We've seen thirty minutes of frustration. We want to see that energy go somewhere" (School of Social Welfare screening).

In conclusion, one thing is sure: while Tasker defined attitudes to the poor as the crux of the problem, neither IDTIMFU nor HNCP changed public opinion about the poor or the superficial ideas that most judgments of the poor – including those of community workers – are based on. In fact, no matter how articulate she was in IDTIMFU, O'Connell projected an image that sparked constant negative responses:[6] "This film, if shown to middle-class people, just confirms their prejudices, that is, it doesn't explain the pile in the kitchen" (a community development worker); "[T]he problem in the film lies with the people: they're dressed funny, ten kids running around, they have no pride" (a low-income housing developer); and "I don't like the image represented of that woman – the sloppiness. I am not like that" (a Calgary public housing tenant). The responses get even worse when viewers critique the technical qualities of the film on the basis of their own misperceptions of poor people's circumstances: "[S]ome articulation was really poor. I couldn't understand it ... That is because a lot of the women had false teeth that weren't fitted right" (Hillhurst-Sunnyside Community screening). From these reactions we can conclude that at the time these CFC films were made, there was still a lot of work to be done, as much to improve the image of the poor held by the general public as to improve the basic housing conditions for the poor in Canada. It is no wonder housing issues remained on the CFC/SN radar for the rest of the program's existence.

---

6 All the following responses to the film are taken from Leila Sujir's "Report on the Promotion of I Don't Think It's Meant for Us," 2–12.

The En tant que femmes Series, the Film *Souris, tu m'inquiètes*, and the Imaging of Women's Consciousness in 1970s Quebec

I2

■

MARIE-ÈVE FORTIN

Amidst the tumultuous political and social climate of Quebec in the 1970s arose the National Film Board's (NFB's) program Société nouvelle (SN), an endeavour both to defend and to engage the political interests of the population while simultaneously promoting the social agenda of the Liberal Party of Canada, in power in Ottawa for the entire stretch of the program's existence, from 1967 to 1980.[1]

Since the beginning of the twentieth century, in keeping with widespread rebellion against social inequalities, women had converged to form a coalition of broad proportions. Through revolutionary and legal battles, proponents of the women's movement systematically acquired for women many of the rights and liberties, such as respect and equality, that were progressively and indelibly woven into the fabric of Canada's Constitution over the course of the twentieth century. Following these efforts, two women at the NFB's Quebec studios, Anne Claire Poirier and Jeanne Morazain, earned the opportunity to produce their own film series made by women, for women, and with women, which they entitled "En tant que femmes" [loosely, "Speaking as women"].[2] Allied with but independent from the program Société nouvelle, En tant que femmes managed to produce three documentaries and three fiction films within a four-year period between 1972 and 1976.

On the one hand, the films were based on extensive research conducted on groups of women representative of all female citizens in Quebec. On the other, both the aesthetics of the films and their themes were carefully chosen by each director to fit her own individual profiles and interests. The gap

---

1 Excerpt for a brief nine-month interregnum in 1979.

2 As Anne Claire Poirier was launching and supervising En tant que femmes via Société nouvelle in 1972, Kathleen Shannon was establishing the Working Mothers series in association with Challenge for Change, which produced ten films. However, while all of the films produced under En tant que femmes are features by various directors, all of the Working Mothers films are shorts, the majority directed or co-directed by Kathleen Shannon. In 1974 Shannon became the executive producer of the first studio designed for women filmmakers, the NFB's Studio D.

between women's ideals and the more concrete aspects of the series may have translated into a disappointing cinematic experience. Some Québécois viewers accused the producers and directors of the series of limiting their focus to general problems experienced by a privileged minority of women. In retrospect, however, the films' status as documentation may have helped to bridge the gap between the social and individual realities depicted in the films and the Quebec population. Criticism notwithstanding, the films were found to be both measurably useful and successful when submitted for a governmental evaluation, although ironically the funding of the series was neither extended nor renewed.

If En tant que femmes unveiled an ethical dilemma engendered by the filmmakers' personalization of the projects, which, in turn, gave rise to questions of legitimacy and truth, the series is nonetheless grounded in history. Following the presentation of each film, a social mediator invited spectators to participate in discussions and debates and thus heightened women's consciousness, the filmmakers initial aim of the series. As a group, the women at the Film Board created a cinematic representation of the female that today is still regarded as groundbreaking.

This chapter proposes to analyse the fundamental elements of En tant que femmes. More specifically, it will endeavour to examine the series's political, historical, cultural, and social attributes, namely its origin, its founders and collaborators, its mission, its production and distribution strategies, as well as its stylistic approaches. This analysis will touch upon the social variables addressed by the series, and will examine its close ties with the political and cultural aspirations of the federal government as well as with the women's movement. Souris, tu m'inquiètes, directed by Aimée Danis in 1973, will serve as an example of what Jocelyne Denault defines as "cinéma documenté" (documented film) and the noteworthy fusion created by En tant que femmes of both fictional and non-fictional components. Denault's work on women's cinematic language in Quebec and Louise Carrière's thesis entitled "La série de films Société nouvelle dans un Québec en changement: (1969–1979)" are among the basic scholarly treatments of this series of films. Articles and promotional material published in the mainstream and local newspapers of the period will also be used to contextualize the series within its broader social framework. It is from a general agreement on the necessity for social change that a women's consciousness was derived, one that was closely bound to the feminist agendas of the seventies. En tant que femmes is thus an essential chapter in the history of Société nouvelle/ Challenge for Change (SN/CFC) in that it provided women with both the opportunity to express themselves and the potential to create a women's cinematic language within the context of newly emerging personal and societal values.

IN THE BEGINNING

Société nouvelle was conceived in 1969 with the intention of providing evidence for two beliefs: first, that citizens were capable of identifying problems inherent in their own daily lives in particular and in society in general, and secondly, that people were capable of finding solutions to those problems (Timmerman 1974). As Carrière explains, it was in this period of economic prosperity that Prime Minister Pierre Trudeau launched his campaign against poverty and for social justice, premised on citizens' participation. Influenced by the Groupe de recherches sociales, the newly born SN program was sanctioned by the cabinet in 1969. Apart from the NFB, it found among its proponents seven of the Canadian government's departments then in existence, including the Departments of Health and Welfare, of Indian and Northern Affairs, and of Resources and Social Development (Carrière 1983, 82).[3]

SN/CFC was intended to instigate a form of involvement and responsibility among the Canadian population through the pragmatic and didactic form of film production. While giving the population an opportunity to reflect on their own reality, the NFB initiated a film practice that was experimental from both a cultural and a political perspective. Although the NFB's mission had always been to act as a visible platform for the inhabitants of both Canada and nations worldwide, it appeared that this film series was deliberately withheld from the international market.[4]

In 1974 Paul Courtier wrote the following in a note to A.G. Vielfaure, an NFB board member: "As you are probably aware, the Department of External Affairs has not been generally in favour of the use of our CFC/SN films outside of Canada" (Carrière 1983, 101). Since then, many questions have arisen about the ambiguous nature of a governmental body providing citizens with the tools necessary to condemn – dramatically – the very power structures that assisted in financing the means by which they can launch such criticism in the first place.

As Carrière explains, the Pelletier and the Nelson reports published in 1973 condemned the program's sectarianism but at the same time endorsed the outcomes of films by scientifically measuring their impact on the popu-

3 Carrière also lists the Departments of Agriculture, Labour, Regional Economic Expansion, as well as the Secretary of State for Citizenship and the Central Mortgage and Housing Corporation. Department nomenclatures have of course evolved with succeeding regimes in Ottawa (Carrière 1983, 82).

4 In a document published about the NFB by the Department of Canadian Heritage in January 1996 called *Une Société nouvelle*, it is mentioned that the Board's "central legislative mandate is summed up in a simple clause: to produce and distribute films designed to interpret Canada to Canadians and to other nations."

lation. Accordingly, the Interdepartmental Committee of SN/CFC suspended program activities for a short period, citing as its reason a so-called over-politicization of its participants.

In the midst of this heated chapter in the history of SN/CFC, a group of women emerged whose ambitions were in accord with the objectives initiated and popularized by the women's movement. It was during this time, in the wake of the aspirations for social emancipation and democratization that characterized the sixties and seventies, that a new feminist politics gained momentum and took hold among certain members of the NFB. At the time, female representation within the staff of the French studio was limited to two women directors out of twenty-one, two editors, no camerawomen, three out of ten animators (including Micheline Lanctôt, who later acted in the films of the series), but many secretaries and receptionists (Carrière 1983, 183). Within this climate, women at the NFB expressed the desire to embrace and celebrate their femaleness through filmmaking. Inspired and encouraged by the rise of a feminist consciousness, Poirier and Morazain instituted a new film series sponsored by SN. Thus began En tant que femmes in 1972.

EN TANT QUE FEMMES AND THE SITUATION OF WOMEN

The seventies saw the rapid growth of feminism, and its reform-oriented philosophy spread quickly to many parts of the world. For Carrière, three important documents were instrumental in bringing about the realization of En tant que femmes: the report of the Royal Commission on the Status of Women, the Bird Report, and the Morazain-Poirier Report. In the previous decade, pressured by some thirty-two activist women's collectives from across the country, the Canadian government had funded the Royal Commission on the Status of Women: "Formed in 1967 to 'inquire into the status of women in Canada ... to ensure for women equal opportunities with men in all aspects of Canadian society,' the Commission was initially greeted with derision. Tabled in 1970, the Commission's report contained 167 recommendations. The recommendations, many based on the public hearings held and 468 briefs received, dealt with issues such as day care, the Indian Act and equal pay for work of equal value" (Library and Archives Canada).

In 1969 Florence Bird, chair of the royal commission and a journalist who had thoroughly followed and written about the women's movement, published the Bird Report, which emphasized women's relation to work, family, taxation, and education. In 1971, hot on the heels of the Bird Report, Poirier and Morazain delivered to the NFB a research report entitled "En tant que femmes." Based on meetings, readings, and interviews conducted with several groups of women from Quebec, the Morazain-Poirier Report expressed the necessity that women produce a representative image of themselves through their own film series.

Poirier and Morazain fought for their cause in the context of the male-dominated administration that had characterized the NFB since its founding in 1939. Their report relies on feminist literature and covers the spectrum, from women's behaviour to the difference between the sexes proposed in several types of films (*Le petit courrier* 1974a). As Carrière explains, their intent was to challenge the NFB's patriarchal work environment through four commitments, which can be summarized as follows: to move away from a system established by others, to work with others as opposed to working for others, to dispute authoritarian work relations, and to transform the workplace into a learning experience based on rotating tasks (Carrière 1983, 184). Through their critical perspective of women's way of life, their expectations towards and valuation within society, women at the Board intended to develop a new social conscience.

After much deliberation, the NFB executives and sponsors finally allocated a small budget to assist in the creation and development of the En tant que femmes series. Solidarity among women became the credo of the NFB women. Under Poirier's guidance, the series produced and distributed six movies between 1972 and 1976 that were meant to illustrate women's general concerns in that time period. The themes and subjects of the films were studied and developed with a view to reaching a certain consensus among the program's participants in particular and the Quebec female population in general. Strongly committed to women's issues, directors Susan Gibbard, Clorinda Warny, Francine Saïa, Marthe Blackburn, Danis, Mireille Dansereau, and Hélène Girard, along with Poirier and Morazain, worked with several groups of women who they felt embodied the general women's community in Quebec. Inspired by the Groupe de recherches sociales, the collaborators consulted youth and seniors associations, retired women between sixty and eighty-four years of age, students from fifteen to seventeen, women aged thirty to fifty from different milieus and social classes, separated or divorced women between twenty-eight and fifty-five, young mothers, as well as professional women, such as sociologists, doctors, psychologists, writers, journalists, and so on, who were friends of the participants in the series – all with the idea of identifying and then focusing on women's preoccupations, desires, and needs (Sarda 1974).

The producers of the series based their selection of participants on people's willingness to engage in a personal as well as a professional investigation (*La voix de l'Est* 1974). The aim of the series was to establish new principles for women based on three levels of awareness: on the individual level, by helping each woman to know and accept herself better; on a collective level, by breaking her age-long isolation; and on the social level, by giving her the means to become active within society (*Le petit courrier* 1974d). On the one hand, the focus taken by the research groups generated inspirational themes for En tant que femmes. On the other, women's lives have always been strongly influenced by the social values and role models that were personalized by the Church, colonialism, and patriarchy to be made uniquely theirs.

Accordingly, on the one side, *Le petit courrier* associated the subject of each film with one of the specific concerns recognized by the seven women's research groups previously mentioned. Parental responsibilities, for example, are discussed in *À qui appartient ce gage?* by Gibbard, Warny, Saïa, Morazain, and Blackburn, while the importance of love in a woman's life is explored in Dansereau's film *J'me marie, j'me marie pas*. The inherent dissatisfaction felt by women who see their lives being sacrificed for those of their husbands and children is the topic Danis chose to communicate in *Souris*. As for Poirier, she directed two films, *Les filles du Roy* and *Le temps de l'avant*. The first looks at women's quest for identity and the multiple roles history has required them to play (see White, chapter 25, this volume), and the second illustrates the dilemmas associated with birth control, the role of the family in society, and the relationship between individual happiness and social evolution. Finally, in a film that subsequently became *Les filles c'est pas pareil,* Girard conducts on-screen interviews with a group of teenage girls who candidly discuss their views on relationships, love, sexuality, and friendship (*Le petit courrier* 1974).

On the other side, the Morazain-Poirier Report observed that women's security was rooted in two transitory moments in their life: the beauty of youth and the sanctified vocation of motherhood (*La voix de l'Est* 1974). Since we can assume that the first may be necessary to secure the other, women failing to fall into either category were branded as outcasts or regarded as women of poor virtue, while those pursuing a vocation or a profession were placed in the unenviable position of having to choose between a career and a family. At the NFB's meeting sessions, three aspects of the existence of a woman were identified as determining factors that weakened their individuality, their identity, and their social pursuit. As *Le nouvelliste* explains: "In childhood, psychological discrepancies are imposed on the child through education and socialization: sex is biological and gender is cultural. Once in high school, when the time comes to choose a career, girls will orient themselves so that they conform to the stereotypes. Incapable of differentiating themselves from social and cultural imperatives, they will pursue careers as 'female' as officework or nursing for instance. The last step finally is motherhood, too often used to fill a vacuum or to conform to the norm" (En tant que femmes: L'ONF n'est plus une affaire d'hommes 1973).

J'me marie, j'me marie pas (1973), one of six films in the En tant que femmes series: translating the reality of Quebec women. Production still.

Clearly, to ensure the obliteration of such stereotypes for women, an alternative cinematic image of the female had to be established. Nevertheless, each woman filmmaker chose to explore through film a subject she felt very close to: "For Hélène Girard, her family responsibilities gave her the insight into the difficulties experienced by teenagers; for a single woman such as Mireille Dansereau, the relationships between marriage and love became more important to redefine, while Suzanne Gibbard and her co-directors focused on questions related to children" (Carrière 1983, 197).

Even though the films reflect themes characteristic of the times, there is a general consensus that most of these themes remain relevant in today's society. If we look closely, some themes run from one film to the next, thus confirming these issues as priorities in any woman's life. Hence, the themes that epitomize women's concerns – marriage, love, the family, and an indefinable uneasiness – are present in all of the films in the series.[5]

According to Carrière, what resulted were films that were more subjective and personal in nature than the ones generated by the SN program, while

---

5 Notable for its absence from the spectrum of En tant que femmes themes are same-sex identities and relationships, though it could be argued that Dansereau tactfully approached the subject towards the tail end of the program in *Famille et variations*.

according to Denault the themes of the films attached the series to their time, giving them an undeniable truth value. Carrière considers the equal integration of the social and the personal aspects in En tant que femmes as problematical, whereas Denault makes a more subtle delineation between the two. For Carrière, the films remain too personal to offer a representative account of women's condition. For her, the directors of the En tant que femmes series deal with the problems of women like themselves who have the means to solve them. She believes that the personal and the social aspects of the films, or rather their subjective and objective elements, are in conflict. As a result, she feels that the films fail to meet the theoretical goals of the series, originally set forth in the Morazain-Poirier Report. In contrast, Denault states that En tant que femmes women "have to be recognized as a group, as filmmakers and as women filmmakers" (Denault 1982, 22). She believes the films reflect specific subjects brought to life by the group discussions. Denault sees the films of the series and more specifically Souris as cinéma documenté in which the juxtaposition of fictional components with nonfictional elements heightens our perception of reality (Denault 1982, 189).

Danis, the director of Souris declares, "During the two or three months of the research, I discovered not ideas but people who impersonate them: that is the revelation" (Nantel 1974). Danis's main character is thus a construct based on many women and subsequently transformed into one, Francine. On the one hand, it is probably right to assume that not only did these manifold ideas reinforce the character's complexity but they also reinforced the complex characteristics of the members of the audience. On the other hand, the film was also very personal and predictably representative of the concerns of the women of Danis's upper-middle-class familial milieu. Indeed, women at the NFB symbolized the first generation of women to be widely educated, which does not mean, though, that they disregarded their less fortunate peers. Conversely, while being relevant to the personal lives of the En tant que femmes directors, the films had the difficult task of both remaining true to various groups of women and being acceptable to the female majority. As a result, while Carrière believes that the series failed to establish a women's point of view because of its lack of objectivity, Denault senses that En tant que femmes sustained a female cinematic language that is as imaginative as it is authentic.

FROM PATRIARCHY TO FEMINISM: A CULTURAL AND A POLITICAL DEBATE

En tant que femmes gave women the opportunity to occupy all key creative positions in each project and thus redefined the existing power structures inherent in a regular film crew. As opposed to many of the SN/CFC films, and

Actress Luce Guilbault as divorcee, Pierrette, in *Souris, tu m'inquiètes* (1973): mixing fiction and non-fiction to create a women's cinematic language. Production still.

partly because of the new restrictions imposed by the departmental committee in 1973 (Carrière 1983, 86–119), most of the films in the series were not only strongly researched, scripted, organized, and planned, but were also followed up by an extensive distribution process and statistical evaluation. But before proceeding with the discussion about the broadcast of the series and related social debates, let us take a closer look at the production processes and their political implications.

Unlike the amateur filmmakers who contributed to SN/CFC, women directors working for En tant que femmes such as Poirier and Danis had already acquired some experience in filmmaking prior to their involvement in the series. Moreover, in some films, the very participation of specific actresses such as Luce Guilbault (*Souris, tu m'inquiètes; Le temps de l'avant*) and Micheline Lanctôt (*Souris, tu m'inquiètes*) assisted in connecting the on-screen portrayal to the social discourse explored by the films: "[T]he casting was made so as to choose contributors or actors that conform in their private and public life to the image the character portrays" (Denault 1982, 112). Guilbault was known for her feminist approach to film and stage acting, most notably in her emphatic refusal to engage in roles that required women to undress. She based the character of Pierrette in *Souris* on the intellectual women who worked for the militant publication *Cité Libre*, but she simultaneously adapted Pierrette's character to her own (Ouvrard 1974). Guilbault portrayed the character of a happily divorced mother who, at the age of forty (incidentally Guilbault's own age), succeeded against all odds (Ouvrard 1974a).[6]

Lanctôt, however, argued that "left-leaning" films were ready-made documents made for the already converted. Unlike her character Francine, at the time of filming the actress was not a mother, not married, not a feminist, and not yet thirty years old. Arguably, she thus managed to maintain the distance from her character necessary to represent her in the most objective possible way. In her personal life outside of film, Lanctôt did not adhere to the women's movement, convinced that her femaleness had not precluded her from achieving both her personal and her professional objectives. Following her experience with En tant que femmes, she resumed her work as an actress and began a filmmaking career.[7] In retrospect, Lanctôt's sensibility vis-à-vis patriarchy would evolve to a point analogous to that described by En tant que femmes participants.

Around the time of *Souris*'s broadcast, it was argued that when the majority of the population associate authority with a domineering government, women perceive men as being the leading force in society – as opposed to women. As much as women wished it was otherwise, men had become their rivals in many ways. They were seen to control and order morality, beliefs, and values and even to define femaleness through multiple mechanisms, such

6 Guilbault often critiqued the entertainment industry for its chauvinism: for example, for always favouring young actresses and having them portray female characters even younger than themselves.

7 Micheline Lanctôt is a prominent figure in Canadian film history. After studying music, fine arts, and theatre, she took art history at Université de Montréal. She started out as a cartoonist at the NFB and then began an acting career, starring in Gilles Carle's *La vraie nature de Bernadette* in 1972. Apart from her work in television, Lanctôt would eventually write four and direct seven feature films. She made her first feature film, *L'homme à tout faire*, in 1980, and three years later, she made *Sonatine*. This film tells the story of two adolescents, Chantal and Louisette, searching for a father figure, for love and understanding. Structured like a musical piece, the film's three movements explore each woman's pursuit of the comforting presence of men. Their experiences fail to provide the warmth and emotional relief they need, leading them to commit suicide. Although the film's success was greater on the international than on the national scene, *Sonatine*'s themes are typically associated with Quebec's cinema and literature (Blain 1989, 137). *Sonatine* won five awards, including the Silver Lion at the Venice Film Festival in 1984 and the Genie for best directing at the Canadian Film Awards in 1985. The film was even recommended for an Oscar nomination for Best Foreign Film.

as politics, publicity, fashion, and the media (*Le petit courrier,* 1974a).[8] These widespread stereotypes formed the basis of lucrative industries that portrayed women as shallow and superficial. If the concepts of freedom, responsibility, self-fulfilment, and independence were legitimate ideals, they were seen to apply more to men than to women – it was a male-oriented society. Accordingly, for SN/CFC the injustice lay in the discrepancies between citizens and their political rulers, while En tant que femmes directors focused the camera on women who rebelled against the patriarchal system in order to address those ideals. This was done by annihilating female stereotypes and creating images that would dignify women in the public's imagination.

On another political level, since the sovereigntist movement in the French studio at the NFB had a few partisans, in addition to which the majority of En tant que femmes participants were French-speaking Québécoises, the nationalist question was often raised during the assemblies. In one specific article published in *Le petit courrier,* the women of En tant que femmes stated that if they had to choose between Quebec and Canada, they preferred Quebec as the country in which to live and raise their children. However, they also understood that any political upheaval would prioritize national identity over any other form of collectivism – that actions around issues related to social class, sexual orientation, and gender would have to be postponed. By comparing themselves to other women in liberated colonies, the NFB women noticed that national rebellion did not equal sexual revolution.[9] On the contrary: "People, like the people of Quebec, who feel that their existence and their survival are threatened, will easily come to give value to maternity, to numerous families and to housewifery" (*Le petit courrier,* 1974a). Accordingly, En tant que femmes participants proposed to update women's values based on a balance between rationalism and emotionalism, at the same time rejecting the fierceness and injustice rooted in competitiveness and domination (*Le petit courrier,* 1974d).

In summary, En tant que femmes' strongest achievements were not limited to the successful creation of a women's collective through political and social actions. Through film, the women of the collective offered cultural alternatives to what they perceived as a male-dominated world. Yet, even though social and political actions were implicit factors in the realization of those objectives, it must be noted that politics per se was not discussed in any of the films of the series (Denault 1982, 52).

8 This edition of *Le petit courrier* included an elaborate article that explains in detail the En tant que femmes project, namely its history and its objectives, as well as its process.

9 Or shall we say, gender revolution.

SOURIS, TU M'INQUIÈTES: A CINEMATIC IMAGE OF WOMEN

For Denault, *Souris* is best described as a "fiction film documented from reality" (Denault 1982, 35). Danis based her story for the film on research conducted with three different groups of women: single mothers, divorcées, and intellectuals. This fictional film was also inspired by Danis's own personal drama, which had not yet been documented. Recognized as one of the first private sector woman filmmakers in Quebec, Danis agreed to develop a narrative about a woman's existential crisis for the public sector series.

The film tells the story of Francine, a housewife and mother living in a Montreal suburb. Francine slowly begins to question her life, her social situation as well as her own identity, when she discovers in herself a nameless uneasiness. She lives a comfortable life, has a beautiful house, a helpful stepmother, and a faithful husband, yet she cannot find happiness. She finds herself suffocating in this no longer rewarding woman's role and embarks on a personal and social odyssey. Francine questions her stepmother's past ambitions and actual achievements as well as her sister-in-law's new way of life following her divorce. She talks to her husband about finding a job and finally decides to leave for Vancouver, telling no one of her departure. In short, *Souris* poses the question: "When a woman has everything to be happy, why isn't she?" To which the reply seemed to be: "Because this everything would never fill the void felt by the one whose existence was defined by her husband and children" (*Le quotidian*, 1974).

As women at En tant que femmes explained, *Souris* depicted women as feeling secondary to others in their search for freedom and sexual liberation. It examined the consumer society and female stereotypes as well as women's invariable dependence on external and social constructs. To avoid confusion about the source of Francine's anxiety, the filmmakers chose her privileged social class carefully to distinguish the problem she felt from any financial or societal problems. Her existential crisis in a typical marriage had to be recognized by as many women as possible. It served to underline the sacrifice women had to make in the name of the family – giving up their identity for the well-being of others. Although *Souris* did not intend to advocate the destruction of marriage, it did point out how this institution perpetuated a state of inferiority and alienation for women. As reported by the series research groups and noted in a series report that will be discussed later, different elements compose happiness for men and for women:

> *Man's happiness*: a job that is praiseworthy; social and professional success; realization of his personal ambitions; autonomy, freedom.

> *Woman's happiness*: material advantages (house, appliances, wardrobe, comfort, leisure); happiness of the husband, the children, and the

family; the husband's professional and social success; self-giving.
(NFB 1974f)

Such gendered conceptions of happiness seem quite conventional for this time period, but they were designated as harmful by the groups of women working with Danis – notwithstanding that most of them appeared in one way or another fulfilled through motherhood. For these women, the consequences of such conceptions led to feelings of physical and psychological discomfort, profound dissatisfaction, and many frustrations. Arguably, however, some of these values are still cherished across the world today, in the same way as they were in the seventies, especially in terms of a man's happiness.

FORMAL STRATEGIES

In *Souris*, Danis proceeded to identify a woman's sense of uneasiness through the use of both fictional and non-fictional formal strategies. This objective-subjective amalgam is significant with respect to what Denault defines as *cinéma documenté*: it allows the director to bring some factual truths to the narrative while simultaneously expressing her creative freedom. While the majority of SN/CFC films utilized the stylistic devices of direct cinema, including 16mm or video formats, in contrast En tant que femmes and *Souris* in particular relied on a hybrid, self-reflexive style that included flat, static frames and freeze-frames, professional and non-professional actors, monologues performed out loud in direct address of the camera, and 35mm format – not to mention women as main characters.[10]

Four scenes in particular were central to establishing the film's aesthetic and the main character's development: the opening scene in the park in which the children talk about the family; the radio show in which single mothers are invited to discuss single-parent-family issues; Francine's monologue by the ironing board; and Francine's discussion with her sister-in-law Pierrette.

The influence of direct cinema is clearly seen in some of the sequences in *Souris*, particularly in the first two scenes. While the children appear to be addressing the camera while answering the director's questions, the radio show is filmed live, allowing the spectators to witness at the same time the debate between the show's guests and its listeners. The third and the fourth scenes are the more obviously scripted. The result mixes improvisation with the rehearsed quality preferred by the actresses Lanctôt and Guilbault, who nevertheless manage to incorporate their own savoir-faire into their respective performances.

10 Master copies of all En tant que femmes films are in 35mm format, while 16mm reels of the same movies can also be found in the National Film Board's film archive.

The stylistic approach of the opening scene also resembles a television vox pop investigation, since even though the parents are nearby, the children speak about them as if they were absent. The radio show with the single mothers discussing with listeners the need for government-managed daycare is actually the one Francine hears while doing her housework. It is edited to fit between two fictional scenes in the film and is as informative as some of the archival or found-footage typically inserted in most documentaries.

The film's most crucial scene comes in the first third of the film. Francine is standing at her ironing board talking aloud of her discomfort as though delivering an interior monologue. As Denault explains, "Her monologue has an objectivity that is both emotional and didactic but its point is only directed to the spectators. The monologue makes them understand Francine's situation and tries to create an effect resulting from the women's situation she represents" (Denault 1982, 120). After first framing Francine in a medium long shot, the camera then focuses closer and closer on her face and we see her stunned expression at close range as the explanation for her dissatisfaction unfolds. Such camerawork builds a form of intimacy between the viewers and the character as well as intensifying the impact of the character's testimony. It also inspires the trust between director and subjects as documentary usually requires.

Finally, the scene in which Francine meets with Pierrette (Guilbault) in her apartment is symbolic of a heightened intimacy between the two women. The tone of Pierrette's voice is gently contemplative when she speaks of her life as a divorcée and of her new sexual experiences. A camera at a distance records this private conversation, respecting its confidentiality (and the actor's personal experience as well).

While most scenes between two women scripted by heterosexual male filmmakers glorify a form of eroticism, this one relies on a heightened femaleness, the expression of women's self-reflexivity. With En tant que femmes, what is elsewhere associated with sexuality is here portrayed as friendship. The film's realistic note is palpable in its subtle detachment, which effectively stimulates an awareness and heightened reflection by the audience. The interplay between the real and the fictional is highly effective in bridging the gap between the concrete world of society and the rather more amorphous singularity of the individual.

EVALUATING EN TANT QUE FEMMES

For the film Souris alone, no less than four documents have been written and archived, addressing all aspects of its history and its impact on its audience. Some of these documents are complete descriptions of the film's history, development, and repercussions, and others act as summaries of one aspect or another. Several strategies were followed to publicize the series. For example, state television (Société Radio-Canada) guaranteed the broadcast of the first four films, and press releases and ads ran in mainstream and local newspapers to describe the series's theoretical and practical intentions.[11] People were hired to survey and document the audience's responses and comments after each showing of the films. A one-page questionnaire was published in major papers, inviting the audience to note their impressions and then mail them back to the Board for analysis.[12]

A closer look at the questionnaire, however, makes it evident that it served to translate the series audience into statistics rather than to create a record of their critical response. In many ways, it also symbolizes the controlled environment that the Interdepartmental Committee established to evaluate SN/CFC's impact. Divided into two parts, the questionnaire first required personal information such as age, gender, level of education, and so on. It then solicited the respondent's evaluation of the film according to fifteen written statements referring to possible physiological and psychological effects. Essentially, the questionnaire focused on the transformations the film might have provoked in the spectator's life, whether social, personal, or intellectual.[13] If such transformations did indeed occur, the film series would have proved itself worthy of its ambitions, at least for the series sponsors.

For *Souris,* most of the NFB's reports consisted of compilations of information phoned in on open lines after the film's broadcast.[14] Eighty-five per cent of the respondents were women and 15 per cent men. No specific questions were posed to the callers, and the data were sorted into three categories: objective data, the audience's reaction to the films, and the audience's attitude towards certain aspects of the films (Lareau 1974). The data in the first category (objective data) suggested that the audience identified with the main character, Francine. Interestingly, most callers were the same age (thirty), had the same lifestyle (married, living in a Montreal suburb), and belonged to the same social class as Francine (upper middle class), and were therefore theoretically susceptible to feeling the same uneasiness that she did.

While *Souris* generated a positive reaction from the majority of its female audience, it generated a negative one from the male counterpart. Indeed, according to the second and third data categories, men feared that the film

---

11 The broadcast dates were as follows: *J'me marie, j'me marie pas,* 9 January 1974; *Souris, tu m'inquiètes,* 16 January 1974; *À qui appartient ce gage,* 27 February 1974; *Les filles du Roy,* 13 March 1974.

12 The NFB received over 1,800 written responses about series.

13 For example: "This film made me curious; This film is very useful; I would like to discuss this film further; This film forces me to rethink my way of life."

14 More than 350 calls were received after the broadcast of *Souris, tu m'inquiètes.*

would create unnecessary discord within couples, awakening an uneasiness within women that they would otherwise remain largely unaware of. Many men were convinced that their wife would never leave her family and husband as Francine does at the end of the film, dismissing such a conclusion as nonsense. In contrast, the female audience sympathized with Francine for her solitude, the lack of appreciation of her husband and family, and her dependence on her male counterpart, all features associated with the life of a suburban housewife and mother. Many women used with the term "commodity" to define themselves and their role within society. They believed that men misconceived women as, if not the secondary player in the dynamic of the family, then certainly subordinate to her male spouse.

Statistically, *Souris* was positively received by 60 per cent of those audience members who commented on the film. For the majority, the film portrayed realistic themes and problems while reflecting women's general position. Forty-seven per cent of the respondents said that the film made them aware of the problems felt by women and that they had reflected further on it; 40 per cent said the film helped them personally; 21 per cent considered the film useful for women; and 40 per cent thought it useful for men. This last group concluded that the film prevented the isolation and individual uneasiness felt by women by promoting a collective identification. For these respondents, *Souris* offered men the possibility of acknowledging women's struggles and helping to find solutions, even though 11 per cent of the respondents wished the film had proposed such solutions to women (Lareau 1974).

Danielle Lareau's reports show that more than half of the respondents' comments concerned the condition of women and their answers were grouped according to specific themes: "Francine; Pierrette; women's role according to women; women's uneasiness; how women sense the way men perceive them; how women sense the way society perceives them; women's liberation; and how women are perceived by men" (Lareau 1974). Answers were diverse but a few examples may help to situate women's feedback. Some people considered that, from a traditional perspective, Francine's uneasiness was normal within a woman's life and privileged housewifery, while others recognized her role as undervalued and dependent upon the family nucleus. Pierrette was perceived both as an idealized character and as a negative influence, yet she was also seen as a liberated woman. Women's perspectives of their role resulted once again in a conflict between a traditional and a more modern way of life. Indeed, most women preferred to raise their children rather than pursue a career, while others tried to find the means through which they could find personal emancipation within the family unit and thus project a new image of women. If some of them felt that society undervalued the role of women, others rejected maternity altogether and chose a professional career in order to benefit from the liberties offered to men. Women's uneasiness was generally associated with the act of sacrifice defined by a life lived according to and for others; a reaction against women's worthlessness, isolation, and dependence; or a belief that men perceive them as a handmaid, an acquired and useful commodity whose feelings are disregarded or mocked. Moreover, they sense that society undervalues them because they hold no monetary power. Those who talked about women's liberation concluded that it is unachievable without equality between the sexes. Finally, men's comments about women indicate that they often see them as housewives and therefore obtuse. In fact, most men privileged women's traditional role in society, and thought that if women felt somehow unsatisfied, a feeling men found questionable, they should find the solution within themselves (Lareau 1974).

In summary, this analysis demonstrates that *Souris* may have succeeded in raising women's level of consciousness at home, at work, and in the world in general. But the film did not stimulate among its audience as a whole a profound re-evaluation of the roles attributed to men and women within those human spheres. If these reports proposed solutions to the problems previously identified by the participants of En tant que femmes, they also validated the general state of mind of Quebec's women. Four major answers suggested what was necessary for social change to actually take shape within women's lives in the 1970s: "to establish an efficient day care system ... ; to share domestic chores with husbands ... ; to change men's way of thinking regarding women in a work environment ... in which their judgment, opinion and ideas would be welcome; to try to find a equal balance between self-fulfilment, love and responsibilities ...," (Lareau 1974).

Apart from the public questionnaires, the open phone lines, and the printed reports, dialogue between the filmmakers and the audience was established by the NFB in conjunction with the screenings of the films; these "social animations" were to keep the feminist debate active and progressive. The Board hired mediators to hold discussions about the themes and subjects of the films following their presentation. In the francophone regions outside of Quebec especially, moderated discussions were organized as soon as the films were released, and followed a methodical process where participants debated the film's posited theories, discussed scenes and characters, examined their own lives, rethought the film's arguments from a global perspective, and suggested a plan of action. Those meetings corresponded to what Scott MacKenzie has presented as the political effects of SN, those "found outside the screening room in what was to be called the 'counter' or 'alternative' public sphere – that is: a public space where voices from the margins could engage in debate in a way that was not sanctified by the dominant institutions of culture" (MacKenzie 1996, 69). Groups of women could then continue to meet together and discuss the main issues of each film. Far from being dark, the screening space was thus redefined as a vital environment where assemblies of women left the virtual isolation of their households for an interactive discussion about women's condition, politics, and art.

CONCLUSION: WOMEN'S CONDITION TODAY

The series En tant que femmes and *Souris, tu m'inquiètes* were deemed to have achieved their goals. Participants in the program clearly identified the problems associated with women's condition while suggesting ways that progress could be made towards a form of liberation. On the one hand, the research groups influenced the films' narratives thematically by reinforcing their truth value with factual elements, ensuring the series's historical significance. On the other hand, each director offered her personality and sensibility to her film, which resulted in unique cinematic representations of women. If the series and particularly *Souris* didn't achieve general consensus among the public because of their portrayal of financially privileged women, it remains doubtful that their theoretical ambitions were not met, as Louise Carrière suggests. It may be fair to assume that disadvantaged women have other priorities than those related to emotional discomfort. However, it is probably wrong to conclude that identity crises such as this "unknown uneasiness" could be completely eradicated and equality between the sexes achieved thanks to social and financial assistance such as daycare and alimony. Quite the contrary.

The realignment of women's situation since the 1960s appears to have assumed an unexpected shape. The concomitant sexual revolution, for example, has increased the pressure on women to conceal their inner selves and their communal force to become instead men's tools in the acquisition of independence, power, and wealth. Now out of their homes and into the streets, women have become not only sexual objects used on newsstands, billboards, and walls, but also productive workforce tools in our ever-expanding capitalist society. Thanks to the women's movement, women finally have jobs and own their own businesses; they can be elected as deputies and ministers and can even join the police force or the military. Nonetheless, even if they have overcome housewifery, women still seem to have to manage their homes, carry out most of the domestic chores, and raise their kids. In other words, in the twenty-first century, the double-edged ideal of the superwoman seems ever closer to reality. Women's new values and social roles are still defined by their sex appeal and their dedication as housewives and mothers, with their career potential now consolidated into the definition.

That being said, women can still be proud of the rights, privileges, and liberties they have gained since the advent of En tant que femmes. In many ways we have succeeded in gaining recognition as an incontrovertible political, social, and cultural force, and even if we have not gained total control of our own images, a great number of women filmmakers, photographers, and artists have acquired the means to propose other ways of looking at the world we live in. To a certain extent, our education and presence in many public spheres allow us to express an even greater radicalism than before. But to say that the battle has been won would be a fallacy. If we reproach the women of En tant que femmes for neglecting the significance of their own socio-economic privilege in their films, we should not also underestimate the importance of the first cinematic representation of women offered by women to Quebec women, an image that both exemplifies and expresses a reality that is uniquely and undoubtedly ours. It may be obvious that social inequalities have persisted to this day despite the desire of the series participants to define themselves *en tant que femmes*. Women are still marginalized with respect to state and social power, and that is all the more evident today. En tant que femmes permits us to wonder – to hope or perhaps to doubt – thirty-five years later, whether it is still simply a matter of time.

13 Le mouton noir: Vidéographe and the Legacy of Société nouvelle

■

SCOTT MACKENZIE

While Challenge for Change/Société nouvelle (CFC/SN) is best known for the series of films made under its auspices at the National Film Board of Canada/Office national du film (NFB/ONF) in the late 1960s and early 1970s, lesser known is the perhaps nonetheless more influential video access program that emerged, in the first instance, as a subsidiary to Société nouvelle: Vidéographe.[1]

Vidéographe was the first independent alternative video production house in North America. Its work in alternative production, distribution, and exhibition became the model on which many other alternative media projects were built among grassroots organizations in the early 1970s. Vidéographe was founded in 1971 by Robert Forget, an NFB/ONF producer with a keen interest in new imaging technologies; this led to his bringing the first Portapak back to Canada from New York in the late 1960s.[2] Forget's academic background had nothing to do with the cinema and technology: he had studied biology and physiology at Université de Montréal. After graduating, he worked as a researcher for educational television before joining the NFB/ONF in 1965. He then worked with Claude Jutra and George Pearson developing what were called "small screen" works at the Board. Some of this research was used in the development of Jutra's documentary on the use of new technologies in progressive education, *Comment savoir* (1966).

Around this time, Forget became a producer. In 1968 he presented a proposal to the Board for a "cinémathèque automatique," which some twenty years later would be realized as the Cinérobothèque in Montreal. The Portapak that Forget brought back from New York was first used at the NFB/ONF

---

1 My thanks to Bernard Lutz for aiding me in obtaining many documents on Société nouvelle some years ago. All translations from French, unless otherwise noted, are my own.

2 Sony introduced the Portapak in 1967. While it was the first portable half-inch videotape recorder (VTR), it was quite heavy nonetheless and more often than not was crewed by two people, one working the camera, the other the VTR.

for parts of Jutra's WOW (1969), which Forget produced; he also used the Portapak for educational films he was working on at the time.

Forget's investigation of new imaging technologies was not simply the pursuit of a techno-geek: his interest stemmed from a conviction that these technologies could be of use in developing democratic forms of media and social justice. In short, Forget was continuously interested in the ways in which emerging imaging technologies could change the means of production, distribution, and exhibition of film and video.

Both Société nouvelle and Vidéographe emerged in part from a research group founded at the NFB/ONF in 1967: Le Groupe de recherches sociales. Run by filmmaker Fernand Dansereau, this group included Forget, Maurice Bulbulian, Michel Régnier, Hortense Roy, and Louis Portugais. In 1971 Forget, by then one of the key CFC/SN filmmakers, buoyed by what was seen as the success of the program, founded Vidéographe.

At first an offshoot of Société nouvelle, Vidéographe was located at 1604 rue St-Denis and was open twenty-four hours a day. Community groups and individuals could drop by with proposals and, if approved, have free access to cameras, editing suites, screening rooms, and distribution. The Vidéographe model emerged from projects already underway in the Challenge for Change/Société nouvelle programs. This centre was a logical extension of the CFC/SN philosophy: through the decentralization of the media, local, grassroots groups in Quebec could not only represent themselves, but also have a space where they could screen their material and engage in discussions and debates afterwards. While Forget stressed the need for what were then called "vidéogrammes" by filmmakers to be considered technically competent, others involved with SN and Vidéographe felt otherwise. Jean-Yves Bégin describes SN producer Normand Cloutier's vision of the mandate of Vidéographe as follows: "The Vidéographe idea fell right in line with Normand Cloutier's enthusiasm for community media ... 'Every consumer is a potential producer or creator,' according to Cloutier. Indeed, video is fascinating as the only audio-visual media operating in both directions – that is, production includes distribution and vice-versa" (Bégin 1996, 100). The technology therefore lent itself to alternative forms of image-making. Bégin goes on to note why Cloutier felt that making images communally was so important: "Cloutier stressed the importance of creating our own images, before being totally invaded by outside images. The progressive democratization of communication media must therefore focus on video – and on community media in general – as the new medium readily lends itself to the endless multiplication of centres for sending and receiving messages" (Bégin 1996, 101).

While, in retrospect, the advent of the Portapak, its use value in making grassroots video, its role as a catalyst for community activism, and its decentralizing of production all seem self-evident, logical extensions of the CFC/SN mandate, that was not the case when Forget first proposed Vidéographe to the Board. In a memo written on 15 July 1970 Forget outlined the problems raised by program committee members, all of which came down to whether the proposal for Vidéographe fell outside the rubric of the NFB Act. Their concerns – that video was not film, that regional and off-site centres were not part of the Board's mandate, that there were no provisions for the creation of screening venues – demonstrated how recalcitrant some members of the Board were to CFC/SN and therefore Vidéographe. Forget responded to these critiques (which he labelled as so much bureaucratic deferral in order to postpone a decision) by claiming to have retooled the proposal, yet arguing that "I am resubmitting the Vidéographe project, as a proposal falling within the NFB mandate, because it focuses on youth, is regionally based and furthers the exploration and democratization of new creative endeavours" (Forget 1996, 99) – in essence, arguing that the exact reasons he was asked to revise the proposal were the reasons why it should go forward. The proposal was passed on 1 July 1971, but this was not the end of the problems Vidéographe faced with some factions of the Board, and these led to its independence in 1973, after a period of sovereignty-association.

Despite the Board's skittishness, the earliest Vidéographe screenings on rue St-Denis were a success, and Vidéographe issued a manifesto of sorts:

CITIZENS HAVE SOMETHING TO SAY
VIDEO CAN GIVE THEM THE MEANS
THERE IS A PUBLIC FOR VIDEO (Bégin 1996, 101)

And, early on, community outreach in the form of video workshops, designed to get media into the hands of the people, were a great success. As an early article on Vidéographe in *Access*, the CFC newsletter, states, "Teams of 'ordinary citizens' are learning how to program up to 60 minutes of television, based on their own program ideas. They are learning to conceptualise, to film, the discipline of editing, and the uses of sound effects, music and commentary as punctuation for their own productions." When these productions were completed, they were screened at Vidéographe: "Evenings at eight, the public pays 55 cents to view a couple of videotapes and have a share of the lively discussion that follows, usually a dialogue with the producers of the tapes" (Prinn 1972a, 18).

The first year and a half of Vidéographe could only be described as a success story. As of 15 March 1973, Vidéographe had received 453 proposals. Out of that number, it had accepted 140 and rejected 313, while 20, because of their subject matter, were given "special aid." These special aid vidéogrammes were made in the spirit of Cloutier's edict that some events – such as the plight of fatally ill asbestos workers – needed to be documented, even if the videos themselves were technically poor. In total, then, approximately 20 per cent of all proposed projects were supported by Vidéographe. And the program was just as successful as an exhibition space: in its first fifteen months, the Vidéothéâtre drew 12,012 spectators, including filmmakers such as Jean Rouch and Dušan Makavejev (both, in quite different ways, interested in process-based filmmaking) (Bégin n.d., 17).

Along with Vidéographe's successful production and screening space, the organization also created, for the time, radically new modes of distribution. Videos, for example, were distributed throughout Quebec, Canada, and the rest of North America for free. As Kirwan Cox notes in an article on Vidéographe in *Cinema Canada*: "All the tape consumer need do is send Vidéographe a blank tape with a request for a certain program from their catalogue. Vidéographe makes a copy and sends it back without charge" (1973, 16). Vidéographe also partnered with a cable system in the Eastern Townships to start a project called Selectovision. As Cox notes, "About 500 subscribers hooked in to a small cable system ... will get a catalogue in the mail from Vidéographe. Then every day between 2 p.m. and 2 a.m. the subscriber will be able to select any program from the catalogue, telephone his selection to the cable station, and see it on his television set. There will be two channels in use with a 'tape jockey' and playlist on one channel in split screen ... The requested tapes will be played on the other channel. The viewer will be able to phone in his reaction to the programs and talk to the tape jockey" (18).

In these two developments, we see the origins of both vHs home distribution and the cable (now satellite and digital) pay-per-view phenomenon, albeit that here these emerging technologies are used for decidedly non-capitalist ends in the service of community outreach, political organization, and social transformation.

THE EARLY VIDÉOGRAPHE AUTEURS: FALARDEAU AND VITALE

While many of the early experiments in vidéogrammes followed on from the participatory democracy model advocated by Challenge for Change/Société nouvelle, in the first few years of Vidéographe, alongside the activist and experimental videos, a form of video auteurship developed. Two videos that stand out as exemplary examples of Vidéographe's "auteur" work in these early years are Pierre Falardeau's *Continuons le combat* (1971) and Frank Vitale's *Hitch-Hiking* (1972). Falardeau's video, an analysis of wrestling in Quebec, picks up where the NFB/ONF's *cinéma direct* classic *La lutte* (Claude Jutra, Michel Brault, Claude Fournier, and Marcel Carrière, 1961) leaves off.

One of the most famous films of *l'équipe française, La lutte* documents a professional wrestling match at the Montreal Forum. The film is divided

Vidéographe: promoting *Continuons le combat*, *Hitch-hiking*, and twenty-eight other videos in the special "Vidéosphère" issue of Société nouvelle's newsletter *Médium-Média* (n.d., c. 1972).

into four parts. The first exposes the artificiality of professional wrestling; the second concentrates on the physical bodies of the wrestlers, turning the spectacle into a grotesque ballet; the third concentrates on the audience's responses to the spectacle; and the fourth returns to the training room, where the losers of the match – who are Russian and Australian – complain that the fight was unfair. In all four sections, *La lutte* examines the construction of a popular national figure, that of wrestler Édouard Carpentier, and how national identity is reaffirmed through the fights this wrestler has in a public space. The filmmakers were greatly influenced by Roland Barthes's *Mythologies* essays, particularly "The World of Wrestling." Barthes writes that "the function of the wrestler is not to win; it is to go exactly through the motions which are expected of him … Wrestling … offers excessive gestures, exploited to the limit of their meaning" (1973, 16). These movements, well known to spectators through repeated viewings, function as catalysts for ritual practices based on mimetic principles connected to the notion of asserting a national identity. Through ritual and repetition, the symbolic battles are internalized to such a great extent that they are fought out in real life. For the francophone working class, who were often made to work in English (the language of the "colonizers"), the symbolic battle on the mat represents, in many ways, the battle then beginning in Quebec. Both the film's and the Forum's audience knows that Carpentier is going to win the battle, but that knowledge, in the end, is not important. What is central is that the emotional highs and lows of identifying with one's imagined community through the symbolic battle fought in the ring allow the individual, as a member of an imagined public, to find a place to voice his or her pride. The aesthetic of the film itself reinforces this notion, as the spectacle is far more important than the sport.

Falardeau's film takes a different approach. Using a wrestling match at the Paul Sauvé Arena (a far more working-class venue) as a metaphor for class and linguistic antagonism, Falardeau strips away the aesthetic pleasure found in *La lutte* to reveal the violent struggle he sees at the heart of the attempt on the part of Québécois to assert themselves. Falardeau claims that while he was first inspired to make films after seeing such ONF productions as Hubert Aquin's *À Saint-Henri le cinq septembre* (1962), Arthur Lamothe's *Les Bûcherons de la Manouane* (1962), and, most profoundly, Michel Brault and Pierre Perrault's *Pour la suite du monde* (1963), he had not seen *La lutte* when he approached Vidéographe about making *Continuons le combat*. Falardeau saw an article in the paper about an organization that was experimenting with video and would lend out equipment to those interested. He recalls the conversation that took place after he had pitched his project to Vidéographe:

VIDÉOGRAPHE: Well the ONF has brought out a film on wrestling. Have you seen it?

FALARDEAU: No, I haven't seen it; I don't need to see it. I'm sure it has nothing to do with the film I want to make.

VIDÉOGRAPHE: Fine, it's good, your project, but maybe you should see this film anyway ...

FALARDEAU: But I don't need to see it, because that's not my project ...

VIDÉOGRAPHE: OK, let's be clear, then: You're going to see the wrestling film! (La France 1995)

Yet, in the same interview, Falardeau goes on to explain that he was inspired to make the film by an anthropology professor at Université de Montréal who taught structuralism, which led him to use anthropological models in the analysis of contemporary culture. When he told the professor that he wanted to study wrestling, he was instructed to read Barthes's essay, and like the *l'équipe française* filmmakers of a decade earlier, he found it of use. Therefore, the question as to whether Falardeau was inspired by *La lutte* is fairly moot; a more profitable approach is to compare how the two works approach wrestling under the influences of structuralism, Barthes, and nationalism. The structure of *Continuons le combat* was inspired in part by *À Saint Henri le 5 septembre* and other diary films where images are juxtaposed with a voice-over, such as Chris Marker's *Dimanche à Pékin* (France, 1956). Unlike *La lutte*, where the images are anchored by music and diegetic sound, in Falardeau's video the images of the match are juxtaposed with Falardeau's analysis of the class and linguistic struggles in Quebec (foreshadowing *Le temps des bouffons* [1985], his scathing indictment of the Anglo and Franco bourgeoisie in the Beaver Club at Montreal's Queen Elizabeth Hotel, inspired in part by Jean Rouch's *Les maîtres fous* [France, 1957]). He does this by juxtaposing poetic, evocative images of the match with a monologue that is in turn sarcastic, humorous, theoretical, and didactic. Unlike *La lutte*, then, *Continuons le combat* can be seen as an act of *détournement*, with far more in common with films like Guy Debord's *La société du spectacle* (France, 1973) than with *cinéma direct*.

Continuons le combat quickly became a bit of a cause célèbre at Vidéographe – indeed it was one of the centre's first "hits." Falardeau was an unknown film- and video-maker at the time, but the screenings of his videos at the rue St-Denis location caused a stir. One evening, a local wrestling promoter came to watch the screening and partook in the discussion afterwards, decrying Falardeau's use of wrestling as a metaphor for the class and linguistic struggles found in Québécois life. Forget argued that if a video made by a then-unknown like Falardeau could generate forty-five orders in no time, then the market for videos by "known" filmmakers was vast; here, Forget prophesied the advent of the VCR.

Frank Vitale's *Hitch-Hiking*, on the other hand, explores the differences between American and Canadian identity through a humorous analysis of what he experienced crossing the American frontier. Carrying a Portapak with him, Vitale traverses the American border, finds out how to hop on a freight train, and is stopped by American police officers for the crime of hitching. Each of *Hitch-Hiking*'s three vignettes is shot in near–real time, exploring both how the Portapak could be used to stand in for the point of view of the participants onscreen and the way in which endurance would come to play a key part in the emerging video aesthetic.[3] To this extent, Vitale's video foreshadows the Dogme '95 movement and the way video can be used to develop a subjective viewpoint that positions spectators in relation to the participants on the screen instead of through the use of passive distanciation achieved by a seamless montage.

POLITICAL INTERVENTION AND FORMAL EXPERIMENTATION

One of the most important aspects of Vidéographe's work by far was the series of political videos it produced in the early 1970s. Marie-Michèle Cron describes the ferment at Vidéographe as follows: "In Montreal, it is Vidéographe that will sign a social contract with video, which had then become a salutatory intervention and fervent militant tool in the hands of individuals and collectives striving to bring about the erosion of dominant classes and the abolition of obscurantist clerical and bourgeois values" (1995, 42). Key videos in this regard include ones that address the plight of striking workers, such as *Grève Campbell* (C.A.C. Chibougamau, 1971), *Les Knock-outés* (Lyse Chagnon, 1971), and *Vous savez ça M. le Ministre?* (Robert Favreau, 1973), all of which give voice to workers' grievances in regard to capitalism, management, and the government. Other videos give voice to the emergent feminist movement and examine the position of women in Québécois culture, such as *Partir pour la famille?* (Hélène Bourgault, 1974), one of the first videos to address the political issues surrounding contraception and abortion; and Louise Noiseux's *Les seins de Louise* (1972), a politically engaged and yet humorous vidéogramme that examines women's feelings about their breasts and the way these same breasts are objectified in patriarchal society.

While a large majority of Vidéographe's work was of a documentary, activist nature, the group also supported experimental works in video feed-

3 To this extent, one can see films such as Warhol's *Empire* (1964), *Sleep* (1963), and *Blow Job* (1963) as the cinematic pre-history of the Portapak aesthetic.

back, such as Charles Binamé's *Réaction 26* (1971) and Jean-Pierre Boyer's *L'amertube* (1974). Gene Youngblood explains video feedback as follows: "If a television camera is positioned too close to its monitor it squeals ... but it squeals visually. This visual noise, like audio noise, is called 'feedback.' Video feedback may be intentionally induced and carefully controlled to produce graphic effects possible only through this technique. The most common effect is the infinitely-repeated image similar to the infinity effect of fun house mirror chambers" (Youngblood 1970, 274). Binamé and Boyer's videos push the specificity of the medium to its limit in an attempt to develop new artistic and political means of representation. Experimentation on the level of both form and content were seen by many as going hand in hand; the aesthetic interests of the art world and the political interests of community action groups were, arguably, more united at this point in Quebec history than at any time since the emergence of the *Refus global* in 1948. Binamé's *Réaction 26* explores, through the use of video feedback, the nature of the video image. Cascading superimposed shapes fill the screen, and the work resembles early abstract, formal, and geometric experiments in film such as Hans Richter's *Rhytmus 21* (Germany, 1921) – indeed, one can see the very echo of Richter's work in the title of Binamé's film. Binamé, who went on to direct popular Québécois features such as *Séraphin* (2002) and *Maurice Richard/The Rocket* (2005), creates a work in the tradition of earlier video pioneers, such as Nam June Paik, and falls firmly within the rubric of what Youngblood first called "expanded cinema." Similarly, Boyer's *L'amertube* explores the way in which video feedback can create medium-specific distortions in visual perception. Other videos – such as Richard Martin's *Métamorphoses* (1972), which layers the image of a dancer nine times through superimposition, thereby creating a similar but distinct video effect comparable to the process printing in such experimental films as Norman McLaren's *Pas de deux* (1967) or David Rimmer's *Variations on a Cellophane Wrapper* (1970) – speak to the analysis of the medium specificity of video that played a key part in the development of video art.

VIDÉOGRAPHE'S PROGENY

Other groups explored the possibility of this synthesis of aesthetics and politics. The community-based principles of Vidéographe prompted the creation of many new groups and video clearance houses in the 1970s. The Montreal art gallery Véhicule Art, founded in 1972, explored the potential relationship between video and the contemporary art world. In 1976 the gallery created its own autonomous video wing – Vidéo-Véhicule – which in 1980 became an independent group called PRIM (Productions et réalisations indépendantes de Montréal). More firmly rooted in the arts community than Vidéographe,

PRIM continues to function as an artist-run centre, supplying video artists with the kinds of facilities needed to support locally based productions.

Political offshoots also developed in light of Vidéographe. In 1975 GIV (le Groupe intervention vidéo) was formed by a group of video-makers that had previously produced videos through Vidéographe. Concerned with returning to the principles of political video-making and interested in setting up a better distribution network, one that would allow their videos to reach wider audiences, GIV attempted to unite political concerns with a rethinking of who constituted its target audience and how this audience could be reached. GIV was also concerned with reuniting video work with the goals of grassroots movements, as there was a feeling that Vidéographe no longer connected with mass publics as it once had. Videos such as *La garderie, c'est un droit* (Louise Gendron, 1975), *Ceci est un message de l'idéologie dominante* (Michel Sénécal and Michel Van de Walle, 1975), and the Vidéographe co-production *Mémoire d'Octobre* (Jean-Pierre Boyer, 1979) connected video production once again with concerns of the left that were quickly subdividing into different areas of interest, some of which were at times at odds with each other – issues of class, feminism, gay and lesbian activism, and Québécois nationalism (for instance, Anne Claire Poirier notes that many Franco-Québécois men saw an allegiance to feminism as a form of treason, betraying the nationalist cause, by putting gender before national identity [MacKenzie 2004, 165–7]). In the face of this splintering, GIV created Vidéo-femmes in 1979, providing a space where images by and for women could be made and seen. Like Vidéographe, it offered on-site screening spaces where video-makers could view their productions and formulate screening programs for schools and community groups.

Groups sprang up throughout Canada in the wake of Vidéographe; these included Western Front in Vancouver, founded in 1973; V-Tape in Toronto, founded in 1980; and Video Pool in Winnipeg, founded in 1983. While these groups differ substantially from each other and from Vidéographe in their history, all were motivated by community-based artists' projects and a desire to set up alternative means of distribution and exhibition.

VIDÉOGRAPHE AND THE POLITICS OF PARTICIPATION

In Vidéographe's 1989 catalogue, Thomas Waugh wrote the following: "Well, in 1989, video has changed the world, but not in the way that I or the NFB's subversive godchild Vidéographe imagined" (1989, 6). While it is true that the utopian dreams of many video activists have not been realized, no one could have predicted just how easily available video technology would be twenty years later. It is possible that the pioneers of video in Quebec overestimated certain aspects of video and underestimated others. While the advent of easily available video technology offered people the possibility of representing themselves through culture's dominant mode of representation, it did not offer the kind of power that typically goes hand in hand with access to such technology, which early video activists believed would necessarily follow. In many ways, the new and rediscovered communities that were founded around video images in the late 1960s failed to take on a life of their own; instead of images functioning as a catalyst for community development, they became the raison d'être of many of these communities. A large part of the reason lay in the fact that access to the technology, and not a new-found coalitional identity, was what brought the people together in the first place. Later in the same essay, Waugh writes that video is now "conceived less as a militant catalytic spark than as a documentary witness" (6). In the age of the camcorder and the DV camera, this seems to be both a more accurate and more realistic goal.

What Vidéographe foregrounded in its early years was the prioritization of "process" over "product." Certainly CFC/SN and Vidéographe were more concerned with the processes individuals go through as they attempt to define themselves and address their problems through images than they were with the nature of the images themselves. But many questions arise from this kind of process: What kinds of communities are formed through the process of image-making? How do groups go from discussion, dialogue, and debate within an alternative public sphere to social action or intervention? What role, in the end, do images play in this process? Can the community survive outside of the highly constructed context of image production? Janine Marchessault has argued that one of the limits of video is that accessibility is too quickly equated with access to power: "Over and again, video is reported to have been greeted with tremendous excitement by different communities. The VTR 'brought the community together' and the television monitor (even if it was closed-circuit) resonated with institutional authority, promising a new form of social communication … Shattering the traditional hierarchies of power implemented by the interview as a formal structure, community members could employ video to interview themselves. Group discussions were to become the dominant representational paradigm for the democratic communication enabled by video" (Marchessault, chapter 33, this volume, p. 360).

Video, then, offered the possibility of representing oneself through the dominant modes of representation of the public sphere without the true power that typically goes hand in hand with such representation. Part of the problem here lay in the power that contemporary culture invests in the image. The image should have been concretized as a starting point, to bring people together, to debate, and to engage in democratic action. Eventually, the image should have fallen away, once the space that the group needed was secured. Yet, this did not happen. To a great extent, once the images were gone, so were the groups. Many of the key "facilitators" – Binamé, Falardeau – went on to careers in video and the cinema, and therefore the same hierarchy was maintained.

The kinds of debates that were engendered by the practices adopted by Vidéographe spoke to the changing face of coalitional and identity politics that followed the Révolution tranquille. As I have argued elsewhere (MacKenzie 2004), as new publics formed around moving images in Quebec, a shift from collective to communal politics was also brought into play to some degree. While the notion of collective cultures within Quebec still existed – and still exist to this day – these cultures could now be brought into contact to debate and explore common goals, beliefs, and biases, and to develop the possibility of social action and the promotion of the common good. One can certainly argue that this kind of dialogism would be of great strategic use to get beyond the neo-racist arguments surrounding "reasonable accommodation" taking place in towns like Hérouxville, Quebec, in recent years. The works of SN and Vidéographe pointed to a shift in both the imagined nature of Québécois culture and the means by which images could be used as a catalyst for political action. Moving away from the *cinéma direct* aesthetic where the images on the screen were a reflection of a collective culture or, alternatively, of a political intervention through the use of Brechtian aesthetics, the works of SN and Vidéographe conceptualized Québécois society as a field of interrelated, yet culturally and economically specific, communities.

POSTSCRIPT: VIDÉOGRAPHE TODAY

What, then, is the legacy of Vidéographe in the contemporary context? One can see often apolitical versions of the Vidéographe process in Youtube and other online forms for sharing moving images. And the video activism of the late 1980s and early 1990s, especially through videos dealing with the HIV/AIDS crisis, also carried on in the spirit of producing images that are debated and contested within the public sphere. And yet if there is one cinematic movement that inadvertently continued on in the tradition of Vidéographe, it is Dogme '95. The explanation is simple: for a variety of reasons, most of which had to do with the problems of shooting 35mm film with a hand-held camera, the first group of Danish Dogme films were shot on digital video (DV). This led to a slew of cheaply shot (and mostly awful) Dogme films worldwide. In the first instance, it would seem that the emergence of "do it yourself" (DIY) movements such as Dogme '95 were antithetical to the kinds of political videos at the heart of the emergence of SN and Vidéographe. While the hand-held, DV aesthetic of Dogme '95 harkens back to the early works of Vidéographe, the Danish Dogme films are largely apolitical. As John Roberts notes, "What is significant about this list [of rules] is its largely technical and formal character; there are no political exhortations, or denunciations of other filmmakers; it is, rather, a kind of low-key DIY guide for aspirant amateurs; the fire of the 1960s avant-garde is tempered by an earnest practicality" (1999, 141).

Yet a recent Vidéographe production calls these default assumptions into question. Pascal Robitaille's *Dogme 41: Lonely Child* (Canada, 2005), the first Canadian Dogme film, is a coming-of-age story about two queer teenagers, Médéric (Dhanaé Audet-Beaulieu) and Maxime (Pierre-Luc Blais), and their older boyfriends, William (Emmanuel Schwartz) and Nico (Francis Ducharme), in Quebec. The hand-held DV camera invokes the *cinéma direct* films of the 1960s and the DIY aesthetic of the early Vidéographe works. The film itself is the simple account of a boy, Médéric, bringing his lover, William, to his home in east end Montreal to meet his family on his birthday. An argument erupts when the latent homophobia of Médéric's mother (Sylvie-Katherine Bouchard) emerges, destroying the sense of family unity that Médéric's sister Vicky (Madeleine Péloquin) had been sure would carry the evening. Following the fight, Médéric and William leave the city and drive to the Eastern Townships to spend time with William's friend Nico and his partner, Maxime (here the film recalls Vitale's first feature, *Montreal Main* [1974]). From the time the boys leave the flat in Montreal, the camera is always in the subjective position of one of the characters – William is the main videographer, as it is his camera (he says he's shooting "memories"), but the camera is passed around among the four characters at different points throughout the film, each of them using it to document their lives and each other. *Lonely Child* charts the relationships between the four boys, their desires, their coming-out stories, their insecurities, their youthful exuberance, and the worries of the two older boys over the perils of dating teenagers on the way out of the closet. Shot on DV and crewed by friends, the film cost Robitaille virtually nothing to make. While it breaks some of the Dogme '95 rules (the film is in black and white, for instance), it is a compelling film – indeed one of the few non-Danish Dogme films that are watchable. Furthermore, Robitaille's film embodies the spirit not only of Dogme, but also that of Vidéographe. While the fusion of Dogme '95 and Vidéographe may seem antithetical, what DV Dogme has allowed is the opening of a space where all one needs is a DV camera and the willingness to intervene in the public sphere in order to make a film. And that, in itself, embodies the notion of getting media into the hands of the people.

14 *The Things I Cannot Change*: A Revisionary Reading

∎

BRENDA LONGFELLOW

Launched with incredible fanfare in a national broadcast on the CBC, 3 May 1967, *The Things I Cannot Change* (TTICC), Tanya Ballantyne Tree's 52-minute, black and white, cinéma-vérité documentary on the poverty-stricken Bailey family in west end Montreal has to go down in Canadian film history as one of the most controversial films ever released by the National Film Board (NFB), one that continues to enrage critics and fellow documentary practitioners up to the present moment.

The first in what was intended to be a series of films about poverty, jointly subsidized by the NFB and the Privy Council, the film was the immediate precursor of Challenge for Change (CFC) and a radical experiment in harnessing a popular medium for the purposes of social activism. As a pilot project, the film represented the enormous latitude that progressive bureaucrats had in the mid-sixties in innovating social programs in response to the social turbulence, radical activism, and bold ideas about social justice that were inspiring new forms of social organizing on both sides of the border. Born out of a progressive impulse, the film nonetheless ended up being demonized as a salutary lesson in documentary ethics and as an abrogation of the very efficacy of film as a tool for social change.

While most of the controversies that ensued at the NFB during the 1960s tended to involve management reacting against the aesthetic or political provocations of renegade filmmakers,[1] in the case of *The Things I Cannot*

---

[1] Implicated among the more prominent controversies were films like *Le Chat dans le sac* (1964) or *Les Raquetteurs* (1958), films whose ultimate style and shape had significantly departed from the original proposals for the films. Most of these "controversies" as such involved filmmakers working on the French side, where political and aesthetic evolution was significantly advanced and where the attitude in the 1960s towards a federal institution was more problematized.

The Things I Cannot Change (1967): an object lesson in documentary ethics gone wrong or a bullshit myth in need of historical context? Production still.

Change, the controversy was played out in completely different terms, in ways that have traditionally exonerated institutional culpability and singularly focused on the ethical breach allegedly committed by the film's young and naïve director, a reading that has curiously held up through the decades. Indeed, as recently as 2002, Matthew Hays (2002) referred to the film in a special issue of *Take One* as "a textbook case of documentary filmmaking ethics gone terribly wrong." In the same issue, Thomas Waugh also referred to the controversy, calling it "an object lesson in problematical ethics for generations to come" (2002a, 46).

Nearly every critical essay and article on the film, from those published in close proximity to the date of the national broadcast to those published recently, formulates an allegation of ethical breach in similar terms. Marie

Kurchak's "What Challenge? What Change?," first published in 1972, asserts that after the film was first broadcast, "the family was exposed to the teasing and mocking of its neighbours" (1972, 121). An interview with George Stoney, published in 1980, expanded on how the Bailey family was brutalized and exploited by the film: "[T]he children became the butts of jokes. The family began to see themselves as other people saw them – as poor people without dignity ... and they literally had to move" (Rosenthal, chapter 15, this volume, p. 177). D.B. Jones in his *Movies and Memoranda* (1981) noted: "After the film appeared on television, the family suffered the ridicule of their neighbours. They were hurt by the film, not helped" (1981, 160). A decade later, Gary Evans, in his monumental history *The NFB: In the National Interest* (1991), refers to the "inexperienced" Ballantyne Tree, asserting that "the unfortunate family suffered dearly for allowing the probing camera to put on display some of their intimate feelings ... [T]heir subsequent notoriety led neighbours to mock the bewildered family " (1991, 159). Janine Marchessault[2] (1995) and Scott MacKenzie[3] (1996) in their provocative rereadings of Challenge for Change (CFC) repeat the allegation to the point where it has now became an apocryphal story, part urban legend, part film community myth. Certainly this was the story I heard as a young anti-poverty activist in Ottawa in the late 1970s. But what were the roots of this particular reading of the film as privacy-invading exploitative sensationalism?

In a recent interview (18 June 2008), Ballantyne Tree claimed that this persistent representation of the family as injured victims was "bullshit," propagated by rumour and gossip and by individuals who failed to actually investigate the reality of the situation. According to Ballantyne Tree, the Baileys did not have deep ties to or friends in the neighbourhood depicted in the 1967 film. They had only lived there six months and were, as documented in her subsequent film on the Baileys, *The Courage to Change* (1985), only too happy to leave what they perceived as a violent and desperate area of the city.

What I would like to attempt here is to go beyond the apocryphal and consider the film in relation to the co-temporaneous institutional, aesthetic, and political contexts that contributed to its complex reception, not the least of which (and largely unremarked in the critical literature) had to do with the

2 Janine Marchessault says of the film: "[W]hile sensitive, [it] only reinforced the hopelessness and futility of the family's situation. Moreover, the family's sense of powerlessness was heightened when, without their being notified, the film was aired on local television. They were subjected to ridicule by neighbours and eventually had to move" (Marchessault, chapter 33, this volume, p. 357).

3 Scott MacKenzie claimed that the family "did not have prior warning that the film was going to be broadcast" and were "so ridiculed by their neighbours after the broadcast that they had to move" (MacKenzie, chapter 31, this volume, p. 329).

particular style of vérité the film adopts as its primary method of exploring the social issue of poverty. As so much of the controversy the film provoked was articulated in terms of the violation of documentary ethics, a consideration of the way aesthetic choices magnified issues of representation and informed consent seems in order. Beyond historicizing the reception of what was surely one of the NFB's most controversial releases, I believe that what makes TTICC an intriguing case study is that it can be seen as a highly volatile, contradictory, and semiotically labile text that complicates issues related to documentary ethics and aesthetics, discourses of poverty, and representation in ways that are still absolutely current.

THE BROADCAST

Let's start with the television broadcast, as it was this new and highly prominent context of exhibition that subjected the film, its subjects, and the filmmaker to national notoriety, far more than the subsequent and extensive circulation of the film did in the NFB's traditional educational circuit of classrooms, community centres, and proverbial church basements.[4] Certainly Ballantyne Tree was under the impression throughout the production of TTICC that her film would be disseminated primarily in the educational market, and by the time of the broadcast on 3 May 1967, she had already left the NFB feeling "too young to commit the rest of [her] life to being a bureaucrat in the Canadian civil service" and in a "wave of youthful iconoclasm" instead married a folksinger and "hit the road" (Ballantyne Tree, 2008).

A memo to John Kemeny dated 2 September 1966, however, indicates that the national telecast date on CBC had already been determined, although it was clearly only one of a range of opportunities envisioned by the distribution office of the NFB. A part of the memo, subtitled Community Distribution Plans, itemizes the intention to lobby the Privy Council to purchase between 150 and 200 prints for distribution through the NFB, public libraries, and film councils. There were additional plans to distribute an information sheet to welfare agencies, universities, churches, and service clubs and to convoke a series of "teach-ins" in the fall of 1967 at major universities; these latter would involve the staging of dramatic debates between, as the memo phrased it, "persons who 'represent the establishment' and also 'persons who represent CHANGE in the community.'" In addition to the national telecast,

4 Ballantyne Tree completed an MA at Concordia, where she conducted an ethnographic study of the film's reception. See Ballantyne Tree, "Formative evaluation of a documentary film on the effects of poverty on a Montreal family," MA thesis, Concordia University, 1989.

there were hopes that the film could be telecast on regional and local televi-sion stations.[5]

Clearly Kemeny and the CBC commissioning producers felt there was something about the film's dramatic subject matter and aesthetic approach that made it appropriate for a one-hour special presentation on the national CBC's premier arts series, *Festival*, and both institutions embarked on what one writer observed as a "colossal promotion." Notices of the broadcast were sent to a mailing list of 80,000, including the Canadian Welfare Coun-cil, the Vanier Institute, the Canadian Labour Council, the Anglican and United Churches, and the Council of Jewish women. A week prior to the actual telecast, screenings were held in closed sessions for the press and members of provincial legislatures. As Rob Shields of the *Toronto Daily Star* noted, "Few Canadian programs have received the buildup that accompanied last night's National Film Board documentary: *The Things I Cannot Change*, shown on *Festival*. The NFB proudly held advance screenings and the CBC plugged it over and over again on the air as 'a shocking documentary on poverty in Canada'" (Shields 1967).

The television clips featured scenes of Kenneth Bailey speaking directly to the camera about the beatings he had received as a child. It seems clear that as the film was fed through the promotional mill, it was being positioned as a sensational exposé of the dark and hitherto obscured realities of poverty in Canada. The CBC *Times*, in tones reminiscent of a Victorian muckraker, noted that "Canada the country with the second highest standard of living in the world has a debilitating, inherited disease sapping her health and potential to an alarming degree: poverty."[6] Almost all of the reviews pointed to the sharp and alarming contrast between the popular conception of Canada as an exemplar of "The Affluent Society" and the "nasty holes" of poverty exposed in the film that could only unsettle the smug belief in the universality of postwar prosperity. The framing of TTICC as an exposé was, of course, facilitated and dramatized by the film's radical observational style, a point alluded to in many of the reviews, which referred to the "intimate," "undirected," and "beyond the statistics" view the film provided into the unabashed reality of poverty. "Nothing is staged, nothing is dramatized. These people aren't actors," remarked the reviewer in the *Winnipeg Free*

5 The "Distribution Plans for Proposed Film on Poverty" bragged that current and back catalogue NFB films had been picked up and screened extensively on regional and local television stations: "During the last 12 months, we have had 6,776 book-ings on television which involve 75 stations out of a total of 88 stations in this coun-try," NFB Archives, 24 March 2008.

6 Quoted in Shields 1967, 26.

Press. "[T]his close-up of the other side of life provides more drama and pathos than most people experience in a lifetime" (*Winnipeg Free Press* 1967).

Under the banner headline "What It's Like to Be Really Poor," the *Montreal Star* of Thursday, 4 May 1967, talked about the film's "enormous sense of humanity, of there but for the grace of God go I" (Pearce 1967, 68). The *Ottawa Citizen*, 4 May 1967, called the film "a portrait, sometimes embarrassingly intimate, of a real-life struggle for survival in a big city" (Penn 1967, 35).

Most of the press reviews (as opposed to the subsequent critical essays) published shortly after the broadcast were, in fact, adulatory. Only Rob Shields of the *Toronto Daily Star* pointed to the "danger" of "camera vérité techniques" as a method of carrying a film he saw as "short on both research and perspective." "We had the uncomfortable feeling," he writes, "that dad was all too conscious of the cameras. Instead of seeing a man tragically ensnarled in poverty we saw self-pity and it failed to move us" (1967).

Oddly, the film was featured at 9:30 PM on Wednesday evening in the CBC's *Festival* series, typically the purveyor of quintessential "high" culture, operas and ballets or "quality drama" from Stratford and successful Canadian theatre. While much of the rest of CBC television was "drowned" in American programs prior to the Canadian-content regulations that would come online in 1970, the *Festival* series was distinguished as an exemplar of the traditional public broadcasting mandate of indigenous cultural production and public service. Moreover, it was not completely unprecedented that *Festival* would feature an NFB documentary. The year before, *Festival* had premiered Roman Kroitor and Wolf Koenig's documentary portrait of Igor Stravinsky, although there the overlap between a performing arts strand and documentary content seemed far more congenial. At a time when the presentation of long-form documentaries as opposed to news shows was intermittent if not absolutely rare, it seemed extraordinary that a slot in a prestige arts series would be given over to a social-issue documentary. However, it was perhaps a prescient move given the topicality of the film's subject matter, its highly telegenic performative and dramatic qualities, and television's subsequent taste for material that featured the no-holds-barred revelation of the private lives of the socially marginal. When broadcast, TTICC received one of the highest audience shares in the history of NFB films.[7]

---

7 Executive produce Robert Allen estimated that *Festival* reached about 900,000 homes in the mid-1960s, and surveys conducted in 1963 on the subject of the program indicated that the show gained audience shares of 17 and 20 per cent in Toronto and Vancouver. Blaine Allen, "Directory of CBC Television Series 1952–1982," http://www.film.queensu.ca/cbc/.

THE WAR ON POVERTY

One can hardly underestimate the growing public concern and interest in issues of poverty at the time. As Ballantyne Tree's original proposal voiced it, poverty was "as topical as the war in Vietnam." Indeed, given the last two decades of neo-conservative dismantling of the welfare state, it seems nothing short of astonishing to think about just how mainstream the belief in the efficacy of the state to address issues of economic disenfranchisement was during the decade of the 1960s.

By the time the film was being conceived, there was a growing awareness that the enormous postwar expansion of the middle class and blue-collar economic advancement via powerful industrial unions were not bringing all members of society into the euphoria of car culture, suburbs, and consumer society. Two enormously influential books, John Kenneth Galbraith's *The Affluent Society* (1958) and Michael Harrington's *The Other America: Poverty in the United States* (1962), were widely disseminated and intensely debated in the public realm. Both aimed to confront middle-class America with the reality that the affluent society had a darker underside of poverty and disenfranchisement. Harrington in particular suggested ways to reform the excesses of advanced capitalism with specific state interventions – ideas that inspired many of the programs launched during Lyndon Johnson's "war on poverty," announced with much fanfare in 1964.

No doubt the war on poverty evolved from a complex genealogy (impossible to detail here) that, given the growing radicalism on campuses and the mass mobilizations of the civil rights movement, encompassed contradictory motivations, from genuine social concern to fear of impending social disorder (see Druick, chapter 32, this volume). In *Race, Money and the American Welfare State*, Michael Brown argues that the "war" in the United States was structured by a deliberate avoidance of the fact that poverty in the U.S. was highly racialized and overdetermined by systematic structures of discrimination (African-Americans being three times more likely to live in poverty than Americans of European ethnicity). The war on poverty, as he writes it, was never intended to be genuinely redistributive or radically disruptive of capital accumulation,[8] and rather than advance the more radical propositions of anti-poverty activists, such as a guaranteed annual income, wages for housework, or genuine job creation, Johnson's program was singularly focused on the liberal provision of "opportunity" as delivered through job training programs.

8 Brown talks about the balance Johnson had to strike between fiscal conservatives, the fear of middle-class backlash, and more liberal inclinations towards social justice.

The American-led war on poverty and a series of crucial statistical analyses[9] proved highly inspirational to radical civil servants attached to the Privy Council in Canada, and Canada's own war on poverty was officially launched in 1965 with Prime Minister Lester Pearson's announcement of $25 million a year to be funnelled to the poor through the Canada Assistance Plan. While this expansion of federal welfare programs might well be read as a corporatist move,[10] it is clear that this policy was partially articulated in response to newly radicalized anti-poverty activism that was making waves in the media and having a marked effect on the broad public debate on poverty. As Margaret Hillyard Little has noted, grassroots anti-poverty activism was burgeoning throughout the sixties, signalling the first substantial mobilizations since the Depression, and included various community and tenant associations and, eventually, innovative and highly radical organizations like the Just Society Movement in Toronto, whose activities – lobbying for welfare rights through occupations and demonstrations – were catalyzing social momentum and evolving a new discourse pertaining to poverty, one centring on rights and social justice (Hillyard Little 2007).

Relying on Nicos Poulantzas's theory of the state as multiple sites of negotiated class struggle, internally contradictory and riven with ideological fissures and divisions, allows for a fuller appreciation of the complexity of poverty demands and policy evolution in the 1960s than a more functionalist or purely instrumental view of the state as a fully administered apparatus of social reproduction (Poulantzas 1978). In that light, the evolution of the war on poverty might be seen as a protracted and complex negotiation between competing demands, those of radical activists and fiscal conservatives, liberal ideologues and elements of the business community and middle class who bore a traditional antipathy towards welfare "dependency" as a means of promoting "sloth and shiftlessness" (Finnegan 2003, 18) and of containing and responding to the growing wave of social turbulence that was collectively interrogating many of the founding myths of liberal capitalist democracies during the 1960s.

Certainly the Privy Council had to be seen as one of the more enlightened state fractions of the time, housing key bureaucrats whose views on social change were seemingly indebted to Saul Alinsky and informed by ideas

9 According to a report published by the Ontario Federation of Labour in 1964, one million Canadians were living in poverty. In 1965 the Canadian Welfare Council conducted a study of rural poverty and found the extent "staggering" (Hillyard Little 2007).

10 This is the provocative argument developed in Zoë Druick's *Projecting Canada: Government Policy and Documentary Film at the National Film Board* (Montreal and Kingston: McGill-Queen's University Press, 2007).

about participatory democracy and self-organizing current in progressive circles. One of its more radical ideas, inaugurated in 1965 as part of Canada's war on poverty, was the formation of the Company of Young Canadians (CYC), which was intended to engage middle-class youth in organizing marginalized communities across the country.[11]

In Gary Evans's well-documented history of the NFB, the idea for a series of films about poverty was first proposed in 1965 by Privy Council representative Gordon Robertson, who wrote to NFB commissioner Guy Roberge. As Evans (1991, 158) narrates it, John Kemeny, one of the executive producers at the NFB, had been searching for innovative projects and immediately seized on the idea. Talks were begun with the Special Planning Secretariat of the Privy Council, whose director R.A.J. Phillips was also a director of the CYC. Kemeny began drafting a working paper on the proposed series; entitled "Proposal for a Program of Film Activities in the Area of Poverty and Change," it was officially submitted 16 February 1967. In the meantime, Kemeny and the Special Planning Secretariat agreed to go ahead and produce a pilot project for the entire series, to be shot in Montreal with a staff director.

Kemeny approached Ballantyne Tree, a young McGill graduate with one film under her belt and into her second year of working full-time at the NFB, with the project and set her the task of knocking on doors at various social agencies in Montreal with the view of finding an appropriate family who would embody the plight of the poor. Ballantyne Tree claims that that was about the extent of the direction she received from Kemeny and that the style, approach, and choice of subjects were left up to her. When she discovered Kenneth and Gertrude Bailey on the other side of one of the many doors she had been knocking on, he with his "tremendous gift of the gab" and she with all those children and the imminent birth of the tenth, Ballantyne Tree instinctively felt that she had found the ingredients "to make something of interest, that would have some drama" (Ballantyne Tree, 2008). Her original proposal, "The Bailey Family: Eleven Going on Twelve," was for a half-hour 16mm black and white film "to be produced for the Privy Council." It was submitted on 13 September 1966, and two weeks later, the shoot had begun.

If Kemeny did not take a hands-on approach to the evolution of Ballantyne Tree's film, it may have been because of his absorption in elaborating the proposal for a whole series of films and innovative film practices that would take the NFB and the social-issue film in an entirely innovative direction.

11 In an almost graphic confirmation of Poulantzas's theory of the internal contradictions of the state, the CYC was almost immediately taken over by leftish and, in Quebec, separatist elements (Gilles Duceppe of the Bloc québécois was a young member), which was, no doubt, why its autonomy was revoked in 1969 and the company disbanded in 1976.

Kemeny's proposal, which would form the core of the Challenge for Change mandate, was clearly produced through extensive consultation, discussion, and collaboration. It is worth reflecting on how some of the key ideas that were being developed in the proposal provided a certain kind of discursive parameter for the Ballantyne Tree film being filmed, edited, and produced at the same time.

It was clear that Kemeny's proposal was animated and inspired by the oppositional movements of the era that were engaged in an ongoing interrogation of the core values and founding myths of capitalist liberal democracies. It was certainly in this spirit that the proposal included the announcement that the proposed films were intended to "provoke basic social change; anything less would be a palliative" (NFB 1967b).

The proposal envisioned three distinctive models of film practice, each with a particular audience in mind, and each involving particular kinds of filmic interventions. Category I films would be addressed to the general public in order to "prepare public opinion for unorthodox attacks on poverty and generate support for government involvement in poverty programs ... without being either shrill or preachy." These would be hard-hitting and profoundly socially interrogative, intended to "deeply lacerate our protective layers of mental and emotional fat." This was especially true, the proposal went on, "where public attitudes are major factors in poverty problems, e.g. attitudes toward public housing, Indians, justice, welfare." The discussion of the parameters of Category I films ended with the advice that only a few of these should actually be made as "[m]ass audiences are unlikely to generate action (the prime need) and a surfeit of them could backfire (an affluent society does not like to be reminded of its sores)" (NFB 1967a).

Category II films would be addressed to people working in the poverty field, to CYC staff, welfare agencies, development officers, Indian Affairs officers, and so on, with the intention of questioning "establishment attitudes" and "conventional approaches" and sparking a far-reaching attitudinal change on the part of state workers. The specific list of suggested topics was fairly narrow and focused on ideas for films on radical social workers, the church and social action, the bias of the justice system, and the social advantages of the cooperative movement. As part of the activities in this category, CYC participants would train volunteers in elementary film techniques in field projects.

The ideas listed for Category III work – "Film Activities among the Poor" – however, were the "most valuable" part of the proposal. As the proposal put it, "Public understanding, wise planning and dedicated field work will have few lasting effects unless the poor *want* to organize themselves, insist on their rights, change their ways of living and working ... We believe that film

activities, radically conceived and imaginatively carried out, could be powerful stimuli for social change in the hands of the poor" (NFB 1967b).

Clearly informed and inspired by the radical discourses of Paulo Freire,
Saul Alinsky, and the models of social organizing pioneered in the civil rights
movement, the ideas and language deployed in the working paper represented a substantial move beyond the traditional paternalism of state welfare
agencies, where the poor were largely considered as little more than victims
or clients of a beneficent state. By contrast, the proposal envisioned that the
work of a state agency in the context of the poverty series was to facilitate
the process of the poor helping themselves, to catalyze "self-perpetuating"
organization, and, ultimately, to withdraw.[12] The proposal concluded with
the weighty admonition that all involved were beyond being "do-gooders."
We must be "hard headed and non-sentimental," the proposal advised,
"accept the possibility of failure" and "be prepared to defend the experimental nature of what we are doing."

OBSERVATIONAL STYLE AND *THE THINGS I CANNOT CHANGE*

One can only speculate how Kemeny and the members of the Privy Council
might have viewed the evolution of Ballantyne Tree's film according to the
discussions on the poverty series that were being carried out at the time. By
virtue of Kemeny having selected a young director with verve and the film
having been originally conceived as a half-hour short, proposed, and moved
into production within a two-week period, TTICC bore some of the experimental characteristics of what would be defined as Category III films. However, given the CBC national telecast and Ballantyne Tree's broad approach
to the subject matter, it is clear that the film was intended to address the general public, which by the time the proposal was completed was judged to be
the least effective and potentially the most likely audience to generate an
adverse reaction.

According to Ballantyne Tree, she was the one who proposed adopting a
"candid" style and dispensing with a conventional format that would have
deployed the requisite expert, pedantic analysis and overdetermined narration, the traditional staples of the educational film. Her original proposal
refers to the many different ways one could approach the topic and references
a CBC documentary apparently in the works that was intended to illustrate
the scope and extent of poverty in Canada, examining some of its socio-
economic causes. By contrast, Ballantyne Tree proposed to "examine poverty

---

12 The proposal envisioned the NFB setting up local film units in communities that
would become self-sustaining within a year, at which time the NFB would "depart."

from the inside … to penetrate as deeply as possible the meaning of poverty in the lives of a few people, in an attempt to discover what it really is to be poor" (1966). As she put it, "When I suggested the method I was thinking of which was just to go there everyday and spend time with those people and document their daily life that seemed to be acceptable. It was surprisingly easy, it was unusually easy, I've never had such an easy time doing films since I left the Film Board" (2008).

Ballantyne Tree had proven herself as an innovator in *Merry-Go-Round* (1966) with its frank depictions of teenage sexuality, her first film as a full-time staffer at the National Film Board. She was well acquainted with the new improvisational style of Albert and David Maysles and with the ground broken in Wolf Koenig and Roman Kroitor's *Lonely Boy* (1962). By the early sixties, direct cinema or vérité was establishing itself via the accessibility of 16mm portable cameras and synch sound equipment as a new and fresh form of documentary art, very much linked to the anti-authoritarian impulse of the time and to alternate forms of knowledge production and art practice that favoured reflexivity, ambiguity, and ambivalence. Appropriating this new language of vérité was a natural choice for a young director who allied herself with aesthetic and political alternatives. Like her closest associates at the NFB, Derek May, Ryan Larkin, and Arthur Lipsett, she was heavily influenced by the cultural revolutions of the sixties. "We were all," she reminisced, "running around with long hair and flowered shirts, listening to music and experimenting with the new morality" (2008).

Filming started 26 September 1966 with an NFB crew including Paul Leach, cinematographer; Bill Brind, sound recordist; and Robert Baylis, production manager. What was captured over the course of three weeks of filming with the family were some extraordinary moments. While not, strictly speaking, pure "fly on the wall" observational cinema (Ballantyne Tree uses sequences from interviews with Gertrude and Kenneth and inserts her own questions as a muted form of interaction), the film's accomplishment rests precisely on its access to the intimate, private, and everyday struggles of the family. The strength of vérité has always been that the characters depicted embody a situation inviting a bond of empathy and identification, and here, the gestures, the body language, the particular verbal "accented" utterances, the exchange of looks, and the personal interactions of the Bailey family with each other and with the police and welfare authorities are drawn with phenomenal poignancy. The viewer is made witness to the daily grind of feeding and caring for the large brood of children, with scenes featuring the children sent to gather stale bread from nuns, the beleaguered Gertrude on her round of visits to her doctor and (off-screen) welfare worker, the charm and spontaneity of the children playing ball from the window of their tenement, sleeping three to a bed. But throughout, what anchors the film and gives it its dynamic centre is the ongoing monologue and performance of the voluble and larger-than-life Kenneth Bailey, narrating his abusive childhood, railing at the punks who were out to get him, passionately extolling his love of his wife and children, and, notoriously, getting punched on the nose in a street fight over six dollars. Vérité has always excelled at provoking our fascination with a real-life character who takes on the complexity, internal contradictions, and idiosyncrasies of fictional counterparts. This is certainly the reading given by British documentarist Basil Wright, who on seeing *The Things I Cannot Change* remarked that the "husband becomes a sort of epic character. He's one of the most odious little people you ever could have met. He's a bully, he's a coward, he's stupid, he's affectionate, he's clever, he's uneducated" (Levin 1971, 49–50).

Indeed, the greatest strength of vérité has been the intimate study of the self-deluding character, and in classics like *Lonely Boy* or *Salesman* (1968) or *Grey Gardens* (1975), the portraits constructed represent the happy coincidence of form and content working together as an extended exploration of the fateful dissonance between performance and self-knowledge. But if this is the strength of vérité, it is also its limitation as a vehicle for political or social commentary, which must extrapolate trends or collective phenomena from the particular. Privileging empathy and pathos over analysis; effects over causes; the present over the past; ambivalence over dogma; drama over discourse; and a bounded and particular world view over a dialogic one, vérité, as Brian Winston argues, "affords a way of apparently dealing with the world ... while running away from its social meaning" (1988, 41).

Certainly the NFB authors of *The Things I Cannot Change* discussion guide acknowledged this limitation, noting that "[t]he particular style of the film may make it difficult to get discussion started." "The film," the guide continues, "does not guide the viewer to any specific response nor to any particular course of action, and its emotional impact is strong enough to leave an audience unsettled and perhaps with conflicting impressions" (NFB 1967c). Because of the emotive power of the film, the guide advised having a break of five or ten minutes following a screening to allow the audience to "recover itself."

The discussion guide, in fact, provides us with a fascinating opportunity to gauge the film's probable reception through its struggle to elaborate potential points of debate among the film's "conflicting impressions." One of the first hurdles was the problem of typicality and exemplification. While the film focuses on the particularities of the white Irish-Canadian Bailey family, who had emigrated to Montreal from rural Nova Scotia, it is clear that the documentary portrait is intended to be read as an exemplar,[13] the original

---

13 This is certainly in line with Druick's observation of the consistent use of typicality as a defining characteristic of documentary realism at the NFB (2006, 27).

promotional one sheet noting that the family represents "the common condition of many people who are short on money and short of hope."

The challenge that the authors of the guide appear to be aware of, however, is that the film might well be interpreted according to a traditional
rhetoric of poverty that blamed the victim, whose alleged moral lapses were
seen to be the direct cause of impoverished circumstance. As the guide notes,
"The audience will want to establish for itself the representativeness of the
film: how much of its situation is due to the particular characteristics of this
man and this family, how much is general ... ?" (NFB 1967c). While it is impossible to determine the multiplicity of readings the film generated with
any kind of accuracy, it is clear from the letters written to the NFB following the national broadcast that at least some viewers were inclined to judge
Kenneth Bailey as the author of his own misfortune. In a review of the film
published in *Canadian Welfare*, William Zimmerman (1967) of the Social
Planning Council in Ottawa wrote that the film presents a "distorted" view
of poverty because the central character, Kenneth Bailey is seen to be poor
not because of "missed opportunity" but because "he is a deeply troubled
guy who literally leads with his chin" (32–3). Zimmerman, in fact, worried
that Kenneth Bailey would actually "represent the danger of expecting the
impossible from social action, since providing opportunities is much easier
than changing people."[14]

The challenge of extrapolating a broader social analysis from the film's
portrait of the family was exacerbated moreover by the prevailing popular
iconography of white poverty that was heavily indebted to Depression-era
images of absolute immiseration, like the famous portraits of sharecroppers
by Walker Evans and Dorothea Lange. The visual evidence of poverty displayed in *The Things I Cannot Change* – the very element that the director
had felt would provide a powerful visceral effect – was, in fact, far more
ambiguous. "The traditional marks of poverty are not too noticeable," the
one sheet observed. "The children are clean and relatively well dressed, the
home is not lacking in the familiar essentials."[15] With little visual or discursive indicators that would connect the family to a community, region,
class, or even neighbourhood, they feel curiously stranded, more anomalous
than representative.[16]

14 *The Things I Cannot Change*, Distribution File at NFB. Of the seven letters on file
from viewers of the broadcast, four in fact honed in on the dilemma represented by
the central character, one claiming personal knowledge of the Baileys and alleging
that Kenneth could not be condemned because he needed psychiatric help. NFB
Archives, 24 March 2008.
15 *The Things I Cannot Change*, one sheet (1967), NFB Archives, 24 March 2008.
16 The choice of an Anglo family in Montreal also raises the spectre of how language

If the ultimate purpose of the film was to provoke support for an innovative reworking and expansion of poverty alleviation programs, as Kemeny's proposal eventually articulated it, Ballantyne Tree's film and the NFB discussion guide remain curiously ambiguous. The film includes long sequences detailing Gertrude's routine interfacing with members of welfare agencies where she is subject to round after round of invasive questioning, to the point where it becomes a parody of an inane disciplinary regime ("What part of the chicken do you eat?"; "How big are your potatoes?"). Nevertheless, the system itself is never taken to task for its humiliations and deficiencies. (In contrast, the system is critiqued gleefully in Terence Macartney-Filgate's *Up against the System* [1969], which ends with a rousing call to revolution on the part of a feisty and undiminished old-age pensioner.)

Like the address of the film itself, the NFB discussion guide presumes absolute ignorance of the issue of poverty and takes a studiously non-political perspective as the appropriate starting point for discussion. Organized around a rhetorical reframing of the film's title, the guide proposes to focus questions around what can be changed, "what causes people to live in this way, and what might be done about it, if anything can or should be done" (NFB 1967c). I call this a rhetorical reframing because the film makes it abundantly evident that the Baileys – the pathologically passive Gertrude, the vulnerable children, and the defensive and pugnacious Kenneth – are incapable of changing their own lives, let alone taking up the revolutionary cause of the immiseration of capitalism's underclass.

But in the absence of any indication as to how the Baileys or subjects like them might participate in a process of change, they remain objects of a discourse rather than subjects, as recipients of middle-class sympathy (or aversion) and state largesse. As Druick has argued, the film's perspective and address, as embodied through key textual elements like the off-screen questions of the film director, remain consistently aligned with the beneficent and paternalistic gaze (and ear) of a state welfare worker (Druick 2006, 141). Things may be done for the Baileys or to them but the real catalyst of change, the film seems to imply, remains elsewhere in the implicit "we" of an affluent professional caste.

politics limited the possibility of extrapolating the general from the particularities of the Bailey family circumstance. Apart from the accented voices of a welfare and police officer, the representation of place is purposefully vague. Certainly if the family had been Québécois and obviously French speaking, reaction to the film might have been very different, given that a Québécois family might take on the additional metaphoric reference as an exemplar of Anglo colonization.

THE MYTH OF INFORMED CONSENT

We started this article by referencing the way in which *TTICC* has accreted a historical notoriety as a textbook example of ethical transgression, and it is worth returning to this point as a final summation of the film's mixed legacy. While many arguments have been made in support of the allegation of ethical breach, some more spurious than others, like the assertion that the crew should have intervened during the fight scene rather than continue filming (the altercation escalates in a matter of seconds), the central case forwarded by the prosecution had to do with the way an alleged invasion of the family's privacy ended by embarrassing them. I've tried to argue that much of the latter was in fact based on an apocryphal tale, but let me suggest that what all of these reservations about the film may be trying to get to is the way in which vérité as a particular language of representation problematizes the issue of informed consent.

As Calvin Pryluck points out, "The essential characteristics of observational cinema will always make it vulnerable to charges of voyeurism and duplicity" (1976, 77). In more traditional forms of documentary like the interview, the formal codes of question and response textually indicate some kind of mutuality and ongoing acknowledged relationship between the interviewee and the crew and director. In vérité, the relationship is more ambiguous because there are no clear textual indicators that consent is being renewed in every situation. We know the Bailey family signed a release for appearing in *TTICC* and were paid five hundred dollars, but did Kenneth Bailey agree to be represented as a pugnacious provocateur in the fight scene, where visual evidence was recorded that could potentially have legal implications (Nichols 1991)? Moreover, a strictly *de jure* interpretation of consent implies that the director or signing authority for the film will have absolute prescience concerning the potential meanings generated by the film in all circuits of distribution and can communicate these to her subjects. Such prescience is clearly impossible, and as I've tried to argue with the case of *TTICC*, the disjunction between the intention of the director and the effectivity and volatile readings of the final film was often particularly acute.

The Baileys were shown the film before the national broadcast and did not raise any objections at that time (Evans 1991, 159) – in fact twenty years later they signed another release and agreed to participate in an update, *The*

17 According to Ballantyne Tree, Kenneth felt there would be further financial benefits for this participation. The family had been paid $5,000 to participate in *The Courage to Change* in 1985, but perhaps what Kenneth's misguided impression points to is the difficulty some subjects have in distinguishing the differences between a low-budget documentary and a Hollywood product.

Courage to Change.[17] But does the strict observance of formal protocol resolve the ethical issues that are so acute in vérité? As Marcel Ophuls has observed, vérité is utterly dependent on the "professional exploitation" of people's "great urge to communicate because of loneliness, because of insecurity, because of bottled up complexes" (Pryluck 1976). Even given the most honourable intention, there will always be an unbridgeable power differential built into the complex negotiation between vérité directors and their subjects, one that stems from the fact that the expectations and goals going into the project may be vastly different.[18]

But even beyond the grey area of negotiated consent, vérité is fundamentally articulated around a power differential that produces an extreme vulnerability for the subject whose life is exposed in phenomenal vividness. While an interview subject may be judged on her sincerity or political opinion, the subject of vérité is judged on his or her character, the tidiness of her house, how he relates to his spouse, how he dresses the children or conforms to stereotypes of the "deserving poor." In other words, vérité functions as a language of representation by reducing and translating the life of a subject into an object of discourse, taking it out of context, putting it on view, and processing it through distinct ideological frameworks of interpretation that, depending on their own ideological formation or class location, may be actively hostile. Perhaps in the end, then, the most important legacy of the film is not how it has served as an object lesson in documentary ethics but how it raises the far more salient point concerning the relationship of observational film to political transformation.

Far from a simple textbook case, *The Things I Cannot Change* represents a fascinating study of converging social, aesthetic, and political trajectories of the mid-1960s and an object lesson in the disjuncture between directorial intention and complex histories of reception and dissemination. As a pilot project for the CFC series, the model *TTICC* developed as a Category I film addressed to a "general" audience was quickly abandoned. As Evans observed, *TTICC* had opened a "Pandora's box" of questions about what documentary does, and all subsequent films on poverty took a very different turn in terms of the language of documentary, targeted audiences, the process of production, and the inscribed relationship with documentary subjects. Interactionist, participatory, process-oriented interventions in particular geographic and community-based locations, the other CFC films attempted to rewrite the power differential between subjects and directors in the interests of the poor as agents and self-representing subjects.

18 This certainly seems to be the case with high-profile cases like *An American Family* (Alan Raymond and Susan Raymond, PBS, 1973), where Pat Loud publicly raised objections after the screening of the notorious television series on her life.

PART 3

Screen Spaces: Spotlight on the Films and Filmmakers

■

PREFACE

The following section offers sixteen capsule chapters focusing either on individual films or groups of films or on individual filmmakers within CFC/SN. These essays remind us how specific documentaries and artists were positioned within the often bureaucratic studio programs and not always progressive political frameworks, and how CFC and SN were the platform for a range of styles, personalities, and politics. These fourteen authors, artists as well as academics, pursue a range of approaches, linking socio-political context to cinematic for, and often incorporating new archival research or oral histories.

The importance of the latter is foregrounded by this section's spotlight on George Stoney, CFC/SN's second executive producer for two years (his service ending in 1970), which is intended to complement the voice of founding producer Colin Low in Part 1. A previously published interview with Stoney from the late 1970s in chapter 15 focuses on the most famous of the CFC First Nations initiatives, *You Are on Indian Land*, while chapter 30 offers an overview of Stoney's entire CFC/SN stint through an interview conducted two decades later by Deirdre Boyle, a leading American media activist/scholar and fellow New Yorker (reprinted from a special festschrift in honour of the then octogenarian documentarist in *Wide Angle*, March 1999).

The other fourteen chapters in this section have various agendas. In chapters 18, 22, and 23, film scholars Thomas Waugh, Liz Czach, and Jeanne Deslandes all focus on major directors from Société nouvelle who have been overlooked by NFB "versioners" and English-language critics and scholars alike – respectively, Maurice Bulbulian, Michel Régnier, and Léonard Forest. Additional light on SN is provided by film scholar Jerry White in his study of Anne Claire

Poirier's influential classic *Les filles du Roy* (chapter 25) and by Toronto teacher-filmmaker Kalli Paakspuu in her comparison of the forgotten "sexual revolution" oddity *Le bonhomme* with a no less personal film from CFC, *Rose's House* (chapter 26). Other neglected regional "discoveries" treated in this section are the Halifax landmark *Encounter at Kwacha House*, dissected by Toronto professor Kass Banning in the light of the late-sixties politics of racial representation (chapter 17); the rural Ontario vignette *Wilf*, treated by Michael Brendan Baker in the light of its exceptional use of popular music (chapter 19); film theorist Jason Lindop's analysis of two "single mom" docs from English Montreal, both by Pierre Lasry (chapter 27); and what is perhaps CFC's final film, *Paper Wheat*, treated by American film scholar Chris Meir in relation to its source material in agitprop farm theatre on the Prairies (chapter 28).

Finally, four familiar corners of the CFC/SN are given new perspectives: the classic film whose repercussions are still being felt in northern Quebec, *Cree Hunters of Mistassini*, by American film scholar Michelle Stewart (chapter 16); the Portapak works that put video into the hands of citizens from Alberta to Montreal, by Calgary researcher Brian Rusted, importing fresh insights from his discipline of performance studies (chapter 20); and the iconic Working Mother series, by Rina Fraticelli, the former head of the women's studio that grew out of Challenge for Change (chapter 29).

You Are on Indian Land: Interview with

15 George Stoney (1980)

■

ALAN ROSENTHAL

People should do their own filming, or at least feel they control the content.
I've spent much of my life making films about doctors or teachers or
preachers that these people ought to have made themselves.
■ George Stoney

INTERVIEWER'S PREFACE (1980)

The essence of George Stoney's thinking is that film can and should be used
as one of the prime tools for social change. This was the key to his role in the
NFB's Challenge for Change program [see also Boyle, chapter 30, this vol-
ume] and is the core of his continuing work in New York.

But what are the responsibilities of the filmmaker in this task? Where
does one place oneself? Is one's main responsibility to society in general, to
the people being filmed, to the network, or to somewhere else entirely? And
how and when should the filmmaker, if ever, yield up control? These are the
questions to which Stoney has been addressing himself over the last decade
and which I tried to cover in our talk.

I met George Stoney in 1961 when he gave me my first real film job. Since
then his ideas have very much influenced my thinking as well as the thinking of dozens of his students in California, where he taught for a while, and
at New York University. Stoney is not just a filmmaker but also a passionately
concerned thinker, doer, and mover who seems miraculously to have time
for everyone.

Most of Stoney's time is now devoted to teaching, but he is in fact one of
the most successful producer-directors in the United States in the field of
sponsored documentaries. One of his main approaches is to develop a ficti-
tious drama to illustrate the way to deal with a certain situation. This method
was used to good effect in *All My Babies*, the best known of Stoney's films,
and in *A Cry for Help* (1962), which was a training film for police dealing
with suicide cases.

Stoney was born in 1916 and minored in journalism at the University of North Carolina. Later he worked as a freelance writer, dealing with socially relevant topics, and contributed to Gunnar Myrdal's 1944 study of blacks in America, *The American Dilemma*.

In 1946 he joined the Southern Educational Film Service as writer-director but in 1950 branched out to form his own company. Since then he has made films on topics ranging from birth control, insurance, and the mentally ill to the nature of the Baha'i faith and, with *How the Myth Was Made*, the making of *Flaherty's Man of Aran*.

In 1968 his independent filmmaking was suspended for a while when he moved to Montreal to become executive producer of the NFB's Challenge for Change series. CFC dealt with a variety of Canadian problems – from the urban poor, to the stricken farmer, to the situation of Canada's Indians. What was fresh about it as a series was its ability to confront and examine the policies of the same government departments that helped fund the program. But the confrontation was done in the spirit of "Let's all learn and understand."

You Are on Indian Land (YAOIL) is one of the "Challenge" films and deals with the problems of the Indians on Cornwall Island [Akwesasne Mohawk Territory] whose land is split between the United States and Canada. Its specific coverage is the one-day blocking of the international bridge across the St Lawrence by Indians protesting unfair customs charges. Among other things, the film pinpoints the crucial difference between the usual media coverage of certain political events, where a small amount of violence is given a distorting, titillating coverage, and the reality of the events themselves (see also Starblanket, chapter 5, this volume; for distribution of YAOIL, see Winton and Garrison, chapter 36, this volume).

Another vital aspect of the film is that it was used by the Indians to examine their situation and actions while the confrontation with the government was still going on. And it is this sort of element that is at the core of Stoney's thinking: that film should be used by different social groups to examine their stands, their actions, and their images. This kind of filmmaking, according to Stoney, is as necessary as ordinary filmmaking for the general public.

ALAN ROSENTHAL: In the late sixties you were living in New York. You then got involved in the Canadian Film Board's Challenge for Change and later became chairman of NYU's undergraduate film division. How did all that happen?

GEORGE STONEY: Frank Spiller, the NFB's director of English programming, invited me to come to Canada to look at the CFC program with the idea that

I might be its executive producer for a couple of years. The Film Board doesn't customarily take people from outside Canada, so this was quite an exceptional experience. I was there for two years, and then I was asked to join NYU. That was in 1970. I really came back home to the U.S. because I thought CFC was a very important concept and I'd like to see it work in my own country. Knowing that it would be almost impossible to do what we were doing in Canada through the U.S. government, I thought maybe a university base might work. So in effect New York University gave me a salary, a place to work, and a licence to hunt for money. Soon I met Red Burns and together we found a large grant to start the Alternate Media Center.

Our mandate from the foundation was to devote ourselves to experiments in the use of cable television, for local programming, particularly public access programming. My own hope was that this would be one small part of a whole CFC approach, using film, videotape, closed circuit, the whole works. But you know how it is with foundations. They have an idea and you have to fit into their idea in order to get the money.

We started working in cable in New York City, and it was a good time because the city franchises were just opening up. For about two years we helped people here in New York and then in a number of other places to get public access centres going. Red, who has, and had, very strong connections with people in the industry, persuaded some cable companies to put up money for these centres at the beginning, and we worked very hard to help the centres raise their own money to match.

AR: When you came to the National Film Board what was CFC doing? What did you yourself do there and how did the experience of CFC affect your own thinking as to what film could or should be doing?

GS: When I arrived, they were making films about a number of things – housing, health, Indian affairs. These were made in response to government requests. There were six government departments subscribing to the CFC program. They would put up half the money and the Board would put up the other half. And these films were supposed to elucidate public problems.

This followed the big Fogo Island experiment. *Fogo* was the first of the big film projects done for CFC. Colin Low was in charge of that one. His idea was to work with people on a remote island off the coast of Newfoundland. Most of the people were on relief because the inshore fishing was dying. It was costing the government a great deal to give them public services – education and so forth – so the government was proposing that they move – just clear off the island after being there three hundred years. And the government had suggested that Colin and the crew go in and see if they could make films to encourage the people to move.

What they found was that a great many of the people didn't want to move and were willing to make changes in their lives and their ways of doing business in order to stay. So a very useful exchange took place between the people of Fogo and the government through this series of twenty-odd films. From that Fogo experience grew a whole theory of Challenge for Change.

When I arrived, the government wanted to do similar films in a number of other places, or I should say, wanted to make similar efforts to use film to promote social change. We soon realized the film crews were too big, the turnaround time too slow, and the costs too high. So Dorothy Hénaut and Bonnie Klein suggested that we use videotape.

AR: How would you characterize this new approach? What did you want to do?

GS: We wanted to film ordinary people and get them to state their positions. Then we wanted them to re-examine their positions as they play the films back, strengthening their arguments for subsequent meetings with officials. It gives officials a clearer view of what people think and what people experience than they would get from the usual official visit. This is a beginning. You usually go through this and then the officials and the people get together.

AR: Probably your most well-known film from your time at the Board is *You Are on Indian Land*. How was that film set up? What had you hoped to do with it?

GS: The way it came about was interesting. I'd only been at the Board a short time. We were working with the Indian Film Crew which had been unfortunately badly set up according to requirements of the Department of Indian Affairs. There were at first eight members, then six as the Indians dropped out. Indian Affairs insisted that they each come from a different tribe – Mi'kmaq on the East Coast to Haida on the West Coast. The only thing that they had in common was that we called them Indians. They came into the Board, were given this very heavy training, and most of them collapsed under it.

One of the few who did well was Mike Mitchell, whose home was close enough that he could live on his own reservation. Mike was one of the young chiefs of the tribe on Cornwall Island in the St Lawrence River. They had been having a lot of trouble down there with the government because their land is all split up between the U.S. and Canada, and the Indians were being charged duty for bringing their groceries back and forth across the border. So there was a mood to strike. A delegation of Indians went to Ottawa to protest. Mike called me up and said, "If we don't get satisfaction, which I doubt, we're coming back and we're going to block the international bridge."

I said, "Well, what do you want me to do?" He said, "If we block the bridge I want a film crew down there."

That was on Friday. Mike would be back the next day, so I immediately went up to the cafeteria and started looking for a crew. Well, this was very unusual at the Board, moving into production so rapidly. That kind of thing is just not supposed to happen. Fortunately I was an outsider. I didn't know the customs yet, so we were able to get a crew down that night. They were with the Indians the next day so that the situation could be recorded from the Indian viewpoint. And it was. They recorded the happenings and they came back after just a few hours of shooting.

Two days later the Indians came up and said, "We need that film." I said, "Don't be foolish, it's in the lab. It's Christmas holidays and we won't even be able to get it synched up till after New Year." And they said, "We can't wait. The tribe is falling apart. The people who got arrested first are accusing the people who got arrested second of not fighting hard enough. The people who got arrested second are saying that Ernie Benedict sold them out when he finally called off the demonstration."

AR: They wanted to use the film to review their own situation while it was happening?

GS: That's right. They said, "We need to see what actually happened." So with the help of the Indians who came up, we were able to put it in synch, and then took it back down unedited, just spliced in chronological order. In the next two weeks it was screened at least ten times, all around the reservation. This clarified what happened for the Indians. Then we said, "All right, now we want to show this to the Royal Canadian Mounted Police and to the other white officials who were involved." The Indians were quite angry about this. They said, "We thought this was *our* film!" I said, "Well, what good is it if you aren't using it with these other people?" So with their co-operation we set up a series of screenings with the RCMP, the local police, and other government officials.

AR: You said before that Mike wanted a crew so that it then could be filmed from the participants' point of view. Now, I seem to recall that this event was also covered by the media. What was the difference between your coverage and the media's coverage in looking at the event?

GS: An absolutely fascinating difference, and it's illustrated by an hour-long film put together by the local TV station called *A Treaty Spurned*. They had gone out there to record the event for quick news coverage. So they had a whole bunch of 2-minute clips of violence. They tied all these together with

Indian Film Crew participant Mike Mitchell in *Challenge for Change* (1968).
Frame enlargement.

some interviews for the long film after the event with the principals. We, on the other hand, did a recording of the full event, and not just the violent moments. So when you see *YAOIL* you notice there are long passages of talk between the moments of violence. You begin to see how the violence happens; you begin to see the nature of the violence, and you see the violence tapering off and some more palaver following. You see what a good job the RCMP did, for example; you see what a wretched job the local police did. Because ours was a more open view, this was even more apparent in the three hours of rushes than it is in the 45-minute edited version.

AR: When you came to New York, how did you start using the ideas that had been developing at the Film Board, and how did those ideas differ from standard conventional documentary filmmaking?

GS: Our fundamental tenet was that people do their own recording. In effect *they* become the filmmakers. We gave them training here on half-inch video, and they went out and did their thing, although we had some facilitators to do some basic teaching of editing. The idea was that people should do *their own* filming, which is the opposite of always doing films for people. I realized that I had spent much of my life making films that doctors ought to have made themselves, that teachers ought to have made themselves, films that preachers ought to have made themselves. And so this gave us a chance to see what it was like when people took a major hand in production. I've since tempered that a bit. I see now that it doesn't matter so much who's handling the camera if the people in front of the camera are controlling the content and *feel* they're controlling the content.

AR: Can you give me any instances of the films made by you or your students in New York where the filmmaker has been caught between his responsibilities to his own group and his desire to make a conventional documentary?

GS: The most obvious case I think is the film called *Godfather Comes to Sixth Street* (1975), a very fine film made by a group from my documentary production workshop led by Mark Kitchell. Mark was a member of the block association on East Sixth Street when Coppola appeared wanting to use their turf for *Godfather Two,* and Mark proposed to make a film from the point of view of the block association. They had the usual hassles with Paramount and the police and the neighbours and so forth, but they managed to get a lot of good stuff on the screen. They got the change in the neighbourhood. They got a beautiful story (and you see it in the finished film) of the neighbourhood's response to the whole mystique of filmmaking.

They also got a parallel story which you do not see in the film. That is, that this was an old neighbourhood, deteriorating. It used to be "Little Russia." Then it became "Little Italy" with some of the Russians still in there, and then some Puerto Ricans started moving in and American blacks. At the time of the filming, the block was about half Puerto Rican.

Everyone wanted to be in the movie. Coppola and his cohorts said, "Yes, we're going to hire people, but they have to look Italian." This seemed to imply very quickly – if you don't look Italian, you're second-rate. And it made a serious breach between the Italians and the Puerto Ricans on the block who had been struggling to find some common ground on which to work together. When the filming began, this division was pointed up by the fact that the Italians were getting the film jobs and the others weren't.

Finally, violence broke out one night when the young Puerto Ricans did about $20,000 worth of damage to the set. We got a little footage of that and put it in the first rough cut. Then Mark realized that he was going to have trouble with Paramount getting permission to release this film anyway and he saw that he had a film that might get a television release – a film that might get him professional notice. He began to see that he had a more general metaphor in his film beyond the happening on East Sixth Street. What had occurred there happens any time a movie crew moves into a neighbourhood. If you put in the fight between the Puerto Ricans and the Italians, it would make it a very *special* case. So he decided that he would leave it out.

He wanted to make a half-hour film anyway and his rough cut was very long. I think that when Mark cut out the sequence he weakened his film, although it's still a very good film.

AR: Where would the responsibilities of a filmmaker lie today?

GS: Well I think there is the conventional road for the documentary, informing the general public, and thanks to television the documentary can get to a wide public. However, my feeling is that the documentary approach is being exploited for entertainment purposes by a great many people, especially on TV. Very often the subject matter is chosen for sensational reasons. It's edited for sensational reasons. It's edited to hold an audience before anything else, though there are many exceptions.

I think that there are other roles for the documentarist. For example, we can go back to Grierson's idea, which was that your first duty was to educate the opinion makers – not so much the opinion makers as the policy-makers. He said many times that if he could get the right dozen people into a screening room to see a film, he was happy.

My own feeling is that we have another duty, and that is to help people to realize the possibilities of changing their own lives, their situations, and to get them to do something about it. And when they get involved in making media (films, videotapes, audio tapes, whatever) about those problems, or those possibilities, they're more motivated to do so.

AR: You told me once, George, that you'd made fifty documentaries. What have been some of the key ethical problems for you as a filmmaker that have come up during these films – situations where you've had to examine yourself internally and not just say "Is this one going to work filmically?"

GS: Well, always there is the question "Is this scene right for the film, or are you doing this because it's going to make you look good?" I think this is the question that always arises. The next thing is always the exploitation of the individual. They perceive it in one way and the viewers perceive it in another way.

AR: Can you give me specific examples here?

GS: Yes. A very early documentary which I think you've seen is called *Palmer Street*. The mother in that film was a marvellous black woman in Gainesville, Georgia. We were an all-white crew, so this was a very strange relationship at the time (1949) but we got to be friendly. Now she insisted on speaking very correct English during the first scenes we were recording, because that's the way she wanted to be perceived at the time. I knew this was going to come across as unnatural, and I was worried about it. I didn't know how to handle the situation – to say, look, you're not talking naturally. I knew it would hurt her. What was I to do? Fortunately her husband got me off the hot seat there, because he came in one day when we were shooting a scene and started making fun of her. And finally she then relaxed and we got much more natural dialogue out of her. But I think you constantly have to be aware of how people want to be seen, and help them feel comfortable with themselves. That was long before "Black is Beautiful" was recognized, before black talk was the way people liked to speak.

AR: Have there been occasions where you knew the fact of filming a certain situation was going to make life extremely difficult for the participant long after you'd gone? That when the film would come up, and the people would be seen in the context of their community, they might be ridiculed or laughed at? Has this happened? If so, did you think that the general good coming from the film was worth the individual problems of that scene?

GS: A good example of what you're describing came out of a very early CFC experience. I was not there at the time but a beautiful, very moving film called *Things I Cannot Change* (Tanya Ballantyne Tree, 1967) was made about a poor family in Montreal – people with nine children. The film recorded the last weeks before they were going to have a tenth child. You realize when that film starts that the last thing that family needs is another child. By the time that child comes you wouldn't, however, want to do away with it. You realize that somehow that family needed this reassurance of itself.

Well, the film was made with great care and was also made the way we ought to make films, by winning the confidence of the people. Any good documentary director sets a climate in which his cast can behave normally. However, often they don't realize what this is going to mean to their futures. And there is no way that you can explain that to them. So *you* have to make the judgments if they're going to expose themselves. And you have this to wrestle with in the editing room.

The young lady who made *Things I Cannot Change*, which was her first film, didn't do that. These people gave her their souls, in effect. She put their souls on the screen. And as I say, it's a very moving film. The first time that family saw that film was on TV, and their neighbours saw it at the same time. The children became the butts of jokes. The family began to see themselves as other people saw them – as poor people without dignity. That's the way the neighbours perceived them anyway, and they literally had to move.

It was a family on the brink of breakup anyway. The father was an alcoholic, mostly unemployed, a kind of bragger. All of this came across in the film. Most of those who saw the film outside the neighbourhood had a very warm reaction to it. Yet the family was deeply hurt by it. Now, my own hunch is that this came about, not because the film was made as it was, but because the film was not introduced properly. The way I would have handled that film (and the way I do handle my films) would have been to show the film to the family in rough cut, and get their reactions and talk to them about it. I help them learn to deal with it. Then I would have set up screenings where they brought in their neighbours and friends and we could have talked about why the film was made. This way they might have begun to see the film in context so that by the time the film was actually seen by the general public, they would know what's there and would have been proud of what they had done, rather than ashamed or betrayed. Because it's usually two sides of the coin.

It's like the Loud family in *An American Family* (Alan Raymond and Susan Raymond, PBS, 1973). You remember, Craig Gilbert who produced that series said the Loud family saw every foot of film and approved it. Of course they did, because they were seeing it completely out of context. They didn't know what the public's response was going to be and they weren't prepared for that.

Now I have a method of preparing myself and other people for films which I've used since 1960. Any time we make a film we do a trial mix of the sound and we take it out in double system and we show it to a lot of representative audiences. We do this first to see what we've got and to feel an audience response. We know if things are misinterpreted then. And at that stage we can always go back and change it. I found that when I take people along in this way, we don't have that kind of problem.

AR: What have you been doing recently on videotape?

GS: Well, I do a lot of videotaping. It's the thing I get the most pleasure out of, because now that I own my own Portapak, I can do pretty much what I damn please. I've never been able to do that with film because of the cost.

What I like about the Portapak is that it's a marvellous way of bridging the gap that develops in the modern world between people. Playback is of course a vital part of this and I always carry along a monitor. I was in Nigeria, for example, and I would go into a remote village, do a little taping, and then hook the monitor up to a battery, take my belt off and hang the monitor in a tree and play it back. People would recognize themselves and usually I could tape anything in the village after that.

But I have found that a great many people are disturbed by their own image. This is not easy to perceive because people *seem* so anxious to see themselves and when they see themselves they always smile. But to say that they enjoy it is very often incorrect. You can't deny your own image. It's there. So you're not going to say you don't like it, though you might say "I look awful." But very often you dread to see it.

For years I used to see myself on film at the end of shots, catching the baby or holding the slate and frowning into the sun, so I always had an excuse for the way I look. But on videotape I began to see myself more and more and there was no escaping it. I am as old as I am. I'm skinny and bald and kind of funny-looking. But then after a long time I realized that nobody seems to mind. They just accepted me anyway. So I've begun to accept myself. But this takes time, and I think that people often need help to do that.

When I go into a place to shoot, I try and put myself or my companions on tape first so they can see that the gun can shoot both ways – that we're not afraid to be on view ourselves. And then I do my best to see how people *like* to be seen. What are they proud of? Perhaps it's a homemade gun like the one I saw in an African village. Or it may be their hairdo or their garden or whatever. And after you tape that, then you come to other things – but what you've done before makes them feel at ease.

It's a trick in a way but also I think it shows a certain amount of respect. What you do is get people coming across more fully themselves. This is quite different from the usual TV reporter's idea of cutting people down, exposing people, catching people off guard – what Geraldo Rivera once described to me as those "golden moments" when politicians' false teeth fall out. This I abhor, whereas the first method is what filming is all about.

16 *Cree Hunters of Mistassini*: Challenge for Change and Aboriginal Rights[1]

■

MICHELLE STEWART

Cree Hunters of Mistassini (Boyce Richardson and Tony Ianzelo, 1974) is perhaps one of the best known films of the Challenge for Change (CFC) era.[2] Upon its release, *Cree Hunters* was broadcast nationally and internationally, earning much critical and public acclaim. For his part, co-director Boyce Richardson has always marvelled at the fact that even though he had never made a film before, he was able to get the word out about the Cree Nation's struggle to protect its culture and territory in the face of Hydro-Québec's James Bay proposal (1971): "With no resources or filmmaking skills, I managed to get out a one-hour film expressing the Cree opposition, more than a year before any of the well-funded agencies, the CBC, the NFB or anyone else was able to utter a word. I owe an enormous gratitude to [Colin] Low and Tony Ianzelo, the superb cameraman-director, who took me along with them" (Boyce Richardson, e-mail communication, 25 August 2005). The circumstances of the production of *Cree Hunters* in a period of budget retrenchment and political uncertainty reveal the commitment of certain CFC members to Aboriginal rights and representation in the 1970s, although National Film Board (NFB) filmmakers and management had frequent disagreements over which styles and strategies would be most politically effective.

Indeed, Aboriginal representation and production played a central role in the debate within CFC regarding which kind of filmmaking best served com-

1 This chapter was developed from a longer piece addressing Aboriginal representation at the National Film Board and offering an in-depth historical analysis of CFC Indian Film Crews (Stewart 2007).

2 Richardson already had a strong record of political journalism and had just begun a film (*Job's Garden*) for the Indians of Quebec Association regarding Aboriginal land claims in Quebec, though *Cree Hunters* was his first film for the Board. Co-director Tony Ianzelo had a long history with the NFB of working on films about Native peoples, having begun his career at the Board in 1966, just before the advent of CFC. Committed to the CFC mission and clearly influenced by Colin Low, Ianzelo was one of the people who worked closely with trainees of the Indian Film Crews.

munities while still fulfilling the NFB's mandate to make films in the national interest. By the late 1960s, the kind of films that were traditionally sponsored, those that explained government services and agencies to citizens, struck many at the Board as a holdover from a bygone era. Thus, Colin Low's non-interventionist documentary approach, an approach that attempted to give voice to the under-represented, appeared as an antidote to the older, more hierarchical model of service. Emerging from Low's twenty-eight films about the inhabitants of Fogo Island (1967), this style of direct-cinema filmmaking was meant to enhance dialogue between government and the governed. The utopian hope emanating from the Board at the time was that filmed communication could spur dynamic social change. Low's experiment represented a more pointedly social interpretation of his direct-cinema experience as a filmmaker in the NFB's Unit B, the English Production Unit from 1948 to 1964. To the direct-cinema practices of scriptless filmmaking, non-intervention, minimization of voice-over commentary, and live synch sound, Low added an ethical and political transformation of Robert Flaherty's practice of screening rushes for subjects and allowing them to decide how and if they wanted to appear onscreen. In early CFC practice, this style of documentary filmmaking became the dominant methodology for "giving voice" to the under-represented. Very soon, however, filmmakers saw the relatively new technology of the portable videotape recorder (VTR) as a more direct and undiluted means for letting communities speak for themselves. A radical, community-initiated activist model, the VTR ethos inspired many involved with CFC.

It was at this time that CFC launched the National Indian Training Program, which brought young Aboriginal men and women to the Board in Montreal to learn filmmaking. Also known as the Indian Film Crews (IFCs), these training programs ran in 1968–70 and 1971–73. The press releases announcing the initiation of the first IFC in 1968 took up the language of the VTR projects regarding community-controlled production. Yet ultimately CFC failed to build sustaining structures for Aboriginal production at the Board or in communities. An autonomous unit devoted to Aboriginal production did not materialize in this period – despite strong proposals from IFC trainees Mike Mitchell and Noel Starblanket, and despite support from national Aboriginal groups (see Starblanket, chapter 5, this volume).

In chronicling the fate of the IFCs, Rick Moore identifies *Cree Hunters* as marking a philosophical turning point for CFC. Notwithstanding the presence of the IFC trainees at the Board, most CFC films touching on Native issues in this period were made for communities by veteran CFC filmmakers. Moore argues that this trend signalled a retreat from the VTR-inspired strategy of using film/video to afford access and catalyze action to a strategy of producing films that generated and displayed "sympathy" (1987, 166).[3] For the producers of *Cree Hunters*, the film represented an important form of advocacy. They saw the film, not as evoking sympathy, but as making good on the original CFC promise – to address and give voice to Cree concerns and to convey a Cree point of view.[4] Proponents of the VTR approach maintained, however, that it is the process of self-representation itself that creates the greatest potential for community organization. A deeper examination of *Cree Hunters* will shed some light on the extent to which advocacy films can contribute to the kind of social transformation championed by supporters of the VTR approach.

Even with outsiders (and government-paid outsiders) behind the camera, "there were powerful forces in Ottawa (in the prime minister's office, some believed) who did not want this [Aboriginal rights] subject broached from a political point of view" (Evans 1991, 170).[5] According to director Boyce Richardson, Colin Low (the film's producer) managed to "outsmart the feds" by selling the program as an anthropological document – hence the working title for the project, "Cree Family" (Richardson, e-mail communication, 25

3 Considering that *Cree Hunters* was made during the drive for regionalization at the Board (1972) and that CFC contributed directly to the move for more decentralized, local production (Dick 1986, *passim*), the failure of CFC to establish the IFCs on reserves at this time, at the very least, constituted a missed opportunity.

4 In the section that follows, I extend the concept of voice, which in the CFC setting, as Burnett (1995a) and others argue, remained rather fuzzy but was roughly equal to "representation." I use "voice" here to indicate both point of view and who is speaking, as well as the multiply determined sense that Nichols gives it: "[I]n the evolution of documentary the contestation among forms has centered on the question of 'voice.' By voice I mean something narrower than style: that which conveys to us a sense of a text's social point of view, of how it is speaking to us and how it is organizing the materials it is presenting to us. In this sense, voice is not restricted to any one code or feature, such as dialogue or spoken commentary. Voice is perhaps akin to that intangible, moiré-like pattern formed by the unique interaction of all a film's codes, and it applies to all modes of documentary" (1988, 50).

5 Richardson's memories of the circumstances surrounding the incident support this view: "[T]he original research for a film on Aboriginal rights was stopped on orders from Ottawa (we assumed, and I was told, the order came from the prime minister, Trudeau). What had happened was that I went, reluctantly, to talk to the Justice Department, whose attitudes towards Indians I abhorred, and was greeted by a fellow called Richmond Olsen, the director of research there, and a friend of Trudeau's. He told me he was on holiday, but had considered the matter sufficiently important to come in and meet me: his message was clear. We should not make this film, because there was not a title or smidgen of legal backing for the concept of Aboriginal rights" (Richardson, e-mail communication, 16 October 2005).

August 2005). The willingness and ability of CFC management and personnel to negotiate conflicting government agendas brought projects like *Cree Hunters* to life. As Richardson explains:

> NFB people like Colin Low, while accepting their role as part of the government structure, did not take kindly to being told what they could and could not make. So Colin, as I said, redesigned my project: instead of being a film about Aboriginal rights, the project was metamorphosed into a series of four half-hour films about the place of Indians in Canadian society. One of those would deal with the Indian attitudes to land. It was pretty clear that Low sold this to the CFC committee on the assumption that this one about land would be of a more ethnographic, rather than political, nature. This was approved by the CFC committee, and Tony Ianzelo and I went ahead just as if we had never been interrupted. (Richardson, e-mail communication, 16 October 2005)

Thus, management often afforded directors a degree of artistic and political autonomy. Yet despite this freedom, Richardson would come to feel that the more overtly political film that emerged from this footage, *Our Land Is Our Life* (Boyce Richardson and Tony Ianzelo, 1974), was ultimately not as engaging as *Cree Hunters*, that the footage of the Cree on their hunting grounds "was rather unique" and perhaps more powerful (Richardson, e-mail, 16 October 2005).

Both *Cree Hunters* and *Our Land* record the same moment in Cree history, and their different rhetorical approaches illustrate the potential value of the well-made advocacy film. The crisis triggered by Hydro-Québec's James Bay project led to the political unification of the Cree Nation for the purposes of resisting the flooding of Cree and Inuit hunting grounds. In recording the Cree Nation's first meetings in response to this crisis, *Our Land Is Our Life* addresses the very political questions the filmmakers were asked to avoid. Nevertheless, while the political struggle of the Cree might be more directly stated in *Our Land* than in *Cree Hunters*, in *Our Land* the voice of the narrator occasionally subsumes that of the subjects. Richardson characterizes *Cree Hunters* as a revelation. He felt "that [the film] made an immensely powerful political point with just a few lines of commentary at the end. No beating the audience over the head. Just a plain statement of the facts as the Jolly family trudged off across the snow-covered lake into the wilderness." Comparing the style of *Cree Hunters* to *Our Land*, however, he adds, "That was an important lesson, although one I never really learned, I'm afraid. *Our Land* is full of heavily ironic juxtapositions designed to irritate right-wingers" (Richardson, e-mail, 16 October 2005). Richardson's insights regarding film style and political impact resonate with the debates within CFC in the late

1960s and early 1970s, though the influence of *Cree Hunters* points to the benefits of a collaborative approach. When the "VTR ethos," stressing self-representation and community organizing, was ascendant, the Fogo-style films – advocacy films made for communities by professional filmmakers – struck critics as a kind of government public relations exercise. In their view, the professionally made films seemed to set the agenda for groups while subtly affirming the government's concern for under-represented communities. At times, the debate reduced the terms of these strategies to autonomy versus paternalism, process versus product (often understood as video versus film), and/or politics versus aesthetics. However, the collaborative filmmaking model employed by some at the Board created the context for more multi-faceted and complex forms of cultural engagement.

During his tenure as executive producer of the CFC program (1968–70), George Stoney saw film and video as tools for organization ("catalysts" or "facilitators," in the favoured terms of CFC's newsletter) first and foremost, and not as ends in themselves. For Stoney, the extent to which a production facilitated community organization and political dialogue was ultimately more important than who held the camera (Stoney, interview with the author, 30 August 2005). And Richardson, though he "had started out rather contemptuous of the NFB pickiness about quality," came to believe that "a high-quality technical production aids enormously in getting your message across" (Richardson, e-mail, 16 October 2005). Anthony Kent, CFC distribution officer for Quebec from July 1968 to March 1969 and CFC producer thereafter until 1971, stressed that "it was essential to involve the people concerned in the social and audiovisual aspects of each project. We were determined to avoid the 'visiting firemen' syndrome, whereby filmmaker activists insert themselves briefly into a community and then triumphantly return to home base without essential follow-up. Every film and video had to be approved by the participants." Further, what was particularly radical in Kent's opinion was that filmmakers often invited those filmed to join the editing process. He considered this an essential enterprise for filmmakers working with Aboriginal communities, where "the different cultural perceptions of the crew members and their eventual audiences had to be respected" (Kent, e-mail communication, 27 October 2005). *Cree Hunters* negotiates these methodological concerns with great sensitivity, perhaps as a result of Richardson's and Ianzelo's ongoing work on Aboriginal rights. CFC films like *Cree Hunters* demonstrate both the variety of strategies open to political filmmakers and the ways in which those at the NFB committed to social change directed their energies, even in an unfavourable political and economic climate.

From the opening of *Cree Hunters*, the viewer is carefully placed within the geographic and cultural space of contemporary Cree reality. Speaking over a map of northern Quebec, co-director Richardson manages to present Cree life as traditional while acknowledging the dynamic nature of Cree culture as it confronts the demands of a modern nation. This map is soon given a body as scenes of a frosty landscape are unambiguously described as Cree and Inuit land. We are told that the Cree and Inuit have hunted here for three thousand years, but that they are now in competition with the white man. Although the voice-over stresses the continuity of Cree existence (they hunt as "they have always done"), the narrative, along with repeated shots of technological implements, underscores the possibility (and tension) of maintaining traditional Indian ways in contemporary Canada.

An unusually lengthy shot introduces the three families and also indicates the somewhat awkward presence of the film crew, the subjects nervously smiling for the crew, camera, and audience. In this manner, viewers are situated as interlopers (not quite voyeurs) via a modified direct-cinema technique.[6] We have been invited, along with the film crew, onto the twelve hundred acres of Sam Blacksmith's hunting grounds. As the filmmakers make apparent the conditions of existence – that the families feed their own from what they catch, that everyone lives in one lodge, that each person contributes to the maintenance of the group – we also come to understand Blacksmith's agenda for the film. When Richardson and Ianzelo asked Blacksmith if they could produce a film on Cree hunting, according to Ianzelo, "Sam went around and checked us out" (quoted in Moore 1987, 155). Since Richardson was well known and respected in the community for his work on Native rights for the *Montreal Star*, Blacksmith accepted. The exceptional nature of the request and Blacksmith's stake in the film are hinted at by the voice-over: "Sam invited us to show the quality of Indian life." It was the first time he had ever had non-Aboriginal people staying on his territory.

The Cree hunters amiably convey to the cameramen and the audience the Cree rationale for hunting and their will to preserve this way of life. In these moments of dialogue with the camera, the Cree voice comes to the fore. At the same time, we come to understand Richardson's strategy in this regard. The dialogue is all in Cree (except for a very limited number of questions asked by the crew). English subtitles translate only key details of Cree relationships or practices, as well as a few conversations that give a more intimate sense of the quality (humour, patience, cooperation) of these interactions. Richardson attributes the somewhat languorous pace of the film – by Hollywood standards – to the editing process, which was conducted in Cree with the Cree directing the selection of certain footage (Moore 1987, 158). Although

6 Modified, in that the directors do not see themselves as flies on the wall but as guests. We are aware of their respectful presence, as they intend to learn from the Cree and to advocate for them.

later we are told that all the children speak English, none of them speaks directly to the camera. The audience is introduced to Cree hunting and daily life mostly by the Blacksmiths (Sam especially) but also by the parents of the two visiting families, the Voyageurs and the Jollys.

Following the rhetoric of an ethnographic film, *Cree Hunters* then presents the audience with what is considered (at least by the director and camera-man) to be a "closed" domain – a world considered generally alien to white society and only "opened" by the presence of the camera and filmmakers. These scenes, which feature interviews with Blacksmith and the other mem-bers of the hunting community, do not serve an indexical function; they do not animate archival footage, nor do they always agree with the narration. Rather, they serve the ends of those who appear onscreen.

As David MacDougall suggests, the question of voice is complicated in films of advocacy; but here, perhaps all the more so. The semi-anthropolog-ical style of the film gives the impression that "the filmmaker is always under instruction, and the ultimate meaning of the film remains with the film's sub-jects" (MacDougall 1994, 33). The Blacksmiths and the other parents place a great deal of significance on teaching, especially on teaching the children how to live "the Indian ways." The film-work highlights the pedagogical relation between the parents and the children and by extension between the Cree and future audiences.

The directors shape the film to emphasize Cree lessons for humanity, a strategy that supports Blacksmith's own agenda. Blacksmith's narrative stresses the severity of winter, the Cree's creative technologies for survival, and his pride in his ability to maintain the land: "I have been hunting on this land for thirty years. This land was given to me after the old man who hunted on it died. I have looked after it well." Sam has worked the land, and in this sense he owns it. Numerous shots of exertion establish this fact and help introduce the Cree philosophy of ownership. The soundtrack records only the sound of their breath as men and women chop wood, paddle down swift creeks, portage canoes, skin game. In Blacksmith's own words, "A man who lives by hunting cherishes the land. A man who lives by hunting truly respects the land. A man who owns the land really cannot because he dies." These relationships between hunter and land, hunter and game, are those of balance and respect. The Cree have special rituals for catching, preparing, and eating game, and thus the message of both the Cree hunters and the white narrator is that this system constitutes a right to the land and also something beyond a right – a cultural force, a spiritual obli-gation – exceeding the mainstream legal meaning of property.

Yet, the emphasis on harmony comes not only from the Cree's self-description, but also from the voice-over and camerawork that underscore the interdependence of Cree life by framing all work in terms of communal labour. The Cree are seldom pictured alone in a frame, and even close-ups develop a relationship of caring or intimacy between two people.[7] The narrator assures the viewer that although each hunter is responsible for the feeding and care of his own family, if one hunter does not do well, other hunters will share their bounty. That the narrative drive to portray a perfect accord hails from the filmmakers (and not the Cree) is revealed by the subtle discrepancy between image and voice-over. In one scene in particular, while the narrator insists that "nothing is haphazard. When your survival depends on it, you can't make mistakes," the image track features the group in the process of raising the teetering main support beam for the lodge. When two of the men try to push the beam in opposing directions, the beam slips and the camera falls with it. Although the lodge does get built, the screams of "Watch out!" and "I don't think it's going to work" seem to undercut the certitude of the voice-over.

The story woven by the Cree and the producers argues that the Cree do not struggle against nature, but live with it in respect and harmony, accepting hard work as part of the equation. The producers, however, put a slightly different spin on this material through the narration and the specific framing of interior shots of the lodge. Suggesting the peacefulness of communal life, Richardson narrates matter-of-factly that three families, a total of sixteen people, lived in this one lodge for months during a cold and hard winter "without accidents, illnesses, or quarrels." What is most revealing in intimate shots of the warm interior of the lodge is not the abundance of plump roasted rabbit or the spirit of communalism, but the good humour and innocence upon which the film dwells. Long takes of smiling teens, girls brushing each other's hair, and children being passed from lap to lap, all appear without voice-over, perhaps echoing (in a less obtrusive way) the romanticism of earlier ethnographic film.

The direction and camerawork of *Cree Hunters of Mistassini* do not alone determine the point of view of the film. Although the lack of narration that tends to characterize a direct-cinema approach is meant to give voice and representation to those who wouldn't otherwise find themselves in front of a camera, the subtle and unobtrusive additions of Richardson and Ianzelo add another dimension beyond the "democratizing effect" of allowing the Cree to "speak for themselves" on film (Barnouw 1993, 262). The voices of both subjects and filmmakers provide parallax views of a shared experience. *Cree Hunters* honours the beauty, ecological prudence, and cultural singularity of the Cree way of life, establishing this difference as a valid basis for

7 It is significant here that in one of the few sequences of individual activity – Sam Blacksmith taking the canoe out to check a trap – Blacksmith indicates the presence of the filmmaker as he looks directly into the camera and chuckles.

Inside the winter tent in *Cree Hunters of Mistassini* (1974): a plain statement of fact with a powerful political point. Production still.

sovereignty. For its beautiful photography and reverent advocacy, *Cree Hunters* has become something of a model for both Native rights and environmental justice films. Yet despite Cree resistance to the massive James Bay project, the Cree were forced to settle with Hydro-Québec.[8] The filmmakers,

8 This settlement, the James Bay and Northern Quebec Agreement (1975), was hailed as a "great victory" and as the "first modern Aboriginal claims settlement in Canada" (Dyck 1985, 28). However, as Bruce Clark notes, "The Aboriginal right of self-government as an inherent and full right was arguably surrendered by these Aboriginal people, in pursuance of these instruments and the corresponding legislation, not because the imperial constitutional law was repealed, but because the natives waived their ability to rely upon it" (1990, 215). The issue of whether these rights were surrendered entirely would again bring the Cree to defend their land against Hydro-Québec in the late 1980s and early 1990s. The Cree continued to contest the ways in which aspects of the agreement were implemented, and many greatly regretted the environmental and cultural consequences of the original agreement and the flooding of La Grande River. When in 1989 Quebec prime minister Robert Bourassa announced a new Hydro-Québec project that would flood the Great Whale River, the Cree successfully organized a transnational campaign that convinced New York State to reject Hydro-Québec power from the project. See *Power* (1996, Magnus Isacsson) for a moving chronicle of the broad-based coalition that the Cree and Inuit of northern Quebec developed to defeat the Great Whale project.

though, believed that thanks to the popular sentiment stirred up by the film the Cree were able to negotiate a small reduction in the scope of the project and receive some financial compensation. Moreover, after several screenings in various Cree communities (including sixty-one facilitated screenings in James Bay and southern Quebec between April and June 1974), many Cree returned to the bush.[9]

Thus, Blacksmith's hopes are partially realized by his appearance in the film. His voice is heard as testimony to the value and significance of Cree hunting life and to the possibility of meaningful cross-cultural dialogue. Although *Cree Hunters* does not elucidate the nature of Cree political power, the film, via Blacksmith's commentary, confirms the basis of Cree sovereignty.[10] *Cree Hunters*, though constrained by bureaucratic demands for an apolitical film, offers a rich and deeply humanist commitment to intercultural understanding, and the recognition of difference.

9 After distributing the film in Fort George and Great Whale, Mark Zannis described the response to the screenings by these two communities (1974): "The impact was astounding. Many of the trappers announced they were making plans to return to the bush in the winter. A study carried out by the James Bay support team [for the case against Hydro-Québec] revealed that an unbelievably great number of families (almost double) were planning to return to the bush for the winter. The reasons given were the film, which revived memories of what that life was like. Members of the support team were unanimous in praising the film and admitting that it was having a profound impact that they had not expected. The film also generated interest in the court case and meetings held in Fort George with the lawyers."

10 Until the hydroelectric project, Cree political life had been organized within the private sphere, through family-based hunting communities (Gagné 1994, 117).

17

"Nation Time" at Kwacha House: The Transitional
Modalities of *Encounter at Kwacha House – Halifax*

■

KASS BANNING

At first glance *Encounter at Kwacha House – Halifax* (Rex Tasker, 1967) offers a straightforward 17-minute black and white vérité snapshot of predominantly young black people in lively debate with community activists about the pressing issues of the day, concerns that shadowed young black Haligonians in the mid-sixties, namely racialized employment, education, and housing practices. The participants heatedly voice first-hand accounts of materialized racism, a modified form of Jim Crow writ large.[1] The merits and utility of the protest strategies enacted by the U.S. civil rights movement, as well as whether these tactics (ranging from moderate forms of civil disobedience, such as economic boycotting, to more militant direct action alternatives) could be successfully adapted to the Halifax context, are also debated. In typical Challenge for Change (CFC) documentary observational shooting style, the conversation offers no rhetorical framing or narration; the contemporary viewer might read the film as if it fell out of the sky, atomized. In the unfolding conversational accounts, the odd first name is mentioned in passing; other than what is discerned as a group of justifiably disgruntled activists and acolytes, the viewer has no idea who these participants actually are. But the documentary footage certainly makes the viewer aware of the particularities of racial disparities and economic disenfranchisement operating in Halifax circa the late 1960s. Yet *Encounter*'s CFC institutional context, as well as its setting, is not as immediately graspable as its politics. Select attention to the film's social and historical contexts, including its varied reception across diverse communities of interest, will hopefully suggest its prescience. Within months of the film's release in the spring of 1968, members of the Black Panther Party were invited to Halifax, which they subsequently visited twice in the fall of 1968 (Smith 1977, 121; Ashe 2005, 106).

1 Jim Crow, broadly defined in its U.S. context, indicates the daily reality of segregation, sanctified by law, in the domains of housing, education, employment, and public services. For a detailed account of racialized law practices in Canada, with a chapter devoted to Nova Scotia, see Backhouse 1999.

At the same time, the "work" of the film is ambivalent, marked by contradictory motives and expectations, behind and in front of the camera. These contesting discourses, including the competing claims about *Encounter*'s role in effecting immediate social change and, by extension and perhaps of more import to local authorities and community elders, and how listening to the participants stemmed impending dissent, could be framed in terms of governmental instrumentality. In fact, the film's key participant, Burnley A. (Rocky) Jones, dubbed by the Canadian press as "our own Stokely Carmichael" (Ashe 2005, 37), was simultaneously being observed (i.e., "contained") by another branch of the state; Jones was under RCMP surveillance for suspected "subversive activities" at precisely the same time that *Encounter* was being shot. Indeed, he had been "monitored" since his arrival in Halifax in 1965 with other SUPA (Student Union for Peace Action) volunteers for the Nova Scotia Non-Violence Project (Ashe 2005, 116; Verral 2006, 127).[2] Yet the film's complexity, both its reception contexts and its textual dynamics, cannot be wholly accountable to the logic of state governmentality, especially given its decidedly supranational dynamics.

Sketching the rich conjuncture that situates *Encounter* might convey why, across the Halifax community, the film was deemed controversial, a hot potato. Timing plays no small role in explaining the logic of *Encounter*. The specific timelines of the 1960s – institutional, governmental, and outernational, specifically pan-Africanism – converged to produce the contradictory terrain in which the film was operating; 1967, for instance, was a key transitional moment in the CFC's refinement of its program policy, as well as in the machinations of black political movements and the ensuing state response, both overt (retribution, policies, and programs) and covert (surveillance), local, and U.S. based.

Viewed today, *Encounter* is not simply a fascinating, regionally specific social document of its time; rather CFC's motivation for the project, the

---

2 Ashe maintains that "the Mounties spied on almost everyone connected with the civil rights movement" (2005, 116), while Sylvia Hamilton's television program on the Jones family, *Against the Tides: The Jones Family,* Hymn to Freedom series, 1994, relates how the Jones family endured harassment of all kinds, including a firebomb attempt on Jones's home. According to Verral, "Jones began working with the Atlanta-based SNCC operations in Canada and SUPA. For Jones there was an obvious alliance between socialist traditions of the New Left and pan-Africanism in the national and international groups he aligned himself with. Inspired by SNCC's Mississippi Summer Projects, SUPA's summer of 1965 action initiatives included the Nova Scotia Non-violent Project" (112). Clarke, however, states, "In 1966, supported by SNCC funds and a grassroots ideology, Jones left the U.S. Civil Rights Movement and returned home to Nova Scotia" (1992, 25).

Rocky Jones listening in *Encounter at Kwacha House – Halifax* (1967):
"visually unexciting talking heads" or goal-attuned catalytic "liveness"?
Production still.

participants' equating segregationist Halifax with the deep South, and
Encounter's various receptions – past and present – are variously informed
by the subliminal weight of our television archive, specifically the iconography and associations of televised civil rights struggles of the 1960s. Television
footage of police brutally subjugating blacks – two infamous instances being
Police Commissioner Bull Conner of Birmingham, Alabama, relentlessly
water hosing peaceful demonstrators[3] and the vicious beating and relentless
tear-gassing of civil rights marchers attempting to cross the Edmund Pettus
Bridge outside of Selma, Alabama[4] – in concert with subsequent footage of
acts of urban retaliation played out in the North and the pervasive images of
Stokely Carmichael, Malcolm X, Fannie Lou Hammer, and a range of black
citizens stirring up excitement for "the Movement," bore upon why and how

3 Footage of Birmingham's firefighters and policemen using firehoses and police dogs
to "subdue" peaceful African-American demonstrators in 1963 remains one of the
civil rights movement's enduring images. Police Commissioner Eugene "Bull" Conner
gave the order to act against marchers who were protesting against the city's segregation ordinances.

4 On "Bloody Sunday," 7 March 1965, six hundred civil rights marchers were clubbed
and tear-gassed on this bridge. The attack by lawmen was caught by a television cameraman and is said to have evoked public sympathy for the protestors, as well as
compel President Lyndon Johnson to sign the Voting Rights Act of 1965.

Encounter was initially conceptualized and subsequently received in diverse contexts. At the same time, not only did the civil rights movement inform the film's subject matter, but its various strategies were also invoked and indigenized throughout. Of more salience perhaps is the fact that key participants passionately *performed* the movement's polemics, *speechifying* on behalf of its more moderate, integrationist, and multiplying black-nationalist branches of the time, directly addressing its audience, the transfixed, embedded studiolike onlookers and film viewers alike.

The opening voice-looped coda introduces shots of a storefront building as a few of the film's participants enter. The coda is comprised of snippets of inflammatory dissent such as, "There comes a time when you can only take so much. You have to vomit if they keep pushing things down your throat. And, the only way to vomit is right back in his face." Apart from this introduction, *Encounter* is shot within the walls of Kwacha (Freedom) House, an interracial youth club housed in the north end of Halifax. Founded in 1965, the initial funds donated by the Quakers rather than the municipality, Kwacha was developed through the efforts of Rocky Jones, the Canadian media's and the RCMP's targeted "black militant," as well as *Encounter*'s primary contributor. While the enclosed one-room set, the tight framing of talking heads and cross-cut glances – let alone the film's topic of racial injustice and redress – might feel contained or bounded, even claustrophobic, *Encounter* decidedly gestures beyond the frame.

On the wider political stage of the U.S. civil rights movement, 1966 marked a seismic shift: SNCC (Student Nonviolent Coordinating Committee)[5] and black power emerge as the significant rhetorical and symbolic force. By 1967 SNCC had formed an alliance with the Black Panther Party; these two organizations were at the forefront of black protest in the United States, challenging the more coalition-building, traditional Martin Luther King–led SCLC (Southern Christian Leadership Coalition) and its white supporters (Williams 1997, 13). The revision of the appellation "negro" to the moniker "black" to signify blackness in the popular vernacular offers the most tangible marker of these seismic changes that reached beyond the immediate internecine power politics of the time. Given these outer-national developments, a temporal dissonance of sorts imbues *Encounter*. The rejoinder of a black youth at the film's end, "I'm a Negro, not a Nigger," meets enthusiastic applause, which suggests how out of synch Halifax youth actually were with pan-African refinements of black identity, issuing from concrete

5 Founded in 1960, SNCC sought to coordinate youth-led non-violent direct action in the South against segregation and all forms of racism. When Stokely Carmichael took over as chairperson in 1966, SNCC became more radicalized, calling for black power, and began to entertain violence as a legitimate form of self-defence.

struggle, that were being enacted at the time, as well as with the aspirations of Rocky Jones and others in Nova Scotia's vanguard. In some ways, *Encounter* indicates the challenge of bringing Halifax youth up to race-consciousness speed; Rocky Jones and his Kwacha House associates, connected to U.S. organizations, attempt to redress this differential temporality. Indeed, the rhetorical logic enacted by Jones and two other black youth workers demonstrates and underscores the modalities of systemic racism. Fuelled on group dynamics of conversational call-and-response patterns that situate examples of local racism in a wider context, such manoeuvres were inspired by SNCC's Mississippi projects to motivate black youth, which could be described as consciousness-raising of a kind (Verral 2006, 112). And *Encounter* itself no doubt could be explained as a template for such rhetorical conversations, suggestive of the optimism of its time, but from the perspective of our jaded moment, this might appear naïve or perhaps dogmatic. Nevertheless such Southern-adopted pedagogical strategies and ongoing contact with U.S. organizations left its residual marks on Halifax: young people were educated, if not transformed.

Yet, diverse accounts suggest that the immediate politicization of Halifax's youth was not as successful as originally hoped for. After their visits to Halifax, the Black Panthers conceded that strategies of direct action and confrontation would not take root in Halifax, that change, in typical British fashion, would take place through more established channels. The Panthers nevertheless maintained that their visits were catalysts for change, attributing to their own efforts a meeting that led to the participation of the Black United Front (BUF), Nova Scotia's black organization, in a human rights conference devoted to "The Black Man in Nova Scotia" (Smith 1997, 121, 144–5). "Furthermore, this discussion resulted in the formation of new government programs and the governmental recognition and funding of several black organizations" (Smith 1997, 121).

Remarkably, CFC makes a similar claim regarding *Encounter*'s immediate effectiveness, to the extent that it adopted a shared self-aggrandisement, characterizing the film (and by association, itself) as a prime catalyst for change. In director Rex Tasker's view *Encounter* "raised a storm and got some direct action" (1969, 10). An earlier report in a CFC newsletter, "The Impact at Kwacha House" by Halifax NFB representative Robert S. Sparks, offers a detailed screening history along with an itemized list of *Encounter*'s invited audiences that is extremely telling in hindsight (1968, 5). Indeed, the selectivity of the guest lists, at Halifax mayor Allan O'Brien's behest, from the first recorded viewing on 25 March 1968 to subsequent screenings is informative. Attending the first screening were members of the African United Baptist Association and various officials, including "Halifax's chief of police, the Chief of the Fire Department, the Chief of Detectives and the superintendent of the RCMP, and many other municipal officials" (5). The third screening included the chairman of the Board of Trade, the chairman of the Nova Scotia Human Rights Commission, the head of the Nova Scotia Association for the Advancement of Coloured People (NSAACP), and various religious leaders, among others. According to Sparks, the film was a catalyst for swift change; briefs were penned and programs implemented, resulting in new jobs for Halifax's black youth. Local officials were prompted to offer various programs and incentives for youth employment, a possible result of a typical liberal white response to black demands, the "cooling out" function of governmentality wherein jobs, for example, are doled out to temporarily "cool" dissent. The threat that racial violence could have erupted in Halifax as in the United States is mentioned several times throughout the report, serving to further underscore the effective intervention that *Encounter* occasioned. Such CFC reports, and CFC newsletter accounts in general, typically adopted a positivist will-to-change lexicon, approximating a messianic bias towards evaluating "results" or immediate eventualities from sources that helped construct the projects in the first place (Kurchak 1972, 127; Burnett 1991, 56). In any case, no doubt both the Panther presence and the *Encounter* screenings engendered a moral panic of sorts across communities. It appears that the underlying roots of this fear were not as deeply interrogated as they might be today.

What now stands as the film *Encounter* features footage that had been shot for a larger project, initiated by Rex Tasker, that focused on a new community organization, the Halifax Neighbourhood Center Project, which was offering initiatives to assist the poor in Halifax.[6] *Encounter* thus grew out of the footage shot for the longer film. In contrast to *Encounter*, *Halifax Neighbourhood Center Project* (HNCP) offers a more extensive "big picture" of poverty in the city, shadowing social workers and clients, employing traditional documentary modes of narration and editorial comment, and explaining the purpose, organization, and validity of the project (see Cammaer, chapter 11, this volume).

While both films fall within Category III of the CFC's original mandate to "film activities amongst the poor" and are in accord with the NFB's newfound commitment to regionalism, the splitting of the two films in the editing stage, decided by a CFC hands-on producer, presumably John Kemeny, rather than the director, is telling (Tasker 1969). In a letter of 28 May 1968 to an aggrieved F.R. MacKinnon, Nova Scotia's deputy minister of public

6 In Tasker's words (1967), "a second film, called *Encounter at Kwacha House – Halifax* was also released – cut from the same material. So – one set of rushes served two films." Here Tasker also states that he was unaware that the material was edited into two films.

welfare, John Kemeny justifies the decision to release two films, claiming, "After filming was done on the Halifax Neighbourhood Center Project, and the resulting footage first shown, material on the project which dealt with Kwacha House was felt to constitute an important enough segment to be made into a separate film" (Kemeny 1968). In other words, because Kwacha was deemed so radically different from the other centre, a separate film was made.

One could conjecture that the CFC was once again adopting U.S. social rhetoric and initiatives, much as Johnson's war on poverty was retooled to initiate Canada's "war on poverty" government program and its mandated Company of Young Canadians (Evans 1991, 157): that is, the decision to separate the two films could have been influenced by the pervasive topicality of race, both in the United States and locally. Following the headlining of Johnson's cry, for example, articles in the popular press – the *New York Times* (1964), *Maclean's Magazine* (Dexter 1965; Bernard 1967), and *Star Weekly* (Fraser 1965), among others – appeared that spotlighted Halifax as Canada's hotbed of racial strife. The relatively liberal Canadian mainstream media could also have been motivated by the growing controversy engendered by the monumental razing of Africville, a centuries-old, mostly black Halifax community.

Another key factor that might have precipitated awareness, resulting in separating and privileging racially informed subject matter, was the residual effect of the mutually beneficial alliance that was struck between television reporting and the civil rights movement. With this new-found relationship, reporters got a dramatic story and the civil rights movement had its gains and losses publicized, thus earning eventual sympathy and support (Gray 1995, 2005; Acham 2004; Torres 2005). This interrelationship ostensibly also grew from advancements in technology. Portable lightweight cameras in particular allowed this unfolding racial drama to be told up close: it made good television. While the CFC mandate was certainly not dictated by sensationalist headlines, there was greater emphasis on region and on a more organic conception of the issues arising from poverty. CFC filmmakers and personnel, no doubt, could not but be affected by immediate social concerns regarding injustice and, in particular, the drama emanating from the South. At the same time, while publicizing "the struggle," television played an active role in mediating how race came to be framed around a "blacks as social problem" agenda. Indeed, the televisual effects of "aliveness" (Doane 1990), a feature – in conjunction with the realist documentary elements of transparency, authenticity, immediacy, and "newness" that characteristically inform the representation of black subjects (Mercer 1992, 57) – is somewhat embedded in *Encounter*. While framing of this kind could be said to have been transferred to CFC, to be fair, CFC personnel generally had a much more protracted and invested relationship with the communities they encountered, as well as a commitment to the larger goals of facilitating long-term social change, than their television colleagues. In short, we could surmise that the CFC's perceived role as benevolent catalyst was informed by the prevailing ethos of community service that has been promulgated in various forms by the NFB since Grierson's tenure in the 1940s.

The reception of both *Encounter* and HNCP was informed by the competing discourses of mild community outrage and a combination of back-slapping and back-pedalling on the part of government. Whereas the trail of "official" letters to department heads and CFC newsletter correspondence can offer only partial insight, responses from local community leaders were generally split between moderates and more radical factions, with fissures drawn mostly along generational lines. Both groups, surprisingly, objected to the films. Alarmed by the vitriolic black power message of *Encounter*, community elders in particular, predominantly church oriented, tried to distance themselves from more strident points of view. Embarrassed by what was perceived as an exposé of the potentially explosive race-relations situation, F.R. MacKinnon, Nova Scotia deputy minister of public welfare, similarly objected to the inclusion of Kwacha footage in the HNCP film, charging that the Kwacha element did not represent the black community, nor were the "right" organizations consulted prior to shooting.

In a letter to the editor of the CFC newsletter, *Encounter*'s key participant Rocky Jones, too, objects to the inclusion of Kwacha footage in HNCP (1969, 10). Apparently, Kwacha participants were unaware of CFC's intention to use Kwacha as a section in the larger film.[7] *Encounter* was shot in the summer of 1967, situated chronologically in the CFC pantheon between *The Things I Cannot Change* (Tanya Ballantyne Tree, 1967) and the celebrated Fogo films. Obviously *Encounter* predates the "Fogo process," a radical approach to filming individuals that was understood to foster participatory democracy by means of granting the filmed subjects control over images of themselves. The fact that the program's policy kinks had yet to be ironed out is woefully apparent in Jones's further concerns regarding *Encounter*'s release: first, not only had the participants not had the opportunity to screen the film before its release as promised, but government officials and social workers had had the opportunity to view the film first; second, the film's editing choices and selected emphasis presented a slanted interpretation of the conversation at Kwacha House, namely by privileging the more vocal youth workers; third, as indicated above, Jones claims that the participants had no idea that the material shot at Kwacha House would be folded into a larger film that did not convey their philosophy, and they would not have

---

7 In his CFC newsletter response to Jones, however, Tasker claims that Jones and his group were aware of the eventual plan for the Kwacha footage (1969, 10).

consented to be filmed had they had prior knowledge; and fourth, and most presciently, Jones concludes his letter by offering the rallying argument that the black community should be offered the means of self-representation in order to make films about themselves.[8] While these responses point to the impossibility of determining a film's reception regardless of intention, they nevertheless rehearse, albeit on a much less publicized scale, the debates that famously dogged *The Things I Cannot Change*, those concerning documentary's *bete noir,* ethics. Gary Evans notes that TTICC marks "the last time that sensationalism played a major thread in the poverty films. From here on, the subjects became involved in the playback and editing process" (1991, 163). In light of the community protests, this tellingly was not the case with *Encounter*. While offering voice, *Encounter* was not party to the participatory stage of the CFC experiment, illustrating once again that the film occupies an interstitial position in the CFC oeuvre: by all accounts, *Encounter* is decidedly transitional.

This in-between designation not only applies to the film's marked lack of participant involvement in the conditions of its release, but it also applies to *Encounter*'s textual and formal properties. Indeed, the film works against the contention of Colin Low, CFC's foremost practitioner and champion, that "high emotion and conflict look good on national television, but ... these two elements hindered the communication process." In his quest for an ethical use of the medium, Low believed theatricality would exacerbate and increase tension, and thereby simplify, in this case, the Fogo experience (Evans 1991, 164). *Encounter*'s televisual theatricality at times places it decisively outside of the CFC philosophy. On the other hand, Evans's statement that *Encounter*'s talking heads were "visually unexciting" would seem to counter the film's evident theatricality (163). As argued above, while indigenizing Southern U.S. topical subject matter, *Encounter* also ingests a televisual camera style to dynamize these "visually unexciting talking heads," thereby generating associations that characteristically attend blackness on the screen.

Shot in a group-circle format, *Encounter* is structured on point of view, relationally sustained by close-ups of either speaking or listening participants. The camera follows each speaker by means of panning or direct cuts. Once a participant speaks, the camera generally adjusts, zooming in for a close-up. Dialogue (passionately conveyed at times) addressed to camera is interspersed with cutaways to individuating close-ups or a small group shot of the mesmerized young audience, often facilitated by a zooming or pulling out to a wider shot. Not only does such shot patterning bind the viewer into the

8 It took twenty years for films authored by black Haligonians to emerge. Even then, owing to NFB guidelines, topics were generally restricted to black heritage or black youth (often pathologized).

space of the room, but the shots of the avid listeners, albeit predominantly silent, function as stand-ins for the viewer, relaying the impact and novelty of the words spoken. One listener in particular, a wide-eyed young woman, functions as the structural lynchpin to this relay of looks, the camera returning to her silent watchful face numerous times throughout the debate.

Rocky Jones, however, takes centre stage as the privileged participant. Not only does Jones receive the most auditory and screen time, but the manner in which he is shot and the specific codes that accentuate his dress and gesture differentiate him further from his more button-down, proper-mannered fellow youth workers. In short, he is codified as revolutionary. Afro-coifed and wearing a polka-dot shirt, his chest exposed nearly to the waist and highlighted through repeated close-ups, Jones initially has a composed demeanour while bearing the marks of militant defiance popular at the time, gesturing with cigarette in hand, negotiating a raconteur and polemical style while speaking. Religiously following Jones's moves, the camera often zooms in for an unmotivated shot of his hands. Once Jones becomes more adamant, sometimes agitated, the camera follows suit. This mode of privileging Jones is accentuated when, near the film's end, the conversation turns to the merits of violence to effect change. While the strengths of Malcolm X's views on violence are heatedly championed over those of Martin Luther King, the camera repeatedly swish pans between Jones and the two other youth workers, and then again swishes around the room to garner reactions. While adopting the conventions of an observational shooting style, this particular moment of formal dramatization nevertheless further imbues these figures – Jones in particular – with the characteristics of "liveness" typical of crisis coverage. And the alarmist message conveyed with impatient urgency, that violence can be considered as a means, further anchors this liveness to the real. That is, the manner in which *Encounter* depicts its subjects in this instance textually weds these participants to normalized or socially constructed notions of black people as a problem, "as seen on TV."

CFC's claim that *Encounter* was a successful catalyst for change cannot be disputed. Following the screenings of *Encounter,* officials were alerted to the potential for unrest in Halifax and short-term opportunities for black youth did emerge forthwith. The fact that these efforts for change could also be attributed to the moral panic that the presence of the Black Panthers engendered in the fall of 1968 is, perhaps unsurprisingly, not on the CFC record. Moreover, the fact that CFC harnessed its efforts to an extant living catalyst for change, Rocky Jones, a transborder activist, is not readily discernible. *Encounter*'s frozen slice-of-time-like properties do not foster disclosure of the rich outer-national relationships that were forged by participants such as Jones, relationships that the state was simultaneously attempting to suppress. While *Encounter*'s institutional, geo-political contexts could be termed liminal, on all counts it bears the marks of transition: access had not yet been extended to the CFC's subject, in this instance, to the black Haligonian. The film's celebrated successful outcomes did not arise from the active participation of its subjects in self-representation. In comparison to Saul Alinsky's CFC films of the period, however, those that depicted labour-related African-American struggles in Buffalo and Rochester, New York, such as *Building an Organization* (Bonnie Sherr Klein and Peter Pearson, 1968) and *From Conflict to Negotiation* (Klein and Pearson, 1968), respectively, *Encounter* is exemplary. While Jones is individuated, he never gets the aggrandized treatment that is afforded Alinsky in all aspects, from framing to screen time. The lack of context afforded to Jones and the film's temporality won't allow Alinsky-like assessments of past strategic accomplishments. The way in which *Encounter* integrates Jones into the larger assembled group at Kwacha House, in my view, indicates a more refined sensibility towards its subjects and perhaps an intention to foster the attainment of the group's goals.

Of more import is the fact that *Encounter* remains contemporaneous to our present moment some forty-odd years later: its topic, combating systemic racism endemic to Nova Scotia, is still applicable today.[9] In this instance, a fervently asked question of CFC – Can film by itself effect social transformation in the long term (and further to this, how can its effectiveness be measured over time)? – is partially answered. *Encounter* documents one black community group's emergent agency. Jones's legacy as a catalyst for change endures – "he brought the Black Panther members to Halifax with him and Nova Scotia has never been the same" (Clarke 1992, 25).

9 At the time of this writing in the summer of 2008, black community leaders in Digby, Nova Scotia, are organizing a protest in response to the arrest and tasering, on 22 June, of two young men by off-duty RCMP officers. The youths were allegedly insulted and provoked by racial slurs made by the officers. See Michael Tutton, "Protesters call for inquiry into police conduct in N.S. street fight," *Canadian Press*, 14 July 2008, http://www.cbc.ca/cp/Atlantic/080714/to71419A.html.

18

The Films of Maurice Bulbulian: Science and Conscience

■

THOMAS WAUGH

Maurice Bulbulian has only recently slowed down his prodigious output as a quiet dynamo of Quebec documentary since the 1960s. Of major Quebec filmmakers, he is perhaps the least known to English-language audiences, and only a couple of his English-language epics on Canadian constitutional quagmires and West Coast native issues in the 1980s and 1990s respectively drew attention from Toronto cinematic tastemakers.[1] Bulbulian officially contributed four films to Société nouvelle (SN) over a six-year period between 1968 and 1974 – *La p'tite Bourgogne* (*Little Burgundy*, 1968, 44 min.), *Un lendemain comme hier* (A tomorrow like yesterday, 1970, 42 min.), *Dans nos forêts* (In our forests, 1971, 89 min.), and *La revanche* (Revenge, 1974, 23 min.). Of these, only the first was made available in English, and five other Bulbulian films made outside of the National Film Board (NFB) program during the seventies fared even worse (despite the fact that two of these, rare focused studies of Unidad Popular Chile before the 1973 coup, are clearly of world historical importance for their subject alone). A book on Challenge for Change/Société nouvelle (CFC/SN) allows us to rediscover unrecognized artists and films and to tap into a cinematic history rich in models of creation and commitment for today, and Bulbulian is a prime candidate.

Born in 1938 to immigrant shopkeeper parents in Montreal's then working-class immigrant district of Plateau Mont-Royal, Bulbulian was bitten by the cinephile bug in church-basement cine-club screenings. He trained as a teacher and first cut his cinematic teeth on scientific audio-visual

---

1 Bulbulian is invisible in almost all canonizing English-language monographs, anthologies, and reference books on Canadian cinema – Gittings 2002; Khouri and Varga 2006; Leach 2006; Leach and Sloniowski 2003; Melnyk 2007; Rist 2001; White 2006; White and Beard 2002; and Wise 2001 – while Clandfield 1987 and Marshall 2001 both offer one (similar) sentence on Bulbulian's *Le p'tite Bourgogne* as an example of Challenge for Change. The two major exceptions to the overwhelming absence of Bulbulian from Canadian film studies literature in English are the interview in Steven 1993 and short summaries of his oeuvre, including his two 1970s features, in Morris 1984.

works at the Board, then on sociologically oriented documentary research with the Group de recherches sociales, a founding body of Société nouvelle. The GRS had anticipated CFC/SN with its grassroots community accountability and empowerment activities in such precursor documentaries as *Saint-Jérôme* (1968). Given these roots, Bulbulian's work has consistently shown, not surprisingly, a didactic, investigative orientation inseparable from its political mission, summed up in his slogan "science et conscience." (Could this irrepressible didacticism perhaps be one of the reasons that English-language versioning committees at the Board systematically passed on his work, thus dooming him to the French-language ghetto?)

Bulbulian's four SN films, which complement his leadership role in Vidéo-graphe and in community video and cable at the same time, show an inspired versatility, encompassing a spectrum of thematic hooks/political contexts, from inner-city renewal to postwar Quebec's monumental rural emigration to the crisis in the forestry industry in remote regions. And all the while he was developing a deep cinematic understanding of citizens struggling with economic, geographical, and cultural displacement and marginality. The five non-SN films made during the seventies would move beyond the SN demographic of (mostly white) working-class Québécois to encounter Aboriginal groups in the North as well as to build cinematic bridges with dispossessed subjects and communities in Latin America. All the works show Bulbulian's intense identification with his subjects of all generations, whether collective or individual, thanks to his mastery of direct-cinema collaborative techniques, the uncompromising rigour of his artistic vision, and his humility and generosity as a community intervener. Réal LaRochelle aptly characterizes his artistic sensibility and mission: "Without vain cries, without demagogy or compromise, Bulbulian makes human rights a stake and a struggle of each moment. This basic theme is served by a cinematic technique notable for its extreme sobriety, discreet and attentive, strongly controlled in the mise-en-scène and editing" (LaRochelle 2006, my translation). All of these factors have ensured that these nine films, albeit less monumentally imposing than the epics of contemporaries of Bulbulian's like Arcand, Groulx, and Lamothe, remain among the most enduring of the decade in their modest lucidity and affect.

La p'tite Bourgogne (1968), Bulbulian's first production for the fledgling CFC/SN program might be considered one of its half-dozen flagship films, a much-loved film on the contemporary city. It is all the more emblematic as virtually the only one of the CFC/SN films to straddle Canada's linguistic barrier, since it focuses on the bilingual Montreal neighbourhood of Petite Bourgogne/Little Burgundy – a depressed, multi-racial working-class community in the historic industrial core, thirteen kilometres southwest of the Board's suburban fortress in Montreal's north end. The district was one of the most conspicuous targets of "urban renewal" during the development frenzy fuelled by Montreal's Universal Exposition of 1967. (Bonnie Sherr Klein [b. 1941], also an activist in the same corner of Montreal, was responsible for the abridged English version of *P'tite Bourgogne*.) The opening shot of the film refers directly to this context, showing the much vaunted Habitat complex, Expo's architectural showcase originally touted as social housing but which epitomizes for the narrator the dehumanizing silence and sterility of urban development.

In 1967 the CFC/SN program's inaugural epic on urban poverty, *The Things I Cannot Change*, also set in Canada's then-largest city the year it hosted the world at Expo, had been controversial for its alleged ethical shortcuts, its victim aesthetics, and the spectacularization of the poverty of its spotlit family (for a persuasive update on the controversy, see Longfellow, chapter 14, this volume). Bulbulian fell into none of these potential traps with *P'tite Bourgogne* thanks at least in part to the radical social-science-inspired, non-voyeuristic methods developed by the GRS. Citizens committees had sprung up when the first wave of demolition notices were delivered to the tenants of a Petite Bourgogne quadrilateral called Les Îlots St-Martin. Bulbulian hooked up with one of the community animators and members of the citizens committee, especially the avuncular Noel Daudelin, a portly grandfather, and the determined, soft-spoken Jeanne Leblanc, a single mother in her thirties. The filmmakers offered not only to record the citizens' push to participate in the political decisions that affected their collective future but also to get them involved in the conception and development of the film. Daudelin and Leblanc and the other committee members, and many other citizen participants, would be named and thanked in the credits, an unusual procedure for the Board up to this time, but one that became an eloquent custom in Bulbulian's subsequent films and indeed throughout the whole CFC/SN period.

The filmmakers' catalytic efforts specifically brought about an encounter between the committee and the leaders of the Montreal administrative council and the provincial ministry of housing, the NFB letterhead turning out to be very effective where the pleas of the citizens groups had always fallen on deaf ears. A key 6-minute sequence thus shows a long in-studio consultation between the citizens committee and the provincial and municipal authorities. Among the latter is the notorious Lucien Saulnier, the authoritarian, "modernizing" technocrat who spearheaded the city's development mania and who rebuffs the citizens' request for a formal consultative role, all the while performing the congenial, responsive politician for the federal cameras. This trope of citizens encountering the state was already becoming another formulaic fixture of CFC/SN's output, its original mandate having to no small extent focused on the job of bringing together citizens to voice their needs to their representatives. The dozens of bureaucrats and politicians preserved for eternity in these films generally put on their best behaviour in the same way as Saulnier does in this film, discreetly protected by their neckties and desks. Such tropes in CFC/SN, one suspects, are sometimes tokenistic efforts to placate ministerial funders and the original program mandate, but local issues were also sometimes resolved in this way. Of course, the larger political and ideological issues were skirted through the de-sublimatory dynamic of the confronting-the-bureaucrat trope and Leblanc's ironic smile at a politician's condescending comment on citizens committees may be a fleeting recognition of the contradiction inherent in the whole CFC/SN process.

Other sequences better exemplify the balance of science and conscience, aesthetics and ethics, that characterizes Bulbulian's work. In contrast to the "silence" of the emerging concrete landscapes of "renewal," Bulbulian juxtaposes the ebullient noisiness of family and community life in Petite Bourgogne's shabby but comfortable streets, stoops, yards, and kitchens. Here the archive of memory and cultural heritage – what one of the inhabitants calls "a whole way of living" – is boisterously captured as it is transmitted by an eighty-five-year-old folksong-singing grandmother to her grandchildren on a creaking backyard swing. Landscape tropes are especially haunting and poetic: the camera glides up and down the evocative street-fronts, running into bulldozers, then imaging first the modest but comfortable brick row houses and then the vacant lots where dispossessed children play among the rubble of their former homes. Bulbulian's gift for encountering and animating stressed social actors is also evident, especially with Daudelin and Leblanc and their families, and with an anglophone black family, the Croxens. Intradiegetic music continues to be used to very stirring effect throughout the film, especially a solo performance of the 1960s folk hymn "Five Hundred Miles," sung by Croxen's daughter, a young female evictee whose fragile but true voice and guitar strums soar out over the entire neighbourhood and its soon-to-be-destroyed streets with their affect of loss and exile "away from home." These poetics of lament over abandoned dwellings and livelihoods would become another hallmark of not only Bulbulian's films but also of CFC film after CFC film, which retroactively come together as a mosaic of ghost towns, ruins, and abandoned homes, farms, and factories.

The contradictions and ambiguities of citizen protest, participation, and co-optation are gently probed in the bittersweet ending to the film: a glitzy parade complete with marching bands, drum majorettes, and clergy marks the ceremony of breaking the sod for the new Îlots St-Martin. The triumphalism is qualified by a typically open and ambiguous finale: Leblanc's oratory about rights to housing and the "human side of development" is eloquent, but the filmmakers return to melancholy travelling shots of the rubble-strewn landscape of the once-vibrant neighbourhood.

Bulbulian's three subsequent "rural" films for sn would deepen the tragic sensibility of *P'tite Bourgogne*. From a traumatized but resilient urban community whose vibrant depiction perhaps reflected Bulbulian's own inner-city roots, the director shifted his gaze towards rural Quebec, a new territory to be discovered. The iconography of the forests is traditionally more strongly rooted in the Quebec folkloric imaginary than urban Montreal of course, and Bulbulian, who had never had a vacation away from the city, was no doubt an outsider to this heritage. Thus his exploration of the boreal hinterland may have first occasioned an outsider tentativeness that translated into an intensely exotic pastoralism – or more properly speaking "sylvanism." With his subsequent films this aestheticizing attitude would be more subdued, though still maintaining its intense affect.

Un lendemain comme hier (1970), a film about the country-to-city migration of the postwar urban industrial proletariat, was inspired by a family he met during the Petite Bourgogne shoot – migrants from Saguenay–Lac Saint-Jean (north of Quebec City) who returned every summer for the blueberry harvest. This work obviously functioned as a bridge between *P'tite Bourgogne* and the two rural films that followed, *Dans nos forêts* and *La revanche*, both of which focused on the crisis-ridden forest industry. The politics of the decline of the resource-based economies of Quebec's northern and eastern regions, namely pulp and paper and lumbering with all the displacements occasioned by this decline, is encapsulated in *Un lendemain*'s portrait of three generations of the Tremblay family. Images of the transplanted family's base in Montreal's working-class district of St-Henri are disproportionately overshadowed in the film by scenes of their ancestral roots in the now economically depressed woodlands. New collaborator Roger Rochat's black-and-white 16mm cinematography[2] constructs the Lac Saint-Jean landscape with an intense visual stylization that expresses the family's longing for their ancestral homeland. The telephoto-captured sequences of the family picking blueberries – the region's iconic activity – are evocative in their blurred close-ups and long-shot processional silhouettes on a moonscape-like terrain (bared thanks either to a thematically apt clear-cut or a burnout). In like vein, the luminous shots of the family patriarch, Marcel, paddling solo across the dazzling lakes in search of moose unfold under his first-person voice-over narration of his history of uprooting and return, or else under the film's extra-diegetic music, a plaintive male-female pop-folkish duet that echoes

2 Rochat would continue to work with Bulbulian on his non-sn Native projects and would be responsible later for some of the most memorable political documentary cinematography of the subsequent decades, most prominently with Alanis Obomsawin.

the film's hetero-conjugal slant. Observational sequences are devoted to visits to surviving lumber mills, like ghost towns with their museal atmosphere, and to comings-and-goings of the clan during the blueberry hunt, community celebrations scored by children's jubilant voices, amid the natural splendour that they annually leave behind on the expressways leading into Montreal. These poetic landscape and observational tropes offer poignant illustration of the sense of loss and ambivalence brought out in the scenes of discussion among the film's subjects. Based on the familiar CFC/SN trope that might be called "focus groups," these scenes do not escape the prevailing aestheticism and are captured in luscious chiaroscuro around a campfire or around an oil lamp. The discussions, whether between the founding couple of the extended family, or in council with the next generation, testify to the family's economic and familial past as well as their anxieties about the future, stories of fulfilling employment on the land, of childbearing and rearing, of unemployment and then displacement and poverty, of difficult adjustment to new urban spaces and livelihoods, and ultimately of offspring becoming strangers to shared histories and spaces, despite the ritual of "we come back each year."

Between the indulgent landscape and observational sequences and the painterly talk sessions, *Un lendemain* is not only exceptionally aestheticized for a SN work, but also leisurely and meandering, unburdened by narration, if not slow and talky. Bulbulian clearly having bonded with the Tremblays, the film stands out also for its interpersonal intimacy in relation to the English or French program standards. He recalls that his efforts to testify to the social changes taking hold at the time through the experience of a single family were misunderstood by the studio brass. They found it too personal as a film because it was allegedly not focused on a collective social problem: "They didn't see the universal in the one family ... That upset me a bit, like a cold shower, because I would have wanted to continue in the voice of familial intimacy. I felt that that was what I wanted to do ultimately. What I like in documentary is the very intimate side. There were three or four of us [in the crew], without any backup. Complete freedom" (Bulbulian 2006, my translation).

Meanwhile, the anglophone cohort of Challenge for Change found Bulbulian lacking in the required pragmatism and discipline that characterized the other side. All of these factors may have affected the decision not to version this film or the subsequent ones for the English market. (One recalls that CFC/SN executive producer George Stoney imposed a re-edit on *Up against the System* because test audiences were identifying with characters rather than issues [Waugh 2009].) On the whole, Bulbulian found the experience disheartening, all the more so since on the Radio-Canada broadcast his cherished leisurely rhythm and unhurried exploration of personal relationships were marred by commercial interruptions. No doubt the series of community screenings of *P'tite Bourgogne* and *Un lendemain*, usually hosted by animators and organized around discussion, was more satisfying on a personal as well as artistic level.

In the light of such misunderstandings, it may not be surprising that Bulbulian's next two films, both shot in 1971 but released in 1971 and 1974 respectively, fulfilled the CFC/SN mandate in a more literal way, focusing more narrowly on the crisis in the forest industry that the Lac Saint-Jean experience had led him to discover first-hand. Although protracted personal testimony remains a vehicle for cinematic investigation, especially in *Dans nos forêts*, there is not the same level of narrative identification and these two films offer a political discourse more explicitly in line with the SN's democratizing mandate (*Dans nos forêts* announcing off the cuff in the opening credits that "this film belongs to forestry workers").

Dans nos forêts, Bulbulian's only feature-length documentary in his SN cycle, has a strong expository focus (endowed even with a fragmentary voice-over narration) ambitiously "based on a circular voyage around Quebec in order to grasp the general situation of the forest and the workers in forestry" (Steven 1993, 106). Despite the close-up portraits that memorably flesh out the film, the generic discourse has shifted, among other things, from microcosmic intimacy to macrocosmic analysis – but without entailing a sacrifice of aesthetics or experimentation. SN permitted its directors considerably more latitude in terms of duration, aesthetics, and format than CFC (for example,

Pointing to our natural wealth in *Dans nos forêts* (1971): a forceful manifesto of collective ownership and forest management. Production still.

while *Dans nos forêts* is only one of eighteen or more ambitious feature-length works to emerge from the French side, only one lonely feature was produced on the English side [*Encounter on Urban Environment*, Roger Hart, 1971]).

With this licence, Bulbulian launched his first feature with a poetic 7-minute prologue that linked the forest theme to a prophetic glimpse of his future preoccupation with Aboriginal issues: an incantation of a Montagnais legend about the creation of the forest species by the wolverine spirit Carcajou, told by François Belle Fleur (and preceded by the French titles translating the legend). The chanting elder's close-up visage is suspended in black space and is followed by unnarrated landscape sequences, highly stylized both visually and aurally – all as if evoking the prehistoric forest that twentieth-century settler capitalism is destroying. The body of the exposition mingles patina-rich archival footage from the heyday of the forest "colonization" (from the NFB's eight-part 1957 docudrama *Les Brûlés*, a staple of much Quebec historical documentary, including another SN work, *Chez nous c'est chez nous* [1972]) with focus-group-type conversations among forestry workers from the five regions where Bulbulian conducted his research, the already familiar Saguenay–Lac-Saint-Jean as well as Abitibi, Témiscouata, the Côte nord, and Gaspésie. The mix is punctuated by observational moments and media reportages of both government prevarication and spontaneous worker protests against the closing down of their livelihoods by the U.S.-owned corporations who had benefited from giveaway provincial concessions. Bulbulian maintains a refrain of aestheticized sylvan landscapes, but now we have the spaces of the forests as transformed by economic exploitation, a poesis of the materiality of logging and the lives of the workers. This sense of the waste of forest riches becomes a prophetic ecological ultimatum that speaks eloquently in the twenty-first century. Perhaps most dramatic is a 2.5-minute long take static shot of a northern highway, the snowy silence punctuated by huge trucks weighed down with the forest's bounty, whizzing past the camera and periodically moving back empty in the opposite direction to pick up new loads beyond the horizon. This demonstration of the power of the documentary long take is followed by another, a monologue of fully five minutes in duration by a trucker shown in black and white, facing the glare of the night shift in his cab hurtling along the same highway, articulately complaining about the worsening economics of his job, without protection of either the state or unions, exploited by corporations that are "stronger than the government."

While with thirty-five years hindsight the politics of *Dans nos forêts* seem lucid and clear, in the context of 1971 with the classic Marxist epics like *On est au coton* still in circulation and available as terms of reference, critics and audiences received the film as a "film-*constat*" (film report) rather than as an explicit political action. It remained for the companion film *La revanche*, a short released three years later, to acquire the aura of a film intervention. Although the subject of workers' cooperatives comes up in *Dans nos forêts*, it is in the next film that Bulbulian moves beyond his diagnostic "sobriety" and "science" to a vision of solutions: "[W]e asked what things would be like if the workers got together to manage the industry, in workers' co-operatives, etc." (Steven 1993, 106). While the literal translation of *La revanche* is of course "revenge," it is much more nuanced in the original context, connoting "answering back," "defiance," or "riposte." No holds barred, the opening titles of the film are a detailed inventory of abuse based on the foreign ownership of the forest industry, an angry denunciation of mismanagement and exploitation, and a call for "solutions that come from the workers." The 23-minute work is a compact reprise of many of the elements of *Dans nos forêts*, shaped around the explicit claim for workers' control as the "revanche." As such, the poetic refrain from the angry Quebec classic novel *Menaud maître-draveur* (1937) is repeated hauntingly in the film over a lumberyard of fresh-cut stacks of timber – "Will we have the courage and the necessary force to take back what we've lost?" This challenge is less an appeal to the Tremblays' futile blueberry-flavoured nostalgia than a forceful manifesto of collective ownership and management of natural wealth.

Bulbulian was far from the most productive of SN filmmakers in terms of output of finished films (his GRS colleague Michel Régnier holds the record for that; see Czach, chapter 22, this volume), and his uneasiness with the program, centred as he recalled on the tension between authorship and collective accountability, led him to leave before the program ran its course. He completed the forest trilogy (*Ameshkuatan – Les Sorties du castor*, 1978) and developed several of his most interesting 1970s works in the main studio of the NFB, not with Société nouvelle.

CFC/SN was clearly winding down by mid-decade, with a return to the "individualist preoccupations" of filmmakers and the erosion of the state's interest in the idea during the late-seventies recession and the troubled last years of the Trudeau minority regime before its 1979 defeat. Bulbulian's strong sense of personal cinematic vision may have been an awkward fit with the CFC/SN philosophy – though no more so than the French program's other star auteurs, from Anne Claire Poirier to Marcel Carrière. In fact, this tension, as well as the dualities of science and conscience, ethics and aesthetics, had arguably informed the enduring artistic and political effect of these works. Whatever the case, the Bulbulian oeuvre of the late 1960s and 1970s, from both inside and outside SN, remains one of our most evocative imprints of 1960s radical idealism and collective resistance – as well as of strategic compromise.

The Curious Case of *Wilf*: Popular Music
19 in Canadian Documentary

∎

MICHAEL BRENDAN BAKER

The National Film Board of Canada can lay claim to a number of ground-breaking (and genre-defining) documentary films on a range of socially and politically engaged subjects. The NFB also participated in the first international wave of documentaries on contemporary popular music subjects, with major Canadian figures like Paul Anka and Leonard Cohen taking centre stage in the films *Lonely Boy* (Roman Kroitor and Wolf Koenig, 1962) and *Ladies and Gentleman ... Mr. Leonard Cohen* (Donald Brittain and Don Owen, 1965). And while the NFB's interest in both political and cultural subject matter continues to this day, rarely have politics and pop music directly intersected in a single film. Consider the curious case of Robert Nichol's short documentary *Wilf: A Study of Rural Relocation* (1968),[1] one of the very first productions of the NFB's Challenge for Change program and the only film from CFC featuring a popular music soundtrack.[2] It provides us with the opportunity to address the significance of the pop soundtrack within the context of the CFC program, to pose questions about the presumed relationship between the socially engaged audience of the CFC series and the emerging singer-songwriter featured so prominently in this film, and to explore the unintended consequence of the soundtrack in terms of *Wilf*'s legacy in Canadian cinema.

1 The production date for *Wilf* is listed in the NFB master catalogue as 1968, but documents available in the NFB Archives confirm that the film was submitted and approved as "completed" on 27 January 1969. And while the film was not exhibited publicly until the spring of 1969, several archived project proposals suggest *Wilf* was among the first films to be formally presented to CFC producers.

2 For the sake of the present discussion, popular music is defined here as those Western contemporary commercial music genres with roots distinct from traditional European art music dating back to the sixteenth century (e.g., baroque, classical, romantic). Phillip H. Ennis identifies the seven main genres of popular music as pop, black pop, country pop, jazz, folk, and gospel. See Phillip H. Ennis, *The Seventh Stream: The Emergence of Rocknroll in American Popular Music* (Hanover: Wesleyan University Press, 1992), 18.

Solitary farmer-hero of *Wilf* (1968): an engagement with seniors, differentiated by a Joni Mitchell soundtrack. Frame enlargement.

Wilf represents an approach to both form and content that is not repeated elsewhere within the CFC series. In contrast to the majority of CFC projects, which gestured towards (or explicitly lobbied for) grassroots, group-based activism, *Wilf* is a poetic meditation on solitary pacifism and the nobility of the family farm in the age of urban sprawl, suburban development, and industrial farming. Most significantly, Joni Mitchell's song "Sisotowbell Lane" plays a considerable role in *Wilf*. The song, a romantic ballad set in a rustic locale – the location is an acronym for "Somehow, in spite of trouble, ours will be ever lasting love" – is re-purposed here as a tribute to the film's namesake and his modest lifestyle, and it is perhaps the strongest formal feature of the film.

Wilf has much in common with the biographic portraits traditionally produced by the NFB, such as Roman Kroitor's *Paul Tomkowicz: Street-railway Switchman* (1953), but it is something of an oddity within CFC. While *Wilf* was originally proposed in July 1967 as a study of rural poverty, the finished film transcends its original focus and becomes both a personal and a political story, addressing the place of the small farm in a rapidly modernizing economy in which an educated workforce is replacing the land as the nation's most valuable resource. Because of its spotlight on the figure of an aging Wilfred Flemming, the sole occupant of a rundown farm near Orillia, Ontario, the film is one of the few CFC projects that directly engages with senior citizens – the other noteworthy film is Richard Todd's *Nell and Fred* (1971).[3] *Wilf* is a thoughtful commentary on the state of the small farm within an

3 *Nell and Fred* tackles the relocation of senior citizens in a completely different arena, namely the personal decision-making process behind moving out of a private residence and into a residential care facility.

ever-expanding world of industrial agriculture, and it spotlights the slim margin between survival and prosperity for those families who choose not to relocate to urban and suburban centres. "[Wilf is] as independent as people can be in today's society," remarks one government representative when asked in an off-screen interview to describe the aging farmer.

In terms of its tone and aesthetic, *Wilf* has most in common with Colin Low's Fogo series, with its fascination with the words and worn faces of the desperate fisherman, but the lack of any onscreen community (save the townsfolk who marvel in voice-over at Wilf's perseverance) distinguishes it from Low's pilot project. *Wilf* shares similar themes and stylistic features with several Société nouvelle films, particularly Léonard Forest's experimental docu-fiction *La noce est pas finie* (1969) and the significant role played by folk song in *Un soleil pas comme ailleurs* (1972). On the English side of things, *Wilf* is a rare aesthetic triumph in a corpus of work often criticized for an absence of artfulness. Nichol displays a gifted eye for composition, while his and Susan Gibbard's editing strikes a balance between poetic black-and-white shots of Wilf's home and directed scenes featuring colour photography of rural landscapes, Wilf carrying out particular tasks on the farm, and Wilf running errands in the city. The whole of the film is structured in such a way as to have Wilf's voice-over assume a particular authority within a soundtrack otherwise populated by policy experts and the casual remarks of neighbours – so much so that the Ministry of Agriculture, responsible for partial funding of the film, felt Nichol did not do enough to explain the benefits of the ministry's proposed farm relocation legislation.[4] It is a pointed continuation of the most progressive, subject-first NFB docs of the 1960s that preceded CFC/SN, and yet the inclusion of Joni Mitchell's song differentiates it from its predecessors and other films in the series.

"Sisotowbell Lane" from the David Crosby–produced *Song to a Seagull* (1968) appears three times in *Wilf*: during the title sequence; at the mid-point of the film, marking Wilf's return to his farm following a trip into town; and at the film's conclusion. Mitchell's song is made to comment on Wilf's lifestyle, emphasizing both his solitude and the contrast between the rustic beauty of his surroundings and the hustle and bustle of the nearby town, which, according to one neighbour, "just moves too fast for Wilf." In the opening verse, Mitchell sings:

Sisotowbell Lane
Go to the city you'll come back again

4 Robert Nichol, phone interview with author, 22 May 2008. There is also anecdotal evidence of the ministry's position on the content of the film in correspondence archived at the NFB (NFB, n.d., production file A80-67, *Wilf*).

To wade thru the grain

…

Come back to the stars
Sweet well water and pickling jars

…

We have a rocking chair
Someone is always there
Rocking rhythms while they're waiting with the candle in the window
Sometimes we do
We wait for you

With the lyrics of "Sisotowbell Lane" afforded the same authority in the soundtrack as Wilf's first-person observations, the music-image relationships within *Wilf* essentially function in the same way: the images are arranged in such a way that the music appears to directly comment upon or assign meaning to those images it accompanies.[5] The opening sequence and the first appearance of "Sisotowbell Lane" best illustrate this dynamic in Nichol's film and establish a context within which the view can consider the significance of the use of Mitchell's song.

Wilf's introductory sequence features scripted narration and an audio collage that mixers interviews with Wilf, policy experts, and neighbours. The image track offers glimpses of the old farmer waking in the morning and milking his cows. This brief scene ends with the sun rising on the farm and a slow pan moving from a static composition of hedgerow across a snowy field populated by rabbits, horses, and grazing cows. Punctuated by the opening guitar figure of the song in question, a screen credit announces "Sisotowbell Lane – Words and Music by Joni Mitchell, etc." and a brief credit sequence begins. Mitchell sings of pickling jars, rocking chairs, steamed kitchen windows, and water pumps as if she is taking an inventory of the images about to appear in the next sequence of the film. Her words and music are meant to lend Nichol's photography a particular nostalgic edge, an authority otherwise absent when the silent frame is occupied by Wilf alone. The sequence concludes with a montage of still photos of Wilf's possessions – a junker car, old photographs, hunting trophies, and a collie dog drinking

5 Siegfried Kracauer, among others, describes the role played by music in this harmonious relationship with the image track as "commentative music," while Michel Chion adopts a range of terms, including "convergence," "punctuation," and "unification" in his theorization and analysis of "simultaneous vertical relationships" in cinema. See Siegfried Kracauer, *Theory of Film: The Redemption of Physical Reality* (London: Oxford University Press, 1960); and Michel Chion, *Audio-Vision: Sound on Screen*, trans. Claudia Gorbman (New York: Columbia University Press, 1994).

out of a coffee cup – but the strains of "Sisotowbell Lane" still echo across these images (such is the power of Mitchell's song), and its authority is reinforced by its subsequent occurrences in the film, where it is deployed in much the same way.

There was no precedent in CFC/SN films for the way commercial popular music was used in *Wilf*, nor did *Wilf* seem to have any direct influence on other films in the program in this regard, although there are a few examples of popular music soundtracks: Colin Low's *Children of Fogo* (1967) with its instrumental rock performance by the Philadelphia Cream Cheese; Michel Régnier's series on urban development (with an electronic score by Alain Clavier); Willie Dunn and Shannon Two Feathers' traditional folk songs in *Ballad of Crowfoot* (Willie Dunn, 1968), *Rose's House* (Clay Borris, 1977), and *God Help the Man Who Would Part with His Land* (George Stoney, 1971); the aforementioned use of Québécois folk songs in the work of Forest; and the appearance of folk song in the English-French co-production *Little Burgundy* (Maurice Bulbulian and Bonnie Sherr Klein, 1969). Importantly, none of these folk songs or contemporary instrumental scores had a life outside the world of the film in the way Joni Mitchell's song is recognized and interpreted within popular culture at large. Screening reports submitted 22 April 1969 following a presentation to fifty elderly farmers include several positive mentions of the song ("it does a lot for the film"), and it seems likely that it made a significant impression upon younger audiences at the time of its release (even if these youth audiences did not necessarily constitute an affinity group in relation to the small farmers and policy wonks to whom the film was addressed).

Mitchell's move to the United States in 1967 after several appearances on CBC television (1965–66), combined with the success of several of her songs as performed by American country and folk artists ("Both Sides Now" and "Chelsea Morning" by Judy Collins; "Eastern Rain" by Fairport Convention; "Urge for Going" and "The Circle Game" by Tom Rush), introduced her to the U.S. music industry and a mainstream North American audience. Equally at home in the New York City–centred East Coast folk music clubs and festivals and the Laurel Canyon–centred West Coast singer-songwriter scene, Mitchell was a household name by the time *Wilf* was seen by the public in spring 1969. In fact, she would win the 1969 Grammy for Best Folk Performance for her *Clouds* LP, released at the time of *Wilf*'s first public screenings.

Based on numerous letters exchanged between Nichol, Robert Fleming (then music director at the NFB), Warner Bros. Canada, Siquomb Publishing Company, and the American Federation of Musicians of the U.S.A., the process of obtaining permission to use the Mitchell song and securing the associated non-exclusive world television and non-theatrical film rights began shortly after the release of *Song to a Seagull* in March 1968. Correspondence dated early April (long before the budget for *Wilf* was established in autumn 1968) marks the start of a three-month process that concluded in early June with the payment of a $500 publishing fee on behalf of the NFB to Siquomb. The timeline of these exchanges suggests Nichol was familiar with the song in advance of its recording and release on *Song to a Seagull*. Moreover, the sequence of events all but confirms that Nichol entered the production phase of the film with the song on his creative radar.

With all of this legal manoeuvring in mind, one should consider why the filmmaker picked this particular song from this particular artist in the first place. In an interview in May 2008, the director explained that he was a fan of the young singer-songwriter, was familiar with her album, and felt strongly that the nostalgic tone of "Sisotowbell Lane" was perfectly suited to the theme and atmosphere of the film he envisioned.[6] While Nichol recognized that this was a different approach from that of other films in the fledging series, he was convinced that the song was an important part of the presentation and central to the film properly reflecting his own experiences on the farm during his three-week stay with Wilf – a visit that had preceded the day-long interview featured within the film. When asked if the song was selected solely for these aesthetic and thematic reasons or if he had a sense that a song from an emerging artist would resonate with young audiences who might otherwise not have connected with the issue of poverty on farms, Nichol admitted he did not appreciate the latter dimension of Mitchell's contribution but suggested this appeal to youth might explain *Wilf*'s popularity on television at the time of its release. (*Wilf* appeared on CBC at least forty-five times in the years immediately following its release, more than any other film from CFC/SN according to undated production documents in the NFB Archives.) In stark contrast to the legal wrangling and layers of go-betweens that characterize the contemporary music licensing business, Nichol simply called Mitchell on the phone after looking her up in the phonebook and asked her permission to seek a licensing agreement for the song. Forty years later, Nichol does not believe that Mitchell has ever seen the film that her song so profoundly influences.

The degree to which "Sisotowbell Lane" is implicitly political or its use inherently political extends beyond a discussion of Mitchell as a singular artist to a larger issue concerning the political status of popular music at large. "While various positions have been adopted with respect [to this] issue," write William Fox and James Williams, "two polar perspectives may be identified: one views contemporary music as essentially apolitical; the other sees it as a significant political medium" (1974, 354). In discussing

6 Robert Nichol, 22 May 2008.

Ron Eyerman and Andrew Jamison's approach to the study of music's politics from the perspective of social movement theory – an appropriate arena in which to discuss CFC filmmakers, participants, and audiences – popular music studies scholar John Street explains that "social movements provide a context within which music is heard and given meaning" (2003, 127). The use of Mitchell's "Sisotowbell Lane" within the context of Nichol's socially and politically engaged documentary, itself embedded in a program like CFC, politicizes the song despite its apolitical romantic subject matter. Both the solo performance and the collective singing of folk songs with political or social content encourage a common consciousness-raising experience. Mitchell's song is not explicitly political (though she herself was positioned within the industry alongside folk singers like Joan Baez and Judy Collins), but the institutional context established by CFC encourages such an interpretation. The use of the song is a clever appropriation of a commercial product in service to the explicitly socio-political, perhaps doubly so if one considers the folk revival's concomitant appeal to youth. Eyerman and Jamison argue that "popular music could provide a sense of belongingness, a sharing in a collective vision, by making use of more emotive language and rhythms" (1998, 138). It is precisely this language and these rhythms for which Mitchell was critically acclaimed and popularly embraced after moving beyond her folk roots and becoming less explicit in communicating her social and political views in her lyrics, and it this sense of belongingness and this appeal to a collective vision that Nichol taps into by associating "Sisotowbell Lane" with his images and narrative.

Unfortunately, the inclusion of "Sisotowbell Lane" had an unintended effect on the place of *Wilf* in the CFC program and the NFB catalogue at large, one that threatens its availability. In the age of DVD releases and online distribution, the mechanical licensing of musical recordings is big business, representing multi-million-dollar transactions, depending on the parties involved. There are any number of high-profile examples to choose from – *The Wonder Years* (ABC, 1988) remains unavailable in digital formats because of the vast number of hit songs from the 1960s and early 1970s that cannot be affordably licensed by its current rights holders – and, apart from its scale, the case of *Wilf* is no different. Like other publicly funded cultural institutions of the era that responded to the pop music boom by featuring it prominently in film and television programming (the BBC, for example), the NFB is now in the unfortunate position of having a catalogue littered with titles it is unable to exhibit or distribute because of long-expired music licences with prohibitively expensive renewal fees. *Wilf* is an example of such a film – another is Robin Spry's hippie demonstration doc *Flowers on a One-Way Street* (1967), which features a song from the Beatles – and for this reason it remains unlikely that *Wilf* will ever be commercially available.[7] The $500 fee paid to Siquomb Publishing in 1968 for non-exclusive world television and non-theatrical rights carried with it no expiry date for the agreement, yet it did not, for obvious reasons, cover home video rights or digital distribution rights.[8] It is this multi-tiered legal murkiness that the current NFB regime appears unable to resolve by way of a new licensing agreement. In a curious way, this situation reintroduces the tension that exists between the commercial (or economic) and the folk addressed by both the film and the featured song, and echoed historically in the commercialization of the folk revival in the late-1960s and in the dissemination of its politics within the mainstream: no matter its origins in a film program geared towards social and political activism or its place in the catalogue of a federally funded film institution, *Wilf* is now just another product to be bought and sold (or left in the archives to rot). That the power of the film is rooted in its simple beauty and the harmonious dance of popular music and the documentary image, however, gives us hope that *Wilf* cannot be silenced.

7 This prohibition on pop in the NFB back-catalogue appears to extend to the institution's online database, which makes no mention of either Joni Mitchell's or the Beatles' contributions, despite the fact that both are credited onscreen and in the official production scripts archived at the NFB.

8 In the current climate of music licensing for film and video, contracts now state that the usage is for "any and all media now known or hereinafter devised." See, for example, the standard Master Use Recording License used by WNBC, http://www.wnbc.com/download/2006/0203/6712917.pdf (accessed 18 May 2008).

Portapak as Performance: VTR *St-Jacques* and VTR *Rosedale*

BRIAN RUSTED

INTRODUCTION

If documentaries pose a critical problem, it is not one tangled in a crisis of representation that tries to resolve whether the art of film impedes its objectivity or how it is that stylistic strategies convince audiences that a given documentary transparently reproduces their notions of the real. The problem is more productively seen as archaeological (Shanks 2004): how to embody documentary texts found resting amongst sedimentations of bygone intentions, aesthetics, social practices, and prior critical readings. Connoisseurship alone does not let a contemporary audience inhabit the spaces of makers or audiences remote in time however much we insist that, by their nature, the media of film and video transcend such dislocations. The critical problem documentaries pose is in restoring or evoking the necessities that occasioned their performance, the bodily engagements of making, viewing, and using documentaries.

Videotape that was used to enact the community development processes of Challenge for Change (CFC) poses such a problem. Despite a revival of the CFC spirit in the NFB's recent Citizen*Shift* initiative and a general recognition that CFC was "the genealogical ancestor of much of what is now called subject-generated media" (Crocker 2008, 72), contemporary viewers share neither the novelty of portable video in the mid-1960s nor the same needs for community development and change.

On its website, the Fogo Island Co-op offers a fragment of an origin tale under the guise of a "company profile": "Following a process of community self-discovery now known worldwide as the Fogo Process, our fishers formed the Fogo Island Cooperative Society, a community based enterprise on which we built the economy of our island" (http://www.fogoislandco-op.com/profile.html). While it may be noteworthy that such an organization traces its roots to a community development process, the absence of any mention of media in that "now known worldwide" process is more intriguing. The omission implies a degree of independence for the process and its media artefacts.

The performance of the Fogo process did things, which in this case – however local, however transient, however dependent on dwindling fish stocks – meant building an economy.

Emphasizing the outcome of the process rather than its media artifacts, the authors of this company profile understand documentary as a performative component of the process. Rather than read the products of CFC as representational texts to be read within critical discourse, this chapter approaches video in the Fogo process as a multi-sensory, non-representational practice (Thrift 2008) that makes "space livelier" (Thrift and Dewsbury 2000, 412), that is "interested in how events are shaped as they happen" (Thrift 2008, 111), and that tries "to counter the still-prevalent tendency to consider life from the point of view of individual agents who generate action" (Thrift 2008, 112). Performance is central to non-representational work and involves an interest in the relational networks of embodied practices (Thrift 2008), in the hybrid performances of technology, and in the materialities of landscape (Haldrup and Larsen 2006b; Larsen 2005). If documentary is approached as non-representational performance, attention strays from the rhetoric of texts to the *practices* of community organizing, the *technologies* of portable video, and the embodied *material relations* that produce a collectively enacted sense of place (Thrift 2008; Larsen 2005). To approach this stratum of Canadian documentary as non-representational performance is to try to see the residue of video texts in the light of the embodied re-enactments of the process.

VIDEOTAPE AND THE FOGO PROCESS

Any Challenge for Change project can be described as a performance of cultural memory, "an activity occurring in the present" to meet the needs of that present (Bal, Crewe, and Spitzer 1999, vii). Challenge for Change has a forty-year history of such descriptions. The CFC initiative helped advance the NFB's institutional mandate to portray Canada to Canadians; it closed the aesthetic gap between media professionals and media amateurs (Watson 1977); it widened the gap between media professionals and media amateurs (Grierson 1972; Marchessault, this volume, p. 354); it gave voice to First Nations and other marginal communities (Stewart 2007); it used technology to other and commodify marginal communities for the voyeuristic pleasures of the middle class (Burnett 1991); it created a climate for participatory democracy and social activism by putting new technology in the hands of people (Crocker 2008; Goldberg 1990); and it promoted a naïve engagement with a new technology that diverted activism and real social change to re-inscribe liberal democracy (Druick 2007; Jones 1981; Marchessault, this volume,

p. 354; Moore 1987). In making a place amidst such a lineage, this chapter can at least query how a technology marketed to enhance "the enjoyment of ... 'home-movie' entertainment" (Sony Corporation) could inspire and fuel such continuous and contradictory descriptions.

Although not present at the inception of the CFC program in 1966, video-tape came to have a decisive impact on the program's mandate "to help erad-icate the causes of poverty by provoking basic social change" (MacPherson 1968, 2) and to apply "audio visual techniques to the task of facilitating communications in spheres where exchanges of any meaningful sort were traditionally at a minimum" (MUN Extension Service, n.d.). The outcome of the program was as much the process of using media for social change as it was the product of representing social change in film and video (Sturken 1984). Introduced in 1968, portable video was a common tool in such pro-jects into the 1970s (Gwyn 1972; Kurchak 1972), contributing directly to the elaboration of the process of community organizing. Work by Hénaut charts some of the evolution of these applications (1969a, 1969b, 1969c, 1970, 1972, 1991a, 1991b).

It is relatively easy to list the contributions of videotape – reduced cost of production, accelerated feedback, diminished technical dependence – but, because of its disadvantages, it is more difficult to account for what appears to be a rapid diffusion of portable video within both the film and the devel-opment communities. Portable video was not of broadcast quality, was not ideal as an archival medium (Gwyn 1972), and it would be a decade before it would be practical for distribution. Portable video, though, did contribute to advances in the application of the "Fogo process," which from its incep-tion had downplayed an emphasis on the actual products: "The screening sessions were deemed to be of the utmost importance. The films per se were worthless, the reactions to the screening of them an integral aspect of the project if the communication was to achieve its true intent as dialogue" (MUN Extension Service, n.d.).

Videotape reduced the time between recording and viewing, and brought community participants more directly into the recording and editing stages (Taylor and Taylor 1973). As Goldberg suggested, two key rules were dis-covered as the process was elaborated: "Any production designed to improve conditions for a group of people and to empower those people requires their consent and active participation in order to be effective ... The process of making the film is as important as the actual film product" (1990, 13). The introduction of portable video made a direct contribution to this,[1] and the idea of process came to dominate the community use of video during its first decade (Boyle 1992; Hopkins, Herman, and Kirk 1972).

DOCUMENTARY AS NON-REPRESENTATION

There have been sporadic efforts to connect documentary practice variously with performance, performativity, and performance studies. Such efforts have approached (documentary) film as evidence of performance (Butler 1993; Muñoz 1995; Phelan 1993) or as a means to understand the subjectively stylized practices of documentary-makers as reflexive (Bruzzi 2006; Nichols 1994). Using performance in this way builds on developmental typologies of documentary styles or modes (Nichols 2001). Performance has also been given a more generative role in anthropological film, where cultural performances can form the basis of "ethnographic 'screenplays'" (Ruby 2000, 246).

Such efforts to connect performance and documentary share an emphasis on the textual and rhetorical features of documentaries. In writing about *Paris Is Burning*, Phelan keeps pulling herself back from discussing what the film has documented to reflect instead on the surface features of the text and its author: "My friend keeps telling me to be sure I keep saying I'm only writing about Livingston's film of the balls and I'm not writing about the balls themselves. My friend knows how tempted I am to take Livingston's film as a perfect unbiased record of the performances. That's where the hook of the film (and perhaps of most ethnographic film) breaks my skin" (1993, 104).

This analysis seems to assume that the subject of the documentary and the subjectivity producing it have not been mutually constituted in a social process. Phelan's ability to step back from the object of analysis suggests that neither have she and her subject. In a similar fashion, Scheibler's discussion of Wenders's *Lightning over Water* recalls Austin's language and ascribes a passive-voiced agency to the film text: "[T]he performative turns on the moment when the film enunciates its own discourse, exclaims its own utterance even as it exceeds it. The performative text passes judgment on its constative self, demarcating the point at which the divisions between fiction and nonfiction, subject and object, begin to waver" (1993, 144). Such analyses help performance travel across critical territories (Bal 2002), but if documentaries do things, their performative force is not confined solely to the surface play of a text. Researchers working within cultural geography (Thrift

1 When Don Snowden gathers a group of social science "experts" to review the experiment, few comments are directed towards the process itself. Despite Druick's observation regarding parallels between social science methods and documentary, the researchers from sociology, education, economics, and political science are more interested in discussing the films as representations of Fogo than in discussing their impact on or parallels with their research methods (Druick 2007). *Fogo Project – Post Mortem* (also titled *Specialists at MUN Discuss the Fogo Films*) captures this exchange. See also Sandra Gwyn's summary of the seminar (1972a, 1972b).

2004; Nash 2000), tourist studies (Couch 2000, 2003; Crang 1997; Larsen 2005), archaeology (Shanks 2004), and even visual studies (Brodsky 2002; Bolt 2004; Mitchell 2005) point to the limitations of a critical emphasis on representation on making contributions towards embodied, sensory, non-representational (Thrift 2008), or "more than representational" approaches to culture (Lorimer 2005). Their dissatisfaction with text and representation often entails an invocation of performance as an alternative research para-digm. Catherine Nash, reviewing non-representational work within geogra-phy, feels that the "value of ideas of performance and practice is their challenge to forms of interpretation which focus on the representation of meaning in visual or literary texts or use textual analysis to understand the world" (2000, 657). Haldrup and Larsen extend this into tourism studies, suggesting that performance "destabilizes semiotic readings where places and objects are seen as signifying social constructs that can be unveiled through authoritative cultural readings rather than in terms of how they are used and lived with in practice" (2006a, 9). Thrift's insistence on "practices" as the focus of such a paradigm is taken up in Larsen's reformulation of "hybridized" practices that intertwine encounters with technology and material culture (Larsen 2005, 419). Approaching documentary as non-representational performance directs attention to its constitutive qualities. The documentary process in this sense is a restoration of behaviour, a performance that adapts and re-enacts a process rather than one that transparently or rhetorically represents it.

VTR AND THE CHALLENGE FOR CHANGE

In the fourth issue of the CFC newsletter, Dorothy Todd Hénaut and Bonnie Klein offer a "video report" on a project involving a citizens group in the St-Jacques area of Montreal. They saw the introduction of video to Challenge for Change as "an attempt to extend to its logical conclusion" (Hénaut and Klein, chapter 3, this volume, p. 24) the program's mandate to create social change by providing access to media tools. Their report back-grounds the project, reflects on the unfolding use of video, and provides an outline of what would become VTR St-Jacques, the NFB film that docu-mented this project.

As with other CFC projects, there was a pre-existing community group – Comité des citoyens de Saint-Jacques – formed with the assistance of a com-munity organizer. The committee's aims resonated with Challenge for Change: they sought access to health care at the community level and greater respon-siveness from different levels of government. The committee saw portable video as an enhancement to their efforts. The NFB-produced documentary film provides a narrative record of the ways video was used in the project. As

Bonnie Klein has suggested,[2] the application of video was balanced by the NFB's need for a film product they could distribute: "Through Dorothy Hénaut, a writer at the NFB, I became aware of Sony's new half-inch portable videotape recorder. So we thought we could do a project in which we used video instead of film and people could make their own material without our intervention. It was a really interesting experiment. George Stoney had been brought from the US to head the Challenge for Change program. Suspicious of video, he told us, 'You can only do it if you shoot a 16mm documenting it'" (Goldsmith 2003, 69).

The viewer is passed back and forth between the NFB crew's film that recorded the video activities of the Comité des citoyens de Saint-Jacques and videotape that was shot and used by the committee during its process. The film charts key moments in the process: the community members learning to use the equipment and exploring its use in the community, debates about the editing process, community members' reactions to viewing the tapes and to the dialogue over issues that arose. These moments of the film are punctuated by freeze frames where members of the committee reflect in voice-over on the process, their experience, and use of video.

The climax both of the film and of Hénaut and Klein's report is an encounter between the committee's VTR group and mainstream journalists during a press conference: "On one occasion, the citizens discovered that journalists, who talk loudly of freedom of the press, consider themselves immune from interviews or cameras; they became angry when they became subjects for the citizens' cameras during the press conference for Operation Snowball" (Hénaut and Klein, chapter 3, this volume, p. 32). This encounter prefigures a commonplace of consumer digital media: alternative accounts are possible because of democratized media access. It also pricks "the myth of objectivity in mass media reporting" (Hénaut and Klein, chapter 3, this volume, p. 31). What makes this a compelling encounter, though, is the struggle on the part of the committee members to articulate the significance of their documentation to the "media." In the midst of recording the press conference and presenting their community project, the members of the information committee gasp for words as they try to respond to a journalist's antagonistic question about why the committee would want to make its own record of the press conference. Why would the committee feel that the journalists' accounts would not be sufficient and definitive? The tension in the cramped room, journalists in suits arrayed against the wall, committee videographers and NFB film crew standing with lenses trained on them, is palpable and compelling. "C'est pour … ah, c'est pour … "

---

2 George Stoney's account of the introduction of video into CFC corroborates this (Sturken 1984).

Although initiated the year VTR *St-Jacques* was released, a film about a parallel VTR project in Alberta's Drumheller Valley – titled VTR *Rosedale* – would not be released by the NFB for another five years. This film documents a mature phase of the use of video in the application of the Fogo process. In a relationship similar to the "Newfoundland Project" (as the NFB documents referred to it; see below in this chapter), the Drumheller VTR project involved a partnership between Challenge for Change and the University of Calgary (specifically the latter's Division of Continuing Education – equivalent to Memorial University's Extension Service – and the School of Social Welfare). This project did not have the initial level of community organizing present in Fogo or St-Jacques. Community worker Anton Karch had been hired and resided in the valley for two months prior to the appearance of the NFB. The project was conceived as an "action research" project from its inception. Although there was a small community action committee in the Rosedale, Alberta, area, video in this case had a more constitutive role in such organizing. Karch had received training at the NFB in Montreal in the use of portable VTR equipment and passed these skills on to members of the community. Two NFB staff brought video equipment to the Drumheller Valley and stayed for a month while the first tapes were made in Drumheller, East Coulee, and Wayne (Karch 1971–72; Baxter 1971). Karch remained in the area for nearly two years and then later returned to the NFB to help with the editing of VTR *Rosedale* (personal communication; see also Baxter 1971 and Taylor and Taylor 1973).

Unlike its counterpart in St-Jacques, VTR *Rosedale* is not a documentary film shot by community members while an NFB crew looks on. As the opening credits indicate, the documentary was made from video that was "transferred to film by shooting directly from a television monitor, in order to preserve for permanent record this early use of V.T.R. as process in a social change context." Although viewers of the film do not see, in the edited sequences, the tapes as they were used in the community in 1969, the film documents the stages of the process with the original raw tapes.[3] An uncredited voice-over narration does address the actions in VTR *Rosedale* to a displaced audience, and although there are no freeze frames of action as in VTR *St-Jacques*, the narration does offer reflections about the process in the transitions between one stage of the project and the next. The film preserves a

3 Karch indicates that nine tapes were made in the East Coulee and Wayne areas, while the Rosedale citizens group made a total of eleven (1971, 9–10). Karch edited the nine tapes for the first public screening in East Coulee, and the Rosedale committee edited their eleven tapes into a one-hour tape for the Rosedale public meeting. Baxter suggests that a total of 150 hours of tape were produced for the Drumheller project, but the material transferred to film for VTR *Rosedale* is all that remains.

Albertan community sees itself on video in *VTR Rosedale* (1974). Frame enlargement.

record of the VTR process, a sense of the quality of the video image from that period, and the aesthetics of the camera practices characteristic of Portapak use. Karch reported on the project and its use of video in issue 7 of *Access* (1971–72), and as with Hénaut and Klein's report, his is essentially a narrative outline of the film itself.

PRACTICES: ORGANIZING

The music track in the opening moments of VTR *St-Jacques* provides a disjunctive, percussive rhythm for the title credits and the shots that establish the film's urban setting. It is not a synchronous sound, and the clanging and trumpeting that greet the viewer appear to have no correlation with the scenes presented by the camera. Later in the film a viewer might connect the memory of this audio bed with the street theatre activities heralding one of the community screenings of the committee's videotapes. The sound track and its corresponding scene suggest the complex layers of practices, events, and performances that are intertwined with the unfolding of the film. A full discussion of the performance practices enacted in and with these videos would look to a genealogy of street performance and the social dramas it catalyzes. In this chapter, mention can be made of practices associated with the organizing process, event structure, and turning-point moments.

From the start, community workers were central to the Newfoundland Project. The "presence of an Extension Service Field Worker" was given as "a final deciding factor" in the selection of Fogo as the site of this first project and was later identified as at the top of the list of "elements ... crucial to the process" (MUN Extension Service, n.d.). This is echoed in the description of the project that appears in the first CFC newsletter: "Foremost among" factors that led to the selection of Newfoundland – Fogo particularly – for the project was "the organization of its Extension Department, under whose auspices Community Development Officers, so essential in this type of experiment, are at work throughout Newfoundland" (1968, 4).[4] Although film crews may have only stayed in communities for a matter of weeks or at most several months, community organizers and Extension Service workers spent several years in the communities participating in these projects. "So that was the beginning. The field worker went into the area, spent time getting to know it well, getting to know the problems and aspirations of the people. We began to know what it was they didn't know and then were in a position to make judgments about the kinds of material and who might be good spokespeople in the area" (Snowden, quoted in Quarry 2006, 488). By the time the Drumheller VTR project had begun, the role of the community worker had shifted from showing films as part of the development process, or acting as host and interviewer in them, to making videotapes in collaboration with the community.

Concurrent and retrospective descriptions of these projects take note of the vocabulary surrounding events that gave structure to the process. "Interviews were recorded every place where people gathered, the hardware store, post office, and both garages" (Baxter 1971, 36) in the Drumheller project, suggesting a context-sensitive approach resonant with contemporaneous notions of verbal art as performance (Bauman 1975). The taping "blitz" (Hénaut and Klein, chapter 3, this volume, p. 27; Karch 1971–72, 9), the "fête populaire" (Hénaut and Klein, chapter 3, this volume, p. 27), public showings (Karch 1971–72, 9–10), and screenings (MUN Extension

4 Despite this emphasis on the role of community development workers, their presence tends to slip away in subsequent descriptions of this film initiative. For example, as head of MUN's Extension Service, Donald Snowden was central to the Newfoundland Project and to the later, inconclusive Farmerville, California, project. He contributed immensely to realization of the potential that Grierson saw for using the Fogo process internationally. While this is readily acknowledged in the development communities, few accounts of Challenge for Change as a documentary process mention him (but see Crocker 2003, 2008; Ferry 2005; Quarry 2006; and Sullivan 2004). George Stoney's own involvement with Oxford University's extension program is also often understated (Druick 2007).

Service) are all occasions whose structure involves the unfolding of an event. The liminal and festive character of these events is also evident: participants feel a sense of "unity and cohesiveness" (Karch 1971–72, 10) and experience the public screenings and discussions as a "place where I can talk freely" (Hénaut and Klein, chapter 3, this volume, p. 29). Marchessault views the reports that video was "greeted with tremendous excitement by different communities" as evidence of the "instrumental logic" of video that is naturalized in relation to power (Marchessault, chapter 33, this volume, p. 356). Yet to view community users as naïve participants in a cargo cult is to dismiss the complex, cultural sensory engagements that produce feelings of *communitas*.

Embedded in the narrative and editing structures are turning-point moments (Denzin 2003) that produce various community transformations as the process unfolds: the sense of unity in Fogo, changes in attitudes to police or, in the case of St-Jacques, to the dominant media, and a "rising spirit" among Drumheller residents (Baxter 1971, 39). Karch explicitly identifies the turning point in the Drumheller project as being when his own role shifts to that of a development worker aiding the community in the use of video (Karch 1971–72, 10).

TECHNOLOGY: VIDEOTAPE

Video entered into the CFC program the year after the CFC newsletter was first published. The significance of adding video to the process was not lost on contemporary commentators. Patrick Watson, writing for the national arts magazine *artscanada* in 1970, noted: "It is one thing to have people participate in planning and even shooting a film about their lives, quite another to involve them in the editing process" (1977, 116).[5] Video made this possible and the impact of portable video technology was decisive: communities participating in the experiment to organize through mediated communication could do the camerawork and editing themselves and have direct control over the life of the tapes following their completion. As Michelle Stewart notes, "the 'VTR ethos' came to suggest self-representation and community organizing, even when film was chosen over video" (2007, 56).

5 Tom Sherman notes that "editing 1/2" video was a nightmare. There were no computer controllers until quite late (Vidéographe in 1972–74, Montreal). Basically you just had to get both machines rolling and then punch the record button when you wanted to chop the new material in. This resulted is an edit somewhere within a couple of seconds of where you wanted it, and often it didn't work and created a messy, noisy edit point. Oftentimes you just had to keep trying until you got the edit to look half decent" (personal communication; see also O'Donnell 1973).

On-the-street Portapak interviewing in *VTR St-Jacques* (1969): enhancing the citizens committee's organizing efforts (Dorothy Hénaut, right foreground). Frame enlargement.

Despite the recognition given the Portapak on its introduction, limited attention has been paid to the social and institutional dynamics that facilitated its adoption or to the embodied experience of its use. It is a commonplace that video technology simply appeared and was immediately and seamlessly integrated into existing practices. As Burris describes it: "Video and Portapak appeared simultaneously. With the 1968 introduction of this first camera-recorder combination priced at a level accessible to individuals and small institutions, video simply exploded on the scene" (1996). George Stoney offers a similar account of this synchronicity with reference to CFC: "I went up there in 1968 when the Portapaks were just coming out. I had used the Ampex video rigs in 1965 and 1966 when I worked at Stanford, but they were so clumsy and full of bugs that I got terribly frustrated with them. When I got to the Film Board, a group wanted to use video and I had to approve the budget" (Sturken 1984).

As already noted, such features as price, portability, ease of use, immediate playback, sharing of tapes, and so forth are frequently listed as the essential (and essentializing) features that made video technology so readily available to artists and activist communities alike. Armes simply says, "The new video system was perfectly suited to certain social applications ... serving as a tool for community action" (1988, 129). Efforts have been made to situate the adoption of video in relation to the art and alternative media practices of the late 1960s (Boyle 1992; Sherman 2002; Willener, Milliard, and Ganty 1976); to the theoretical and critical discourses of information systems and participatory democracy (Hill 2002); to the art world negotiations with late, modernist aesthetics (Burris 1996); and to the later development of cable community television, artist-run production cooperatives (Bégin 1996),[6] and the broader issues of access (Engleman 1990; Goldberg 1990; Kellner 1992; Surman 1994). Such accounts seem to call out for an elaboration of the social practices that enabled video's adoption within these "scenes," and of the experiential qualities of the use of the technology.

In clarifying the myths of agency that surround the introduction and early adoption of video as a medium in the art world, video artist and educator Tom Sherman noted that Sony introduced its first half-inch studio reel-to-reel deck in 1965 but that a battery-operated model was not released in North America until 1968 (2007).[7] He notes that, instead of a rapid process of adoption, "initially the product had few takers … ½ inch video was inconsistent technically from machine to machine and often couldn't be regularized (through time-base correctors)" (personal communication). Such limiting features were bound up with the experience of using the technology. *VTR St-Jacques* conveys some sense of this with its discussions of the need to wrap the recording deck in a diaper to protect it from the cold, along with shots of the team trying to disentangle the various cables connecting microphone to deck and deck to camera. Sherman notes: "The adoption was slow because the technology was so modest. Heroic but very slow. The batteries on the Portapak lasted about twenty minutes in cold weather. The first Portapaks weighed a ton and the cables between the camera and the decks were always failing. The light-sensitive vidicon tubes were destroyed easily, leaving a black streak, a 'burn,' on all subsequent images. Video shot in low light was flat and grey with little contrast and the audio was terrible" (personal communication).

Despite the disappointing reality of the first truly portable systems, using Portapaks did contribute to new ways of seeing, as is conveyed in the voice-over of *VTR St-Jacques*: "You know, I walk around here every day and I pass by things without even noticing them and when I look through the camera I really see." In a preface added to their video report when it was reprinted in

---

6 Sandra Gwyn's account of the rural and urban uses of video and the Fogo process gives a good indication of the early proliferation of video practice in Montreal, Toronto, and Winnipeg in particular (1972a, 1972b).

7 The Experimental Television Center's Video History Project contains a useful resource section describing the features of early models of Portapaks (http://www.experimentaltvcenter.org/history/resources.html).

the first issue of *Radical Software*, Hénaut and Klein note that community members "can use the camera to view themselves and their neighbourhood with a new and more perceptive eye" (Hénaut and Klein 1970).[8]

The real-time experience of viewing video was as important as the experience of making video. The cybernetic discourse of feedback was frequently noted as a prominent aesthetic feature of video (Boyle 1992; Burris 1996), one that both offset the technical limitations of image quality and blurred "the distinction between representation and performance through the involvement of real bodies in everyday time" (Palmer 2004, 32).[9] Those reporting on the St-Jacques project noted that the use of a camera and a microphone increased the likelihood that people in the community would respond to questions (Hénaut and Klein, chapter 3, this volume) and also enhanced people's sense of self-worth and individuality. This novelty factor contributed to the Drumheller project as well (Baxter 1971, 37), particularly with respect to the young people in the community (Karch 1971–72, 9). Karch suggests that one of the reasons the community attended the screenings was "to come to see and hear their neighbours" (1971, 9). The collective reception experience offered a heightened encounter with both video and community, and as Sherman noted regarding the initial use of portable video, "Everyone could feel the potential, and the instant replay or 'live' closed-circuit image was magic, but the first machines were so primitive technically" (personal communication).

Sherman has suggested that the "Sony Portapaks probably had a useful life of about a year and a half" (personal communication), given the technical problems (e.g., tape and recording-speed incompatibility across different models) and the wear and tear on mechanical components. Their product life was also brief, but this was due to the complex interweaving of market demand for portable broadcast-quality gear (met initially in the early 1970s when Sony introduced its U-matic three-quarter-inch format) and the rapidly changing engineering goals when it came to reliability and image resolution. The shortened product life reflected a contradictory element in the community use of portable video: the desire for access to broadcast outlets for wider distribution. Narrowcasting in closed-circuit systems did not limit half-inch

8 Most attempts to chart the development of community video rely on *Radical Software*, first published in 1970. Because it reprinted articles published several years earlier in the Challenge for Change newsletters, attempts to chart the chronology of portable video that rely on *Radical Software* risk diminishing the degree to which early community video work was modelled on Challenge for Change (Boyle 1992).

9 This betwixt and between approach to video is one way to respond to Phelan's influential assertion that performance is "representation without reproduction" (1993, 3).

portable video. It was the essence of the process aesthetic. Despite the frequent recognition that the video product should not overshadow the video process, the desire to have tapes reach beyond the local, closed-circuit setting shortened the product life of the Portapak. In the later years of the CFC project, the program's newsletter was renamed *Access* in recognition of this conflation of distinct notions of access: access to technology and access to broadcast outlets of cable television.

Although Challenge for Change was focused on creating social change and facilitating community organization, its process also produced a sense of place among those involved.

MATERIALITIES: SPACE

In the iconic projects, the people in the communities in question were under pressure to abandon their homes, relocate, or no longer identify as a place owing to political neglect (St-Jacques), changes in government policy (Fogo), the depletion of natural resources (Rosedale), or impending development (Mistassini). Starting with the Newfoundland Project, these projects were identified spatially. The Newfoundland Project was described locally as the "Fogo Island Film and Community Development Project" (MUN Extension Service), and the film *VTR Rosedale* was known as the "Drumheller VTR Project" (Baxter 1971, 3).

If place is "a knot tied from the strands of the movements of its many inhabitants" (Thrift 2006, 141–2), then portable video also performed "island," "valley," and "neighbourhood." In *VTR Rosedale*, the sensory, embodied, relational engagement with the materialities of place (Haldrup and Larsen 2006b) is evident in the follow-up footage that appears at the end of the documentary: the cleanup of the town, the making of a park, and so forth. Although the film footage interwoven in *VTR St-Jacques* represents place (the alleys, the welfare office, the street corners, etc.), it is in the final scene, when the tapes are screened for the community, that the sense of place is performed. It is not simply "one of downtown Montreal's many poor areas" (Hénaut and Klein, chapter 3, this volume, p. 25). As the voice-over reflects, "The people identify with the people on the screen. They feel at home."

Assessing the impact of the use of media in the Fogo process, Stephan Crocker has suggested that its legacy was in creating an image of people through enabling them to create an image of themselves (2008, 73). The process, however, did not create an image of people so much as it created a bodily engagement with place.

CONCLUSION: RE-ENACTING PROCESS

In an essay dealing with the body in documentary, Bill Nichols considers embodied experience from the point of view of representation. For a documentary-maker, the problem posed by embodiment is one of presenting "a realistic likeness," particularly of "historically located individuals" (1993, 175, 176). In constructing a cinematic version of events, the documentary-maker must endeavour "to restore specificity to an historical figure or event. Representing the subjectivity, perspective, style, and perceptions of people is no simple matter of offering likenesses, or providing "stand-ins" who propose these qualities to us" (177). Nichols's essay looks to the variety of solutions that documentary-makers resort to in trying to represent prior embodied experience. The testimony of witnesses and archival footage are examples, as is the "once accepted convention" of re-enactment, which "observational styles all but destroyed" (176–7).

The representational problem with re-enactment, as Vanessa Agnew notes, is that it eclipses "the past with its own theatricality" (2004, 335). It has a "body too many," as Nichols says (1993, 177), meaning the body referenced *by* the text and the body represented *in* the text. For the historian, re-enactment resorts to a "body-based discourse" (Agnew 2004, 330) that confuses knowledge with individual experience. The bodily, sensory facts of re-enactment are problems to be overcome if representations are to be authoritative or authentic.

Nichols considers the instability of re-enactment strategies in the texts of films by Morris, Trinh, Mallet, Ruiz, and others in terms of the three orders of the body in documentary: the absent subject of the documentary; the subject's narrative presence as a character; and the ahistorical body that "serves as the object of both desire and identification" (1993, 184). The common ground of the documentaries Nichols considers is that they all call "into question the conventions of historical representation" (1993 187). Such questioning suggests a complex of strategies that answer Nichols's question about how representations might "restore that order of magnitude which characterizes lived experience when it can only represent through evocations what lies beyond its own bounds" (1993, 188).

In dismissing a body-based discourse of re-enactment, one overlooks another way of approaching the practices of documentary, especially those based in a process aesthetic. This other way is a form of re-enactment that does not evade the representational needs of documentary to recreate a past. "Performance," says Joe Roach, "stands in for an elusive entity that it is not but that it must vainly aspire both to embody and to replace" (1996, 3). The VTR tapes, the films about them, and the process they record are also re-enactments. Each textual instance re-enacts a glimmer of the place-based, local elaboration of the process. Each successive project stands in for those prior performances of the process. They are not representations of bodies in a process. The making and the use of the videos are bodily re-enactments of the process. As technological and material practices, they are multi-sensory performances of the process of social change. The "films per se may be worthless" but the process they perform is not.

Does such an observation enliven these documentaries? Does it make the tingling flecks of magnetic emulsion dance? Does it reposition these videos among sedimentations of always newer technology, of higher definition? Perhaps only long enough for another community to stand in their place and for others to realize that they are not the audience of these documentaries.

21 Bonnie Klein, Saul Alinsky, and the American Experience

■

STEPHEN MICHAEL CHARBONNEAU

In 1968 Bonnie Sherr Klein directed a series of five films for Challenge for Change (CFC) entitled "The Alinsky Approach: Organizing for Power." Arranged thematically from *People and Power* to *A Continuing Responsibility*, this series attempted a form of filmic pedagogy aimed at outlining Saul Alinsky's theories of social transformation. In fact, these were not the first films produced by CFC that sought to illustrate Alinsky's ideas. Three earlier films – *Saul Alinsky Went to War* as well as *Encounter with Saul Alinsky, Parts I* and *II* – were directed by Peter Pearson in 1967 and similarly functioned to disseminate Alinsky's views on the centrality of community organization in promoting social change. The attraction to Alinsky in these early CFC projects was not without controversy. On the one hand, there was the question of the validity of Alinsky's approach, which was viewed by Colin Low as "fundamentally cynical" (Evans 1991, 165). On the other hand, there was also the question of applicability. To what extent was Alinsky's organizing methodology relevant to an array of local circumstances that could be considered uniquely Canadian or – at the very least – different from the American cityscapes in which Alinsky had been entrenched?

The handing over of the directorial reins to Klein – an expatriate American filmmaker – served to mediate the latter concern. Klein showed an interest in demonstrating to Canadian audiences "how Alinsky's organizing techniques might be grafted on to the Canadian trunk" (Evans 1991, 165). As a displaced American living in Canada, Klein could potentially assist in the dissemination of Alinsky's ideas across the border. The concern over the validity of the Alinsky approach was, perhaps, similarly mediated by notable points of overlap between Alinsky's method of community organizing and the very principles which animated the CFC agenda. Such principles included a broad address to the "powerlessness" of average citizens and the subsequent need to bolster their capacity to "explore their own problems and arrive at their own solutions" (Boyle, chapter 30, this volume, p. 314). This emphasis on civic agency was reinforced by filmmaker Raymond Garceau's commitment to giving "common people the chance to express their frustrations and hopes on camera," a sentiment that reverberated in the work of other filmmakers, like that of Michel Régnier, as well as in the Challenge for Change/Société nouvelle (CFC/SN) program as a whole (Evans 1991, 161–2).

Alinsky's theories of social change dovetailed with these principles in a variety of ways. The concern with a disenfranchised citizenry exhibited by the CFC/SN ethos is reproduced in Alinsky's division of society into the "haves" and the "have-nots." In fact, his classic treatise on organizing – *Rules for Radicals* – opens with a comparison between this text and Machiavelli's *The Prince;* the latter "was written ... for the Haves on how to hold power," while the former was "written for the Have-Nots on how to take it away" (Alinsky 1971, 3). This common alliance with a broadly constituted class of citizens who were excluded from the reins of political and economic power made Alinsky a natural CFC subject. Furthermore, this alliance – for both Alinsky and CFC – was attuned to the facilitation and harness of marginalized voices as a means towards effecting social change. Both Alinsky's thought and CFC/SN's aims sought to stake out a democratic terrain – through organizing or making use of media – in which otherwise marginalized voices could be constituted as political actors. Such activation carried a significant amount of existential weight for Alinsky, who wrote: "To lose your 'identity' as a citizen of democracy is but a step from losing your identity as a person" (1971, xxvi).

In addition to their affinity with marginalized sectors of society, Alinsky's political program and CFC/SN often prioritized explicitly local forms of community over broader trans-regional or national identities. A bottom-up sensibility, rooted in an ideological preference for the local, permeated both Alinsky's rhetoric and CFC/SN's. In Alinsky's case, an emphasis on acting locally is evident in his writings as well as in his past history as an organizer in Chicago. In his response to "young radicals" reeling from experiences like the 1968 Democratic Convention in Chicago, Alinsky places a premium on *home:* "Go home, organize, build power and at the next convention, *you be the delegates*" (Alinsky's emphasis; 1971, xxiii). A bottom-up ethos is underscored as Alinsky lays out a narrative of social change that is initiated at the local level. This emphasis manifested itself in Alinsky's experiences in Chicago, where he "searched for local solutions" to what was considered "the most intractable problem faced by his native Chicago in the years following the war: [namely] racial segregation" (Santow 2007, 29).

The early films of CFC were also decidedly local in terms of content and orientation. *Encounter at Kwacha House – Halifax* (1967) documents racial tensions in a storefront community centre between young blacks and white Nova Scotian society at large (see Banning, chapter 17, this volume). *Pow-Wow at Duck Lake* (1967) portrays a heated discussion in the town of Duck Lake on problems facing Aboriginal peoples in an educational system insensitive to their cultures and histories. While the tensions displayed in such films were undoubtedly applicable to a wide variety of circumstances across Canada, the localized nature and specificity of these situations was often prioritized in the films themselves – frequently leaving the question of broader applicability ambiguous and open to debate (Evans 1991, 163–5).

Such points of overlap made Alinsky and his ideas about community organizing a logical fit for CFC. As mentioned earlier, Klein's status as an expatriate American was understood as an asset in the propagation of an American organizer's ideas to Canadian audiences. Klein herself had been politically active for many years. In fact, her involvement in the civil rights and anti-war movements in the United States, coupled with her "passion for theater," led her to documentary filmmaking as a profession. When her partner received a draft notice, they married and moved to Canada, where she subsequently found work at the National Film Board, specifically for CFC (Goldsmith 2003, 66). Her own politicization, together with her tutelage under documentarist George Stoney, steeped Klein in a tradition of socially conscious non-fiction filmmaking. Undoubtedly, her experience with the civil rights movement in the United States granted her a degree of familiarity with Alinsky's form of bottom-up community organizing and minority rights.

The five films that make up the Organizing for Power series represent a substantial elaboration upon the three earlier works about Alinsky produced by CFC. Encompassing an expository presentation of Alinsky's ideas and methods as well as scenes of their application in various localities, this follow-up 1968 series attempts to construct a uniquely cinematic seminar that blurs the lines between theory and practice. After an overview of the Alinsky approach in *People and Power*, the series proceeds to show this approach as it is taught to a gathering of citizens in Dayton, Ohio (*Deciding to Organize*). From here, subsequent films draw the viewer further out into the field as efforts to organize in Buffalo, New York (*Building an Organization*), Rochester, New York (*Through Conflict to Negotiation*), and Chicago, Illinois (*A Continuing Responsibility*), are documented. The last of these works underscores the Woodlawn Organization's success at taking on a life of its own after the departure of Alinsky, a development that is implicitly represented as disentangling the method from the man, the ethos from the persona.

Now that we have reviewed the points of contact between CFC and Alinsky, a closer look at the films that make up Organizing for Power will grant us insight into how some of these commonalities were registered in terms of both form and content.

The first film of the series, *People and Power*, allows Alinsky to be a kind of "voice of authority" – an onscreen commentator who directs the flow of information to the viewer (Nichols 1991, 37). This introduction to Alinsky's philosophy is presented in his own words. For the most part, this presentation is channelled in two directions: to the viewer of the film as well as to an

U.S. community activist Saul Alinsky addressing the camera in
Building an Organization (1968). Frame enlargement.

onscreen observer. Scenes of Alinsky interacting with First Nations youths on
the Rama Indian Reserve in Ontario, lecturing to an audience at the Episco-
pal Theological School in Boston, and dialoguing with the U.S. secretary of
labour serve to convey the central tenets of his ethos but also demonstrate a
presumed dynamism on his part. By juxtaposing such scenes (taking the
viewer back and forth between these kinds of sites), the film metaphorically
argues that the Alinsky model, and indeed the man himself, is a flexible entity
that can function in the halls of the state (secretary of labour), in the arena
of religion (theological school), and on the front lines in oppressed communities (Indian reserve). Such flexibility serves to underscore the practical basis
of Alinsky's methodology, encouraging the viewer to perceive the Alinsky
discourse as one that is grounded in the realities of decision-making and
capable of yielding results for the have-nots by linking grassroots organizing
to the instruments of the state. This radical pragmatism on the part of
Alinsky also stresses immediacy, siding with the necessary impatience of victims. "What do you tell a mother?" asks Alinsky in the film. "That it will
take time?"

To a degree, these qualities resonate with a CFC/SN program that makes
use of the democratic mechanisms of the state to address and redress social
inequalities. However, the emphasis placed on Alinsky as an expert, as a
purveyor of a model of organizing that seemingly lends itself to a variety of
circumstances, rubs against a CFC ethos that is more inductive, prioritizing
the collective expression of localized hopes and frustrations over the delivery of answers from experts. Indeed, if the film were not contextualized
within an overall series, the Alinsky approach as it is presented in *People and*

Power would appear overly personalistic and schematic in light of a film-making program that sought to let the "common people" find their own solutions. Additionally, the emphasis placed on immediacy by Alinsky could be seen as in conflict with the CFC approach, which places greater value on process and expression. Nevertheless, this first film serves to anchor the viewer, as he or she is presented, in subsequent parts, with a series of case studies in which the methodology that has been espoused is seen "in action" in a variety of locales.

In the second film, *Deciding to Organize*, a "voice of God" explains that a "group of concerned citizens looking for a method to attack poverty" have gathered for a ten-day course at a training institute in Dayton, Ohio, to learn strategies and tactics from Alinsky. Like the first film, *People and Power*, this instalment centres on the pedagogical project of teaching the viewer about the specifics of Alinsky's form of community organizing. However, it gently ventures beyond the first film by tethering the viewer to the space of the institute's classroom in order to focus on how the method reviewed by Alinsky in the opening film is received and understood by organizers grappling with unique challenges at the local level. *Deciding to Organize* formally encourages the viewer to identify with the organizers seen onscreen with Alinsky, and it does this by, on the one hand, frequently cutting to reaction shots of the organizers listening to Alinsky and, on the other, making use of shots that frame Alinsky in such a way that he appears to be addressing the camera directly. In this latter shot, the dual address to an onscreen as well as an off-screen audience, mentioned earlier, is explicitly evoked and is registered in both the editing and the shot composition. To a certain extent, this identification of onscreen and off-screen audiences seems to reproduce the messianic qualities of the first film: Alinsky and his approach are presented in a relatively unproblematic fashion to audiences that seem to be represented as passively receptive to the ideas espoused. Nevertheless, this is subtly complicated throughout *Deciding to Organize*, as the attendant organizers at the institute punctuate the flow of rhetoric from Alinsky with their own accounting of particular on-the-ground problems.

However, the conclusion of *Deciding to Organize* subverts the personalistic tenor of the first film even more emphatically than such moments of exchange and interaction. Following the end of the teach-in, the camera stays with the organizers in the absence of Alinsky. One organizer asks, "Are we selling community organization or Saul Alinsky?" Another wonders if there is a "more valid" or "up to date" approach. In spite of these questions, a concluding sentiment exclaims that "we must admit … he's helped us." Ending on such a scene lends a reflexive quality to the film that is reminiscent of Jean Rouch and Edgar Morin's seminal documentary *Chronique d'un été* (*Chronicle of a Summer*, 1961), which concludes with a discussion of the film by the participants. Given the affinity established between the onscreen and off-screen audiences for Alinsky's teachings, this concluding exchange among the organizers seems to cue viewers on the kinds of questions to be considered in the wake of a screening of *Deciding to Organize* as well as of the series as a whole. The Alinsky persona and approach are posited as finite and open to the questioning and applications of the organizers and the audience. Indeed, these same questions can be turned around and directed at the films themselves.

The final three films of the series take the viewers further with depictions of community organizing in Buffalo, Rochester, and Chicago. In many ways, the series' relatively observational approach – the film crew largely assumes a non-interventionist posture and documents events as they unfold before the camera – is continued in these films but is opened up to include a greater number of on-camera interviews, a heavier use of narration, and more lively exchanges in the various communities depicted. In the final film, *A Continuing Responsibility* – which will receive the bulk of the attention here – Alinsky is present primarily to continue his overview, provide historical context, and respond to criticisms of his form of community organizing. This final instalment of the series reviews Alinsky's organizing efforts in Chicago and the role of his Industrial Areas Foundation in the aiding of the Temporary Woodlawn Organization (later referred to as the "Woodlawn Organization," or TWO) in the sixties. Here the Alinsky approach is grounded in a specific historical and political situation with agents and witnesses who can and do testify on camera about the impact of Alinsky's organizing efforts as well as their own. In this sense, the Alinsky approach becomes less about Alinsky and more about a particular ongoing struggle in Chicago's South Side over racial segregation, urban renewal, and the dearth of economic opportunities for Chicago's African-American communities.

In *A Continuing Responsibility*, the have-nots in Alinsky's discourse are explicitly racialized, being subject to the conjoining of racial and class-based oppression within an American urban setting. Testimony in the film from the president of TWO at the time, Reverend Arthur Brazier, compares and contrasts life in Chicago's South Side before and after the establishment of TWO, noting a transition from a prevailing sense of "defeatism" to one of empowerment "to change the face of our community." Additional historical context for the viewer is provided by voice-of-God narration as well as by Monsignor John Egan, who recounts the establishment of TWO as well as Alinsky's arrival to assist in the community's fight against urban renewal programs that forced the poor out of their homes. It is evident from the recounting of this history that TWO's story is one of conflict with both the city and the University of Chicago, which was seeking to expand its campus into the Woodlawn community. This narrative of struggle between powerful institutions and a subjugated class resonates with and, undoubtedly, informs Alinsky's emphasis on confrontation in his model of community organizing.

The film crystallizes the debate over Alinsky's approach by featuring the comments of Philip M. Hauser, a sociologist at the University of Chicago, who repeatedly criticizes Alinsky for engendering "hostility" and "bitterness" in the community by virtue of his organizing methods. Hauser is shot in a seminar space and is frequently filmed speaking with students about TWO. Similarly, the film presents the criticisms of Julian H. Levi, a city planner and professor of urban studies at the University of Chicago. The presentation of these white authority figures in academic settings contrasts with the scenes of African-American organizers and activists in the streets. Levi's complaint that Alinsky is irresponsible for stepping aside once a community is organized – when, as Levi puts it, the "ballgame just begins" – is critiqued by Alinsky himself when he asks, "Am I the great white father?" Here the film presents a moment of self-consciousness on Alinsky's part pertaining to his role as a disseminator of a model of community organizing. In this sense, the film works to attenuate the degree of ownership frequently ascribed to Alinsky in the formation of organizations like TWO. The dominant role played by Alinsky's persona in the first film of the series is, by the latter films, overturned through the emphasis placed on the organizers and activists themselves, who had to appropriate, adapt, and work with Alinsky's ideas in conjunction with their own.

Alinsky's critique of the "white father" complex is part of an overall sophisticated treatment of race by the film. One scene depicts Leon Finney and Tony Gibbs, a pair of staff directors from TWO, planning a campaign against the neglectful policies of a corrupt landlord. At the conclusion of the scene, asking whether or not the landlord is white, Finney notes that it is "easier to organize against a white man." In this moment, there is recognition of the complicated ways in which a race-based narrative of black versus white overlaps with Alinsky's paradigm of the haves vs the have-nots. While the racial dimensions to the structural inequality faced by residents of Chicago's South Side is recognized as very real, this scene illustrates the importance of narrativizing or – as Alinsky would say – cutting an issue in such a way that citizens are mobilized and energized.

By the end of the series, viewers are presented with an example of community organization – TWO – that has persisted long after the departure of Alinsky and the assistance of his Industrial Areas Foundation. While the series opens with a review of Alinsky's model that is very much tied to his charismatic persona, it closes with a more complex entrenchment of his approach within a political context overwrought with racial and class-based inequalities. In this sense, the series grows somewhat schizophrenic towards the end as it tries to balance the pedagogical aim of illustrating Alinsky's approach with the documentary aim of representing activities of specific organizers and activists that may or may not clearly reflect the principles reviewed. The CFC ethos of providing the means for local people to "explore their own problems and arrive at their own solutions" is evident in the representation of Alinsky as merely one player out of many in the final film. While the movement beyond the personalistic focus on Alinsky is evident at the end, there remains the question of how these case studies and the methodology behind them relates to Canadian experiences. Like the organizers at the end of *Deciding to Organize*, the viewers of this series are left to contemplate the applicability of the localized examples depicted on screen.

22   Michel Régnier's *"Films-Outil"*

■

LIZ CZACH

In neither the histories of the National Film Board (NFB) nor those of the Challenge for Change/Société nouvelle (CFC/SN) program does film director Michel Régnier figure prominently. His absence is particularly troubling considering he was the most prolific director working on either the French- or the English-language side of CFC/SN. Credited with twenty-five films during his association with the program, Régnier directed two large-scale projects: Urbanose, a series of fifteen black-and-white, half-hour films exploring urban development issues in Montreal; and Urba 2000, a series of ten hour-length, colour films addressing urban issues in various cities across the globe.[1]

Why then, despite his prodigious output, has Régnier remained a marginal figure? This omission may be partially attributed to the fact that his more radical and polemical films of the Urbanose series were never translated into English. Furthermore, the impact of the Urbanose films might be muted when viewed individually, rather than in the context of the more sustained arguments that the series as whole systematically puts forward. Yet, while these are no doubt contributing factors, perhaps a more pertinent reason for Régnier's marginalization is that his SN films diverge from the process-oriented, cameras-in-the hands-of-the-people filmmaking that has come to define the program (Marchessault, chapter 33, this volume). Régnier's films do not follow the principles of self-representation as a form of participatory democracy that dominates the history of CFC/SN.[2] This is not to suggest that the Urbanose or Urba 2000 series don't respond to the program's mandate or are apolitical; on the contrary, the films merely highlight that the CFC/SN filmmakers did not have a singular approach to their task of advocating for change via filmmaking. Régnier, like his CFC/SN contempo-

---

1 Régnier considers Urbanose to have been a thirteen-film series, counting the two-part films *Concordia* (1972) and *Où va la ville* (1972) as single films; my own preference is to consider them separately. Two of the Urba 2000 films – *Basingstoke – Runcorn – British New Towns* (1974) and *Grenoble – La Villeneuve: The City Conceived Anew* (1974) – were feature length.

2 For example, Colin Low's series on Fogo Island.

raries, was committed to making films that were socially useful, and he saw film as a tool in making change possible – a belief that is evident in his method of filmmaking, an approach he termed *films-outil*.[3]

Born in France in 1934, Régnier worked as a photo-journalist in France and the Ivory Coast before arriving in Canada in 1957. He quickly found work at the National Film Board, and after several years of working as an assistant on over a dozen documentaries, he left to freelance. Régnier directed films for both the NFB and Radio-Canada and returned to the NFB in 1967. He stayed on as a director for seven years, first working with the Groupe de recherches sociales and then with the SN program (NFB-Portraits, http://www.nfb.ca/portraits/michel_regnier/en). After his departure from the NFB, Régnier continued directing political documentaries for the next thirty years.

While the CFC/SN filmmakers shared many goals, "it is a mistake," as Scott Mackenzie has pointed out, "to look at them as interchangeable" (Mackenzie, chapter 31, this volume, p. 325). While the impetus for the CFC program is constantly traced back to the poor reception of Tanya Ballantyne Tree's *The Things I Cannot Change* (1967) (see Longfellow, chapter 14, this volume), the formative influences on the French-language directors at the NFB must be attributed in large part to SN's predecessor, the Group de recherches sociales (GRS). The *cinéma direct* films of director Raymond Garceau, an agronomist who made documentaries on Quebec rural life, influenced this group of filmmakers – Michel Régnier, Maurice Bulbulian, and Fernand Dansereau. Garceau's films, and other *cinéma direct* films such as *Les Raquetteurs* (Michel Brault and Gilles Groulx, 1958), were groundbreaking in their filmmaking technique, but also helped stimulate a growing sense of Quebec nationalism. However, the GRS filmmakers would depart from Garceau's concerns in two principal ways: one, their focus would be on the urban milieu; and two, they would adapt *cinéma direct* techniques, moving towards a more calculated, and less random, selection of images.[4] One of the first documentaries to meld a depiction of an urban milieu with adapted *cinéma direct* techniques was Hubert Aquin's *À Saint-Henri le cinq septembre* (1964), a day-in-the-life portrait of a working-class Montreal

3 See *L'oeil et le coeur: Une passion de cinéma documentaire* (Régnier 2000, 147). Régnier's *films-outil* literally translates as "tool films" or "film-as-a-tool," although "useful film" better expresses his intention (Régnier, interview with the author, 29 October 2008). Gary Evans has translated it as "functional cinema" (1991, 162). All translations from Régnier's memoir are my own.

4 As Scott Mackenzie has noted, Quebec films of the 1960s began addressing a "complex notion of Québécois identity in transition – from rural to urban, from parochial to secular, and from apolitical to radical" (MacKenzie 2004, 12).

neighbourhood. However, the response to this film was less than the film-makers expected. As Fernand Dansereau noted, "When the film went into distribution and was televised, it provoked an astonishingly violent negative reaction from the people who had been filmed" (Dansereau, chapter 4, this volume, p. 34). This catalyzed the filmmakers to reconsider their approach, and their next film, *Saint-Jérôme* (Dansereau, 1968), was produced with community participation and feedback. This participatory model is also apparent in Maurice Bulbulian's *La p'tite Bourgogne* (1968), a film that doc-uments citizen involvement in the redevelopment of their Montreal neigh-bourhood (the same area in which *The Things I Cannot Change* was filmed), and in Régnier's 1968 feature documentary *L'École des autres*, a GRS film on underprivileged children at school.[5] The lessons and interests of GRS were carried over to the SN films – for Régnier, the concern with the urban, and with Montreal more specifically, became a central focus.

That Régnier takes Montreal as the subject matter for his SN films is of little surprise given that his passion for the city was indicated as early as 1961 with the publication of *Montréal: Paris d'Amérique*, a book of poems (by Régnier and others) and photographs celebrating the city. The charac-terization of Montreal as the Paris of North America clearly situates the city as a crossroads between Europe and North America, a position Régnier takes up again with the Urbanose project. As the films make clear, Montreal's position as a mid-point between Europe and North America is precarious. Montreal may retain its European charm and character, or it may devolve into the kind of urban nightmare evident in failing American cities. Which of these fates awaits it?

The prosperity of the postwar period, the end of the Duplessis era, and the burgeoning of Quebec separatism fuelled Montreal's rebirth as a centre for Quebec's modernization. In the 1960s Montreal emerged from the poverty and oppression that had characterized it for decades, and was rap-idly being transformed. All across North America, cities were changing in fundamental ways with the demolition of older neighbourhoods, the expan-sion of highways, the construction of skyscrapers, and other monumental architectural undertakings. In Montreal, two key events defined the city's urban development, Expo '67 and the 1976 Olympics.[6] These monumental undertakings helped focus citizen attention on the issue of redevelopment.

5 The lessons and interests of the GRS dovetailed so seamlessly with the priorities of SN, that Régnier considers *L'école des autres* his best SN film despite its being produced under GRS auspices (Régnier interview, 29 October, 2008).

6 For Régnier, the lack of attention to Montreal urban problems following Expo '67 was particularly deplorable. He notes: "This shamed us in the days following our beautiful international exposition Expo-67" (2000, 144).

Régnier's Urbanose and Urba 2000 series, released in 1972 and 1974 respectively and falling chronologically between these two major events, palpably address Montrealers' anxiety over the city's modernization. Would Montreal's "progress" compromise the city's viability and livability?

URBANOSE (1972)

The films in the Urbanose series were shot in eighteen weeks, from January to July 1971, with an allocation of $165,000 – a miniscule budget for the scope of the project.[7] Each 27-minute film in the fifteen-part Urbanose series addresses a specific urban issue facing Montreal. The purpose of the series, notes Régnier, was "nothing other than to sound the alarm" (2000, 142). The films are thematically titled to indicate the subject matter under consideration. For example, *L'automobile* examines the repercussions of increasing car ownership for Montreal's downtown urban fabric; *Le labyrinthe* investigates the labyrinthian complexity of municipal bureaucracy; slum landlords are exposed in *Locataires et propriétaires* (Tenants and landlords); and lack of river access for ordinary citizens is discussed in *Les rives* (Riverbanks). Each film is numbered as part of the series, and they are structured in a similar manner. The films begin with the same musical theme, Alain Clavier's rather bleak and somewhat ominous synthesized music. This is followed by a number of Yukari Ochiai's black-and-white woodcuts. The woodcuts vary from film to film but always depict characteristic scenes of Montreal urban life. For example, the woodcuts at the beginning of *Où va la ville?* (Where is the city heading?) represent a typical Montreal walk-up, skyscrapers, the Métro (subway), the Habitat housing complex, and an aerial view of a maze of highways. The films in the series also display a consistency in execution, engaging techniques uncharacteristic of most CFC/SN films: they employ music and narration (although minimally) and rely heavily on interviews with "experts," a practice disparaged by most CFC/SN filmmakers who favour allowing people to represent themselves. In his memoir *L'oeil et le coeur: Une passion du cinema documentaire* (Eye and heart: A passion for documentary cinema), Régnier notes that his approach was heavily criticized "for having privileged experts, specialists, and builders over average citizens" (Régnier 2000, 152). Although Régnier relies on experts, such as engineers, architects, city planners, developers, and sociologists, it must be noted that

7 "To prepare, shoot, and finish thirteen telefilms for that money, including the travel of a four-member team to six countries, at that time, was a utopian dream, and for some colleagues, an aberration. I could have, following the criteria of very critical colleagues, decided to use the entire budget for a one-hour technically slick documentary" (Régnier 2000, 142).

many civil servants of 1960s Quebec had become highly politicized in conjunction with the radical swing to the left that had emerged simultaneously with a growing sense of nationalism and separatism.

Régnier took the title for the Urbanose series from a poem he published in the collection *Génération* (1969). Urbanose (urbanosis), a neologism of Régnier's creation, is defined as "an urban cancer, caused by the individual or combined operations of rural/urban migration, property speculation, and the primacy of private investment on the public sector, the suffocation, to some degree and form, of numerous large cities" (Régnier 2000, 141). The films in the series are structured as a debate, gathering together a variety of experts occupying a range of positions across the political spectrum. Régnier claims to have, as an organizing principle for the films, "privileged thoughtful debate over all other criteria" (2000, 142). The opinions expressed vary widely on what form Montreal urban planning should, or should not, take, and they generate a series of polemical and contrary positions regarding Montreal's future. The films can, at times, be maddeningly ambiguous and cannot be described as essayistic, as Régnier does not seem to be taking a clear side or making a consistent argument. Nor are the films journalistic – that is, they do not claim to offer a balanced report of opposing views. They are, for lack of a better word, agitational. The films are effective in offering a series of opposing views on the status of the city's future and challenging the viewer to take both a position and action.

The two-part film *Concordia 1* and *Concordia 2* perfectly illustrates Régnier's unique *films-outil* approach. Here, Régnier could have easily included a participatory model but didn't. Residents of the Milton-Parc area organize and form a committee to oppose a proposed redevelopment (Cité Concordia) that will see low-rise residences destroyed to be replaced with a high-rise tower. Rather than give cameras to the members of the Comité des citoyens Milton-Parc or engage them in the process of making the film, Régnier simply documents their meetings and protests. However, he counterposes this documentation with interviews he conducts with other residents from the area. He talks to people on the street and storeowners who support the development and argue that it is beautiful and will be economically beneficial. Although the Milton-Parc community protest wasn't completely successful – part of the proposed mega-project was constructed – it did "galvanize public opinion and turned the city away from megaprojects requiring demolition and massive rebuilding in favour of projects that addressed the urgent social and urban issues of the city" (Lambert 2004, 18) Yet, rather than take a role in clear support of the protestors, Régnier opens up the terms of debate and consequently encounters, and represents, a wider spectrum of citizen opinions.

The polemical structure that Régnier adopts is also clearly expressed in the two-part film *Où va la ville?* The film's tone is set by the introductory

Montreal streetscape in *Concordia II* (1972): a non-participatory forum for opinions on demolitions and development. Frame enlargement.

narration, which rather apocalyptically questions Montreal's future. The narrator asks whether Montreal will address the urban problems it faces or whether it will become a city without character, half dead, where the minority profits while the majority lives in squalor. The dramatic and somewhat alarmist narration suggests that Montreal might be "lost," a sentiment that recurs in a number of the films. Repeatedly, the urban decay of Washington, New York, and Philadelphia (with the emptying out of downtown cores for the suburbs, and the ensuing devaluation and ultimate demolition of property) is held up as a cautionary tale of what might happen in Montreal. Alternatively, European cities, particularly Scandinavian ones, are positioned as models to emulate. There, we are told, they have laws that dictate what can and cannot be demolished. In an interview, two young female residents of Stockholm extemporize on why their city works. Régnier rather starkly juxtaposes cities that are working (Scandinavian examples) with those that are tragically failing (American ones). Will Montreal, positioned as both American and European, succeed or fail?

If Régnier errs on the side of filming more interviews with "experts" than with ordinary citizens, this practice is made most evident in *Entretien avec Henri Lefebvre* (Interview with Henri Lefebvre). Released in 1972, the interview follows the publication of the French sociologist's *La révolution urbaine* (1970) and precedes that of his seminal work *La production de*

Woodcut graphics as part of an alarmist polemical structure in *Où va la ville? 1ʳᵉ partie* (1972). Frame enlargement.

l'espace (1974). Lefebvre, one of the most influential thinkers on urban space, is seated in a garden facing the camera while Régnier is, as always, off-camera asking questions. Régnier's decision to interview Lefebvre is not surprising, as both men are attempting to rethink the question of urban space through a Marxist, or at least leftist, lens. Yet the interview is a curious juxtaposition of Régnier's pragmatism and Lefebvre's abstraction, or what Régnier characterizes as Lefebvre's "idealism" (2000, 143). A structure based on expert opinion and citizen opposition is again established, but here between interviewer and interviewee, who offer contrasting positions on where to find the answers to the question of urbanization. This is highlighted when Lefebvre suggests that poets and philosophers – not architects and developers – provide the means to think through urban issues. Lefebvre proposes that Nietzsche, Heidegger, and Bachelard are better suited to the task of thinking about urban space than bureaucrats and functionaries. This suggestion stands in stark contrast to the hours of interviews that Régnier has himself conducted with urban planners, city officials, developers, and architects. While both Régnier and Lefebvre approach the question of urbanism from the left, they clearly differ in where they search for answers.

URBA 2000 (1974)

In 1973 Régnier embarked on Urba 2000, taking a feature film budget of $373,000 and stretching it to produce a series of ten one-hour films. Like its predecessor series Urbanose, the intent of Urba 2000 was to stimulate debate on the state of urban living. As Régnier notes, the defined objective was to "create a series of films that did not offer 'the solution,' since none existed " (2000, 148). It is within this series that *New York – Twin Parks Project – TV Channel 13*, Régnier's only English-language film, appears. This Urba 2000 film begins typically enough with the exploration of a revitalization project, the Twin Parks project in the Bronx, New York. The film documents the coming together of various clergy to spearhead the project and interviews with families that have moved into the new buildings. Then the film radically shifts focus. At a community meeting of residents who oppose a seniors' centre out of a fear of falling property values, the film switches to documenting the television crew from the educational television station WNET Channel 13 who are also present at the meeting. Interviews with television producer Penny Burnstein inform us that the WNET coverage is attempting more community-oriented models of production. Location shooting is advocated over working in the studio; local citizens are interviewed; and viewers are encouraged to call in and respond to shows. As Burnstein puts it, "You've got more reality on location, whereas in the studio you get experts." She sees the show as presenting a model for how citizens could communicate with each other, moving in a direction that is "more open forum, less structure." This is precisely the model of participatory practice that CFC/SN championed. Interestingly, Régnier's most obvious engagement with the participatory model was to make an English-language film, under the auspices of SN, about participatory filmmaking in the United States.

Thirty-five years after their release, the films of Michel Régnier are still strikingly relevant – most of the issues that threaten the viability and livability of urban centres remain the same. Long before the threat of global warming, films such as *L'automobile* (1972) and *Centre-ville et piétons* (*City Centre and Pedestrians*, 1974) presciently argued that our dependency on cars could not continue. Yet these films, produced as tools to stimulate debate, discussion, and change, were and continue to be marginalized in CFC/SN's history. Unlike many of the NFB staff directors of his era, Régnier preferred to work quickly and cheaply, taking a budget that could easily be spent on a producing a single film over several years to create multiple films that he considered simple but effective. Reflecting on the impact of the Urbanose series, Régnier maintains "that these simple films, costing less than $12,000, have more impact than chrome-plated productions costing $200,000" (2000,

146–7). Although he found a sympathetic audience among the public as well as the mainstream media and intellectuals, the simplicity of his films and his non-adherence to the participatory model were frequently criticized for under-representing ordinary citizens and being uncinematic. Régnier recalls that some of the harshest critiques came from his fellow directors: "[F]or some amongst my profession, I was fit to be shot." He recollects a public screening at which his films were denounced by a filmmaking colleague as "'the shame of the NFB because they are not cinema'" (2000, 145).

If the films of Michel Régnier have been omitted from the canonical works that define the CFC/SN program, it is not for lack of relevance. Régnier's film-making is as passionate and political as that of other CFC/SN directors, but his model of advocacy through his *films-outil* reflects an alternate strategy to the preferential participatory mode of his CFC/SN contemporaries and ultimately accounts, in large part, for his undeserved marginalization.

23   Léonard Forest and Acadia

■

JEANNE DESLANDES

At the National Film Board of Canada, Léonard Forest was more than simply a filmmaker. Directly involved in over 150 films during a thirty-year career, he was first a scriptwriter and translator and later became a script editor, director, and producer. In 1957 he became the director of the French Production Branch (Déléas 1998, 31–4). In 1970 he took charge of the re-structuring of the NFB team, Groupe de recherches sociales (GRS), which, while joining the Challenge for Change (CFC) program in the institutional sense, acquired its own identity as Société nouvelle (SN), retaining its own ideology in its focus on social change and giving a voice to the underprivi-leged (Déléas 1998, 114). In 1974, while still at the NFB, Forest created a regional program for French production outside of Quebec called Régional-isation Acadie, and outside the NFB he was the founding president of the Syndicat général du cinéma et de la télévision (Déléas 1998, 92). Despite this workload of administrative and executive responsibilities, he remained a filmmaker of vision and importance.

Long before his participation in CFC/SN, Forest was making films *with* his subjects. It began with docudramas such as *La femme de ménage* (1954) and included films featuring non-professional Acadian actors from New Bruns-wick and Nova Scotia (*Les Aboiteaux* [Dikes], 1955; *Pêcheurs de Pomcoup* [Fishermen of Pubnico], 1956). His key contributions to SN consist of a docudrama, *La noce est pas finie* (1969), and a documentary, *Un soleil pas comme ailleurs* [*A Sun like Nowhere Else*] (1972), and each demonstrates an experimental edge unique within the program's corpus.

That Forest immediately followed his documentary *Les Acadiens de la dispersion* (1968) with *La noce est pas finie* makes perfect sense. During the production of the earlier film (a feature-length documentary about Acadians spread out all over the world), Forest met many successful Acadians and dis-covered that those from northeast New Brunswick were often suffering under large debts.[1] Because CFC/SN focused on giving a voice to the underprivi-leged, Forest once more saw a need to get involved with the community and chose to shoot a film with the people of Gloucester County.

The title of the film uses slang. It should read "La noce n'est pas finie." By omitting the negation of good French grammar, the title itself speaks the language of ordinary people.[2] In addition, Forest wanted to emphasize the voice of Gloucester County: "I thought for some time about making a film on a story being played by actors who would stop now and then to discuss what they were doing and why they were doing it, and did it 'feel right' – did what they were doing correspond in any way to their own real feelings?" (Prinn 1971, 18).[3] His original idea involved professional actors, in a manner recalling Pirandello, staging actors whose performances are incorporated into the fiction (Bégin n.d., 5). However, Forest went beyond Pirandello and even beyond the accepted ideology of the CFC/SN program. He did not simply give a voice to the underprivileged people of Gloucester County, he endeavoured to have them write the entire film as a collective.

The production of the docudrama was unconventional. When Forest headed to Gloucester County for the first phase of this project, he attended a meeting in Tracadie. "They called it *'le congrès des pauvres'* meaning 'don't tell us any more lies – we're 'poor' and this is our congress,'" Forest recounted (Prinn 1971, 18). He was amazed to see that they were already talking about the issues, but even more so to find out that all the regions shared the same problems.[4] After attending this meeting, Forest was positive that the community had something to say and that this voice would speak for the entire county, but he was unsure about what step to take next. He could not just propose a script to the NFB, since the script was intended to be a collective creation by the local community. Forest couldn't even submit an outline of the project, since the subject matter was to be the choice of the community. In the end, Forest leveraged his credibility within the NFB at large to secure approval and funding for this ambitious project. The budget was generous but the timeline was restrictive, six weeks of pre-production and four and half weeks to shoot the film.

1 In the section of *Les Acadiens de la dispersion* focusing on Caraquet, New Brunswick, a priest explains how "ordinary" Acadians struggle with credit. The northeast area of New Brunswick was one of the underprivileged regions designated by the government (Forest 1969a, 1969b).

2 Furthermore, the title uses the word "wedding" (*noce*), which also refers to the general convivial meaning of "party." Consequently, "The Party Ain't Over" would be a fair translation of the French title and partially explains the open ending of the film.

3 All translations are the author's.

4 In an interview for *L'Évangéline* in March 1969, Léopold Laplante, the spokesman for CRAN (Conseil régional d'aménagement du Nord-Est [regional development council]), said that the population was "not ready to speak out" and that it needed to be awakened to the concept of democracy (Forest 1969a, 5).

Forest left Montreal to meet people from two citizens committees in Lamèque and Shippagon. He would use the six weeks of preparation time to find his actors and work with them to prepare a script and plan the shooting (Prinn 1971, 20). Hostilities existed between these two localities (they had quarrelled for over two centuries), but Forest was firm in his resolve to help them coordinate a common project. He wanted them to work together as non-professional actors, improvising their own lines.[5] And so, with their help, the new citizens from the virtual locale of Lachigan were born.[6]

Forest decided to experiment with psychodrama. His belief in fiction as an ideal context for generating catalysis and his desire to provoke consciousness-raising explains this choice (Bégin n.d., 5). Psychodrama is an in-depth method of psychotherapy originated by J.L. Moreno in the 1920s.[7] Upon first screening *Noce*, I inferred a definite Brechtian influence, especially because of Forest's unique structural use of music.[8] And although Forest conceded that the "narrative succeeds in both narrating the story and proposing reflections on this very story" (Forest 1969b, 11), he never actually mentioned Brecht, but instead declared an inspiration from Pirandello and Moreno.

5 Forest comments on the quality of the acting: "They made the dialogue as we shot each scene and they brought to it everything that they know about their own milieu. They were expert on the milieu. We re-shot only a few scenes with the sophisticated parts; we might do a sequence for a second time after a rest" (Prinn 1971, 20). Furthermore, the collective writing allowed the community members to avoid exposing any one aggressor or victim specifically. According to Forest, "Fiction thus written allowed people to say some things which they could not have said directly" (author's translation; Forest, quoted in Faucher 1971).

6 In French, Shippagon is spelled "Shippagan." The combination of Lamèque and Shippagan results in "La-shi-gan" – or "Lachigan." This exercise in virtual geography vividly expresses Forest's desire to blend these two communities together.

7 Moreno used drama in therapy to investigate past, present, and future life. Psychodrama offers one the opportunity to see oneself from outside, practise new roles safely, gain insight, and change behaviour accordingly. The director of the drama helps the group explore new solutions to old problems. The "actors" participate as significant others and share how they personally relate to and learn from the presenting of the issues. In his autobiography, Moreno compared himself to Freud: "[He] analyse[s] their dreams. I give them the courage to dream again. [He] analyse[s] and tear[s] them apart. I let them act out their conflicting roles and help them put the parts back together" (Moreno 1985, 163.

8 For Forest, music was "a means to push the image beyond its simple ordinary signification, beyond its non-signification, and then extend the possible meanings, the possible correspondences" (Déléas 1998, 43). This remark from Forest regarding a film

In accordance with the ideology of psychodrama, Forest saw himself as an intermediary. He would be a catalyst, not the initiator. He kept asking the group for a topic: "Is it going to be the conflict between generations? Is it going to be the Pill? Is it going to be Love?" After much discussion, he discovered "that it always came back to the same basic theme: the feeling of being impotent because of political powers, the feeling that they could never take any initiative because if they [did], it was blocked" (Prinn 1971, 20). Citizens sensed that a reign of terror – a system of oppression based on fear – was taking over the county, especially after a series of suspicious fires (set, for example, in several schools, a municipal garage, and private property) served as sufficient warning against their participating in any initiative like the one led by Forest (Rousselle 1971, 1). The goal of *Noce* was to instigate and accelerate the indispensable process of change by challenging the status quo. The project developed into a fable about the awakening of the Acadian consciousness to change, and soon *Noce* was recognized within the community as the perfect argument to defend change (Saint-Jean 1971, 3–6; Déléas 1998, 75–9).

With *Noce*, the founding principle of CFC/SN advanced a step further. It was no longer simply a matter of making films with citizens, but actually one of offering them the chance to make their own films. Forest sought to help participants articulate their own views. Understanding that different communities have their own way of speaking and their own vocabulary, Forest asked the non-professional actors to improvise their lines. He also expected them to establish the subject matter. His idea of collaboration differed from that of other directors in the program. Forest erased his authorial presence and focused on putting his skills at the service of the actor-citizens.

Although the open ending of *Noce* suggests a sequel, Forest confided, "The only thing I *can't* do right now is to make a sequel of that film; there is no point in making another film on the same level. What I hope is that these people will be ready soon … to invent their own future" (Prinn 1971, 22). The local community felt the project should continue with a sequel, but Forest would not hear of it. His interest in psychodrama was leading him in another direction – towards developing a docudrama about the future of the region in order to get the community to think long term (Perreault 1972, 5). Instead of a sequel, Forest applied for an emergency budget to capture events

score is typically Brechtian. The music in *La noce est pas finie* has an alienating effect in coordination with the actors' own interruption of the flow of action. They allow the spectator to step back and, hopefully, gain awareness regarding the facts exposed. The film score was performed by musicians from the area under the direction of Flora Chiasson and inspired by the themes of Georges Langford, the actor who played the role of the teacher who causes havoc (Kermoyan 1971, 30).

in northeast New Brunswick on film, and this resulted in the documentary *Un soleil pas comme ailleurs*.

On 16 January 1972, the unions of New Brunswick organized a "Day of Concerns." During this demonstration, the citizens refused to let the politicians and authorities make speeches and shouted the slogan, "We don't want to listen to you." The Acadians had had enough of being told they could easily find work in Quebec or Ontario. They did not want to be exiled; they simply wanted their overdue unemployment insurance. Forest, alerted to this exceptional demonstration, rushed to New Brunswick with his crew. Within a month, he had completed ten days of shooting and editing. He was ready to return to the region to show the film – along with screenings outside of the region in Moncton, Edmundston, and Fredericton. Forest posed the following questions to his test audience: What should be changed? How useful would this film be in your region? How should it be distributed? The citizens agreed that no changes were required, yet these dress-rehearsal sessions produced the blueprint for Forest's next project, an intensive film distribution initiative called "Opération Nord-Est 2000."

This distribution *opération* was an exceptional accomplishment at the NFB. Never before had a province-wide distribution campaign been undertaken. Not only was it intensive (it was carried out over six weeks), but it unfolded with the filmmaker on hand at each screening (Brunette 1973, 3, 21). Each locale designated an animator to lead the discussion following the screening, and screenings took place in Bathurst, Moncton, Fredericton, and Edmundston (Archambault 1973, 2). After each of the eighty-three screenings, the audience had a discussion in Forest's presence. All these discussions were captured on video. In total, more than half the Acadian population saw the film at one of these screenings or on television. It was broadcast on CHAU-TV (Bathurst) and Canal 10 (Fredericton), as well as on CBAFT (Radio-Canada in Moncton), followed each time by a live call-in discussion with Forest (Archambault 1973, 4, 9). In the annals of the NFB, this joint exhibition-broadcast plan remains the most remarkable feat of distribution, as well as the most remarkable feature of this documentary. Giving a voice to citizens on the screen led in turn to giving them a voice in smaller discussions in reaction to the documentary.

A crucial feature of this film is its Acadian overtones. Forest adopts a tone that aims at calming the angry citizens. Seeing their frustration over not receiving their overdue employment payments, Forest takes the opportunity to build upon a sense of community, one with a more conciliatory tone. This position is made explicit in the editing of *Soleil*. Following a scene of violence at the unemployment office, Forest cuts to a rendering by Marie-Reine Chiasson of the Calixte Duguay song "Tout doucement." The mellow song plays on the soundtrack while a panorama of the snow-covered city gives way to Chiasson herself, continuing her performance of the song onscreen. This sequence is followed by a scene in which the demonstrators discuss police violence and other things and subsequently by an account from Mathilda Blanchard, who sheds light on the entire situation.[9] The impact of this montage softens the rebellious tone of protestors and shifts the emphasis from threats of violence to facts, suggesting a path to understanding and reconciliation.

Often presented as a cohesive entity, French Canadian cinema actually consists of different schools. Acadian committed cinema has a tone and an ideology quite different from its Quebec counterpart. In Quebec, French-language dissident cinema is assertive, while in New Brunswick it is soft and sanguine.[10] This difference in tone reflects the differences in the cultures (Brunette 1973, 25; Archambault 1973, 12). Forest prefers reconciliation and optimism over claims of victimization and injustice. His ideal of committed cinema is realized most completely in the manner *Soleil* was distributed.[11] Unlike *Noce*, *Soleil* is not exceptional in terms of its form as a film; its value is most evident in terms of its distribution.

Nonetheless, in both of these productions Forest's personal style is present. He lends a very poetic touch to his films. Musical performances are featured to help release emotion, a strategy for gaining the understanding of the audience. His aesthetic has a lot to do with addressing a question to the brain of the viewer while at the same time making the viewer vibrate to the rhythm of emotion, cementing the process of understanding.

9 Mathilda Blanchard was often compared to Michel Chartrand in Quebec because of her public activism. The NFB documentary *Mathilda, la passionnaria acadienne* (Ginette Pellerin, 1997) recounts her career.

10 For example, Forest did not approve of *L'Acadie, l'Acadie* (Michel Brault and Pierre Perrault, 1971). Unlike the Québécois, who see a fundamental linguistic dispute in their cultural claims, Acadians conceive their predicament differently (Bégin n.d., 4). In 1972, in an open letter to Pierre Perrault, Forest voiced his criticism by telling him that "Acadie has no need for grave-diggers" (1972, 1). The strong stance Forest took against *L'Acadie, l'Acadie* was political; he rejected the linguistic legitimation, arguing Acadians were not victimized for speaking French, and felt strongly that the province needed its own solutions to using film in service to the citizens – not those developed in Quebec.

11 The budget for the distribution for *La noce est pas finie* was almost equal to that of the production, and the film was screened for only nineteen days (Prinn 1971, 14–21). It seems safe to assume that the production/distribution budget for *Soleil*, which was screened eighty-three times, had a larger share designated for distribution than for production.

Léonard Forest: rebellion but also reconciliation in *Un soleil pas comme ailleurs* (1972). Production still.

As a filmmaker, Forest is experimental, not radical. It is in his nature to be articulate yet soft-spoken, to negotiate rather then to raise controversy. To the question "What is cinema?" Forest answers that cinema is similar to language. It is everything yet nothing. It is what you make of it. He conceives it as a modern means of expression still to be explored. And even though some may think that cinema has tried everything, he holds that there is still a lot to experiment with and to perform (Fillion 1971, 25).

In the postwar era, sociology and psychology were in a ferment of discovery. It is therefore not surprising that these evolving sciences would provide the theoretical framework for CFC/SN production. Forest drew upon psychology more than his colleagues did, but at the same time he hoped to increase sociological awareness and trigger a collective self-analysis by rummaging around in the group's *imaginaire*, a process tailored specifically to the needs of the people. In keeping with the tradition of psychodrama, Forest believed that fiction was the ideal format for generating catalysis.

Noce's cultural impact was tremendous. The film encouraged citizens to embrace their community and their region, and its use of drama was truly in tune with Acadian culture. It gave people a chance to talk about real issues without exposing their own personal biographies. Cinema being a myth industry, a new myth emerged to compete with the prevailing ancestral legend of *Évangéline* in the francophone community of New-Brunswick.[12] Now, in turn, *Noce* is the historical document of a fable, that of Acadian citizens coming together, grasping their future, and making responsible choices as a community.

Soleil offers a different historical legacy. It epitomizes the NFB's growing awareness of the importance of distribution. CFC/SN distribution officers showed exemplary creativity in exploring new modes of dissemination, enacting their mandate to ensure the embrace by the population of their own films. In that respect, *Soleil* was a precursor of what would follow. It was the first film for which a radical, experimental model of broad, intensive distribution was applied – in many ways, this application was the apex of distribution practice within CFC/SN.

12 *Evangeline* (E.P. Sullivan and H. Cavanaugh, 1913) was the first feature film produced in Canada. Adapted from a poem by Henry Wadsworth Longfellow, it narrates the betrothal of an Acadian girl named Evangeline to her beloved Gabriel. When the British deport the Acadians, the diaspora causes their separation. She spends years looking for him. She is an old nun when she finds Gabriel among the dying during an epidemic. He dies in her arms. This legend is pivotal in the Acadian culture. Consequently, in *La noce est pas finie*, when Georges Martin (the Québécois protagoniste) sings a song at a wedding about a nun giving a "French kiss" to Gabriel "the alcoholic," some are shocked, and a fight ensues.

24 Filmmaker as History: The Interventionist Films of Martin Duckworth

∎

MICHAEL LITHGOW

Martin Duckworth is one of Canada's hardest working filmmakers and has been for over forty years. He has directed more than twenty-five documentaries and served as director of photography (DOP) on another sixty film projects. He has received over twenty awards for his film work. He is an important Canadian documentary storyteller, and he attributes the direction of his film career to early work he did with Challenge for Change (CFC).

Duckworth's filmmaking can be roughly organized into four phases: (1) his early "experimental" work (arguably, a kind of filmmaker's *juvenilia*); (2) his films about place, captured through the political struggles of the people who live there; (3) his anti-war films; and (4) his portraits of artists and their art, especially musicians. At the core of his documentary work are two complementary tensions: an interest (in his own words) in "poetic truth" and a commitment to the subjects of his films that complicates the authorial/ directorial distinction between subject and object.

Duckworth's films (the ones made during and after participation in CFC, especially his films about place) are interventions in history. They record events but are also inextricably bound up in those events. Interventionist films make history in their making – at least, this is their claim; they are a kind of filmmaking that shapes history in addition to preserving it. This was the *modus operandi* of the CFC project where Duckworth first encountered the idea. Martin Duckworth is one of the pioneering voices of interventionist cinema in Canada.

When I finally catch up with Duckworth in 2008 at his Montreal home, he is as busy as ever – shooting later in the week for Alanis Obomsawin's new project; preparing to travel to Bhutan as DOP for Erik Allgoewer's film *Gross National Happiness;* and having just finished his own documentary, *La Bataille de Rabaska* (2008), which he co-directed with Magnus Isacsson, about a small Quebec community's struggle against the development of a natural gas plant. He is helping a friend edit a short film about his friend's return to Haifa, Israel, after forty years of self-imposed exile, and he is trying to raise money for a new documentary project about an East Coast anti-war artist. Duckworth celebrates his seventy-sixth birthday this year, and he shows no signs of slowing down.

Duckworth's career started at the National Film Board (NFB). He was among a generation of Canadian filmmakers paid to learn to make films. He says, without a hint of irony, that making his first film was like being in love. Between 1963 and 1972, Duckworth completed five short-film projects.[1] These films were personal and impressionistic, mostly interested in the medium as opportunity for expression and visual pleasure.

In 1972 Duckworth was invited by CFC to take a camera into Collins Bay Penitentiary in Ontario. The goal was to work with the guards and inmates using film as a tool to help resolve ongoing difficulties and tensions in the prison.[2] It was a strategy that had succeeded in other settings, but according to Duckworth, the hostilities were too great at Collins Bay, and so the project fell apart. But in the attempt Duckworth met a prisoner who wrote poetry and who Duckworth thought would make an interesting film study. He proposed spending a night in jail with his camera. The result, *Cell 16* (1972), is a jarring, intense, and intimate portrayal of one man's experience of the existential nightmare of being imprisoned. A collage of disjointed images and sounds from inside the prison is accompanied by a fury of words written and recited by the prisoner, Peter Madden. Partly because of Duckworth's film, Madden was granted early release. He went on to a celebrated career as a playwright and remains a close friend of Duckworth's to this day. *Cell 16* signalled a new direction for Duckworth. He had discovered the power of film to influence social and political outcomes.

The second and the only other film that Duckworth directed for CFC was *Temiscaming, Québec* (1975) about the efforts of a group of workers to reopen and run a pulp and paper mill in rural Quebec. "I saw it as a chance," Duckworth explained, "to use the techniques of CFC to help make it [the reopening of the pulp mill] happen and to help the workers achieve their aim of establishing Canada's first co-ownership plant." Duckworth and his film crew moved to Temiscaming and became an integral part of local efforts to convince provincial authorities to invest in the project.

1 *Half-Half-Three-quarters-Full* (1970), *Passing through Sweden* (1970), *Untouched and Pure* (1970), *The Wish (1971)*, and *Accident* (1972).

2 The idea was to allow guards and prisoners to document their experiences and concerns. These films would then be shared through public screenings as a way to open discussion between the two groups. CFC/SN had pioneered film and video as a tool for engaging divided communities in dialogue. What could not be said face-to-face could be said to a camera and could be witnessed or listened to without the affective disturbance of the "other" being in the same room.

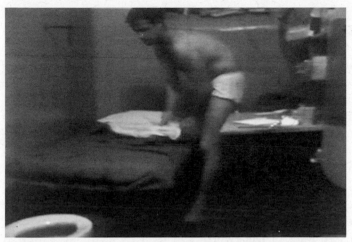

Cell 16 (1971): Martin Duckworth's "intense and intimate portrayal of one man's experience." Frame enlargement.

One of the qualities that sets CFC productions apart from other approaches to filmmaking is the aggressive narrowing of the gap between subject and object – between filmmaker and those being filmed. Process is as important and often more important than the final outcome. The emphasis is on allowing those being filmed creative input into how they are represented. "At every stage of the film," Duckworth says, "we had screenings in the community. They were held in the union hall and shown as part of union meetings. I brought a Moviola [a portable 16mm film-editing system] up from the NFB and rented a house for five months. I would do 'first assembles' and then show the results in the meetings." The screenings became part of the ongoing dialogue within the movement. "It encouraged them to keep going," Duckworth says, "and provoked debates about what steps to take next." The filmmaking process also had an impact on the notoriety of the story. "State officials were very aware of what was going on – aware that the NFB was making the film and making it a public issue. They had to help out. It was very exciting. It made you feel like you were putting your art to some use."

The relatively short two-part film (64 minutes) offers a visceral glimpse inside the workings of capitalism, but from the unique perspective of labour mobilizing – first, to maintain its industrial base and then to run it. The worker cooperative model was a pioneering idea that brought labour as owners into a complex relationship with private investors and the state. Duckworth's documentary tells the story from inside the political and social spaces inhabited by the townspeople. We witness the tensions of a blockade, but from within the protest, as anti-riot police advance towards the camera and against families and townsfolk. We celebrate in the local taverns when things go right. And we follow along as the euphoria of initial success gives way to the difficulties of managing the mill, securing orders in the global marketplace, and keeping production costs competitive and efficient. Tensions surface between the cooperative's management and workers as the community struggles to find creative strategies for including worker participation in corporate decision-making. The documentary tells a story about capitalism rarely told – about labour taking over the managerial reins (at least in part) and having to learn from the inside how best to realize capital's industrial potential. Today, the mill is still in operation as a profitable workers co-op (see Waugh, chapter 18, this volume, for a darker version of a similar northwoods narrative in Quebec).

The place-based films of Duckworth can be read surprisingly well in terms of current discussions in the field of geography that address the tension between uninhabited spaces and their transformation through human experience. It is with caution, Massey suggests, that we should approach any notion of "place" as dependent on human engagement. The danger is twofold: a "romanticisation of place ... can bring in its train both exclusivities and resistance to change, and through the distinction it can engender between space (abstract, meaningless) and place (meaningful) [it] can all too easily play to a political localism or local centredness" (Massey 2005). Massey rejects both an essentialized model of place as distinct (and therefore corruptible) from outside influences and the neoliberal "wish image" of place that is reduced to an open-bordered, unstructured, unbounded globality where capital, people, goods, and culture can flow unimpeded and endlessly – that is, the obliteration of place distinction altogether. Rather, place is conceived as a "co-existence of distinct narratives, as the product of power-filled social relations" where what makes place unique is derived from the relationships between actors within a dynamic of local, regional, and global influences (Massey 1999). Duckworth's films help shape even as they reveal the "geometries of power" (to use Massey's phrase) that influence the ways in which people live, work, and play. Massey argues that the concept of "place" when seen in terms of relationships reveals a politics of relations and that where relationships adversely affect places and the people who live in them – for example, the adverse impacts of capitalism – they must be "attacked ... by strategically employing identity claims – geographic and social – that are knowingly constructed" (145). Duckworth's films allow those who live somewhere (small-town pulp mill labour, prisoners, Métis street youth, Cape Breton miners) to redefine their identities through stories about how where they live shapes their lives – not only the landscape, but the industrial and social relationships that have emerged from a shared interest in the landscape. David Harvey describes this dynamic between biography and place as "geographic imagination" (1973, 24). An understanding of place confronts the landscape, but it must also encounter the imaginative geography that emerges through human experience. Castree argues that geography at some level involves "a cognitive mapping with political intent and material effectivity" (2004, 139), or in other words, demonstrates the qualities of geographic imagination. "Thus," he writes, "rather than asking whose geographic imaginations are correct, we need instead to ask: *who has the power to construct what geographical imaginations and with what effects?*" (emphasis added) (139). This is in essence one of the lines of questioning posed by the CFC modus operandi and in Martin Duckworth's films about place-making in Canada.

Duckworth liked feeling that his art played a practical role in the social and political outcomes of the subjects he was shooting. After directing only two CFC productions, he found that the experience had changed how he thought about filmmaking. "CFC," he says, "brought me into films about social issues." His next film, *12,000 Men* (1978), constructs an epic tale about coal miners in Cape Breton and their efforts to secure dignity, safety, and fair wages in their struggle against the United Steel Company of Montreal. *A Wives' Tale* (1979), which he co-directed with Sophie Bissonnette and Joyce Rock, tells the story of a six-month strike at the Sudbury nickel mine and shows how the miners' wives were key to the eventual success of the strike. The film was made during the strike, and the crew lived with the miners' families in their homes. Money for the production was raised with the help of the union, churches, and feminist organizations across Canada.

Temiscaming, 12,000 Men, and *A Wives' Tale* are portraits of certain parts of hinterland Canada that are central to dominant constructions of Canadian heritage – the pastoral of rural Quebec, Maritime folk cultures, and the resource-based wilderness of Northern Ontario and Quebec. Rarely, however, are these cultural and geographic places portrayed through the lives of workers – through the experiences of the men and women who live in these settings as they struggle within industrial contexts to improve the quality of their lives.

The much later film, *Riel Country* (1996), similarly offers an intimate portrait of place, this time through the struggles and experiences of Métis youth on some of Winnipeg's meaner streets. And more recently, in *La Bataille de Rabaska* (2008), Duckworth and his camera become part of a rural community under siege, trying to protect itself in the face of industrial transformation. These are, in my viewing, Duckworth's films about place – which really means about the people who inhabit the places and how their struggles for better lives shape the landscapes they live in. Public art practitioner and feminist Lucy Lippard has written that *space* becomes a *place* when we become a part of it (1997). Duckworth's Canadian landscapes are recognizable only through the lives of the people who live closest to the land and through the political struggles they endure.

In 1981 Duckworth made the first of his anti-war films. *Back to Kampuchea* (1981) follows a U.S. Cambodian émigré as he returns home two years after Pol Pot's exile (at the time, Pol Pot was still actively lobbying for the international recognition of his regime as Cambodia's legitimate government). In 1986 Duckworth completed *Return to Dresden* (1986), about a Canadian soldier returning to the city he helped fire-bomb during the Second World War. Also in the 1980s Duckworth directed *No More Hibakusha* (1983) and *No More Hiroshima* (1985), which, at the height of the Cold War, follow survivors of Hiroshima to New York, where they participated in peace marches demanding an end to nuclear proliferation.

With *Our Last Days in Moscow* (1987), Duckworth entered the fourth phase of his filmmaking with a crossover film about war (the Cold War), musicians, and art.[3] *Last Days* was followed by *Crossroads* (1988), *Oliver Jones in Africa* (1990), and *Shared Rhythms* (1991) – all of which focus on musicians and their performances.[4] And in 1994 he directed *Brush with Life*, a film about painter Diane Lenoir and her troubled journey as she transitioned from living in a mental institution to living with her family and being an artist. One senses in these films the filmmaker's own search for creative sensibility, an albeit understated self-reflexive inquiry into the creative process. More recently, Duckworth's films draw on all three of these influences – place, peace, and art. *Referendum Take Two* (1997) documents Quebec's second referendum on separation; *Acting Blind* (2006, mentioned earlier) is about a theatre production with an all-blind cast; and his most recent film, *La Bataille de Rabaska – Chronicle of an Environmental Conflict* (co-dir. Magnus Isacsson, 2008), chronicles community resistance to a methane tanker terminal (2008).

When I asked Duckworth about the role of the filmmaker in society, he suggested that the kind of filmmaking that he does plays a role in helping

3 In 1991 Duckworth also made *Peacekeeper at War*, another anti-war film, about his outrage at Canada's apparent shift in foreign policy from international peacekeeping to support of U.S. interventions in the Gulf War.

4 *Crossroads* (1988) weaves together performances by jazz pianists Leonid Chizhik, Oliver Jones, and Jean Beaudet along with their conversations about the roots and meaning of twentieth-century jazz. *Oliver Jones in Africa* (1990) follows Jones as he travels and performs in Africa and is welcomed into cultural settings that have played a role in the foundations of modern jazz. *Shared Rhythms* (1991) documents an international music festival that brings together artists from West Africa and Quebec.

people achieve a sense of self-worth. He described the struggles of the small community during the production of *Rabaska*. "The film helped them to stay alive as a movement, a resistance," he said. "They had a sense that we were with them every step of the way for three years. It helped keep their spirits alive. We became part of the movement. They let us in to all their meetings, which is something you can't do if you're a news crew." For Duckworth, making a film is about commitment – commitment to a community, to a movement, to a family, or to an individual. *Riel Country* and *12,000 Men* were only possible, he said, because of the months spent in the communities before filming, getting to know people and building up trust. It is a commitment that extends beyond the film frame into private lives. "A good film comes about from intimate relations between the filmmaker and main characters," he explained. "You choose your characters not only according to their relevance to the subject, but their willingness to let you into their lives, [to] open themselves up. And once that happens, you become good friends, you stay friends – for the rest of your life, really."

When I asked about truth in documentary, Duckworth turned to poetry. "I think poetic truth is a more honest truth than religious truth or political truth," he said.[5] "Statistical truth is useful. But we have to have revelatory truth to survive as a human race. We have to know which facts are relevant, how to interpret them, and what to do with them. That kind of truth is up to artists to convey." In the same breath, he talked about his love for the work of Canadian painter Jean-Paul Riopelle. "The Group of Seven reveal the beauty of nature," Duckworth commented, "but Riopelle reveals the beauty of the human imagination." And it's this – the human imagination – that Duckworth values most. "The human imagination has to save us from the decline our world leaders and industrial leaders have put us in. We can't resist unless we keep our imaginations alive."

5 Duckworth is not unfamiliar with the politics of truth. In the late 1970s he was working on *As Friend and Foe* (1982), a film about wage and price controls under the Trudeau administration. It was, in Duckworth's hands, an aggressively pro-union film critical of the way strikes were outlawed under wage and price controls. He had discovered that William Lyon Mackenzie King (Canada's tenth prime minister) had worked for J.D. Rockefeller during a particularly brutal labour dispute. King was Rockefeller's public relations secretary at the time of the Ludlow Massacre, a coalminers strike in Ludlow, Colorado, that ended with twenty members of a strikers' camp, mostly children and miners' wives, being shot down by the National Guard. In the documentary, Duckworth made connections between King, Rockefeller, and Trudeau's wage and price controls. It was too hot for the NFB brass, who took Duckworth off the project after they saw the rough cut. The film was completed without Duckworth and without the criticisms of Mackenzie King and Trudeau.

Truth in documentary – poetic truth or otherwise – is a troubled notion. Documentary may have its beginnings in the idea of a truth project, but it is an idea much complicated by evolving positions on the nature of truth and its representation in film.[6] As Nichols writes, "The comfortable accepted realism of one generation seems like artifice to the next" (1998, 17). Along these lines, Nichols identifies four major styles of documentary that have emerged in response to shifting perceptions of truth and how to show it: direct address (truth in the authoritarian voice-of-God narration); cinéma-vérité (truth in the supposed absence of authority and absence of narration); direct address via interview (truth in testimony); and self-reflexive documentary (truth in express examination of the filmmaker's role in the narrative). Cinéma-vérité, for example, would have the filmmaker step out of the frame altogether, arguing that less interference equals greater truth. But in the interview documentary, the filmmaker plays a more obvious and active role in constructing the story by eliciting the testimony of witnesses and experts. These films (films that rely on testimonials) not only valorize truths from multiple voices, but are also organized around the "direct encounter of the filmmaker with the subject of the documentary" (Sport 2003, 147). Interventions on the part of filmmakers can be as simple as conducting an interview or as complicated as joining a political movement. It is this latter kind of commitment (what Waugh in fact calls "committed" filmmaking), the making of films about, with, and by people engaged in political struggles, that describes the kind of filmmaking that took place under CFC and more generally the filmmaking of Martin Duckworth (Waugh 1984, xiv).

Rabinowitz argues that these more overtly polemical documentaries emerged from the need to historicize certain kinds of experience, the fragments of reality captured through cinéma-vérité that in fact begin to "alter the relationship between subject and object" towards what has been described as a "third cinema" – a phrase first used by filmmakers Fernando Solanas and Octavio Getino in their manifesto of the same name to describe the use of film in the decolonizing movements of the global south. This is cinema that intervenes in history – in Rabinowitz's words, a "cinematic self-determination" that acknowledges its role in becoming part of history through the actions of its own making (1993). If, as many commentators have suggested, the Hollywood film constructs a subject of desire, then "[b]y contrast, one might suggest that the political documentary – the documentary that seeks to intervene in history – mobilizes a subject of agency, that is, a subject who becomes an actor in history" (Rabinowitz 1993, 128).

6 Even documentary's origins as a truth project are suspect, especially in light of Robert Flaherty's manipulations in the making of *Nanook of the North*, considered by many to be the first documentary ever made (Rothman 1998).

Trinh T. Minh-ha has argued that what is usually put forth as truth in documentary is actually "meaning" – that in the face of truth as Protean substance, what remains (in the documentary) are the meanings we make of what is no longer there (1990). And Trinh argues that, to the degree that this tension is not addressed in documentary practice, documentary suffers from an unexamined reification of subject/object dualism: "At the core of such a rationale dwells, untouched, the Cartesian division between subject and object that perpetuates a dualistic inside-versus-outside, mind-against-matter view of the world. Again, the emphasis is laid on the power of film to capture reality 'out there' for us 'in here'" (83).

Trinh focuses on the moment of appropriation and consumption where what occurs is not, she argues, an unadulterated exposition of the real but rather a "repetitive, artificial resurrection of the real, an operation whose overpowering success in substituting the visual and verbal signs of the real for the real itself ultimately helps challenge the real" (1990, 83). Duckworth's films (in particular, the CFC films and his films about place) suggest this in not so many words – that is, that what is real is challengeable and changeable, that the "out there" real depends on the "in here" real. Or in other words, that history is a collaborative affair.

Trinh remains critical of socially oriented filmmaking that does not overtly and self-consciously address the construction of truth at the representation/exhibition stage onscreen. She argues that to not do so, even in the case of the activist filmmaker who purports to speak on behalf of those who have no voice, allows authority to persist. Films made about "the common people," she writes, if they do not address the filmmaker's authority, merely perpetuate the status quo.

What remains largely unexamined in all this is the role that the *process* of filmmaking can play in complicating the subject/object dichotomies. This is the territory that CFC occupied with its blurred distinctions between filmmakers, subjects, and audiences – where subjects participated in making films about themselves or were taught to make their own films, and where audiences watched themselves on screen. Emphasis on the we/they, inside/outside distinction at the moment of representation and consumption alone fails to consider that in the case of interventionist (i.e., activist, or socially engaged, or committed) filmmaking, the subject/object distinction has already been challenged long before the images make it to the screen. When the subject of a film is invited into the production process and when subjects are transformed into filmmakers, the subject/object gap is radically altered.

This is not to say that when the images do reach the screen, that the complications raised by Trinh won't apply. But her assurance that the replacement of "one unacknowledged authority with another" will "perpetuate the Master's ideological stance" must be tempered with an awareness that the

Master's stance may have been complicated at an earlier stage of collaborative production (1990, 89). This is in fact the challenge that CFC production techniques present to traditional documentary filmmaking.

Duckworth's deference to poetic truth reveals an interesting and surprisingly contemporary quality at the heart of even some of his earliest documentaries. He suggests that facts need poetry to approach revelatory truth, to give meaning to statistics, to help us determine priorities and what actions to take next. His poetry is one of collaboration, an approach to filmmaking that is a persistent challenge to the filmmaker's monopolization of authority and one that he first encountered forty years ago working for Challenge for Change.

25 *Les filles du Roy*

■

JERRY WHITE

Someone looking at Anne Claire Poirier's *Les filles du Roy* (1974) might not immediately know that it was produced as part of Société nouvelle (SN), the French-language sister program of Challenge for Change (CFC). The film is a meditation on the history of Quebec and an attempt to intervene in that historical understanding by giving a central place to gender politics. It is an eccentric, slightly brooding film, one that does not connect to any specific community beyond that of *les Québécoises* since the 1600s. I am not, of course, the first person to point out the degree to which its formal, political, and historical concerns place it well outside the idealism of Société nouvelle. Scott MacKenzie, for one, sees *Les filles du Roy* as embodying the distinctly non-Challenge-for-Change-y sense of that program. Recalling the degree to which SN collectively lost interest in a collaboration-centred approach to filmmaking, MacKenzie writes: "Notions of process and interactivity fell by the wayside, as video replicated many of the same viewing patterns as cinema. While SN went on to produce a variety of politically engaged films, such as Anne Claire Poirier's *Les filles du Roy* (1974) and the En tant que femmes series, these works moved closer to the traditions of politically engaged European art cinema and away from the early principles of SN" (MacKenzie, chapter 31, this volume, p. 334).

There is indeed little question that the gap between *Les filles du Roy* and, say, *Saint-Jérôme* (1968) and *VTR St-Jacques* (1969) is huge, to say nothing of the gap between *Les filles du Roy* and *Introduction to Fogo Island* (1967). Yet, while it may seem clear that *Les filles du Roy* is not part of a tradition of collaborative filmmaking, this is a slightly more complex matter than it may appear. The film has a credit for "scénario et texte / Marthe Blackburn; avec la collaboration de Jeanne Morazain / Anne Claire Poirier." When I spoke to Poirier by phone on 16 July 2008, she told me that the text for the film was, in essence, written by all three of them together. Furthermore, the credits also list eight names under "Avec la participation de": Catherine Deer, Danielle Ouimet, Marie-Josée Da Silva, Suzanne Gervais, Hélène Girard,

Nicole Lebreton, Monique Fortier, and Berthe Latraverse-Poirier. These are women who are present in the film, representing some form of "La Québécoise." Deer is the Aboriginal woman at the beginning of the film. Ouimet is the actress who plays the woman who is unveiled to stand naked before the camera; she is of course also the actress who played the title role in the pioneering soft-core feature *Valérie*, made five years earlier (Denis Héroux, 1969), transforming the scene, among everything else, into a critique of Quebec film history – as well as into a conversion narrative not at odds with CFC/SN as a whole or with its offshoot Studio D! The other women appear in some form as various representations of Quebec women (*la figuration* is the term that Poirier used to describe their role in the film). This is also true of Latraverse-Poirier, the director's mother, who is seen talking with a few younger women midway through the film. Some of these women were filmmakers (such as the NFB animator Gervais), but Poirier made it clear that they were not co-filmmakers, so to speak, but people who were involved with the film.

Indeed, *Les filles du Roy* strongly evinces Poirier's cinematic voice, and recognizing that voice helps us see the degree to which *Les filles du Roy*, like all of Poirier's films, is very clearly part of an international (and very strongly francophone) tradition of "women's cinema." This matter of taxonomy is the defining "problem" that the film presents. Three other problems raised by the film lead us there: structure, visuals, and politics.

One aspect of *Les filles du Roy* that can scarcely be understated is the degree to which it is defined by strikingly composed visuals. An early prominent example of this tendency comes in the film's opening sequence, when the camera tilts down onto a high-angle long shot of five women in black robes, prostrate in the snow. Poirier cuts to a close-up of one of these women but then zooms back into long shot and tilts up into the icy expanse. This is, of course, a way of using immediately recognizable Catholic imagery (the allusion here is to the ceremony in which religious make their final vows to the Church, prostrating themselves before the altar) to illustrate the level of commitment expected of the *filles du Roy* (they are, in essence, making their vows to the territory, prostrating themselves before the landscape).

The film's semi-Brechtian closing sequence, shot on a cluttered sound stage, works in a similar way. A mummified woman is slowly unwrapped, projecting an image that Joan Nicks calls "a powerful sign of returning humanity to the forgotten woman in Quebec's Quiet Revolution and of reconfiguring la Québécoise in feminist terms. Unveiled by Poirier, the naked woman remains standing in well-lit view of the camera, as the female voice-over dismantles the hitherto male look at *la Québécoise* as a 'porno' figure" (1999, 230). I take the point here, but it is important to note that it is not only the voice-over that does this. This is a single shot, one that moves from long shot to close-up and back to long shot, only to slowly open the iris and fade to white that harks back to the icy landscapes of the opening sequences. It is a highly composed, highly artificial image that strongly resists easy identification on the part of the viewer.

Les filles du Roy's ordered but open structure is quite clear in the sequence where Poirier shows women working as nurses in a hospital. This part of the film opens with a shot of a woman cleaning an office, the soundtrack picking up the quiet sounds of her work in a more or less synchronous (and clearly diegetic) way. This is followed by a sequence of three shots showing a nurse tending to a baby in a hospital crib; then by a shot of a nurse turning over a young girl on a backboard; and finally by two shots of a pair of nurses tending to a baby's surgical wounds. This set of nursing sequences is followed by a sequence of two shots (and several zooms) of a woman working behind a bar, mixing drinks. On one level this is all fairly straightforward documentary material. Indeed, unlike most of the film, all of these sequences use only diegetic synch-sound rather than voice-over. But their juxtaposition, and moreover their common visual rhythms (sequences of two or three shots and a slow, fairly deliberate camera movement), like their common use of synch-sound, make them all feel very much of a piece. Hospital work, office cleaning, and bartending are all forms of labour that are in many ways invisible, part of the labour of everyday life that is rarely explicitly recognized as essential or even worthy of the word "labour." Poirier is making this argument about women's labour – and about the connections between various forms of that labour – visually, not via the voice-over. Indeed, the voice-over throughout the film (like the visuals, really) tends towards the poetic, not the expository. This sequence on the invisibility of women's labour leaves a fair bit for the viewer to do in terms of bridging gaps in meaning, as the voice-over doesn't explain the connection between these images. But that connection is there, and Poirier is working pretty hard via the sorts of visual motifs that I've explained to make that clear. This sequence is poetic, open; it is also argumentative, in an ordered way.

This sense of ordered openness is also evident in the film's opening sequence, which shows a series of images of the snowy Quebec landscape. These images are not, however, still images. The film's first shot appears to be a white screen, but Poirier zooms out to reveal the snowy, ice-covered St Lawrence River; the camera then pans left along the trees and low hills. This is followed by a series of shots of snowy landscapes, shots that all combine zooms, pans, and tilts. After an image shot off the back of a boat, Poirier dissolves to a close-up of a young woman standing in a snowy landscape. She then cuts to that same women in medium shot, with a second woman in the background walking towards the foreground. Then we see that second woman in close-up as well. This sequence is typical of the film's structure.

There are several key motifs in these images – Quebec's distinctive landscape, the sense of struggle that was central to simple existence in the territory, the way that women are simultaneously absent and present – and the connection between these motifs is not so difficult to ascertain. As in the sequence with the nurses, then, Poirer resists the temptation to draw connections explicitly or to make didactic arguments about these connections. Instead the images flow into each other visually. There are more dissolves here than cuts, and camera movements, zooms, and set-ups are often repeated or echoed (such as the composition of the two women in the snow or the counter-clockwise pan across snowy hills that is directly followed by a clockwise pan across snowy hills). The argument is clear: women were always present in this brutal land-scape, and they bore the brunt of its brutality just as much as the storied voyageurs. But that argument does not unfold linearly; it emerges elliptically. The opening sequence makes it clear that the film will speak the language of poetry, not of prose. *Les filles du Roy* may feel like an essay film, but really it is in the form of an elegy. And that elegy, rendered through an elliptical, highly visual structure, departs even further from the CFC/SN project because of its politics. *Les filles du Roy*'s political project is twofold: gender-based and nationalist. Really, though, they are one and the same political project.

While *Les filles du Roy*'s desire to reinscribe women into the historical and present-day understanding of Quebec may seem to be easily consistent with the generally progressive political project of CFC/SN, there are some important differences here. Indeed, it would also be easy to see *Les filles du Roy* as consistent with the broad contours of the then-emergent Studio D (founded in 1974, the year *Les filles du Roy* was produced). But Poirier was actually a producer in an SN sub-series called En tant que femmes, and Bill Marshall writes about how "she refused the model of the English side's women-only unit, Studio D" (2001, 215). But she was also clearly refusing the pan-Canadian quality of the NFB's overall project. Canada does not figure into the historical project of *Les filles du Roy* at all. This is not to say that Canada has been explicitly rejected in favour of Quebec; it is simply absent. The film is very explicit about the connection between gender and nation-building – the voice-over in the opening sequences marvels at the hubris of trying to raise children to create a nation in such a landscape – but that nation is obviously, unproblematically Quebec. In this way, the film is, as Nicks writes, very much a product of the Quiet Revolution. It is the specifics of the Quebec nationalist project that are at issue here. Poirier con-fidently takes for granted the reality of Quebec national belonging as such.

If *Les filles du Roy* is (like a lot of French-language NFB films of the sixties and seventies) rejecting the pan-Canadian assumptions of the NFB project, it is also rejecting the assumptions of feminist documentary that were prominent at the time. It is true that 1974 was the year that Studio D was

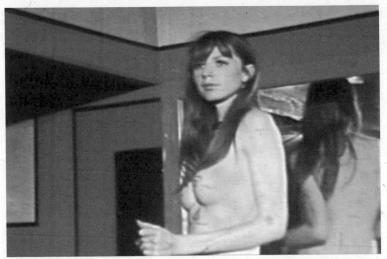

Erotic entertainer as forgotten Québécoise worker in *Les filles du Roy* (1974).
Frame enlargement.

founded and that *Les filles du Roy* was released, but 1973 was the year that
Claire Johnston published "Women's Cinema as Counter-cinema," and 1975
was the year that Akerman released *Jeanne Dielman, 23 Quai de Commerce,
1080 Bruxelles* and Laura Mulvey published the famous article "Visual
Pleasure and Narrative Cinema." It is more genuinely illustrative of what is
going on in *Les filles du Roy* to see it not in the light of 1974 and the NFB's
emerging interest in women-centred documentary practice, but as part of the
continuity of a formally adventurous, politically radical form of feminist filmmaking that began to emerge in both the anglophone and francophone Euro-
American world of the early 1970s.

Although Mulvey's article "Visual Pleasure and Narrative Cinema" is
mostly discussed in terms of its importance to an understanding of classical
Hollywood cinema, it also reflects on the political and formal characteristics
of an alternative form of filmmaking. Mulvey writes that cinema "has
changed over the last few decades. It is no longer the monolithic system based
on large capital investment exemplified at its best by Hollywood in the
1930s, 1940s and 1950s. Technological advances (16mm and so on) have
changed the economic conditions of cinematic production, which can now be
artisanal as well as capitalist. Thus it has been possible for an alternative
cinema to develop ... The alternative cinema provides a space for the birth
of a cinema which is radical in both a political and an aesthetic sense and
challenges the basic assumptions of mainstream film" (1989, 15).

Les filles du Roy is certainly an example of a film that comes out of a
more or less artisanal context. Shot on 16mm, it was made in a way that
indeed bore very little resemblance to the industrial production methods of

commercial cinema. It also has radical aspirations in terms of both form and content. I have tried to spell out these aspirations above: namely the degree to which Poirier is critiquing the already-insurgent Quiet Revolution, and the degree to which she is doing this by an associative, rather than didactic or even linear, structure, one that rejects the narrative-driven literalism of conventional cinema in favour of a more centrally visual language.

In addition, though, the manner in which this visual language unfolds is quite consistent with Johnston's 1973 call for a fully thought through feminist aesthetic. Critiquing what she saw as the reductionism of cinéma-vérité, Johnston writes: "Clearly, if we accept that cinema involves the production of signs, the idea of non-intervention is pure mystification. The sign is always a product. What the camera in fact grasps is the 'natural' world of the dominant ideology. Women's cinema cannot afford such idealism; the 'truth' of our oppression cannot be captured on celluloid with the 'innocence' of the camera: it has to be constructed/manufactured. New meanings have to be created by disrupting the fabric of the male bourgeois cinema within the text of the film" (1976, 214).

Again, as I tried to illustrate above, this sort of skepticism with respect to simple realism, with the consequent favouring of engaged artificiality, is quite consistent not only with *Les filles du Roy* overall but with the way that the film uses synch-sound, vérité-ish documentary footage. Vérité had, by the 1970s, become a sort of "house aesthetic" for the NFB, in no small part because of the enormous contributions that NFB filmmakers had made to the emergence of the form. This was especially true of the francophone contingent. But Poirier is using that *form* here as part of a larger strategy of, as Johnston says, construction/manufacture. The synch-sound sequences – nurses flipping a young woman on her backboard, a woman behind the bar mixing drinks and making chatter with the men on the bar stools – are mere elements in a larger montage, a montage that mounts the argument that women and the work they do have been excluded from Quebec's understanding of its history and its contemporary transformation. It is Poirier's centralization of a montage aesthetic – and that aesthetic's concomitant subjectivity and polemical sensibility – that disrupts the fabric of vérité aesthetics specifically but also that of documentary aesthetics overall. Poirier does not turn to documentary out of a sense of innocent feminist idealism; rather, she uses documentary as an occasional formal gesture in the service of creating new meanings. She uses it to create a new interpretation of Quebec history.

This rewriting of cinematic codes – and especially of realism's codes – is not only consistent with English-language film theory of the 1970s but also a crucial part of women's cinema in the francophone world. The seminal example is clearly the work of Chantal Akerman. Ivone Margulies has written of the interplay between Akerman's work and the realist film theory of

André Bazin, stating that "[s]eemingly democratizing reception (as Bazin does in advocating the long take), the hyperbolizing homogeneous texture of Akerman's cinema makes it impossible to forget one's condition as a spectator" (1996, 59). This combination of Brechtian self-awareness and Bazinian realism is indeed the characteristic quality of Akerman's cinema, and such a combination is equally characteristic of *Les filles du Roy*, with its long takes and complex camera movements or its use of documentary footage on the one hand and its images of women staring directly into the camera against snowy landscapes or being unwrapped on sound stages on the other. There is no doubt that a crucial difference between a filmmaker like Akerman and one like Poirier is the matter of hyperbolizing. Akerman's *Jeanne Dielman* has a sort of relentless quality that Poirier's *Les filles du Roy* simply does not (although that is less true of later Poirier films such as 1979's *Mourir à tue-tête*). But what these films share is an embrace of the intellectual and political project that Mulvey saw for an alternative cinema: "The satisfaction and reinforcement of the ego that represent the high point of film history hitherto must be attacked. Not in favour of a reconstructed new pleasure, which cannot exist in the abstract, nor of intellectualised unpleasure, but to make way for a total negation of the ease and plenitude of the narrative fiction film. The alternative is the thrill that comes from leaving the past behind without simply rejecting it, transcending outworn or oppressive forms, and daring to break with normal pleasurable expectations in order to conceive of a new language of desire" (1989, 16). Akerman is a bit more on the attack than Poirier, but it is Poirier who is more engaged with the complex work of leaving the past behind without simply rejecting it. What these filmmakers share, though, is their search for a new way of representing the lives of women, a way that both challenges and rewards an engaged viewer. What they share is their quest for a new language of desire.

Overall, then, it is important to understand *Les filles du Roy* not only as an example of the way that a lot of sn films seemed to move away from the nfb's internal Challenge for Change aspirations (as MacKenzie reasonably does), but also as a key example of how many of these films moved towards internationally important movements in political and formally adventurous filmmaking. The early 1970s was an exciting time for feminist cinema, both in terms of theorizing and practice.[1] Poirier's films, especially *Les filles du*

---

[1] Patrice Petro, in her 1999 Martin Walsh Lecture at the conference of the Film Studies Association of Canada, gave a nuanced discussion of the pitfalls and possibilities of nostalgia for this period in film theory. This was published as "Film Feminism and Nostalgia for the Seventies" in the *Canadian Journal of Film Studies* (Petro 1999). (This issue also has an essay by André Loiselle on Poirier's 1979 film *Mourir à tue-tête*.) I particularly agree with Petro's statement that it is "remarkable that both

Roy, should be seen as work that was very much on the front lines of this movement, as work that was in a complex conversation about the connection between form, gender, and politics.

Mulvey and [Tom] Gunning's work has tended to inspire, not further analyses of independent films or the avant garde, but extended discussions of Hollywood cinema itself" (17). This is indeed a singularly curious fact of anglophone film studies. As I have tried to show here, a Mulveyan world view is much closer to a film like *Les filles du Roy* than it is to contemporary Hollywood.

In Praise of Anomaly: *Le bonhomme* and *Rose's House*

26

■

KALLI PAAKSPUU

INTRODUCTION

Two bold films from Montreal and Toronto, respectively *Le bonhomme* (Pierre Maheu, 1972) and *Rose's House* (Clay Borris, 1977), emerged within the context of 1970s political activism and aesthetic confrontation as part the National Film Board's (NFB's) politically charged Challenge for Change (CFC) and Société nouvelle (SN) programs. Both films were anomalies within their respective program, each going beyond the programs' mandate to provoke public policy debates and empower citizens to deliver atypical and highly personal reflections on the countercultural shifts and minority and subcultural formations in Canada's two metropoles. Maheu (1939–79) pushed the legacy of direct cinema to probe the crisis of traditional marriage and national identities in the face of alternative sexual/social ideals. Five years later Borris (b. 1950) hybridized Colin Low's community development process with an artisanal, semi-autobiographical aesthetic to produce a short feature that is the anglophone CFC's unique venture into narrative cinema. It is worth considering these atypical products together, both of them produced in the heyday and at the tail end of the CFC/SN programs, so as not only to rescue two unique films from undeserved oblivion but also to illuminate the larger cinematic grain against which they rubbed so creatively.

The legacy of direct cinema, with its legendary lightweight cameras and portable equipment, was the backdrop for both films. This stylistic idiom was born of massive socio-economic transformations in an urbanizing and laicizing postwar Quebec and participated in the Quiet Revolution's revision of the province's self-image and alteration of its social values and media culture. Meanwhile, the style had a parallel history in English Canada, marked by its own innovations and specific cultural trajectories of possibility. Allan King's *A Married Couple* (1969) was for some its apogee, a film that uncannily anticipated aspects of both 1970s films under study here, most notably with its strong narrative appeal to audience members to identify with characters negotiating their lives together or apart. These two unusual films allow us to take stock of how direct cinema was ready by the 1970s to be pushed –

intrusively or daringly, depending on your take – by Maheu into the existential domain of identity, desire, and rupture, and by Borris into personal narrative and family history. How both experimental documentaries were brought to fruition by maverick directors on the Canadian taxpayers' tab, thanks to the aegis of Société nouvelle and Challenge for Change, is a fascinating chapter in the momentous story that this book is undertaking to write, a chapter rich in the discourses of regional geography and historical memory, the beautiful and the abject, ethnography and melodrama.

LE BONHOMME

When Pierre Trudeau, in his 1968 book *Federalism and the French Canadians*, railed against the "separatist counter-revolutionaries" who called the National Film Board and Radio-Canada home, he might have been talking about Pierre Maheu, except that it was only the next year that Maheu was to enter the federal studio. Maheu had been a founder of *Parti pris* as well a contributor to *Cité Libre*, the intellectual journals of the Quiet Revolution that had been hosting pleas by prominent NFB filmmakers like Jacques Godbout, Gilles Carle, Gilles Groulx, and Denys Arcand for a personal national(ist) art cinema in Quebec. For his part, Maheu did not hesitate to label the NFB a colonial institution and fifth column in the heart of Quebec (Kinik 2007, 10). Perhaps Maheu's movement over to the federal institution in 1969 was a decolonizing gesture, but in any case, along with producing several epochal films, he directed two documentaries there before his accidental death at the age of forty in 1979.

Maheu's *Bonhomme* (loosely translated as "the ordinary guy") offers an eschatological meditation on francophone traditionalism. Microscoping private encounters between a working-class heterosexual couple from Saint-Henri, Maheu transposes the gendered power relations into a metaphor for the Quiet Revolution's reordering of Quebec's institutions. The officially accepted reality of the family is the crucible for an existential hero who defies all standards. The cinematic narrative begins with a traditional church baptism intercut with husband Claude's motorbike ride under a reddened sky. We then follow Claude around a commune in the Laurentians where he goes nude canoeing with a female commune member (also nude), ending up in carefree, drug-enhanced skinny dips where "Alleluia" is graphically written on a rock face. "Alleluia" becomes a swimmers' chant for an alternative redemption. *Bonhomme* counterposes a twenty-year marital battleground with a utopian alternative.

Husband and wife argue in a ripping, painful-to-watch verbal tango that stalemates over his pension and other differences. *Le bonhomme* gives us a glimpse of an earlier harmony between a beautiful couple through photographs that unsettle by their contrast to the gritty marriage standoff. The wife growls from her throne chair positioned next to the gas stove (was this the usual position?) and chain-smokes as she negotiates a new deal. Towards the end she doesn't bother to change out of her black lingerie. Her husband flits around the room and invites his teen daughter to the commune. She rejects the offer, for she'd rather have a smoke, which she lights off the gas stove. In the next dimly lit room the daily laundry hangs.

Le bonhomme exposes too vividly the pain of marriage dissolution in the working-class Saint-Henri neighbourhood of Montreal. After marriage at eighteen and ten subsequent children sired with Yolande, husband Claude reinvents himself in the commune in the Laurentians. The film's moments of inarticulate confusion invite us to consider what beyond these two individuals needs to change. Is it the Church in the opening scene? Do social expectations between married partners change through time? Is this couple representative of a general social malaise within post–Quiet Revolution Quebec? Is this a social critique of Quebec nationalism, of the commune counterculture, or simply an existential narrative?

Unacceptable conditions of married life outpour in dialogue that shows a private life turned inside out. The evening that Claude takes Yolande to the strip show backfires into another battle, and Yolande's closing words to her daughter and to us indirectly as her film audience sum up the shifting terrain of allegiances: "Pis quand ton pere est pas icitte, je m'ennuie de lui, pis quand y est icitte ben y me damne encore. Fait que c'est rien que de l'ennui que j'ai. N'importe qui me désennuirait." [When your father is not here, I miss him, but when he's here he puts me through hell. In fact, it's only loneliness that I'm feeling. Anyone at all could save me from that.] At the same time that cinema reconstructs a phenomenal world, private encounters get extended through technology into performances that animate public outrage or sympathy.

Maheu may well be interpreting the slogan "Maîtres chez nous," or "Masters in our own house," through a rejection of federalist intrusions, but in his film there is no "chez nous," no place – certainly not the home – that is stable. Husband Claude describes his goal as "Me faire brûler sur une planche en l'air là au soleil-là." [I just wanna toast in the sun on a board there.] Nation is implicated in the gender power impasse and vice versa. However unsympathetic Yolande's growling is, the film provides a rare window on how sexist countercultural politics really were. Whereas Claude and Yolande bring up too much and excoriate each other endlessly, Maheu's Toronto counterpart Borris would discreetly leave us wanting to know more of his mother Rose's story.

Le bonhomme (1972): countercultural hero Claude tree-hugging in the Laurentians. Production still.

ROSE'S HOUSE

A New Brunswicker of Acadian descent transplanted to Toronto, Clay Borris's own initiation and later practice as a filmmaker echoes the CFC philosophy. An early dropout, the young Borris hung out at the Central Neighbourhood House and then joined the free school called Point Blank, founded by the educational reformer and boys worker George Martell,[1] who became Borris's mentor in life and art. Like CFC filmmakers in other contexts, Martell introduced his students to film technology to give them a different role and agency in their community. Borris credits him with steering him into his life work:

> We were all the dropouts from Cabbagetown and we would get together twice a week ... George used to say to me, "You know. Clay, you should make a film ... Just come up with an idea. Something that you can do in the neighbourhood."

1 Martell was also founder of *This Magazine Is about Schools* (later *This Magazine*), the bible of 1960s radical pedagogy.

So we used to drive in the car and George used to take us to go for hamburger or something like that. One night on the way home ... we were teenagers sixteen, seventeen. I had quit school at that point. I got kicked out for hitting a teacher ... I was a dropout like everyone else. I'm in the car. Young George is driving. [I said,] "I got an idea for a movie ... This kid comes home from school and he's walking through the neighbourhood. Three tough guys are standing at the street corner. They don't like the way he looks at them so they chase him through the neighbourhood. They beat the shit out of him and then they walk away as if nothing happened." George stopped the car and he goes, "Wait a minute. Whoa! What'd you say? I asked you to do something about the way you see your neighbourhood. That's the way you see it?" I said, "Yah. Guys are always chasing me. I'm always chasing them. That's the way I see it. Yah." ... So he got me a Super 8 camera and I shot the film on weekends with the guys in the street gang that I was in ... Everybody in the film was in a gang. And John Phillips who was a friend of George's, who taught me photography ... [He] showed it to somebody in the Department of Education, Youth Branch. They said, "We like this film. Why don't you make it over again in 16 mm with a cameraman?"

I shot the first one myself handheld. I'm like, "Wow ... okay." We shot this film in 16[mm]. There was no talking or anything. So the whole film was a chase basically through the neighbourhood in Cabbagetown. And, of course, in my version, it was like twenty minutes long because it was my first film and I thought you had to show the whole neighbourhood to get to where you were going. I didn't realize you could cut. (Borris, interview with the author, 29 July 2008)

Borris was soon making an impression with his short early documentaries. These offered rare evidence of working-class life (Morris 1984, 38) and were constructed on an artisanal level with the networks of family and friends he had maintained since his days at the free school. His 1971 short *Paper Boy* got his foot in the door at the NFB. Cinematographer Phillips, one of the original CFC Newfoundland collaborators, offered him a formative co-production partnership, and they brought the Fogo ideal of "shift[ing] 'the voice' from the outside to the inside of a community" into the mean streets of Toronto artisanal filmmaking (Phillips, e-mail communication, 12 August 2008).

Borris then developed a more ambitious project based on family history, a personal narrative of the challenges faced by an Acadian francophone family moving to Toronto, nursing a dream of homeownership and respectability, and seeking educational opportunities for their deaf daughter. It was also to be a frank portrait of Rose, Borris's mother, who was to play herself in her own environment, raising a family in a rooming house, cooking and cleaning in a Cabbagetown neighbourhood rife with gangs and bootleggers. The film would also be a vivid deconstruction of the social institutions that supported newly arrived "minority" families in Toronto – and of the gaps in that support.

Borris and Phillips formed Cabbageroll Productions and got the film to rough-cut stage through Canada Council and Ontario Arts Council support, but above all through "network contributions." Phillips shot the film, and Rose re-enacted scenes from her life raising four children in a rooming house. Borris wrote the screenplay together with poet friend Paulette Jiles, who also plays a supporting role as a boarder. In addition to Rose, a whole network of family and friends, mostly from New Brunswick, played various characters, including a party-loving waitress and a gay bootlegging couple. Borris's father's parents Down East put on their Sunday best to wave goodbye to the young couple leaving in a sixties sedan weighted with worldly possessions – wintry Canadiana at its most stunning. As they scrambled for post-production funding, Phillips's connections with the NFB led to the studio's financial involvement, and their personal project exceptionally ended up as part of the CFC catalogue of social issues and community activist films.

CFC was clearly running out of steam in the late seventies, and the recruitment of fresh blood and new projects, however apparently peripheral to its mandate because of its feature aspirations, must have seemed like the right thing to do. After all, *Rose's House* was approaching certain social issues familiar to other CFC films through the vehicle of improvised narrative anecdote. For example, the climax of the film is Rose's confrontation with a bureaucratic social worker who would seem at home in any of the program's early documentary output (e.g., *The Things I Cannot Change* or *Mrs. Case*; see Lindop, chapter 27, this volume). Paradoxically enough, the social worker was played by Martell, who clearly took much pleasure in haranguing Rose about her son, who has just had his first scrape with the law over a stolen bike, spending a night in juvenile jail. Martell's involvement not only encapsulates his opposition to policies that place children outside the history of their people, ethnicity, and class – an expression of seventies educational activism – but also turns the audience's sympathies to the mother. Martell's improvised professional jargon deliberately antagonizes Rose and sparks her emotionally wrenching performance. This performance gets an unusual edge when the then illiterate Rose states, "I learned more English when I was fighting with people." In a memorable cat-and-mouse dialogue she turns the conversation into a challenge to the social worker, who insists that the criminal justice system provides the best discipline for her son. This scene unmasks the

Clay Borris (left) and schoolmate making Super8 ancestor of *Rose's House* (1977), Cabbagetown c. 1968. Production still courtesy of photographer John Phillips.

system's Kafkaesque bureaucratic logic that American Frederick Wiseman had just exposed in his direct-cinema works like *Welfare* (1975).

Rose's House, as with Société nouvelle's more numerous experiments with hybrid docu-fiction at this time, produced a self-reflexive awareness of cinematic culture. Direct cinema enabled the filmmaker's consciousness to inflect the cinematic form and meaning given to amorphous objective reality: "Instead of effacing his presence, the filmmaker will affirm it. Instead of rendering the technical process transparent (supposedly), he will emphasize its materiality" (Clandfield 1984, 113). For example, Borris intentionally left in the off-camera French exchange in which Rose tells him she's finished in the scene – just in case the viewer thought the re-enactment was a documentary reality.

Borris's *Rose's House* is a rare enactment of Cabbagetown culture through a mother's negotiation of domestic and public space in the management of her family. Rose articulates core ethics and values of Toronto's working-class – homeownership, unity of family, and family networks are central vehicles for survival – and as a byproduct offers a proto-feminist critique of the inadequacies of patriarchal justice system. Seemingly in tune with CFC/SN's national networks of communities grappling with the challenge of self-representation, Rose declares, "First, I don't want to be somebody else. I can be myself," and her son's rejoinder might have served as a slogan for the whole movement: "The hardest thing to play in movies is yourself." *Rose's*

House was exceptionally well received, at least by critics and the film industry establishment, who showered it with Canadian Film Award nominations (but no prizes in the era of the Capital Cost Allowance!).[2] Borris went on to play himself in his feature debut film, *Alligator Shoes* (1981), the only Canadian film that year at the Director's Fortnight at Cannes.

Interestingly both Maheu's and Borris's films feature celebrity musical talent, fully in tune with NFB practice since the early 1940s of using music as a vehicle of community self-realization (though not all CFC/SN films continued the practice). *Le bonhomme* commissioned music by American jazz artist Red Mitchell and Quebec pop *chansonnier* Luc Cousineau, and the music underscored the motorbike and pastoral commune scenes with a new world consciousness. *Rose's House* commissioned native activist and CFC veteran Willy Dunn to write the film's theme song – "Rose's House is our house. A place where you can survive. A story not being told."[3] Music was one of CFC/SN's eclectic measures for immersing the public into local issues from the inside (see Michael Baker, chapter 19, this volume).

After more than thirty years, *Le bonhomme* and *Rose's House* still resonate with a self-conscious and risk-taking ethic/aesthetic of confronting issues that contemporary reality television has never achieved. Each film in its unique way extends the culture of citizenship by inclusive practices and a critique of dominant culture (Stevenson 1997, 42). These two anomalous films, perhaps more than any other among the CFC/SN catalogue, belie the myth that the program produced politically ambitious, black-and-white documentaries that abdicated artistry and faltered both aesthetically and ideologically. Interestingly, neither of these two films, despite their rich local histories of Montreal and Toronto in a turbulent decade, is available in the other official language.

2 The 1978 Canadian Film Awards saw both Borris and Jiles nominated for Best Screenplay and award-winning poet Jiles also nominated for Best Supporting Actress as the female boarder. Phillips was nominated for Best Photography, while Rose Maltais-Borris was nominated for Best Actress. No awards were received.

3 This was Dunn's second collaboration with Borris after the NFB short *Paper Boy* (Clay Borris, 1971).

27

Getting Close and Staying Far: Pierre Lasry and the Solo Moms

■

JASON LINDOP

Documentary representations of the historical world sometimes interact with filmmaker-centred tactics of self-legitimization, as considerations of accuracy are measured in relation to how such tactics will reflect on the film. Desired impressions of empathetic closeness or interrogative competence may be achieved through valorizing their human subjects, or at the price of degrading them. The two English-language documentary shorts that Pierre Lasry made about Montreal-based single mothers, as part of the National Film Board's (NFB's) Challenge for Change (CFC) series, illustrate such contrasting tendencies.[1]

Mrs. Case (1969, 14 min.) reveals the economic difficulties of an impoverished mother of five and focuses on a philanthropic agency worker who is condescending rather than supportive. By aligning itself with Mrs Case and addressing important aspects of her situation ignored by the bureaucrat, the film foregrounds its sympathetic connection to the subject and ethical clarity of vision. *Laurette* (1969, 20 min.) focuses on the subjective adjustment to single life undertaken by a comparatively comfortable mother of one. While Laurette expresses empowerment in her status as a solo parent, the film works to frame these expressions as her attempt to mislead the crew regarding her more fundamental conjugal desires. This presentation highlights the film's ability to reveal a truth the subject is attempting to conceal. These two women may have been selected for their ability to provide a cross-section of the kinds of problems faced by this marginalized segment, but the

---

1 Pierre Lasry (b. 1938, Morocco) had come to the attention of the NFB on account of *The Drifter* (1966), a fiction feature he had produced and edited, which was shown at Expo '67. He had also acquired technical knowledge though work in the adult film industry (Lasry, interview with author, May 2008). It was under the CFC banner that he would direct his first works with the NFB, beginning an association that would span eight directed films over twenty-nine years. According to the NFB website, "[h]is work as an independent filmmaker and with the NFB has often focussed on the relationship of the outsider to the world: single parenthood, unemployment and mental illness are some of his subjects." http://www.nfb.ca/portraits/pierre_lasry/en/.

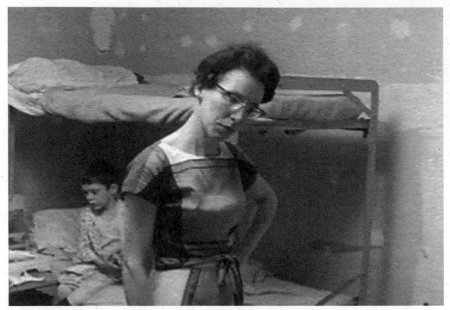

The eponymous single mom of *Mrs. Case* (1969): the caseworker victimizes her but CFC tries to understand her without judgment. Frame enlargement.

most striking thing about Lasry's diptych is the different attitudes taken towards the subjects.

Rather than a coherent outlook across both films, I find a significant divergence: the rhetorical design of *Laurette* echoes the approach of the agency social worker so maligned in *Mrs. Case*, as film design and historical actor adopt interrogative stances in exercising their own power to construct. During each of her visits to the University Settlement, the agency social worker's philanthropic home base, Mrs Case is accused of committing some form of deception and is pushed to take some course of action. During one visit, she is criticized for falsely maintaining that she is in contact with her husband, the children's father, and is advised to do the right thing by telling her kids that he has in fact deserted them. At another meeting, the agency worker implies that Mrs Case is making more money than she reports. Stopping short of an overt accusation, the social worker takes steps towards outing this truth in time for their next visit. In *Laurette*, an interrogative approach arises by way of structural and stylistic devices. Through suggestive editing, it is implied that Laurette refuses to acknowledge the challenges imposed by a child. However, the more problematic instance of getting past false stories and constructing another occurs in relation to coupling. The arrangement of scenes and manipulation of the images give the impression that the filmmaking process helped Laurette move away from self-delusional narratives of self-sufficiency and towards a climactic epiphany regarding the necessity of men. She is assigned a dramatic arc in which her true thoughts are revealed, certainly to the film crew and possibly to herself as well. While the agency worker may not have had much success in determining Mrs Case's behaviour in the historical world, Laurette is made to undergo a transformative experience at the level of representation.

This resonant affinity between bureaucratic social worker and government filmmaker constitutes a variation on a tendency noted by Zoë Druick, who wrote that many CFC films "took the speaking position of privileged state workers' investigation of others' marginalization. A common trope in NFB films found the filmmaker standing in for state representatives, especially in the realm of welfare provision" (2007, 140). While the designs of *Laurette* and the agency social worker in *Mrs. Case* both adopt interrogative stances in their attempts to construct others, these broadly similar tendencies work on different registers. The agency worker's attempts to control her subject occurred in the historical world and were driven by ethical considerations. Taking a charitable view, one could say that the enquiries about money were presumably made in relation to the need for an equitable distribution of limited funds. Similarly, the advice on informing the kids seems to have been motivated by ideas about proper child-rearing. The rhetorical aims of *Mrs. Case* also work towards ethical ends when the social worker is criticized for taking an aggressively one-sided approach in dealing with her client. *Laurette* operates in a different sphere by cultivating a pleasure at the level of the representation, a pleasure that in places crosses over into the erotic. The gradual uncovering of Laurette's private thoughts is framed as an act of seduction, her final confession of desire laced with connotations of consummation. The film process that reveals her true feelings becomes a palpable character that moves in at the moment she comes to terms with her desire. It is as though the film set up her awakening for its own pleasure. The relation between these films gives way to an unsettling irony. While *Mrs. Case* poses an ethical criticism in relation to the misuse of power in the historical world, *Laurette* indulges a perverse enjoyment in the manipulations of an image.

The agency worker's attempts to control her client's behaviour arises in relation to the story Mrs Case tells her children, who are led to believe that she is in regular contact with their father and that he asks how they are doing. The social worker urges her to tell them that he is not returning, saying they will lose trust in her when they discover the truth from someone else. Mrs Case responds that the "time will come when they will know, but by then they will not be interested anymore." Moments later, her defiance softens into ambivalence, and she asks, "How can you tell them when you don't know yourself." The agent ignores this attempt at open communication and continues to press her agenda, the impression being that following her directive would increase her client's chances of receiving additional help. Mrs Case's comment about not knowing what to tell the kids could be taken to indicate either that she believes her husband may return or that if her kids knew their father was gone for good, their ensuing questions and stress would require attention that would be difficult to satisfy, given the financial situation. The social worker seems indifferent to these possibilities, and while it may be good advice to tell the kids, her rigid stance undermines her credibility. The film, by calculated contrast, derives moral authority through its effort to understand its protagonist without passing judgment.

Their other interaction indicates the agent's desire to distribute limited resources equally, as she implies that Mrs Case is not reporting all of her income and, for this reason perhaps, should not be entitled to additional funds. Asked if she has made money with a typewriter, likely provided by the agency, Mrs Case replies that her health difficulties have prevented it (she suffers from leukemia and/or diabetes). The skeptical social worker requests hospital documentation, adding that they are "just for our records." Clearly exceeding the requirements of perfunctory record keeping, this request seems to be motivated by a desire to unmask the deception and justify withholding additional assistance. After briefly indicating the difficulty of obtaining such records, Mrs Case lists a number of her important but unmet needs, such as clothing for her kids. Operating on an equally subtextual level, her inventory of difficulties seems intended to justify the non-reported income and argues the need for additional assistance. The agency worker and Mrs Case talk in veiled meanings, a request for hospital documents suggesting incredulity and the listing of difficulties justifying a deception. The likelihood of these subtextual meanings is reinforced in a subsequent scene in Mrs Case's kitchen, where she tells the camera crew, with a sly grin, that "the typewriter pays good."

By delaying this revelation of monetary subterfuge until after the interview, the film increases viewer sympathy for Mrs Case, for the social worker's distrust is highlighted rather than the accuracy of her suspicions. If the viewer were to watch the interview with the knowledge that Mrs Case had profited from the typewriter, there would be a risk that the agent's cross-examination would be validated. Indeed, the editing temporarily supports Mrs Case's claim – that she is too sick to work – by following the interview with a scene in which she is at the hospital undergoing extensive tests. This sequencing also suggests that the extra money is irrelevant compared to her difficulties, a point that echoes what she implies when, in response to the social worker's implied accusation about hidden funds, she lists her children's difficulties. Because our sympathy for Mrs Case is established early on, the revelation of unreported income can occur later without the risk that our allegiance will shift to the social worker.

The delayed clarification also highlights the film's ability to bring intelligibility to what would otherwise remain an ambiguous exchange. During their interview, Mrs Case and the social worker talk past each other, and it is a few moments before the dynamic of accusation and resistance becomes clear. The subsequent revelation of illicit income confirms this reading and reveals who was correct, albeit, as has been mentioned, in a way that avoids giving credit to the social worker. The film would be easier to follow if viewers learned about the money made before the interview, as they would not need to mentally revisit and amend their previous reading of the interview. The subtext would be readily apparent. Rhetorical tactics of self-legitimization are worked into a cinematic design that heightens our sympathetic response and showcases the film's ability to access hidden information.

Much as the agency worker does in *Mrs. Case,* the format of *Laurette* adopts an oppositional stance in its efforts to complete inadequate statements and structure another person. In one example of this, the editing highlights how Laurette's language conceals the economic difficulties having a child imposes on her. She says, "[N]ow I feel paralyzed, one has to agree, mainly because of money. You're so tied down, you can't go anywhere." While Laurette is careful not to link her child to increased costs and reduced mobility, the editing does exactly that with a shot of her daughter immediately after she makes this observation. The connotation is enhanced by the context of the interview, which takes place at Laurette's Outremont apartment on an evening when her daughter is playing with another single mother's child, an arrangement she tells us allows them, the single parents, to take turns going out. Later on, at work, Laurette notes that the challenges of being a single provider leave her without money after she has covered all her expenses. In the next scene, she enters her apartment and happily calls out the name of her daughter. The child is framed as a cause of difficulty for the second time, more prominently here because of the break in location.

Such implied commentary constitutes an oppositional position because Laurette does not make this association, although she does say that "if I did not have my daughter, I don't know if I would want to live that badly." While she positions her child as a saving grace, the film suggests that her daughter is the cause of her difficult position. This is not to say that her comments don't produce something of a paradox, as the depression she alludes to was triggered by her status as a solo parent and would not have arisen, perhaps, without the child who now provides her with the only reason to live. Regardless, Laurette presumably avoids the connection in order to avoid blaming her child. The film works against this protective instinct by trying to present the child in a light the mother wanted to avoid. The film's game of cat and mouse bears traces of the dynamic between Mrs Case and the agency worker, especially with regard to the concealed income.

Closing in on single mom *Laurette* (1969): erotic connotations that some viewers did not miss. Production still.

An interrogative stance is taken in *Laurette* through the direct manipulation of images. In response to her account of how she left her husband, Lasry says, "I see more pain than that," and presents her laughter in slow motion and facial expressions in freeze-frames. Such stylistic flourishes attempt to reveal the pain she is trying to mask and would have been too brief to notice without the camera being used as a scientific surveillance device. The impression of a secret revealed is most strongly created by the film's conclusion. Discussing older independent women she has worked with, Laurette says that they seem unable to love men and that she does not want to end up like that. Her final musings elaborate on the idea that "it is a man that makes a woman, there is no question about it." In these moments, the audio is desynchronized from the image and can be heard as she drives, the road shown from her point of view and her comments taking the aura of subjective thoughts. Her words are foregrounded by an image track that is reduced to black, a move that figuratively evokes the confessional and heightens the significance of her words. Lasry whispers, "Cut," a performative power utterance that positions him as the grand inquisitor who, having enabled Laurette to realize her truth, can terminate his session. Her comments receive further emphasis through pride of place. Plantinga has summarized the structural importance of endings: "The *overarching* function of the ending is epistemological rather than dramatic. Formal endings guide the backward-directed activity of the spectator in comprehending the film. The ending may fill in gaps, sum up main points, or suggest a 'correct' frame by which the previous data can be interpreted. This backward-directed activity can be achieved by 'retrospective additional patterning,' by which the end adds to or alters the epistemological framework constructed earlier in the text" (1997, 131).

This ending alters a previous framework in which Laurette indicated an equivocal empowerment in her life as a single mother. Despite a painful initial adjustment and the lack of any assurance that her position would be temporary, she seems sincere in saying that living alone has benefits and is "a good way to be." A different impression would have been created had the film ended with her statement "I feel I can make it, I really do." An ending that strongly emphasizes the primacy of men raises the disappointments of singlehood above the advantages of independence and, more subtly, repositions ambivalence as deception. It is as though her comments on the benefits of being single were an attempt to mislead the film crew, and possibly herself along the way. *Laurette* partakes in a game of subject possession that culminates in a forced concession of desire, a rhetorical peripeteia that contains her attempts at independence and valorizes the film's revelatory powers.

The tendency to minimize Laurette's agency extends to the film's surrounding documentation. While she clearly indicates in the film that she left her husband, the NFB catalogue entry states that the film is "a portrayal of a young woman left alone to cope with family problems" (NFB website). This suggests she was left by her husband and reinforces the sense of her reduced power that runs through the film. Just as some of her final comments about men are framed in a way that raises connotations of uncovered secrets, her victim position is enhanced to provide a sense of dramatic relevance. This characterization brings *Laurette* closer to *Mrs. Case* by emphasizing, or indeed outright manufacturing, a victim position in line with the project's ethical or political agenda.

The film's ending constitutes the most unsettling marker of male-centricity. Sexual connotations surface during the shrouded conclusion when the film closes in on Laurette, ready to have its epistemological way with her. Erotic connotations were not missed on late-sixties viewers. As Lasry says, "People kept saying to me 'Did you screw that woman, it's in the dark, are you in her bedroom screwing her?' That is what people used to say" (2008, interview). It seems unlikely that people would have posed such lurid questions without other elements pointing to the gap between a female subject and an all male crew. One such element is Lasry's tone of voice. He constantly whispers to Laurette with a coaxing softness, almost a romantic paternalism, which highlights her status as a single woman. This tone, like the film's various structural and stylistic manipulations, recall Foucault, who in his characterization of the history of sexuality as a prolonged game of sado-masochism discusses "the pleasure that comes of exercising a power that questions, monitors, spies, searches out, palpitates, brings to light" (1978, 45). In an overlap of the film's conclusion, Foucault also suggests that the confessional prefigured subsequent power dynamics that would involve sexuality and power.

The final scene also connects with a number of ideas developed by Bill Nichols. One of these is vivification, a term he uses to indicate representational strategies that help overcome the gap between representation and represented. During such moments, "the sense that this reality now comes before us, as though for the first time, remains powerful. This is largely because reality is represented with an eye to the text's own project, its own argument" (1991, 232). In *Laurette*, vivification aids the impression of a film that brings us elusive truth. The freeze-frames of Laurette's hidden expression are examples of this, although this impression is created most forcefully at the conclusion, during which the film becomes a living process that, in revealing the concealed, seems to unfold as we watch. Lasry takes this one step further, however, by applying this effect to the thought processes of a character within the film, as Laurette is made to voice her concealed desire as though for the first time. Vivification in *Laurette* also connects with Nichols's comments on pornography, in which "knowledge and objects cannot simply be acquitted or taken; the act or process of knowing/possessing must itself be described and documented in far greater detail than what any plot requires" (1991, 215). The aura of the confessional suggests part of the process at work in *Laurette*. In the film, however, vivification does not produce a less-mediated sense of life but, on the contrary, emphasizes the process of representation over the primacy of the represented and evokes a pleasure that undermines the work's objectivity.

Despite contesting Laurette's claims of independence, her relatively comfortable position also led to greater possibilities for, and therefore more emphasis on, her future options. At numerous points in the film, she discusses where her life may be going. These kinds of speculations are largely unheard from the comparatively marginalized Mrs Case. Her past history and future desires receive minimal attention, though the film does end with a bleak commentary as the camera pans from the back porch of her Little Burgundy apartment to rest on the image of a dead end, an emblematic shot implying the terminal nature of her situation. Perhaps the most inadvertent reinscription of agency occurs in the parallel but distinct etiologies of the films' titles, both of which were taken from scenes in the films. Laurette states her first name to a friend in a conversation in which she has power. Mrs Case has her last name spoken to her by the agency worker during one of their guilt sessions. Both films have eponymic titles, but only *Mrs. Case* is an aptronym, being a "name that fits the nature and character of a person and/or their occupation" (Cuddon 1991, 55). Surely this was the result of either coincidence or irony, although as a sign of reduced agency it resonates with the films' contrasting assumptions regarding their subjects' future options.

Single mothers were covered in other CFC films, the most sustained English treatment being Kathleen Shannon's eleven-film Working Mothers series (1974–75), which helped prompt the development of Studio D, the Women's Unit (see Fraticelli, chapter 29, this volume). Two of Shannon's films take up similar themes to those explored in *Mrs. Case* and *Laurette*, but are instructive in their contrasting approach to representation and subject agency. *Would I Ever Like to Work* (1974) is about a single welfare mother with seven kids. In contrast to *Mrs. Case*, the entire film consists of a direct interview and explores the mother's subjective history, asking how and why she married so young and had so many children. The disappointment of not being able to live a different life is made explicit. Addressing the subjective desires that surround children and marriage, " ... *and They Lived Happily Ever After"* (1975) looks at the social forces that idealize the traditional family and encourage premature marriage. It does this though a direct deconstruction of glossy media images that position marriage and baby-making as a woman's most rewarding prospect. A variety of individuals comment directly on the glossy pictures, and the film makes no attempt to qualify, frame, or undermine their comments. Shannon's films reduce the presence of the filmmaker and increase the agency of the subject. *Laurette* does the opposite.

One of the major concerns of the Lasry team in making *Mrs. Case* and *Laurette* was that the films might exploit the poor. Referencing early NFB misfires, Lasry noted that "at the National Film Board we had a program called Challenge for Change, and we managed to fuck up the lives of so many people by going six weeks into a neighbourhood, and nobody would speak to them afterwards" (Lasry interview, 2008). Thus, in addition to limiting the shooting time to about two days per subject, he avoided an exclusive focus on the poor (Lasry interview, 2008). The desire to avoid the pitfalls that sometimes happen when the privileged investigate the marginal is also evident in an archival statement of purpose, a pre-production palimpsest: "[T]he three filmmakers decide to take the problem away from their middle class point of view and go and research the problem by taking their camera and recorders to the ~~poor~~ people" (NFB, "Single Parent Family," 1968). That the word poor was written and removed suggests the tenacity of this class-based perspective, for despite efforts to the contrary this bias managed to surreptitiously infiltrate the final products.

Such an influence, however, does not appear to have operated in the way suggested in Lasry's quote or in the pre-production statement of purpose. Rather, it was the representation of *Laurette*, clearly the better off of the two subjects, that seems to have gone off in a questionable direction. Perhaps her social standing, in being perceived as closer to the filmmakers, provided a comfort level and confidence that enabled the final product to end up as a New Wave exercise more concerned with the interesting than the accurate. Indeed, the treatment of Mrs Case suggests that her poverty functioned as a firewall against the suspiciously creative.[2] With regard to *Laurette*, the attempt to avoid one form of exploitation may have provided the filmmaker with the false sense of security needed to engage in another. During the long nights when the director-editor was alone in the editing room, working with the image of a young woman, it is possible that guards were let down, that liberties were taken, and that a film that prided itself on being able to entrap its subject was itself caught in the seductive but ultimately destructive lure of representational authority.

2 Interestingly, Lasry maintained contact with both his "single mom" subjects – with Mrs Case until she returned home to the Maritimes in the late 1980s and with Laurette to the present day. According to Lasry, the latter, NFB documentary filmmaker Laurette Deschamps, best known for the Studio D productions *On Our Own* (1984, also about previously married women), and *No Longer Silent* (1986, on women in India), credits him with helping her break into documentary (Lasry, e-mail communication, 2 May 2008).

28 *Paper Wheat*: Alternative Theatre Meets Alternative Filmmaking

■

CHRISTOPHER MEIR

This kind of theatre is really new. To all of a sudden have a show about them, when they've been hearing about British and American plays, and now all of a sudden there's a play about them. "No one makes plays in Saskatchewan, and if they do, it [*sic*] can't be very good." And then they come and it's dynamite. It's not just good, it's more that good; it's like boom, click and there's a spark and they connect.

With these words, spoken near the end of the film *Paper Wheat* (Albert Kish, 1979), Andras Tahn, creative director of the 25th Street Theatre, expresses the excitement that had surrounded the stage play of the same name. Released in 1979, *Paper Wheat* was one of the last films produced for the Challenge for Change/Société nouvelle (CFC/SN) program. The film was also one of the program's most popular productions, having been broadcast on the CBC in 1979 and subsequently excerpted for the NFB film *Scenes from Paper Wheat* (Rita Roy, 1981). Tahn's words specifically refer to how the stage production of *Paper Wheat* attempted to revolutionize both the content of Saskatchewan theatre and the way it addressed its audience. The play, assembled largely from interviews with members of farming communities across the province, reached out to local audiences and told them their own stories in a way that mainstream theatre at the time simply did not do. Such innovative production methods and unprecedented attempts to reach local audiences grew out of the 25th Street Theatre's embrace of the "really new" kind of theatre that Tahn describes above, a movement that has come to be known in the history of world and Canadian drama as "alternate" or "alternative theatre."[1]

This chapter offers an account of the alternative theatre movement in Canada as a vital historical and cultural context for *Paper Wheat*. In so doing, it demonstrates how the form of the film itself adapts the formal and

1 Following Usmiani (1983, 28), I will use "alternative theatre" instead of "alternate theatre," as the latter term refers to Toronto-based manifestations of the movement, whereas the former is more pan-Canadian and international in scope.

political concerns of the play while also documenting an important moment in Canada's and Saskatchewan's cultural history in its attempt to make a positive intervention in the life of the nation and the province. Finally, it elucidates the shared concerns of this theatre movement and the ethos behind CFC/SN; given historical hindsight, it is more than fitting that a major work from this movement should end up being the subject of a CFC/SN film.

CONTEXTUALIZING *PAPER WHEAT*: TOWARDS A CANADIAN NATIONAL THEATRE AND ALTERNATIVE THEATRE IN CANADA

In what is one of the many parallels between the different forms of the national media, Canadian theatre, like Canadian cinema, has had great difficulty establishing itself as a distinct entity on both the national and the international scene. Up until the 1960s, a distinctly Canadian theatre in terms of artistic traditions or national audience base was non-existent. As Mark Czarnecki has argued, the causes of this were numerous and included logistical factors such as Canada's small population density relative to its large geographical size, with even the major urban centres spread out over great distances (1985, 35–6). Czarnecki points to the preferences of Canadian audiences – which he terms "unconsciously colonized audiences" – for productions from the United States, Britain, and France as a major obstacle in the development of an indigenous Canadian theatre (36). The absence of a truly national theatre led in the early 1960s to the commissioning of a Canada Council report on ways to foster such development (35–6). The report's major recommendation was the establishment of a regional theatre system that would provide government support for theatrical centres across the nation. While the regional system was later scrapped, it nonetheless helped to lay the foundation for what would come to be known as Canadian alternative theatre.

The alternative theatre movement was global in scope and began in the early 1960s in both Europe and the United States. From its inception, it sought to change both the aesthetic practices of the theatre and the place that the medium holds in public life. It was overtly political, producing left wing–oriented works such as the anti-Vietnam War musical *Hair*, which became the most internationally famous product of the movement and was later adapted to the cinema. Alternative theatre in Canada absorbed many of the distinguishing characteristics of its global counterpart, a number of which are central to an analysis of *Paper Wheat*. These include (Usmiani 1983, 2):

■ A distinct system of production featuring companies outside of the mainstream theatrical establishment. The conservative, pseudo-colonial theatrical establishment in Canada is typified by the Stratford Festival.

▪ Aesthetic tendencies that were overtly revolutionary and experimental in nature, often modelled after the practices of Bertolt Brecht and the privileging of theatrical process over finished product.

▪ Overtly revolutionary social and political ideology that acted in tandem with those aesthetic practices.

▪ A commitment to making theatre a popular and indeed populist medium rather than an elitist, high art institution. James Garrard, founder of one of the most important alternative theatre companies in Canada, Theatre Passe-Muraille, often said that he wanted to make theatre "as popular as bowling" (44).

▪ Production methods that were collaborative and collective in nature. As Usmiani puts it, alternative theatre rejected the traditional hierarchy between playwright, actors, and audience in favour of a model in which the entire company was responsible for assembling a script and staging a performance, with actors researching and preparing their own roles (46).

▪ Finally, Canadian alternative theatre distinguished itself from similar productions around the world by its commitment to national and local concerns, as it overtly sought to comment on Canada's history and cultural identity (2; Usmiani 1985, 49).

It is perhaps easy to see a number of parallels between different alternative theatre productions in terms of production practices, political sympathies, and institutional contexts.

Within English-speaking Canada, the most influential early practitioners of alternative theatre were found at Toronto's Theatre Passe-Muraille (literally translated as "theatre without walls"). On the strength of a string of highly successful productions, including *The Farm Show*, *The Immigrant Show*, and others, the company achieved an unprecedented degree of celebrity for a Canadian theatre company outside of Stratford. Theatre Passe-Muraille went on to inspire a number of companies across Canada, among them the Mummers Troupe in Newfoundland, Theatre Network in Alberta, the Tamahnous Theatre in Vancouver, and the 25th Street Theatre in Saskatoon, the creators of *Paper Wheat* (Benson and Conolly 1987, 85). In addition to establishing the precedent and providing the inspiration for these companies, Theatre Passe-Muraille also provided the personnel who founded and/or shaped the artistic direction of many of these theatres; for example, actor Paul Thompson of the company would move west to the 25th Street Theatre.[2] The stage version of *Paper Wheat* was a particularly successful production within this movement in Canada, touring much of the province and ultimately the

2 "25th Street Theatre," in *Canadian Theatre Encyclopedia*.

Paper Wheat (1979): Challenge for Change echoing the ethos of the alternative theatre movement. *Right*, CFC director Albert Kish. Production still.

nation. It was eventually seen in over thirty locations by over sixty thousand people.³ Such a successful run on stages across the nation led eventually to the documentary produced under the auspices of CFC/SN.

DOCUMENTING *PAPER WHEAT*

The two main goals of the film *Paper Wheat* were the documentation of the phenomenon of the stage play, specifically, and alternative theatre in Canada, generally, and the interrelated and overlapping goal of adapting the play itself, its major themes, and its social message to another medium. The film thus presents *Paper Wheat* and alternative theatre as cultural and social phenomena.

Featured at the beginning, middle, and ending of the film are images of the play's cast loading their van and heading to the next destination. The film's narrative is thus punctuated by reminders that in some ways it is the 25th Street Theatre Company, and not the play per se, that is focus of the film. When we first see the cast, we are introduced to them and to the production by means of a radio broadcast that tells the listening audience about each cast member (with the film cutting to the individual actors as the radio announcer describes them), as well as about the historical subject matter and

3 "*Paper Wheat*," in *Canadian Theatre Encyclopedia*.

unique production methods of the play itself. By using a radio broadcast instead of the convention of scripted narration, the filmmakers emphasize the popularity of the play. Not only does the announcer literally tell the audience that the play is popular, but the radio broadcast itself serves as a reification of the word-of-mouth buzz that surrounded the production at the time.

Talking-head interviews make up a large portion of the film and are very important to its strategy of documenting the production. At various points in the film, members of the company's creative team talk to the camera about alternative theatre and the production itself. The director of the production, Guy Sprung, and the artistic director of the company, the aforementioned Tahn, provide particularly important interviews in this vein. At one point, Sprung explains the unique working methods that went into the making of the play, specifically the collaborative techniques characteristic of alternative theatre – which saw the actors research and devise their own roles – as well as the structure for the play – a three-act exploration of the settler history of the province, the founding of the wheat pools, and the ongoing challenges that face the Saskatchewan wheat farmer. Aside from this segment, it is Tahn who provides the bulk of the exposition within the film, offering historical background and outlining the aesthetic goals of the play. While making his way across the countryside handing out posters for the play, Tahn explains the historical background of the wheat pool movement and the reasons that the company chose to make this the focus of the play. Later, in the passage of dialogue that appears in the epigraph above, Tahn provides the most succinct (and impassioned) description of the aims and goals of the play within the larger context of the approach to the medium taken by alternative theatre.

Tahn's short speech on the virtues of alternative theatre and *Paper Wheat* follows a sequence in which we see the cast reading aloud from, and commenting on, a newspaper piece on the contemporary vogue for "Canadiana," a zeitgeist of which the play, the alternative theatre movement, and the film itself were all part. This short sequence reminds us of the buzz surrounding the production (much like the radio commentary that opens the film) and reiterates the national and local import of what we have seen throughout the film. The film is interspersed as well with moments of fly-on-the-wall observation that collectively document the artistically and politically progressive nature of the play, its creators, and its creation. These moments include backstage interactions between actors, actors speaking to audience members, and, of course, scenes from live performances of the play.

There is more to say about this final category of observational moments, where the strategies of simultaneously documenting and adapting the play coalesce most forcefully, but for now it is important to observe how these scenes relate to the concerns of alternative theatre. In a scene midway through the film, we see two of the company's actors, Lubomir Mykytiuk and David Francis, discussing Mykytiuk's feeling that his depiction of a Ukrainian settler is inauthentic, stereotyped, and clownish. He fears that the local audience may recognize the representation as false, since they are familiar with the real-life equivalents of the character. Such reservations from Mykytiuk convey the actors' concern over representing their subjects fairly (an issue very familiar to CFC/SN filmmakers), as well as their commitment to researching their roles and making sure that their audiences can relate to their characters. This scene is a counterpoint to a later scene in which Mykytiuk meets an elderly member of the audience who is clearly of Ukrainian descent. When the two men begin speaking cheerfully in Ukrainian, we are led to think that the performance was in fact well received by the audience it sought to simultaneously entertain and give voice to.

It is the observational footage of live performances of *Paper Wheat* that makes up the largest portion of the film. While this footage acts as a document of the play, preserving it in a way that anthologizing the script could not accomplish, it also allows the filmmakers to adapt it for the viewing audience, finding filmic equivalents for the play's unique achievement within its own medium. Viewers of *Paper Wheat* are given a number of the play's most entertaining and memorable scenes, but more importantly they are given passages that are emblematic of what was new and interesting about the play in terms of stagecraft and its political message. Among these are depictions of the hardships faced by early settlers (captured memorably in one scene by means of a sliding tablecloth), the rather complex economic principles behind the wheat pools (illustrated by, among other things, a tap dance duet, with each dancer wearing one shoe), and the economic fragility of the farmer today (conveyed by Mykytiuk juggling an ever-shrinking ball of bread that represents the farmer's profits from bread production). The ways in which these passages are edited also helps to drive home the importance of the play and the alternative theatre movement. Intercut with each extract from the performances are three kinds of footage: shots of a visibly appreciative audience, often composed of people old enough to have living memories of the historical moment depicted in the play; archival footage and/or photographs from the historical period in question; and, finally, segments of interviews with audience members, farmers, and other people with first-hand experience of the issues represented in the passages from the play.

The film audience is first introduced to this structure by way of the on-screen introduction of the play's audience. As a live audience watches the play, a matching shot of a crowd is introduced, in this case an archival photograph of a prairie theatre audience. This juxtaposition, arriving so early in the film and emphasizing as it does the aforementioned elderly demographic of the audience, immediately conveys the idea of bringing a collective, living history to the stage. This idea is crucial to both the play and the film, as it speaks to the unique connection that alternative theatre sought to make with its audience. Subsequent sequences continue to employ, and expand upon, this editing structure. An ironic musical number from the play (in which a farmer, in song, equates his reliance on his wife, "Bessie," with the way he relies on other beasts of burden) is intercut with laughing faces of older women in the audience, archival photographs of prairie women, and interviews with women who grew up on the prairies during the settler years about how difficult life was when they were young. Here, the editing once again underscores the living-memory aspects of the play, not only by means of the archival photographs but also by means of the interviews, which feature first-hand accounts of the grim realities of the period that the song's humorous tone is meant to contrast.

The structure also displays the extent to which the actors researched their roles. The interviews verify and add depth to the representation, and the photographs often accentuate the accuracy of the portrayal of the play's characters and authenticity of the costumes. A photograph of a prairie wife, for example, is matched by the actress playing Bessie who is dressed in the same fashion. Nearly every extract from the play is adapted in a similar manner. For example, a series of archival photographs illustrates the grain elevator system as retired farmers explain how speculators and grain companies used "paper wheat" to manipulate markets and exploit the farmer, leading to the need for the wheat pools.

This structure is employed most poignantly in the juggling sequence near the end of the film. As previously discussed, this sequence is concerned with the metaphoric depiction of the continuing difficulties farmers face. Here, in a style distinct from the rest of the film, the montage features contemporary rather than archival footage and interviews with both young and old people discussing the generation gap that left contemporary farmers alienated from the cooperative system. As an older farmer talks about the ignorance of today's farmers and younger farmers discuss their own cynicism about the pools, the selected footage depicts both the continuing danger of corporate farming concerns (a menacing shot of a Cargill silo, matched with a speculator character from the play who praises the ethos of free enterprise) and the continuing presence of the co-op in contemporary life (by way of endless images of co-op–branded products and shops). In the final sequences of the film, which seek to adapt the play itself, the goals of the play and those of the alternative theatre movement, the film, and the CFC/SN program at large coalesce in the form of a plea to those working the wheat fields today: remember your heritage, embrace the cooperatives, and collectively change your own futures as well as those of the province and the nation.

ALTERNATIVE THEATRE AND THE CFC/SN ETHOS

The juggling sequence demonstrates the logical convergence of the alternative theatre movement and the ethos of the CFC/SN program. The parallels include a production context that remained outside of the mainstream (in terms both of CFC/SN's marginal status within the NFB and of the Board's role as a minor player in the U.S.-dominated Canadian mediascape) and one that emphasized collaboration and collective production over individual artistry or accomplishment. An additional parallel in terms of production circumstances is the reversal of the audience/artist dynamic. For alternative theatre, this reversal meant involving audiences in the creation of plays as well as in individual performances; for CFC/SN, this often meant giving editorial control to the subjects of films (e.g., Colin Low's production methods during the making of the Fogo Island films [see Wiesner, chapter 10, this volume) or giving the camera to the subjects themselves (e.g., VTR St-Jacques/ Opération boule de neige, Bonnie Sherr Klein, 1969 [see Hénaut and Klein, chapter 3, this volume]). The two movements attempted to break the aura surrounding their respective media and chose to empower their audience, efforts that reflected the Brechtian influence often evidenced in the works of each movement, both of which sought to foreground process over content in a variety of ways. Alternative theatre's dedication to exploring Canadian culture and history, particularly for regions that had been marginalized within Canadian society, is paralleled by the CFC/SN's mandate and indeed by the mission statement of the National Film Board/Office national du film as a whole. Understanding these parallels between alternative theatre and CFC/SN, one might perhaps be surprised that more plays from the period were not taken up as objects for adaptation or experimentation by the program. Nonetheless, *Paper Wheat*, both in terms of its concept and content, demonstrates the powerful links between the alternative theatre movement in Canada of the 1960s and 1970s and its artistic and politically active contemporaries in CFC/SN.

"Would I Ever Like to Work": The "Working Mothers" Films and the Construction of Community

■

RINA FRATICELLI

AUTHOR'S NOTE

When I joined Studio D as executive producer in March of 1987, Kathleen Shannon, its founding executive producer, had been gone for over a year. Screening the studio's formidable body of work, beginning with the "Working Mothers" (WM) films, was one of the ways of orienting and connecting myself with the founding vision and philosophy of the already-legendary studio. Then, as now, I was struck by the enduring power of these eleven short films and, in particular, by the political intelligence and narrative impact of the seven deceptively simple one-woman films in the group.

I

The woman stands at her kitchen sink washing dishes, her seven hyper kids at the table behind her, alternately inhaling their lunch and making mayhem with it. We hear the voice of the filmmaker off-screen casually ask, "Would you like to work?" The pure longing in the answer, "Oh, would I *ever* like to work," packs a punch, providing the film with its title.

Would I Ever Like to Work is one of the eleven short films that make up the 1974–75 Working Mothers films.[1] This groundbreaking collection of films captures some of the most enduring and salient features of early second wave feminism and provides a sobering reminder of the continuing relevance of its key issues. They speak, on the one hand, to the entrenchment of women's second-class status via specific political and economic strategies;

1 Each of these films was subtitled "Part of a Group of Films about Working Mothers." As Doris Mae Oulton put it in an e-mail exchange with the author, the term "series" was studiously avoided because it was seen to falsely suggest that "more would follow or that the stories would follow one another. We saw these (films) as a group with discrete stories with no relationship to one another except in the sense that they are all about women and work but there was no attempt to link them – i.e., serialize them" (Oulton, e-mail communication, 23 August 2008).

and, on the other, to the liberating tension inherent in the linking of personal narrative to collective experience. What has changed most in the thirty-five years since these films were produced is not, sadly, the status of women or their marginalization in our film culture, but the willingness of government to acknowledge and address this reality.

Kathleen Shannon produced and directed the series within the National Film Board of Canada's (NFB's) legendary Challenge for Change/Société nouvelle (CFC/SN) program (1967–80). Part of a wide-ranging and generously funded federal strategy, CFC/SN sought to identify communities at risk of being left behind in Canada's exciting new knowledge-based society and proposed "to help them understand and participate in the changes occurring in their social environment through the combined utilization of film and other means of audiovisual communication" (Cabinet Document 622, 11 June 1969). While the WM films were a natural fit with CFC/SN's objective of using film, in the words of the government film commissioner Hugo McPherson (1968), "to help eradicate the causes of poverty by provoking basic social change," the eleven films bore a deeper allegiance to the core politics and strategies of 1970s feminism.

As Elizabeth Anderson describes it, throughout the late sixties and early seventies, women were coming together to lay the foundation for a wide-ranging spectrum of initiatives that would build feminist culture over the next decade: "One should not underestimate the way an active and visible North American women's movement and burgeoning international film movement contributed to a climate more receptive to the importance of women's cultural production at the NFB" (1999, 43). In Canada, government initiatives like the Royal Commission on the Status of Women, independent collectives like Women's Press (Toronto) and Women in Focus (Vancouver), and lobby groups like the National Action Committee on the Status of Women had been evolving throughout the mid-sixties to early seventies. More specifically, Anderson cites San Francisco Newsreel's 1971 *The Woman's Film*, which "focused on social structural definitions of women's issues and intercut footage of interviews from several different women's lives. This format, a blending of the individual and collective, the personal and political, was replicated in Shannon's 'Working Mothers' series ... Both the individual and the collective approaches, in their attempt to balance the stories of individual women's lives with an analysis of how all were defined and delimited by socio-political structures, served as prototypes for other feminist documentarists" (44). Reproductive freedom and the allied demand for affordable childcare constituted the ground zero of second wave feminism, much as legal personhood and the right to vote did for the earlier suffragette movement.

Tapping into the primal duality of power/fear inherent in women's biology, the Working Mothers films spoke to Everywoman. The duality was a great leveller, uniting women of every class, race, and region, from puberty to menopause and beyond. Joy, a research biologist, and the subject of *Mothers Are People*, another of the Working Mothers films, puts the matter more bluntly: "To have a child is just a biological happening. It does not have to be the end of your life, for heaven's sake; you don't have to be punished because you just happen to be the sex which bears them!" If women are being punished for being the child-bearers, the films tell us, it is not their biology that is to blame but the specific and systemic ways in which that biology is read and constrained by patriarchal society. For mothers who had experienced their frustrations or limitations in that role as personal failings, seeing these films – particularly in the context of an intimate screening followed by an engaged discussion with other women – was liberating.

II

When Shannon set out on the Working Mothers project, she was making a single film about an overarching issue. The federal "partner" for this project, the Department of Manpower and Immigration, had requested a fifty-one-minute film that would provide the "definitive answer" to the puzzle of women's absence from the labour force (Oulton, telephone interview, 12 August 2008). Why were working women not rejoining the labour force after motherhood? What obstacles were they encountering? Why were there wage discrepancies between men and women?

Once Shannon began to edit her interviews, however, it became clear that no single film could do justice either to the individual women's experiences or to the issue as a whole. Doris Mae Oulton, who had been brought into the CFC/SN program as a distribution consultant, recalls being in the editing room as Shannon struggled to wrestle these individual vignettes into a cohesive whole. "They were little gems," she recalls. "It was clear they needed to stand on their own" (Oulton, telephone, 2008). Together they began to conceive a different approach to the project, one that would provide a distinct cinematic space for each woman and allow a larger female narrative to emerge through the aggregation of these specific voices.

The decision had significant and enduring consequences. To counter resistance to the proposed new format from both the NFB and its federal sponsor, a team of filmmakers, distribution staff, and community workers were dispatched across the country to conduct a series of test screenings of rough cuts of the films with small groups of women in a range of local community settings. "It was what some of us had always wanted to do: undertake an experiment in Challenge for Change distribution, where the starting point was the 'disadvantaged group' featured in the films rather than the NFB distribution system" (Oulton, telephone, 2008).

The biggest question was how could women be reached where many of them actually were, in their homes, in offices, in factories, in restaurants (rather than through the usual clubs and associations that use NFB films). What evolved was the "multiplier" workshop for a cross-section of community women with energy – and contacts (Shannon et al., chapter 7, this volume).[2] Oulton describes the results: "Wherever we went, the response was overwhelming. It confirmed what we had all sensed in Kathleen's editing room. Women wanted to talk about what they'd seen and heard in the films, and the length of these films was perfect for that. They were succinct conversation-starters" (Oulton, e-mail, 2008).

These intimate screenings, followed by discussions and facilitated workshops, were well suited to the political times and the growing practice of women meeting in small "consciousness-raising" groups. "The term had been coined by an American, Kathie Sarachild: women would meet regularly and talk from their own experience. It was to have nothing to do with gossip; groups set out to explore both what women had in common and the issues that divided them. The overall aim was to begin to understand private fears and discontents in a wider context, to discover, through 'sharing, recognizing, naming' their political implications. As Juliet Mitchell remarked, 'women come into the movement from the unspecific frustrations of their own private lives, and find [that] what they thought was an individual dilemma is a social predicament'" (Walter 2005, 112).

The unequivocal success of the screenings led to approval of the format change, but the experience of travelling with the films to gatherings of small groups of women across the country had an even greater effect on Shannon. Watching the impact of the films – the quality of dialogue they unleashed, the personal validation and sense of community they engendered among those present – confirmed her conviction that the films were incomplete in themselves and could be completed only by viewers in discussion with each other: "People who come to see the films expecting to be told 'where the women's movement is at' will be disappointed. The women's movement is wherever a group of women meet together as women. I like to see the films in that context, used as ways to get people communicating. Such an approach shifts the focus in an important way. The people coming together are the event and the films become a contribution to that event" (Shannon et al., 1975, 6).

2 A special edition of *Access*, the CFC/SN newsletter (no. 14 [Spring 1975]), was devoted to the Working Mothers films. In addition to the conversation reprinted in chapter 7 of this volume, the issue also includes a number of personal reflections by Shannon and a discussion with Rosemary Sullivan, as well as a number of unattributed quotes.

This philosophy – emphasizing the primacy of the audience's needs, the role of women's media as a means rather than an end, and the value of test screenings – not only set the distribution strategy for the WM films, but also became a founding principle of Studio D's approach to filmmaking and distribution. In fact, the network of local women's groups cultivated by the WM distribution team would continue to play an important role in the work of the studio throughout its life (1975–96).

Emphasizing film as both core content for a neglected constituency and as a vehicle for social interaction was far from exclusive to the NFB or to the early days of Canadian feminist media. In Lisa Steele's short history of women's video art production in Canada, Sara Diamond, describing the prodigious output between 1981 and 1983 of Amelia Productions, the Vancouver-based feminist video co-op, says: "You did the work to get it out, to represent, because a voice had to be given. There wasn't a lot of discussion about how it could be better. We just had to do the work. There was always something to record. If we didn't do it, it wouldn't be done. The only conscious choice was to be nontraditional in terms of documentary. By that we meant we wouldn't have a voice-over" (Steele 1987, 50). The WM films had the same sense of urgency to capture and communicate the undocumented reality of women's lives in the most direct and unmediated manner possible. The film subjects speak directly to the camera/Shannon, who is occasionally present onscreen but more frequently present only through the sound of her voice, asking questions. Shannon plays the role of an engaged listener and witness to each woman's account, standing in for the eventual audience and anticipating the dynamic of the screenings. It is an effective device, creating a sense of formality that validates the subject's voice and experience within an atmosphere of intimacy and confidence.

III

The Working Mothers films were created and distributed at a particularly propitious historical moment, just far enough into the second wave of feminism (or women's liberation movement as it was then more commonly known) to be informed by this small but rapidly expanding grassroots and intellectual movement but before it had become engaged in the exhausting (though critically necessary) debates and divisions that would absorb it a few years later.

The 1960s New Left world of Vietnam protests, civil rights activism, and Saul Alinsky's war on poverty saw a generation of educated, politicized, and committed young women working long, heady hours as community organizers alongside their activist boyfriends and "comrades" only to find themselves considerably less welcome on the podium and in the editorial committees. A few years later, a great many of them would find themselves at home and isolated, raising children and, as likely as not, working part-time outside the home to subsidize their partners' further education or careers. But unlike the generation of women before them, who had been summarily ejected from their workplaces at the end of the war, this generation would come together to break out of the disempowering solitude of the nuclear home and found a revolution.

Not Joan, though.[3] The welfare mother in *Would I Ever Like to Work* is in her twenties with seven children under the age of twelve, four of them preschoolers. She "had to" get married at sixteen to her nineteen-year-old boyfriend, she tells us, and her Catholicism, along with her fear of losing her children, kept her tied to a physically abusive husband for far too long: "Oh, would I ever like to work. As a waitress, I could live better ... get away from these monsters. I'm a lousy homemaker. I can't take the noise of those kids anymore; they get on my nerves ... fighting all the time ... running in and out. Mummy this and mummy that; I lose my temper. I'm swatting when they shouldn't be swatted. They shouldn't be beaten all the time. I would be a better mother if I could get out of the house." The childcare that might take her out of this situation for even a few hours a day is unaffordable on the wages of an unskilled woman with four preschool children, even if it were available; so the dreamed-of "work" would elude her for a few more years at least.

Each of the eleven films in the series approaches its theme from a different vantage point. Ten are documentaries and one is animated. Three of the documentaries explore the subject through group discussions; these provide a general overview, a little context, and a general introduction to the subject of the working mother. The strength of the series, though, lies in the seven films that focus on a single individual who relates, usually directly to the audience/camera or to our surrogate (Shannon), the particulars of her situation.

In *Mothers Are People*, Joy, a Jamaican-Canadian research biologist and widowed mother, is still pained and embarrassed by the lie she had to tell – that she would *never* allow her children's needs to interfere with her job – to secure her position.

Cathy, the head of a university department, describes herself as a "tiger on a tight leash" – the title of her film. While she appears to be the best off financially of all the women, her situation makes it very clear that there is "no such thing as security in the question of child care" for either mothers or

3 None of the seven subjects of the individual profiles was identified in the films. All but one, Alanis Obomsawin (*Our Dear Sisters*), were later identified – by their first names only – in the Spring 1975 *Access* devoted to the WM films.

Would I Ever Like to Work (1974): a small boy helps his welfare mom do the dishes in the most famous of the Working Mothers series. Production still.

caregivers. "The society we live in doesn't accord much prestige to house-keepers and babysitters," she points out dryly, and that reality leads to insecurity for both the mothers and the childcare workers. As an educator, Cathy sees the impact of women's double workload on her students: "Insecurity is, I think, very marked in the adult student. They tend to be the best and brightest, having the life experience as well as the academic credentials; but they don't have enough leisure. They lack peace of mind. The result is that they don't work as creatively as they could if it were possible to free their mind for a certain period during the week when all they had to think about was their studies. Learning is a question of having the time to think ... the mind is inevitably divided."

Joy and Cathy, like the other working mothers in this group, undermine the notion of a "working mother" as singular fixed identity. Their narratives expose the multiple layers of being that this role obscures: the moral being, the intellectual being, the creative being, the sexual being. They reveal, in a word, the complex, multi-layered female person behind the role.

It is the two Aboriginal women in the group who most clearly frame mothering and work as a problem only as it collides with mainstream Canadian culture. In *Our Dear Sisters*, Abenaki performer and filmmaker Alanis Obomsawin, a single mother, takes her child with her wherever she performs, confident that the child will be welcome and included. Rose, the Métis mother in *Like the Trees*, describes how she came to reject the contradictions and tensions between motherhood and personhood, Native and European, so pronounced in urban Canadian society, for a life informed by the more practical and generous rigours of nature. Cathy concludes: "If there are going to be institutions taking over the mother's role, [women] must invent them ... but the working mother hasn't the time, energy, power to do that; it's not yet seen as being in the national interest."

Over the next decade, and especially in the eighties, this notion of the universality of women's experience would largely give way to "identity" politics, moving feminism into a very different stage. African-American writers Audre Lorde and bell hooks, among others, would remind feminists that women with radically different life experiences could not be presumed to have identical interests and priorities. As bell hooks writes in her 1984 essay "Margin to Centre," "liberation means the freedom of a mother finally to quit her job – to live the life of a capitalist stay-at-home, as it were ... To be able to work and to have to work are two very different matters" (cited in Walter 2005, 102).

For Joan, the mother in *Would I Ever Like to Work*, though, it is relief from the isolating, unremitting job of being the ever-present sole parent to seven young children that she seeks, even more that the wages which would barely replace welfare; that, and her belief that a few hours a day away from her children would make her a better mother to them.

IV

This takes us back to the Working Mothers collection's relationship to the Challenge for Change/Société nouvelle program as a whole. Official rhetoric about CFC/SN provides an invaluable glimpse of the optimistic and expansive vision of Canada that prevailed within the public sector at the time – a Canada in which the regrettable gap between the haves and have-nots would speedily be dispatched through a muscular combination of governmental will and community empowerment. Within CFC/SN, the WM initiatives (and their French-language counterpart, En tant que femmes [see Fortin, chapter 12, this volume]) provided belated, if vital, recognition that women as a group were exactly the sort of constituency this program had been designed to serve.

The notion of working with and through communities, as opposed to individuals, lay at the heart of the entire CFC/SN program. CFC/SN targeted problems that affected communities as a whole and was premised on the conviction that the remedies lay within the community itself (not with experts

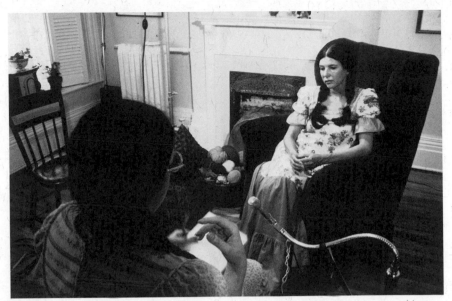

Our Dear Sisters (1975): emerging filmmaker Alanis Obomsawin as documentary subject
In the Working Mothers series. Production still.

outside it) if only it had the tools necessary to access and fully exploit its
resources: "The program employs the medium of film and videotape to help
Canadians identify situations in need of change. It teaches people to use communications techniques so that they themselves can find the solutions to their
problems. The program seeks to make people aware of their problem-solving
capacity, and to give them a voice in shaping decisions that affect their own
lives" (NFB/ONF Annual Report, 1970/71).

A more perfect description of the premises and principles of the women's
movement would be hard to find, yet nowhere in the plethora of enthusiastic reports, memoranda, and newsletters celebrating the early successes of
CFC/SN is there any indication that women had ever been considered as one
of these disadvantaged communities worthy of the program's resources. This
in spite of the fact that the Royal Commission on the Status of Women had
been (however reluctantly) struck in 1967, a formal and public acknowl-
edgment that women's status had to be redressed.

Instead, CFC/SN's target communities were described in very general
terms (the disadvantaged, the poor), sometimes in terms of their occupations
(fisherman, gold and uranium miners, migrant labourers), and occasionally
with reference to specific political events ("the growing racial question in
Halifax and the Indian blocking of the Cornwall Island Bridge" [NFB/ONF
Annual Report, 1970/71]). It would be well into the mid-seventies before

women would make it onto the CFC/SN agenda, and then only at the prompting of staff with the federal Department of Manpower and Immigration (Oulton, telephone, 2008).

Indeed, as Gail Vanstone describes in *D Is for Daring*, it is unlikely that the NFB would have accepted Shannon's 1974 proposal for the creation of a women's unit, in spite of the groundswell of interest and support the Working Mothers films had unleashed. Once again it would take direct pressure from the federal government to move the NFB to take steps to address the gender imbalance within the organization: "[A]s Shannon often claimed, the NFB had no real wish for a women's studio and no financial commitment, establishing it only in compliance with a federal directive. Such suspicions are borne out by a memo circulated between NFB executives André Lamy and Bob Verrall detailing a telephone conversation with government officials: 'The government is considering proposals for International Women's Year … They said we should be expected to "reorganize our priorities" and provide a special program that would be really "special." They are looking for convincing evidence that the NFB considers women's programs important'" (Vanstone 2007, 38).

And yet the Working Mothers project was arguably the most significant achievement of the program. The films and film workshops spread like brushfire across Canada, leaving their audiences with print and other media resources to use in their continuing discussions. The flourishing numbers and vitality of the network generated specifically for the distribution of the WM films became an important resource for Studio D, and its members continued to be strong and vocal advocates for women's initiatives not only within the NFB and other media organizations, but in every aspect of Canadian public life.

V

In the twenty-first century, after decades of feminist effort, women continue to constitute the largest disenfranchised group in Canada and, it seems, the easiest group to dismiss. Women continue to make, on average, one-third less than men and to be concentrated in the least powerful positions in all professions. In media industries, women remain radically over-represented in support roles and under-represented in the content-determining positions of writer, director, and executive producer. This gender imbalance behind the scenes, inevitably, is reflected in the gender stereotypes on screen, with ever-intensifying results.[4] To paraphrase prominent feminist filmmaker Aerlyn Weissman, while women were typically ignored or patronized in the mass media of seventies, today they are brutalized. Hypersexualization of women and young girls of a sort that would have been considered pornographic then is now routine primetime/anytime fare.

If the leadership at the NFB in the seventies was slow to recognize and respond to women's demands for equality, if the federal Department of Manpower and Immigration was naïve in its request for a definitive answer to the puzzle of women's absence from the labour market in fifty-one minutes, by contrast with the current political culture, that era was a feminist utopia.

As Doris Mae Oulton, director of status of women and human rights for the Canadian Federation of University Women, put it in describing the current political culture: "We have a government that comes in and takes 'equity' out of the mandate of the Women's Directorate – it is almost beyond comprehension – and that they get away with it is scandalous" (e-mail, 16 August 2008).

The cutbacks in social and cultural programs since the late 1980s have increased dramatically in recent years; not surprisingly, they have had a disproportionate impact on women, rolling back many of the gains of earlier decades even as the economic and political conditions have worsened for the most vulnerable sectors of society. What's more, public and private institutions increasingly obscure the extent and specificity of women's marginalized status, burying it within the more amorphous category of "diversity," making the assault and its costs more difficult to track.

Public consultation was part of the culture of the public sector in the era of CFC/SN; this, if nothing else, held the promise that independent community voices might eventually be heard. Today, by contrast, the governing culture of the federal government and its cultural agencies is rigidly and proudly centralized, and decidedly male, making the likelihood that we could look forward to a similar era of grassroots, community-determined initiatives sadly unlikely.

4 Studies in 2007 and 2008 by women's groups like Realisatrices équitables in Quebec (www.realisatrices-equitables.org) and Please Adjust Your Set Campaign (www.please adjustyourset.com) in British Columbia underscore the persistence and even increases in labour inequities, particularly in content-determining roles.

30   O, Canada! George Stoney's Challenge (1999)

■

DEIRDRE BOYLE

In a career that has spanned continents and centuries, George Stoney has become a legend. Having researched his life to write a broad-strokes profile of him for the *Independent* in 1997 (Boyle 1997, 10–18), I was curious to know more, especially about his two-year stint as executive producer of the Challenge for Change (CFC) program at the National Film Board of Canada (NFB). On his return to the United States in 1970, Stoney went to New York University, where he co-founded the Alternate Media Center, launching a national public access movement in cable television that continues to this day, arguably his greatest professional accomplishment. How had those two years in Canada contributed to Stoney's vision of community-made media? With several assumptions and lots of questions, I went in search of answers from the man himself and several of his closest NFB colleagues (see Rosenthal, chapter 15, this volume).

In 1968 Stoney was invited to be CFC executive producer by Frank Spiller, then head of the English program at the NFB. CFC was created "to help eradicate the causes for poverty by provoking basic social change." Focusing on issues of powerlessness, the lack of control that citizens had over their lives, the CFC proposed to use film and other media as a tool in social change. The CFC enlisted filmmakers as technicians rather than auteurs, facilitating community projects that enabled ordinary people to explore their own problems and arrive at their own solutions. Stoney would replace John Kemeny, who had helped start CFC with Colin Low, Fernand Dansereau, and Robert Forget. Kemeny could deal with the filmmakers, according to Stoney, but he could not handle those "cantankerous" community organizers. The solution was hiring an outsider who could come in, make tough decisions, and take the lumps for a couple of years. Stoney agreed to be that outsider.

On his return from an around-the-world tour with the International School of America, Stoney realized he wouldn't prosper back at Stanford University because they wanted him to raise money and he didn't believe in

Originally published in *Wide Angle* 21, no. 2 (1999): 48–59.

having students dragooned into doing things for money. Instead, he decided to finish some films in New York, where Spiller found him. No one can recall how Spiller spotted Stoney, but Stoney's former Stanford student Bonnie Sherr Klein, who was then working at the NFB, was one of those who recommended him. Stoney went up to Montreal and encountered contention before he even arrived at the office: the two staffers who met him at the airport drove him into the city while discoursing on who he'd have to fire. Stoney knew that if he took the job "*those* are the two I have to get rid of first." He agreed to come for two years – no more, no less – because he was not a very good expatriate but people should know they were stuck with him. It proved rougher than he expected.

Conflicts between the French and English units were on the rise. The French unit worked under the banner Société nouvelle and the English unit, Challenge for Change. Eight departments of the Canadian government put up $100,000 each and the NFB matched that, so Stoney had a budget of $1,600,000 that had to be divided between the two units. He was answerable to a board composed mainly of representatives from these departments, and the board had final say on how to allocate the budget. The French unit sized Stoney up and decided they no longer wanted to get one-third of the budget; they wanted half because they had endured three centuries of abuse and the like. Stoney replied, "B – s – ! You have less than one-third of the population all in one province, you should get only one-fourth of the budget because you don't need to spend money on travel." No one had ever dared be that confrontational before. It was not the Canadian way. The French budget stayed at one-third.

Next Stoney upset the English unit. After being shown a film about a French community group that he thought was great, he said they ought to do an English version of it. The English unit revolted, and he found how hostile the English could be. Stoney thought all he needed to do to reconcile the units was just put the two crews together, send them to the Prairies, and they'd do fine. He discovered that the French sound crews, "who could have joined the English crews," were afraid of going to the Prairies, where they expected to be ostracized, stigmatized, or worse.

Stoney inherited a French-speaking secretary, and whatever he was doing was immediately being passed on to the French unit. When he asked that she be removed, the leak stopped, but then he had no secretary. He claims he didn't realize how much tension he was under during the first year, but he drove to Long Island every other weekend during his first winter, "twenty hours round-trip," just to be with friends and family for a few hours. That first year was a very lonely time. The second year was different: his teenage daughter came up to study French. Stoney enrolled her in an all-French school and found her a place in the home of French-speaking civil servants with four young children. With ties with the Québécois better established and his daughter near for frequent visits, his life changed for the better.

One of Stoney's first projects involved the Indian Film Crew that was part of the Company of Young Canadians. The crew was trained by the NFB but selected by the Bureau of Indian Affairs. As a result, there were eight men from eight different tribes – from Mi'kmaq to Haida. Some were traditional enemies; all they had in common was the label "Indian." Mike Mitchell, one of the traditional chiefs of the Mohawks, was a member of the Indian crew. He lived on the Akwesasne Reserve near Cornwall, Ontario (then called St Regis), sixty miles from Montreal. One day in December 1968 he called in to say he wasn't coming to work because he was leading a delegation to Ottawa to protest the actions of the new border superintendent, who was charging them duty on the groceries they bought in the United States. The reservation was cut by the U.S./Canada border and by the Ontario/Quebec border; people had to cross regional and international borders to traverse their own land. The Indians claimed the Canadian authorities were dishonouring their rights to duty-free passage according to a treaty dating from 1794. The Mohawks were united against the border police, and because Mitchell expected little in Ottawa, he wanted a crew awaiting the delegation when they returned, thinking this was where the real confrontation would come. Stoney reminded him that the rest of the Indian crew was in the Midwest. "I don't care what colour they are so long as I can tell them what to do," was Mitchell's rejoinder. Stoney went up to the cafeteria, stood on a table (an unheard-of liberty), and announced bluntly, "The Indians are in trouble, and they want some help." A few people volunteered to shoot and take sound, violating all the rules for how such things were done at the NFB. Later that day a crew was waiting with the police for the Indian protesters to return. *You Are on Indian Land*, edited by Kathleen Shannon, was shown numerous times to the tribe during the conflict, which helped pull them together when solidarity flagged, and at Stoney's behest, it was also shown to the Royal Canadian Mounted Police and the local police. Both sides were disappointed that there was so little violence in the film, having been conditioned to expect it from the local TV news coverage, which recycled a few highly charged moments, distorting and inflating the nature of the events (see Starblanket, chapter 5, this volume; Winton and Garrison, chapter 36, this volume).

Stoney had insisted on showing the film to both sides as soon as possible. Luckily, he found a distribution person with vision who supported him. The conventional wisdom at the NFB at the time was that once a film was made, the distribution people would decide how to get it out. If it had a theatrical future, it would be kept out of any other distribution for a year, offered to television, and then finally be made available to groups and individuals. Stoney believed this was absolutely backward for any CFC/SN program, which should be going up the chain, not down. Dorothy Hénaut, editor of *Access,* the CFC newsletter, carefully promoted the film. *You Are on Indian Land* was used not only by the Mohawks of Cornwall Island but by other tribes. The idea of grassroots distribution had been pioneered by John Grierson, one of the founders of the NFB, but it had fallen out of favour at the Board when filmmakers more eager for theatrical notice than social change prevailed.

Stoney became involved with another film that proved confrontational. One of the CFC's government advisors suggested making a film on the "attitude of relief recipients." Stoney thought it a wonderful idea, but Hénaut and others bristled. None of the CFC staff was interested, so Stoney invited Terence Macartney-Filgate to come back to the NFB to shoot the film because Filgate's camera looked people straight in the eye and "there was no room to look down." Stoney had worked with Filgate in New York when he was exploring the cinéma-vérité style of filmmaking. Filgate agreed to shoot the film and decided to set it in Ontario, where he knew the minister of welfare and many welfare rights activists. His first cut was about thirty-two minutes. Stoney disliked the insider jokes and suggested they set up test screenings with average viewers. After three such screenings, Filgate reported he didn't need any more: people only talked about the characters, not the issues. He recut the film to nineteen minutes, and *Up against the System* began to work.

Stoney brought the fine cut to Toronto to the minister of welfare because he needed to explain why they had not used any of the interviews with officials. And since the film blasted the welfare system, he felt as the outsider he could "get by." Stoney was immediately struck by how open Canadian public officials were. The minister's first response was clear but polite: "I think you could have spent your nineteen minutes on the screen to better advantage." Then he asked, "When will it be ready?" He asked Stoney to hurry the chaps because he wanted to premiere it at the regional conference. Why? Because the ministry needed to know the criticism that was coming. *Up against the System* was shown at all the regional welfare conferences across the country. It made everyone aware that people had real gripes about problems within the system, and it helped in the setting of new public policy.

When some staffers from the U.S. Department of Housing, Education, and Welfare (HEW) came up to the NFB to see what was going on, Stoney showed them *Up against the System,* and they invited him to come Washington, D.C., to show it. Thirty mid-level bureaucrats came to the screening. Stoney first explained to them the Film Board's mission "to present Canada to Canadians." The first question after the screening was: "Why did you make this? It doesn't promote any program." Stoney explained the whole process again. No one got it. Finally, someone asked, "Does the government really *know* you're making these films?" "Know?!!" Stoney exploded. "They're paying for it!" "How long do you think you'll get away with it?" was the final parry.

"By and large this was the response I got whenever we showed our films in the States," Stoney recalls. "The whole business of conciliation before confrontation was lost and not just with the government. The community activists here were critical too: it was too soft; there just wasn't enough yelling." What worked in Canada was not valued in the United States, where fostering antagonism was a more popular organizing methodology than building consensus. Stoney assumed that when people understood, they would change. "That's a great big assumption," he remarks now, laughing.

Audience testing was a crucial part of the *You Are on Indian Land* and *Up against the System* projects. Stoney was absolutely adamant on the importance of pre-screenings, especially for the citizens who were the subjects of the films. He wrote an editorial for *Access* based on the experience of a film titled *The Things I Cannot Change*. It is a powerful film about a dysfunctional English-speaking family in Montreal. Filmmaker Tanya Ballantyne Tree presents the mother, who was expecting her ninth or tenth child, and her husband, an unemployed alcoholic, with great sympathy such that by the time the baby came home from hospital, viewers sympathized with the father and understood how loved this new child was. But the family saw the film for the first time when a neighbour told them it was airing on TV that night; afterwards, covered with shame, they hurriedly moved out of the neighbourhood. Stoney noted that this should never have happened and wouldn't ever again (for a new take on this episode, see Longfellow, chapter 14, this volume). Screenings with participants had been part of the Fogo Island project that had launched CFC, but it remained a largely isolated case until Stoney arrived. It would provide the backbone for another project that proved historic for other reasons.

Dorothy Hénaut and Bonnie Sherr Klein came to Stoney with the idea of doing a project with a citizens' committee in a poor neighbourhood in Montreal. Klein's husband, a physician, volunteered at the St-Jacques Medical Clinic; she knew the committee and thought their organizing might benefit from media. Klein and Hénaut proposed to Stoney that they use the new portable video equipment just on the market. Unlike film, which took time to learn and years to master, portable video was easy to use, the perfect tool for non-professional filmmakers. No one can remember now whether Stoney ordered three dozen half-inch video rigs or whether they had already been purchased by the NFB, but video was provided with the caveat that Klein make a 16mm film to document the process. Stoney had had a disappointing

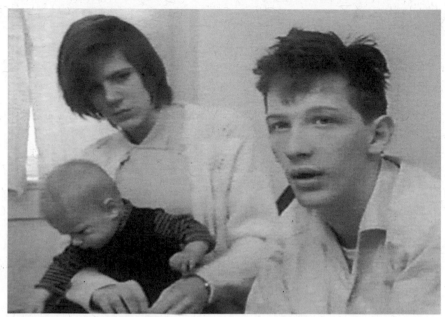

Up against the System (1969): exploring the culture of poverty. Frame enlargement.

experience at Stanford using Ampex one-inch video equipment. The tapes often wouldn't play back on the machines. It wasn't until the Japanese models and standardization that one could reliably play tapes on any machine. Given his doubts about video, he was counting on the filmic record to offer evidence that something had been accomplished.

VTR *St-Jacques* is a record of Klein and Hénaut's success in training community residents to use video to assist in their organizing process and in educating local administrators about the need for locally available and affordable medical care. The film is amazingly fresh to this day and offers a textbook example of the joys and woes of community-made video (see Hénaut and Klein, chapter 3, this volume; and Rusted, chapter 20, this volume).

Klein remembers that they were all on equal grounds of ignorance when it came to video. Hénaut recalls that it was her eleven-year-old son who helped her figure out how to use the new video equipment. She had a background in publishing and this was her first experience producing video or film. She learned editing the hard way, first using a razor blade and then mastering the frustrating, unpredictable, manual backspace editing method. For the duo, being on the cutting edge was a literal, not a symbolic, statement of the truth. Stoney gave them full support, fostering the first community video project in Canada, a model that would travel across the county, inspiring major projects in every province, then down to the lower forty-eight, spurring a powerful movement of community-made video that reverberates to this day.

Stoney, who had come to filmmaking as a scriptwriter, had never been entirely comfortable around a film camera. Cameramen jealously guarded their turf, and it was not until Stoney met Filgate that he found a collaborator who would call him to look through the lens and choose a shot. Video made it possible for Stoney, Hénaut, and others untrained in the use of a camera to wield one with ease, pleasure, and purpose. Stoney's confidence as a film director grew with access to this new tool that welcomed everyone. And video would prove to be the medium that would catalyze the community media movement back in the States.

Although Canada was wired before the United States for cable television, it was slow in developing any notion of public access. Most subscribers wanted cable so that they could receive the signals of commercial U.S. channels. The idea of watching local programming did not enter the picture. According to Hénaut, since Canadian cable companies were large and powerful, a cash cow from the very beginning, they found no incentive to give citizens any access and so never provided funding, equipment, or studio time for the production of community-made work. Because the government never forced them, the cable companies never gave up any of their control. Hénaut's brilliant utopian vision of community television appeared in *Access* and was later reprinted in *Radical Software* (no. 1 [1970]), the alternate video movement's chief publication in the United States. "Television as Town Meeting" soberly acknowledged the obstacles to success, proving Hénaut's astute grasp of the issues. Stoney would be more successful than Hénaut in putting these ideas and insights into practice because U.S. cable companies were temporarily less than giants and the Federal Communications Commission (FCC) was still a force to be reckoned with.

By the time Stoney's contract was up at the NFB, he could have easily been persuaded to stay, but by then Leo Hurwitz, head of New York University's graduate school in film, and Dean Oppenheim had offered him a job to head up the undergraduate division. Stoney's experience juggling conflict in CFC was just what NYU needed. NYU had been under siege by students angry at a university that exploited undergraduates in order to foster the graduate school. The students struck and imprisoned the remote and elegant dean in his office for several hours. When Stoney agreed to return to New York, it was because NYU officials thought video might help to slake the fires of student protest.

Stoney, asked today what might have happened had he stayed on at CFC/SN, looks thoughtful. He admits it didn't do very well after he left. It had been well launched before he arrived, and he got to take the credit for all the successes without being held accountable for its demise, further evidence of Stoney's "dumb luck" theory about his life. But regardless of how disappointing CFC/SN may have been in its final years, its newsletter alone had eighteen thousand subscribers at the end, reaching every country in the world, from Botswana to the Seychelles, and influencing a whole new generation of producers interested in using video for social change. Had he stayed, he wouldn't have been at NYU to join forces with Red Burns to create the Alternate Media Center, a unique enterprise that forged a relationship between the cable companies and socially engaged public-access proponents. Burns wooed the cable operators and Stoney hatched a plan, with the help of the fledgling National Endowment for the Arts, to create an internship program that placed talented, energetic public-access programmers in cable systems around the country. In a few years time, the group morphed into an independent association, the National Federation of Local Cable Programmers, which continues today under the title Alliance for Community Media.

Stoney had been steeped in the ideas of community media from his days travelling with the Farm Security Administration, reaching people in churches, union halls, and Rotary Clubs. He carried those ideas to Canada, where he had to handle community conflicts in an unfamiliar, linguistically polarized society. For a southerner tutored in the realities of racial inequality, Canada's struggles remained elusive yet familiar. He found a culture that valued conciliation over confrontation, which helped him feel more at home, yet he was never truly at home in Canada, always an outsider. His experiences at CFC/SN would influence his own film projects; this was immediately apparent in his film about St Peter's Church, *Pastor of the Night Flock,* a powerful glimpse of what it took to sustain a New York jazz congregation in its move to a new church building. It would also influence him to devote the lion's share of his time for many years to fostering community-made video and public access to cable TV. Who can say which element of those two years was the most significant – developing an intimate ease and love for the camera; building consensus and understanding in a culturally unfamiliar environment; enduring the loneliness of being an outsider; or working with two young women whose interest in video catapulted him into a brave new world of video production? The goals of CFC/SN meshed with Stoney's lifelong commitment to championing the rights of ordinary people. Ever versatile as an administrator, Stoney found himself in the right place at the right time. He incorporated Canada's liberal ideas about governmental support for media promoting social change back home, where it was still possible to move government agencies to protect the public's right of access to communications media. Once an outsider, Stoney quickly became the great insider of the public-access cable movement and a global ambassador for social activism. And he is still at it.[1]

1 The author is grateful to Dorothy Hénaut for sharing a copy of her unpublished essay "The Hammer and the Mirror Machine: Video and Community"; and to Stoney, Hénaut, and Klein for their generosity in granting stimulating interviews in June 2000. For further reading, see Hénaut 1991a and 1991b, Sturken 1984, and Evans 1991.

PART 4

Discursive Spaces: Theorizing Challenge for Change/
Société nouvelle

■

PREFACE

This section brings together six robust chapters that all tackle complicated, controversial, and enduring theoretical questions surrounding Challenge for Change/Société nouvelle. This critical analysis
probes the ideological and epistemological currents of the program,
troubling their conceptual frameworks – or in some cases the lack
thereof. These seven authors (chapter 36 is co-authored) cut through
the rhetoric and hype of CFC/SN and present provocative perspectives on the initiative's theoretical flashpoints: knowledge/power,
cultural citizenship, access/agency, participatory democracy, the
public sphere and counterpublics, praxis, identities, and the holy
grail for activist media, community. Taken together, these six contributions engage critically with the "big ideas" of media, democracy,
and power while carefully connecting the particular historical
moment of CFC/SN to issues that persist to this day.

In chapter 31, "Société nouvelle: The Challenge to Change in
the Alternative Public Sphere," Quebec film expert Scott MacKenzie
interrogates theories of the public sphere as they relate to Société
nouvelle's development of cinema-fuelled counterpublics in 1960s
and '70s Quebec. Writing in 1996 while preparing his doctorate
at McGill University on the Quebec cinematic public sphere,
MacKenzie troubles the valorization of access but is also interested
in how debate and discussion fostered by SN projects might actually
have moved towards social action and intervention. In chapter 32,
"Meeting at the Poverty Line: Government Policy, Social Work,
and Media Activism in the Challenge for Change Program," Vancouver-based professor and NFB authority Zoë Druick continues
the discussion of the public sphere by situating CFC/SN films on
work and poverty in the context of 1960s public discourse. Druick
shows how a certain Canadian history of welfare, as well as a governmental logic around social work and poverty, inflected CFC/SN,
ultimately leading to problematical and contradictory outcomes.

Chapter 33, Janine Marchessault's "Amateur Video and the Challenge for Change," first published in 1995 in her influential anthology on Canadian video, *Mirror Machine: Video and Identity*, examines the complex power relations between CFC/SN filmmakers, their subjects, and state funders and bureaucrats. Now a York University research chair and Marshall McLuhan expert, Marchessault tempers the project's original unfettered enthusiasm, reminding readers of issues such as lack of self-reflexivity by content makers, production without distribution, the coupling of technology and nationalism, and her principal theme, "access without agency." A similar skepticism was taken up the following year by her then colleague at McGill University Ron Burnett, now Emily Carr University of Art and Design president and prolific author on visuality and education, in chapter 34, "Video: The Politics of Culture and Community." Burnett approaches CFC/SN and its claims rigorously and unsentimentally with a dissection of assumptions around "community," "pedagogy," "change," and "effect." Focusing on empowerment and pedagogy as well as on the global historical trajectory of video as a tool for social change and "development," Burnett urges a closer look at the dynamic between theory, practice, and outcome.

Norwegian researcher and teacher Marit Kathryn Corneil shifts the critical lens to ethics in chapter 35, "Winds and Things: Towards a Reassessment of the Challenge for Change/Société nouvelle Legacy." Corneil revisits two of CFC/SN's most famous (or infamous?) works and teases out the implications of the ethics of responsibility (of the filmmaker), the ethics of access, and the ethics of representation. Her discussion also bears on the political aesthetics of the program and on tensions between performance and representation. While Corneil argues that the CFC/SN initiative overcame – to a certain extent – the ethical dilemma of representation, Ezra Winton and Jason Garrison, in chapter 36 – "If a Revolution Is Screened and No One Is There to See It, Does It Make a Sound?" – close the section with a look at the dilemma of distribution in relation to social change. PhD student, activist, and curator Winton and "culture hobo" Garrison, both Montreal-based, discuss grassroots distribution, community media, and revolution by returning to themes broached in chapters 31 and 32 – those of power and the public sphere. They apply the concept of hegemony to film and video distribution and interrogate how CFC/SN facilitated community-based counterpublics, considering the program's implications for contemporary initiatives in alternative cinema and media democracy, such as the Montreal-centred documentary exhibition network Cinema Politica.

31 Société nouvelle: The Challenge to Change in the Alternative Public Sphere (1996)

■

SCOTT MACKENZIE

In the late 1960s, the direction of Québécois filmmaking undertook a dramatic shift. Sidestepping attempts to build a united collectivity behind the notion of the French-Canadian nation-state that characterized much of the *cinéma direct* movement, Québécois cinema and video, under the auspices of the National Film Board of Canada/Office national du film (NFB/ONF), began to explore the means by which these organizations could get media into the hands of the people. These goals were to be achieved at the Board through the creation of two programs: Challenge for Change and its francophone counterpart, Société nouvelle. While in many ways the programs were united in their goals, it is a mistake to look at them as interchangeable. Thus, the current work focuses almost exclusively on SN and its predecessor, Le Groupe de recherches sociales, their development, and their strategies as they pertained to Quebec.

The work of SN points to a shift in the means by which images could be used as a catalyst for political action. Moving away from the *cinéma direct* aesthetic – where images on the screen were seen as a reflection of Québécois national identity – the films of SN conceptualized Québécois society as a field of interrelated, yet culturally and economically specific, communities. While the notion of a collective Québécois culture still held a great deal of sway, this culture and others inhabiting Quebec could be brought into contact to debate with one another in order to explore common goals, beliefs, and biases and develop the possibility of social action and the promotion of the common good. Further, questions could be raised about the francophone experience outside Quebec, allowing, via the cinema, a typically neglected dialogue to take place between Canada's francophone communities. In short, SN filmmakers attempted, through image-making, to create the kinds of communities, collectivities, spaces, and dialogues imagined as central to the new cultural and political landscape of an independent Quebec. Filmmakers such as Fernand Dansereau and Robert Forget contended that what was needed in the cinema were not only "accurate" images of Québécois identities – which were increasingly fragmentary and in conflict – but representations that would allow both audiences and filmmakers to imagine a new and egalitarian way of living and interacting.

To understand what kind of break in documentary practice SN represented, one only needs to compare these works to the *cinéma direct* films of the ONF's *l'équipe française*. The goals of both *cinéma direct* and SN were to create a new sense of Québécois identity. However, what distinguished the two movements was their focus: while *cinéma direct* concentrated on Québécois cultural issues, SN was concerned with how cultural politics related to questions of class and social inequality. SN's critique of class structure reflected a central concern of Québécois nationalists at the time. SN posited that images could be used to create a new, national imagined community that disassembled hierarchy and opened up debate and discourse within the public sphere. Of special concern was the attempt to find a way by which to circumnavigate the ethnographer's dilemma of obliterating the culture in front of the camera through the process of rewriting it; this concern was especially felt by the image-makers who were attempting to address social and political concerns such as chronic unemployment and poverty. To this end, viewers themselves would participate in the creation and dissemination of images, allowing the "voiceless" of society to produce their own representations of themselves, in order to bolster their own sense of community while *also* providing a means to address larger publics. The political "effect" of these image-making practices, then, would be found outside the screening room in what has recently been termed the "counter" or "alternative" public sphere, a public space where voices from the margins can engage in debate in a way that is not sanctified by the dominant institutions of culture (Negt and Kluge 1993; Hansen 1991; Fraser 1992, 109–42). These emerging desires coalesced around SN. Dorothy Hénaut, one of the early filmmaker/activists of the program stated that filmmakers such as Forget and Dansereau "saw a need to give a public voice to those that did not have one, and they proposed a project to use film as a tool for social change that would help disadvantaged communities organize themselves and take control of their own destinies … If we really believed in people's right to express themselves directly, then we needed to eliminate ourselves from the process and find a way to put the media directly in the hands of citizens" (1991a, 48–9).

Making video became as important as watching video, as the *process* of production was the basis of the new-found sense of community. Letting *the people* – an intuitive but ill-defined notion – make videos that addressed their interests fostered the sense of both a local community with specific concerns and an emerging "public voice." Nevertheless, the conceptualization of this new public voice and its actualization were two different issues, and the tensions that lay between theory and practice were foregrounded throughout SN's existence.

It is this sense of a specific notion of what it means to be part of a "public" – and the tensions that ensue when the attempt is made to create "publics" – that I wish to explore presently. The notion of "publicness" supported by SN's attempts to provide the disenfranchised of Quebec a voice mirrors the reconfigurations of the public offered by critics responding to Jürgen Habermas's influential model of the public sphere put forth in *The Structural Transformation of the Public Sphere* (1991). I wish to address why SN's attempts at constructing an alternative public sphere in some ways fail, and how this very failure helps us see what Fraser has called, in her reconsideration of Habermas's notion of the public sphere, the "limits of democracy." By doing so, I wish to explore how the contradictions that governed SN's goals graphically point to the difficulty of constructing and maintaining the notion of community at the margins of culture.

RECONSIDERING THE PUBLIC SPHERE

The model of the public sphere offered by Habermas is straightforward in its conception. He claims that in the seventeenth and eighteenth centuries a shift took place that fundamentally changed the division of power in Europe. Through a series of interrelated developments, including the rise of literacy and the emergence of English coffee houses and French *salons*, which provided spaces for individuals to congregate, a new notion of the public emerged, one that was relatively autonomous from both state and capital. He describes this new public as follows: "The bourgeois public sphere may be conceived above all as the sphere of private people come together as a public; they soon claimed the public sphere regulated from above against the public authorities themselves, to engage in a debate over the general rules governing relations in the basically privatised but publicly relevant sphere of commodity exchange and social labour. The medium of this public confrontation was peculiar and without historical precedent: people's public use of reason" (1991, 27).

Habermas's project, in the first instance, is a return to Kant's belief that, for "enlightenment, however, nothing is required but freedom, and indeed the most harmless of all things to which this term can be properly be applied. It is the freedom to make public use of one's reason at every point" (Kant 1784, 86–7). Indeed, Habermas is one of the few critical theorists of the late twentieth century who attempts to revitalize Kantian notions of rationality. For this reason, Habermas's analysis of the bourgeois public sphere has come under attack, most often for its exclusions and for its valorization of rationality and the Enlightenment project. Specifically, his work has been attacked by theorists such as Arthur Kroker because of Habermas's reinscription of a Kantian-derived rationality into the critical theory of Theodor Adorno and the Frankfurt School (Kroker and Cook 1991, 235–61). Kroker writes: "Habermas's philosophical importance has been that of a firebreak, transforming the radical critique of the self-liquidating tendencies of the Enlightenment into its opposite – the Kantian-inspired theory of communicative rationality so ridiculed and as a hermeneutics so decisively abandoned in *Dialectic of Enlightenment*" (Kroker and Cook 1991, 255).

The idealist notions that guide both Kant and Habermas certainly need to be questioned, as it is indeed true that the over-valorization of the rational-critical project leads to political dead ends; the inability to plan the creation of a public sphere for rational-critical debate in the manner of a Weberian ideal–type points towards this. Further, Kant's belief that the public use of reason frees the people and thereby "affects the principles of government, which finds it to its advantage to treat men, who are now more than machines, in accordance with their dignity" (Kant 1784, 92), seems like a naïve if not self-destructive vision if applied to the current relationship between public and political spheres of contemporary society. Nevertheless, in spite of these critiques, an inescapable fact of contemporary existence is that the very principle of rational-critical debate is striven for and that there is a common belief that these principles ought to guide public life, even if they often never do. Indeed, it is the utopian belief in the possibilities that rational-critical debate offers that have guided many models of radical political practice and also guided SN. Therefore, it seems essential not to dismiss outrightly Enlightenment rationality, but instead to examine the considerable gap that so often exists between these ideals and the *realpolitik* of political practice. It is to these gaps that I now wish to turn.

BUILDING PUBLICS: SOCIÉTÉ NOUVELLE

The story of the origin of both CFC and SN is by now quite familiar (Watson 1970 [1977]). In 1966 the Canadian Privy Council asked the NFB/ONF to produce a film to fight the war against poverty. Tanya Ballantyne Tree proposed making a cinéma-vérité film about the poor in Montreal. After doing some research, she found a family, the Baileys, who were willing to have her film them in their apartment for a period of three weeks. The film that emerged from this experiment fundamentally changed the direction of the French and English units of the NFB/ONF over the next few years. Titled *The Things I Cannot Change* (1966), it caused positive and negative ripples throughout both the Board and community action groups in the Montreal area. The film was shot in the Point St-Charles district of Montreal, an area of chronic poverty and unemployment. Further, it documented the Baileys' struggle to live at even a subsistence level. At the end of the film, Mrs Bailey says that she has only enough baby formula and food to feed the family for two or three days; she does not know where the food for her and her eight children will come from next.

Ballantyne Tree's film caused quite a scandal (for a contemporary view, see Longfellow, chapter 14, this volume). The main points of contention around it were that it was broadcast without prior warning to the Baileys and that they did not have final say as to what appeared on the screen. When the film was broadcast on CBC, the family was so ridiculed by their neighbours that they were forced to move. But the larger issue here was that by not having a say in how their image was constructed and distributed, they lost control of the image itself. Similar problems arose when *l'équipe française* attempted to make films about the Montreal underclass. A case in point is Hubert Aquin's *À Saint-Henri, le 5 septembre* (1964), which was criticized in much the same manner as *The Things I Cannot Change*. Fernand Dansereau wrote that the response to *À Saint-Henri* was "astonishingly violent": "[The people of Saint-Henri] felt debased by our *outsiders'* observations of them. Worse yet, certain people who played a role in the film felt deeply and personally hurt. One of the families that had been filmed, for example, was overcome with a sort of shame so great they decided to remove their children from the local school" (Dansereau, chapter 4, this volume, p. 34). Because of these experiences, the desire of Dansereau and other NFB/ONF filmmakers was to overcome these boundaries of representation; in order for this to be done, not only did the people need to be able to make their own images, but they also needed to be able to debate and contest the nature of the images on the screen and what they meant.

In response to these critiques, raised by filmmakers and community activists alike, the NFB/ONF directors and producers set up the Groupe de recherches sociales in 1967, which led in part to the formation of CFC/SN in 1969. These programs were attempts to allow the working classes and the disenfranchised to create images of themselves for themselves. Yet, the mandate of CFC/SN went beyond the desire to make accurate representations of the poor, the disenfranchised, and the voiceless; instead the programs strove to radically redefine the way in which communities and audiences were built around films and videos. NFB/ONF directors became facilitators whereby they would demonstrate and supervise the technical aspects of film- and video-making, but the final film or video would be under the control of the community groups. CFC/SN, then, had the primary goal of having the working classes film, view, and re-edit the images shot of themselves, by themselves, in order to build a community base for activism. This was accomplished by screening the finished films and videos in union halls and community centres.

Dansereau employed this new approach when he directed one of the earliest CFC/SN films, *Saint-Jérôme* (1968), which was set in a mid-sized, economically depressed city forty kilometres north of Montreal.[1] He became a

---

1 For an overview of this project, see Hénaut, "Channelling Change in Quebec: Fernand Dansereau's Saint-Jérome," *Challenge for Change/Société nouvelle Newsletter* 2 (1968): 10.

facilitator more than a director or auteur. With this film, he essentially attempted to give control of the film over to the people depicted in it. At any point between shooting and the final cut, participants could decide to remove their image from a given scene if they no longer liked it or changed their mind about what they had said or done. At first he worried that the two-hour film would only make sense to the community of Saint-Jérôme, but it soon became clear that it was well received throughout Quebec. He claimed that this was because "the sort of liberation in language and reflection that the film provokes seems to have come at the right moment" (Dansereau, chapter 4, this volume, p. 36). Dansereau was intuitively aware of the limitations of the form and attempted to readdress this problem by making the film interactive. To do so, he made twenty-seven reels of what he called "satellite films." These films were made of outtakes from the original shoot. When audiences had a question about a certain event on the screen – whether they wanted more information or thought that Dansereau was biased – Dansereau would recommend a satellite film that expanded on the issue being addressed. To some extent, however, this ended up defeating the purpose of the SN program, as the image became the reflection of culture, the end product, and not the starting point for a larger community action. There was the illusion of interaction, though, as each satellite film expanded on the premises of the first; this process abstracted community action further and further away from concrete reality and more and more towards the world of images. And in this move towards the world of images, process quickly divorced itself from the real.

This movement can be seen in SN film about the process of making films in local communities. Bonnie Sherr Klein's film *Opération boule de neige* (VTR *St-Jacques*, 1969) offers a fairly accurate portrait of the kind of community action that was undertaken by SN in the early years. The Board provided the Comité des citoyens de Saint-Jacques with videotape recorders, which they then took into the streets to record the complaints, concerns, desires, and opinions of the people who lived in the neighbourhood. The committee itself edited the different tapes together, debated what would be shown, and then screened the material on four television monitors at a local community centre. People from the neighbourhood came to the centre, saw the images of themselves, and debated the representations on the screen. In doing so, they began to discover what their common concerns were, where they differed, and what they believed could be done to improve life in the community. Images functioned only as catalysts to establish a public that would debate the concerns of the local community. In the end, the meaning of the image was supposed to become secondary to the sets of relations that emerged in the public forum. Nevertheless, the potential meanings and effects of the films were debated a great deal; a scene in *Opération boule de neige*, for example, shows two committee members deciding what their video could not show, imagining that the wrong response might be generated in the audience.

These new image-makers were right to be concerned about the effects of their videos, but the results were not the kind the makers might have expected. Images often took precedence over content, and the real power of the process lay not in the discourse produced, but in the public nature of the discourse itself. The effects of the videos often had little to do with the actual content of what is said onscreen, as can be seen in some of the comments generated after the screenings:

> We were not very interested in ourselves when we started.

> But it helped me a lot to know myself. You see how you function. Could we have stopped people on the street and questioned them, the same way, if we had not had a camera and a microphone? I don't think so. It's a good pretext for talking to them. (Hénaut and Klein 1969, 5)

These responses point to the kind of valorization of discourse that takes place when the private is made public. By offering the people of St-Jacques a forum, what they say becomes important if only because of its status as media-image. Here, the public sphere does not have an effect because of the persuasive powers of rational-critical debate, but because in the age of mass mediation the public voice is, *a priori*, equated with the voice of reason.

Fulfilling the quite understandable desire of the disenfranchised to experience a public voice for the first time became the central goal of SN facilitators in the early years of the program. Léonard Forest's *La noce est pas finie* (1971) demonstrates the often contradictory processes of community action and image production as understood by SN (see Deslandes, chapter 23, this volume). Set in Acadia, the film combines fiction and documentary practices and, at first glance, seems to have more in common with late sixties European art cinema – especially the work of Godard – than it does with the Portapak activism taking place in Montreal. The film developed from workshops and subcommittees set up by citizens groups in order to determine the future of Tracadie, a small town in New Brunswick. Forest was moved by the process of public debate the local inhabitants partook in, even after inviting members of Parliament and government officials who never materialized. After this experience, he obtained a small budget and a six-week schedule to produce the film. At the outset, he and a group of locals met and discussed what the film could be about while another local took notes. The notes became the basis for the script of the film, which dealt with the chronic poverty and abuse that took place in Acadia (Forest, chapter 6, this volume; Hénaut 1971–72, 18–22). The film premiered in Bathurst to an audience of sixteen hundred people and then went on the road throughout northeastern New Brunswick. The response to the film was varied, ranging from incomprehension as to why anyone would wish to make a film like this – a point of view held by older viewers – to jubilation on the part of the young, who wanted to see more films made in this way in different places throughout New Brunswick. Discussions following the screenings ran from fifteen minutes to two and a half hours (Prinn 1972a, 17). The film seems to have served as a catalyst by generating community-based action to remedy many of the area's problems. Yet in many ways the prioritization of the positive effects of filmmaking became the focus. Forest's follow-up film, *Un soleil pas comme ailleurs* (1972), arose when Forest was asked to return, as local organizers, in his words, "thought there was a need for some other film input; they didn't quite know what" (Prinn 1972a, 14).

After returning to New Brunswick and shooting more meetings, Forest states: "Having done the shooting, having evaluated the material when I came back, I realized that there was enough substance for a film, because of the point that their own reflections had reached, and the consensus that came out of these *tables rondes*. Perhaps the people had not realized from group to group that they were thinking along the same lines but I found a great similarity of ideas. It occurred to me that it would be extremely useful to them if I edited the material and issued it. It would reflect their ideas back to them, to help their own process of reflection" (Prinn 1972a, 14). Here, we see the need to produce images as the fulcrum upon which community action becomes based. Local groups continued to need an external, and highly public, catalyst that they believed validated the process of social transformation. Faced with these kinds of dilemmas, SN had to ask itself, how can we privilege process over all else and still intervene socially?

A spirit of vitality, of imagining that images were instigating change, led to experiments where process was all that mattered. A case in point is the SN experiment in cross-cultural communication. Addressing the mutual alienation and distrust that many young francophones and Jews felt about each other, two cultural workers within these communities attempted to see if video could "initiate an audio-visual system of communication wherein both groups, given their newly emergent values, could convey genuine feelings in order to break down traditional defense mechanisms that hamper profound rapprochement and sincere dialogue" (Cohan and Levy 1974, 20–1). There were ten participants – five Franco-Québécois, five Anglo-Jewish – who were directed not to make documentaries on the other group's culture, but to record their own subjective impressions of the other culture. The tapes were filled with humorous versions of many of the stereotypes in common currency, but when the two groups got back together to screen the tapes, they laughed at one another's jokes and felt closer to one another, not because of the nature of the images per se, but because of the common experience of going through the process of video-making together. Indeed, as the report on the project states, "In the final session, there was more rapport and even anxiety about separation after the project. This led to a commitment by the group to continue meeting" (Anon., "VTR," 1974, 21). Despite the happy ending this seems to be, the limitations of SN are also made apparent in this experiment in cross-cultural communication. The separation anxiety felt by the participants has far more to do with the intensity often felt during the production process than with a new understanding of the other culture. The weak link in the process had to do with the question no one wanted to ask, as no one could answer it: how do new-found publics maintain their coherency once image-making falls away as an organizational catalyst?

THE DISPERSAL OF THE PUBLIC SPHERE: COMMUNITY AND CONTINGENCY

Nancy Fraser, in what is the most valuable re-evaluation of the public sphere, outlines what would be required of a model of contemporary late-capitalist publics. It is with reference to Fraser's work that I wish to turn back to the question of how the public sphere may be of use in our understanding of SN, video activism, and getting media into the hands of the people. Fraser contends that four of the key points in Habermas's model of the public sphere are highly contentious and need to be rethought if an adequate model of an "actually existing democracy" is to be developed. She states that the "bracketing" of social status is not enough and that one must eliminate social inequality; that a multiplicity of publics allows for a greater range of publics to engage in debate and therefore to effect the "actually existing democracy"; that what is deemed private is often masculinist in its ideology and should be included in the public sphere; and that both strong and weak publics must be allowed to coexist in the new, post-bourgeois conception of the public sphere (Fraser 1992, 136–7). Fraser does not remove from the public sphere the principle of rational-critical debate; instead, she makes space for alternative voices and concerns to enter the fray without having to fully embrace the paradigm of publicness put forth by Habermas. In undertaking these reconsiderations, Fraser allows for the possibility that contesting and contested publics coexist within a given society, that these weaker publics constitute alternative public spheres that gain strength through their alternative status and function as critiques of the dominant order. It is to the building, on the part of SN, of these kinds of alternative public spheres through the process of getting media into the hands of the people that I wish to turn to now.

What SN's early projects point to is the prioritization of process over product in the creation of publics. In this light, Fraser's notions of the alternative public sphere and of multiple publics open up many possibilities in relation to the question of film and video spectatorship. One could contend that, as a public space of imagining a cultural identity, the cinema, albeit in an illusory manner, eliminates social inequality during a screening, as the audience is engaged in a shared cultural experience that is accessible to all. Further, the public nature of the event sanctions the events taking place on the screen as valid both to the people the film represents and to the people it imagines to have cultural authority. Yet, this process raises many questions: Can one transcend the limits of the screening and take this imagined social equality outside the screening room and into the realm of lived experience? How does one turn a viewer into a producer of images? How does one bridge the gap between production and consumption?

Indeed, there seem to be far more questions than there are answers. While it is obvious that the cinema cannot by itself eliminate social inequality, film does offer the viewer and the public the chance to imagine a radically reorganized notion of public life. This possibility of social imagining is not solely determined by the image on the screen, but also by the potential communities that can arise around the images and the contexts in which these images are seen. For a brief moment, Québécois film provided a new discursive space within the public sphere for Québécois audiences. This space allowed viewers to re-imagine themselves and their culture, and it seemed, briefly, that these utopian imaginings could be carried over into the realm of lived experience through social intervention. Screens became sites where culture was not simply represented, but was questioned, created, recreated, and demythologized. In short, the tensions of representation that were introduced into Québécois cinema by SN made it possible for film to become the site where meanings of intuitive, yet fuzzy, concepts such as culture, class, ethnicity, and identity could be negotiated by image-makers and audiences alike. Certainly, SN was more concerned with the processes individuals go through as they attempt to define themselves and address their problems through image production than it was with the representational nature of the images themselves.

Many questions arise when one prioritizes process over product: What kinds of communities are formed through the processes of image-making? How do groups go from discussions, dialogue, and debate within an alternative public sphere to social action and intervention? What role, in the end, do images play in this process? Can the community survive outside of the highly constructed context of image-making production?

In the case of SN, the answers were not as uplifting as one would have hoped. Notions of process and interactivity fell by the wayside, as video replicated many of the same viewing patterns as cinema. While SN went on to produce a variety of politically engaged films, such as Anne Claire Poirier's *Les filles du Roy* (1974) and the En tant que femmes series, these works moved closer to the traditions of politically engaged European art cinema and away from the early principles of SN. But one is still left with the question as to why the original impetus of SN – to radically redefine the means of image production while constituting a politically engaged image-making practice – faded away.

Video may have changed many things, but it still hadn't changed the world, at least not in the programmatic, utopian manner imagined by many. There are many reasons for this. Janine Marchessault has argued that one of the limits of video is that accessibility is too quickly equated with access to power: "Over and again, video is reported to have been greeted with tremendous excitement by different communities. The VTR 'brought the community together' and the television monitor (even if it was closed-circuit) resonated with institutional authority, promising a new form of social communication" (Marchessault, chapter 33, this volume, p. 359). Yet, as Marchessault goes on to note, video offered one the possibility of representing oneself through the dominant modes of representation of the public sphere without the true power that typically goes hand in hand with it. Part of the problem here lies in the power that our culture invests in the image. Community groups and filmmakers alike should have seen images as a starting point, to bring people together, to debate, and to engage in democratic action. Eventually, the image should have fallen away, once the space that the group needed was secured. Yet, to a great extent, this did not happen. Once the images were gone, so were the groups; there was no other infrastructure to maintain the publicness of these alternative publics.

The problem SN engendered in attempting to shift from working-class audiences watching images of their collective identities to audiences taking part in the creation of their own often-contradictory images lay in an over-investment in the power of the image to transform culture, and not the audiences around it, to bring about social and political transformation. Ron Burnett writes about the program's failure to bring about cultural transformation: "These processes of transformation may not naturally open up discursive spaces for audiences and may not lead to the kinds of exchanges and interchanges that produce the possibility of social, cultural and political change. In fact, an argument can be made ... that the medium itself may not have the importance that is so often attributed to it by social and cultural commentators, analysts and practitioners" (1991, 60).

The ideal of SN – to create public spaces where ideas could be debated and critiqued – was a valiant attempt to revitalize a notion of publicness that previously had not been a part of video culture, but in this attempt, the image was not only over-valorized, but in the end was given priority over the individuals who were to make up these new publics. The new and rediscovered communities that were founded around video images in the late 1960s failed to take on a life of their own once government money dried up. The attempt to formulate a public sphere around images should have precipitated the development of further notions of community. Yet this did not occur. A large part of the reason lay in the fact that access, and not a new-found coalitional identity, was what brought the people together in the first place and that simply getting media in the hands of the people does not in and of itself transform the public sphere.

The SN program attempted to develop a new notion of identity in Quebec, one based around community. It failed, in part, because of its over-investment in the image, but also because of the stronger pressures in Québécois culture that were coming to the forefront at the time. The experience of SN points to the large gap that exists between the ideals of the democratic public sphere put forth by Fraser and the contingencies and contradictions that govern actual actions within a public. Indeed, the contradictions that Marchessault says lie at the heart of CFC and SN – notions central to the ideals of liberalism (the ability to guarantee individual freedoms while supporting the common good) – also constitute the tensions that tear at the notion of a public sphere centred on rational-critical debate (Marchessault, chapter 33, this volume). By the early 1970s, it was not just the utopian notion of community activism through image-making that was disintegrating; the disintegrating community spirit could also be felt out on the streets. At the very time that SN was reaching its peak, Québécois national identity was going through its most trying period – the terrorism of the FLQ and the October Crisis of 1970. By the end of the month, Prime Minister Pierre Trudeau had tanks and infantry in the streets of Montreal and Ottawa. In many ways, it was a turning point for Quebec. It was at this moment that the political possibilities and utopian ideals of egalitarianism and social democracy that were central to Québécois nationalism – and a key part of Société nouvelle – faded in the face of the *realpolitik* of government.

Meeting at the Poverty Line: Government Policy, Social Work, and Media Activism in the Challenge for Change Program

ZOË DRUICK

There appears today to be a growing consensus amongst not only politicians and students of Canadian social issues but also the public as a whole that poverty is a major national problem which must be solved.
■ W.E. Mann, *Poverty and Social Policy in Canada* (1970, 345)

In the course of its own work and its work for government departments and agencies, the National Film Board has come to believe that programs intended to eliminate causes of poverty in Canada could be greatly strengthened by a coordinated program of film activities. The eradication of poverty demands unorthodox ideas. Support for these ideas, and for radical measures based on them, demands new concepts of communication. For this purpose, film – used imaginatively and unequivocally – is the best medium of communication.
■ "Proposal for a Program of Film Activities in the Area of Poverty and Change," 16 February 1967

Challenge for Change [was] a program designed to use film as a catalyst in various social programs to improve the lot of Indians, poor fishermen, mothers on welfare.
■ George C. Stoney, "The Mirror Machine" (1971–72, 9)

The Challenge for Change/Société nouvelle (CFC/SN) program at the National Film Board (NFB) marks one of the institution's most notable undertakings. Established in 1967 and producing nearly 250 films over a more than ten-year period, the program continues to emblematize the possibilities of a kind of filmmaking that is at once radical and public. The NFB itself utilizes the positive legacy of this moment to convey core values associated with newer initiatives, such as its Citizen*Shift* program. The films made in the CFC/SN program constitute a unique and valuable archive, expressing a kind of political engagement rare on Canadian screens. The "Fogo process" – using video to create community consensus – has been credited with inspiring participatory video projects in many places around the globe (Crocker 2003). Yet, this sense of respect and awe for CFC/SN, especially its filmmakers and its producers, can overshadow the bigger picture in which the program took on its form.

In this chapter, I situate the influential films of the Challenge for Change/ Société nouvelle program in relation to the public discourses of the 1960s, including those concerning urbanization, the centralization of the welfare system, the new politicization of ethnicity, and the rise of radical social work. Focusing on a number of the films made between 1967 and 1969 that deal with welfare, I examine the logic governing their production and analyse their perspectives in relation to government policy. I suggest that the rise of federal powers and the shifts at work in employment and economic structures were not necessarily coterminous with the more radical objectives of the citizens committees, social animators, and film- and video-makers who found themselves involved with the program. Despite widespread discussion of ideas of community and communication across the political spectrum, the contradictions between different agendas around anti-poverty politics paradoxically led to a range of productive outcomes. In what follows I give a brief history of welfare in the Canadian context, with an emphasis on the policies of the 1960s, especially regarding employment. I consider the politics of the CFC/SN program itself and look at the diverse styles apparent in a range of films about poverty and welfare made under its auspices.

WELFARE IN CANADA

Industrial societies are reliant upon massive divisions of labour that create conditions beyond each individual's control. In order to accommodate this compromise to the liberal ideal of free will, welfare provisions have consistently included basic care for the poor. These provisions have taken many forms, from the poor laws of eighteenth-century England to charitable works by religious organizations, to the state-run welfare provisions that have taken hold since the Depression. The British North America Act of Confederation (1867) limited federal duties to defence and the economy. All social expenses, from education to welfare and health, were the responsibility of local governments (Strain and Hum 1987, 350). This local regulation of welfare tended to employ a strong moral aspect delineating deserving from undeserving poor. The cause, rather than simply the condition, of penury was often assessed, and some poor were deemed more worthy of help than others. As we will see below, the debate about the deserving and undeserving poor runs throughout the welfare discourse of this period, as does the question of the radical or conservative implications of "community."

In Canada, piecemeal welfare programs instituted by churches and local governments became increasingly centralized and managed until, by the 1940s, the apparatus of the modern welfare state had begun to take shape. A number of postwar programs, such as Family Allowance (1945), Old Age Assistance and Security (1951), Unemployment Assistance (1956), the Equalization Program (1957), the Canada and Quebec Pension Plans (1965), the Canada Assistance Plan (1966), the Medical Care Act (1966), and the Guaranteed Income Supplement (1967), gradually shifted welfare responsibilities to the federal government (Chappell 2006, 346–7; Ismael 2006, 27–9; Strain and Hum 1987, 351). Although the centralization of powers was for the most part a gradual process, in the mid-1960s things accelerated quickly. A war on poverty was declared in the Liberal throne speech of 1965 (mirroring President Johnson's policy in the United States), and the introduction of the Canadian Assistance and the Canadian Pension Plans were both announced.

One of the effects of these developments was a corresponding growth in the field of social work (Gripton and Irving 1996). Another was a shift in the register of citizenship from the local and the provincial to the national level, an important aspect of nation-building. As Canadians became modern, urban citizens, they simultaneously became more national in orientation. According to historians Finkel and Conrad, "following the Second World War, government policy and economic activity were focused on bringing every Canadian into the modern age. Subsistence survival by farming, fishing, and hunting was deemed unworthy, and rural life, unless fully commercialized, experienced a rapid decline. As a result, many communities became ghost towns, while cities experienced unprecedented growth" (2002, 376). Urbanization was so rapid that where at the end of the Second World War more than one-quarter of Canadians lived on a farm, thirty years later fewer than one in fifteen farmed (377).

A macroscopic view of the impact of technological change on Canada's future took hold and was reflected, among other places, in the theme of Expo '67 – "Man and His World." The federal state took more and more responsibility for dealing with the social problems posed by rapid modernization, including poverty, devising for that purpose the "low-income cut-off" (LICO) as an economic indicator of poverty in the late 1960s – the so-called poverty line (Ismael 2006, 10).

Although Canada did not experience race riots and radical First Nations politics in the sixties, Canadians were well aware of these events south of the border. According to Leslie Pal, the years 1965–66 saw much talk about community development and social action "building principally on the American civil rights and student movements. The focus was not language, ethnic groups, or women, but the poor, urban renewal, students, and Native

Indians. In the American context, the links among poverty, class, race, and urban power were easy to make, because of the civil rights movement's concentration on the problems of poor blacks in inner cities. The first wave of community development and citizens' participation that came to Canada consequently also focused on youth and poverty and local control" (1993, 106).

In many ways, Quebec's policies were as formative with respect to the federal vision as were American examples. Not only did the Quebec government turn to culture before the federal government in the 1960s, but its increased assertion of provincial autonomy led to the hearings of the Bilingualism and Biculturalism Commission through the mid-1960s and the release of its reports in the late 1960s (Pal 1993). Quebec also led the way in the field of *animation sociale*. Michel Blondin was the first social animator in an urban setting in Canada. In 1963 his team of social animators at the Conseil des oeuvres de Montréal (Social Development Council of Montreal) spawned what became known as citizens committees.[1]

Animation sociale is not exactly the same as social work, although it is related to it. While social workers are often functionaries of the social welfare system, animators are social organizers who attempt to bring people to an awareness of the issues that affect them and the things they can do about their situation.[2] They are facilitators, especially for those who don't already have a sense of entitlement around their own social participation. Given its prominence on the social welfare front, it was perhaps inevitable that social animation would come to play an important role in the CFC/SN process.

Change and the challenges – and possibilities – of the future were on everyone's mind. Mainstream 1960s social thought was preoccupied with questions related to the future of work and the impending post-industrialization of the Canadian economy. A major and recurring question concerned society's ability to maintain human values in a rapidly technologizing environment. NFB films about education from the period explore this question of student and worker in the new automated environment (see, for example, Morten Parker, *The Skilled Worker* [1958], and Mort Ransen, *Teacher: Authority or Automaton?* [1961]). In English Canada, John Porter's *Vertical Mosaic* (1965) emphasized the ethnicization of class in Canadian society and

---

1 Changes in Quebec society led to an air of radical possibility in the province. According to social activist Blondin, writing in 1971, "During the past five or six years, Quebec has been going through a period of soul-searching and self-examination, in a desire to develop its potentialities and gain control of its destiny. Thus Quebec is willing to face up collectively to the changes of every kind that are radically transforming it ... Everything is being challenged, re-examined and reassessed" (164).

2 Radical social workers in the 1960s recognized social work as part of the conformist aspects of the welfare state (Rein 1970, 13–14).

created a stir by challenging Canada's myth of equality. In the same year, the Massey Lectures delivered by University of Toronto political theory professor C.B. Macpherson challenged Canadians to think about democracy in a much more expansive way than liberalism, with its focus on the individual, allowed. Adaptation to the challenges of a new economy dominated public discourse to the degree that terms such as "challenge" and "change" became clichés.[3] Indeed, environmental activist Patrick Watson, a strong supporter of the CFC/SN program, mocked the name as sounding like a "grade-eight-social-studies-textbook" (1977, 112). Citizen participation, communication, community, and dialogue were the buzzwords of the day; their political valence was usefully ambiguous. A variety of political positions took different participants in this configuration – from bureaucrats to filmmakers, from citizens committees to the poor, and from cable TV activists to video artists – in often quite divergent directions.

THE POLITICS OF CHALLENGE FOR CHANGE/SOCIÉTÉ NOUVELLE

The origin of CFC/SN is linked, then, to government policy, from the war on poverty to the Company of Young Canadians (Kurchak 1972 [1977], 121). This linkage can tend to imply the radical orientation of the state, for if the films were deemed to be politically left wing, so too must be the state that financed them. In this section I want to explore that relationship. The exact connection between government policy, the films that were made, and the ways they were circulated is not entirely transparent. We do know that a government organizing committee vetted all the proposals and took the first look at all the films. At the same time, a range of groups – whose "orientation ranged from cultural ... to militant" – found a supportive environment in CFC/SN (Kurchak 1972 [1977], 124). Perhaps historian of public media Ralph Engelman has put it most succinctly: "[I]ncompatible agendas – liberal, McLuhanesque, and leftist – coexisted uneasily" in the program (1996, 234).

---

3 A selection of titles from the 1960s is illustrative: M. Carter McFarland, *The Challenge of Urban Renewal* (1962), a series of lectures delivered in Ottawa under the auspices of the Central Housing and Mortgage Corporation; Leslie Tom Morris, *Challenge of the Sixties: 3-point Program for Canada* (1964), addresses to the Communist Party of Canada; United Church of Canada, *The Challenge of Change to the Rural Church* (1965); Rae Murphy, *Canada's Trade Union Movement: Change and Challenge* (1967); Lister Sinclair, *Change Comes to Canada: Challenge of the Changing Times* (1967); B.Y. Card, *Trends and Change in Canadian Society: Their Challenge to Canadian Youth* (1968); and Economic Council of Canada, *The Challenge of Growth and Change* (1968).

The NFB proposed the CFC/SN program to the Privy Council and Secretary of State using language engineered to resonate with the prevailing anti-poverty policies. The report that proposed the CFC program in 1967 fitted into the war on poverty and divided potential film audiences into three distinct groups: the "general public," "those involved in the poverty field," and "the poor." In each case, the objective was to acclimatize different groups to intervention by the federal government. "Films for the general public could develop understanding of and concern for poverty problems, prepare public opinion for unorthodox attacks on poverty, and generate support for government involvement in poverty programs ... Mass audience films are unlikely to generate action (the prime need) and a surfeit of them could backfire (an affluent society does not like to be reminded of its sores)." Possible criticism of the state was anticipated and sanctioned. Films for those working with the poor were to "question conventional approaches to social problems and the 'establishment attitudes'" developed to deal with them ("Proposal for a Program of Film Activities in the Area of Poverty and Change," 1967, n.p.).

NFB communiqués to the government in the late 1960s repeatedly insist that democracy can be enhanced by new technology: "The technology is here – it has been for some time. The society which incorporates in the fabric of its institutions a two-way dialogue and debate will counteract the tendency towards dehumanization that seems to go with ever-increasing size and complexity of our institutions. Democracy is based on participation and debate. The citizen must be brought back to the agora by the very technology that tends to screen him from the center of that vital discussion involving his survival and fulfilment on this planet" (Nemtin 1968, n.p.).

This message about technology facilitating dialogue and citizen participation – what Marchessault (1995a, 1995b; see also Marchessault, chapter 33, this volume) characterizes as the program's technological determinism – was palatable to a state used to technological solutions for social and political problems (Charland 1986). But others were more interested in the possibilities of radical democracy. To appreciate the extent of the divergent views, let us consider two distinct uses of the word "change," one in a government report on the CFC program, the other as used by media activists working within it. *Report of Activities for the First Year of the Experimental Program Challenge for Change/Société nouvelle: 1970–1971* positions the program as "intended to create awareness of the nature of change and of the need which citizens and institutions have of understanding it and working with it" (5). This language is connected to the idea that Canada was undergoing a structural shift towards a post-industrial and post-resource-based economy. By contrast, in the CFC/SN newsletter the language is not about responding to change, but rather about provoking it. The epigraph found at the head of the table of contents of all the newsletters describes CFC/SN as "[a] program designed to improve communications, create greater understanding, promote new ideas and *provoke* social change" (emphasis added).

The government program was intended to entail the making of films and videos within communities where interventionist policy could be productive. Poor inner-city and rural communities without much political clout that were dealing with concrete issues such as relocation or housing were good case studies. Yet in the CFC/SN newsletters from 1969 to 1975, one can see the progression from this kind of targeted film- and video-making towards a more radical kind of community media developed by CFC/SN employees and the affiliated groups starting up in cities across Canada, such as Intermedia, Video In, and Vidéographe, as well as by Aboriginal and community broadcasting initiatives. Although the program began with an emphasis on film, as video technology was introduced into the program, the newsletter increasingly turned towards a focus on public-access video as a means of constituting active citizen participation. In fact, CFC/SN became a flashpoint for many people involved with community broadcasting, both television and radio (Peter Anderson, personal communication, 2008). There is an important difference, I submit, between the public officially imagined by the CFC/SN program at the outset and that foreseen by community media activists as the program progressed. One envisioned a closed-circuit dialogue loop between decision-makers and the poor and disenfranchised, while the other saw the formation of widespread, grassroots publics. These two divergent approaches to issues of inequality were maintained in the CFC/SN program in uneasy balance. One sustained a focus on ways to help the poor help themselves by conveying their needs to the state (Evans 1991, 175; Marchessault, chapter 33, this volume). The other opened up a more radical vision of participation outside of the state, where the lines between audience and media-maker were not so clearly drawn.

RURAL RELOCATION

I have argued elsewhere (2007) that the NFB was an important instrument for envisioning the process of the welfare state in Canada. As more and more features of social life were taken over by the state in the postwar period – becoming "governmentalized," in Foucault's terminology (Foucault 1991; Dean 1999) – film became one of the many educational and promotional processes used to convey the new role of the state in administering people's lives. In Canada, because the constitutional division of powers allocated education (along with welfare provision) to the provinces, the National Film Board arguably became a way to convey messages about the federal state to the general population – ultimately it became an advocacy tool for federalism itself. We shall see below how this process operated in the Newfoundland case of the films about Fogo Island.

As other contributions to this volume describe, the CFC/SN films were characterized by their use of hand-held cameras and especially their experimentation with Portapak video. Many of the films were considered to be process rather than product oriented. Where a film such as *Man and His Resources* (Donald Fraser, 1961) utilized the lecturing model to teach about the need to reallocate global resources, films made in the wake of *The Things I Cannot Change* (1967) followed the more modern style of direct cinema and correspondingly seem more current and youthful. In their focus on being on hand during events, utilizing ordinary people, and providing depth to the statistics by showing the "faces" of poverty, the films demonstrate a different kind of storytelling. Immediacy takes the place of context and interpretation, with the corresponding sacrifice of analysis and broader perspective.

The celebrated Fogo Island films are examples of the application of film to local decision-making. They document and contribute to the process of resettlement that characterized Newfoundland's Confederation experience. Let us consider them in context. Between 1955 and 1975, twenty-eight thousand people were relocated from outport communities to "growth centres," and people with fishing skills became test cases for employment retraining schemes. Many of the unemployed collected some form of government assistance, and the Newfoundland government turned to the federal government for help. In 1964 Newfoundlanders started the rural development movement in order to organize locally in communities too small to have municipal governments: "With no forms of local or regional government there to express their interests, people in rural areas felt that planners and bureaucratic decision-makers in St. John's and Ottawa were uninformed and insensitive to the local potential which was, in fact, available for regional, rather than centralized, forms of economic development. The simple and straightforward solution was to band together to identify opportunities, seek financing for local development projects and lobby for improved services" (Fuchs 1987, 195).

Beginning in 1965, the federal government began to contribute financial assistance to the resettlement programs as part of its war on poverty. This fiscal relationship continued through to the mid-eighties, when a cost-sharing program was established with Newfoundland. Throughout this period, elected Rural Development Councils around the province constituted a province-wide representative council in Gander under whose auspices they worked closely with the province's Department of Rural, Agricultural and Northern Development (RAND) as well as other government agencies (Fuchs 1987, 208).

It is against this backdrop that the Fogo Island process films were made. When the film crews arrived, a number of communities – Fogo Island, Port au Port, Great Northern Peninsula, Eastport, Green Bay, and Bell Island – had already been involved in negotiations about resettlement for a number of years. Social animators were being trained by RAND, and the process of determining what to do with outport communities would continue on with local organizations for fifteen years after the process films. As the welfare of Newfoundlanders was taken over by the transfer payment legislation connected with the centralization of the welfare state, their fate became an important barometer of the success of the new federal system. While the films granted a new, and respectful, platform to Newfoundland's poorest communities as they attempted to negotiate the province's "great modernization," they could also be seen as acts of interpellation into national citizenship.

A report on the process by NFB coordinator Bill Nemtin illustrates the degree to which it was hoped that film might clarify decision-making regarding the community's future.

> The Fogo Island Project was designed to investigate the reactions of a community when its people and its problems were filmed in depth and the results played back to them for discussion and criticism. Our role was to facilitate communication between individuals and between communities and to assist in transferring information from one segment of the community to another. By this simple process we hoped to generate confidence in people to formulate and express their problems as they saw them, for it was felt that the expression of problems is a step towards understanding and solving them. Furthermore, it was believed that the playback of these expressions in the community could reveal the contradictions in individual attitudes and also in group attitudes. It could be a beginning in modifying attitudes, achieved not through dissemination of information or propaganda but through real participation which has the potential of creativity. (1968a, n.p.)

The NFB played to the state agenda to resolve the welfare issue brought about by the economic shift away from fishing. Nemtin reflected that welfare was a touchy issue that might have been handled better. "We might ... have covered certain issues differently," he wrote in 1968. "The most sensitive one was welfare, and although we waited until we had been filming for four weeks before treating it at all, when that time came, we confronted it head-on. Though sixty per cent of Fogo Islanders are on welfare, we have unfortunately shown only those who do not receive welfare discussing its effect upon those who do ... [W]e screened for our first showing at Seldom a local merchant describing the detrimental effect of welfare – and many in the audience walked out" (1968a, n.p.).

Indeed, the films *Discussion on Welfare* (Colin Low, 1967) and *Brian Earle on Merchants and Welfare* (Colin Low, 1967) are both quite harsh on the topic of welfare, and although they use the language of eradicating "blocks to communication," they are more provocative than conciliatory. Both are quite engaged with the deserving/undeserving poor question, noting, as one participant does in *Discussion on Welfare*, that there is "a heckuva lot of relief" and that it may negatively affect those who receive it by destroying their initiative – "squelching their spirit" is the memorable phrase – while simultaneously creating resentment in those who do not. Solutions proposed include using welfare money for industrial development to create jobs instead of handouts. The idea that some in the community think that the "welfare state has gone too far in Newfoundland" comes across clearly. Although the films are left unresolved and open-ended, the over-utilization of people critical of those on the dole is perhaps telling of the filmmakers' orientation towards the state's interests and of the type of cooperation they received. There was no doubt that they were government representatives.

URBAN POVERTY

Other films about poverty focus on urban centres – Toronto, Montreal, and Halifax – and explore the changing Canadian city and the plight of victims of the class system. I will discuss a number of films that explore the so-called culture of poverty – the conditions that trap people in penury for generations – and cast a critical eye at the welfare apparatus itself. I will briefly look at the problems as set out in the films, the solutions proposed, if any, and the aesthetic strategies used by the filmmakers. *The Things I Cannot Change* (Tanya Ballantyne Tree, 1967), *Up against the System* (Terence Macartney-Filgate 1969), *A Young Social Worker Speaks Her Mind* (Terence Macartney-Filgate, 1969), *World of One in Five* (Jim Carney, 1969), VTR *St-Jacques* (Bonnie Sherr Klein, 1969), *Halifax Neighbourhood Center Project* (Rex Tasker, 1967), and *Mrs. Case* (Pierre Lasry, 1969) all scrutinize aspects of the dehumanization inherent in the administered system and also, in line with much postwar social thought, in the anonymous urban environment itself. A number of these films were made in the wake of an amendment to the National Housing Act of 1964 that allowed for the commercial redevelopment of urban lands purchased with federal funds. According to one historian of welfare, this created "a frenzy of garish urban renewal schemes that resulted in 'the brutal clearance of low-income families from their cherished neighbourhoods'" (Ismael 2006, 27).

The Things I Cannot Change, the pilot film made to raise people's awareness of the war on poverty and screened on CBC, takes the strategy common to direct cinema of finding a built-in narrative in a real situation. In this case, it is the impending birth of a new baby into an already very large and very poor family. The film is famous for having embarrassed the Bailey family by naming them and exposing their poverty for all to see, but there are a number of mitigating factors that should be considered. First, according to Rick Clifton Moore, the family was paid for its participation, a sum so large that it would have helped them considerably ($500 in 1966 ≅ $3,200 in 2008 dollars) (1987, 52). Second, the decision to follow a single family and to make a longer film (55 min.) allowed the filmmakers to profile them with a fair amount of depth. The family is desperately poor, but they are also by turns smart, talented, funny, sad, dignified, incensed, scared, and hopeful. In a moment of stress, Kenneth Bailey opens the door to his apartment and clearly asks the director, Tanya Ballantyne Tree, and her crew to leave, offering a moment of self-reflexivity about the filmmakers' complicity in the very system that is victimizing his family. The film successfully highlights the impossibilities that the poor must live with; every day is a new struggle just to survive. The film crew is shown to be just one more indignity to be borne.

By contrast, and in direct response to the controversy stirred up by *Things*, *Up against the System*, *World of One in Five*, and *Halifax Neighbourhood Center Project* adopt an anonymizing strategy by showing fragments of the lives of many different people caught in the welfare trap. We don't get to know any of them very well, and without names they are more likely to become two-dimensional representatives of their plight. Of course, each film approaches the problem slightly differently.

Up against the System makes extended use of the trope of abjection.[4] The film repeatedly characterizes welfare as an institutional attempt to deal with the class differences produced by capitalism. Capitalism creates poverty; poor people are then treated as filth, as the excess baggage of the system that produced them. The capitalist system, then, is also a meaning-making system, bestowing value on middle-class subjectivity, defined by the dominant practices of education, types of work, and styles of leisure, while simultaneously criminalizing, pathologizing, and patronizing working-class and non-working people. The image of filth is evoked numerous times. Shots of garbage and broken windows visually underscore the abjection of people forced to live in

4 Abjection functions as a structural metaphor in the work of Mary Douglas (1966), Julia Kristeva (1982), Barbara Creed (1993), and others to delineate all that is dirty from all that is clean. It operates as the basis of social meaning making, differentiating self from other and proper subjectivity from debased materiality.

substandard conditions. The film sounds out many voices, all of them recognizing that the system as it stands needs rethinking, but none agreeing on what is to be done. In editing together the voices of the poor and disenfranchised, as well as the voices of those who work with them, the film addresses the population at large, asking people both to consider the wounds caused by the affluent society and to think about possible changes, such as guaranteed income and social housing.

A longer interview with the articulate young social worker who appears in the film, Joanna Stern, can be found in *A Young Social Worker Speaks Her Mind* (1969). Significantly, although she is very thoughtful and well spoken, her analysis of the solution to poverty is much less rousing than that of the pensioner whose words end *Up against the System*. *Young Social Worker* ends with a freeze-frame on Stern, but rather than a call for revolution, she has just articulated the view that she doesn't foresee the poor organizing in Canada the way they have in the United States, because race isn't a significant issue in Canada.

Stern gets to the crux of the contradiction at the heart of welfare policies in Canada. A critique of poverty leads inevitably to an assessment of the values of industrial society, including an emphasis on rewards for the industrious (Rein 1970, 16). Yet, to extend the notion of the essential value of human beings to individuals regardless of their market productivity would be to radically challenge the values of the market system. While welfare grapples with the contradiction by providing a punitive form of aid, a more progressive perspective would see welfare as a means to challenge the values of the system

Up against the System (1969): tropes of abjection?
Frame enlargement.

itself. The social work profession was riven in the 1960s by the issue of allegiance to client or system. Radical social workers saw their work as a sort of community organizing, while others saw themselves as functionaries on the lookout for fraud by welfare clients (see Wagner 1989, 267–8). Into this ideological knot waded the filmmakers of the CFC/SN program.

Stern's view on race in Canada is somewhat contradicted by *Halifax Neighbourhood Center Project* (1967), directed by Rex Tasker. The film is a compelling example of the engagement of a variety of voices on the question of poverty, in this case with respect to racism in Nova Scotia. The voice-over narrator makes comments straight out of war on poverty discourse, such as "the poor are still with us." He conveys that their numbers are growing because of the cycle of poverty. "Do things really change?" he asks cynically. The film also includes an independent voice, that of journalist Frank Filmore, who is shown watching the film and who makes comments throughout. The film also uses snippets of interviews with impoverished people, usually families, living in substandard housing in Halifax's north end.

Halifax illustrates new initiatives that were undertaken to deal with poverty; for example, a Manpower office was opened in the neighbourhood and agents were hired to study and catalogue the situation of the local population. The film also includes a long sequence in which black youth discuss racism in Halifax and violent civil rights struggles in the United States. This discussion is intercut with a scene where white church ministers wonder aloud why the black community doesn't appreciate their attempts at outreach. Filmore warns that the "black power" confrontations of American ghettos may find their way to Canada if racism and poverty are not curbed. The film features an intelligent and sympathetic social worker, Marvin Burke, who is attempting to organize residents of public housing into tenants associations that can make coherent and forceful claims on the city.

Made in the same year, *World of One in Five* represents the combination of the new and the old NFB. Narrated by Stanley Jackson, who had been making films at the NFB since the 1940s, and produced by Gordon Burwash, the narrator of *Man and His Resources*, the film was directed by Jim Carney for broadcast on CBC. *World of One in Five* utilizes a narrator throughout, but it encompasses a number of observational sequences in a variety of institutional settings – welfare office, homeless shelter, doctor's office, job centre, orphanage – as well as on the streets. Like the others, the film identifies the current issues of the "culture of poverty" and its multi-generational traps. But the tone is much more removed and less visceral. The film makes use of a vision of a rapidly modernizing society, one that has created its own victims, by using shots of the brutal urbanization underway in the Toronto landscape in the 1960s, including the completion of the raised Gardiner Expressway. In the final shot of the film, a troubled child met earlier at the orphanage is shown as a tiny figure dwarfed by the expressway running through his east-end neighbourhood. However, all discussion of anti-expressway protests is left to another film, one not part of the CFC/SN program, entitled *City Limits* (1971).

World features a number of striking sequences, particularly the travelling shots down dreary apartment hallways that are used as transitions between stories of a number of destitute families, and the travelling shot through a welfare office that imparts a similar sense of the massive numbers of people victimized by poverty. Like the others, the film ends with a sense of open-ended anxiety. Something needs to be done, but nothing particular is suggested. Although open-endedness certainly can be an aesthetic strategy to provoke thought and discussion on the part of the viewers, it can also be the mark of a retreat from politics common to work that attempts to achieve objectivity. (The memorable critique of the journalists in *VTR St-Jacques* who claim to have no point of view is "What are the reporters afraid of?")

Pierre Lasry's *Mrs. Case* is a fascinating example in the CFC/SN poverty films. While the title suggests the use of the anonymous strategy, it actually turns out to be the name of the single mother of five on welfare profiled in the film. The film treats the same problem as the others – the culture of poverty and the injustices and inhumanities of the system. Mrs Case is extremely artic-ulate and pragmatically struggles with her lot. However, Lasry defamiliarizes the observational footage that in other ways so closely resembles that of the other films in the series by repeating it with a loop-based aesthetic and deploy-ing other forms of non-naturalistic editing. It is made abundantly clear that the case worker assigned to Mrs Case is, in her words, "hindering" her and that the system is set up to scrutinize the poor rather than give them mean-ingful aid. These are the points made by Joanna Stern in *Young Social Worker*, but they are more clearly illustrated here than elsewhere.

Two sequences exemplify this. The first takes place during what at first appears to be a straightforward observational sequence in which Mrs Case makes lunch for her five children. Mrs Case's assessment that her caseworker doesn't do anything for her is underscored by the repetition of a number of images showing her doing things for herself and her family. When looped, the scenes of her washing carrots, spreading cheese on bread, sewing, and disci-plining her children all begin to take on a larger existential tone, not unlike the image of the woman perpetually walking up the stairs with her water jug in Fernand Léger's *Ballet méchanique* (1924). Daily actions here take on the feeling of a more abstracted experience of everyday life. But, more than that, the sense of frustration that Mrs Case is expressing is manifested for the viewer to feel as well as hear.

In another sequence, where we meet the frustrating social worker our-selves, the filmmaker has intercut scenes of Mrs Case being interviewed (or interrogated) with a scene of her undergoing an X-ray at the hospital. The indignities of scrutiny inside and out could not be clearer. Adding a layer of self-reflexivity to this sequence (not unlike what Tanya Ballantyne does in *Things*), Lasry includes his own question, repeated a couple of times, about what she does on Thursdays. The film's willingness both to explore the culture of poverty and to experiment with disruptive editing remains an exciting remnant of the combination of experimentation and social purpose associated with the CFC/SN moment. In their different ways, all of the films leave the issues open in their attempt to create disquiet and invite discussion and response.

VTR St-Jacques is an example of an activist film. It illustrates the bridge between two different streams within the program by using film to document the use of video. As with many other CFC/SN films, *VTR* sets up the "culture of poverty" issue and points out that progressive politics must work to give the poor something they do not have: the power to control their lives. In a report on the film, Klein and Hénaut write: "The VTR project in Saint-Jacques is an attempt to extend to its logical conclusion the conviction that people should participate in shaping their own lives, which means among other things directing and manipulating the tools of modern communication necessary to gain and exercise that participation ... Their experience with video – conceiving, shooting, editing and presenting their own programs – made the citizens particularly aware of the myth of objectivity in mass media reporting and sensitive to conscious and unconscious manipulation. They have become a less gullible public" (Hénaut and Klein, this volume, p. 31).

Shot in a poor francophone neighbourhood of Montreal, the film also documents the citizens committees discussed by Blondin. People on the St-Jacques committee use the video equipment supplied to them by the NFB to clarify their own positions on issues that affect them, to enable them to approach people on the street, and to generate interest – and possibly larger membership – in their group. Interviewing people coming out of welfare agencies, the citizens committee finds white men angry at the government but also angry at immigrants and women for having jobs they perceive as rightfully theirs. The film thus wades into the difficult subject of rifts within the working class. After the VTR screening shown in the film, the topic of conversation among the citizens is, as in *Halifax Neighbourhood*, *The System*, and *World*, inadequate housing.

VTR St-Jacques represents a bridging text in the CFC/SN archive in that it suggests in ways both direct and indirect that the next step for this use of media in social activism is broadcasting, not closed-circuit TV. The film, co-directed by Dorothy Todd Hénaut (see Hénaut and Klein, chapter 3, this volume), is thus closely connected with ideas finding expression in the CFC/SN newsletter, edited by Hénaut, as it moved into discourses about community broadcasting (e.g., February 1971 issue).

CONCLUSIONS

The films discussed in this chapter are vivid and exciting evocations of the changes going on in the late 1960s and of various filmmakers' attempts to work within the ambit of the state's attempt to study, interpret, and remedy poverty. As I have tried to suggest, the reasons behind the state's motivation to bring filmmaking into communities as a form of social animation or mediation may have been different from those that inspired the tactics of educators, organizers, filmmakers, and media activists who did the actual work. While the various players may have all been concerned about poverty and inequality – and while there may have been some agreement around the idea of communication and mediated social fora as preliminary steps in the solution of social problems – there the similarities ended. The state's focus appeared to be on making invisible citizens appear – albeit in mediated form – to their state representatives and on using technology to stimulate problem-solving at the community level. At the most, the state envisioned open-ended "objective" shows made for broadcast on CBC (to which end an ambiguous observational style could be quite effective). For their part, social activists and media producers seemed more intent on bringing about a radically democratic public sphere and on using media to provoke change – including in perception through the use of formal experimentation – as opposed to simply adjusting to it once it had occurred.

One implication of the discussion in this chapter is the presence of polyphony in the films and social policies alike. Depending on the prevailing policy language, a variety of groups can presumably find a place in relation to dominant discursive parameters. In the 1960s, much as today, people and groups with radical political ideas worked alongside – and in and out of – the spaces produced by government policies (see Pal 1993). The difference is – and it is a profound one – that the government discourse of the 1960s paid lip service to an engagement with change and the production of meaningful lives in just communities. This humanist discourse can be utilized by people and groups with left of centre politics in a way that neoliberalism, with its emphasis on the unhampered competition of isolated economic actors, cannot.

The idea that some people are victims of structural change, or systemic inequality, has seemingly fallen out of the mainstream, as has the discussion of human values or the public good as the basis for political and economic decisions. Today's neoliberal social policy has reintroduced the notion of deserving and undeserving poor, and the charitable sector has begun to replace the residual state in the provision of welfare (Ismael 2006, 13). Current social policy is deeply invested in a technological discourse as well, but with notable differences from the 1960s. The Internet features prominently in current discussions of media access, and in this regard Citizen*Shift*, the online inheritor of the progressive mandate of the NFB, is instructive. The program off-loads production to individuals (there is no money for production) and provides a forum for blogging in the place of the screening/meeting model. Where before social workers, activists, and the general public were the intended audience and filmmakers worked in conjunction with members of the communities they had targeted as needing help, today's filmmakers are independent social investigators, choosing projects that interest them – and for which they presumably can find some kind of funding – rather than ones that meet with government social policy objectives or combine with organized social and media activism. It is difficult to assess the kind of public(s) constituted by this type of online media sharing. One thing is certain, CitizenShift will not create the community media institutions that were such an important legacy of CFC/SN. Nor does it constitute a policy issue – such as public-access broadcasting – that could be used as a rallying point.[5]

As in the past, the current configuration is rich with contradictions. As cultural productions in modern industrial capitalist society, especially ones with the progressive aim of exposing the un- or underexposed, these films and videos express a continued faith in the possibility that a politicized viewing public might bring about change. Certainly, the attempt to turn social process, politics, and policy into mediated form continues to be an important practice – as well as an enduring problematic in communication studies. Whatever the shortcomings of the Canadian state's anti-poverty policy of the1960s, the current neoliberal version seems far less hopeful. Looking back on the complexities of the Challenge for Change/Société nouvelle program, we are reminded of the perennial questions concerning the relationship between welfare and cultural citizenship and perhaps are given some insight into strategies for the future.

5 These are points of particular relevance given rumours of the project's demise in 2008/09.

Author's Note: Thanks to Peter Anderson for sharing with me his collection of Challenge for Change newsletters and his experiences with community media and activism in Vancouver in the 1970s. Thanks also to Bernard Lutz of NFB Archives, Mirfat Habib of SFU Media Bookings, Laurynas Navidauskis, and Tom Waugh for help with research sources.

33 Amateur Video and the Challenge for Change (1995)

■

JANINE MARCHESSAULT

AUTHOR'S PREFACE (2008)

This essay was written in the early 1990s when the effects of the Internet and the rise of digital culture were barely visible. Would a different essay have been written today? No. And of course, yes. My chapter offers a critical perspective on one aspect of Challenge for Change: the way the program underplayed structures of power by emphasizing the immediate and seemingly unmediated nature of the forms of communication that were being animated by the National Film Board filmmakers involved in the project. The technology of video in particular was employed as a simple recording device – or mirror – that enabled people to speak to each other, to have a voice, to have access to the means of production. There was, the essay argues, a lack of critical reflexivity on the part of the NFB filmmakers in terms of the overall government involvement in the project and in controlling its potential impact. This lack is a serious shortcoming and can be seen to have sown the seeds of the program's demise.

This critique is by no means intended to underestimate the extraordinary nature of this experiment in all its diverse articulations as a landmark moment in the history of social and media activism. Nevertheless, I remain convinced that the liberal ideology underpinning the project obscured the political economic structure that enabled and defined access for communities and the material complexity of communication. This becomes evident when we examine the failure of the project to set up a structure for any kind of sustained connection to cable television or to other circuits of distribution. In the end, I maintain that the project instituted access without agency – or, put another way, the age-old Canadian problem, production without distribution. While we cannot deny the excitement that many participants must have felt in learning to use different media for the first time and in viewing new kinds of community communication, any discussion of the project must be tempered by an awareness of its limitations.

Contemporary incarnations of Challenge for Change's aspiration to embed media in marginalized communities have both been inspired by the NFB's innovative fostering of community media and been carried out with a more developed critical acumen (see Miller, chapter 37, this volume). Challenge for Change needs to be situated within an archaeology of the media radicalism of the 1960s, which includes the solipsistic process-oriented films of Andy Warhol alongside the McLuhanesque visions of media democracy found at Expo '67 – the multi-screen architecture of the NFB's *In the Labyrinth* project, which Colin Low had conceptualized in the early 1960s, is perhaps the ultimate expression of this optimism. From this perspective, we can see that Challenge for Change's experiments with media democracy and social justice activism are important precursors to the diy (do it yourself) aesthetic and the networked cultures of digital media around the world. Such networks are grounded in localized circuits of communication and action that in turn have a global effect. In the context of networked, locative, and distributed media, we can appreciate the importance of the feedback loop that was the basis of the Challenge for Change methodology. Although the critique of liberal ideology found in this chapter continues to be a vital one, the very logic of the feedback loop encompasses a conceptualization of production as always already intrinsically tied to consumption and circulation. That is, as Walter Benjamin put it in 1934, the use of the apparatus in this manner proposes the "author as producer," which is then the challenge for change.

Once the dispossessed and powerless have access to the means of information they can no longer be misled by Establishment bullshit. And that is in itself a revolution.
▪ Patrick Watson 1970, 20

Nineteen hundred and sixty-seven was an important year for Canada. As a centennial celebration of Confederation, Expo '67 (Montreal) saw the convergence of technology and nationalism as never before. IMAX, the largest screen in the world, could, we were told, only have been invented in Canada. The spectacular five-screen cinematic feat, devised by the National

Film Board of Canada's (NFB's) Unit B, epitomized the image of nationhood: technological mastery, natural abundance, and an open multi-accented democratic participation. Its theme, in the Unit B tradition, was the wonder of human life. Cognitive and technological development were harmoniously synchronized in a symphony dedicated to McLuhan's favourite metaphor, the labyrinth. The United Nations theme of the fair, "*Terre des hommes*/Man and His World," announced official bilingualism and "the multicultural Canada in a multinational world" promoted by the Liberal government (Wilson 1991, 162–8).

Nineteen sixty-seven also saw the birth of a new program at the NFB: Challenge for Change (CFC). Initiated with subsidies from seven government departments, the program gained almost instant international recognition. Much like IMAX, it reinforced the image of Canada as an advanced democratic nation. The project's aims were simple: give the disenfranchised and marginal communities of Canada a voice by giving them access to the media (film and later super 8, video, and cable television). This was intended "to encourage dialogue and promote social change" mostly around issues of poverty (Hénaut 1991a, 49; see also Hénaut and Klein, chapter 3, in this volume). By the time the program began to lose momentum (i.e., to lose government subsidies owing to fiscal restraint) in the mid-1970s, it had produced hundreds of films and videos, and hundreds of hours of unedited "process" videos.

Although Challenge for Change defies simple evaluation (there are differences not only between the English and Quebec – Société nouvelle – versions of the program but between the various projects within each program),[1] I wish to draw attention to a particular teleology at its core, one that came to dictate the way video was used as a "mirror machine" for the people, implementing non-hierarchical forms of authority and consolidating the identity of difference. I am especially interested in the way "media for the people" exhibited a highly instrumental view of cultural development. D.B. Jones has pointed out that this view – and CFC on the whole – reflected the Liberal's twofold policy to democratize and regionalize culture, a strategy largely aimed at integrating the margins into the mainstream of Canadian life (Jones 1981, 171–2).

Unit B director Colin Low, heavily involved in the IMAX sensation, would pioneer the participatory techniques that gained Challenge for Change its reputation as one of the cornerstones of the alternative media movement. The participatory process was conceived as a means to counter both the objecti-

---

1 Société nouvelle, the Québécois counterpart of the project, was set up in 1969. Growing out of Le groupe de recherches sociales (1966–69), whose members included Robert Forget, Claude Jutra, and Fernand Dansereau, Société nouvelle placed far less emphasis on process film and video.

fication of earlier ethnographic approaches and the aestheticism of an emerging auteurist tendency at the NFB (mainly in Quebec).

The CFC pilot film, Tanya Ballantyne Tree's *The Things I Cannot Change* (1967), lacked an essential political imperative. The cinéma-vérité portrait of a poverty-stricken family in Montreal, while sensitive, only reinforced the hopelessness and futility of the family's situation. Moreover, the family's sense of powerlessness was heightened when, without their being notified, the film was aired on local television. They were subjected to ridicule by neighbours and eventually had to move – so the story goes.

In the aftermath of *The Things I Cannot Change,* an ethical dimension was incorporated into the documentary process. For Low and others, the CFC film would seek to "engage the people on the screen as partners in the film-making process" (Hénaut 1975). Thus, the aims of a project could no longer be subsumed to the self-expression of an individual director. Turning away from his earlier formal inclinations – *Corral* (1954), *Universe* (1960), *Circle of the Sun* (1961) – Low resolved to break "the illusion that I can communicate, that I am effecting social change" (cited in Gwyn 1972, 12). Rather than making films about disadvantaged groups, he sought to make film with them. This approach presented an alternative to the paternalistic and authoritarian mandate of Grierson's NFB: "to interpret Canada to Canadians and to the rest of the world and to make films in the national interest" (while diminishing sectionalism). Challenge for Change would confront the NFB's technocratic elitism, seeking to transform the government-sponsored film into a public platform for "the people."

PARTICIPANT OBSERVER

The first prototype films were produced in 1967 on Fogo Island, just off the northeast coast of Newfoundland. For long-time CFC worker Dorothy Todd Hénaut, the principles informing what has since been called the "Fogo process" would be fundamental to the development of "a community process, media by the community" (this volume, p. 77). Low's notion of subject participation paralleled the Liberal interpretation of cultural development (i.e., "help them help themselves") and would play an essential role in the state promotion of community culture in Canada.

Unable to sustain their livelihoods owing to the corporatization of the fishing industries, the five thousand islanders who made up the different communities on Fogo were about to be relocated by the government. Despite their geographical isolation from each other, it was their intention to resist the relocation. To increase communication between the communities and not to impose his own interpretation on their views, needs, and histories, Low opted to film interviews with different members from each community. The members not only chose the topics they discussed but viewed the rushes afterward and could demand the omission of any material that did not properly reflect them. Often the interviews were screened to other island communities and Low would record their reactions, creating a series of vérité observational or feedback documents.

Refusing to make an overall film about the Island,[2] Low produced what he calls "vertical" films. Somewhat akin to the home-movie archive, vertical films consisted of one community event (e.g., *Jim Decker's party,* 5 min.), an everyday occurrence (*The Mercer Family,* 10 min.), or an interview where one issue was discussed (*Tom Best on Cooperatives,* 10 min.). Editing was kept to a minimum and intercutting between people on the basis of issues was eliminated altogether. This practice, according to Low, functioned to keep the filmmaker's interventions and value judgments to a minimum, facilitating more self-directed community expression and democratic communication (Gwyn 1972, 5).

While anthropology's nefarious "participant observation" seeks to resolve power relations by positioning the observer inside the field to be investigated, the Fogo process sidestepped power altogether. It inscribed not a self-reflective gaze, one that takes account of the observer's contradictory status of belonging, but a self-reflective observation that eliminated boundaries altogether. Using film, participants could observe their own behaviour on the screen *a posteriori*. Low theorized that the media – film and, as we shall see, especially video – could be made to function as a collective mirror, enabling communities "to view themselves, discover their strengths and bring their ideas to better order." Thus, what came to matter was not so much the final product but the use of media "as a sparkplug for process" (Low 1973). Aimed at strengthening community communications, the process involved building consensus and advocacy around particular issues.

Historically, the participatory approach to documentary filmmaking is not a stylistic but an ethical engagement with the process of representation. At the very least, it entails some involvement with and accountability to those lives that were being depicted. It is a mode of gathering information that can produce very different results and is certainly no guarantee of political acumen. As a methodology, it enabled the staged realities of Flaherty's *Nanook of the North* (1922) to gain ethnographic currency, just as it was fundamental to the tenement dwellers' direct address in Edgar Anstey and Arthur Elton's *Housing Problems* (1935). Yet subject participation in the CFC films became synonymous with an ethical rejection of style in favour of direct

2 *Children of Fogo* (1967), *The Winds of Fogo* (1969), and the follow-up film *A Memo from Fogo* (1972) are circulated as general interest films for the public.

speech. The twenty-eight films produced on Fogo embodied a dominant aesthetic trope – or anti-aesthetic – that would come to characterize a majority of CFC films and videos: the talking head or the talking head viewing the talking head. D.B. Jones has commented on this: "[A]s if, in the words of Guy Glover, 'simple quotation were the only guarantee of veracity.' Ironically, the self-expression that Grierson had abhorred, and which he noticed in some of the Board's work when he visited Montreal in 1964, and which Challenge for Change had meant to counteract, was re-emerging. Only it wasn't the filmmakers who were expressing themselves, it was 'the people.' Challenge for Change, which sprang in part as recoil from the aesthetics of self-expression, got rid of aesthetics, but not the self-expression" (1981, 168). While subject participation was intended to counter the ethnographer's distant gaze, it was being delimited in terms of the filmmaker's detachment from the processes of representation.

VIDEO

From 1969 onwards, video became the choice technology for the participatory practice. Not only was it cost-effective but it could, ostensibly, provide an automatic – instantaneous and simultaneous – record, a mirror machine that needed no operator. Hénaut recalls: "[A]n aspect of the process was bothering us. These people were dependent on our equipment and goodwill – in short, our own power – for access to the instruments of communication. As intermediaries, we were nevertheless cumbersome. If we really believed in people's right to express themselves directly, then we needed to eliminate ourselves from the process and find a way to put the media directly in the hands of citizens. Fortunately, a half-inch portable video called 'Portapak' was released onto the market in 1968" (1991a, 49).

Video redefined the film director's role. No longer an authorial agent, the director became a social animator whose chief function was to provide technical training to select communities. In the late 1960s and early 1970s, through the CFC project, several video access centres were set up across Canada (Vidéographe, Trinity Square, MetroMedia, and Teled among others) to encourage community culture and communication of which video linked to cable television was a central feature. Indeed, many of these access centres – arguably some of the most productive initiatives of the entire project – continue to exist very constructively as artist-run organizations.

Over and again, video is reported to have been greeted with tremendous excitement by different communities. The videotape recorder (VTR) "brought the community together" and the television monitor (even if it was closed-circuit) resonated with institutional authority, promising a new form of social communication (Karch 1971–72). Able to transcend the mediated facets of film production, video's technical accessibility enabled citizens "to express themselves directly." Shattering the traditional hierarchies of power implemented by the interview as a formal structure, community members could employ video to interview themselves. Group discussions were to become the dominant representational paradigm for the democratic communication enabled by video – the disembodied authority behind the camera seemingly absent from the process.

VTR *Rosedale* (1970), a film documenting the use of video and the Fogo process in the rural community of Rosedale, Alberta, echoes this enthusiasm. Challenge for Change animator Anton Karch trained the Rosedale Citizens' Action Committee to use video with the aim of assessing community needs. The film's soft-spoken female voice-over tells how the citizens interviewed by the committee were able to watch themselves immediately after on the playback monitor: "They were impressed by how clearly they had expressed themselves." Cut to a town meeting where the edited version of the interviews, which includes watching the playback, is presented to the community and videotaped once again. Here, the utilization of video to implement the Fogo process produces an astounding observational regress: a displacement of the apprehending gaze that screens and deflects relations of power. The modalities of power inherent in the process become less and less tangible as the frame appears to open forever outward. There is no outside, no semiotic interference in the mimetic process upon which identity construction depends. The refracted gaze makes the community – in true Foucauldian fashion – both the subject and the object of knowing. This observational paradigm at once mirrors and obliterates VTR *Rosedale*'s institutional framework: the state-sponsored program becomes a community initiative. Thus, the impression prevails that the communications technology is unregulated; it is merely a recording apparatus servicing the community.

While *Labyrinth* sought to answer the nineteenth-century quest to overcome the exclusion of the spectator from the image, the video Portapak promised to overcome the viewer's exclusion from television. The same technological determinism pledged interactivity in the form of an immediate and empowering transport, from the mundane disconnected experience of the everyday to the social nexus of the screen. Fostering processes of equivalency and unification, this engagement would multiply the order of meaning and, as McLuhan theorized, move the world (or at least Canada) towards universal harmony.

Yet the interactivity and participation that video delivered instituted access without agency. It instituted a particular form of self-surveillance rather than transform the actual institutional relations of production and knowledge. If empowerment came from demythologizing the technological and social institutions of television by the very fact that anyone could be on television, that television could be used to make a difference, then it also served to reinforce the difference television makes. Video projected television's generalized fantasy of transparency, immediacy, and extension through that contradictory bifurcation of *being on TV*. And most of the community experiments with video never went beyond this initial positivism, beyond this social reproduction.

Community videos produced through Challenge for Change, although emerging from a diversity of communities, tended to look the same. According to producer Boyce Richardson, the problem with the Portapak was that its "easy to operate" façade did not encourage anyone to actually learn about or experiment with its use. Instead, black-and-white "glitchy" images, unfocused and barely edited, were glorified as "a manifestation of honesty and directness" (NFB 1980, 19). Videographic reality appeared to have an ontological edge over film; video, unlike the chemical processing needed for film, was a *tape recording* able to "feed back," to mirror, the reality of difference directly.

In this way, the formal characteristics of community video were delineated in opposition to art and to the mediating subjectivity of the auteur. Video was an antidote to indeterminacy – the more ordinary and transparent, the more authentic. Community video and television were intended – were funded – to provide a document of community experience and need, increasing the internal coherence of the community. Although "process" video was supposed to work against any finished product, ultimately its goal was to bring ideas to better order. The "authentic" expression of community was made to replicate the instrumental discourses of the state. More often than not, community video was synonymous with the transparency and certainty of public service information.

PROCESSING DIFFERENCE

Foucault has encapsulated the power/knowledge problematic in the following way: "[W]e are subjected to the production of truth through power and we cannot exercise power except through the production of truth" (1980, 93). The equation of community video with public service information is not surprising, since the very cohesion of those community identities – dispossessed, black, Aboriginal, working mothers, the welfare class – was constituted by the state in the first place. The institutionalization of cultural difference defines the project of multiculturalism not only to manage and integrate difference, but to make it at once separate and identical. This construction creates a common other whose solidarity is made impossible under the burden of difference.

Here, the "people" or the "community" are defined negatively by exclusion, by the participation, wealth, and access to power that they do not have. John Frow has argued that the reduction of difference to an "antagonistic duality" (people/state or community/society) cannot "break the cycle of the power because it is never more than its mirror image." It will only produce "a repetition of the Same" as difference (1992, 30). The category of the people, Frow maintains, is a "fact of representation, rather than an external cause of representation." Similarly, he rejects the concept of "the popular" because it is theorized in relation to this "singular entity." The "strategic value" of these terms is found in the way they maintain dominant perceptions of how cultural space is organized and valued: "The point is to describe this normative function rather than accept it as given" (32–3).

Challenge for Change sought to enlarge the public sphere to include voices marginalized by, and excluded from, civic discourse. Certainly, this project was extremely important to the inception and growth of Canada's alternative video culture – both for art and community video production. Yet to what extent was the culture produced through the program limited to fulfilling a binary conception of "media by the people"? To what degree were established structures of authority recognized and challenged?

Infused with the radical aspirations for the new media that characterized the late 1960s, Hans Magnus Enzensberger's landmark essay "Constituents of a Theory of the Media" (1970) proposed a socialist strategy – a cultural revolution – that would do away with "the contractions between producers and consumers." The "emancipatory potential" of the media was to be "released" from the grips of capitalist production. Correspondingly, "the masses" needed to "organize themselves" and use "the new productive forces" to "secure evidence of their daily experiences and draw effective lessons from them" (1970, 14–23). Although sympathetic to Enzensberger's political aims, John Hartley has criticized his proposal for maintaining an implicit distinction between the "vanguard intellectual" and the "masses": "Enzensberger's notion of the 'masses' is contradictory, wanting them to be active and self-determining, but only if such action is organized along existing political lines, to support existing (socialist) strategies, and only if it is *mass*. Evidence that populations are not masses, and that the new media technologies suffuse popular culture in ways that challenge socialist orthodoxies, is dismissed as the result of corporate manipulation, leaving a view of the masses as, by default, passive, depoliticized and in need of organization" (1992, 24).

Certainly far less radical in its scope than Enzensberger's proposal, Challenge for Change suffers from a similar contradiction: the voice of change must emanate from the community that is "in need of organization." The participatory process was intended to overcome this contradiction. Yet this process – the Fogo process, the process of enabling a community to come to voice, the process of putting the media directly in the hands of the community – could not challenge an authority that it worked to obscure. Instead, the Fogo process consolidated a version of community identity largely determined by the directive of Liberal reform.

One of the main criticisms of Challenge for Change has been that it worked to diffuse direct action, to contain and stabilize the potentially explosive effects of difference. It is easy to see how CFC is entangled in that web of coercion and consent, technologies of domination and technologies of the self, which define the functioning of power in the liberal democratic state. As Chantal Mouffe has remarked, liberalism continuously denies its own limits in order to maintain political legitimacy, its foundation in civil society (1993). Discourses of access and participation often work to conceal the institutional conditions of access and the political limits of coming to voice.

Yet in times of crisis, limits do become apparent. At the height of Challenge for Change in 1970, the Liberal government imposed the War Measures Act on Quebec, arresting citizens without due process and censoring the media to protect the Quebec population from the threats of FLQ (Front de libération du Québec) terrorism. The video Portapak was used by the government for the purposes of monitoring and surveillance, purposes that defined its historical usage.

Video, Stuart Marshall has underlined, is a product of the information age. It is part of "a vast investment in commercial, military and managerial technology ... in a process entirely committed to extending institutional control and efficiency" (1985, 66). Delimiting that concern for "effect rather than meaning" typical of McLuhan's "electric time," the globalizing processes of the telematic media convert history into information. New information technologies make it difficult to locate institutional assumptions and structures of power because the actual source of a transmission is blurred within the new economy of the user. The emancipatory ambitions of Challenge for Change were circumscribed and contained by this complexity. It is just such a complexity (the thrill of access) that so often precludes us from taking into account the dialogic nature of access and participation: what are we being given access to and what are we participating in?

THE PEOPLE'S AUTHORITY

While Challenge for Change served as a model for thinking about community television around the world, it was a model that failed in Canada. There are countless reasons for the individual failures in Thunder Bay, Vancouver, Roosevelt Park, and Winnipeg. One impediment rested with CFC's neoliberal interpretation of the media's role in community development, as the following report summarizes: "The emerging pattern, if one examines the generation of projects beginning with Fogo, is that of gradual withdrawal from active social intervention in specific communities to a policy of provision of service and information" (Taylor and Van Every Taylor 1973, 68).

This "emerging pattern" reflects the technological determinism at the very heart of the program: the ahistorical conflation of new communications technologies with democratic participation. Thus, cable television was introduced to various communities as a service. The economic and institutional interests that fuelled this service were overshadowed by the National Film Board's euphoria of access and participation – a rhetoric supported by the public service history of television in Canada. Although the Canadian Radio-television and Telecommunications Commission (CRTC), in the early seventies, encouraged cable companies to open time slots for community programming, only one-third of them actually did (Berrigan 1977, 87). Moreover, cable managers and owners were free to impose restrictions on community productions. Except in Quebec, where community television has enjoyed some success, no state funding has ever been made available for community-access television. According to Marc Raboy, community broadcasting has remained marginal in Canada because it "was not seen as a new sector to be fully developed so as to meet the needs that could not be filled by either national public broadcasting or commercial private broadcasting. The possibility of community-controlled cable *systems,* as opposed to community access channels within privately owned systems, was never seriously explored" (1990, 203).

While not without problems, the model has been far more successful in the United States, perhaps because the market-driven institutions of television are more readily apparent. National Federation of Local Cable Programmers, founded as an advocacy association for public-access and community programming on cable television, has sustained a strong cablecast network. No such organization was ever deemed necessary in Canada.

The "people" harboured a new empiricism for the NFB – an amateur culture whose seeing was without intentionality, a neutral ground of everyday truth, totally transparent and uninformed. Video was the amateur technology *par excellence.* This might explain why many of the "people" (and the NFB in general) lost interest in making videos, getting involved instead in authoring film. This is also why, until recently, art video and community video have been mutually exclusive terms. Video artists have had to distinguish their work as art – video art – by linking it with the non-utilitarian concerns and institutions of high art in order to procure funding. Video activism, especially around AIDS, challenged this historical distinction.

Funding for the arts and subsidies for community culture – the arts and community culture traditionally being separate bodies in Canada – are also being redefined. Agencies are being made to rethink the ideologies that have defined art in modernist terminology and community in terms of development and preservation (i.e., craft).

The lessons that can be learned from Challenge for Change are tied to the contradictory impulses of liberalism, to the incompatibility of its dominant aims: to guarantee pluralism (individual freedom) while implementing a notion of the common good. The political avant-garde, and video-makers perhaps especially, have long been suspicious of those liberal claims that have served to mask the institutional structures of television. In effect, if alternative video production has worked to produce social change (increasing reciprocal understandings, actively producing rather than reflecting meaning), it is not through any notion of the "good life" but through a sense of justice – which is precisely where a radical concept like community materializes.

34   Video: The Politics of Culture and Community (1996)

■

RON BURNETT, RCA

AUTHOR'S NOTE (2009)

This article was written in the middle of the 1990s well before the Internet began to transform not only the manner in which video is distributed but also discourses about social networking and community. Many of its core assumptions remain extremely pertinent, including questions about the programmatic nature of videos oriented towards political change. The assumption that a well-thought-out message, carefully crafted in accordance with community needs, will not only be effective but may also produce change continues to have a profound hold on twenty-first-century video-makers. One of the challenges is the rather loose manner in which the word community is used as a trope for transmission, communications, and understanding.

A community can be many things to many people. It can be the set of boundaries that a particular culture uses to distinguish itself from others, boundaries that can be physical and symbolic as well as psychological. It can be a certain identity that has been gained over time through historical, social, and cultural processes and that symbolically unites different peoples in a shared sense of connection and interdependence. At its most basic, community stands for common interest.

What is most important here is the relationship between community and the symbols, images, and communicative instruments that communities use to define their activities. To what degree can outsiders capture that complexity? For example, a farming community is largely defined by a shared economic activity that is underpinned by social and cultural interactions. The people in the community don't have to tell themselves what they share; they know what unites and divides them by virtue of their everyday lives and through a set of tacit understandings. On a smaller scale, a kinship system brings diverse people together under the heading of family and in concert they form a community of interest. Some families use religion as a unifying force, as do some communities. Others may use a shared historical experience, a traumatic event, or even music to bring meaning to what connects them. In other words, every social formation has a variety of communities within it and an often unpredictable way of portraying the ways in which these communities operate.

The best way to understand community is to examine people's experiences within the communities that they share. And one of the most important activities that communities concern themselves with is learning. It doesn't really matter what form that learning takes, or whether it is formal or informal. The important point is that learning is seen as a central activity. It is also seen as a crucial indication of whether the community has the vision and organization necessary to communicate its historical, technical, and cultural knowledge to its members. Communities have always made use of a fairly complex set of communicative tools. The challenge – and it is an analytic as well as anthropological one – is to understand many of the already existing cultural patterns within communities. This was one of the great contributions of grassroots film and video creators – to engage with communities and to try and discover what made them tick. Problems arose when that knowledge was then connected to social change, and a template of requirements and expectations was laid onto communities in order to judge whether transformative movements could be put into place.

Political video-makers continue to see communities through rather limited lenses, referring to notions of participatory democracy for example, as if participation and learning are one and the same. Notwithstanding the richness of contemporary work in video compared to what was produced in the 1980s and 1990s, one of the key elements of this article is its effort to make sense of the many contradictory assumptions about learning that video-makers invoke to explain their work with communities. As I say in the article, giving a voice to people may not empower them. This fundamental problem remains a major challenge today.

Portable video use has exploded worldwide. Since its appearance in the late 1960s video has become the medium of choice for larger and larger numbers of people from a variety of diverse constituencies. Community, gay, and feminist organizations, environmental and social advocacy groups, nongovernmental organizations in developing countries, and mainstream and alternative political and cultural formations in North America and Europe have made active use of video for information gathering, political agitation, artistic experimentation, and the distribution and dissemination of local and transnational debates and ideas.

In southern or developing countries, video has been embraced in much the same way radio was by a previous generation, as a technology for training, education, organizing, information gathering, political agitation, and cultural preservation (see Mulay, chapter 38, this volume). Even more importantly, the appropriation of video has been seen as a key way for economically deprived communities to gain some measure of democratic control over information and communication sources now controlled either by the state or multinational corporations. These grassroots activities have had a profound influence on the way in which very different communities in many parts of the world have thought about communications, change, and the political process.

At the same time, these activities in the developing world have many contradictory elements because of the profound transformations these societies are undergoing as a consequence of this involvement with new and emerging communications technologies. The links between the old and the new, between societies in transition and communities undergoing a variety of complex changes, alter the landscape within which communication technologies operate and affect their potential influence on political change.

However one puts it (the shift from the modern to the postmodern, the movement from the colonial to the post-colonial), the many uses of video (among a number of additional technologies) have overwhelmed the critical and analytical approaches that one can take when trying to analyse their impact and importance. The process of engagement with new technologies is so challenging that far more work is needed, not only in critical theory, but also in the history of communication technologies and the impact of their introduction into differing social contexts.

In fact, and notwithstanding the complexities involved in introducing any technology to traditional societies, the unfettered use of communication technologies for a variety of different purposes has been advocated as a constitutional right, to be written into the legal framework of all countries (MacBride Commission 1980).[1] The commission called for "structural changes to equalize and balance the legal structure under which communications technologies operate. Such balance is necessary, according to its proponents, if development – economic, political, social and cultural – is to be effectively

---

1 See the International Commission for the Study of Communication Problems (MacBride Commission), *Many Voices, One World* (London: Kogan Page, 1980), and *World Communication Report* (Paris, France: UNESCO, 1989). The latter lists a long series of reports that have come out of various countries and constituencies.

promoted. This approach sees communications technologies as the infrastructure for economic growth, and thus, development" (Mowlana and Wilson 1990, 58).

In what follows, I will argue that most of the categories in place for analysing the video work that has grown out of twenty-five years of activity, exploration, and experimentation have not been examined with the critical depth that is needed for one to understand their impact. From notions of participatory democracy (i.e., community collaboration defines the production of ideas and images), to the horizontal nature of collective work with video, to the various paradigms for understanding the role of mainstream media (as different from the work produced through the efforts of the community), the categories used for analysis have been weak. There has been a lack of critical and evaluative work done on the videos themselves, although there are many descriptive examples that end up justifying the use of video as a tool of community development and consciousness-raising.[2]

There are now hundreds of video centres, some independent, some run by NGOs, others run by universities and museums, all engaged in activities that have legitimized video as a preferred medium for a variety of creative and often innovative endeavours. The advent of multimedia in the mid-1980s has increased the hybridization of video and computer technologies and has brought a variety of information systems together, with even greater potential for experimentation and research. One of the central presuppositions of this activity is that the base of participants who use and watch the medium of video will grow, because video incorporates so many different technologies and potential viewing sites and experiences.

In fact, in many discussions about the medium and its impact, the term "video" seems to stand for any electronic device that displays images. In that sense, it encapsulates all other media. As a result, the often-profound differences among a variety of media, differences that can sometimes be explained and other times not, are obscured through the rather vague global use of the term "video." This error would be of less consequence were it not for the fact that video-makers assume that there is a specific and direct link between the ways in which video images communicate and what is understood by viewers. The communications paradigm at work here needs close, critical examination because the relationship between viewing and understanding is neither direct nor a function of the technology in use.

Another important point is that the deeply felt antipathy on the part of grassroots video activists to ubiquitous and often dominant forms of popular culture leads these activists to assume that experimental and political

2 See in particular the essay by Chinyere Stella Okunna, "Communication for Self-Reliance among Rural Women in Nigeria," *Media Development* 39.1 (1992): 46–9.

video is a good alternative for achieving the goals they set for themselves. Although there are many potential and important ways in which such videos could connect to the society as a whole, their mode of distribution (small scale), as well as their carefully nurtured marginality, has kept these works from being seen by larger and more heterogeneous audiences. The political use of video to make a statement or provoke discussion and possible change is fraught with these challenges, which are at the core of any communications process. However, notwithstanding what I have just said, there is a deep commitment to the medium as a vehicle for communications intended for broad and diverse groups. This central concept of networking for social change forms the basis for much of what I will discuss in this essay.

At another level, the advent of cheaper and cheaper camcorders giving near professional results (especially with Hi-8 and now digital cameras) has encouraged the proliferation of informal networks of communication and exchange, altering the landscape for the use of communications technologies as a whole. An example of this is South Africa's Video News Service, which operates through the placement and exchange of videocassettes in small communities throughout South Africa. These cassettes have become a precious commodity, as they are often the only source of alternative news for groups of people with limited access to broadcast technology. Another example is Video SEWA in India, which is a unique example of the grassroots applications of lowcast forms (like video, local radio, local cable access, and Internet access [Burnett 2009]) to community activism: "Video SEWA is the video cooperative of the Self-Employed Women's Association, trade union of some 30,000 poor, self-employed women in Ahmedabad, India" (Stuart 1989, 45).

Vidéazimut, or the International Coalition for Audiovisuals for Development and Democracy (which is located in Montreal, Canada), is a large and well-funded group that brings a diverse collection of activists together. This organization has grown dramatically during the 1990s. It works on the premise that alternative sources of information will encourage dramatic cultural, personal, and political transformations in the societies and among the people that make use of new technologies (it is now actively pursuing satellite and broadcast media to enlarge the distribution base for its work). Vidéazimut is made up of well over twenty organizations worldwide, from Peru and Mozambique to India and Hong Kong. These organizations often represent regions rather than countries, and they are associated with a large number of smaller groups. Vidéazimut has become a clearinghouse for the distribution of hundreds of videotapes shot by these groups (although I must make it clear that very little time is spent analysing the content that has been produced).

There is a need to more fully explore why this type of investment is being made in video and whether it reflects an idealism for which the criteria of evaluation and critique are often self-serving. The active implication of nongovernmental organizations in these efforts to spread the use of video must be analysed as a Western phenomenon, very much related to notions of development, aid, and economic support. Most of the NGOs in the field are supported by Western governments and aid organizations. They are managing video in much the same manner as they might approach a project on educating peasant farmers in the better use of their land. In other words, the medium is being treated as if it can serve the function of a formal and informal educational tool. In addition, video, like radio, is often described by NGOs as one of the most important vehicles for giving a voice to the disenfranchised.[3] The educational and media model in place here is derived from Paulo Freire and his work on the problems of literacy with South American peasants.[4]

The philosophy of "giving a voice" was recently critiqued in an editorial in the newsletter *Interadio,* which is produced by the World Association of Community Radio Broadcasters (also an NGO and is also known as AMARC):

> More than any other mass communication medium, radio is accessible, affordable and easily appropriated by groups of people whose demands have traditionally been ignored by the mainstream media. Many marginalized groups are turning to community radio as a forum for expression, by passing the corporate and state media rather than fighting to access them. Community radio often speaks of the need "to have a voice" and of the necessity of establishing community stations as independent voices. Community radio has also become known as the "voice of the voiceless" in many parts of the world. However, while the term voiceless may well refer to those who have traditionally been denied access to the media, labelling community radio as the voice of the voiceless demeans the very essence of community radio. The phrase voiceless overlooks centuries of oral tradition that preceded radio technology (traditions which are especially strong in Asia, Africa and among indigenous populations). It can also be interpreted as implying that people do not have a voice in their communities and in their everyday lives unless they have some kind of access to the media. (Vinebohm 1993, 2)

3 See Ad Boeren, "Getting Involved: Communication for Participatory Development," and Manfred Oepen, "Traditional and Group Media Utilization in Indonesia," in *The Empowerment of Culture: Development Communication and Popular Media,* ed. Ad Boeren and Kes Epskamp (The Hague: Centre for the Study of Education in Developing Countries, 1992), 47–60, 61–78.
4 See Paulo Freire, *Education for Critical Consciousness* (New York: Seabury Press, 1973).

This is an important caution, but the issues it raises are generally over-looked, if not subsumed in the ongoing need to keep producing videotapes and radio shows. In order to more fully understand how traditional cultures in transition interact with new technologies, the communities affected would have to "educate" the outsiders who bring the technology to them. Yet even the distinctions in operation here between the inside and the outside have been undermined, if not overcome, by the rapid spread of communications technologies worldwide. The result is that few societies are now without some experience of video, television, and radio. The various distinctions of "otherness" that have guided the introduction of video have changed almost entirely. The resulting social contexts in which communities have developed sophisticated media strategies at an aesthetic and political level are often far removed from the concerns of the NGO groups that bring the media with them. Many of these challenges cannot be dealt with unless a new paradigm is developed that accounts for the introduction of media technologies into non-Western societies.

There is also more to the notion of voice than what Vinebohm suggests. One of the guiding assumptions in the development process is empowerment. Voice stands in for all of the processes that supposedly lead to enhanced notions of community control of information and knowledge. As Goldberg writes, "Dialogue is at the very heart of community access television. For this is a medium that is (or is supposed to be) interactive, user-defined and operating horizontally. A sharp contrast indeed to the centralized, one-way, top-down flow pattern of conventional media. This alternative communications system ... has enormous potential to liberate the public from the controlled flow of information, experience and thought" (1990, 6). This quote summarizes many of the concerns of the alternative video movement in both the South and the North. Aside from the conventional bow to the hegemonic influences of mass media (which foregrounds the notion of dominance, control, and democratic response), there is the key thought of liberation from control, the opening up of hitherto closed spaces of experience, and the unveiling of different (and hopefully politically effective) ways of thinking. Goldberg is referring to the process of community control, though she rarely defines the meaning of community, and to the resulting sense she has that people, once empowered in the use of the medium, will gain a new under-standing of their own views of the world, if not of their politics. Why and how does the experience of images create the openings that Goldberg proposes? "Like the medical treatments of the barefoot doctors, community television was a shared tool belonging to a community of equals. However, in the community TV model, the distinction between 'doctor' and 'patient' breaks down. The medium becomes a tool of community self-healing" (10).

Empowerment begins with the presumption that something is missing either in the community or in people's lives. The intervention of the video-makers, accompanied by the use of the medium on the part of "ordinary" people, supposedly leads to shifts in identity and further claims of self-determination. How different is the creative use of the medium for communicative purposes from traditional political work in the community? Do many of the contingent factors that govern the production of meaning in a video contribute to or inhibit the sense that meaningful exchanges can take place? What blockages are there to learning? Is the concept of horizontal participation an idealized projection on the part of the community workers who use video? To what degree does participation suggest anything about learning?

In asking these questions from a negative rather than a positive stand-point, I in no way want to belittle or even underestimate the importance of community efforts to use video. Rather, my aim is to show how little research time is spent by video-makers on the issues of empowerment, participation, democratic control, and communication – albeit that these words are used in an almost continuous fashion to construct the discourse surrounding video activism. I believe that, given the fundamentally intercultural nature of many of the productions now circulating, these issues must be dealt with if there is to be a more profound understanding of the political implications of the work. Yet, I also believe that even after nearly twenty-five years of effort, the utopian presumptions underlying the community use of video have not been evaluated in great depth. To what degree are communities likely to respond positively to a technology that from the outset could potentially reconfigure their own modes of communication, some of which may have been around for centuries? Have the proponents of this technology brought a critique with them? How well have we understood video from within our own cultures? Given the "newness" of video, it is somewhat ironic that the critical analysis that should precede the introduction of the technology has not played a more significant role in its placement and use in developing countries.

Part of the problem I have faced in researching the organizations involved in using and promoting video as a political tool is that so much of what is being made is treated as information in the most ephemeral sense of the word. Although there is some discussion of aesthetics and form, the discourse is generally quite limited, in part because there seems to be no critical vocabulary with which to examine and analyse the material produced. Videotapes circulate and are shown to audiences, but the evaluations that follow are short-lived and rarely followed up. In addition, the arguments that have been developed to describe and analyse the production of community or political videotapes are often not concerned with how or whether images communicate meaning and to what degree analytical tools were and are in place for explaining the various relationships between different forms of cultural production and discourse. This resistance to theory and to critical practices, suffuses, if not dominates, the video movement. Can a video stand on its own as a way of dealing with community concerns? Can the "message" be transparently clear, even if the audience the video is addressing does not necessarily share the premises of the communication? The videotapes depend upon the electronic image to do the work of revealing, if not creating, discursive spaces within which questions of identity and self can be raised. But can images play that role without a creative pedagogical strategy that extends far beyond the boundaries of the image, its mode of distribution, and its display? How can that strategy be enacted without a careful reflection on the history of the medium, on its aesthetic characteristics and formal properties, and on its place within the circulation of traditional and popular cultural forms?

Kelly Anderson and Annie Goldson addressed some of these problems in a recent article, "Alternating Currents: Alternative Television Inside and Outside of the Academy" (Anderson and Goldson 1993). The authors bemoan the lack of contact between academics and video practitioners. They make the claim that there is very little interest on the part of theorists in examining the history and development of alternative media in the United States as well as elsewhere.[5] Although they clearly underestimate the research that has been done, they pinpoint a serious gap in the thinking about community and alternative media. There is an underlying moral imperative to the notion of alternativity that locates critique and analysis within a framework of opposition to nearly all aspects of mainstream culture, including research within the university community. This oppositional approach becomes the centrepiece of an evaluative strategy that is then applied to the videotapes that are produced in a community context. For example, a badge of honour for alternative video-makers is to overemphasize the difference between their

5 The authors seem not to be aware of the work of John Downing, whose *Radical Media: The Political Experience of Alternative Communication* (Cambridge, Mass.: South End Press, 1984) attempts precisely to link historical and theoretical concerns with practical experience. Various monographs (Francis J. Berrigan, *Community Communications: The Role of Community Media in Development* [Paris: UNESCO, 1979]; and *Access: Some Western Models of Community Media*, ed. Francis J. Berrigan [Paris: UNESCO, 1977]), short articles (Terence Turner, "Visual Media. Cultural Politics, and Anthropological Practice: Some Implications of Recent Uses of Film and Video among the Kayapo of Brazil," *Commission on Visual Anthropology Review*, Spring 1990), and the work coming out of the *Group Media Journal* in Germany reflect an ongoing concern with various issues arising out of the alternative use of the media. Also see Roy Armes, *On Video* (New York: Routledge, 1988).

aesthetic and that of conventional media. The assumption is that there is something inherently wrong with mainstream work, and although this may well be true, that assumption has to be based on more than a superficial analysis of what traditional broadcasters create. It is not possible, or even desirable, to isolate the critique of culture in general from what alternative video-makers themselves create. The latter are inherently a part of the same circle of activity even if the ideologies are different.

To what extent, then, is there some clarity with respect to the idea of alternativity? Anderson and Goldson suggest a number of different approaches. Their first assumption is that community-based alternative television has a "precarious though binding relationship to the dominant economy of media production" (Anderson and Goldson 1993, 59). Here they are referring to the various strategies that alternative producers and practitioners, as well as community workers, engage in with respect to funding and the acquisition of resources and equipment. Funding in itself is a fascinating area, because it is at the root of an economic activity that is rarely, if ever, measured. A number of objections could be raised here to the suggestion that we are dealing with alternative production processes. The first is that lowcasting now makes use of increasingly sophisticated equipment. Although not as costly as conventional broadcast technology, the investment can be considerable. Second, any effort to go beyond the immediate availability of basic resources involves grant requests to government or local agencies, corporations or foundations. This issue has been debated before and the argument always is that public or private aid pollutes, if not skewers, the political track of advocacy that governs so much of the production at the community level. Yet, what seems to be at stake here is precisely the idealizations of the "alternative" that sees itself outside of the very institutions to which it is beholden. This is a circuitous route, full of potholes, but the most important point to keep in mind, is that the terrain of practice that can be opened up cannot rely solely on vague notions of alternative politics as the measure of effectiveness or impact.

Yet this could become a more dialogic process, and it could be more sensitive and aware of the institutional nexus within which it must operate, if there were not such a strong dependence on the central idea of a dominant culture. There is no question that monopolies – from Time Warner to News Corporation – control the media marketplace, and recent moves towards consolidation on the part of telephone and cable companies in the United States presage even more complex, though not necessarily uniformly similar, worldwide corporations. This is indisputable. But the terrain of communications, the place within which meanings as such are exchanged, interpreted, worked upon, is within the very communities that video activists want to politicize. If the model of dominance were to operate at the level, and with the intensity, suggested by the relationship between mainstream and alternative, then the very people who inhabit those communities would not be accessible (or perhaps even interested in seeing anything different). It is because there is an economy of scale involved in the activity of community video that we can begin to talk about the grassroots and define with much greater precision what community means. And when we do so, the convenience of the opposition I have been discussing would dissolve and political activists would see their work within a continuum of which popular and local cultures are simply one of a number of different elements.

There are so many aspects to a community's activities that traverse the boundaries between what is acceptable and what is not, so much heterogeneity in the relationship between institutions and people, that questions of power and how to address the powerful cannot be answered from within the hazy traditions promulgated and supported by the easy dichotomy of alternative and mainstream. In some respects, this opposition carries the same weight as the superstructure/base opposition that did so much to undermine creative, theoretical, and critical work on culture from within the Marxist tradition. The simplicity of the opposition cannot be sustained any longer. It is perhaps more necessary than ever to unmask the weaknesses of an approach that cannot account for desire, pleasure, and the contradictory politics of incorporation that, it must be remembered, can be simultaneously experimental, even radical, *and* co-opted. A more comprehensive and perhaps more subtle set of distinctions needs be introduced, distinctions that will reinvigorate the meaning of all kinds of media practices without locking them into an intellectually convenient binary structure. This can only be done by recognizing how heterogeneous the work of the media is, how it is possible for a film like *Wayne's World* (Penelope Spheeris, 1992) to present an analysis and critique of community-cable television and be, at one and the same time, irreverent and part of the mainstream, a money-maker, and a joke on American cultural values.

In a work that addresses some of the issues I am raising, Lili Berko suggests that the advent of the Portapak in the late 1960s broke the hold of broadcast television and allowed people to use the technology of electronic images in new and unpredictable ways:

> The coupling of the portable videotape recorder (Portapak) with the advent of the videocassette offered artists and social activists alike an opportunity to participate in the production of images that were to shape their culture. The most revolutionary aspect of the Portapak was its mobility. Through the Portapak, television production was not locked into a studio and the confines of the codes of such mediated experience. Through video, the mystique of production was shattered and the streets became equally important sites of textual inscription.

> Video soon became the vehicle through which the social world could
> be easily documented, the vehicle which would record the voices and
> the images of the Newark riots, or a Mardi Gras celebration; as such
> it proclaimed the public sphere to be its own. (Berko 1989, 290)

The changes launched by the advent of portable video certainly foregrounded the need for a re-evaluation of the ways in which mainstream
broadcasters operated. A conversation was generated – within the institution
of television (primarily the networks at that point) and outside it – between
radically different conceptions of the public sphere and, substantively, although
these were not fully articulated differences, with respect to processes of communication and interchange.

Berko's analysis of the differences between broadcasting and lowcasting
and the reclaiming of a territory seemingly lost to mainstream media summarizes the approach of an entire generation of writers and practitioners in
the field of media studies and communications, from the mid-1960s through
to the middle of the 1990s. There were few texts or articles on video that did
not make the same set of claims for this break between the mainstream media
and its alternatives (all of this resonated with the symbolism of the sixties
and was most fully represented by the work of Nam June Paik and Michael
Shamberg, both of whom combine a political and experimental approach to
video).[6] Much remains unexamined in this strategy. The most important
point is that the analytical framework for the study of video was at that time
in its infancy. In fact, there were very few film departments in universities, let
alone media or cultural studies departments. There were, however, a number
of crucial "university sites" where media were analysed, and for the most
part they were dependent on communications and cultural theory as it had
evolved from the 1930s.[7]

I make this point because the attitude towards mainstream television that
underlies Berko's approach is based on a hegemonic view of the role of the
media, with the result that Portapak activity is analysed as if the practice of
image creation was itself a sufficient, if not utopian, reclamation of lost territory as well as being a critique of that dominance. This occupation of a new
space was seen as a political act with an immediate impact upon the environments in which videos were used and shown and the upon the people in those
environments. Yet, the absence of contexts for the analysis of mainstream

6 See Michael Shamberg, *Guerrilla Television* (New York: Holt, Rinehart and Winston, 1971), and *Illuminating Video*, ed. Doug Hall and Sally Jo Fifer (New York:
  Aperture Foundation, 1990).
7 Two of the most important were at the University of Pennsylvania (the Annenberg
  School of Communications) and the University of Chicago.

media in the late 1960s (which was in part a result of the newness of electronic images) suggests that the initial shift to a populist view of portable television technology was based on a fragmentary and often reductive presumption about mass forms of entertainment and learning.

This oppositional framework continues to be the premise of much of present-day video practice and theory, which still does not grapple explicitly with the problems of audience, performance, and learning with regard to media production at the local, national, and international level. There is, therefore, a measure of continuity to the debate and a historical underpinning to the contrasting attitudes that have been taken towards media technologies that address both large and small audiences. In addition, many of the definitions of impact and change that underpin notions of grassroots activity and democratic access (most of which are rather ephemeral if not superficial) have been used to give credibility to the practice of narrowcasting with video. These presumptions need to be dramatically rethought.

It is estimated that there are about four hundred groups working in popular video in South America, with a predominant number, two hundred, working in Brazil. Luiz Fernando Santoro, a professor at the University of São Paulo, has observed that for the most part these groups make use of video in three ways: "Historically, there have been three distinct moments in video work: the first was the use of video to share information within the movement (video as a self-organizational tool); the second, video used as counter-information (video as a tool for constructing discourse within the movement); and the third, present moment, where video is used to present an alternative view of the world to the collectivity at large" (Roy and Thede 1992, 3).

One might ask, with respect to the first category that Santoro describes, how information is shared. What are the public and private "locations" within which richly endowed discursive interactions can be developed in a self-reflexive way? This is, of course, a question of pedagogy, of learning, a question of how important political issues can be raised and then discussed, if not acted upon, within contexts that are open and unthreatening. The utopian ideals of the video movement are based upon this desire to share information, and they reflect both a need to jumpstart the learning process and an aspiration to create open contexts for communication and exchange. There is also the presumption that if video is made in local contexts, the images will reflect the genuine needs of the people who participate and, as a consequence, channels of communication will be opened in a natural way and change may indeed eventuate.

Video is promoted by Santoro as perhaps the best way of democratizing processes of communication and providing access to the media, particularly for those presently excluded from power or from the conventional networks for the production and exchange of information. Ironically, the literature on video is often apprehensive about its complexity as a creative medium and yet eagerly embraces its potential with regard to communications, interaction, and learning. In other words, the creative process is the real challenge and what happens afterwards must be left to chance.

Underlying Santoro's third point about presenting local interests to the broader world community is the notion that video has become a tool to reach larger and larger numbers of people. Yet this means that video has changed from a lowcast medium to a broadcast medium. If this is true (and I am not convinced it is), then the underlying impulses and strategies I described above will have shifted. This means that the perceived need to reach more and more people will change both the aesthetic approach and fundamental assumptions about the technology. This need will professionalize what up until now has been informal, and as Santoro puts it, "The accent is on making more complete programs in order to get them broadcast" (Roy and Thede 1992, 14). This premature movement into broadcasting may not happen with the rapidity suggested by Santoro. Even if it did, all the questions of communication, learning, and social change would remain the same.

In many southern countries, training videotapes are used to make education more accessible to large numbers of people. Examples abound from the most basic forms of education (images that show people how to make use of supplies of clean water) to more complex (how to develop communal structures for economic growth and diversification). The videotapes are meant to fit into the formal and informal networks of learning already in place. But who makes these videotapes? Where do the assumptions of learning and education come from? How are cultural differences dealt with? In fact, how are the issues of intercultural communication integrated into the videotapes when they are presumably used by a wide variety of people with different interests?

These questions are usually answered with the assertion that local people know and control the relevance of the videotapes and often contribute to their content even if outsiders actually make them. If community members are adequately informed and involved, then the videos will be seen as relevant and will perhaps have an even profounder influence on the community as a whole. But this remains a supposition, because as the history of educational video in developed countries suggests, learning from video is a very complex matter. Without delving deeply into this issue just now, I will say that it is not that clear how people learn from images or even whether they do. This is not to suggest that viewers don't learn, but that the evaluation criteria for whether learning has taken place remain vague and more attached to an imputed and easily comprehended content than anything else. This rather complex relationship between viewing and learning haunts the use of videos for political purposes. There is no easy or direct link between what images may mean and the many and often contradictory ways in which they are understood (which may explain why the vast majority of image productions, from video through to the cinema, fail to find audiences).

Approaches to these challenges range from the formal to the informal. One example is the approach taken by a communications network called Zebra, with headquarters in Paris, which is heavily involved with Africa and has one or two workshops in video production running every week in a number of countries. These workshops are community based and are intended to provide local people with the tools they need to work with the medium. Most of the workshops are run with the purpose of improving the technique and craft ability of creators (how to make videotapes, how to use the equipment, etc.), thereby invoking a pedagogy that is rarely examined but when it is, the evaluation is usually based on vague notions of empowerment through the use of video. In other words, although the aim is to generate more and more instances in which local information will be produced and distributed, Zebra has not yet developed a conceptual framework that would permit it to evaluate the pedagogical work it is doing. In a sense, it faces a conundrum well known to ethnographers and anthropologists. Outside observers and participants with the best of intentions and the most rigorous notions of the local, or the indigenous, are nevertheless *not* members of the communities with which they get involved. This obviously has an impact on the pedagogical methods that are chosen for training purposes, but an examination of the literature produced to date shows little awareness of these challenges, which are fundamentally intercultural in character. How can critically informed methods of training be developed with respect to video? Is the terminology wrong to begin with here? What are the historical origins underlying the assumption that to learn a technology, you have to be trained in it? Are we dealing with craft-oriented approaches here and what are the implications of this for critical analysis? What are the biases of trainers and how do those biases translate into teaching and learning models and with what effect?

Yet, while these contradictions seem to be very much a part of video use, I must also stress the positive side. Some of the preliminary research I have done on such projects as the Integrated Rural Project in Education, Health and Family Planning in Honduras suggests that, with limited tools and cheap technology, video has been useful in opening up hitherto untapped venues for learning and debate. In this instance, video and sound cassettes were used to provoke discussion on the health and welfare issues of central concern to Hondurans living in small and impoverished villages. This encouraged an open exchange of ideas, and the participants began to make tapes of their own and exchange them with other villages. Similar projects in Kenya, Senegal, and Bolivia point towards the potential strengths of this approach. Another major effort is the Village Video Network, co-sponsored by the United Nations University and Martha Stuart Communications (now called Communication for Change). The network is non-profit and has many participants from a number of African and Asian countries. "Women are a primary target and beneficiary of Village Video Network activities and women's groups (such as the Self-Employed Women's Association of Ahmedabad, India) are active participants in the workshops and exchanges made possible by the network" (Mowlana and Wilson 1990, 142).

The German Foundation for International Development has been involved in a large number of projects in the South. They held a series of seminars on community communications between 1986 and 1990. A report on these seminars was written up in the *Group Media Journal*, published in Munich. Manfred Oepen invokes three categories to describe a new paradigm for the use of media in the community: "They have gone from information diffusion *for* people to information seeking *by* and *with* people. Here, problem and practice-related information is generated through local or regional community processes and fed into existing media networks horizontally and vertically, to inform both central decision-makers and community groups respectively" (1990, 4). Oepen goes on to describe three key concepts of community communication: "access, participation and self-management" (4).

These three aims were also the foundation upon which the Challenge for Change (CFC) program was developed at the National Film Board of Canada (NFB).[8] In the late 1960s and early 1970s, CFC was created to engage with processes of social change through the use of video and film. Broadly speaking, this desire to use the medium as an instrument for an activist relationship to Canadian society grew out of the recognition that the Film Board, as well as politically committed cultural workers, needed to be involved in more than the production of films or videotapes. They needed to connect with, and better understand, the audiences and communities they were addressing. The aim was to extend the process of creation and production from an institutional nexus to a decentralized model, based on an idealized version of community involvement. "Films can teach, they can explain and they can move people to great depths of emotion. Having done all of these things, is it possible for films to move people to action? There is no question for most social scientists that carefully constructed presentations, films for instance, can produce changes in attitudes in those who adequately receive the com-

8 For additional information on Challenge for Change, see Ron Burnett, "Video/Film: From Communication to Community," in *Video in the Changing World*, ed. Nancy Thede and Alain Ambrosi (Montreal: Black Rose Books, 1991), 54–60.

munication. The use of adequately is of course a conscious one in that we know that people tend to mis-perceive that which they hear and see, and go through fairly complicated strategies of selective attention and selective perception" (Hénaut 1969a, 3).

In fact, the audience became an obsession at the Board, and specific people at the institution were assigned to develop polling methods and questionnaires for distribution to the populace at large. After certain films or videotapes were shown on television for example, the Film Board phoned people at random to see if they had watched and to pose questions to viewers who were willing to participate. The premise of this community-oriented work was pedagogical, political, and cultural, and it influenced an entire generation of activists devoted to the use of visual media for political purposes. This issue of connectivity to the viewer, to the community – of the relationship between production and distribution – is what distinguished the efforts of the Film Board from many similar organizations elsewhere. The traditions developed during the heyday of the CFC period were improved upon in the late seventies when the NFB decentralized and opened up a series of regional centres across Canada in an effort to build closer ties to the communities it was serving.

The idealism of Challenge for Change was based on notions of democratic access, the rallying call for anyone seriously interested in promoting the use of video in the community. The history of that period has not yet been written in great detail, and suffice to say that one of the most interesting aspects yet to be explored is the relationship between the social work movement in Quebec in the early 1960s and the accelerated movement towards media use for educational purposes. The level of advocacy in both education and social work was very sophisticated, with tie-ins to provincial government departments and local municipalities. The use of video for the purposes of empowerment was embedded in a particular political context and surrounded by debates within Québécois culture about the role of the media. The specificity of this situation not only affected the videotapes being made, but the institutions that promoted them. The claims of this period and the video activism that followed were not as easily transferable to other contexts as was presumed at the time. In fact, it is startling to read the anecdotal comments about Challenge for Change by modern-day proponents of community video[9] and the decontextualized analyses of the films that were made. It is also surprising that the history of the National Film Board is so poorly understood; few know, in particular, that many of the films were the site of conflicts

9 See a number of the essays in Alain Ambrosi and Nancy Thede, eds, *Video in the Changing World* (Montreal: Black Rose, 1991).

between the English and French sections of the NFB (which had a definitive impact on what the Film Board meant by "community"!).

Rick Moore, who wrote, "Canada's Challenge for Change: Documentary Film and Video as an Exercise of Power through the Production of Cultural Reality" (this is one of the few sustained efforts at an analysis of the relationship of the NFB to CFC), quotes one of the members of CFC: "All across Canada (often with the help of Challenge for Change), citizens are picking up half-inch VTR cameras and learning to speak through them" (1987, 119). Moore then goes on to say, "The assessment was not an exaggeration, geographically speaking. Challenge for Change had begun numerous projects across the country in which the primary emphasis was citizen access. Over twenty-three major projects were eventually completed, some in urban areas such as Vancouver, Halifax and Toronto. Some were done in rural areas such as Drumheller, Alberta. In many of these communities, Challenge for Change staff took on new titles. For example, 'directors' were no longer directors, but 'media counsellors' in charge of helping the local citizens use the media most effectively" (119).

Guided by a vague concept of change, firmly believing in the potential of video as a technology to empower people to talk to each other, engaged in the legitimation of a public sphere with a hierarchy of discourses that CFC workers rarely examined, the program nevertheless produced many important experiments in the field of community video. But the operative word here is *experiment* – and in some senses people and their communities became the site within which many different ideas of democratic involvement were tested. The problem was that the targets for these experiments were as much the members of the community as the video-makers and what they created. And the often-expressed frustration of CFC workers was that no other form of communication adequately responded to the needs of the people as they understood them. But this is a confusion of levels. Experimenting with the image, testing its effectiveness with regard to change, is already fraught with contradiction. Applying these ideas to the relationship between the image and spectator, the image and the community, just confuses the issues even more.

If it appears as if I am referring to a historical situation that may not be relevant anymore, here is what a recent article by Deirdre Boyle had to say: "Nearly 30 years since the video Portapak launched an independent television movement in the United States, a new generation of video activists has taken up the video camcorder as a tool, a weapon, and a witness. Although the rhetoric of guerrilla television may seem dated today, its utopian goal of using video to challenge the information infrastructure in America is more timely than ever and at last practicable. Today's video activism is the fulfilment of a radical 1960s dream of making 'people's television'" (1992, 67).

Boyle goes on to talk about the three components of video activism – "[t]o be a tool, a weapon and a witness" – as they have coalesced in the 1990s (1992, 78). These three categories are as constitutive now as they were in the late 1960s and early 1970s. Their longevity is enframed by the concept of empowerment. Yet, an examination of the literature and research that has been produced in relation to video reveals very little with regard to empowerment as a process. Terms like "democratization" and "control by the community" appear over and over again, but these are assumed from within the activities of portable video use. There is very little about audience, about the ways in which video images work as devices of communication, if at all, or the connections of representational issues to empowerment and so forth.[10]

Care must be taken in discussing the effects of portable image-based technologies on users and viewers. The evaluative tools we have for examining how these technologies have been appropriated and then how they are understood by audiences cannot simply be reduced to an instance of the technology itself, and while it is true that hundreds of groups started to use video in the late 1960s and early 1970s, this by itself does not suggest very much. Nor should too many radical conclusions be drawn from the way camcorders are used today, since much of the usage is devoted to constructing a catalogue of familial memories and may have no links to agendas for social change or innovation.

Critical analysis in this area needs to account more fully for the difficulties that one encounters in researching the subjective relationships that practitioners and viewers develop with video images. Is it true that advocacy video changes the ways in which people both analyse and act upon the social contexts of which they are a part? There is little but anecdotal evidence to suggest what these changes are actually about, to what degree and with what depth viewers and/or communities work upon the images they watch or create. This is as much a methodological problem as it is a theoretical and practical one, and is very closely related to how community is defined, both as a concept and as a lived experience. All the various problems of conflating class, ethnicity, colour, and gender come to the fore here in a notion of community that seems to rise above all the contradictions and conflicts that are a part of any individual's history within a community.

By now it should be evident that I am concerned with the relationship between the history of a technology and activist assumptions about how that technology can be used and responded to. I am also concerned with presumptions of impact and various hypotheses about change as they are refracted through the shifting parameters of technological growth and innovation. To what degree, for example, does the appearance of video coincide

10 These questions are addressed, albeit all too briefly, in Berko 1989, 289–307.

with the desire to enlarge the market for electronic goods? Does this explain the rapid acceptance of the medium by many different sectors of our society? Do the camcorder and the palmcorder presage a historical shift in the way electronic images will be watched, understood, and created? If we go back to Sony's invention of the half-inch black-and-white Portapak, will we be able to delineate the social, cultural, and economic factors that led to the appearance of this new technology? In retrospect, it now seems clear that Sony was setting the stage for the video cassette recorder (VCR), having made the judgment that spectators would eventually want to control their own viewing experiences and turn their homes into private viewing environments.[11] What led Sony to this hypothesis and is it valid in the mid-1990s? How did the Sony Corporation come to the conclusion that both recording shows off television and purchasing videotape copies of films had the potential to be a major industry? Why did an American firm, the Ampex Corporation, which invented video recorders in 1955, ten years before Sony introduced the Portapak, not grab the opportunity in the same way? These are questions that this essay will not be able to answer, but they are part of a history that needs to be developed in any discussion of video if we are to broaden our understanding of technological change and the role of video images in cultural, social, and political development and transformation.

There is a "history" that can perhaps account for the new circuits of communication that have been put in place by the advent of video. In particular, one would have to develop an analysis of the implications of more and more people of vastly different backgrounds becoming comfortable with video as a device in the home. We would have to explore the link between the technology as a structure of possibilities in the political arena and its location within a postmodern context in which new kinds of histories (public and private) are being created in rather nonlinear ways. At first blush, it appears as if video permits a massive set of variables to be introduced into a world of endless disjuncture where there is no clear or level playing field for the construction and maintenance of specific meanings. It may be the case that electronic images created for very specific political reasons will allow for an interchangeable flux of meanings to be sustained by hitherto undescribed modes of linkage.

11 Akio Morita, the founder and head of Sony, said of the VCR: "[It] will revolutionize television. It will change the concept of prime time so that *any* time can be prime time. Before the development of video recording, television was too fleeting. While it has been outstanding for conveying information, providing entertainment, and improving our culture, the sad fact exists that once a program is off the air it is gone forever for the TV viewer. Newspapers, magazines, and books can be read and kept for future reference. But this had not been so with TV programs seen in the home." Quoted in Lyons 1976, 211.

The often-expressed desire of video activists to bring the people in the communities they work with together for the purposes of change and social cohesion is situated in a concept of community that is both naïve and under-theorized. Even aside from the difficulty of gaining access to the rather complex and multi-layered aspects of community life, the very notion of community is based on a denial of difference and on a vague conception of conflict resolution. As Iris Marion Young has put it, "The ideal of commu-nity, finally, totalises and detemporalises its conception of social life by setting up an opposition between authentic and inauthentic social relations. It also detemporalises its understanding of social change by positing the desired society as the complete negation of existing society" (1990, 302).

Young goes on to talk about the efforts of political activists to radicalize and politicize the communities they work in. She claims that the notion of face-to-face relations "seeks a model of social relations that are not mediated by space and time distancing. In radically opposing the inauthentic social re-lations of alienated society with the authentic social relations of community, moreover, it detemporalises the process of social change into a static before and after structure" (1990, 305). The implications of Young's arguments for doing political work in the community with video are quite dramatic. They suggest that the assumptions of involvement and participation that video activists so vigorously pursue may have contributed to a static model of human relations on which it would have been difficult, if not impossible, to build new paradigms of political and cultural activity, let alone translate all of that into productive actions towards change.

The desire to bring people together around the practice of making video-tapes has an initial ring of authenticity to it. In the literature of community video, the results are described positively, as though the introduction of the technology produces positive outcomes irrespective of content. The effect is doubled when the images that have been shot are shown back to the com-munity, the explicit presumption being that images provide a mirror for self-reflection that would otherwise be unavailable.

Within this environment, the topography of ideas that are used to clarify or support political media activities needs to be carefully thought out. Although often discredited both from within and outside academic circles, the high culture/low culture dichotomy remains at the centre of presump-tions about what works as political communication and what does not. Low culture or popular culture is seen as a distortion not only of truth but also of the needs of community members. In this context, the arguments presently in place for the activities of viewing are strung out along a very thin border between conflicting conceptions of passivity and non-passivity that mirror the high culture/low culture model. This dichotomy cannot account for the complexities of televisual viewing. I believe we need an entirely different model. I bring this up because in the context of the arguments that have been developed around the legitimacy of video as a political tool, it is television, and by extension all of popular culture, that is named as the site of a lack, an absence that the community use of video or video advocacy will somehow fill. It is in the context of this notion of a loss of power to the mainstream media and to the potential for technological innovation to overcome impediments to clear and progressive thinking that the notion of empowerment through watching or engaging with video draws its strength. Yet the question of empowerment cannot be answered from within the negative parameters of a cultural opposition that promotes such a mechanical model of communication and exchange. So, perhaps the very idea of empowerment as it has been theorized up until now needs to draw upon different sources that incorporate many more forms of cultural activity, and that accept the diversity of needs, desires, and political priorities that communities, groups, and individuals create and respond to as they face the challenges of change.

Underlying the approach taken by the community video movement is a rationalist ideology of communication, centred on ideas of citizenship, identity, and empowerment through participatory media-based activities. In fact, there is a need to move beyond generalized metaphors of the media to perhaps address the following question as it is posed by Nicholas Garnham, "Can we identify cultural forms or types of media practice that favour the formation of democratic identities and others which undermine such identities?" (1993, 264). In one respect, this seems like a naïve question. In another, it is at the core of the political assumptions that both guide and enframe the use of video as a pedagogical and political tool. These points are not articulated by the organizations that have become the most important purveyors of video activism, and there is an assumed link between radical media practice and the public sphere within which responses are articulated. The assumption is that images will contribute to the growth of social movements – viewers will also fit what they see into what they think about, both with respect to their own identities and with respect to their sense of themselves as public and private personae (the contribution they can make to the social context in which they live). This notion of a "public subjectivity," a term articulated by Benjamin Lee (1993), is essentially proposed as a holistic practice that moves citizenship beyond the narrow parameters of the community or nation-state. In this respect, public subjectivity comes to stand for a public sphere and a public culture that stretches far beyond the physical and psychological boundaries of community as we presently define it. It also stands for strategies of spectatorship that are dependent on intercultural and therefore more hybridized conceptions of what works as communication and what does not.

The appropriation of video leads to forms of cultural expression that mix many different aspects of historically differentiated types of information. The problem is, to what degree can these histories be accessed when their specificity is both overwhelmed and diluted by the movement of ideas across many, often distinctive, cultures in one country or many countries? What are the attractions of different publics for the videos presented to them? To what degree and with what depth can public spaces be constructed where the videos can be evaluated? Can viewers gain access to their own and their neighbour's experience of media images? Even more importantly, since so much of the viewing of electronic images is bound up with desire (the desire to know, sometimes combined with, and other times offset by, the desire to be entertained) and since the discursive articulation of desire is neither easy nor, generally speaking, public (and may even be antithetical to the culture involved), what kind of access can we gain to the way viewers learn from, and experience, video images?

It may be that Garnham's question merely reinforces the idea that instrumental forms of communication can be constructed to promote political involvement and change. Surely the time has come to alter, if not recreate, this kind of argument. Some gay and feminist video-makers have moved beyond the restrictive boundaries of instrumentality, and this has led to an intense and sometimes explosive experimentalism. (In particular, I would cite the extraordinary experimental work of Sadie Benning.)

Video advocacy, particularly in developing countries, is in deep trouble. Community video has rarely moved beyond the initial parameters of the debates that established the movement. The time has come to examine these closed systems of thought and discourse and reflect on why they have played such a dominant role in grassroots work with video and why they have been used as the foundation upon which so-called alternative media institutions have been built. If the heterogeneity of "community" and the richness of the "local" can engage with the genuinely important shifts of emphasis represented by video and other emerging technologies of communications, then it may just be possible to redefine the meaning and breadth of alternativity at the creative, political, and discursive level. And these redefinitions may lead to not only to less instrumental notions of communications, but to genuinely different forms of participatory democracy.

35

Winds and Things: Towards a Reassessment of the Challenge for Change/Société nouvelle Legacy

■

MARIT KATHRYN CORNEIL

Forty years after its inception, twenty-eight years after it was laid to rest, the legendary National Film Board of Canada/Office national du film (NFB/ONF) program Challenge for Change/Société nouvelle (CFC/SN) is raising its sleepy eyes to look anew at the world. The program was in many ways a political project, one that put the means of media production into the hands of citizens and, so the legend goes, overcame the ethical dilemmas of representation, liberating minority groups from becoming the victims and stereotypes of both media and government. But today the inheritors of this project encounter a world where access to the means of creating and distributing media has proliferated well beyond the traditional media institutions. They see a world also where the social problems that CFC/SN was meant to address, poverty and inequality, appear to have become more exacerbated, complicated, and global. In some ways, the idea of CFC/SN has carried on after the institution, but the problems have multiplied – resource depletion, over-consumption, climate change, pollution, species extinction, war – the list goes on. After two decades of neoliberalism and suffering the long-term effects of Reaganomics, the question of politics is back on the agenda for many people. Something must be done – but what? That was the question then. That is the question now. As documentary filmmakers, what can we do?

In 1967, the NFB/ONF set about doing something. Challenge for Change/Société nouvelle was one of a number of government programs aimed at alleviating poverty and "giving voice" to marginalized segments of society so that they could air their grievances directly to the people in charge, to university experts and to government officials. CFC/SN did this by making cameras and training available to community groups in different parts of the country. The goal was to open up a media dialogue that would assist in improving representative democracy and transforming it into a more participatory form of government. The outcome of the program revealed, on the one hand, the almost explosive potential of the camera in the hands of the people, the camera as a tool to expose injustice and human rights violations, and on the other, the increasing institutionalization of public communication in the form of community television on cable, the dispersion of social activism into the production of government service information, the petrifaction of community agency under the burden of minority difference, and, at the extreme end, self-surveillance by some communities during the October Crisis of 1970 (Corneil 2003; Marchessault 1995b).

Forty years later, the time is ripe for a re-evaluation of the program and its history. This is because of renewed interest in activist documentary in the last few years and growing public interest in the genre more generally. This interest comes with the streamlining (and stretching out) of the media industry by what has been called Reality TV where, in the span of a few years, film and TV crews have been cut back and production turnaround time sped up.[1] Remarkably, we have also seen the increasing popularity of the independent theatrical documentary on the big screen as well as a growth in scholarly research on documentary and realism, with a proliferation of conferences and festivals devoted to documentary filmmaking.[2] More importantly, perhaps, in the context of this volume, the NFB, along with a host of other media-makers, has brushed the dust off this old legend and is administering artificial resuscitation with the help of new digital technologies. And the revival is looking promising.[3]

So it seems very crucial at this time that we put on our forty-year anniversary glasses and look back at the history and re-examine the events, the films, the effects, and evaluations that were made at the time. It is also time to reassess the legend as it was consolidated within film studies in the three decades after the demise of the program. Beginning with a look at the reception of the first CFC film, *The Things I Cannot Change* (Tanya Ballantyne Tree, 1967), and an examination of the only colour film to be made on Fogo Island during those first years of the project, *The Winds of Fogo* (Colin Low, 1969), in what follows, I will discuss what this reassessment means and the implications for the discourse on documentary ethics, aesthetics, and politics as we experience these in retrospect, these forty years down the road.

---

1 In Norway, the late 1990s inaugurated the era of the "DV video-producer," and more recently the film union introduced the category of the "documentarist" – the trend has gained ideological overtones. See Guant 2008.

2 See Chanan 2007 for a recent discussion of this development.

3 The NFB has recently revived the program with its Filmmaker-in-Residence, Blog on Burgundy, and Citizen*Shift*. These projects arrived after a new strategic plan was implemented for 2001–06 in which CFC/SN figured prominently. But the revival is not limited to the NFB, and many filmmakers and activists are attempting to implement similar strategies. See, for example, workingfilms.org, localfilms.org, and witness.org.

THE LEGEND

The story goes something like this. In an effort to address the ongoing problem of poverty in a prosperous Canada of the late 1960s, a film "product" was commissioned by government officials on the subject. This film – *The Things I Cannot Change* – was an example of observational/ethnographic-style documentary, where the filmmakers immersed themselves in the daily lives of a family that was struggling with a number of chronic problems associated with poverty: ten children, unemployed father, isolation within the community. After the film was broadcast on national television, the family underwent further alienation and ostracism, eventually being forced to move from the neighbourhood where they lived (see Longfellow, chapter 14, this volume). The outrage this caused at the National Film Board inspired some producers and filmmakers to rethink the ethics of documentary filmmaking in the context of community development, and this became the agenda for the experimental program in ethical documentary at CFC/SN. The Fogo Island project, which used a process method of making films in, for, and with a local community, became the exemplary model of community media for a whole generation, one that went on to develop what came to be known as the "access movement," which resonated among community mobilizers throughout the world and across the decades to follow.

The story, told in this way, appears occasionally in the gradually amassing literature that came to be academically instituted as documentary studies.[4] Eric Barnouw's history from 1974, *Documentary: A History of the Non-fiction Film*, under the chapter entitled "Catalyst," begins with a recounting of Jean Rouch's film practice, "the filmmaker as catalyst," and the anthropological project that sought to register what the Navajo people would do with a film camera in the work of Sol Worth and Jon Adair, and follows with what he calls the "activity" at the NFB called "Challenge for Change," with the projects *You Are on Indian Land* (Mort Ransen, 1969) and *VTR St-Jacques* (Bonnie Sherr Klein, 1969) as examples of work that catalyse social change. Barnouw writes, "As members of the community saw themselves and others in discussion, subtle shifts of opinion took place. The tapes thus stimulated and improved intra-community communication, as well as serving as a bridge to officialdom outside the community" (1974, 260).

Barnouw's early registration of CFC/SN's achievements as shifts in public opinion, the stimulation of community communication, and a bridge between community and government should not be underestimated. These seem still to be the primary achievements of the experiment. However, and perhaps

4 A selection: Nichols 1981, 1991; Winston 1995, 2000; Evans 1991; Engelman 1996; and Boyle 1997.

unfortunately, the program went down in documentary and film studies as having accomplished what amounts to the impossible – that is, as having overcome the ethical dilemma of representation. This dilemma is a dilemma for documentary studies, but by extension it is also a dilemma for media and for democracy more generally. If the public requires adequate information in order to participate in – or to elect viable representatives to decide upon – the important issues facing us at any given moment, how can the representations made by the media overcome the problems associated with audio-visual techniques that are so vexed by ethical issues? And as such, these claims made by documentary theory in its kindling years need interrogation now, as we, even more than ever, are facing ethical problems in media generally, in these times of global terrorism and corporate machination, of the digital image.

THE LEGEND IN DOCUMENTARY THEORY AND HISTORY

In *Ideology and the Image* (1981), one of the first analytical scholarly works on documentary within film studies, Bill Nichols names CFC/SN as an example of an attempt to overcome the ethical dilemma of representation (1981, 237). In this book, as in many other accounts, Ballantyne Tree's film is seen as the catalyst for a debate on documentary ethics. A fundamental ethical difficulty that the documentary filmmaker faces when he or she sets out to represent reality arises from the relationship that he or she establishes with participants as subjects. Filmmakers had been struggling with the sometimes-negative consequences that filming individuals had on their lives. The NFB had been experimenting with direct-cinema practices, developing lighter equipment that would allow more discreet filming of reality, of individuals going about their daily business. The goal was, after all, to show Canadians to themselves, and in John Grierson's words, "make peace as exciting as war." According to the majority of accounts, the ethical debate was brought to a head in Canada when on 3 May 1967 *The Things I Cannot Change* was broadcast on public television across Canada.

When Grierson saw the film, he said he "hated it for revealing a person's private life without that person deciding that he or she be fully known." Colin Low, a key figure in CFC, also disliked the film. "Low thought it was unforgivable that a documentary film which purported to be sympathetic to the subjects had exacerbated a family situation" (Evans 1991, 159; see also Low, chapter 2, this volume). Low had said in commenting on earlier Unit B Candid Eye documentaries that "there was however, the problem of invasion of privacy and personality, that is, the destructive elements that were possible." He thought that "documentary had no business playing the voyeur; it was a thin line indeed between Cartier-Bresson and his love of his subjects and those who wanted to look under a rock to see the helter-skelter of creatures" (Evans 1991, 79).

In retrospect, it is possible for us to see that the film underwent a scrutiny that most observational projects of the time did not. The filmmaker was held accountable in a way that by today's standards seems excessive, not only against the measure of the ethical debaucheries regularly committed by producers of Reality Television (one wonders what *Nanny 911* would have done with the Baileys) but against that of even more respectable longitudinal documentary projects (i.e., films where the filmmaker embeds with his or her subjects across periods of time), like Michael Apted's *7 Up* series. Ballantyne Tree was criticized primarily for what she did *not* do – pre-screen the film, leave out potentially defamatory scenes, protect the father from self-harm, intervene in a violent situation. Yet all the things she *didn't* do, in the end, tell us very little about what she *did* do.[5] At the very least, the project was an attempt to do something about chronic problems associated with poverty, and to do this by bringing the issue before the public eye, being the film with the largest television audience to date for any NFB documentary (Evans 1991, 158). In this sense, the film was a success and was the catalyst, not only for a subsequent debate about ethics within the Film Board, but perhaps, more significantly at the time, for garnering financial support from government for the new program.[6]

But regardless of the moral condemnation of Ballantyne Tree's treatment of her subjects, there remains a question as to whether the subsequent use of the film in the critiques of observationalist documentary practices still holds up in hindsight. Ballantyne Tree's film has commonly been framed as a strictly observational project, practising the so-called non-obtrusive "fly on the wall" techniques typical of the American direct cinema. Upon closer examination of the film, we find that there is a strong participatory element at work, as we clearly hear the filmmaker's soft voice behind the camera sympathizing, questioning, and gently prodding her subjects throughout

5 For example, George Stoney is quoted as saying: "What should have happened – the film should've been screened for the family, in their apartment, privately, with just a few of the crew around. All the response would be sympathetic and understanding. Then, with the family itself doing the inviting and deciding who should come, it could've been screened at the church, at any group where the family had connections and where people would start from a friendly base" (Watson 1970 [1977]). See also Kurchak 1972 (1977), 121.

6 See chapter 2 of Rick Moore's unpublished PHD dissertation, "Canada's Challenge for Change: Documentary Film and Video as an Exercise of Power through the Production of Cultural Reality," University of Oregon, 1987.

much of the film. The other *voice-off* to occupy the screen acoustically – "acousmatically" (to borrow the term from Michel Chion, that potent cinematic voice that "has one foot in the image" [1994, 4]) – is the voice of Mr Bailey, who is established in this way from the very beginning as a competing subjectivity.

That the film later came to be the focus of the ethical critique in film theory of observational modes of documentary does not harmonize with the reflexive aspects brought about by the aural presence of the filmmakers. Nor does it address the performative aspects of the interactions between the family members and the filmmakers with their filmmaking (their performances, as it were) that are contained in the film's mode of presentation.[7] In addition, the film remains one of the most successful films that the NFB ever produced, as it lives on as material for discussion in academic fields also outside the confines of film studies, notably in anthropology and sociology. In both these fields, the questions surrounding the filmmaker's ethics are very often eclipsed by the discussion of Mr Bailey as a social type, a discussion that has been going on since the film's release.[8] In this sense, Mr Bailey has been framed as the typical victim of the social documentary.

THE VICTIM IN DOCUMENTARY THEORY

In *Representing Reality*, Bill Nichols describes the ethical dilemma of documentary in the following way: "When both filmmaker and social actor coexist within the historical world but only one has the authority to represent it, the other, who serves as subject of the film, experiences a displacement. Though bodily and ethically absent, the filmmaker retains the controlling voice, and the subject of the film becomes displaced into a mythic realm of reductive, essentialised stereotype, most commonly romantic hero or powerless victim" (1991, 91).

7 There is some dispute within documentary studies as to what is meant by the terms "performative" and "performance." For lack of space and not wanting to contribute to further obfuscation, I refer the reader here to Anne Jerslev's clarification of terms in her chapter "Performativity and Documentary" and Sami Saif's and Phie Ambos's chapter "Family and Performativity," both in Rune Gade and Anne Jerslev, eds, *Performative Realism* (Copenhagen: Museum Tusculanum Press, 2005), 85–115.

8 To witness the ongoing currency of the film, see Matthew Hays, "On Ethics and Aesthetics: *The Things I Cannot Change* and *Courage to Change*," in *Take One,* July-August 2002, a condemnation of the filmmakers for their continued exploitation of the family in the follow-up film *Courage to Change* (1989); and a review of the film by Kenneth Stoddart in *Teaching Sociology* 17 (January 1989), which describes the usefulness of the film in teaching sociology at an undergraduate level.

It was Brian Winston who in 1988 developed the concept of the Griersonian "victim" in his essay "The Tradition of the Victim in the Griersonian Documentary." Later, in his book *Claiming the Real* (1995), Winston elaborates: Grierson's movement represents an institutionalization, or internalization even, of the realist documentary. Grierson and his followers hid behind the rhetoric of a leftist position, while in actual fact they represented the conservative status quo when they channelled their filmmaking through state and private capitalist institutions.[9] Their films were an attempt to represent social conditions without examining cause or effect, something that would have threatened their sponsors. Winston sees this as a "flight from social responsibility." They did this by concentrating on both the subject as social victim and the "problem moment," an approach that later became the concept of balance in TV news coverage (Winston 1995, 40). Winston is critical of Grierson and his followers for institutionalizing a kind of film practice that denies any true engagement in the social reality it is claiming to represent (96). The lack of clarification about what the term "documentary" could mean – a "clumsy formulation but let it stand" – was paramount to the ethical problems that documentary film practice would eventually face (Sørenssen 2001, 13). Direct cinema inherited the problem and the ethical dilemma intensified: "Now they could really gather evidence, film life as lived, shoot 'events as they happened.' The new equipment did not just bolster and protect documentary's truth claim; it enhanced it and magnified it" (Winston 1995, 147).

The NFB's CFC program marks a transition from direct cinema/cinéma-vérité over to the more personal, subjective, reflexive, and targeted uses of documentary film that were became increasingly prominent throughout the 1970s and 1980s. For Winston, CFC/SN, particularly as it developed experiments in "process" and community and social advocacy filmmaking, represents the only road towards solving the victim problem of the social documentary and creating a more ethical documentary practice. He writes, "Advocacy by the subject means the end of the documentarist as artist but, perhaps just as significantly, it also means the end of the victim as subject – a necessary development if this ethical mess is to be cleared up" (1995, 258). More recently, he has continued to insist that the primary concern in documentary ethics is the concern shown by filmmakers towards their subjects, although he knows that any restrictions on filmmakers would hamper free-

9 See Malek Khouri's *Filming Politics* (2007) for a recent counter-argument to Winston's critique of Grierson, as well as of Joyce Nelson's *The Colonized Eye* (1988), which links Grierson to emergent global corporate capitalism. In Khouri's account, Grierson and the NFB were far more influenced by and involved with the progressive labour movements of the early 1940s, evidenced in the counter-hegemonic representations of workers in the early NFB films that had previously gone unexamined.

dom of speech (Corneil 2008, 243). Winston argues for a personal ethic, a "duty of care" along journalistic lines, for documentary filmmakers: "This is perhaps at base nothing more than a call for an ethical consciousness, an appeal for responsible behavior (especially a concern for others), and is the best we can do. It certainly supports the view, which I come more and more to believe, that the attitude and sensitivity of the filmmaker to the subject and the relationship they establish are the clue to ethical filmmaking, albeit one – like authenticity itself – that cannot be read off the screen" (Winston 2007).

In any case, the debate that arose after the screening of *The Things I Cannot Change* became the seedbed for ideas about a more ethical use of documentary (Kurchak 1977, 121; Evans 1991, 160). The primary goals of the CFC/SN program as it was developed were to train community action workers in the use of film and video, to reach out to the community and bring it together in order to empower citizens, to improve communications among citizens and with government, and to effect social change. Here we can hear echoes of Grierson's original mission in pre-television Britain in 1937: "It is worth recalling the British Documentary group began not so much in affection for film per se as in affection for national education. If I am to be counted as the founder and leader of the movement, its origins certainly lay in sociological rather than aesthetic aims" (1937 [1979], 78). There was frustration with the ineffectiveness of the social documentary in actually helping the people who participated, as well as with the resultant exploitative quality of the final product. This frustration with the inability of the social documentary to create social change led to a desire to experiment with more expanded applications of filmmaking within community development and with more ethical modes of documentary practice. The Fogo Island experiment was the first of these (Kurchak 1977, 121).[10]

THE FOGO ISLAND PROJECT

In May of 1967 John Kemeny sent Colin Low to Fogo Island, a rocky island off the coast of Newfoundland, to do "reconnaissance" – to find out if it would be a suitable community for the CFC program. They picked Fogo Island because it was a small community of five thousand people living in ten port communities, such as Joe Batt's Arm, Seldom Come By, Tilting, and Fogo,

10 See Hénaut 1968 on the use of film as an instrument of social change. Both Waugh 1984 and Gaines 1999 raise questions about the mythical status of the relationship between documentary and social change. Svenstedt 1970, Kurchak 1972, Moore 1987, and Burnett 1996 complain of how CFC/SN never defined what was meant by social change, and there has been very little assessment of the actual societal impact of documentary films and videos. Some exceptions are Whiteman 2002 and Hill 2007.

that were in danger of disappearing, threatened by the government's relocation plans. Sixty per cent of the people were living on welfare, fishing techniques needed modernizing, and there were few prospects for the future. At the time, the provincial government was trying to formulate a policy to deal with this situation, which centred on the idea of relocating communities to more centralized and inhabitable areas. Fred Earle, a local and a Memorial University community development worker, had already been organizing the islanders and had helped them form a development committee. It seemed to be the perfect project for the new program. Hence, Colin Low, in association with the Memorial University Extension Department, conducted the "Fogo Island Communication Experiment," which involved the production of a series of twenty-six short films from 1967 to 1968.

Swedish film scholar Carl Henrik Svenstedt learned about the process through interviews he conducted with the filmmakers in 1969–70. According to Svenstedt, Low was initially not very inspired by the films. He couldn't see the value of doing anything more than one or two documentaries about work and environment. It was Fred Earle as organizational advisor who was responsible for the structure of the shooting process. Three main lines of thought were clearly in place when the filmmakers went to stay on the island for the five weeks of shooting: (1) interviews would be focused more on people than on issues; (2) candid camera techniques were forbidden, as obtaining the islanders' full confidence in the filmmakers was a prerequisite for getting a good result; and (3), filming, editing, and screening would happen in open format with maximum influence from the islanders as to their form. Svenstedt writes: "Even though Colin Low didn't give a clear indication of it, it is most likely that he had little motivation for the project. It would be a boring film. At this stage, he made his first ingenious maneuver: he stepped back and listened, let Earle and the Islanders steer the work themselves and made himself available for technical advice" (1970, 81).

Most filmmakers would have wanted more control, and the first films indicate that Low was tempted: "The temptation was there in the beginning, which is reflected in one of the more 'descriptive' films, *The Children of Fogo*, where Low made a conventional documentary film, with intercutting, commentary and 'ambient shots'" (Svenstedt 1970, 81). Low showed the films as a cycle, opting for a vertical model of presentation. According to Svenstedt, this was simply because Low didn't know what to do with the twenty hours of footage and decided to leave the films as free-standing units "related to a given theme but that each maintained their integrity as much as possible" (82). But this was a small revolution: "The decision had a great significance for film ethics: through this construction and by maintaining the films in two track form (sound and picture) the films themselves were given the last word in the editing process" (82).

Svenstedt describes the evolution of the Fogo project as somewhat hap-hazard and instinctual – not consciously pre-planned. The community planning expert from Memorial University, Fred Earle, played a much greater role in how the program evolved than he had been given credit for elsewhere. The film's overall role in the experiment thus takes a lesser position and becomes only one step in a complex process (Svenstedt 1970, 83). Indeed, there are indications that the presence of the filmmakers hampered parts of the process. The camera often stymied discussions among community members, though likely only temporarily, as discussions probably carried on once the camera was removed. This makes it difficult to attribute the events that followed to the films alone. In the end, Svenstedt is quite critical of the Fogo project, and of Canadian sociology of the time more generally, for not being empirical enough, for not going far enough in examining social problems at a structural level, for focusing too much on the quest for local solutions, rather than going after structural problems and creating (Swedish-style) social revolution.

So far, we have seen how, upon closer examination, the two major elements in the CFC/SN legend – the ethical dilemma of representation and the ethics of access as the solution – are not as cut and dried as they have previously been portrayed. In the remainder of this chapter, I want to explore the implications of this for documentary ethics and aesthetics today, especially considering the political (activist) approach of CFC/SN as a model for documentary filmmaking.

A POLITICAL ETHICS FOR CFC/SN

In their introduction to *Feminism and Documentary*, Diane Waldman and Janet Walker describe how the "image ethics" discourse rests on a privileging of the filmmakers' position, the "us" of the filmmakers and the "them" of the subjects. In reference to Calvin Pryluck's (1976) essay "Ultimately We Are All Outsiders: The Ethics of Documentary Filming," in which he says, "[W]e can take our gear and go home," while "they have to continue their lives where they are," Waldman and Walker describe how the us-them duality is in turn replicated in the critique being offered here. They write: "Our point here is that the image ethics discourse echoes this pattern – at a theoretical level. True, the point of the ethics discourse is to find ways to level out or ameliorate the inegalitarian power relations it correctly identifies, but by concentrating on what the filmmaker can do to protect the rights of the subject ('the image maker's obligations to his/her subject'), this discourse actually reiterates the very power imbalance it seeks to redress" (1999, 14–15).

The authors are referring in part to Thomas Waugh (1988), who early on pointed to this problematic in his article "Lesbian and Gay Documentary:

Minority Self-imaging in Oppositional Film Practice, and the Question of Image Ethics." While other image ethicists discuss the responsibilities of the filmmaker towards audiences (the right to know) and towards their subjects (the duty of care), they neglect two other important responsibilities, or "accountabilities," that, in the case of what Waugh calls "minority oppositional film practices," must include collective and autobiographical modes of filmmaking and can even take precedence: accountability to the self and accountability to one's own constituency. Waugh writes: "Gay and lesbian cultural workers share their accountability to their constituency with all minority and oppositional activists. In fact, mainstream media workers and journalists are also accountable to a constituency – white middleclass heterosexual men – though of course this accountability is unacknowledged and masked by the media's claims to be speaking for society as a whole. My notion of accountability to the self is more distinctive, in fact unique to lesbians' and gays' identity as an invisible sexual minority" (1988, 253).

Waugh's interrogation of the ethics of responsibilities to these two other categories is especially useful – crucial, I would argue – in relation to an examination of CFC/SN, as the primary aim of the program was the political project of bringing minority groups into visibility within a Canadian media landscape that had neglected them heretofore. But it would also be extremely useful to speak in Waugh's expanded terms in light of the much-needed re-evaluation of the "filmmaker-victim" paradigm as it has been discussed in film theory. For Brian Winston, Bill Nichols, and others, CFC/SN was on its way to overcoming the ethical dilemma of documentary by allowing the subjects to have control over their own images; the "ethics of access" was seen as a means of eliminating the problem of the victim. This position becomes a difficult pill to swallow for filmmakers generally when we take into account that when the filmmaker gives up control, or becomes a mere facilitator, this eventually becomes a form of self-annihilation – there will be no more profession, which is one of the reasons the CFC filmmakers backed off from the process films in the end.

Not all subjects are in a position to represent themselves, nor should they always try.[11] Bill Nichols has more recently tried to address this issue, implying that a different code of ethics applies for people in positions of power who manipulate the media: "When power flows the other way – when

11 See Burnett, chapter 34, this volume, for a critique of the notion of "giving voice" in community video and of the assumption by filmmakers that community video will lead to empowerment ("community self-healing"). This assumption relies on the presumption that the community is missing something from before, that it is lacking a voice, which seems absurd when one is talking about communities with long oral traditions (Burnett 1996, 287).

subjects are not dependent on the filmmaker to have their story told – the ethic of responsible encounter gives 'getting the story' a 'higher priority'" (2006, 32). But how can this work? How can one set of ethics apply to one group of people but not to another? And more importantly, especially with the ethical problems associated with *The Things I Cannot Change* in mind, we might in hindsight question whether or not, when the subject of the film is in control, it may become a form of self-victimization just as easily as it can be liberating or therapeutic, for communities as well as for individuals.

If we use Waugh's four categories for a closer inspection of the ethics of representation involved in documentary filmmaking – the filmmakers' accountabilities to the self, to their constituency, to their audience, and to the subjects – perhaps we might be able to move beyond these problems. But new questions arise. What does it mean to be accountable? What would be the limits of this accountability? We would also have to understand what we mean by "constituency" here, which Waugh is very clear about. Is the constituency some particular source of funding? If so, it could ultimately (and probably mostly) eclipse the other three accountabilities in the minds of all involved. Is the constituency also the film's intended audience, and where does the ethical responsibilities of the audience figure into this scheme?

Vivian Sobchack claims that it is up to the spectator to evaluate the ethical reactions of the filmmaker, reactions that operate as "sign vehicles," where the ethical response is inscribed in the filmmaker's viewing activity or "gaze." Here we see "human behavior visibly encoded in the representation to signify the particular embodied situation of the filmmaker and thus his or her capacity to affect the events before the camera lens" (2004, 249), especially in the cameraperson's visible reaction to, for example, the taboo or transgressive, such as the sight of death.[12] This "ethically inscribed space" produces a "documentary consciousness" in the viewer that can occur at any moment in his or her viewing of a film and also within fictional representations. It is a personal ethic of care that arises from a specific subjective experience of the historical context. But how do the ethics of truth-telling

12 "Those visible 'sign vehicles' that function to make death seemingly visible on the screen most significantly signify the manner in which the immediate viewer – the filmmaker with camera – physically mediates his or her own confrontation with death: the ways s/he ethically inhabits a social world, visually responds in and to it, and charges it with an ethical meaning visible to others. As well, such sign vehicles are the means by which the mediate viewer – the spectator of the film – immediately and ethically inhabits the theater and visually responds to it ('do we shrink in our seats or lean forward?')" (Sobchack 2004, 244). For a less philosophical and more empirical approach to this topic, see Annette Hill's recent research on audience reception of documentary (2007, 2008).

come to visibility in the context of CFC/SN? Put another way, what were the (political) aesthetics of the program?

THE POLITICAL AESTHETICS OF CFC/SN

In the opening scene of the film *Winds of Fogo* (Colin Low, 1969), the only film shot in colour in the Fogo Island series, we see the Wells family pile into a car in their Sunday best, only to discover that the automobile won't start. In this highly stylized scene with its well-directed acting, sound-scaping and continuity editing, the filmmakers set up a romantic contrast between the symbolic aspiring land-legs of the younger generation, who dream of automobiles and progress, of leaving the island, and the more stalwart older generation. For this generation, the boat is the only sensible means of existence, and from there, fishing, kite flying, and boat-building, as the only realistic or viable future for existence and, in the words of William Wells, happiness on the island.

The symbolic status of the car and the boat matches the status of the kite near the end of the film. The recently adopted Canadian flag – turned into a kite – against the blue sky, symbolizes the continuity of the colours of the Union Jack as well as the youth and hopefulness of the Maple Leaf. According to Jerry White, *Winds of Fogo* undermines the dominant impression that the films produced in this era had no cinematic value (2006, 76). White is addressing here the misrepresentation of CFC/SN as the equivalent of poor-quality community television on cable, dominated, for example, by the implication that the "talking heads" aesthetic allows the films little lasting value (see Marchessault, chapter 33, in this volume). White points to the political aspects embedded in the visuals and sounds, in the affective and aesthetic dimensions: "The fact that this film, and for all practical purposes this series, closes with an image of the Canadian flag unpretentiously soaring (it has been made into a kite after all) over Newfoundland, points to its inseparable connection with a revitalized, and modernizing, Canadian nationalism. That it makes this link through the language of images is entirely consistent with the way that the film emphasizes both the political and the visual, both the communication and aesthetics, and refuses to sacrifice one for the other" (2006, 78).

While we value the aesthetic and affective dimensions of the Fogo films, the films also suggest a rethinking of the different ways in which documentary films may communicate knowledge. In one of the films, *Specialists at Memorial Discuss the Fogo Films* (George Stoney, 1969), experts from the government and Memorial University comment on the Fogo films. The minister of social development questions the subtle influence of the filmmakers on content when he asks whether the subjects were giving answers that they thought the interviewer wanted to hear. The sociologist asks if there couldn't be more socially stratified interviewing and questions the absence of the clergy. The geographer marvels at the "sense of environment" that the films offer. The economist questions the usefulness of the film at the level of content: "representative" is an ambiguous term, the film can't give a macro view, but it can give a feeling of participation and may be used together with other kinds of material. These questions, and the way they are framed, contribute at an aesthetic level, the dimension of reflexivity to the project.

But just as these various categories of expertise abstract different forms of knowledge from the films and their context (the project), if we take into account the structure of *Specialists at Memorial* as a whole (whether stumbled upon or designed), we might be able to understand the significance of Fogo in broader terms than as simply having inspired the access movement. The film cycle allowed for a variety of different kinds of communication to run in tandem. This was a remarkable leap forward in the thinking about documentary ethics. By including the feedback loop showing various audience reactions, the project incorporated the ethical space of audience reception, an important space where meaning is ultimately generated, into the ethical space constructed between filmmakers, subjects, the community, and the authorities.

Here I want to stress the importance of taking the entire cycle and its broader context into consideration when evaluating the experiment, in order that we may conceive of the Fogo project as an approach to documentary that contained a multiplicity of practices: aspects of narrative, *cinéma direct*, performance, participatory and reflexive modes, as well as interview and testimony. In this sense it was a documentary project that matched the scale and scope of the IMAX prototype *In the Labyrinth* project of Expo '67. By extension, the multiplicity of ethical and aesthetic approaches conceived under the umbrella of CFC/SN, that in fact ranged all the way from pre-screenings, to training citizens groups in production, to citizens writing and performing in fictions, demonstrates the rich legacy of the program as an experiment in a new political use of documentary, both in its French and English versions.

CONCLUSION

The political dimension of CFC/SN that would, after this foray, appear to remain entirely inseparable from the ethics and aesthetics at work in the various projects that were produced in the series demonstrates the continued value of the films and a pressing need to re-evaluate the legend. The ambitious project undertaken by the editors of this volume in presenting this collection of work on the program reflects the range and scope of the program itself and inspires such a re-evaluation. Can we as filmmakers overcome the ethical dilemma of representation by stepping back, by allowing subjects to represent themselves? Does this solve the problem of the documentary victim described by Brian Winston? My answer is probably no. But maybe this concept is dated to the point where it is no longer useful for us. When we are speaking of representation of a community, when autobiographical and collective modes of filmmaking come to be increasingly predominant under the spread of media access in the four decades that followed Fogo and particularly since the advent of digital media, a new model of ethics is required. As Waugh concludes, "The problematic of the collective and the constituency contradicts ... the traditional individual focus of (image) ethics ... There is no ethics for gay/lesbian cultural activism, of our oppositional self-representation, separate from its politics. For us, as for all oppositional cultural workers, the ethical, like the personal, is ultimately the political" (1988, 271).

In addition, the separation of process from product ultimately led to a dispute among filmmakers at the Board that brought the program to an early death in the beginning of the 1980s (Moore 1987). The Fogo project, which ambitiously combined both process and product, demonstrated the effectiveness of the two in combination. As Jerry White puts it, "The Fogo Island series offered an aesthetically open-minded, socially engaged vision for Canadian cinema at a crucial time in Canadian history. That Canadian cinema as a whole basically decided not to follow its path does not make it any less important" (2006, 79). Indeed, the project points in the direction of more recent activist media production that uses feature documentary filmmaking as part of a broader campaign that also makes use of the Internet and more traditional community-based organizing techniques. As inheritors of the CFC/SN legacy, we would do well to look back at the program to examine more closely the many experiments that were conducted under the political banner of facilitating change and building a new, more egalitarian society. I hope this chapter has shown that issues of ethics and aesthetics cannot be abstracted from the political dimension of this aspiration.

Acknowledgments
Thanks to Professors Thomas Waugh and Knut Ove Eliassen for their comments on this text. And thanks also to Professor Bjørn Sørenssen and the folks at the Concordia Documentary Center, as well as to the Norwegian University of Science and Technology's Internasjonal Seksjon and bilateral programs of the Research Council of Norway's Contact Committee for Immigrants and the Authorities, which have kindly supported this research.

"If a Revolution Is Screened and No One Is There to See It, Does It Make a Sound?" The Politics of Distribution and Counterpublics

■

36

EZRA WINTON

JASON GARRISON

What *Entertainment One* understands is that the profit and power centre of the film and television business is distribution – the access to the market-place – in which having scale and leverage matter in order to elbow your way in between the giants ... This has always been a distribution-driven business. Anyone who doesn't understand that, master it and live by it religiously is doomed. There's never been an exception.
■ Robert Lantos, quoted in Pachner 2008, 62

INTRODUCTION

There are many dirty little secrets swishing around the film industry, but the least-glamorous and most academically overlooked one happens to involve the very foundational measure of success the whole structure rests upon. Ask any independent filmmaker, they'll tell you: it's the distribution, stupid. And so, while film and video technology simplifies and reduces in size and cost, and while cameras and their power to document the world have fallen into the hands of the citizenry, radical changes in production alone do not put the full power of cinema at the ready. Distributive structures shape the cinema we see (and are even aware of) and the audiences film producers have access to, predominantly along lines of commercial viability. Important films – political and activist films that explore under-represented narratives – often fail to find an audience because of the indifference of exclusive commercial distribution channels. But not only is analysis of distribution generally a neglected area of film and communication studies, the majority of scholarship focuses more or less exclusively on Hollywood and mainstream commercial distribution. These works ignore alternative modes of grassroots/community documentary distribution and exhibition, or counterpublic spaces (Fraser 1990) that animate discussion and facilitate action in community-based venues and the larger public sphere, rather than enriching the bottom lines of media cartels. Today, developing and supporting counterpublics, or "myriad and diverse spaces where discussion and dissent occur" (Rennie 2006, 19), that empower communities and democratize public spaces while avoiding the pitfalls of myopic digital enthusiasm, depends on understanding past attempts. Proactive Canadian policy-makers in the 1960s tried to achieve social transformation through the Challenge for Change/Société nouvelle (CFC/SN) program, imbuing documentary cinema with radical participatory impulses, at the levels of both production *and* distribution, creating "a revolution in community organizing and development of communications which continues to this day" (Erin Research Group 2005, 5). The aim of this chapter is to look at grassroots distribution of documentary as it was engendered in CFC/SN and as it relates to digital and current community material iterations.

WHY DISTRIBUTION?

Popular rhetoric suggests there is a revolutionary marriage of documentary and democracy springing forth from the wells of technology and human experience. Filmmaker, documentary advocate, and writer Peter Wintonick gives the zeitgeist shape when he writes: "We are now living in the 'hear and now' of an evolutionary wave, the digital revolution, where everyone, literally, can become a filmmaker" (2005). The implication is that everyone and anyone can find a camera, point it at the world, stitch together a story on a cheap computer, and take pride in their new title as "documentary filmmaker." But while documentary films and filmmakers continue to be associated with qualities of democracy and civic action, such as "explorer, reporter, advocate, bugler, prosecutor, observer, catalyst" (Barnouw 1993), the spaces created out of the efforts to distribute and exhibit documentaries remain largely overlooked in favour of mainstream/commercial feature distribution. Unfortunately, these channels tend neither to distribute much documentary nor to produce or sustain dialogue on the connected issues. Dissent may be the engine of change, but without distribution it doesn't get very far at all.

Following the success of *Fahrenheit 9/11* in 2004, which alone brought in $119 million, a critic spoke of an "onward and upward" trend in documentary (Deutchman 2005, 60). But this enthusiasm collapsed soon enough when only three documentaries broke the one-million-dollar barrier in 2007 (Harvey and Wilson 2008, 54). The North American market seems to have sufficient enthusiasm for only one big documentary every year, and consequently documentary remains a mere morsel in the income coffers of the media conglomerates. Lacking a measurably positive trend, risk-averse distributors will stay away, and titles they do pick up are as likely to be family fare (*March of the Penguins*) or pop-culture focused (*Leonard Cohen: I'm Your Man*) as they are to be political/activist documentary (*Darwin's Nightmare, Super Size Me*). Most independent documentary filmmakers are squeezed out of the mainstream commercial distribution network, left clawing past one another at festivals to secure the few commercial spots the system opens up every year. It is easier for the majors and their "alternative" studios to cherry-pick than to fund proposed productions. The majority of socially conscious documentaries find limited or no commercial theatrical release, and must hope instead to secure an afterlife in DVD sales and – if nothing else for these neglected labours of love – elicit distribution in that ever-expanding vacuum of media space, the World Wide Web.

Yet many are not lost. They are salvaged through grassroots efforts that bring cinema's under-represented stories to interested communities and social networks. Film festivals, film clubs, non-profit indy theatres, café screenings, advocacy series, radical film nights, activist conferences, cinema collectives, and campus groups, all provide a lifeline for political/activist documentaries. These modes of distribution and exhibition generate and sustain alternative *spaces between* (Bhabha 1994, 25) the box office numbers, summer blockbusters, and mega-plexes that dominate cinema distribution. They are counterpublic spaces that encourage not only a culture of cinema-going, but dialogue and action in response to compelling narratives urging social change. Two counterpublic spaces, or moments, we will examine in this chapter are Challenge for Change/Société nouvelle and, to a lesser extent, the student-run project and network Cinema Politica (CP).

With the lion's share of scholarly attention going to the commercial mainstream cinema spaces and to production minutia or content analysis, ample opportunity exists to discover, examine, and theorize grassroots distribution and exhibition of documentaries. This inquiry is concerned with contributing both to the amelioration of independent documentary communities and to the "democracy project." In other words, we map grassroots practices that create spaces conducive to access and inclusiveness, participation, and responsiveness (Barney 2005, 10). In concert with Clemencia Rodriguez, we are conducting a "theoretical analysis that attempts to capture the essence of alternative media and/or to explain the importance of these media as processes of communication and democracy" (Rodriguez 2001, 11). However, before we get to the details of CFC/SN and CP, let's theoretically examine the notion of commercial distribution as a hegemonic structure and what alternative/grassroots distribution provides by way of rupturing this structure or posing alternatives.

"HOLLYWOOD HEGEMONY," DEMOCRACY, AND COUNTERPUBLICS

Media consolidation in the film industry has led to medium-sized studios being gobbled up by larger ones (Miramax to Disney, New Line Cinema to Warner Brothers, etc.) and formerly "alternative" or "independent" distributors being colonized by the big studios, leaving almost nothing in the realm of truly independent cinema (Spaulding 2004, 52–3). Commercial distribution itself in North America is collapsed with production, marketing, exhibition, and retail as a totalizing operational system that flows from – for example – investment firms in Germany, studio management and talent in Hollywood, stand-in locations and tax breaks in Canada, and cheap labour in Southeast Asia. Transnational media cartels orchestrate every stage of the shelf life of a cinema product line from inception, spinning money in perpetuity from TV, VOD (video on demand), DVD sales, sales to foreign networks, spinoffs, cellphone ring-tone downloads (Pachner 2008, 61), and even plastic toys in overpriced breakfast cereal. Commercial distribution has expanded its scope far beyond the older system of charting courses for canisters of celluloid. If, as Janet Wasko argues, the two "hidden" elements of the commercial cinema industry – financing and distribution – together contain all the machinations of power and control (Wasko 2003, 33), it is not unfair to say that the major studios enjoy a *hegemony* over cinematic consumption in North America.

The "Hollywood hegemony" (Miller and Stam 2004, 269) that grips the Canadian film industry (Beaty 2006, 149) is the matrix of cultural and financial forces described above, joined at the hip to a larger discursive hegemony Bourdieu describes as "The Tyranny of the Market" (Bourdieu 1998a). The prevailing "common sense" (Peet 2002, 56; Bourdieu 1998b) of this hegemony is the orthodoxy of neoliberalism. The linkage between the hegemonic structure of commercial film distribution and neoliberal ideology means our cinematic social conscience lives and dies on the possibility of financial return and little else. Inherent to this economic ideology of open markets, free trade, and the accumulation of capital is the process of commodification and control of resources, including media resources (Leys 2001, 2, 108), especially as they are concentrated in media cartels. As states and large transnational corporations consolidate costs through processes of privatization and trade deregulation (Leys 2001, 108), some spaces open up while others close. The spaces for companies to trade "commodities" like fresh water, for example, open up, while the spaces for an independent documentary challenging the privatization of water become more restricted as commercial cinema cannibalizes alternative distribution channels.[1] The world may be at a crucial crossroads, but as citizens we cannot expect commercial studios and their commercial distribution networks to get the message out when the risks they

---

[1] The importance of issue-directed films is meaningless to business except as such matters are part of commercially viable trends, trends transnational companies and governments are happy enough to see evaporated, as when the transformative potential of *An Inconvenient Truth* (2006) is diffused by the foolish idea of filling our gas tanks with ethanol, maybe for a last tour of civilization.

are most concerned with are financial. Yet there seems to be little alternative for reaching people, with commercial distribution and marketing dominating the landscape.

A hegemonic structure is a shaping of society by dominant groups using the vast resources they have amassed to raise their way of seeing and experiencing the world to the level of common sense. It was originally used by Lenin, was then theorized by Gramsci to explain the failure of Marxism to organize the working classes (Day 2005, 57), but has been extended more recently by the theorists of radical democracy such as Ernesto Laclau and Chantal Mouffe (Torfing 1999). In its original form, bourgeois hegemonic formations established a capitalist status quo to be opposed and then shattered by counter-hegemonic formations produced by a revolutionary vanguard, naturally that of the Communist Party (Day 2005, 59). The image here is that of Godzilla vs Mothra battling for the unified hearts and minds of the masses, with the "free" citizen defined as the individual properly owing allegiance to the hegemonic force. In the post-Marxist theorizing of Laclau and Mouffe, hegemony is not a vast block of power, but is by nature a fractured and polyvalent assemblage of metonymous structures and modalities always on the move. The collapse of Marxism and the rise of the new social movements (feminism, gay liberation, black power, etc.) forever de-centered the battle for social justice away from the ideology of the proletariat to a diversity of revolutionary subjects, united not by the destiny of history but by similar-enough ideas, language, and values that could challenge the status quo. Hegemony therefore admits of continuous and yet unknown possibilities of rupture, deformation, and growth in new directions.[2]

As we think about distribution, we need to keep in mind both the limiting character of the "Hollywood Hegemony" and the continuous possibilities for undermining, intervening, and appropriating those structures for the socially conscious distribution networks of the future in order to (re)open cinematic space to diverse representation outside the norm, thereby increasing the scope of a culture of democracy. As Mouffe argues, "The constitution of democratic individuals can only be made possible by multiplying the institutions, the discourses, the forms of life that foster identification with democratic values," and these need to focus on "the types of *practices* and

---

2 This flexibility is observable even within the "Hollywood Hegemony," since some socially critical documentaries do make the commercial cut, and a handful of these – *Fahrenheit 9/11* (2004), *An Inconvenient Truth* (2006), and *Super Size Me* (2004) – have indeed set mass media "dialogue" in motion. Nevertheless, the inadequacy of commercial hegemony in film distribution leaves us cold, not only because these films tend to make very limited critiques of culture, but because the bulk of socially conscious documentary remains on the delivery room table.

not the forms of argumentation" (2000, 11). Grassroots initiatives that focus on the collective values of "small groups" (CFC/SN project parlance used in contradistinction to "mass audience") in the material world (as opposed to virtual worlds) and articulate a sense of community and the public sphere (over mass media and commercially controlled private property) are part of the multiplying factor Mouffe speaks of. In the domain of cinema, democratizing production must meet with democratizing distribution, while de-linking from the logic of the "Hollywood Hegemony" and neoliberal discourse.

As the next section will explain in more detail, CFC/SN provided an experimental framework for artists and citizens to de-link by actively confronting hegemony and by forming not just their own heterogeneous content, but also diverse spaces, schedules, and channels of content sharing and flows. The CFC/SN project is instructive for imagining and realizing a democracy capable of fracturing the present landscape of globalizing liberal cultural articulations reflected in commercial cinema systems. The "fissures in the mediascape" (Rodriguez 2001, 1) that were created during screenings of *You Are on Indian Land* (discussed below) and scores of other CFC/SN films therefore contribute to the building of new possibilities for counterpublics and cultural participation.

CHALLENGE FOR CHANGE/SOCIÉTÉ NOUVELLE

Challenge for Change/Société nouvelle approached the percolating social issues of the sixties and seventies with a bold shift in film production and distribution. The National Film Board (NFB) was already known as a "world class propaganda-maker during World War II" (Walz 1997, 132), but beginning in 1967 it would undertake to be the propagandist of sorts for the marginalized and under-represented, bringing disaffected youth and those negatively impacted by urbanization, unemployment, poverty, discrimination, and poor health policy into a more direct and fair dialogue with government policy-makers, who had a great part in determining – and changing – their lives. It would do so through a twin movement: by bringing both production and distribution to "the people."

CFC/SN did not invent community distribution *ex nihilo*,[3] but carried over many of the ideas and activities begun by its parent, the National Film Board. Early on the NFB was mandated to exhibit films to communities across Canada, the audience the nation as a whole, at a time when reaching distant communities was difficult. Too many citizens were located in regional pockets,

3 A CFC/SN source points also to socialist and Communist film distribution networks that were disrupted by the efforts to mobilize for WWII, the labour-activism disrupting effect of the New Deal, and the witch-hunting of the Cold War (NFB 1977, 3).

without a sense of nation, thus posing difficulties for mobilization during the Second World War. NFB projectionists travelled throughout Canada on regional film circuits projecting films, providing prints, giving technical and organizational advice to community groups, and sending back monthly reports to head office. Audience discussion of the films was an important element, leading to the development of "discussion trailers" intended to guide the audience response to the film. Although community distribution was to create a "two-way flow of information between government and citizen" (Druick 2007, 81), this communication was, it seems, mainly intended to reinforce the idea of nation in communities across Canada by, among other things, normalizing the idea of government programs.

After the Second World War, the film circuit structure shifted to film councils. These local organizations, whose volunteers "saw themselves as community activists, improving themselves and those around them" (Druick 2007, 86), acted "as a co-ordinating body, [promoting] the production, distribution and effective use of informational visual material for the general welfare of all peoples" (Charles W. Marshall, cited in Druick 2007, 82). The audience was no longer the nation as a whole, but split between those thought to be in need of social welfare programs and the helping class – the professionals, social workers, and charity workers. Foreshadowing the CFC/SN program to come, a report on pre-screening discussions stated that people will "do something about a problem [only] if they have discussed it and convinced themselves what needs to be done, and feel they have made the decision themselves" (*Getting the Most out of Your Film Screening*, cited in Druick 2007, 84). The didactic function of these discussions is reinforced by the joint production of the discussion guides by the NFB and the Canadian Education Association (Druick 2007, 84).

Although Druick states that the film councils were aided "by newly established film libraries and regional depositories" (2007, 83), a CFC/SN internal document from 1977 suggests that the establishment of a regular NFB distribution system, namely through these libraries, caused a "collapse" of grassroots distribution and "a diminution of active field distribution of films and an ever widening gap between production and the audience" (NFB 1977, 2). Through greater institutionalization, the emphasis on projectionists was replaced by one on distribution officers, who "assisted local libraries and film councils and sold prints to a wide variety of audiences" (Mintzberg and McHugh 1985, 183). By the 1960s, they used a pink card system "to keep track of when and where the film was shown, and how many people saw it. Every month [they] had to send those cards in to the head office in Montreal. [Their] performance ... was judged by the number of pink cards [they] sent in" (Walz 1997, 138). Performance evaluation here is linked to feedback about audiences, but apparently the NFB at this time did not view the audience as being particularly important as an origin of ideas. After continued shifts in the distribution landscape with the advent of television and some changes in government, including a pre-Expo funding increase for the NFB, the late sixties saw a window open for new government programs.

Taking up the views of Marshall McLuhan, many media activists of the sixties believed that "by gaining access to new communications systems, the disenfranchised minorities ... could gain social power" (Ryan 1988, 42). In January 1967, a proposal titled "Challenge for Change" circulated in the NFB for "an Action-Program of Film activities" at the Board "to help eradicate the causes of poverty [and] provoke fundamental social change" (NFB 1967b, 1). It was suggested that previous attempts to eradicate poverty failed in part because of a "problem of informing and involving" (NFB 1967a, 1) those who were affected by the programs and a lack of self-awareness that led to "a cycle in which apathy is bred and transmitted from one generation to the next" (NFB 1967b, 11). Both problems could be addressed by cinema. Film would help involve citizens in the pre-planning stages of policy-making by bringing their lived concerns to government and program administrators, and the mirroring power of cinema would enable the disenfranchised to become more self-aware and to develop and maintain self-perpetuating, self-help initiatives.

In less than a year from the first proposal, the focus of CFC/SN quietly shifted from eliminating poverty to facilitating "social change" (NFB 1967b, 7), which was ambiguously defined. The power of deciding *who* needed to respond to the government and *why* shifted more directly into the hands of filmmakers and community activists. Now social problems and conflicts formerly unknown or ignored appeared on the screen. Issues uncomfortable for the average white, middle-class, male bureaucrat like native rights, black power, and women's issues got a seat at the table formerly set for "legitimate" social hygiene, educational, nationalization, and war-time mobilization projects. What was most radical about the early energy of CFC/SN was the notion of a government-sponsored film production and distribution network tasked specifically with criticizing government initiatives. Bill Nemtin put it well when he declared that "[a]nti-government feeling, even when based on misinformation, must be allowed expression. This is essential for the community and for the government" (1968b, 18). Indeed, shining a critical light into the dark corners of regressive or failed government policy was the undercurrent to many of the CFC/SN films.

To accomplish the facilitation of social change, production and distribution were welded together. Filmmakers acted as animators of grassroots community interests, working with citizens and activist groups to present issues from the point of view of those experiencing said challenges. The subjects and audience of the film would be the same, citizens in need (NFB 1967b, 7), and because the "[p]rime accountability [was] to the users of the program" (Roberts 1974, 4), the audience would be extended to other groups only if authorized by and in the interests of those depicted. In principle at least, mass audience films were rejected, since they were "unlikely to generate action [and] could cause unsympathetic reactions" (NFB 1967a, 3). As much as possible, the raw footage would be shown to the community while the production process was underway. As Ches Yetman put it: "We'd sit some people down and get them talking about bad housing. We'd videotape it and then take the videotape next door and show it to the neighbours. Then we'd videotape them talking about their bad housing. And so on" (Walz 1997, 138). Rough cuts of the films were to be shown to the citizens involved, with their response feeding back into the editing and distribution choices. A community-approved film in hand, the CFC/SN filmmaker would screen the film for other activist groups, the government or expert communities – teachers, social workers, public health nurses – and other interested communities. Given the simpler Portapak single-system video cameras available in the late 1960s, distribution officers and filmmakers would also be able to film audience reactions to the film screenings they organized. It was hoped that distant distribution points might act as true two-way communication nodes, between the competing interest groups the film presented (NFB 1967b, 8). Process replaced an emphasis on pre-defined end products (Roberts 1974, 3), with some projects resulting in no distribution of footage outside of the communities themselves. Although CFC/SN leveraged the existing NFB distribution networks, with its access to theatres and television, these aspects of distribution were not stressed by the program. One film, *Pikangikum* (John Gould, 1967), was withheld from community distribution for six months because it was set for commercial theatrical distribution (Kemeny 1968, 4), but this was not the norm.

FILMS FOR "INDIANS" AND DISTRIBUTION

Native groups became explicit targets of film production, distribution, and support under CFC/SN. Early film project proposals included a wide diversity of topics about Natives, suggesting a mixture of governmental, white social activist, and Native interests – the multiplicity of conflicting perspectives that would characterize the CFC/SN program as a whole. Various proposals were made during the program to extend film distribution to First Nations reserves (Kemeny 1968, 7), to formerly underserved areas like northwest British Columbia (Kent 1970, 2), or to improve distribution in difficult-to-reach areas like the Far North (NFB 1975, 8). Other proposals focused on connecting to already-existing First Nations organizations and activist groups. Films such as *Cree Hunters of Mistassini* (1974) were being co-distributed within the Native community by its own organizations, in this case the National Indian Brotherhood (NFB 1974a, 2).

There can be little doubt that these developments had a positive effect. In 1973, the 2,276 bookings of films on Native issues comprised 26 per cent of the total of CFC/SN bookings of 8,725,[4] when 14 per cent would have been proportional to the number of films (9 to 62) (NFB 1974a). Of these, one film, *Ballad of Crowfoot*, comprised 7.3 per cent of the total bookings for *all* of CFC/SN (NFB 1974a). Although, the impact of these numbers diminishes when we consider that CFC/SN bookings in 1975 were only 4.4 per cent of total NFB bookings, that is quadruple the percentage of CFC/SN titles (1.2 per cent of NFB titles). Even more impressive is that sales of CFC/SN titles accounted for 25 per cent of total NFB sales. Whether the "disproportion" of Native film bookings carried over to sales is unknown by these researchers. But that CFC/SN, and Native CFC/SN, titles punched above their weight in terms of distribution is indisputable. This imbalance of representation can likely be attributed to the efforts of CFC/SN distributors to bring these films specifically to the attention of Native and therefore stakeholder communities.

Yet, the "good news" about a growing representation of Native communities faced a persistent problem: one of the functions of the NFB before CFC/SN was to "[provide] a visual representation of [Natives] for the wider society to understand its relationship to them" and to define them as "part of the Canadian state plan" (Druick 2007, 110) as a manageable population. As Noel Starblanket said in 1968, "Eighteen films have been produced about Indians by the National Film Board, and all of them have been made by *outsiders* looking in on the situation" (Starblanket, chapter 5, this volume, p. 38). A number of CFC/SN films seem to continue this tradition. For example, the audience is invited to gain "insight into the origins of economic backwardness of Indians" by watching *PowWow at Duck Lake* (1967) (Kemeny 1968, 12), and the synopsis of *Indian Dialogue* (1967) informs the audience that Indians do "not worry about their white neighbours," and invites them to marvel at the "essential democracy" and "spiritual riches" of the Indian way of life (Kemeny 1968, 12). Many people of the First Nations, suffering as they have for centuries under the aggression and indifference of foreign governments, could not but look at the CFC/SN program with cynical

---

4 *Ballad of Crowfoot* (1968), *Indian Dialogue* (1967), *PowWow at Duck Lake* (1967), *These Are My People* (1969), *Encounter with Saul Alinsky, Part 2* (1967), *You Are on Indian Land* (1969), *Indian Relocation: Elliot Lake* (1967), *God Help the Man Who Would Part with His Land* (1971), and *Pikangikum* (1967); missing were *Loon Lake* (1969) and *North American Indian Travelling College* (1968) (NFB 1974a).

eyes, seeing these descriptors as those of the outsider/colonizer, the helping professional, the white liberal who pities the "Indian" and would like to "understand" if only it could be put in their own terms.

Michelle Stewart in chapter 16 of this volume writes, "Indeed, Aboriginal representation and production played a central role in the debate within CFC regarding which kind of filmmaking best served communities while still fulfilling the National Film Board's mandate to make films in the national interest." But the CFC/SN program was a result of multiple interests, and its radicalism – carried out in the typically sedate Canadian way – sometimes had surprising result of eluding government influence and the dead weight of NFB bureaucracy. When a project was rejected by government sponsors because it touched on Native rights (Moore 1987, 152), Colin Low repackaged the proposal in terms of ethnography and, when it was accepted, put no restrictions on the filmmakers at all, effectively producing funding for the project the government had originally rejected, the eventual result being one of the best-loved CFC/SN films, *Cree Hunters of Mistassini* (1974).[5] Those who analyse CFC/SN need to be aware of multiple sites of resistance, even within a bureaucracy developed in conjunction with government.

An attempt to reposition Native film within a Native perspective came in the form of the National Indian Training Program (1968–71), initiated by the NFB and aided by the Company of Young Canadians (CYC). Gathering seven young Native people from across Canada, NFB experts successfully trained them in the techniques of film production, with the hope they would initiate film projects of their own. Unfortunately, CYC funding dried up, making independent Native filmmaking practically impossible without the help of the NFB. Yet the Native film students had not been trained to "deal with the bureaucratic mechanisms of the Film Board" (Moore 1987, 151). The films involving these individuals were organized and directed by non-Natives, the one exception being *You Are on Indian Land*, which was for the most part initiated, produced, and distributed by the Native people themselves, perhaps most powerfully expressing the principles CFC/SN was created to uphold.

YOU ARE ON INDIAN LAND (1969)

Exemplifying the shifting articulations of power dynamics while illustrating alternative methods of production and distribution is the 36-minute *You Are on Indian Land (YAOIL)* (Mort Ransen and Mike Mitchell, 1969).[6] The film is about Mohawks who blockade an international bridge near Cornwall,

5 A film, by the way, that Rick C. Moore insists isn't really a Native film at all, since it was organized by outsiders, not the First Nations groups being filmed (1987, 161).

You Are on Indian Land (1969): filmmaker-activist Mike Mitchell forgot the Scotch Tape for the blockade notices. Frame enlargement.

Ontario, in pursuit of the rights promised to First Nations by the Jay Treaty of 1794. As officers haul away old and young agitated Mohawk activists aware of earlier media moments when the same warning had rung internationally, a protester yells to the camera, "The whole world is watching!" Untrue to be sure, but Ransen and Mohawk organizer Mitchell were both there to document the event and ensure that if not the world, then at least many communities would bear witness to the struggle.

That this film was made at all is accidental. Mike Mitchell, a Mohawk of the Akwesasne Reserve (then called St Regis), called George Stoney, then the executive producer of the CFC/SN program, and told him of an imminent blockade of the road connecting Canada and the United States. As Rick C. Moore describes it, it was because of the willingness of Stoney to circumvent usual NFB rules that he was able to throw together a crew in under twenty-four hours, in time for the blockade (1987, 139). In this sense, the film is an exception within CFC/SN, which itself is an exception to the usual

6 While Ransen is officially given exclusive directorial credit, the filmmaker always maintained that *YAOIL* was made in complete collaboration with Mike Mitchell of the NFB's Indian Film Crew, who is also one of the film's main subjects and its narrator. From the NFB site: "[T]he Aboriginal voice is central to the storytelling. Hearing a narrator using terms like 'we,' 'many of us,' 'our land, our people' is much more intimate and inviting than the detached, observational, anthropological narration that can only say, 'the Indians ... '"

NFB operations – a gap within a gap that made a truly confrontational representation and documented moment of oppression possible despite government funding.

Alan Rosenthal, in speaking of YAOIL's impact, asserts, "This steadfast refusal to engage film and video as mass media, by insisting first and foremost that they circulate locally, back into the communities which they are documenting, as vehicles for collective self-examination is central to Stoney's distinctive approach" (quoted in Ginsburg 1999, 66). In keeping with the CFC/SN objective of making films *with* communities, and not merely *about* them, raw footage was made available within twenty-eight hours to Mitchell and his activists (Stoney 1969, 1), and a two-hour rough cut was hastily put together within days of shooting the film. For his part, Mitchell set out with the two 16mm reels to the affected community, where the conflict was still percolating, unresolved. He remembers that "there were about a dozen screenings, and members of the First Nations community represented in the film gave feedback for the final edit and used the film as a springboard for discussions on future actions, plans, and tactics to resolve the conflict" (Mitchell, personal interview, 2007).

Reports on these very early screenings were not readily available at the NFB Archives; they begin for 2 January, about two weeks after the shoot. One early reaction – from a strong-willed female protagonist, Kahn-Tineta Horn – was concern about what would happen if the footage fell into the hands of the police. Thirty-five protesters had been arrested at the blockade by Cornwall police and were awaiting a 25 March court date, and there was worry that the film might be used as evidence against them. On 3 January, two hundred people watched the film in a school basement, and on the 4th, between fifty and a hundred people saw the film, including most of the constitutional Longhouse chiefs of the Six Nations. Noel Starblanket noted that because most of these people were not from Akwesasne, reactions were not linked to the recognition of the people involved but to a more general enthusiasm as the action of the film progressed (1969a, 3).

The line between CFC/SN filmmakers, distributors, and activists, already blurred at the birth of this project, remained indistinct as Mitchell and Starblanket got involved themselves "at the Longhouse for Kahn-Tineta's border crossing" on 5 January (Starblanket 1969a, 4). On 10 January, after Mitchell tried to dissuade other Mohawk activists from following Kahn-Tineta Horn's attempt to instigate another blockade, a rough cut was shown in Toronto to about thirty people connected to the Canadian Civil Liberties Association. Disappointingly, the screening was evaluated as having "little purpose" because most of the individuals – "hobbyists about Indians" – "feel that they are magnanimously donating their valuable time ... rather than being genuinely involved" (Shannon 1969, 1). The Natives in the crowd responded more enthusiastically.

On the 11th, there was a screening at Ohsweken (on the Six Nations Reserve near Brantford, Ontario). Starblanket recorded a message from Chief Joe Logan to the people of Akwesasne and an English translation of two Native treaties (Shannon 1969, 1). Asked to give some prefatory comments before the film, Logan remarked, "The Jay Treaty didn't give us rights, it re-affirmed them." Although there were two hundred people there, the room was silent, no laughter and no applause. The film reminded the audience of the police brutality the community had experienced in 1960 at a previous Native protest.

On 16 January, a VTR (videotape recording) transfer of the rushes was screened for about fifteen Cornwall municipal officials. One commented that the film crews were "a nuisance to the police." Another said, "I think we've heard enough of her," and asked for the film to be fast-forwarded. The screening resulted in expressions of sympathy, but no solutions. Polite for-mality closed the discussion – "We certainly appreciate your concern in invit-ing us," and "[I]t was a very orderly demonstration" (Starblanket 1969c, 1). Later that day, the film was screened before RCMP and Indian Affairs, the lat-ter of whom snuck in after the second reel. In describing the reaction of the police officers, Starblanket noted their attempt to show no emotion but also that the film affected a number of them. The Indian Affairs officials laughed nervously when someone in the film called the old chiefs "puppets" (Star-blanket 1969c, 2). The police made no substantial contribution during the discussion, but Mitchell was successful in winning over the crowd.

On the 17th of January the film was shown to an audience of sixty people at Hogansburg Methodist Church. The young people present suggested the church host a benefit and speak-in with Iroquois orators to raise money for their cause (Starblanket 1969c, 2). The next day, a screening at the same place was held for fifteen steelworkers. On the 19th, the distributors went to Toronto where Indian Affairs was holding a meeting to change the Indian Act. A joint protest by the "Urban Indians" and the Akwesasne Mohawks took place, and it was for these people that reels 2 and 3 were shown on the 20th. Starblanket records that the chiefs who "sold out" to Indian Affairs were in attendance and describes their emotional reactions, which perhaps suggested their shame for how one of them reacted in the film. Some people in the audience suggested a shorter edit of the film. On the 21st, the rough cut was shown at an NFB Distribution Region meeting before twenty-five to thirty delegates. According to Starblanket, they were "astounded" and supportive (1969c, 5).

Thus ends the archival record of the immediate community-wide distri-bution of *You Are on Indian Land*. On 3 February, Starblanket proposed a

You Are on Indian Land (1969): arrested Mohawk demonstrator Kahn-Tineta Horn surrounded by police and blocked cars. Frame enlargement.

screening for the lawyers involved in the defence of the thirty-five arrested Mohawk activists and for the Grand Council of the Six Nations Chiefs of the Iroquois Confederacy on the 9th. In making his request, Starblanket cited the "indication of support and solidarity [of] the NFB" (Starblanket and Mitchell, 1969, 1) in aiding their defence, but little did he know how far they would have to go, as both the Crown and Kahn-Tineta's defence lawyers tried to grab the film – probably the first and last time an NFB film was booked via subpoena. On 18 March, Deputy Chief of Police Poirier sent the NFB a request to have the film shown at the courthouse for the 25 March trial (Staecy 1969, 2). The Crown tried to subpoena the film for the prosecution, but those named could not be found (Stikeman 1969, 2). The next day, Kahn-Tineta's defence lawyer obtained a subpoena for Anthony Kent to produce the unedited footage to – ironically given her previous opinion of the film – vindicate her before the court. By the 25th of March, all the charges had been dropped except those against seven activist leaders, including Mike Mitchell and Kahn-Tineta. NFB representatives attended the trial, with canisters in their car, and almost rushed back to Montreal when they thought the film might be shown, but the it never made it to the trial. Eventually all the charges were dropped.

Mitchell, who recently retired as grand chief at Akwesasne, describes touring with the film in Canada and the United States, speaking at over a hundred screenings within a six-month period. He says that many screenings were the result of universities inviting him to come and discuss the issues raised in the film. Mitchell insists that First Nations issues were barely on the map in North America at that time, and so, as he says, firmly, "it was a big deal" (Mitchell, personal interview, 2007). In his opinion, the CFC/SN films were circulated and exhibited in as grassroots and community-oriented a way as they were produced (involving subjects and communities in the process): "I travelled all over the continent, visiting First Nations reserves, community centres, schools, and prisons, using the film to raise awareness about the Mohawk struggle." Mitchell goes on to say that it was crucial to "really push the theme of CFC by implementing discussion, creating dialogue, and generating a buzz around the documentary so that local media would cover the grass roots screenings, and in turn, the larger issues of First Nations rights" (Mitchell, personal interview, 2007).

Mitchell argues in the same interview that by "using media as a tool," the initial grassroots efforts "amounted to many points of discussion, focus meetings, and it was ultimately a prelude to the wider distribution – it created interest in the film." *You Are on Indian Land* was not shown in Canadian commercial cinema houses, but had a national presence through the NFB distribution system, of which CFC/SN was a part. Released as a 37-minute 16mm film in 1969, within five years it had been booked 1,199 times across Canada and had been on TV a total of forty-five times, more than all but three other CFC/SN films (NFB 1974b, 5).

Mitchell credits the grassroots movement and the sharing of the film as "bridging a communication gap" between antagonistic groups, including First Nations protesters and the police. He believes that a direct outcome of the community circulation of the film was that the charges were dropped against the protesters. An important effect, according to Mitchell, was that the film's distribution throughout North America, at universities and other community locations, led to international interest. As he puts it, "it was the first time First Nations issues began to surface, it helped put the pressure on Canada" (Mitchell, personal interview, 2007). Screenings were small-scale, and stakeholder groups were invited to discuss issues raised in the film, with the Board having little overarching control. Indeed, the film's movement was powered by the politics and passion of those closest to its central issues. It had wide dissemination not because of a mass-marketing campaign but because of the dedication to connecting audiences (no matter how small) to the work in settings that were public, politicized, inclusive, and participatory. And so, the edges of early counterpublic spaces became visible in this documentary history.

VIRTUAL VS MATERIAL DEMOCRACY AND CINEMA POLITICA

The year 1969 is ancient history in terms of visual culture distribution, given the advent of video, home computing, home theatre, video cameras, and Internet distribution, among other things. Needless to say, the CFC/SN model is long gone. In an attempt to excavate inert material and reconnect with the mobility of an emergent "democratized and globalized" cinema culture, today's contemporary Film Board has announced a massive unsealing of sorts – by distributing over the next several years all 10,000+ NFB titles via the World Wide Web, *You Are on Indian Land* among them. This turn to digital distribution signals the NFB's inclusion in the techno-orgy of the post-analogue world of media dissemination and consumption. Is digital the true heir to grassroots distribution like CFC/SN?

If you follow the hype, it is a world of revolutionary technologies and experiences, combining the wildest fantasies of consumerism with the mirages of limitless democracy. A recent report on the film industry in Canada ecstatically shouts from the page: "[T]echnology is handing the scheduling keys to the consumer" (Canadian Film and Television Production Association 2007, 5). The rise of personal technologies – realized in TV, home video, VOD (video on demand), Internet programs, torrent software, and streaming content sites, etc. – permits the end users to obtain and exhibit moving images in their own home or mobile device, apparently erasing the need for community distribution like that of the NFB and its CFC/SN offspring. Problems of cinema distribution appear to reduce to those of (1) how to get people into theatres for first-run films for a big opening window, or (2) how to get consumers media they can "plug and play" at home and "on the go," mainly through DVD sales and rental and online downloading and streaming. Digital distribution is sold as the next great frontier for empowered individualization.

Indeed, we should not deny the power of digital distribution. YouTube not only enables the easy distribution of already-finished works, but creates novel cultures of production, particularly for kid-produced videos. In this "viral" culture, one exciting video – Galipoka's "Jaeger Report" video (Jaeger-Rydall 2006) for example – leads to virtually endless remakes by other kids. Producers are, by and large, also the audience. The entry cost to the amateur is small, with the (cheap) camera, (free) editing tools, and the (free) means of distribution falling into the hands of individual kids.

Nevertheless, this digital collapse is very different from CFC/SN. The atomization at the heart of the home-theatre experience carries over to the Internet, despite its culture-establishing power. As in the culture of TV-watching, kids who produce their own videos are encouraged to stay in the house, the thin channel of computerized text and video providing the only connection to this new virtual "outside" world. Counterintuitively perhaps, since hegemony tends to bring to the imagination an image of groups of people occupying shared ideological space, *isolation* is a prevailing framework within neoliberal capitalism: individual consumers, rich in rights and possessions, guard over their home-theatre system or home computer and their ability to choose what they desire. Isolation reduces not only our ability to imagine shared horizons of concern, but also our ability to imagine shared horizons of action, at a time when this kind of mobilization is sorely needed. Isolation reinforces the gaps between perceptions of threat, personal moral obligations, and our real activity. It is precisely here that *non-virtual* distribution and exhibition has a place – that is, within real spaces and among real bodies ("meatspace" in cyber-tongue) – by grounding communities of perception, feeling, and action. If, for example, the environmental threat is real – and the recent aggressive moves by Arctic powers to negotiate the melting boundary lines is an important indication that it *is* real for government policy-makers as well as for environmental whistle-blowers – then we need to bring all our powers to bear upon it, including and especially the power of cinema to real groups in material spaces.

ENTER CINEMA POLITICA

What is lost in the virtual is the face-to-face connectivity among audience members themselves and between the audience and filmmakers. The experience of elbow-to-elbow audiences and the space of shared social experience collapse in virtual distribution, replaced with isolated individuals looking at private screens. Cinema Politica (CP) takes up this aspect of distribution. CP (founded by one of the authors of this text, Ezra Winton, in 2003) is a largely campus-based grassroots distribution and exhibition non-profit network for independent political film and video, located (at the time of writing) at over forty sites across Canada, with satellite locals situated in Europe, Asia, South America, and the United States. It is run by volunteers and until recently received no state or private funding (2008 marked the first year the project received support from the Canada Council for the Arts). The project is organized around providing a central screening pool of mostly documentary works (with a significant Canadian provenance) at the beginning of each school semester. Titles are selected by one programmer, Winton, but this hierarchical structure is being addressed with plans for an online programming-choice function for audiences on the CP site. This is a compromise between recognizing the skill and experience of a programmer and adopting the more democratic process of audiences "choosing" – and therefore distributing – films. Locals then choose from the screening pool to determine their own lineup for exhibition. Locals are semi-autonomous, creating their financial structures, political mandates, and programs. However, they also agree to some guiding principles set down by the centralized CP group in Montreal, and in 2008 some began paying membership fees to maintain access and screening rights to the CP library of over three hundred films and videos.

One of the first huge CP screenings was *The Corporation* (2003), an event that resonated with co-director Mark Achbar as a positive community experience complete with audience feedback and debate around the issues of corporate power and culture. Achbar points out that regardless of how many millions of torrent downloads the Canadian documentary sensation has undergone, he will still revel in the experience and memory of his years of touring with the film and screening it in First Nations communities, at raves in the middle of British Columbia forests, and in musty basements, classrooms, churches, and other non-commercial venues (Achbar, personal interview, 2007). *The Corporation*, unlike most CFC/SN films, also enjoyed a commercial run in theatres in Canada and the United States, but this activity was measured in numbers (dollars and eyeballs), not the communal feelings that surrounded the film in hundreds of grassroots screenings. This spatial bias, this political commitment to physical place, is the focal point for the Cinema Politica project.

Another anecdote may serve to illustrate the above points of difference. At a screening in 2006, journalist and filmmaker Kevin Pina was flown out of Haiti after his life and that of his colleagues had been threatened verbally and with violence, and was brought to the Cinema Politica space at Concordia University. Pina literally came from the airport with the never-before-seen DVD of his recent hard-hitting documentary *Haiti: Harvest of Hope* (2006) tucked deep inside his luggage. The screening, like many CP events, was co-organized and co-presented by a community stakeholder group, in this case Haiti Action Montreal. The campus auditorium was filled to capacity at nearly seven hundred people, many if not most of whom were part of the Haitian diaspora located in Montreal. Pina gave a short introduction and the film played – a feature-length exposé of chaos, brutality, and human suffering. Graphic images of Haitian citizens being shot in the face by police as they crawled through streets hung on the forty-foot screen like horrific portraits of a very near and present reality. The audience responded with emotion. Crying, shouting, and wailing filled the room as the images confronted the spectators. At the end of the film, a shell-shocked Pina admitted to never having seen the film on a large screen and apologized for any trauma that he may have incited. Some audience members left in tears, obviously affected by the film in quite visceral ways.

But the discussion that ensued inside the auditorium harnessed the power and violence of the images, combined the spirit and emotion of the audience, however precarious, into a structure of feeling (Williams 1977) that can be accounted for with one word: community. The audience of individuals became rooted in the material space of debate as they stood at their seats and debated in English, French, and Creole across the aisles, sometimes engaging with Pina at the front. The space was open and participatory, an environment where one could cry, shout, scream, laugh, and sob. It was a space that was constructed by a politicized community constituted by this powerful media event, in contrast to the media-nourished mainstream configuration of both Haiti and Haitians (as victims, as lacking agency, as invisible, etc.). Here was a counterpublic enabled by Cinema Politica away from the narrative machine of Hollywood fiction, the sterile mega-plex, and the virtual media *multiverse*. And it is no small point to say that Pina's films are not commercially distributed, rather smuggled out of conflict zones and dusted off for community screenings as they are, sight unseen.

As cinema screens become more private (whether a cellphone screen on the subway or a large flat-screen "home theatre"), the residue of a democratic platitude like "scheduling keys" is transferred onto something the consumer has control of, even owns, such as cars and homes. In contradistinction to such proprietary keys is the social-material community screening practice that sustains the CP network. By emphasizing increasingly corporatized Canadian campus spaces as sites, and by consciously creating inclusive, pluralistic, and politicized spaces within the university fortress, CP dangles active and charged shared experience, not keys, in front of participants. The endpoint is not the screening itself and certainly not the number of eyeballs represented on a spreadsheet, but the process of constructing the space of a counterpublic. Western democracy has its imperial limitations as well as its violences, but the striving towards the fulfilment of democratic and political ideals (marked as it is equally by discord as by resolution), through the material realities of cultural participation among other strategies, may not only strengthen a public sphere but help to construct viable radical democracy.

CONCLUSION

Challenge for Change/Société nouvelle was a program that urged (and urges) a closer look at the spaces between commercial distribution and exhibition. The initiative highlights the importance of documentary practices beyond production, and reveals the ways media can be harnessed through citizens creating and sharing public cinema spaces and practices. The use of media as an agent for social change helps citizens to imagine and articulate community in the face of so many other forces, among them neoliberal-inspired materialism. In short, what CFC/SN produced, with its films and its distribution and exhibition practices and spaces, were counter-narratives and counterpublics to dominant systems, regimes, and ideologies. It is crucial for us to analyse those spaces where media is produced *and* disseminated with a view to building community and a democratic public sphere, and to understand past attempts to achieve social transformation. There are many examples of the use of documentary film towards such ends, but few come close to the CFC/SN experiment in terms of breadth and historical vitality or of its unique, exemplary record of collaboration among state bureaucrats, artists, community activists, grassroots media organizers, and spectators.

As media scholars concerned with progressive social change, we could not possibly re-imagine the spaces media and community can inhabit within Canada's physical and psychic borders without revisiting the spaces created by CFC/SN, and more recently, Cinema Politica. In the new techno-babble rhetoric of multi-platform delivery systems, digital downloads, and hyper-consumerism, one mustn't forget the central tenet of a program ambitiously created to bridge the gap between government and governed, between the haves and the have-nots, the dominant and the fringes. If tangible social change is still on the drawing boards for policy-makers and documentary filmmakers, then they might do well to shift some attention away from production notes and away from the commercial theatre system and set their sights on those spaces in between, the dynamic, fertile, and, dare we say, promising spaces of grassroots distribution and exhibition. Change only comes about through dissemination – like dissent itself.

Authors' Note: This chapter is taken, in part, from the larger Media Studies master's thesis "The Spaces Between: Grass Roots Documentary Distribution and Exhibition as Counterpublics," by Ezra Winton, Concordia University, 2007.

PART 5

Conclusion: Contemporary Reincarnations

■

PREFACE

In this section, two current participatory media projects are examined in relation to the ethos of Challenge for Change/Société nouvelle, with similarities and divergences highlighted in each chapter. In both cases, the participants themselves describe video (or visual media) as a tool for advocacy, as a bridge for communities and issues, and as a pathway for the articulation of social justice and human rights issues. While CFC/SN may have lived out its exciting and rocky moments some four decades prior to the publishing of this book, we offer these parting glimpses of contemporary renewals to demonstrate how this bold National Film Board project has influenced and infused media practices and theories to this day. While the first example is more directly linked to the original, the second shows that people's capacity to harness media towards goals of participation, equality, and justice is a social phenomenon not restricted to any culture or context. If anything, these two contributions remind us that CFC/SN was a project that tapped the perennial human desire for mutual understanding and community – a cultural impulse that may be teetering but has never yielded to the steady forces of turbo-capitalism and neoliberalism.

In chapter 37, "Filmmaker-in-Residence: The Digital Grandchild of Challenge for Change," documentarist, professor, and activist Liz Miller interviews her fellow activist media-maker Katerina Cizek, their conversation linking current praxis with the distant past. In their discussion of Cizek's recent NFB project, Filmmaker-in-Residence (FIR), the two filmmakers interrogate the difficult spaces of video advocacy – from representation, identity, audience, and collaborative methodologies to the big question, "What is storytelling?" This conversation sees FIR – a joint project between a Toronto hospital and the NFB to address health, poverty, gender, and enfranchisement within an interventionist action research framework – as a modern offspring of the CFC/SN project.

In chapter 38, "Thirty Years and Twelve Thousand Miles Away ... ," activist, teacher, and filmmaker Vijaya Mulay compares CFC/SN to the ongoing participatory community project Community Media Trust (CMT) in the southern Indian state of Andhra Pradesh. Mulay describes how the two projects share common ground despite their obvious separation in time and geography. She finds that goals of empowering citizens around political issues like gender, poverty, and social justice are present in both articulations. However, Mulay also examines the differences between CFC/SN and CMT, raising the key variable of literacy, for example, and pointing to possible reasons for the NFB project's demise and, in contrast, for the ongoing success of the women farmers, organizers, educators, and media-makers of CMT. This last chapter of the book is an appropriate and fascinating look towards the future of media democracy, with at least one eye kept on past endeavours.

37 Filmmaker-in-Residence: The Digital Grandchild of Challenge for Change

■

INTERVIEW WITH KATERINA CIZEK BY LIZ MILLER,
11 MAY 2008

INTERVIEWER'S PREFACE

Katerina Cizek is the National Film Board of Canada's Filmmaker-in-Residence (FIR), based in an inner-city hospital where she is passionately re-envisioning Challenge for Change in the age of the digital revolution. Under the auspices of this experimental initiative, conceived of as "an alternative model of media-making" (http://filmmakerinresidence.nfb.ca/) and fully funded by the NFB, Katerina has been collaborating with doctors, nurses, researchers, and patients at St Michael's Hospital, a teaching university affiliated with the University of Toronto's Faculty of Medicine, one of the largest medical schools in North America. With a background in anthropology and an established practice of making engaged documentaries, she makes media to educate, investigate, and change policies. The film she directed with Peter Wintonick, *Seeing Is Believing: Handicams, Human Rights and the News* (2002), has won numerous awards and is now a staple in college classrooms around the world.

Katerina and I first met at a collective session in New York to work on *Video for Change*, a book she co-wrote and edited for the non-profit organization Witness, whose mandate is to train human rights activists in video advocacy. As a filmmaker invested in advocacy filmmaking and collaborative work, I have been in conversation with Katerina since she began working for FIR four years ago. Katerina has initiated an impressive array of projects and exploded the boundaries of documentary by engaging with so many different media forms. To date, the projects include *The Bicycle*, a short documentary about an inspiring public AIDS worker in Africa whose innovative approach to fighting AIDS is a model for future programs; *I Was Here*, a sixteen-month photo blog and installation project that has powerfully brought the experiences and needs of young mothers who have lived in the streets into the public sphere; *Unexpected*, a video-bridge film that creates a candid filmic dialogue between young mothers with experience living in the streets and the medical staff who help deliver their babies; *The Interventionists*, a half-hour vérité film that profiles a desperately needed mobile mental-health crisis-intervention team as they respond to 911 calls in inner-city Toronto; and finally, *Drawing from Life* (2008), a half-hour documentary-animation hybrid film following a twenty-week group-therapy program for people who have attempted suicide more than once.

Each of the projects is featured on the interactive web documentary site at http://www3.nfb.ca/filmmakerinresidence/, which has won numerous awards, including a Webby Award, known as the "Oscars of the Internet," for the best online documentary series. And while the Filmmaker-in-Residence program continues to gather international acclaim for its combination of stunning aesthetics and political relevance, what is especially important for this collection of essays are the collaborative frameworks and the powerful advocacy components of the FIR projects. Each one has involved a participatory approach to involving collaborating partners in a transformative process. And while the partners are not included in this interview, Katerina was careful to acknowledge the shared authorship and invaluable contributions of all of her collaborators.

To conduct this interview, I met with Katerina in the midst of Hot Docs, the Canadian International Documentary Festival in Toronto, where Katerina had been chosen as a mentor for makers of upcoming non-linear digital documentaries. Katerina is a mentor for many of us, and in her four years as FIR she has challenged and informed many of my ideas about participation and advocacy. The digital revolution has provided new opportunities to grapple with ethics, collaboration, and agency – some of the same issues that informed the earlier National Film Board (NFB) experiment, Challenge for Change (CFC). The Filmmaker-in-Residence program has pushed the boundaries of collaborative practice, community advocacy, and documentary in the digital age, and a close look at it is an ideal way to end this unique reflection on the impact of the landmark Challenge for Change project.

LIZ MILLER: I filmed an interview with you and George Stoney a year ago (for another project) in which you asked him for a definition of Challenge for Change and how it is different from other social documentaries made by the NFB. I'm wondering if you have your own definition of the Challenge for Change method?

KATERINA CIZEK: Well, to give the fifteen-second version to people in terms of what's unique about the work that we do, I actually use his definition because it's just so succinct and really gets at the heart of what Challenge for Change means, which is that we don't make documentaries about people, we make media projects with people.

LM: Has your concept of CFC changed since you started this project four years ago?

KC: There are three rivers that influence Filmmaker-in-Residence, and one is definitively Challenge for Change. It's what the National Film Board came to me with when they were considering bringing it back as a stream of methodology in the time of the digital revolution. The second river is video advocacy and the work that I've done with Witness. Peter Wintonick and I co-directed a film called *Seeing Is Believing: Human Rights, Handicams, and the News*. And after that, I ended up, along with you, working on a book with Witness called *Video for Change*. Throughout that process, I learned even more than while making a film. I had an incredible opportunity to interview human rights activists, journalists, filmmakers, and community members from around the world talking about the ethics of editing and how things change when it's specifically for advocacy – that is, what storytelling is when the focus is moving to action. And then I did a chapter on safety and security, working in difficult, high-risk situations. So those three chapters really help me to redefine and rethink what's at stake when the work is about human rights and actually changing the conditions in the lives of people rather than making a nice story. And then the third river came from the partners that I have been working with at St Michael's Hospital. I started meeting people who had a very similar approach in medicine and in health care to what we do over on the media side, which they call intervention research and others call participatory action research.

The idea behind that kind of research is to challenge some of the conventional notions of academic research within medicine – for example, where people can try a drug or a form of intervention and spend ten years studying it and then another five before they publish it without giving back to the very communities that they work in. The distance between the laboratory and the bedside is very long for numerous reasons. Intervention researchers thought, "This is too long and we need to give back and work much more closely with the communities that we're involved in." And to me that was really inspiring. I drew parallels with the work that we're trying to do with Challenge for Change within the digital revolution, keeping our work close to the community and responsible to the community. It doesn't mean that the community becomes the filmmaker, there's all sorts of different nuances and sophistications in terms of understanding what participatory media is. Everybody brings to the table a certain kind of expertise. For example, in Filmmaker-in-Residence, we retain 100 per cent editorial control over the work, and that's a really strong element for me. We're not making corporate or public relations videos, whether it's for the hospital or for the front-line workers, but we're collaborating and respecting each other's expertise.

LM: Tell me more about retaining the editorial control. When you begin a project, how do you explain the degree of collaboration to the participants?

KC: I would say that, for the most part, I think people want it. The partners that we develop projects with at the hospital, they are not media savvy. They understand the role that media can play but they don't necessarily know how to do it. I do not have the background in health care to tell somebody how to deliver a baby. For example, with the project *I Was Here,* there is a real respect on all sides: between the young women and the expertise that they bring in terms of their own lives, the health care professionals that we had in the room, and the media. It was a three-prong triangle and I think that's what made the project really egalitarian and interesting for all of us.

LM: Were there ever any tensions in that collaborative process or times when you had a difference of opinion between one of the participants and yourself?

KC: Yes, absolutely. We had differences of opinion all the time. Sometimes people think collaborative work is supposed to be consensus but it's actually much more about respecting differences and respecting diversity of opinion. We've been running for nineteen months now and the dynamics have really changed from the beginning to now. At first, the biggest issue was privacy and confidentiality. When we developed *I Was Here,* we decided to develop it as an academic project and go through the research and ethics board at the hospital as any social science or medical research would do at a hospital. As documentary filmmakers, we like to think that we do ethics so well. I really learned that we don't. The process and the dialogue that we were able to have and the capacity to actually change the terms of the project based on the hypothetical situations that we walked through in the process of writing up that ethics document was huge. I had never gone through that kind of rigorous process.

Traditionally as filmmakers or as the National Film Board, if we're going to be investing money into a project, we would assume that we need media, something at the end of the day to show Canadian taxpayers what we've done with their money. So there's a tension between a film agency of the Canadian government mandated to make media to Canadians about Canadians and an institution that's dealing with life and death situations and the

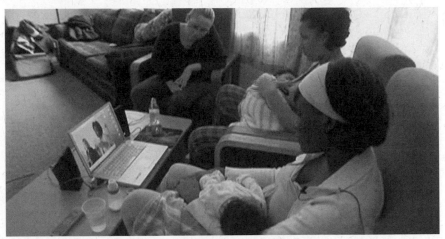

Frame from Filmmaker-in-Residence video *Unexpected* (2008): a dialogue between health care workers and young mothers who have experienced homelessness. Frame enlargement.

confidentiality and the privacy of the patients. When you do a research project in an academic setting, participants have the right to anonymity and the right to withdraw at any time. So how do you reconcile that with a media project that essentially puts somebody's identity out into the public realm? Once you've published something, whether it is on the Internet or a film or in the newspaper, you can't take it back. It's out there. And the participants in our group were in such a vulnerable position. Any kind of information that goes public could potentially be used against a woman to take her child away from her. That's a lot at stake there.

So what we decided to do after lots of discussion and consultation with other people was create a group where people could enter and provide informed consent at many different levels. The first level was to use a pseudonym, learn how to use a still camera, and have your own photo blog online that's accessible by username and password. You remain completely anonymous to the rest of the world. Most of the women, in the beginning, that's the term they chose. A lot of the women were very reticent about the project, about having their images shown, about even identifying as homeless. We spent hours just thinking about what does homelessness mean, the stigma and the taboos attached to that word, the dangers associated with it for women, pregnant or parenting. We added this extra level of technology with the computers, and it was a little bit fussy at the beginning for everything that we were dealing with in terms of all the privacy and life issues, and that made us question, have we gone too far with the technology? But in the end it worked out. When you look at the women now, their confidence with the technology has radically shifted. We learned a lot from them and the downsides of this kind of technology. What is the digital divide in our own city here of Toronto? I've spent many years thinking about the digital divide across the oceans, north and south, but it's right here in our own city.

Once the women started feeling comfortable and seeing not only their own work but each other's work, they started sharing their photographs and their stories. At one point, one of the women said, "Well are we ever going to show this to the public?" It's the whole point of communications, to develop your voice but then hopefully somebody will listen as well. And that's when we started talking about a public exhibit and we moved to the next stage of consent. At that point, we started developing the idea of a public photo exhibit of the photo blogs. The process by which we chose the photographs was in consultation with the women, but we curated the show and to this day the women talk about how they wished that this photo had entered or that photo had gone in. We did play a curatorial role and I don't regret that at all. I think it's what helped make the exhibit strong. We wanted to have an individual story within each woman's set of photos but then also a group story, a group narrative that worked. It wasn't 100 per cent participatory. I defend that position because I think that the exhibit spoke very loudly and really moved people in a way that I'm not sure it would have if we had just let each woman choose her photos – it would not have been as strong.

LM: You might have had a different concept of audience in mind while you curated.

KC: That's a really good point because I think when everybody started, their first audience was a woman and herself. It was like a private journal and at first it was frustrating because we wanted the women to relate to one another more. We had been warned by a woman from a fantastic youth health centre in town that does health care work and support work for youth on the streets who said, "In a lot of the workshops that we run with young women, the women don't really relate to each other much in the group, so be ready for that." It's going to take a while to build that trust and that totally happened in our group. I think all of us have agreed that this program is pretty unique in terms of the philosophy, the methodology, the kind of space that we created and the relationships. I was really astounded at how little opportunity they had in their lives to just reflect on their own situation, on their own identity. People need to be given certain things to be able to develop and reflect on their situation. When you have food, when you have a shelter, when you have a roof over your head, when you have the support of people in your life that can take care of certain things ... making art is a real privilege and it should be a right.

LM: Tell me more about how you have thought about audiences for this project?

KC: One of the initial motivators for the project was to actually use photo voice as a way to teach health care professionals about how to do their work better in terms of providing health care for young parents with no fixed address. So the hospital was a natural audience for that. We thought an art gallery would be great to situate it in an art context, and we wanted to do the National Film Board because of the relationship with Filmmakers-in-Residence. Then we asked, "Where's the most political place we could use this?" and we thought City Hall. And why not invite the mayor to host the reception? We started thinking, "I don't think it's a good idea to just invite the mayor to say a few words, having never met the women." So we asked the mayor's office for an hour of his time in the week prior to the opening of the exhibit and he consented and it's one of the most interesting political meetings I've ever witnessed. It was transformative for everyone in that room, including the mayor, the women, including us as media-makers and the health care professionals. Each of the women had rehearsed and thought through what they wanted to tell him about their lives and the realities that they face living in this city and he was blown away. It's one thing to hear it or read about it in a report or in the newspaper but to actually sit down and meet Adrienne, Jess, Meghan, and Keneisha and meet their babies and see their artwork is another thing altogether. There is a relationship between media and its context that creates room for political dialogue. The mayor says it has informed some of his policy decisions. Homelessness and housing is such a critical issue in this city but the idea of talking about young women who are either pregnant or parenting has not really been high on the agenda.

At the speak-out that we did at the end of the exhibit, we invited over sixty young parents from across the city to the NFB. The young women from *I Was Here* hosted a three-hour speak-out on eight issues. We asked the women and the parents in the audience to give solutions, and we recorded the session and spent ten months with the women transcribing and putting together a fifteen-page key-recommendations document that identifies some of the key issues and then presented it to the mayor. And it's full of great ideas from people with first-lived experience. So that's still circulating and I think it's the art that helped it get there.

The emergence of the digital revolution and the huge tradition with community-based media has been around for a long time. The good part of it is that everybody gets a chance to use this technology and tell their story. The bad part about it is that there is a cacophony of voices that are screaming, and there's just so much noise that nobody is really heard or listened to. The work that we have ahead of us is not just about putting the technology in the hands of the people who don't get a chance to touch it. The second part of it is really getting it to the eyeballs of the people that can do something about it. That's the creative part of what we do, thinking, "What is the story and also who do we want to get the story to?" That's really the basics of video advocacy. The higher up you're going in power to try and tell a story, probably the shorter your piece has to be. In the documentary world there's so much focus on the feature-length documentaries. In fact, as the digital revolution matures, it's clearer and clearer that short is probably the political reality.

LM: Could you talk about other projects and forms of collaboration you have developed?

KC: For *The Interventionist* (2006), I spent eighty hours in the back of a police squad car of a specially trained team. It's a psychiatric nurse and a specially trained police officer that respond to 911 calls dealing with emotionally distressed people. And this is a unit that was developed specifically at St Michael's in reaction to the death of Edmond Hugh, a man diagnosed with schizophrenia, who was homeless at the time of his death. He had an incident occur in a streetcar, the police responded and the situation escalated. He had a plastic hammer in his hand and they shot him to death. These kinds of incidents have been happening across North America in tandem with the de-institutionalization of psychiatric institutes across the continent. One of the answers that has come out of inter-city hospitals is to take the psychiatric nurse out into the community and have a response immediately on-site. So how does making a film with people rather than just a film about them, how does that work in that context? We certainly can't put a camera into the hands of a mental health nurse who is de-escalating a critical situation in the field. So we worked out a great relationship. I was always ready in the back of the squad car, and if they ever needed to use the squad car to bring someone to a hospital or to the police station, I would actually just remove myself on-site and take a cab.

We also worked out some important ethical issues. If somebody's having that kind of crisis, can they really make an informed decision about being seen in public? Number two, should we even be asking them that? Is it appropriate? We decided no, and my producer Gerry Flahive had the brilliant idea to try a specific shooting style that leaves the participant somewhat out of frame or to use obstacles as a tool to keep identities hidden. And that was a nice idea because with the digitization of faces there's a trope of criminal-ization. It was on Helen, the nurse, to ask whether the person would agree to have the nurse and the police officer filmed. The film is about how they do their work. So in that sense it's a conventional, *vérité* film, but if you understand the way in which we came to making that film and the way the film has been used, it's very much Filmmaker-in-Residence.

LM: Can you tell me about how the film's been used and who's seen it?

KC: Sure. For one thing it's been used as a teaching tool for academics. Dr Ian Dawe, who's the head of psychiatric emergency at St Michael's Hospital, he's travelled extensively with the film. He was at the World Congress of Psychiatrists in Australia and showed the film to hundreds of psychiatrists from around the world, and it was real hit because it tells the story in a way that numbers and reports and statistics don't. The power of documentary, it hits you on a different level. And we also presented it to the Police Services Board in Toronto with Dr Ian Dawe, who made three recommendations – all of which have been adopted. The first one is that the service should become available across the city. Number two is to extend the hours, as it only runs from 2 PM to 11 PM when the most EDP (emotionally disturbed persons) calls come in. But regardless, there are a lot of calls they miss earlier and later in the day. And then thirdly, to use the film as an awareness tool within the Police Services Board because a lot of the police don't even know about the existence of the mobile crisis intervention team. You know police aren't trained to deal with mental illness and it's not why they enter the force. And so it is important for them to understand that there are resources that they can draw on, that make their lives safer and also the lives of the people in the community safer in an immediate way.

LM: One thing that comes up a lot in a project like this or alternative media projects is how to evaluate the success of a project aimed at social change. Is evaluation something that you were thinking about?

KC: Yes, absolutely. That's been really important to me and really important to the academic partners. Most of the projects have an academic research framework, and long before we started we were identifying our barometers of success or evaluation. So each project has its own protocol for methodology, for parameters of privacy and confidentiality and also evaluation.

LM: A lot of times, personal transformation is not taken into account or the project is evaluated once it's out in the world but not throughout the process. Is that important for your evaluation?

KC: It's number one and we had many goals. We had almost a page of things that we'd hoped to accomplish with the project *I Was Here*. Part one was with the photo voice and part two was the video bridge. For the video bridge, the idea was to train the young women in the group on video technology and then have them interview each other and other young parents about their experiences within the health care system with regards to natal care. Concurrently what we did – the filmmaker team and the health care team, but not the young parents – was to go to the hospital and interview health care professionals about their challenges and attitudes – their own reflections. It's not just young parents that don't get to reflect on their lives and their role in society, it's a lot of us. And especially in the health care system. We have a huge nursing shortage in this country. So the pressure on health care professionals is huge. So what we did was go to the health care professionals and interview them about what it's like to try to deliver the baby of a woman that they have no relationship with. Someone who comes in with no history, no background, and who potentially has nowhere to live, nowhere to take the baby. It's considered one of the most beautiful moments of a woman's life, at least that's how it's stereotyped, and yet it can turn into the most traumatic experience. So we filmed both sides and then we showed the footage back to each other to see how people would respond. I was inspired by the Fogo Island process and I think it actually turned into something else all together.

LM: What elements of the Fogo Island experiment were you inspired by?

KC: The idea of people speaking to a camera, getting a chance to see themselves speak and then giving people the chance to respond to each other through the technology rather than face to face, that this will produce different results. In the Fogo Island case, it did. I thought this might be a really interesting context for that. Health care professionals are required by law to report any high-risk individuals, just that very fact makes the relationship very tense. The trust is difficult to establish on both sides. As an anthropologist, I'm interested in how a clinical setting, a cultural setting, will define a relationship and the way two individuals interact. What happens when you actually take people out of that clinical setting and give them a chance to listen and speak and understand each other in different ways? And really quickly what I saw emerge was a dialogue between two sets of people who have very little control of what's happening in their work situation or their lives or in the clinical setting of the interaction. There was a lot to learn from each other but then the bigger political picture was, who else needs to be part of this dialogue? It's clearly not going be resolved by young parents and health care professionals. This is something that we all as a society need to think about and address. And so that's how the idea for the "Hand-Held

Un-conference" [a FIR-organized event combining video and digital story-telling with conventional conversation, involving young mothers who have experienced homelessness engaging with the health care system] came to be. Who else needs to be part of this dialogue and what kind of setting and what kind of context can we create to have that dialogue? In the Fogo Island context, it was provincial decision-makers that were able to actually make changes, whereas health care professionals don't have that much power. Very quickly it became evident to us that these are not the only players and I think in the Fogo Island case, the players were right there, at the camera.

LM: In the video bridge *Unexpected*, I was very struck by Eva, one of the nurses you interview. She is so honest on camera and she makes it evident that we all carry around a set of prejudices and stereotypes. How did other health care representatives respond?

KC: I think there's a resistance to being open and honest for fear of public scrutiny, for fear of looking like the bad guy. One health care professional, high up in the federal agency, told me, "I'm really concerned about how the public will perceive us doctors after watching this film." I said, "That's really interesting because I've actually spoken to a lot of people and they admire Eva for being honest and for being open and for actually listening and feeling moved by what she herself acknowledges are the limitations of a clinical setting, how little time she's given to interact with people as human beings. She learnt from that experience and that humility turns her into a hero." And then the doctor said, "I'm glad to hear that." I find that's very central to the work that I've done with many communities. I think there's often people, especially people in power who are concerned about a certain level of honesty within documentary. It is uncomfortable and challenging, and they don't know how to read it themselves because it's too close. It's only after they hear other people's reactions that they get it. And that's happened to me over and over again in this work. There's been a lot of teaching that we had to do. Not just myself as a media-maker, but also patients and people that are closer to the grassroots that understand the sophistication of a medium that actually doesn't have all the answers and has a lot of questions and gives people a space to talk. There's no right answer. It's in the dialogue, the process that we're going to come up with new ways of thinking. If we always think we have the answers, that's not really documentary. That's not the power of a medium that's transformative.

And I really wish the camera had been on for one of the young women's reactions to Eva, because this had been a woman very critical of health care professionals from her own personal experience. After watching Eva's reaction, she said, "I guess it really is so hard for health care professionals. They only have so much time. What if the woman that has come in before me really is a drug addict?" I'd never heard her step outside of her own experience and be able to understand what the situation must be like on the other side of the table. This piece really is meant to be the start of a dialogue. And we were creating it, in the end, for the Hand-Held Un-conference where we brought together people from all walks of life, people with first-lived experience of living in the streets, the women in our group, and other people we thought might be able to contribute to the dialogue: policy-makers, health care professionals, heads of hospitals, bureaucrats, decision-makers at the city level, at the Ontario level, federal level, academics, other media-makers, and journalists. We spent the day in four breakout sessions, with eight to ten parallel sessions. We organized Hand-Held in the un-conference model, out of the open-source technology movement. Everybody said the most important part of conferences was the coffee break. Somebody came up with the great idea of making the whole thing a coffee break and of allowing participants to devise ideas for breakout sessions as we go along. Everybody has the responsibility of being an expert and contributing, and if you're not contributing to a session, if you're bored, then you just go to another group. So, we brought in an expert in this facilitation process. We spent a lot of time just figuring out how the day would best work. We also hired a policy analyst to spend the day with us and then go through all the transcripts for the day. There were note-takers, and then we followed up with key participants on their ideas for policy recommendations and ideas that would come out of the day. And then we invited people from the un-conference to go back into their respective communities to distribute and disseminate some of the ideas that came out of it.

LM: People might make the assumption that un-conferences aren't planned out. What are some of the specific things you thought through to make that day as successful as possible?

KC: The biggest part of it is managing the guest list and inviting people. We spent hours and hours making lists of different silos and categories of people and trying to get the right balance, making sure there weren't too many of one or another group in the room. Also tailoring the way that the day would flow, and because it was about participatory media, we thought about how to include the media within the day. We showed *Unexpected* in the beginning as a way to get as many people to meet at the start of the day with real conversations. Right away, you're discussing with strangers your reactions to this very intimate and powerful film. That's a great conversation. The way our facilitator has worked before is he poses three key questions that are central to the day. So, that was the first question. For the second, we showed another clip about participatory media – [from] *I Was Here* – and the question was, "How can this be used in other settings?" The idea was to pose a question that would stimulate a provocative dialogue. That's really what the conference was about: eliminating titles and silos and hierarchies and making people come together in a non-structured way, where everyone has something valuable to say. Some people found it uncomfortable.

LM: Tell me more about who was uncomfortable.

KC: We had so many reactions, but the very interesting one I had was from a fairly authoritative health care professional who felt that it was biased in favour of young parents. She felt that there wasn't enough dialogue about the reality of having to take children away. There is a reason Children's Aid exists. My reaction to that is that we're not questioning Children's Aid. We're not questioning whether there should be a police force in *The Interventionist*. It's just about addressing and understanding the nuances from all sides, thinking about it in new ways. What happens when you make an equal space is the powerful lose some of their power in order for the less-advantaged to actually have space to talk. That makes some people feel uncomfortable. Dialogue isn't always comfortable and you have to work hard for it. You can't assume and take the status and the place you're used to assuming, whether that is being quiet or being really loud. As the facilitator explains, when you're in a group and there are eight people, then, seven-eighths of the time you should be listening.

LM: I would like to talk about how the Internet and online dialoguing are new to the Challenge for Change model. How have you been using the Internet as a means of facilitating dialogue/conversation? Has this online potential opened up avenues for new kinds of conversations?

KC: From the beginning, the Film Board was really interested in seeing a feature film come out of Filmmaker-in-Residence that would tell the bigger story, the bigger narrative about what it is that we're doing. We started talking very quickly about instead of doing a feature film, why don't we put that responsibility into another medium, the Internet? Why not tell a feature documentary through the World Wide Web? It is not a companion site, or a place to dump stuff that you couldn't put in the film, but it actually is the documentary. It tells the philosophy and drive behind all the different projects and the spirit in a way that individual projects can't or shouldn't. It's a free, easy, accessible way to learn that story. It's a fairly linear narrative, but it's immersive. It takes full advantage of full-frame photography, audio, text, and some video, delivered in a very simple flash structure. There's interactivity in the sense that you can choose which stream you want to follow. I don't think it is as interactive as a game, or those very trendy interpretations of interactivity, but I had a very specific purpose for the website and for the flash-based narrative structure: to tell a story that no other media could tell. I didn't want to do it as a feature film, because I don't think we could have filmed a lot of it. There's no way we could have ever brought a video camera into *I Was Here*. To put that kind of pressure onto the group, it would have fallen apart. I'm convinced of it. Documentary doesn't have to be on a camera. There's so many other ways of telling documentary stories, and that's what I wanted to do with the website. I think we did it.

LM: Another difference between the past and the present is this idea of using so many media at the same time, your many media approach. How do you come to the decision of which media to use for each project?

KC: It's huge because the documentary world tends to focus on video and linear storytelling as being the epitome and the highest epitome is the feature-length film. When I think of the pattern that my life has taken, I've actually not been committed to any media, I'm pretty agnostic and I always have been. I came out of photography, I was behind the barricades at Oka, I ended up writing a book. Then I really got into newspapers and helped start a newspaper in northern Quebec. It's almost like many or any media, and it's what best reaches and challenges the audience. And every medium has its advantages and its limitations. Still photography as opposed to video was a choice in *I Was Here*. It's a decision about not letting the technology get in the way of the story, and video technology often does in participatory media because you just end up worrying so much about the camera, and editing is not as glamorous as it's made out to be. We used audio for the *Street Health Stories* – which we haven't talked about. The idea was to create these large self-standing light boxes, 36 by 36, lit from behind, gorgeous portraits with headphones and you put the headphones on and you listen to somebody's story for three to five minutes – and their experiences, their health, and their access to health care. There's something so permanent about it in a way that a movie isn't. We have a lot of clichés that we use in the documentary form, and a lot of it, in the Canadian context, has been driven by the power that television has had in terms of funding documentary for close to twenty years. It's a challenge but it's also an opportunity right now with so many forms of media at our fingertips – why wouldn't we explore the boundaries? I'd say take the handcuffs off the documentary linear form and just blow that out of the water and have fun, experiment.

LM: What is next for you and the Filmmaker-in-Residence program?

KC.: What we're hoping to do now is create a long piece in filmic form that tells the story of Filmmaker-in-Residence and the films we've made. We've had a lot of requests from universities and high schools, so I've done a lot of outreach to journalists, documentary-makers, communications students. The biggest message that I am trying to communicate from both Challenge for Change and the Filmmaker-in-Residence program is [that] there has [developed] a formulaic approach to teaching documentary and passing on the documentary tradition which is troublesome for me. So what I'm really interested in doing is challenging the documentary world and our relationship with subjects. I think that's what we really need to work hard on because I think it's been very colonialist and I think the technology can really decolonize the relationship.

LM: Is there anything that I haven't touched on or something that you want to add in terms of framing this incredible project?

KC: The manifesto would be really important for me to talk about. Until the website came up, there was a lot of misunderstanding about the work. One morning I got up and I thought, well, I'm just going to write out the ten guiding principles of Filmmaker-in-Residence. So number one really challenges that notion of auteur filmmaking. The ideas for projects come from the community partners. And then number two: it's the filmmakers and the documentary-makers, it's their responsibility to create an appropriate documentary response to that idea. It's not about a public relations arm or an audio-visual arm, but how does the principle of documentary-making become part of the process of approaching and challenging ourselves to tackle the social issue at hand. I think the manifesto's helped a lot in terms of helping people delineate and understand the process by which we go through.

LM: Well, it's also your legacy. In your interview with George Stoney you asked him about his thoughts on replicating Challenge for Change.

KC: He said it didn't work in the States and that really stuck with me. That really helped me understand what's Canadian about this project. Specifically, the *I Was Here* project. He said that, time and time again, after leaving Canada and returning to the States, his homeland, he tried replicating the model, developing a dialogue between civil servants and the people they serve, and he said it failed every time. The notion of civil servants in the States is not the same as in Canada, and when he told me that, I kept an eye out for it. It's something that we can really be proud of – that we have a civil service that is open to criticism, open to hearing from the people that we're serving about how we can work better, and that's expected of the system in Canada.

Whenever we present this project in the States, there are two things that come out very quickly. One is they can't believe a National Film Board exists, and [that] a cultural institution with a historical legacy exists to fund a project like this. Number two, because of our context, the inter-city hospital, a lot of Americans tend to talk about our medical system. "Oh my God, you have universal health care!" Americans are really blown away by the project and one of my favourite reviews of the website is by a U.S.-based blog that said, "This website almost made us want to move to Canada." There's something about Filmmaker-in-Residence that is uniquely Canadian in so many ways – both the NFB and the health care system and then also this very deep notion of what it means to have a public system, to have a civil service that engages and has a responsibility to the public.

38 Thirty Years and Twelve Thousand Miles Away ...

■

VIJAYA MULAY

INTRODUCTION

"Let good thoughts and ideas come to us from all over the world," says the *Rigveda*,[1] the most ancient text of India. The Challenge for Change/Société nouvelle (CFC/SN) program undertaken by the National Film Board of Canada from 1967 to 1980 was one such good idea, one that has reappeared in many avatars in other parts of the world. Though different in many ways and influenced only indirectly by CFC/SN,[2] the Community Media Trust (CMT) program of the Deccan Development Society (DDS) of Hyderabad in India, started in 1996, is, in my opinion, much closer to the ideology, passion, and processes of the original CFC/SN than many others.

What I propose to do in this chapter is to provide a very brief profile of the DDS, explain its participatory media program, and highlight how it continues the pioneering work of CFC/SN in a different context in a world now much changed by communications technologies and predatory corporate globalization. The features of CFC/SN that are maintained are autonomy over media by people who are closely concerned with the issues in a film (or a radio/audio program), complete commitment to democratization, and two-way or even multiple communications. I will also point out how DDS differs from CFC/SN and why in the twelve years of its existence it has become sturdier than CFC/SN, which ceased to exist after doing some very good work in the same span of time.

A BRIEF HISTORY OF THE DECCAN DEVELOPMENT SOCIETY

In 1983, some committed professionals got together in Hyderabad, the capital of the southern Indian state of Andhra Pradesh (AP) and founded the DDS as a non-governmental organization (NGO). They were particularly concerned

---

1 First Mandala, hymn 89. The Sanskrit text says, "Aa no kratavaah yaantu vishvataah."
2 P.V. Satheesh, founder member of DDS and its director since 1988, refers to this indirect influence of CFC and direct cinema of Canada and the United States (e-mail communication, 3 August 2008).

with the plight of people living in the remote semi-arid area of Telengana, frequently visited by famine, because over several decades, its fragile ecosystem had been devastated by the destruction of forests, neglect of topsoil, and so on. The result was reduced productivity not only of small peasants (with holdings averaging about two acres) but also of big farmers (with thirty to forty acres). As productivity declined, the big farm owners preferred to let their lands lie fallow, as the return from land would be far less than what they could get from other activities. The early strategies of DDS were to combine ecological and employment parameters to regenerate the livelihood of people through a number of activities, such as trenching, adding topsoil, water conservation, and greening the area through planting on the village commons. Another objective was to apply people-oriented technologies to housing, such as adopting a permaculture way of organic farming and using solar energy. DDS activists soon discovered that although non-literate people had deep reserves of knowledge about farming, forestry, ecology, biodiversity, and the sustainable management of natural resources, the process meant a two-way transfer of knowledge.

Gender and social justice being its creed, DDS decided to work with the most marginalized people, namely Dalit (low caste) peasant women, mostly non-literate and often the main breadwinner of their family. They were hard working and willing to try anything. Initially, DDS assured these women wages for a hundred days in the year, and the women spent these days improving their lands. DDS also negotiated with the owners of fallow lands to let the women work collectively on their farms in return for some agreed-upon return to the landowners. It encouraged women to set up cooperatives (*sanghams*). These sanghams continue to be the basic work structure of DDS in this area. About five thousand women in seventy-five villages work in them.

Education being a high priority, DDS ran intensive workshops for adult women as and when they were needed; it also ran village night schools for out-of-school children. Over the course of years, it has set up *balwadis* (preschool institutions for village children, now forty in number) and a green school (*pachasaale*) for working children. The latter combines formal learning with life skills in its curriculum and redefines education for its relevance to rural children. It also prepares children who have dropped out of school to qualify for the state secondary school examination, an important service since passing that exam is the gateway to higher education or to jobs in the public sector.

What the sangham members have achieved is equally impressive. From 1985 onwards, their grain production has gone up from half a million to three million kilos every year. The alternative public distribution system, started a little later, takes care of those families that need the grain most. Right from the beginning, the sangham members preserved their seeds, and later they set up community seed banks. Their farming practices enshrine indigenous knowledge about preserving biodiversity and the sustainable cultivation of food crops. They have improved their natural resources in many ways, for example by designating small areas of land as watersheds and by regenerating over a thousand acres of common land in and around their villages by planting neighbourhood forests. In thirty village commons, they are growing over sixty species of medicinal plants. One of the sanghams has won a prestigious national award (Friends of Trees) for its work.

At the heart of all their activities is the issue of the autonomy of local communities in every sector vital to their survival – be it food production, marketing, seed conservation, or management of natural resources. Management of natural resource includes the reclamation of species of crops suitable for the area's rocky soil and dry climate; these are species that had almost disappeared from the area because of anti-people market forces. The sangham members understand that in order not to be crushed by unseen but powerful global forces, local communities must become autonomous. They are clear about the role that corporate globalization plays in the lives of citizens, though they may express it in their own way. Following a screening of their films at the Mumbai International Film Festival for Documentaries (MIFF) in 2004, for example, the women met the press at a special press conference. On learning that some of them had visited farms in the West, journalists asked in the state language, Telugu, whether they would not prefer to have big farms that produced bigger produce per acre. The women smiled and one of them answered:

> Yes, the farms are very big and produce much more per acre. In Canada, I visited a three hundred–acre farm. Since machines did most of the work, there were only three people working on the farm, which had no relationship with the nearby village. The farmer owned no animals, and the biggest surprise was that he did not even eat his own produce. It was all sold to a faraway firm that told him what crop he should produce and bought it. After spending a lot of money on fertilizers, seeds, machines, repairs, etc. to produce a big crop for some firm, he was still in debt. I have only a two-acre farm; I produce all that my family needs and have some left over for sale and I have no debts. I am my own master and prefer it that way.

MEDIA AUTONOMY

Autonomy in media came later than autonomy in other sectors, more as a solution to the women's need to communicate with other women like themselves and with the outside world. They were also dissatisfied with the way outsiders looked at their problems and made films about them. So, when in 1995 UNESCO approached DDS to see if it wished to participate in its program entitled Learning without Frontiers (LWF), DDS suggested that the program be done somewhat differently. To discuss and design the nature of this program, a three-day meeting was organized in which, in addition to DDS activists, UNESCO representatives, some state officials, and seventy-five sangham women members participated. The women strongly asserted that the LWF program should be designed in such a manner that they could overcome the barrier created by literacy to communicate with the outside world, as learning to read and write was a slow option.

P.V. Satheesh had considerable experience in making documentaries. In fact, he gave up his job in public television to join DDS and became totally committed to the philosophy and work of DDS. He firmly believed that with the user-friendly video technology these women could communicate the concerns of their communities to a much wider audience. The training began in 1996 with a series of four-day workshops, spread over eight months. The first batch had ten women. Of these, two were students, six were non-literate farm workers, and two were DDS workers. In addition to Satheesh, the training team included one cameraman-producer and a local Dalit youth who had, as an apprentice in a video production house, learnt video production and editing. For equipment, the team had one digital video camera, two VHS cameras, and a makeshift editing set-up. Games like hopscotch were used to bring home the concepts involved in taking a shot – image size, camera distance, heights, and angles. Participants also did group analysis of everybody's work. In the course of training, the women coined their own glossary in Telugu for technical terms like "low-angle shot" or "overhead shot," all based on their experiences. The terms "landlord shot," "slave shot," "sangham shot," and so on describe how a landlord sees a serf, how a serf sees a landlord, and how sangham women see each other – not up or down but at eye level.

In films related to their training, the women have explained why they wanted to learn filmmaking: agricultural work has to be filmed at specific times because of its seasonal nature, but sometimes an outside filmmaker might not be able to come; and filmmaking allows them to tell news to or discuss their issues before a wider circle and to spread the idea of autonomy through sanghams to other villages not yet in the program. One of the women, Narasamma, said exactly the same things that the CFC/SN filmmakers have said – namely, that their filmmaking meant depicting the truth as best as they could and involving in the process the people concerned with the issues depicted in the films. She said, "Outsiders come and ask questions; we answer them in our language. We are never sure about what they have understood, nor do we know what finally has gone into their films and

The Community Media Trust in action in Andhra Pradesh, India: agricultural worker Lakshmamma demonstrating camera use. Production still courtesy of the Deccan Development Society.

whether what we said has been correctly portrayed." She therefore felt that if they themselves were to make films in their own language, they would be truer in depiction and would be understood easily by their kind of audiences.[3] The films were also seen as a tool that could be used for advocacy with authorities and other groups. The women in this first workshop were the founding members of the Community Media Trust, which was set up in 1996. Now more have joined.

The initial funding for CMT came from UNESCO. Then the Bernard Von Leer Foundation of the Netherlands, which works on issues related to early child development and had previously given some funding to DDS for starting *balwadis,* wanted the *balwadi* program to be documented. The foundation liked the idea of women recording the progress of the program on video and agreed to provide some money for video equipment. Initially some seed money was needed from donors, but since then CMT has been making films and buying the required equipment with what it earns. It is now self-sufficient.

3 Interviews of the trainees are featured in their first two films: *Ten Women and a Camera* and *Sangham Shot.* By now they have made more than 150 films (www.ddsindia.com and www.ddsindia.org.in).

Who buys its films or commissions the CMT to make them? Actually, even as its training program was going on, the public television channel used the footage it had shot to show what harm a heavy rain at the wrong time of year could do to a millet crop. The fact that the filmmaker was standing in the mud of her field to show how her millet crop was ruined brought the tragedy home. Both the public and a private Telugu channel have been using CMT films or film clips in their rural programs. However, most of the funds CMT generates come from commissioned films or sales of CDs to groups in India and abroad that are interested in promoting biodiversity and sustainable rural development, protesting the introduction of genetically modified (GM) crops, and so forth.

CMT makes three kinds of films: those that are meant for sangham women and other villagers; those that are commissioned by DDS; and those commissioned by other Indian or international organizations. However, CMT does not accept film projects that go against its credo around the autonomy of local communities and sustainable development. The gist of its trainees pledge at the end of their training is as follows: "We will not use our filmmaking skills as an income earning skill. We will make films only for those things and issues in which our community and we believe. We will not work for commercial institutions but only in the interest of our people as well as other institutions who share our concerns and ideologies." And CMT has remained steadfast in its resolve. For example, after seeing and being impressed by the CMT film *Millet, the Miracle Grain*, the commissioner for agriculture of the AP government wanted CMT to make a film to promote Bt cotton (grown from Monsanto GM cottonseed) for the AP government. The CMT refused. Its budgets are modest even by Indian standards. On average, a budget comes to about 100,000 rupees (about $2,500 Can. [2008]) for a film of twenty minutes. The biggest donation ($34,450) it has received has been from a European organization for a thirty-minute film made in 2005 and titled *A Disaster in Search of Success: Bt Cotton in the Global South*. The film was shot in West Africa, South Africa, Southeast Asia, and India. The films CMT makes for DDS's own communities are generally single-concept films of eight to ten minutes and cost about $500. The sizable kitty that DDS has built up provides funds for its community films and for running CMT. DDS forms teams of two or three persons to make these films; each team is committed to make one film per quarter; the issues and specific themes of the films to be made are decided upon in a meeting. To use the CFC/SN terminology, some of their films (e.g., *Sooremma Makes a Film*, 2004, 13 min., about a fifty-five-year-old village woman learning filmmaking) are vertical, like the Fogo Island shorts, and deal with just one person or one theme. Others, like *Why Warangal Farmers Do Not Like Bt Cotton* (2002, 24 min.) are horizontal, picking up material from different sources and putting it together to make a coherent story. This latter, much-appreciated film shows that these women are now well versed in the language and grammar of filmmaking. (In their film *In the Lap of Paccha Mama*, about training Quechua Indian women in Peru, I even saw one aerial shot!) It begins with angry farmers cursing Monsanto Corporation for its false promises; it then systematically builds up the case against genetically modified seeds by date-wise field records, interviews with farmers and agricultural researchers/experts, and market transactions that spell disaster for farmers, driving many to suicide. The film ends exactly as it began, but now the viewer understands why GM seeds, despite claims from the corporate sector, have indeed been a disaster. The awareness that this film and its fuller version brought about in farming and village communities, as well as the widespread suicides by heavily indebted farmers reported in national and local papers, was a factor in getting the AP government to put a temporary ban on Monsanto GM cottonseed.[4]

HOW CMT DIFFERS FROM CFC/SN

One major difference between the CFC/SN and CMT is that the CMT women do not see themselves as filmmakers per se; they see themselves as family members, peasants, community activists in their sanghams, and also filmmakers. All of them continue to work on their lands, some more than others. They certainly eat and dress better than they did before the DDS program began, but this has much more to do with their accomplishments in sangham work than with their CMT work per se. Their living standard is not much different from that of other sangham women except that they travel more than the others. This is so because DDS ensures that sangham women attend state, national, regional, and international meetings to which the DDS is invited, to encourage their direct contact with the outside world so that they learn that many of their issues are global and thus need to be tackled internationally. Moreover, as the CMT women are often asked to provide training

4 However, the battle continues, as the corporate monster has once more raised its Hydra-like heads. Soon after the AP government ban, on 12 November 2005, India and the United States signed the Joint Declaration of the India–United States Knowledge Initiative on Agricultural Education, Research, Service and Commercial Linkages. Then president Bush, a good friend of the corporate world, named Monsanto as one of its members. A 2008 documentary *The World According to Monsanto*, co-produced by the NFB and Wide Eye Cinema, has ably exposed the penetration of Monsanto into U.S. public offices. It shows how the firm is involved in all kinds of clandestine operations and is instrumental in suppressing vital information, not to mention harassing farmers in the United States and elsewhere who would not buy GM seeds.

for women like themselves in countries of the South (Bangladesh, Nepal, Pakistan, Sri Lanka, Peru, etc.) and their films are shown at different film festivals around the world, they travel.

I have known these women for the last fourteen years and have seen them develop without losing their spirit of cooperation and innate good sense. They have learnt to speak to the point (probably a skill transferred from their editing training). If a child being nursed has to travel with its mother, the mother has several willing helpers. The exchange of camera and child happens quite smoothly. (In Canada, ace camerawoman Susan Trow of Studio D used to strap her child behind her back as she handled her camera; two working mothers from two different cultures solved a similar problem in different ways – one more social and the other more individualistic.) They value the respect and dignity that they have gained. It was amusing to see that Lakshmamma, who earlier, as a poor Dalit peasant, had to sit outside the portals of the landlord's house, was asked by the same landlord to film a big *pooja* (prayer) ceremony in his house. Lakshmamma walked straight to the "sanctum sanctorum," and when she found that the blaring television noise interfered with her work, without hesitation she ordered the landlord's son to turn it off. They also value the broadening of their horizons and their new learning. Consequently, CMT is free of the elitism and careerism that often enters many participatory media projects. Colin Low has said something extremely pertinent in this connection: "There is an assumption in all elitist filmmaking that the filmmaker *knows* what the changes in institutions should be for the betterment of people and society. History demonstrates this to be crap" (emphasis in the original). He is also wary of careerism, which could be quite harmful if it penetrates filmmaking about a community: "A sustained career of filmmaking alone is a very artificial activity over several decades, if it is not a *real* part of the community we belong to" (quoted in Jones 1981, 151–75).

There seems to be very little danger of either elitism or careerism entering into the work of the CMT. Its films are not likely to win any Oscar, but they are well shot and well edited; the quality of the sound is good; and, most important, they are appropriate for the purpose and audience for which they are made. This is not to say that auteur documentaries are not important; exploring many dimensions of film art is certainly important. But community media are designed as tools for a program of social change and are not ends in themselves. At the time of CFC/SN, video technology was in its infancy and was not as user friendly as it is now. A CFC film like *You Are on Indian Land,* for example, needed a trained 16mm filmmaking team that would honestly express the plight, concerns, and views of Mohawks to officials and the public. It is to the credit of CFC filmmakers that they abdicated their roles as filmmakers and let the people concerned not only have control over the editing or what was said in a film but also approve what was to be shown to the public. Such an intermediary role was needed before video technology developed. CMT women now use media in the way that Dorothy Todd Hénaut and Bonnie Sherr Klein (who both worked first in CFC and later in Studio D) and many others had hoped and had tried to use video in CFC/SN (see Hénaut and Klein, chapter 3 this volume).

The second major difference between CFC/SN and CMT is that for CFC/SN there was only a general directive of poverty alleviation and participatory democracy. For CMT, there is a definite program on the ground for enabling people to gain community autonomy in various areas. Film becomes more useful as a tool only if it is part of a system with a medley of strategies, designed for achieving certain well-defined goals for social change. The Fogo films were successful because they effectively brought the scattered communities of the island together and placed the views of the community before the authorities, who were sensible enough to listen and act.[5]

Another crucial difference between the CFC/SN and CMT programs is that after initial help the CMT has become self-financing. CFC/SN (and the NFB too, of course) was always dependent on public funding that depended on the direction the political winds blew. George Stoney, who worked as the producer for CFC/SN for two years, has said that CFC/SN was possible because there was a more welfare-conscious government in power in Canada at that time – it works only when there are people who are willing to try mediation before confrontation. He tried to do similar work in the United States and found that in his country trying mediation was almost considered cowardly; the officials concerned did not even find time to see the films made by people under Stoney's guidance. Ann Michaels, an official in the (now defunct) U.S Office of Economic Opportunity, also tried to use the Fogo process and invited many of the CFC filmmakers to help her in setting up projects. Finally, presumably in despair, she said, "The crazy Canadians were new to the confrontational style of American politics and failed to comprehend the extent of distrust of government at grass roots levels" (Wiesner, chapter 10, this volume).

But there are limits to what any government, however liberal, will allow. The truth is that one would never be allowed to touch the sacred cows of mainstream society. The story of two very good films about the Crees who were

---

5 I am aware of difficulties that later developed with the Fogo program. In my opinion, the fault lies in thinking of development as a one-shot affair. It is a continuous process, with the very first step changing the dimensions of the situation, which demand different strategies and approaches. CFC/SN provided media autonomy but had no mandate to provide other autonomies or a much-needed total development and functionally flexible plan for all-round sustainable development.

soon to lose their lands to the James Bay hydroelectric project, made almost towards the end of the CFC/SN years, illustrates this point (see Stewart, chapter 16, this volume). The first film, *Our Land Is Our Life,* is very direct about the land rights of the Crees, while the second, *Cree Hunters of Mistassini,* does it more gently by first showing the Crees' environment-friendly way of life and how they cooperate and share their natural resources with other families to let their lands recover. At the beginning and at the end, *Cree Hunters* refers to the James Bay project and points out that this way of life will end soon. It was shown on the public channel and it received many kudos. The other, more direct film was never aired. The Crees had the Hobson's choice of taking money for land they did not want to sell to the corporation because they knew that they would lose it in any case. The sacred cow in this respect was the insatiable need of mainstream Canadian society for cheap power and what is considered to be "progress." But what is progress? Ronald Wright questions the currently dominant idea of progress, pointing out that within ten thousand years of civilization we have reduced the earth to a point of no return and that the twenty-first century will probably be the last century for humankind.

WALKING IN THE SAME DIRECTION

When asked about the return of CFC/SN, Low states that it will happen in less affluent, if not depression, times, when people rediscover community and recognize that mass media as practised today is fundamentally an opiate, manipulated by corporate interests. Could one say that the CMT's media work of the DDS fulfils Low's expectations to some extent? Seventy-five villages and five thousand women are a drop in the ocean. Billions of silent revolutions must happen all over the world to set things right. Will it happen? As I sometimes despair, some lines from a book by two Indian Jesuit priests often make me hope again. These are:

Who can tell us whether what we hope for, exists or does not exist?
It is with it as it is with roads on the earth.
First there are no roads, but they come into existence.
When many people walk in the same direction.
And then it becomes a road.

Challenge for Change/Société nouvelle:
The Complete Filmography

■

Note: Film titles and their official translations appear in *italics*. Titles appearing in [brackets] are unofficial translations provided by the editors. Abbreviations: DIR (director); PROD (producer); CAM (camera); ED (editor); NARR (narrator); MUS (music)

■ *The 80 Goes to Sparta,* 1969, 45 min.
DIR: Bill Davies; SCRIPT: Bill Davies; CAM: David De Volpi, Don Virgo, Jacques Fogel; ED: Alan Davis; SOUND: Claude Champagne, Ted Haley, Claude Hazanavicius, Michel Hazel, Leo O'Donnell, Hans Oomes
A representation of the Greek community's diverse and politically divided composition in Montreal during 1969, with an emphasis on cultural and economic problems encountered by new immigrants. The title refers to the bus on Avenue du Parc, in the Greek neighbourhood.

Montreal Greek-Canadian senior stares back at CFC in *The 80 Goes to Sparta* (1969). Frame enlargement.

▪ *Activator One*, 1969, 58 min.
DIR: John Spotton; PROD: Barrie Howells; NARR: Bill Davies;
CAM: Don Virgo; SOUND: Jacques Drouin
A film about the late Dave Pellan of Vancouver and his philosophy of human behaviour. Activator "converts" employ his methods to help others with their social problems.

Activator One (1969): Vancouver social activists learning from Dave Pellan. Production still.

▪ *Alchimie nouvelle* / See original English version, *The New Alchemists*.

▪ *... and a Broom Factory*, 1970, 12 min.
DIR: Chad Hannah; ED: Willa Breakey; SOUND: Grant Bardsley;
COMMUNITY PARTNER: Town Talk
Roller hockey, drag-racing, flying, gymnastics, hunting, shooting, fishing, and making hand-made brooms are some of the activities of the Massaro family of Thunder Bay, Ontario. This film was made by students of the Thunder Bay Community Film/VTR project – a collaboration between the Challenge for Change/Société nouvelle program and Town Talk, a citizens group from the Lakehead.

▪ *Andrew Britt at Shoal Bay*, 1967, 14 min.
Series: Newfoundland Project
DIR: Colin Low; PROD: John Kemeny; CAM: Robert Humble;
ED: Dennis Sawyer

This film discusses the issue of fishermen's cooperation, the need for a fish plant, and adult education. *See chapters 2, 10, and 32.*

▪ *"… and They Lived Happily Ever After,"* 1975, 13 min.
Series: Working Mothers
DIR/PROD: Kathleen Shannon; DIR/ED: Irene Angelico, Anne Henderson; CAM: Robert Nichol, Don Virgo; SOUND: Gui Bernardes, Claude Delorme, Ted Haley
A long, hard look at marriage and motherhood as expressed in the views of a group of young girls and married women. Their opinions cover a wide range. At regular intervals glossy advertisements extolling romance, weddings, and babies flash across the screen, in strong contrast to the words that are being spoken. The film ends on a sobering thought: the solution to dashed expectations could be as simple as growing up before marriage. *See chapters 7 and 29.*
Awards: AMER Golden Eye Award, Annual AMER Film Awards (Association of Media Educators in Religion), Dubuque, U.S.A. (1979)

▪ *Anthony Mazzocchi Talks about Chemicals and the Workers,* 1978, 09 min.
Series: Occupational Health and Safety
DIR: Boyce Richardson; PROD: Andy Thomson; SCRIPT: Boyce Richardson; CAM: Don Virgo; ED: Mike Goddard; SOUND: Bev Davidson
"Every human being should have the right to make a product without having to put a piece of his life into that product." Anthony Mazzocchi, vice-president of the Oil, Chemical and Atomic Workers' Union in the United States, discusses the political and social reasons for so much occupational disease. Chemicals are coded, which means that the worker doesn't know what he is exposed to in the environment. Factories are not properly maintained because that costs time and money. Productivity is the main goal.

▪ *Après 5 ans* [After 5 years], 1974, 57 min.
DIR: Jean Coutu; ED: Annick de Bellefeuille
This film assembles excerpts from approximately thirty films realized within the Société nouvelle/Challenge for Change program. These selections have been organized in order to underline the series's principal themes of social intervention: the marginalization of individuals, the desire to belong, the conservation process, the need for communication, the familial environment, the organization and structure of committees in society, the experiences of women, the city, and the organized activism that has social change as its goal.

▪ *À qui appartient ce gage?* [To whom does this pledge belong?], 1973, 56 min.
Series: En tant que femmes
DIR: Marthe Blackburn; Susan Gibbard, Jeanne Morazain, Francine Saïa,

Clorinda Warny; PROD: Jean-Marc Garand, Anne Claire Poirier;
CAM: Jacques Fogel, Thomas Vamos; SOUND: Richard Besse;
MUS: Maurice Blackburn, Alain Clavier
A cry for help for women and children that emerges out of the debate over state-sponsored daycare centres. Women refuse to bear the burden of child care and call for a more egalitarian sharing of parental responsibility among couples. We hear from parents in three different Montreal environments, all endowed with accessible daycare facilities: a working-class environment, an underprivileged area, and a neighbourhood marked by the anti-establishment message of teenagers. *See chapter 12.*

À qui appartient ce gage? (1973): a cry for help from working mothers over the burden of child care. Production still.

▪ *L'attitude néerlandaise* [The Dutch attitude], 1972, 26 min.
Series: Urbanose
DIR: Michel Régnier; PROD: Normand Cloutier; CAM: Pierre Mignot;
ED: Michel Régnier; SOUND: Serge Beauchemin, Richard Besse;
MUS: Alain Clavier
Hemmed in by the sea, the Dutch have acquired such a unique form of experience, scientific knowledge, and wisdom concerning the cultivation of the earth, urban planning, and accommodation that a film had to be dedicated to the subject. The interests of a community are embedded within every aspect of this culture. In the lower regions of the country, where land has always been a rare commodity, we find the inhabitants of its cities to be the most prepared for the twenty-first century. *See chapter 22.*

▪ *L'automobile* [The automobile], 1972, 26 min.
Series: Urbanose
DIR: Michel Régnier; PROD: Normand Cloutier; CAM: Pierre Mignot;

ED: Michel Régnier; SOUND: Serge Beauchemin, Richard Besse;
MUS: Alain Clavier
A denunciation of Montreal's forced subjection to private transportation, for which we destroy neighbourhoods, demolish thousands of good dwellings, and displace entire populations. Ultimately, all of these actions fail to resolve the general problem of urban transportation. Likewise, plans for the Autoroute Ville-Marie highway threaten to destroy most of the city's Hochelaga-Maisonneuve neighbourhood. Led by Michel Bourdon, the Common Front against the Expressway must come up against Lucien Saulnier, the president of the Montreal Urban Community. *See chapter 22.*

■ *The Ballad of Crowfoot,* 1968, 10 min.
DIR/SCRIPT/MUS: Willie Dunn; PROD: Barrie Howells
An examination of Aboriginal peoples' situation in North America through the figure of Crowfoot, the legendary nineteenth-century Blackfoot leader of the Plains. A rapid montage of archival photos, etchings, and contemporary newspaper clippings is married to the words and music of an impassioned ballad written by Mi'kmaq singer and songwriter Willie Dunn. *See chapter 5.* Awards: Atlantic Film Festival, Halifax (1987); SODRE International Festival of Documentary and Experimental Films, Montevideo, Uruguay (1971); American Film and Video Festival, New York (1970); International Film Festival, Chicago (1969).

■ *Basingstoke – Runcorn – British New Towns* / See original French version, next entry.

■ *Basingstoke – Runcorn – villes nouvelles britanniques,* 1974, 86 min. / English version, *Basingstoke – Runcorn – British New Towns*
Series: Urba 2000
DIR/NARR/ED: Michel Régnier; PROD: Nicole Chamson, Jean-Marc Garand; CAM: Laval Fortier; SOUND: Claude Lefebvre; MUS: Alain Clavier
Great Britain was the first country to plan the establishment of "new towns" to house the overflow from rapidly expanding industrial centres. Today these towns number over one hundred. This film examines the operation of two of them. *See chapter 22.*

■ *Before the Time Comes* / See original French version *Le temps de l'avant.*

■ *Billy Crane Moves Away,* 1967, 17 min.
Series: Newfoundland Project
DIR: Colin Low; PROD: John Kemeny; CAM: Robert Humble;
ED: Dennis Sawyer

In this vertical film, Fisherman Crane tells why he is being forced to find employment in Toronto. *See chapters 2, 10, and 32.*

■ *Bologna: An Ancient City for a New Society* / See original French version, next entry.

■ *Bologne – une ville ancienne pour une société nouvelle*, 1974, 56 min. / English version, *Bologna: An Ancient City for a New Society*
Series: Urba 2000
DIR/NARR/ED: Michel Régnier; PROD: Nicole Chamson, Jean-Marc Garand; CAM: Laval Fortier; SOUND: Claude Lefebvre; MUS: Alain Clavier
Exemplary in its town planning and administration, Bologna has been transformed into a city that is avant-garde, both socially and culturally, yet still preserves its historical roots. *See chapter 22.*

■ *Le bonhomme* [The Guy], 1972, 58 min.
DIR: Pierre Maheu; PROD: Normand Cloutier, Jean-Marc Garand; CAM: Martin Duckworth; CAST: Chris Castle, Lise Cousineau, Luc Cousineau, René Hébert, Red Mitchell; ED: Claire Boyer; SOUND: Jacques Drouin, Pierre Maheu, Jean-Guy Normandin; MUS: Luc Cousineau, Red Mitchell
An observational *vérité* portrait of the familial tension found within the marginalized Montreal neighbourhood of Saint-Henri when a husband discovers nature and liberty. Ending twenty years of conflict and alienation, Claude, a father of ten children, abandons Yolande and opts for a communal life in the Laurentians. As a result of this choice, Yolande confines herself within her household as she increasingly voices her indignation and yields to hopelessness. As a radical search for happiness within "modern culture" through the audacious examination of the private sphere, this film questions many of the founding beliefs of consumer societies. *See chapter 26.*

■ *Les Borges* [The Borges], 1978, 60 min.
DIR: Marilú Mallet; PROD: Jacques Gagné; CAM: Roger Rochat; ED: François Dupuis; SOUND: Richard Besse
A portrait of a Portuguese community composed of approximately 30,000 members who have all established themselves in Montreal; in particular, the family of Manuel Borges, arrived in 1967. The film thus exposes the numerous problems linked to the lives of immigrants and demonstrates how the latter can adapt in a country that they seek to make their own.

■ *Brian Earle on Merchants and Welfare*, 1967, 10 min.
Series: Newfoundland Project
DIR: Colin Low; PROD: John Kemeny; CAM: Robert Humble; ED: Dennis Sawyer

Les Borges (1978): a lively *ruelle* in Montreal's Portuguese community.
Production still.

A vertical look at the relationships among the Fogo Island merchants and
fishermen and at the demoralizing effects that welfare has on them. *See chapters 2, 10, and 32.*

▪ *Building an Organization,* 1967, 10 min.
Series: The Alinsky Approach: Organizing for Power
DIR: Peter Pearson, Bonnie Sherr Klein; PROD: Barrie Howells, John
Kemeny; CAM: Tony Ianzelo; ED: Roger Hart; SOUND: Hans Oomes
A depiction of the obstacles encountered by a new community action organ-
ization in Buffalo, New York, led by legendary organizer Alinsky, as it begins
to work for recognition. *See chapter 21.*

▪ *A Bus – For Us,* 1972, 14 min.
Series: Urban Transportation
DIR: Rex Tasker; CAM: Tony Ianzelo; ED: Rex Tasker; SOUND: Gui Bernardes
After repeated attempts to obtain service from the public transportation au-
thorities, these suburban Ottawa residents finally decided to do it themselves.

▪ *Cell 16,* 1971, 14 min.
DIR/CAM/ED: Martin Duckworth; PROD: Colin Low; NARR: Jim Morrison;
SCRIPT: Peter Madden; CAST: Peter Madden; MUS: Eugène Grandmond
Set in Ontario's Collin's Bay Penitentiary, an experimental portrayal of in-
carceration's effects on the individual. Prisons, the film shows, lock men in

themselves, depriving their minds of normal life experiences, confiscating their humanity ... but prisoner poet Madden resists.

▪ *Centre-ville et piétons*, 1974, 56 min. / English version, *City Centre and Pedestrians*
Series: Urba 2000
DIR/SCRIPT/ED: Michel Régnier; PROD: Nicole Chamson, Jean-Marc Garand; CAM: Laval Fortier; SOUND: Claude Lefebvre; MUS: Alain Clavier
This film focuses on the approaches that several cities have taken to one problem. Through various examples, it examines the implications and options for a pedestrian-oriented city core. *See chapter 22.*

▪ *Challenge for Change*, 1968, 24 min.
DIR: Bill Reid; CAM: David De Volpi, Jean-Pierre Lachapelle; ED: Jacques Bensimon; SOUND: Jacques Drouin, Hans Oomes
A summary of the Challenge for Change program after its first year in operation: what role can film play in participatory democracy? *See chapter 10.*

▪ *Charley Squash Goes to Town*, 1969, 04 min.
DIR/SCRIPT: Duke Redbird; NARR: Isaac Beaulieu; CAM: Wayne Henwood, Kjeld Nielsen; ANIM: Marie Claire Bérubé, Yvon Mallette; MUS: Alanis Obomsawin
An animated film, based on an Aboriginal comic-strip character created by Duke Redbird, which tells the story of a young First Nations individual who leaves the reserve to make his way in the city. Eventually he returns to the reserve and the ways of his people. *See chapter 5.*
Awards: International Festival of Short Films, Philadelphia (1971)

▪ *Chasseurs cris de Mistassini* / See original English version, *Cree Hunters of Mistassini.*

▪ *Chez nous, c'est chez nous* [Where we live is where we live], 1972, 81 min.
DIR: Marcel Carrière; PROD: François Séguillon; CAM: Réo Grégoire, Pierre Letarte; ANIM: Clorinda Warny; ED: Monique Fortier; SOUND: Jacques Blain
The filmmaker illustrates the impact of Quebec's socio-economic restructuring plan on rural areas. Eleven villages are demolished in the lower regions of Saint-Laurent and Gaspésie, notably Saint-Octave-de-l'Avenir. Intercut with archival footage, the resulting document functions as a warning: will this practice expand in a manner that would demolish other villages, rural parishes, and country lifestyles all in the name of technocratic profit? Aren't there human values that justify the survival of an inhabited countryside, away

from the city's "for-profit" spaces where human beings are increasingly stuck?

Chez nous, c'est chez nous (1972): the Fraser family and friends in the soon-to-be-demolished community St-Octave de l'avenir. Production still.

▪ *The Children of Fogo Island,* 1967, 17 min.
Series: *Newfoundland Project*
DIR: Colin Low; PROD: John Kemeny; CAM: Robert Humble;
ED: Dennis Sawyer
Given the problems the people of Fogo Island must contend with, what keeps them committed to the land? In this exceptionally lyrical and non-didactic film, we witness, through the eyes of children, some of the magic of this barren island that keeps its inhabitants clinging stubbornly to its shores. *See chapters 2, 10, and 32.*
Awards: Certificate of Merit, Conference on Children, Washington (1970)

▪ *Citizen Discussions,* 1967, 28 min.
Series: Newfoundland Project
DIR: Colin Low; PROD: John Kemeny; CAM: Robert Humble; ED: Dennis Sawyer. COMMUNITY PARTNER: Memorial University of Newfoundland
A group discussion on efforts to obtain provincial support for the United Maritimes Fisheries Co-op to run the Seldom fish plant, and comments on the subsequent decision by the Newfoundland government in favour of the Yellow Fish Company. *See chapters 2, 10, and 32.*

▪ *Citizen Harold,* 1971, 08 min.
DIR/ANIM: Hugh Foulds; PROD: John Taylor; ANIM: Wayne Morris;
ED: Luke Bennett; MUS: High Street Band
One of the rare CFC/SN animated films explores one man's attempt to bring changes to his community through his participation with fellow citizens and the local government. A trigger film with a dual ending, it is directed at groups exploring methods of bringing about change.
Awards: Chris Bronze Plaque, International Film and Video Festival, Columbus (1973); Diplomat of Merit, International Film Festival, Melbourne (1973); Certificate of Merit – Category: Education, International Animation Film Festival, New York (1972)

▪ *Citizens' Medicine,* 1970, 30 min. / French version, *La clinique des citoyens*
DIR/PROD/ED: Bonnie Sherr Klein; CAM: Réo Grégoire; SOUND:
Richard Besse; COMMUNITY PARTNER: St-Jacques Citizens' Committee
In Montreal, the St-Jacques Citizens' Committee set up a community health clinic, aided by volunteer doctors, nurses, dentists, and medical students. This film shows discussion, planning, and the clinic in operation, and presents its problems and advantages as seen both by medical workers and by local residents. Committee members participated in the filmmaking, from original planning through filming, selecting, and editing.

▪ *Citoyen nouveau: Services juridiques communautaires* / See original English version, *The Point: Community Legal Clinic.*

▪ *City Centre and Pedestrians* / See original French version, *Centre-ville et piétons.*

▪ *La clinique des citoyens* / See original English version, *Citizens' Medicine.*

▪ *Community Action Theatre on Tour,* 1973, 23 min.
DIR: Tom Shandel; PROD: Barrie Howells; CAM: David De Volpi; ED:
Homer Powell; SOUND: Richard Besse
A group of welfare recipients from British Columbia choose theatre to express their discontent with the welfare system and the general attitudes persisting towards those receiving social assistance. On a tour of Vancouver Island, the "actors" perform skits before a variety of audiences – and the audiences react. An exploration of theatre as a tool in organizing for social change.

▪ *Concordia I,* 1972, 26 min. / original French production
Series: Urbanose

DIR/ED: Michel Régnier; PROD: Normand Cloutier; CAM: Pierre Mignot; SOUND: Serge Beauchemin, Richard Besse; MUS: Alain Clavier
Shot in Montreal's scarred but resilient Milton-Parc neighbourhood, an account of the tension between a technocratic, modern, and authoritarian conception of progress and the interests of residents who desire to preserve an old neighbourhood with a "humanist" outlook and modest housing. Confronted with this conflict, questions about democratic participation in urban progress are asked: "How do we change cities?" *See chapter 22.*

▪ *Concordia II,* 1972, 26 min. / original French production
Series: Urbanose
DIR/ED: Michel Régnier; PROD: Normand Cloutier; CAM: Pierre Mignot; SOUND: Serge Beauchemin, Richard Besse; MUS: Alain Clavier
The conclusion to this essay film on one of Montreal's historic citizens-vs-developers battlegrounds. *See chapter 22.*

▪ *A Continuing Responsibility,* 1968, 42 min.
Series: The Alinsky Approach: Organizing for Power
DIR: Bonnie Sherr Klein; PROD: Barrie Howells, John Kemeny; CAM: Tony Ianzelo; ED: Roger Hart; SOUND: Hans Oomes
As demonstrated by the Woodlawn Organization in Chicago – African-Americans resisting the encroachment of an elite university on their turf – Alinsky's technique creates sustainable community organizations. *See chapter 21.*

▪ *Co-op Housing: Getting It Together,* 1975, 23 min.
DIR/NARR/SCRIPT: Laura Sky; PROD: Kathleen Shannon; CAM: Carol Betts, Joan Hutton, John F. Phillips, Nesya Shapiro; ED: Ginny Stikeman; SOUND: Aerlyn Weissman; MUS: Laurent Coderre
People, housing, funds, and expertise: getting them together isn't easy, but it can be done. The film deals with the planning and procedures involved in setting up a co-op, whether that means building one or buying and rehabilitating existing housing. Individuals living in different kinds of co-ops talk about them and how they function.

▪ *Co-op Housing: The Best Move We Ever Made,* 1975, 23 min.
DIR/NARR/SCRIPT: Laura Sky; PROD: Kathleen Shannon; CAM: Carol Betts, Joan Hutton, John F. Phillips, Nesya Shapiro; ED: Ginny Stikeman; SOUND: Aerlyn Weissman; MUS: Laurent Coderre
The housing crisis in Canada: the definition of cooperative housing and its possibilities, as described by some of the people living there today. Here, housing is owned and operated by people as users, not as investors. The film

emphasizes an alternative in housing, with owners valuing security and mutual aid.

▪ *Cree Hunters of Mistassini,* 1974, 57 min. / French version, *Chasseurs cris de Mistassini*
DIR/CAM: Tony Ianzelo; DIR/NARR/SCRIPT: Boyce Richardson;
PROD: Colin Low; ED: Ginny Stikeman; SOUND: Richard Besse,
Jean Guy Normandin
During the winter since times predating agriculture, the Cree of Mistassini have gone to the bush of the James and Ungava Bay area, threatened by hydro development, to hunt. Three hunting families agreed to meet an NFB crew, who filmed the building of the winter camp, the hunting, the relationship to the land, and the rhythms of Cree family life. This film expresses the ecological principles that are the foundation of Cree lives, and ethnography acquires a political edge. *See chapter 16.*
Awards: Etrog for Best Documentary over 30 minutes, Canadian Film Awards (1975); Silver Boomerang, International Film Festival, Melbourne (1975); Robert Flaherty Award, British Academy of Film and Television Awards (1975)

▪ *Cree Way,* 1977, 26 min.
DIR/CAM: Tony Ianzelo; PROD: Peter Katadotis, Mark Zannis; NARR: Earl Pennington; CAM: Buckley Petawabano; ED: Gérard Sénécal; SOUND: Jean-Guy Normandin, Gordon Polson
Teachers at the Indian Affairs school at Rupert House, James Bay, have initiated a curriculum development project using local people and resources. The teaching materials are drawn from Cree folklore, are written mainly in Cree, and make use of old photographs, artifacts, and books that are written and printed in the community. The school year is organized so that pupils have time to go hunting and fishing with their families. This innovative approach makes local control of education a reality in native communities. *See chapters 5 and 16.*

▪ *A Crowded Wilderness,* 1972, 08 min.
DIR: Grant Kennedy; PROD: Roger Hart; CAM: Réo Grégoire, Douglas Kiefer, Don Virgo; ED: Ginny Stikeman; SOUND: Bev Davidson, Jacques Drouin, Michel Hazel
Canada's national parks are in crisis, facing demands on their resources without a continuing program of extending the parks system. Wilderness may, in fact, be the greatest heritage this generation of Canadians can leave to future generations. The problems, and the need to act now, are well defined in this film by cabinet minister Jean Chrétien and concerned conservationists.

▪ *Dan Roberts on Fishing*, 1967, 16 min.
Series: Newfoundland Project
DIR: Colin Low; PROD: John Kemeny; CAM: Robert Humble;
ED: Dennis Sawyer
This vertical film looks at the success of the longliner and the problems
encountered in obtaining and running it as a solution to the crisis in the Fogo
fishery. *See chapters 2, 10, and 32.*

▪ *Dans nos forêts* [Within our forests], 1971, 89 min.
DIR: Maurice Bulbulian; PROD: Normand Cloutier; CAM: Guy Desbiens;
ED: Marc Hébert; SOUND: Claude Delorme, Claude Hazanavicius,
Jean-Guy Normandin; MUS: Philippe Gagnon, Dominique Tremblay
A representation of the emerging political consciousness and revolt of people living in Quebec's forest regions. An investigation of the abusive and
alienating exploitation of forests by corporations solely concerned with the
maximization of profit. A plight for the forest as a provider for the majority
and for an environment that is essential to the dignity and happiness of
humankind. A film that gives a voice to the people. *See chapter 18.*

▪ *Débarque-moué au lac des Vents* [Drop me off at the Lake of the Winds],
1974, 71 min.
DIR: Michel Gauthier; PROD: Jean-Marc Garand; SCRIPT: Robert Tremblay;
CAM: Pierre Letarte, Jocelyn Simard; ED: Fernand Bélanger; SOUND:
Michel Descombes, Benoît Fauteux; PARTICIPANTS: Léandre Chabot,
Arnold Potvin, Lorraine Potvin, Adrien Tremblay
For a long period, Chibougamau was a meeting place for First Nations people in northern Quebec. Now a city, Chibougamau remains a meeting place,
but now between two cultures, two lifestyles, and two types of individuals.
Explorers, fur traders, and elderly loners like prospector Adrien Tremblay
coexist with miners and skilled workers, all of whom had established themselves in the middle of the woods and built a city. Numerous other locations
similarly exist near the frontier where untouched nature meets post-industrial
civilization.

▪ *Deciding to Organize*, 1968, 34 min.
Series: The Alinsky Approach: Organizing for Power
DIR: Peter Pearson, Bonnie Sherr Klein; PROD: Barrie Howells,
John Kemeny; CAM: Tony Ianzelo; ED: Roger Hart; SOUND: Hans Oomes
A look at a group of concerned citizens from Dayton, Ohio, meeting and
consulting legendary organizer Alinsky on the means of creating an effective
organization. *See chapter 21.*

Deciding to Organize (1968): Saul Alinsky (right) with Ohio community activist. Frame enlargement.

■ *De grâce et d'embarras* [Of grace and trouble], 1979, 94 min.
DIR: Marcel Carrière; PROD: Jacques Gagné; CAM: Pierre Letarte; ED: François Labonté, Louise Surprenant; SOUND: Richard Besse, Alain Corneau
Outside of Sorel, the daily life of Henri Letendre, farmer, and Déovic Saint-Germain, a hunter of muskrats, both residents of the Île d'Embarras, reflects the inherent contradictions of a rural environment increasingly shaped by the city. One of the pioneering direct-cinema sound recordist's two films directed for SN.

■ *Discussion on Welfare*, 1967, 06 min.
Series: Newfoundland Project
DIR: Colin Low; PROD: John Kemeny; CAM: Robert Humble;
ED: Dennis Sawyer
A focus group on the effects of welfare on Fogo Island residents. *See chapters 2, 10, and 32.*

■ *Do Your Thing*, 1973, 29 min.
PRODUCTION TEAM: Bev Davidson, Jean-Pierre Joutel, Colin Low, Pierre Letarte, Donna Nichol, Robert Nichol, Richard Todd, Dorothy Todd Hénaut
On the evening of 24 January 1970, the National Arts Centre in Ottawa was crowded with public housing tenants seeking to see the final performances of their own contest. This was the first time they had used the prestigious national space, and for many, it was the first time they had been near it. The film captures the behind-the-scenes organization and the on-stage talent.

■ *Dr. Epstein Talks about Chemicals in the Workplace*, 1978, 07 min.
Series: Occupational Health and Safety
DIR/SCRIPT: Boyce Richardson; PROD: Andy Thomson; CAM: Don Virgo;
ED: Mike Goddard; SOUND: Bev Davidson

Dr Samuel Epstein, professor of occupational and environmental health at the School of Medicine, University of Illinois, feels strongly that the worker should have the right to know what chemicals he or she is exposed to. A recent American government report has estimated that 80 per cent of the chemicals in the workplace are as yet unidentified. Dr Epstein suggests what workers should do if they want to avoid being carelessly exposed to dangerous chemicals.

▪ *Dr. Epstein Talks about Distortion of Information*, 1978, 13 min.
Series: Occupational Health and Safety
DIR/SCRIPT: Boyce Richardson; PROD: Andy Thomson; CAM: Don Virgo; ED: Mike Goddard; SOUND: Bev Davidson
Dr Epstein believes that democracy is threatened by distortions in the database on which decisions are made. He describes incidents that prove his argument.

▪ *Dr. Epstein Talks about the Chemical Explosion*, 1978, 08 min.
Series: Occupational Health and Safety
DIR/SCRIPT: Boyce Richardson; PROD: Andy Thomson; CAM: Don Virgo; ED: Mike Goddard; SOUND: Bev Davidson
Dr Epstein describes how, since the 1930s, the world has accommodated a virtual explosion of the use of chemicals, perhaps bringing with it more dangers than benefits. Failure to regulate environmental carcinogens is proving more costly than the costs of the diseases themselves, because what happens in the workplace vitally affects the people outside the workplace.

▪ *Dr. Selikoff Talks about the Latency Period*, 1978, 06 min.
Series: Occupational Health and Safety
DIR/SCRIPT: Boyce Richardson; PROD: Andy Thomson; CAM: Don Virgo; ED: Mike Goddard; SOUND: Bev Davidson
Dr Irving Selikoff, a leader in the identification of the health hazards posed by asbestos, describes how workers can suffer many years later from overexposure to metal dusts, chemicals, and other dangerous substances. We have not yet decided that people's health should no longer be deliberately endangered.

▪ *Düsseldorf – Balanced Urban Growth* / See original French version, next entry.

▪ *Düsseldorf – équilibre urbain* 1974, 56 min. / English version, *Düsseldorf – Balanced Urban Growth*
Series: Urba 2000

DIR/ED: Michel Régnier; PROD: Nicole Chamson, Jean-Marc Garand; CAM: Laval Fortier; SOUND: Claude Lefebvre; MUS: Alain Clavier
Individualized for profit, yet harmonious in its whole, Düsseldorf has met and largely conquered the conflicting demands of economic growth and a humanist environment. *See chapter 22.*

■ *Encounter at Kwacha House – Halifax,* 1967, 17 min.
DIR: Rex Tasker; PROD: Barrie Howells, John Kemeny; CAST: Rocky Jones and others
A vociferous discussion among black youths at their storefront club in Halifax that touches upon racial discrimination in employment, housing, education, and interpersonal relations. Violence seems a tempting solution for some. *See chapter 17.*

■ *Encounter on Urban Environment,* 1971, 108 min.
DIR/ED: Roger Hart; CAM: David De Volpi; SOUND: Hans Oomes
A look at an urban community, stimulated by a panel of specialists from different fields who met with members of every level of the Halifax/Dartmouth community during a week-long session to consider the future of the area and the responsibility of the citizens and government in planning the future.

■ *Encounter with Saul Alinsky – Part 1:* CYC *Toronto,* 1967, 28 min.
DIR: Peter Pearson; PROD: Barrie Howells, John Kemeny
This is a lively confrontation between Saul Alinsky, a professional activist from the United States, and several members of the Company of Young Canadians. Doubts are expressed about the means and the costs of securing social change, about the challenge facing all socially engaged people, and some Canadian-American cultural misunderstandings emerge. *See chapter 21.*

■ *Encounter with Saul Alinsky – Part 2: Rama Indian Reserve,* 1967, 32 min.
DIR: Peter Pearson; PROD: Barrie Howells, John Kemeny; CAST: Alinsky, Duke Redbird, and others
An examination of the conflict between Alinsky's pragmatic ideas and the idealism of some First Nations youths. Against their arguments for a revision of the hundred-year-old Indian Act by peaceful persuasion and culturally rooted values, Alinsky advocates the more direct deployment of political power. *See chapter 21.*

■ *Entretien avec Henri Lefebvre* [Interview with Henri Lefebvre], 1972, 34 min.
Series: Urbanose
DIR/ED: Michel Régnier; PROD: Normand Cloutier; CAM: Pierre Mignot; SOUND: Serge Beauchemin, Richard Besse; MUS: Alain Clavier

Encounter with Saul Alinsky – Part 2: Rama Indian Reserve (1967): Indian Film Crew member Duke Redbird (left) and Alinsky in dialogue. Production still.

Henri Lefebvre, the famous French sociologist (1901–1991), delivers the essential points of his views on the city and contemporary urban living. Denouncing the reign of the automobile, the commercialization of everything, and a superficial conception of progress, he illustrates that, within the modern period, our civilization has dramatically missed an essential turning point for the industrial revolution, and he presently recommends, after agrarian reform, urban reform as a corrective. *See chapter 22.*

■ *Extensions of the Family,* 1974, 14 min.
Series: Working Mothers
DIR/PROD/ED: Kathleen Shannon; CAM: Robert Nichol;
SOUND: Ted Haley
An exploration of alternatives to the prevailing nuclear family. A self-selected "family of 13" buys a Vancouver house and shares responsibilities. Originally, four adults held the mortgage. Since this vivid colour film was made, two of the original members moved on, necessitating new arrangements for sharing equitably with other people who have joined the group. *See chapters 7 and 29.*

■ *Famille et variations* [Family and variations], 1977, 75 min.
DIR/NARR: Mireille Dansereau; PROD: Anne Claire Poirier; NARR: Marthe Blackburn, Pierre Huet; CAM: Roger Rochat, Michel Thomas-d'Hoste; CAST: Ginette Paris; ED: Jacques Drouin; SOUND: Joseph Champagne; MUS: Marie-Michèle Desrosiers, Robert Léger

Alternative Vancouver family in Kathleen Shannon's *Extensions of the Family* (1974). Frame enlargement.

Rural Québécois alternative family in *Famille et variations* (1977). Production still.

SN's version of the English-language film in the previous entry, this four-part feature immerses itself within four widely different families: a family with a disabled child, a rural commune, a single mother, and, finally, two urban divorced women cohabiting with their children. The director had just made Canada's first private-sector fiction feature by a woman, *La vie rêvée*, but is an attentive and sensitive documentary listener in this her second SN film.

▪ *Les filles c'est pas pareil* [Girls are not the same], 1974, 57 min.
Series: En tant que femmes
DIR: Hélène Girard; PROD: Anne Claire Poirier; CAM: Susan Gabori;
ED: Hélène Girard; SOUND: Esther Auger, Joseph Champagne, Roger Lamoureux; MUS: Maurice Blackburn
Six teenaged girls, between fourteen and sixteen, allow their intimate universe to be recorded by the camera. Their challenges push them to the limit: precocious sexual experiences, peer-group identification, parental relations,

The forgotten women of Quebec's Quiet Revolution in *Les filles du Roy* (1974). Production still.

social tolerance, friendship ... Despite obstacles, they manage to live out their adolescence each in her own unique manner. *See chapter 12.*

▪ *Les filles du Roy,* 1974, 56 min. / English version, *They Called Us 'Les Filles du Roy'*
Series: En tant que femmes
DIR/PROD/SCRIPT/PARTICIPANT: Anne Claire Poirier; PROD: Jean-Marc Garand; NARR: Dyne Mousso; SCRIPT: Marthe Blackburn, Jeanne Morazain; CAM: Georges Dufaux; ANIM: Jean-Thomas Bédard; CAST: Danielle Ouimet; ED: Claire Boyer; SOUND: Joseph Champagne; MUS: Maurice Blackburn; PARTICIPANTS: Marie-Josée da Silva, Katherine Deer, Monique Fortier, Suzanne Gervais, Hélène Girard, Berthe Latraverse-Poirier, Nicole Lebreton
Under cover of a love letter, this is an impressionistic history of the women of Quebec down through the ages: the First Nations woman, the *fille du Roy,* the nun, the settler's wife, the soldier's wife, and, finally, today's woman, who examines her traditional role as mother and wife and contrasts it with her new place in the labour force. *See chapter 12.*

▪ *Fishermen's Meeting,* 1967, 27 min.
Series: Newfoundland Project
DIR: Colin Low; PROD: John Kemeny; CAM: Robert Humble;
ED: Dennis Sawyer
In this vertical film, some of the problems discussed are the lack of fish and the inability to market any species but cod. *See chapters 2, 10, and 32.*

▪ *The Fogo Island Improvement Committee,* 1967, 13 min.
Series: Newfoundland Project
DIR: Colin Low; PROD: John Kemeny; CAM: Robert Humble;

ED: Dennis Sawyer
Committee members discuss the building of a speaking platform for the anticipated visit of the Newfoundland premier. *See chapters 2, 10, and 32.*

▪ *Fogo's Expatriates,* 1967, 15 min.
Series: Newfoundland Project
DIR: Colin Low; PROD: John Kemeny; CAM: Robert Humble;
ED: Dennis Sawyer
Individuals who have moved "away" express their opinions on the Island's life and problems. *See chapters 2, 10, and 32.*

▪ *The Founding of the Cooperatives,* 1967, 21 min.
Series: Newfoundland Project
DIR: Colin Low; PROD: John Kemeny; CAM: Robert Humble; ED: Dennis Sawyer
A record of the Fogo Island Ship Building and Producer Cooperative's founding meeting. *See chapters 2, 10, and 32.*

▪ *Fuir* [Escape], 1979, 73 min.
DIR/SCRIPT/ED: Hélène Girard; PROD: Jacques Gagné; SCRIPT: Claire Wojas; CAM: Pierre Mignot; ED: Babalou Hamelin; SOUND: Jacques Blain; MUS: Yves Laferrière; PARTICIPANTS: Janine Claussmann, Hélène Mercier
Two approaches, a fictional mode and a more documentary-like method, convey the intense moments of anxiety that precede a suicide. The film attempts to make the audience understand suicide as a call for help.

▪ *George Dionne, un Mineur de L'amiante* / See original French version, next entry.

▪ *Georges Dionne, un mineur de l'amiante,* 1978, 11 min. / English version, *George Dionne, un Mineur de L'amiante*
Series: Occupational Health and Safety
DIR/SCRIPT: Boyce Richardson; PROD: Andy Thomson; NARR: Jean Groulx; CAM: Don Virgo; ED: Mike Goddard; SOUND: Bev Davidson
Georges Dionne started working at ten cents an hour sweeping up asbestos dust. Drinking water came out of a bucket covered with this dust. Now retired because of asbestosis after many years in the asbestos mines of Thetford Mines, Quebec, he talks about his experience as miner, union militant, and concerned citizen.

▪ *God Help the Man Who Would Part with His Land,* 1971, 46 min.
DIR: George C. Stoney; PROD: Tom Daly, Colin Low; CAM: David De

Thetford Mines, Quebec: asbestosis-stricken retired miner tells all in *Georges Dionne, un mineur de l'amiante* (1978). Frame enlargement.

Conflict over disputed land ends in handshake between Mohawk activist Mike Mitchell and white cottager in *God Help the Man Who Would Part with His Land* (1971). Frame enlargement

Volpi, Tony Ianzelo; ED: Bill Reid; SOUND: Bev Davidson, Hans Oomes; MUS: Shannon Two Feathers
The Mohawk of the Akwesasne Reserve near Cornwall, Ontario, contest the land claim of white people to two islands in the St Lawrence that are being developed for summer cottages. A film of the dispute is shown to Indian Affairs in Ottawa, and representations are made by the Mohawk themselves. *See chapter 5.*

■ *The Greenlanders*, 1973, 37 min.
DIR/CAM: Hubert Schuurman; NARR: Strowan Robertson, Niels Henrik Lynge; ED: Marion Meadows; SOUND: André Galbrand; MUS: Donald Douglas
The Native people of Greenland were centralized along the coast of their island so that Denmark, the country they are a part of, could more readily provide them with housing, health, and other government services. This film was made for Canadian Aboriginals and government agencies concerned with the development of the North.

▪ *Grenoble – la Villeneuve – réinventer la ville,* 1974, 116 min. / English version, *Grenoble – La Villeneuve: The City Conceived Anew*
Series: Urba 2000
DIR/NARR/ED: Michel Régnier; PROD: Nicole Chamson, Jean-Marc Garand; CAM: Laval Fortier; SOUND: Claude Lefebvre; MUS: Alain Clavier
The "La Villeneuve" project in the Swiss mountain city aims at the genuine creation of a total community in the city core. It is a remarkable undertaking, both in its comprehensiveness and in its dependence on real collaboration between the public and all levels of government. *See chapter 22.*

▪ *Grenoble – La Villeneuve: The City Conceived Anew* / See original French version, previous entry.

▪ *Griffintown,* 1972, 26 min. / original French production
Series: Urbanose
DIR/ED: Michel Régnier; PROD: Normand Cloutier; CAM: Pierre Mignot; SOUND: Serge Beauchemin, Richard Besse; MUS: Alain Clavier
Griffintown, an ignored and devastated area of Montreal two steps away from the city's centre. A small, but very opinionated population struggles to survive. A professor of architecture from McGill University has established a class there and contributes to the struggle of the citizens' committee. The poor conditions of this neighbourhood, tyrranized by developers, prefigure a threat to the entire urban fabric. *See chapter 22.*

▪ *Halifax Neighbourhood Center Project,* 1967, 33 min.
DIR/ED: Rex Tasker; PROD: Barrie Howells, John Kemeny; CAM: Jacques Fogel, Paul Leach; SOUND: Ted Haley
Shows a campaign launched in Halifax in 1967 to probe the core of poverty in that city – low incomes, ill health, and inadequate housing affect more than 12,000 people in the central area. The project showcases the combined efforts of both local and government agencies in order to alleviate these conditions. *See chapters 11, 18, and 32.*

▪ *Les héritiers de la violence* [The heirs of violence], 1977, 56 min.
DIR/CAM: Thomas Vamos; ASSISTANT DIR: Micheline Charest; PROD: Anne Claire Poirier; CAM: André-Luc Dupont; CAST: Raymond Cloutier, Denise Courtois, Murielle Dutil, Rita Lafontaine, Ginette Robitaille; ED: Yves Leduc; SOUND: Serge Beauchemin, Claude Hazanavicius; PARTICIPANTS: Gilles Allard, Louise Boire, Marc G. Gagnon, Gloria Jéliu, Carmen Langlais, André Masse, Louise Repper, Louise Vigneault
Violence in all of its shapes within the familial realm affects children and influences their development. Not an accusation, this film, through several hon-

est first-hand accounts, seeks to find the source and causes of violence in our society.

▪ *Homer Séguin Talks about Radiation at Elliot Lake,* 1978, 08 min.
Series: Occupational Health and Safety
DIR/SCRIPT: Boyce Richardson; PROD: Andy Thomson; CAM: Don Virgo;
ED: Mike Goddard; SOUND: Bev Davidson
Homer Séguin, staff representative of the United Steelworkers of America in Elliot Lake, Ontario, describes the radiation tragedy among uranium miners in the new uranium boom town. Lung cancer caused by radiation must be prevented because it cannot yet be cured, he says.

▪ *"I Don't Think It's Meant for Us ... ,"* 1971, 32 min.
DIR/ED: Kathleen Shannon; PROD: Colin Low, George C. Stoney; CAM: David De Volpi, Don Virgo
Tenants of public housing in Ottawa express some of their concerns and perceptions of the public housing positions of the federal, provincial, and municipal levels of government that make and administer policies that negatively affect the tenants' lives. *See chapter 11.*

▪ *Indian Dialogue,* 1967, 27 min.
DIR: David Hughes; PROD: John Kemeny; CAM: D'Arcy Marsh, Douglas Kiefer; ED: Kathleen Shannon; SOUND: Hans Oomes
First Nations people discuss many problems, particularly the threat to their own culture by a dominant white society. The younger generation is the most forthright, more aware of the poverty and the spiritual deprivation in their communities. *See chapter 5.*

▪ *Indian Relocation: Elliot Lake,* 1967, 29 min.
DIR: David Hughes; DIR/CAM: D'Arcy Marsh; PROD: John Kemeny;
ED: Christopher Cordeaux; SOUND: Sam Chandler, Michel Hazel.
An experiment to prepare Native people for city life through vocational and academic education for families who were moved to Elliot Lake in northern Ontario from neighbouring reserves. The film listens in on classes and discussions, and interviews several families who stayed and other families who went back. It offers insight into the sort of adjustments that First Nations face within this kind of "programmed" integration. *See chapter 5.*

▪ *Introduction to Fogo Island,* 1968, 16 min.
Series: Newfoundland Project
DIR: Colin Low; PROD: John Kemeny; CAM: Robert Humble; ED: Dennis Sawyer

An introduction to the Newfoundland Project series and its experimental ethos of communication and social change. Basic facts about Fogo Island and its selection for the pilot CFC project. *See chapters 2, 10, and 32.*

▪ *Introduction to Labrador,* 1970, 23 min.
PROD: Harvey Best, George C. Stoney; NARR: Stanley Jackson; ED/CAM: Joe Harvey; SOUND: Randy Coffin; COMMUNITY PARTNER: Memorial University of Newfoundland, Extension Service Media Unit
An analysis of the problems affecting the remote communities of the Labrador coast – particularly the relocation of families to more populated centres that offer better employment opportunities as well as superior school and medical facilities. The role played by the Labrador Film/VTR community development project is outlined.

▪ *It's Not Enough,* 1974, 15 min.
Series: Working Mothers
DIR/PROD/ED: Kathleen Shannon; CAM: Robert Nichol; SOUND: Gui Bernardes, Ted Haley, Jean-Pierre Joutel, Ron Seltzer
An introduction to the Working Mothers series. Considering the kind of jobs available to them, most women work because they must. However, there are other reasons. *See chapters 7 and 29.*

▪ *Jim Decker Builds a Longliner,* 1967, 19 min.
Series: Newfoundland Project
DIR: Colin Low; PROD: John Kemeny; CAM: Robert Humble; ED: Dennis Sawyer
How one of the Fogo Islanders built a longliner with the help of his friends, overcoming the problems of financing and the lack of tools and government support. *See chapters 2, 10, and 32.*

▪ *Jim Decker's Party,* 1967, 06 min.
Series: Newfoundland Project
DIR: Colin Low; PROD: John Kemeny; CAM: Robert Humble; ED: Dennis Sawyer
A rollicking party on Fogo Island, music and jigging. *See chapters 2, 10, and 32.*

▪ *J'me marie, J'me marie pas* [Do I marry or not?], 1973, 81 min.
Series: En tant que femmes
DIR: Mireille Dansereau; PROD: Anne Claire Poirier, Jean-Marc Garand; CAM: Benoît Rivard; ANIM: Jean-Thomas Bédard, Vartkes Cholakian; ED: Claire Boyer; SOUND: Claude Lefebvre; PARTICIPANTS: Linda Gaboriau,

Folk culture serves as resistance on Fogo Island in *Jim Decker's Party* (1967). Frame enlargement.

Francine Larivée, Jocelyne Lepage, Tanya Mackay
What value – regenerative or destructive – do women attribute to love in their lives? Can the choice of marriage fulfil them completely? Can maternity be disassociated from a relationship with a man? Refused? Four women aged twenty-eight to thirty discuss these issues and illustrate how various modes of living and types of relationships are possible for women ... and for men. *See chapter 12.*

▪ *Joe Kinsella on Education,* 1967, 07 min.
Series: Newfoundland Project
DIR: Colin Low; PROD: John Kemeny; CAM: Robert Humble; ED: Dennis Sawyer
Joe Kinsella talks about the problem of young people leaving Fogo Island after they finish their education. *See chapters 2, 10, and 32.*

▪ *Labrador North,* 1973, 37 min.
DIR: Roger Hart; CAM: Andreas Poulsson; ED: Roger Hart
A film on the government relocation of the Labrador Inuit and the effects this has had on their culture and social structures.

▪ *Le labyrinthe* [The labyrinth], 1972, 26 min.
Series: Urbanose

DIR/ED: Michel Régnier; PROD: Normand Cloutier; CAM: Pierre Mignot; SOUND: Serge Beauchemin, Richard Besse; MUS: Alain Clavier
An essay on urban bureaucracy and dysfunctional urban decision-making. Absurd administrative divisions compromise present and future struggles. Despite these obstacles, the public interest is gradually making itself heard. Interviews with numerous urban experts and government officials of Quebec, Montreal, and Ottawa, including one with Laurent Saulnier, president of the Montreal Urban Community. *See chapter 22.*

▪ *Laurette,* 1973, 37 min.
DIR/ED: Pierre Lasry; PROD: Nicole Hamann, Thérèse Haselsteiner, Barrie Howells, Dan Leithman; CAM: Paul Leach, Jean-Jacques Parent, Richard Todd; SOUND: Jacques Drouin
Portrait of a single mother left alone to cope with family problems. Laurette, a young secretary, separated from her husband, with a daughter to bring up, lays bare her thoughts, feelings, and fears. *See chapter 27.*
Awards: Certificate of Merit, Conference on Children, Washington (1970)

▪ *Un lendemain comme hier* [A tomorrow like yesterday], 1970, 41 min.
DIR: Maurice Bulbulian; PROD: Pierre Maheu, Paul Larose; CAM: Roger Rochat; SOUND: George Croll
A family from Lac-Saint-Jean moved to Montreal to escape unemployment. The parents, never fully at home in this environment, return every year to their "lost paradise" with their children for the region's iconic blueberry-picking. Through the prolonged dreams of the parents and the growing distance of the next generations from their roots, the audience experiences a tragic disparity between different cultures and generations. *See chapter 18.*

Transplanted city-dwellers returning to blueberry-picking on the land in *Un lendemain comme hier* (1970). Frame enlargement.

▪ *Like the Trees,* 1974, 14 min.
Series: Working Mothers
DIR/PROD/ED: Kathleen Shannon; CAM: Robert Nichol; SOUND: Ted Haley
Rose is a Métis from northern Alberta, a woman who has lifted herself out
of an anguished existence in the city by rediscovering her roots among the
Woodland Cree. "I've left everything ... I'm just being myself ... Like the
trees, we belong here." *See chapters 7 and 29.*

▪ *Little Burgundy,* 1969, 30 min. / See original French version, *La p'tite
Bourgogne.*

▪ *Locataires et propriétaires* [Tenants and landlords], 1972, 26 min.
Series: Urbanose
DIR/ED: Michel Régnier; PROD: Normand Cloutier; CAM: Pierre Mignot;
SOUND: Serge Beauchemin, Richard Besse; MUS: Alain Clavier
Is housing a human right or simply "a commodity like any other?" A group
of disenfranchized tenants are told that the law is on their side, but they still
fail to obtain justice against a landlord. Bolstered by a new-found political
awareness, these tenants choose to contest the system and demand a new
kind of lease. *See chapter 22.*

▪ *Luckily I Need Little Sleep,* 1974, 07 min.
Series: Working Mothers
DIR/PROD/ED: Kathleen Shannon; CAM: Robert Nichol; SOUND: Ted Haley
Kathy worked as a nurse in Greece and then came to Canada. She and her
family live in northern Alberta, where they are developing a farm. Kathy
works outside the home as a nurse, sews for the children, maintains the
house, and helps with the farm work. *See chapters 7 and 29.*

▪ *Madawaska Valley,* 1967, 26 min.
DIR: John Ormond; PROD: John Kemeny; SCRIPT: John Ormond; CAM:
Paul Leach; ED: Christopher Cordeaux; SOUND: Hans Oomes; MUS:
Robert Fleming
The extraordinary beauty of the Madawaska Valley, northwest of Ottawa,
masks the hardship in which many bushmen and their families live out their
lives. Now some of these people are working together to try to improve their
conditions.

▪ *McGraths at Home and Fishing,* 1967, 11 min.
Series: Newfoundland Project
DIR: Colin Low; PROD: John Kemeny; CAM: Robert Humble; ED: Dennis
Sawyer

Shot at the sea and in the kitchen, a discussion about Fogo Island fishing, with some criticisms of the longliners. *See chapters 2, 10, and 32.*

■ *A Memo from Fogo,* 1972, 41 min.
DIR: Roger Hart; PROD: Colin Low; CAM: David De Volpi; ED: Roger Hart; SOUND: Randy Coffin
A retrospective look at Fogo Island, Newfoundland, four years after the original Newfoundland Project series was made. This is an assessment of the value of the programs initiated and of what film can do to help spark new life in a fading community. *See chapters 2, 10, and 32.*

■ *Le menteur (1re partie) – l'alcoolisme: La maladie* [The liar (first part) – alcoholism: the disease], 1977, 82 min.
DIR: Robert Séguin; PROD: Anne Claire Poirier; NARR: Colette Beauchamp; CAM: Thomas Vamos; ED: Pierre Lemelin; SOUND: Richard Besse
Alcoholics discuss the origins of their disease, its development, and the growing irresponsibility that resulted from their dependency. They speak of their hallucinations, their solitude, and the source of their present desire for a new life. Doctors describe the different phases of the disease that precede this life-changing decision.

■ *Le menteur (2e partie) – l'alcoolisme: la thérapie* [The liar (2e partie) – alcoholism: therapy], 1977, 82 min.
DIR: Robert Séguin; PROD: Anne Claire Poirier; NARR: Colette Beauchamp; CAM: Thomas Vamos; ED: Pierre Lemelin; SOUND: Richard Besse
Specialists evaluate the physical damage caused by alcohol. This second part also deals with the spiritual and moral development that contributes to an individual's physical recovery, as well as with the importance of patients' ability to depend, at all times, upon a friend, a former alcoholic, a therapist, or any individual who is willing to love them and help them accept themselves.

■ *The Mercer Family,* 1967, 09 min.
Series: Newfoundland Project
DIR: Colin Low; PROD: John Kemeny; CAM: Robert Humble; ED: Dennis Sawyer
The Mercer family discusses the pressures that force the young people to leave Fogo Island and their families. *See chapters 2, 10, and 32.*

■ *The Merchant and the Teacher,* 1967, 13 min.
Series: Newfoundland Project

DIR: Colin Low; PROD: John Kemeny; CAM: Robert Humble; ED: Dennis Sawyer
A vertical film about the role of merchants on Fogo Island and the feasibility of cooperatives. *See chapters 2, 10, and 32.*

▪ *Montréal – retour aux quartiers*, 1974, 56 min. / See English version, next entry.
Series: Urba 2000
DIR/NARR/ED: Michel Régnier; PROD: Nicole Chamson, Jean-Marc Garand; CAM: Laval Fortier; ED: France Dubé; SOUND: Claude Lefebvre; MUS: Alain Clavier
Along with integrating new, low-rent housing into old neighbourhoods (either on vacant land or as a replacement for slum housing), the city is now restoring older apartments through direct action and government subsidies. *See chapter 22.*

▪ *Montreal – The Neighbourhood Revived* / See original French version, previous entry.

▪ *Mothers Are People*, 1974, 07 min.
Series: Working Mothers
DIR/PROD/ED: Kathleen Shannon; CAM: Robert Nichol; SOUND: Gui Bernardes, Ron Seltzer
Joy is a research biologist, a consultant to a large company. She is also a widow with two school-age children. In discussing her own dilemmas, she speaks for many other women: "The powers that be know that women *do* work, but they turn a deaf ear." Apart from "discrimination against women," Joy sees the absence of universal daycare as a loss for children too. *See chapters 7 and 29.*

▪ *Mrs. Case*, 1969, 14 min.
DIR/ED: Pierre Lasry; PROD: Nicole Hamann, Thérèse Haselsteiner, Barrie Howells, Dan Leithman; CAM: Paul Leach, Jean-Jacques Parent, Richard Todd; SOUND: Jacques Drouin
Mrs Case is a deserted welfare mother who is bringing up her five children alone in a poor Montreal neighbourhood. The film shows the particular problems of a single parent, her involvement in community affairs, and her constant worry over medical and other expenses – plus her cat-and-mouse struggles with her social worker. *See chapter 27 and 32.*
Awards: Certificate of Merit, Conference on Children, Washington (1970); Best Black and White Cinematography given to Paul Leach, Canadian Film Awards (1970)

▪ *The Nearest Point to Everywhere,* 1978, 27 min.
DIR: Roger Hart; PROD: Barrie Howells; NARR: Howard Ryshpan;
SCRIPT: Michael Bryans, Gary Toole; CAM: Andreas Poulsson; ED: Roger
Hart; SOUND: Roger Hunt
Cape Breton Island, rich in coal, has been the scene of the most bitter labour
dispute in Canadian history because the development of its resources has
largely been determined by political and economic forces from outside the
Island. This film illustrates the efforts of the Nova Scotia and federal gov-
ernments, through the Cape Breton Development Corporation (DEVCO), to
stimulate and diversify the economy and to create jobs.

▪ *Nell and Fred,* 1971, 28 min.
DIR/CAM: Richard Todd; PROD: George C. Stoney; ED: Malca Gillson;
SOUND: Michel Hazel
Two charming seniors consider the pros and cons of entering a "home." Do
old-age institutions fit the needs of those they are designed to help?
Awards: Blue Ribbon Award – Category: Social Comment, Itinerant, Amer-
ican Film and Video Festival, New York (1973); Honorable Mention,
National Council on Family Relations, Minneapolis (1972)

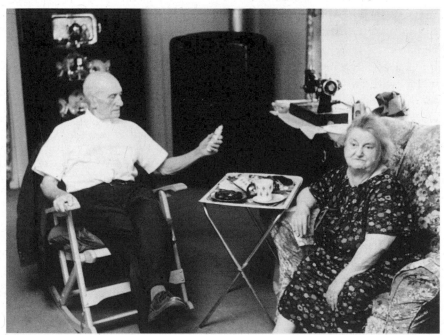

Two Montreal elders at a crossroads in one of CFC's most popular films, the prizewinning
Nell and Fred (1971). Production still.

▪ *The New Alchemists,* 1974, 28 min. / French version, *Alchimie nouvelle*
DIR: Dorothy Todd Hénaut; PROD: Colin Low; NARR: Stanley Jackson;
CAM: Martin Duckworth; ED: Torben Schioler; SOUND: Hughes Mignault;
MUS: Marsha Johnson, Robert Karstens, Joe McIlvine, Mary Lou McIlvine
At a farm in Massachusetts, a small group of people, including some scientists, explore possibilities for more humane, self-sufficient lifestyles involving
interrelated food-producing systems and small-scale solar and wind technology. Their work is a model for others with the vision of a greener, kinder
world and a taste for inventing the future. "Think small," say the New Alchemists. "Look what thinking big has done."

▪ *New York – Twin Parks Project – TV Channel 13* / See original French
version, next entry.

▪ *New York – twin parks project – TV channel 13,* 1974, 56 min. / English
version, *New York – Twin Parks Project – TV Channel 13*
Series: Urba 2000
DIR/NARR/ED: Michel Régnier; PROD: Nicole Chamson, Jean-Marc Garand;
CAM: Laval Fortier; ED: Michel Régnier; SOUND: Claude Lefebvre; MUS:
Alain Clavier
In a city that has become a symbol of urban disaster, two projects indicate
an important reorientation of priorities: in a particularly dilapidated part of
the Bronx, a cooperative citizens movement tries to rejuvenate urban life;
WNET-TV uses its television programming as an open forum for the public de-
bate of urban problems. *See chapter 22.*

▪ *Nishnawbe-Aski: The People and the Land,* 1977, 27 min.
DIR: Phyllis Wilson; PROD: Graeme Ferguson, John N. Smith; CAM:
Graeme Ferguson; ED: Brenda Gibson; SOUND: Phyllis Wilson; COMMU-
NITY PARTNER: Graeme Ferguson Ltd
An exploration of change and how it affects the Cree and Ojibwa of the
Nishnawbe-Aski region. Four of their communities illustrate the different
ways people are reacting to change. *See chapter 5.*

▪ *La noce est pas finie* [The wedding ain't over], 1971, 85 min.
DIR/ED: Léonard Forest; PROD: François Séguillon; CAM: Pierre Boucher;
SOUND: Michel Hazel; MUS: Georges Langford; PARTICIPANTS: Émilienne
Basque, Elphège Chiasson, Alban Duguay, Jean-Louis Gauvin, Georges
Langford, Carmen Le Breton, Raymonde Le Breton, Micheline Losier,
Eddy Mallet, Édouard Robichaud, Gildard Savoie, Patricia Savoie
A citizen-scripted docudrama, unique in the SN catalogue. As imagined and
performed by francophone citizens of Gloucester County, New Brunswick,

an outsider arrives with his guitar and shakes up a rural community. *See chapters 6 and 23.*

▪ *Nos terres, source de vie* / See original English version, *Our Land Is Our Life.*

▪ *Occupation,* 1970, 46 min.
DIR/PROD/ED: Bill Reid; CAM: David De Volpi, Jean-Pierre Lachapelle; ED: Albert Kish, Pierre Lasry; SOUND: Jacques Drouin, Jean-Guy Normandin; MUS: Tex Koenig
Concerned with the democratization of their university, striking political science students occupy the offices of the Political Science Department at McGill University. The issue: greater student control over the hiring of faculty. The film crew lives with the students and follows their action through confusion, argument, dissent, and negotiations with faculty members.

Occupation (1970): McGill politics majors make demands in a rare CFC film about late sixties student activism. Frame enlargement.

▪ *Opération boule de neige,* 1969, 26 min. / English version, VTR *St-Jacques*
DIR: Bonnie Sherr Klein; PROD: George C. Stoney; CAM: Réo Grégoire, Roger Rochat; ED: Ulla Ryghe; SOUND: Richard Besse
An experiment in using videotape recording (VTR) and closed-circuit television to stimulate social action in a poor district of Montreal. A citizens committee, formed in the downtown neighbourhood of St-Jacques, was given a VTR unit, which they used to record people's problems and concerns. After viewing the edited tapes, people recognized their common problems and began to talk of joint solutions. In trying to change what needed changing, they ran into resistance, but the effectiveness of this means of promoting joint action had been tested and proved. *See chapters 3, 21, and 32.*

▪ *Original Sin,* 1973, 04 min.
DIR: Tom Shandel; MUS: Jake Lieberherr
In this rare CFC "musical," a troubadour sings his song called "Original Sin"
while the camera takes in the audience members.

▪ *Our Dear Sisters,* 1975, 14 min.
Series: Working Mothers
DIR/PROD: Kathleen Shannon; CAM: Joan Hutton, Robert Nichol; ED:
Donna Nichol; SOUND: Esther Auger, Ted Haley
At the start of her prolific career as a documentarist, Alanis Obomsawin, an
Abenaki woman, talks about her life, her people, and her responsibilities as
a single parent of an adopted child. *See chapters 7 and 29.*

▪ *Our Health Is Not for Sale,* 1978, 25 min.
DIR: David Newman; DIR/SCRIPT: Boyce Richardson; PROD: Andy
Thomson; NARR: Bronwyn Drainie; CAM: Don Virgo; ED: Ian Rankin;
SOUND: Bev Davidson
In the 1970s workers all over Canada began to realize that instead of leas-
ing their labour, they were selling their health. By recalling some of the more
infamous strikes of the decade, this film examines the plight of workers who
frequently have no right to know what health hazards they are exposed to.

▪ *Our Land Is Our Life,* 1974, 57 min. / French version, *Nos terres, source
de vie*
DIR/CAM: Tony Ianzelo; DIR/SCRIPT: Boyce Richardson; PROD: Colin
Low; NARR: Walter Massey; ED: Ginny Stikeman; SOUND: Richard Besse,
Claude Delorme, Jean Guy Normandin
In March 1974 the Cree people of the Mistassini area in northern Quebec
meet to discuss their long-term future. After 300 years of minimal contact
with Europeans, they have been offered "compensation" by the government
of Quebec for the effects of the James Bay power project. But they decide that
nothing, neither jobs nor money, means more to them than their land. The
film presents the issues under these headings: The Conflict, The Hunting Culture, The Schools, The Villages, and The Fight for the Land. *See chapter 5.*

▪ *Où va la ville? (1ʳᵉ et 2ᵐᵉ parties)* [Where is the city heading? (first and
second parts)], 1972, both parts, 26 min.
Series: Urbanose
DIR/ED: Michel Régnier; PROD: Normand Cloutier; CAM: Pierre Mignot;
SOUND: Serge Beauchemin, Richard Besse; MUS: Alain Clavier
The problems of the entire country can be found in the city. Will Montreal
follow the model of declining American cities with their bedroom suburbs?

Or discover the diverse array of choices that exist? We will have to confront the city's problems head on, and cure, at its roots, its cancer so that we can recreate an entity conducive to humanity's happiness. *See chapter 22.*

▪ *Overspill,* 1970, 28 min.
Series: Swedish-Canadian Co-productions
DIR: Mort Ransen; PROD: Tom Daly, John Kemeny; SCRIPT/ED: Roger Hart; CAM: Martin Duckworth; SOUND: Tommy Bergh
A film about Norrbotten, in northernmost Sweden, where industrial and agricultural patterns have changed and people are being relocated in industrial towns. Interviews with people who have known the dignity of independence and who have suddenly become welfare cases. How can we reconcile human values and economic needs?

▪ *Paper Wheat,* 1979, 57 min.
DIR/ED: Albert Kish; PROD: Adam Symansky; CAM: Barry Perles; CAST: Sharon Bakker, Michael Fahey, David Francis, Lynne Hostein, Skai Leja, Lubomir Mykytiuk, Bill Prokopchuk; SOUND: Claude Delorme
Based on the play of the same name, the film depicts the harsh lives of early Saskatchewan settlers and the foundation of the co-op movement on the Prairies. The 25th Street House Theatre troupe brings to life an era in Canadian history – the development of the West. *See chapter 28.*
Awards: International Film Festival, Hong Kong (1980); Chris Statuette-Category: Business and Industry, International Film and Video Festival, Columbus (1979)

▪ *Penticton Profile,* 1971, 28 min.
DIR: Peter Jones; PROD: George C. Stoney; COMMUNITY PARTNER: Simon Fraser University student project
A colourful look at the rich farming and tourist area in the Okanagan Valley, British Columbia, and at the diverse people who pass through it in the summer.

▪ *People and Power,* 1968, 17 min.
Series: The Alinsky Approach: Organizing for Power
DIR: Peter Pearson, Bonnie Sherr Klein; PROD: Barrie Howells, John Kemeny; CAM: Tony Ianzelo; ED: Roger Hart; SOUND: Hans Oomes
Conflict and controversy are an integral part of Alinsky's approach to organizing communities. Here he talks about his philosophy and the dynamics of organization. *See chapter 21.*

A First Nations film uses drawing and speech rather than live-action documentary cinematography in *Pikangikum* (1967). Production still.

▪ *Pikangikum*, 1967, 09 min.
DIR/ANIM: John Gould; PROD: John Kemeny, Robert Verrall; CAM: Raymond Dumas, Kjeld Nielsen; ED: Kathleen Shannon; SOUND: Hans Oomes
In this film, made originally for theatrical use, the mood of the Pikangikum First Nation Reserve in northern Ontario is evoked through snatches of dialogue and drawings.

▪ *The Point: Community Legal Clinic,* 1972, 28 min. / French version, *Citoyen nouveau: Services juridiques communautaires,* 1972, 27 min.
DIR: Grant Kennedy; PROD: Roger Hart; CAM: Jean-Pierre Lachapelle, Pierre Letarte, Pierre Mignot; ED: Peter Raymont; SOUND: Jacques Drouin, Bill Fowler
Citizens of Point St Charles, a bilingual working-class district in Montreal's inner city, found a solution to the lack of adequate legal aid in their community by forming a legal clinic with salaried lawyers and student volunteers from university law faculties. Citizens and volunteers talk about the project, how it was initiated, and how it now serves residents' needs.

▪ *PowWow at Duck Lake,* 1967, 14 min.
PROD: David Hughes; CAM: Douglas Kiefer, D'Arcy Marsh; ED: Kathleen Shannon; SOUND: Hans Oomes
A discussion at Duck Lake, Saskatchewan, of First Nations and Métis problems, before a gathering of Aboriginals and whites. Among matters discussed are the kind of schooling available to individuals of First Nations and the limitations of education that restrict their opportunities to develop in ways best

for themselves. As the residential school era comes to a close, an eloquent glimpse.

▪ *The Prince Edward Island Development Plan, Part 1: Days in September,* 1969, 61 min.
DIR/ED: Roger Hart; PROD: Barrie Howells, George C. Stoney; CAM: David De Volpi, Jean-Pierre Lachapelle; SOUND: Jean-Guy Normandin
The first of two films dealing with the comprehensive social and economic development plan for Prince Edward Island. In essence the films are a study of the dynamics of the plan, the relationships and communication between the planners and the planned-for, and between the planners and the governments involved. This first film shows the events, over a ten-day period, that led up to the plan.

▪ *The Prince Edward Island Development Plan, Part 2: Days in March,* 1969, 51 min.
DIR/ED: Roger Hart; PROD: Barrie Howells, George C. Stoney; CAM: David De Volpi, Jean-Pierre Lachapelle; SOUND: Jean-Guy Normandin
Filmed six months later, this second part is a four-day follow-up that occurs at the time of the signing of the development plan. This is democracy in action, a laborious though persistent process.

▪ *Priory, the Only Home I've Got,* 1978, 28 min.
DIR: Mark Dolgoy; PROD: Tony Karch, Anne Wheeler; CAM: Doug McKay; ED: Christopher Tate; SOUND: Ralph Parker; MUS: Geoff Venables
The Priory is a public extended-care hospital in Victoria, British Columbia, for people suffering from chronic geriatric illnesses. Treatment is innovative, based on the theory that even the ordinary activities of a patient's life contain elements of therapy. Patients are encouraged to do as much as they can for themselves despite their confinement to wheelchairs.
Awards: Red Ribbon Award, Itinerant, American Film and Video Festival, New York (1980); Genie Award for Best Documentary under 30 Minutes, Genie Awards (1980)

▪ *Promises, Promises ... ,* 1973, 29 min.
DIR: Reevan Dolgoy; PROD: Roger Hart; CAM: Mark Dolgoy; ED: Anne Wheeler; SOUND: Allan Stein
The problems and the potential of small towns in Alberta's Drumheller Valley. Citizen participation is generated in the region by the Task Force on Urbanization and the Future, but lessons are learned when the task force is curtailed.

Confronting urban renewal: citizens committee leader Noel Daudelin
(foreground, white helmet) and Montreal Mayor Jean Drapeau (upper right)
meet the media and police in a soon-to-be demolished *P'tite Bourgogne*
(1968). With camera, Michel Régnier, CFC/SN's most prolific director.
Production still.

■ *La p'tite-Bourgogne,* 1968, 43 min. / English version, *Little Burgundy*
DIR/ED: Maurice Bulbulian; DIR: [Bonnie Sherr Klein]; PROD: Robert
Forget; NARR: J. Keable; CAM: Claude Larue, Michel Régnier; ANIM:
Clorinda Warny; ED: Jacques Gagné; SOUND: Michel Hazel; COMMUNITY
PARTNER: Comité des Îlots Saint-Martin
The context is Expo '67 "urban renewal" mania, and a vibrant, bilingual,
and multi-racial working-class neighbourhood is being demolished to make
way for a new low-rental housing development. What can residents do to
protect their own interests? This film reveals such a situation in the Little
Burgundy district of Montreal. The citizens committee makes effective representations to City Hall, but the ending is bittersweet. *See chapter 18.*

■ *La p'tite violence* [Small violence], 1977, 71 min.
DIR/ED: Hélène Girard; PROD: Anne Claire Poirier; CAM: Pierre Mignot;

CAST: Jean-Claude Couture, Albert Dumas, Brigitte Dumas, Jean-Marc Dumas, Gilbert Sicotte; SOUND: Richard Besse

Through meetings with workers of diverse occupations and professions, this film essay, going beyond standard statistics and analyses, displays the role of work in human development. An obtained right, a social necessity, or a cause of alienation, what is the true range of choice that work offers to human beings?

▪ *Québec à vendre* [Quebec for sale], 1977, 58 min.
DIR/SCRIPT: Raymond Garceau; PROD: Anne Claire Poirier; CAM: André-Luc Dupont; ANIM: Yvon Mallette; ED: Jacques Jarry; SOUND: Joseph Champagne, Yves Gendron; MUS: Alain Clavier

The crisis in the organization and management of arable land faced by Québécois society at large. Can the survival and development of agriculture in Quebec be assured by public policy?

▪ *Qu'est-ce qu'on va devenir?* [What will become of us?], 1971, 40 min.
DIR/ED: Michel Gauthier; PROD: Normand Cloutier; CAM: Claude Larue; ED: Raymonde Pilon; SOUND: Richard Besse; MUS: Robert Charlebois

Crisis in Quebec's down-river tourist centre of Baie Saint-Paul. The ground is no longer profitable. The sea is polluted. The young are leaving and the adults remain unemployed. However, life continues: a cooperative of craftsmen, a summer festival ... What future awaits these resilient individuals who, refusing to exile themselves to the cities, have resolved to remain in similar environments because they love to live there?

▪ *The Question of Television Violence*, 1972, 56 min.
DIR: Graeme Ferguson; PROD: Colin Low; NARR/SCRIPT: Patrick Watson; CAM: Don Virgo; ED: Malca Gillson; SOUND: Bill Fowler

A report on the hearings of the United States Senate Subcommittee on Communications investigating the effects of television violence. Four days of intensive debate in Washington, recorded by the NFB, establish that there is a correlation between violence on the screen and violence in real life.
Awards: Chris Statuette-Category: Documentary, International Film and Video Festival, Columbus (1973)

▪ *Raison d'être* [A reason for living], 1977, 78 min.
DIR/ED: Yves Dion; PROD: Anne Claire Poirier, Robert Forget; CAM: André-Luc Dupont; SOUND: Yves Gendron

Two individuals, diagnosed with cancer, have accepted to live their last months in front of a camera. For Micheline, it is a positive experience: she lives her death as if an adventure. For François, it is negative: how does he

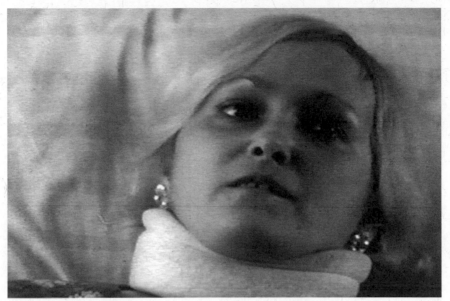

Micheline living her death from cancer as an adventure in *Raison d'être* (1977).
Frame enlargement.

make his real needs understood by a society that perceives death as a taboo? In the face of death, individuals need to live life to the fullest and find a reason for their existence. A philosophical work by a young auteur who emerged towards the end of the SN period.

Awards: Grand Prize Festival international du film documentaire et de Court Métrage, Lille (1977); Silver Sesterce, Visions du Réel / Festival international du cinéma documentaire, Nyon (1977)

▪ *Regina Telebus*, 1973, 19 min.
Series: Urban Transportation
DIR: Rex Tasker; CAM: Douglas Kiefer; ED: Rex Tasker; SOUND: Hans Oomes
A report on Regina's successful experiment with dial-a-bus, a flexible service, midway between bus and taxi, that provides passengers with front-door-to-destination transportation.

▪ *Réhabilitation des habitations* [Restoring homes], 1972, 26 min.
Series: Urbanose
DIR/ED: Michel Régnier; PROD: Normand Cloutier; CAM: Pierre Mignot; SOUND: Serge Beauchemin, Richard Besse; MUS: Alain Clavier
Instead of destroying an existing city in order to make room for "newly

polished slums," a new practice gives new life to old houses, renewing irre-
placeable assets such as their foundations, their architecture, and their environment. The restoration of housing takes different forms in places such as
Montreal, London, and Boston, but everywhere the resultant quality of life
is preferable to wide-scale demolition. *See chapter 22.*

▪ *Rénovation urbaine* [Urban renewal], 1972, 26 min.
Series: Urbanose
DIR/ED: Michel Régnier; PROD: Normand Cloutier; CAM: Pierre Mignot;
SOUND: Serge Beauchemin, Richard Besse; MUS: Alain Clavier
Urban renewal, a notion presently under attack due to various urban catas-
trophes and shared frustrations, usually means the demolition of housing
and the displacement of populations, all in the name of the sacrosanct imperatives of development and commerce. However, civilians are now waking
up and increasingly demanding to be consulted about the "progress" that
affects them. *See chapter 22.*

▪ *La revanche* [Revenge], 1974, 22 min.
DIR/ED: Maurice Bulbulian; CAM: Guy Desbiens; ED: Yves Dion; SOUND:
Jean-Guy Normandin; MUS: Philippe Gagnon, Dominique Tremblay
Popular revolt in the forest regions of Quebec. Exhausted by their exploitation, workers declare the end of bosses, foreign owners, and governments
for sale. In Cabano and Maniwaki, among other locations, they demand
joint management and workers' control. The ending borrows a plaintive note
from Félix-Antoine Savard's novel *Menaud, maître-draveur* (1937). *See chap-*
ter 18.

Angry forestry workers
in *La revanche* (1974).
Frame enlargement.

▪ *Les rives* [Riverbanks], 1972, 26 min.
Series: Urbanose
DIR/ED: Michel Régnier; PROD: Normand Cloutier; CAM: Pierre Mignot;
SOUND: Serge Beauchemin, Richard Besse; MUS: Alain Clavier
Montreal, constructed on water, does not have access to water: the boundaries of the water are private. When it is not the exclusive privilege of the few,
water serves to lubricate the wheels of commerce and industry. However,
water should serve everyone, as in Switzerland where all shorelines are public. *See chapter 22.*

▪ *Robert Sass: Workers in Saskatchewan,* 1978, 09 min.
Series: Occupational Health and Safety
DIR/SCRIPT: Boyce Richardson; PROD: Andy Thomson; CAM: Don Virgo;
ED: Mike Goddard; SOUND: Bev Davidson
Saskatchewan is a leader in legislation for a cleaner workplace. Robert Sass,
director of the Provincial Occupational Health and Safety Division, describes
how workers must depend on their own efforts, and not on those of "experts," to clean up the workplace. He feels that unions have been too concerned about "time away from work, not time at work."

▪ *Rose's House,* 1977, 57 min.
DIR/ED: Clay Borris; SCRIPT: Paulette Jiles; CAM: John F. Phillips; CAST:
Albert Borris, Garry Borris, John Brown, Edmond Charest, Paulette Jiles,
Magella Joseph, Ronald Maltais, Rose Maltais-Borris, George Martell;
SOUND: John F. Phillips, Chris Terry, Arla Saare; MUS: Willie Dunn
Based on the young filmmaker's memories of his mother's boarding house in
gritty Cabbagetown, Toronto, this rare CFC docudrama revolves around
Rose and how she runs her establishment. In her countercultural household,
the marginal mix with the straight and Rose hands out her own brand of
justice for bootlegging, violence, and stealing. For all the scripting and performance, Rose has a very-CFC-like run-in with a social worker. *See chapter 26.*

▪ *'Round and 'Round,* 1978, 57 min.
DIR: Barbara Greene; PROD: Tom Daly; CAM: Douglas Kiefer; ED: Ginny
Stikeman; SOUND: Joseph Champagne
When Alex Lawson, minister, came to Moose Jaw, Saskatchewan, he recognized the need for a family self-help program. In cooperation with his
parishioners, he organized the Minto Family Life Education Program.
Through group meetings, they are learning new skills to help them restruc-
ture their lives and resolve personal problems. While the people participating in this program live in a small Prairie town, their concerns are universal

and include issues like raising children, adolescence, loneliness, marital strife, and alcoholism.

▪ *Sapporo – croissance planifiée,* 1974, 56 min. / English version, *Sapporo – Planned Growth*
Series: Urba 2000
DIR/NARR/ED: Michel Régnier; PROD: Nicole Chamson, Jean-Marc Garand; CAM: Laval Fortier; ED: France Dubé; SOUND: Claude Lefebvre; MUS: Alain Clavier
In contrast to the unplanned sprawl of industrialized cities in southern Japan, Sapporo, on the Island of Hokkaïdo, today appears to be one of the best-planned large cities in the world, combining growth and technology with town planning and the preservation of green spaces. *See chapter 22.*

▪ *Sapporo – Planned Growth* / See original French version, previous entry.

▪ *Saskatoon – la mesure,* 1974, 56 min. / English version, *Saskatoon: Land and Growth Control*
Series: Urba 2000
DIR/NARR/ED: Michel Régnier; PROD: Nicole Chamson, Jean-Marc Garand; CAM: Laval Fortier; SOUND: Claude Lefebvre; MUS: Alain Clavier
In the city of Saskatoon, an effective government policy of controlling land investment prevents speculation, keeps land prices down, and provides a good balance between commercial, residential, and public areas. *See chapter 22.*

▪ *Saskatoon: Land and Growth Control* / See original French version, previous entry.

▪ *Saul Alinsky Went to War,* 1968, 57 min.
Series: NFB Presents
DIR: Donald Brittain, Peter Pearson; PROD: Barrie Howells, John Kemeny; CAM: Tony Ianzelo; ED: Edward Le Lorrain; SOUND: Hans Oomes
Saul Alinsky, controversial community organizer, goes to war against the conditions that keep the poor poor. The film shows how he helped people in the black ghettos in the United States find an effective, non-violent method of fighting for their rights. *See chapter 21.*
Awards: Chris Award, International Film and Video Festival, Columbus (1970); Hans Oomes, Best Sound Recording, Canadian Film Awards (1969)

▪ *Schumacher: Une société à la mesure de l'homme* / See original English version, next entry.

▪ *Small Is Beautiful: Impressions of Fritz Schumacher,* 1978, 29 min. /
French version, *Schumacher: Une société à la mesure de l'homme*
DIR/PROD/NARR/SCRIPT: Donald Brittain; DIR/PROD/ED: Barrie Howells;
DIR/PROD/CAM: Douglas Kiefer; SOUND: Fraser MacAninch; MUS: Brian
MacLeod, Yehudi Menuhin, Yehudi Menuhin Youth Orchestra
Up to age forty-five, Fritz Schumacher, economist, technologist, and lecturer,
was dedicated to economic growth. Then he came to believe that the mod-
ern technological explosion had grown out of all proportion to human need.
Author of *Small Is Beautiful: A Study of Economics as If People Mattered*
and founder of the London-based Intermediate Technology Development
Group, he championed the cause of "appropriate" technology.

▪ *Un soleil pas comme ailleurs,* 1972, 47 min. / English version, *A Sun like
Nowhere Else*
DIR/ED: Léonard Forest; PROD: Jean-Marc Garand; CAM: Benoît Rivard;
SOUND: Jean-Guy Normandin, Ron Seltzer; SONG: Marie-Reine Chiasson,
Calixte Duguay; PARTICIPANTS: Rose-Hélène Aubé, Mathilda Blanchard,
André Boudreau, Aristide Chiasson, André Dumont, Arthur Landry,
Rodrigue Pelletier, Fernand Savoie, Yvon Sirois
In this film, Acadians speak for themselves – about their feelings towards
governments wanting to relocate and urbanize them, about present-day
"tragedies" in their communities, and about their hopes for a productive
future. *See chapters 6 and 23.*

▪ *Le sol urbain* [Urban land], 1972, 26 min.
Series: Urbanose
DIR/ED: Michel Régnier; PROD: Normand Cloutier; CAM: Pierre Mignot;
SOUND: Serge Beauchemin, Richard Besse; MUS: Alain Clavier
American cities destroy themselves as many, if not more, times than they are
constructed. There are more vacant areas at the centre of Montreal in 1972
than in 1950 and it is not even a time of war! Questions concerning the private control of land and speculation begin to arise. Is urban planning really
possible in a capitalist country? In the Netherlands, the word "speculation"
is banned, but it is not the same in Montreal. *See chapter 22.*

▪ *Some People Have to Suffer,* 1976, 42 min.
DIR/PROD/VID: Christopher Pinney; NARR: Boyce Richardson; CAM: Doug
McKay, Ron Orieux, Tony Westman; VID: Laval Fortier; ED: David Wilson;
SOUND: Ralph Parker, Richard Patton, Larry Sutton
A community's struggle to survive in the face of government indifference and
the political and financial clout of industrial developers. In 1953 the resi-
dents of Bridgeview, British Columbia, were promised sewers; after years of

debate, frustration, meetings, and verbiage, construction started in 1977. The residents state their opinions frankly both to the camera and at meetings. When the film was shown at the Habitat conference in Vancouver, 1976, press coverage noted: "The Third World is merely twenty miles from the site of Habitat."

▪ *Some Problems of Fogo,* 1967, 21 min.
Series: Newfoundland Project
DIR: Colin Low; PROD: John Kemeny; CAM: Robert Humble; ED: Dennis Sawyer
Some of the problems discussed concern the fishermen's unions, the fish plant, able-bodied men on welfare, education, and the consolidation of schools. *See chapters 2, 10, and 32.*

▪ *The Songs of Chris Cobb,* 1967, 07 min.
Series: Newfoundland Project
DIR: Colin Low; PROD: John Kemeny; CAM: Robert Humble; ED: Dennis Sawyer
Fogo Islander Chris Cobb sings his own songs and recites his poems about the old days and the recent changes in Fogo. *See chapters 2, 10, and 32.*

▪ *Souris, tu m'inquiètes* [Smile, you are worrying me], 1973, 56 min.
Series: En tant que femmes
DIR/SCRIPT: Aimée Danis; PROD: Nicole Chamson, Anne Claire Poirier, Jean-Marc Garand; CAM: Daniel Fournier; CAST: Louis Aubert, Luc Durand, Antoine Gélinas, Geneviève Gélinas, Philippe Gélinas, Luce Guilbeault, Micheline Lanctôt, Yves Létourneau, Bonfield Marcoux, Olivette Thibault; ED: Claire Boyer; SOUND: Jean-Guy Normandin; MUS: Pierre F. Brault
This film looks at the loss of self experienced by women who live only to support their husband and children. Facing an "unnamed sickness" that affects her, Francine, played by Lanctôt in her second starring role, is compelled to leave her husband and children in order to discover who she is. This film, interweaving dramatized scenes and non-fiction material, ultimately reveals a middle-class Québécois woman's unique experience. *See chapter 12.*

▪ *The Specialists at Memorial Discuss the Fogo Films,* 1969, 26 min.
PROD: George C. Stoney; COMMUNITY PARTNER: Memorial University of Newfoundland
As a follow-up to the 1968 Newfoundland Project, a group of sociologists, economists, educators, political scientists, and fieldworkers from Memorial

Determined to stay, resourceful Fogo Islanders have restored a boat in *The Story of the Up Top* (1967). Frame enlargement.

University and the Newfoundland government discuss and evaluate the films made on Fogo Island. *See chapters 2, 10, and 35.*

▪ *The Spring and Fall of Nina Polanski,* 1974, 05 min.
Series: Working Mothers
DIR: Joan Hutton; DIR/ANIM: Louise Roy; PROD/MUS: Kathleen Shannon
In this rare CFC animated film, Everywoman Nina marries amidst much fanfare and photo-snapping, and settles into a domestic routine of cooking, washing dishes, ironing, and babies. Eventually she becomes the very machines she uses every day, until one day she walks into the woods and takes back her old self. *See chapters 7 and 29.*

▪ *The Story of the Up Top,* 1967, 08 min.
Series: Newfoundland Project
DIR: Colin Low; PROD: John Kemeny; CAM: Robert Humble; ED: Dennis Sawyer
The story of how one Fogo Island family managed to raise an old passenger boat from where it had been sitting for four years and renovate it for use as a fishing boat, despite a lack of capital and government aid. *See chapters 2, 10, and 32.*

Les taudis (1972): Montreal "slums" in one of Régnier's twenty-five documentaries on the ailing contemporary city. Frame enlargement.

■ *A Sun like Nowhere Else* / See original French version, *Un soleil pas comme ailleurs.*

■ *The Superior Scrapbook,* 1970, 20 min.
DIR/PROD: Jim Farrell, Bill Lemmon, Donna Mikeluk, Ron Spence; MUS: Bill Houston
Made by students of the Thunder Bay Community Film/VTR project, this film records the social history of the Lakehead from 1880 to 1913 through the use of old photographs.

■ *Sur vivre,* 1971, 57 min. / English version, *"There Are Others Worse Off Than Us ..."*
DIR/ED: Yves Dion; PROD: Normand Cloutier; CAM: Roger Rochat; SOUND: John Yanick
This is a look at the daily life of a young couple. Both wife and husband suffer from cerebral palsy. Although every day is a struggle, they are fed up with consoling discourses of science and charity, and choose to marry, to have a child, and to derive strength and courage from each other. An early treatment of the politics of disability and a challenge to the middle-class takeover of the mind. (The title is a pun meaning both "survival" and "living.")
Awards: Grand Prize-Gold Sesterce, and Award of the International Federa-

tion of Cine-clubs, Visions du réel / Festival international du cinéma documentaire, Nyon, Switzerland (1972)

■ *Les taudis* [Slums], 1972, 26 min.
Series: Urbanose
DIR/ED: Michel Régnier; PROD: Normand Cloutier; CAM: Pierre Mignot;
SOUND: Serge Beauchemin, Richard Besse; MUS: Alain Clavier
An essay film on slums, a spectacular urban cancer, probes a system where housing is not an essential human right but rather a commodity. Facilitated by shameless speculation, slums impact on hygiene, unemployment, criminality, self-esteem, and political enfranchisement. *See chapter 22.*

■ *Temiscaming, Québec,* 1975, 64 min. / French version, *Témiscamingue, Québec,* 1977, 64 min. DIR/ED/CAM: Martin Duckworth; PROD: Len Chatwin, Dorothy Todd Hénaut; NARR: Michel Garneau; CAM: Serge Giguère; ED: Michael Rubbo, Gérard Sénécal, Virginia Stikeman; SOUND: Benoît Fauteux, Hughes Mignault; MUS: Bob Robb
The story of a town's struggle to survive after its main source of employment, the CIP mill, was closed down by its U.S. owner. Part I tells what steps the workers, townspeople, and ex-CIP managers took to reopen a mill co-owned and co-managed by the workers; Part II explains the new corporate ownership of the mill, how it works, and its growing pains. This is a film about ownership of the Canadian economy and industrial democracy.

Workers take over the abandoned pulp mill in *Temiscaming, Québec* (1975). Production still.

▪ *Témiscamingue, Québec,* 1977, 64 min. / See original English version, previous entry.

▪ *Le temps de l'avant* 1975, 87 min. / English version, *Before the Time Comes*
Series: En tant que femmes
DIR/PROD/SCRIPT: Anne Claire Poirier; SCRIPT: Marthe Blackburn, Louise Carré; CAM: Michel Brault; CAST: Angèle Arsenault, Paule Baillargeon, Nicolas Dufresne, J.-Léo Gagnon, Roger Garceau, Paul Gauthier, Pierre Gobeil, Luce Guilbeault, Manon Jolicoeur, Jean-Pierre Légaré, Jean Mathieu, Viviane Neya, Catherine Potvin, Marisol Sarrazin; ED: Jacques Gagné; SOUND: Joseph Champagne; MUS: Maurice Blackburn; SONG: Angèle Arsenault
One of the first Canadian films on reproductive rights, this docudrama examines the question of contraception and abortion through the story of a woman, happily married, with three children, who, with her husband, must make the agonizing decision of whether to give life. *See chapter 12.*
Awards: Conseil national des femmes belges, International Festival of Women's Films, Brussels (1977)

▪ *That Gang of Hoodlums?* 1972, 29 min.
DIR: Robert Nichol; PRODUCTION TEAM: Ken Colby, Bev Davidson, André Galbrand, Ted Haley, Roger Lamoureux, Pierre Letarte, Robert Nichol, Barry Perles, Kathleen Shannon, Ginny Stikeman, Richard Todd, Rudy Wolf
Two kinds of protest demonstrations. Filmed during the 1971 federal-provincial welfare ministers' conference in Ottawa, the film shows militant and non-militant protests and the degree of government response to each. The title is from a comment by one of the protesters about the people who run things on Parliament Hill.

▪ *"There Are Others Worse Off Than Us ... ,"* 1972, 57 min. / See original French version, *Sur vivre.*

▪ *These Are My People ... ,* 1969, 13 min.
DIR/CAM/SOUND: Roy Daniels, Willie Dunn, Michael Mitchell, Barbara Wilson; PROD: George C. Stoney; ED: Noel Starblanket
Made by the Indian Film Crew, training under the CFC program, this film was shot at Akwesasne. Two spokespeople explain historical and other interwoven aspects of Longhouse religion, culture, and government. They reflect on the impact of the European's arrival on the Aboriginal way of life and on what the future may bring. *See chapter 5.*

▪ *They Appreciate You More,* 1974, 14 min.
Series: Working Mothers
DIR/PROD/ED: Kathleen Shannon; CAM: Robert Nichol; SOUND: Gui
Bernardes, Ron Seltzer
Aliette lives in Montreal with her husband and three children. Since both
Aliette and Pierre work outside their home full-time, they share household re-
sponsibilities. This development has changed them as individuals and, they
think, has affected the dynamics of their family – for the better. *See chapters
7 and 29.*

▪ *They Called Us 'Les Filles du Roy,'* 1967, 55 min. / See original French
version, *Les filles du Roy.*

▪ *The Things I Cannot Change,* 1967, 55 min.
DIR: Tanya Ballantyne Tree; PROD: John Kemeny; CAM: Paul Leach;
ED: William Brind; SOUND: Roger Hart
Considered to be the forerunner of the NFB's Challenge for Change program,
this observational film is a look at a Montreal anglophone family in trouble.
There is the trouble with the police, the begging for stale bread at the con-
vent, the birth of another child, and the father who explains his family's
predicament. An anatomy of poverty as it occurs in North America is seen
by a camera that became part of the family's life for several weeks. A sequel
to this film was made in 1986, under the title *Courage to Change,* showing
what happened to the Bailey family eighteen years later. *See chapters 14, 33,
and 35.*
Awards: Certificate of Merit, Conference on Children, Washington (1970);
Diploma, International Short Film Festival, Oberhausen (1968); Golden Gate
Award for Excellence in Network Presentation, International Film Festival,
San Francisco (1967); Special Mention-Category: Medium-Length Films,
Festival of Canadian Films – Montreal International Film Festival (1967)

▪ *Thoughts on Fogo and Norway,* 1967, 16 min.
Series: Newfoundland Project
DIR: Colin Low; PROD: John Kemeny; CAM: Robert Humble; ED: Dennis
Sawyer
A discussion on the methods of fishing, marketing, organization, and welfare
in Norway, with reference to the situation on Fogo Island. *See chapters 2, 10,
and 32.*

▪ *Through Conflict to Negotiation,* 1968, 45 min.
Series: The Alinsky Approach: Organizing for Power
DIR: Peter Pearson, Bonnie Sherr Klein; PROD: Barrie Howells, John Kemeny;

American role model for Canadian community organizers: Alinsky and Rochester, New York, activist in *Through Conflict to Negotiation* (1968). Frame enlargement.

CAM: Tony Ianzelo; ED: Roger Hart; SOUND: Hans Oomes
A community action group in Rochester, New York, confronts the community's largest employer on the issue of corporate responsibility and the employment of minority groups. *See chapter 21.*

▪ *Tiger on a Tight Leash,* 1974, 07 min.
Series: Working Mothers
DIR/PROD/ED: Kathleen Shannon; CAM: Robert Nichol; ED: Kathleen Shannon; SOUND: Ron Seltzer
Cathy, mother of three, is a university department head in a Maritime city. She speaks of the insecurity she experiences because of unpredictable daycare arrangements and of the reflection of the same difficulty in the work of her married students. "They don't work as creatively as they could." *See chapters 7 and 29.*

▪ *Tignish Cooperatives,* 1969, 27 min.
PROD: George C. Stoney; COMMUNITY PARTNER: Memorial University of Newfoundland
An investigation of the producer and consumer cooperatives and the credit union of the people of Tignish, Prince Edward Island, and what these entities have done to improve their living conditions.

▪ *Tom Best on Cooperatives,* 1967, 12 min.
Series: Newfoundland Project
DIR: Colin Low; PROD: John Kemeny; CAM: Robert Humble; ED: Dennis Sawyer
A discussion of the problems and efficacy of a fishermen's cooperative. *See chapters 2, 10, and 32.*

▪ *Tout le temps, tout le temps, tout le temps … ?* [All the time, all the time, all the time … ?], 1969, 115 min.
DIR: Fernand Dansereau; PROD: Robert Forget; CAM: Gilles Gascon;
CAST: Raoul Béliveau, Lionel Blanchet, Francine Boivin, Denyse Chagnon, Polydor Chagnon, Serge Clément, Jeanne Dupuis, Jeanne Joly, Lionel Joly, Ghislaine Lemieux, O'Neil Lemire, Diane Séguin, Yvonne Tremblay; ED: Raymonde Pilon; SOUND: Michel Hazel; MUS: Robert Charlebois, Le Jazz libre du Québec
A Québécois extended family reunites in the country at Sainte-Théodosie, underneath the roof of Raoul Béliveau, where its members discuss the importance of love, a deeply satisfying life, the need for liberty, and society's imperfections. This film was produced with the collaboration of thirteen citizens from Montreal's east end.

▪ *Travelling College,* 1968, 09 min.
PARTICIPANT: Ernest Benedict
Produced by the Indian Film Crew for exhibition to First Nations audiences across North America, this film demonstrates the concept of self-help of the Travelling College, an educational venture designed to teach students what they want to know, be it business knowledge, handicrafts, or marketing.

▪ *Two Cabinet Ministers,* 1967, 18 min.
Series: Newfoundland Project
DIR: Colin Low; PROD: John Kemeny; CAM: Robert Humble; ED: Dennis Sawyer
A discussion between Eric Jones, MPP for Fogo Island, and John Crosbie, minister of municipal affairs and housing, on the role of the Fogo Island Improvement Committee and the feasibility of supra-island government. *See chapters 2, 10, and 32.*

▪ *Two Union Leaders Talk about Workers and Health,* 1978, 09 min.
Series: Occupational Health and Safety
DIR/SCRIPT: Boyce Richardson; PROD: Andy Thomson; CAM: Don Virgo; ED: Mike Goddard; SOUND: Bev Davidson

Jim Fill, director of legislation and community affairs of the United Auto Workers in Canada, and Dave Patterson, president of local 6500 of the United Steelworkers of America in Sudbury, Ontario, describe briefly how workers are trying to get more control over conditions in their places of work. Patterson says that the worker used to have only two rights: the right to disease and the right to death. In two provinces, workers now have the legal right to refuse a job they consider hazardous.

▪ *Unemployment: Voices from the Line,* 1980, 53 min.
DIR/ED/SCRIPT: Pierre Lasry; PROD/SCRIPT: Mark Zannis; NARR: Stanley Jackson; CAM: Barry Perles; SOUND: Jacques Chevigny, Michel Hazel, Jean Pierre Lefebvre
A reflection on the effects of unemployment on people and their families – not solely economic. It exposes the harsh realities of unemployment and graphically depicts situations that contradict the notion that unemployment insurance takes care of the problems experienced by the jobless. The film illustrates that most unemployed persons prefer to work and that the real cost of unemployment is human suffering.

▪ *Up against the System,* 1969, 19 min.
DIR/CAM: Terence Macartney-Filgate; PROD: George C. Stoney; SOUND: Russ Heise
People on welfare are rarely heard. What do they go through? How do they feel? How do concerned social and welfare workers feel about the welfare system? What is welfare supposed to do? In this film, welfare recipients and social case workers talk about the problems of being "up against the system." *See chapters 15, 30, and 32.*
Awards: Exceptional Merit, International Festival of Short Films, Philadelphia (1971)

▪ *Urbain and Arthur Leblanc on Cooperatives,* 1969, 29 min.
PROD: George C. Stoney; COMMUNITY PARTNER: Memorial University of Newfoundland
Set in Prince Edward Island, a one-time cooperative worker and a member of the United Maritime Fishermen talk about why co-ops succeed and fail.

▪ *Varsovie – Québec – comment ne pas détruire une ville,* 1974, 56 min. / English version, *Warsaw – Québec: How Not to Destroy a City*
Series: Urba 2000
DIR/NARR/ED: Michel Régnier; PROD: Nicole Chamson, Jean-Marc Garand; CAM: Laval Fortier; ED: France Dubé; SOUND: Claude Lefebvre; MUS: Alain Clavier; PARTICIPANTS: Fernand Caron, Bernard Cleary,

Andrzej Cosma, Ewa Garber, Vianney Guindon, Jacek Jedynak, Zbigniew Filipow, Boleslaw Malisz, Claude Paulette, Andrzej Rajgrodzki, Halina Skibniewska, Zygmunt Skibniewski, Val Tessier, Hanna Welecka, Stanislaw Wyganowski, Jan Zachwatowicz
Is it possible to provide the amenities required by modern life without destroying the socio-cultural heritage of past generations? In this film, two historically preserved cities present contrasting examples of contemporary growth. *See chapter 22.*

▪ *Vous êtes en terre indienne* / See original English version, *You Are on Indian Land.*

▪ *Les vrais perdants* [The real losers], 1978, 93 min.
DIR: André Melançon; PROD: Jacques Gagné; CAM: Pierre Mignot; ED: Josée Beaudet; SOUND: Claude Beaugrand, Richard Besse
Problems in children's education and upbringing within our competitive society. While they are helping their children to develop their talents, whether they are linked to hockey, gymnastics, or music, are parents or trainers consciously seeking to project their dreams and their need for competition upon their children? This film listens to children on this important subject.

Kids being initiated into the competitive adult world in *Les vrais perdants* (1978). Production still.

▪ VTR *Rosedale,* 1974, 31 min.
PROD: Len Chatwin
Rosedale, once referred to as "the rear end of Alberta" by one of its frustrated citizens, pulled itself together as a community. It formed a citizens action committee, cleaned up the town, built a park, and negotiated with the government to install gas, water, and sewage systems. It all happened within five months. The catalyst of this development process was the use of VTR equipment by the citizens themselves. *See chapters 20 and 33.*

▪ VTR *St-Jacques* / See original French version, *Opération boule de neige.*

▪ *The Wages of Work,* 1978, 27 min.
DIR/SCRIPT/ED: David Wilson; PROD: Adam Symansky; CAM: Savas Kalogeras, Barry Perles; SOUND: Joseph Champagne, Claude Hazanavicius, Michel Hazel
Three working-class families on limited incomes discuss how they cope with the high cost of living. As it turns out, the figures quoted by Statistics Canada as being adequate for a family to maintain a decent standard of living fall short of reality. These families must resort to food and housing co-ops, extra jobs, overtime, and clothing exchanges to make ends meet.

▪ *Warsaw – Québec: How Not to Destroy a City* / See original French version, *Varsovie – Québec: comment ne pas détruire une ville.*

▪ *A Wedding and Party,* 1967, 10 min.
Series: Newfoundland Project
DIR: Colin Low; PROD: John Kemeny; CAM: Robert Humble; ED: Dennis Sawyer
Two Fogo Island festivities: a Roman Catholic wedding in Joe Batts Arm South and a party with music and dancing in Joe Batts Arm North. *See chapters 2, 10, and 32.*

▪ *"When I Go … That's It!"* 1972, 11 min.
DIR/PROD: Ron Alexander, Colin Low, Dennis Sawyer, George C. Stoney; COMMUNITY PARTNER: Memorial University of Newfoundland
Ex-fisherman Billy Crane in Brampton, Ontario, at an industrial job with regular hours. Here, he tells why he left Fogo Island and says he has no regrets.

▪ *Where Do We Go from Here?* 1973, 22 min.
Series: Urban Transportation
DIR/SCRIPT: James Carney; PROD: Rex Tasker; CAM: Douglas Kiefer,

Michel Thomas-d'Hoste; ED: Ginny Stikeman; SOUND: Richard Besse
Toronto as a case study in the mechanics of urban transportation, but also
of underlying political and economic tensions.

▪ *Who Will I Sentence Now?* 1978, 28 min.
DIR/SCRIPT: David Newman, Boyce Richardson; PROD: Andy Thomson;
CAM: Don Virgo; ED: Ian Rankin; SOUND: Bev Davidson
A grim document about workplace diseases. The film takes us to Sudbury,
Thetford Mines, Elliot Lake, and St. Lawrence, Newfoundland, and shows
workers, widows, doctors, and a union leader throwing light on a social
problem that is only now beginning to emerge from the carefully preserved
obscurity of the modern industrial workplace.
Awards: Second Prize – Category: Prevention/General, World Congress of
Rehabilitation International Film Festival, Winnipeg (1980)

▪ *Wilf,* 1968, 20 min.
DIR/CAM: Robert Nichol; PROD: Barrie Howells; ED: Susan Gibbard;
SOUND: Jacques Drouin; SONG: Joni Mitchell
Filmed near Orillia, Ontario, this film shows that farm life is changing and
that for some farmers the future looks bleak. The conclusion to this portrait
of an elderly, solitary holdout is that while a new trade and a new location
in town may be better for some, for those who make that move, there will
be much to miss. *See chapter 19.*

▪ *William Wells Talks about the Island,* 1967, 11 min.
Series: Newfoundland Project
DIR: Colin Low; PROD: John Kemeny; CAM: Robert Humble; ED: Dennis
Sawyer
William Wells defends the viability of Fogo Island and expresses his appre-
hension about the exodus of young people. *See chapters 2, 10, and 32.*

▪ *The Winds of Fogo,* 1969, 20 min.
DIR: Colin Low; PROD: Tom Daly; CAM: Robert Humble
Not officially part of CFC or the Newfoundland Project, this colour documentary, exceptional for its lyrical take on CFC's Ur-location Fogo Island,
should not be overlooked in the context of the program because of its obvious link to both place and project director Low. In this film, William Wells,
fisherman, and his two sons take a day off from the nets for a journey to the
gannet colony on the Funk Islands, fifty miles farther out to sea. There are
exceptional close-up views of enormous flocks of seabirds swarming on the
cliffs and in the sky. *See chapter 35.*

▪ *A Woman's Place,* 1967, 16 min.
Series: Newfoundland Project
DIR: Colin Low; PROD: John Kemeny; CAM: Robert Humble; ED: Dennis Sawyer
Two women discuss the roles and problems of women, education, and shopping on Fogo Island. *See chapters 2, 10, and 32.*

▪ *The World of One in Five,* 1969, 27 min.
DIR: James Carney; PROD: Gordon Burwash; NARR: Stanley Jackson; CAM: Eugene Boyko, Martin Duckworth, Richard Leiterman; ED: Jacques Bensimon; SOUND: Roger Hart, Michel Hazel, Hans Oomes
A fifth of Canadians live at the subsistence level. Filmed across Canada, this is a look at that world where the street is home, and where poor shelter, poor food, poor schools, and poor health are the only certainties of life. Children, old people, the sick and the drifters are caught in it. *See chapter 32.*

▪ *Would I Ever Like to Work,* 1974, 08 min.
Series: Working Mothers
DIR/PROD/ED: Kathleen Shannon; CAM: Robert Nichol; SOUND: Gui Bernardes
A kitchen-sink encounter with Joan, a welfare mother with seven children. Originally from the Maritimes, this Montrealer would like to work as a waitress and feels she'd be a better mother if she could. But daycare costs more than she can afford. *See chapters 7 and 29.*

▪ *You Are on Indian Land,* 1969, 36 min. / French version, *Vous êtes en terre indienne*
DIR: Mort Ransen, [Michael Mitchell]; PROD: George C. Stoney; CAM: Tony Ianzelo; ED: Kathleen Shannon; SOUND: Hans Oomes
One of CFC's most treasured films, a documentary account of the wintry 1968 protest demonstration by the Mohawk of the Akwesasne Reserve near the international bridge between Canada and the United States near Cornwall, Ontario. By blocking the bridge, which is on the reserve, protesters draw public attention to the violation of their treaty rights. The film shows the confrontation with police and the ensuing action. *See chapters 5 and 15.* Awards: Etrog: Special Award given to the Challenge for Change Unit, Canadian Film Awards (1970); Blue Ribbon Award, Itinerant, American Film and Video Festival, New York (1970)

▪ *A Young Social Worker Speaks Her Mind,* 1969, 24 min.
DIR/CAM: Terence Macartney-Filgate; ED: Kathleen Shannon; SOUND: Russ Heise

Joanna Stern's "talking head" diagnoses the welfare system in *A Young Social Worker Speaks Her Mind* (1969), spun off from *Up against the System*. Frame enlargement.

In this spinoff from *Up against the System,* Joanna Stern tells of her experience as a welfare worker, exposes her personal inside view of the welfare system and how it affects the people trapped in it, and raises the question of alternatives. An extended monologue. *See chapter 32.*

▪ *You're under Arrest!* 1979, 15 min.
DIR: Don Arioli; DIR/CAM/ED: Wolf Koenig; PROD: Adam Symansky; SOUND: Jean-Guy Normandin; MUS: Max Chamitov
Supported by animated drawings, Claude-Armand Sheppard, a Montreal lawyer, discusses citizens' rights in dealing with the police. He uses an authentic case where trumped-up charges were twice laid against a citizen. The citizen went to court, was acquitted, and then sued for damages. Failure to do so would eventually lead to the erosion of civil rights.

INDEX OF CHALLENGE FOR CHANGE/SOCIÉTÉ NOUVELLE SERIES

The Alinsky Approach: Organizing for Power series (Bonnie Sherr Klein)
Building an Organization
A Continuing Responsibility
Deciding to Organize
People and Power
Through Conflict to Negotiation

En tant que femmes series
À qui appartient ce gage?
Les filles c'est pareil
Les filles du Roy

J'me marie, J'me marie pas
Souris, tu m'inquiètes
Le temps de l'avant

Newfoundland Project (Fogo Island project) series (Colin Low)
Andrew Britt at Shoal Bay
Billy Crane Moves Away
Brian Earle on Merchants and Welfare
The Children of Fogo Island
Citizen Discussion
Dan Roberts on Fishing
Discussion on Welfare
Fishermen's Meeting
Fogo Island Improvement Committee
Fogo's Expatriates
The Founding of the Cooperatives
Introduction to Fogo Island
Jim Decker Builds a Longliner
Jim Decker's Party
Joe Kinsella on Education
McGraths at Home and Fishing
The Mercer Family
The Merchant and the Teacher
Some Problems of Fogo
The Songs of Chris Cobb
The Story of the Up Top
Thoughts on Fogo and Norway
Tom Best on Cooperatives
Two Cabinet Ministers
A Wedding and Party
William Wells Talks about the Island
A Woman's Place

NFB Presents series
Saul Alinsky Went to War

Occupational Health and Safety series (Boyce Richardson)
Anthony Mazzochi Talks about Chemicals and the Workers
Dr. Epstein Talks about Chemicals in the Workplace
Dr. Epstein Talks about Distortion of Information
Dr. Epstein Talks about the Chemical Explosion
Dr. Selikoff Talks about the Latency Period

Georges Dionne, un mineur de l'amiante
Homer Séguin Talks about Radiation at Elliot Lake
Robert Sass: Workers in Saskatchewan
Two Union Leaders Talk about Workers and Health

Swedish-Canadian Co-productions series
Overspill

Urba 2000 series (Michel Régnier)
Basingstoke – Runcorn – villes nouvelles britanniques
Bologne – une ville ancienne pour une société nouvelle
Centre-ville et piétons
Düsseldorf – équilibre urbain
Grenoble – la Villeneuve – réinventer la ville
Montréal – retour aux quartiers
New York – Twin Parks Project – TV *channel 13*
Sapporo – Croissance Planifiée
Saskatoon – la mesure
Varsovie – Québec – comment ne pas détruire une ville

Urbanose series (Michel Régnier)
L'attitude néerlandaise
L'automobile
Concordia I
Concordia II
Entretien avec Henri Lefebvre
Griffintown
Le labyrinthe
Locataires et propriétaires
Où va la ville? (1ʳᵉ partie)
Où va la ville? (2ᵉ partie)
Réhabilitation des habitations
Rénovation urbaine
Les rives
Le sol urbain
Les taudis

Urban Transportation series
A Bus – For Us
Regina Telebus
Where Do We Go from Here?

Working Mothers series
"... and They Lived Happily Ever After"
Extensions of the Family
It's Not Enough
Like the Trees
Luckily I Need Little Sleep
Mothers Are People
Our Dear Sisters
The Spring and Fall of Nina Polanski
They Appreciate You More
Tiger on a Tight Leash
Would I Ever Like to Work

Comprehensive Bibliography

∎

Acham, C. 2004. *Revolution televised: Prime time and the struggle for black power*. Minneapolis: University of Minnesota.

Agnew, Vanessa. 2004. Introduction: What is reenactment? *Criticism* 46:327–39.

Alinsky, Saul. 1971. *Rules for radicals: A practical primer for realistic radicals*. New York: Random House.

Anderson, Elizabeth. 1999. Studio D's imagined community. In *Gendering the nation: Canadian women's cinema*, ed. Kay Armatage, Kass Banning, Brenda Longfellow, and Janine Marchessault, 41–61. Toronto: University of Toronto Press.

Anderson, Kelly, and Annie Goldson. 1993. Alternative television inside and outside of the academy. *Social Text* 35:56–71.

Anonymous. 1968. Channelling change in Quebec: Fernand Dansereau's *Saint-Jérome*. *Challenge for Change/Société nouvelle Newsletter* 2:10.

– 1972. Chez nos voisins acadiens, "Un soleil pas comme ailleurs." *La Patrie*, 18 November.

– 1973. En tant que femmes ... as women: A Société nouvelle project by and for women. *Access: Challenge for Change/Société nouvelle Newsletter* 12:24–7.

Archambault, Jocelyne. 1973. Rapport d'évaluation: *Un soleil pas comme ailleurs*. Challenge for Change folder. Cinémathèque Québécoise (19 April 2009).

Armes, Roy. 1988. *On video*. London: Routledge.

Armitage, Andrew. 1975. *Social welfare in Canada: Ideals and realities*. Toronto: McClelland and Stewart.

Ashe, Robert. 2005. *Halifax champion: Black power in gloves*. Halifax: Formac Publishing Company.

Backhouse, Constance. 1999. *Colour-coded: A legal history of racism in Canada, 1900–1950*. Toronto: University of Toronto Press.

Bal, M., J. Crewe, and L. Spitzer, eds. 1999. *Acts of memory: Cultural recall in the present*. Dartmouth: University College Press of New England.

Bal, Meike. 2002. *Travelling concepts in the humanities: A rough guide*. Toronto: University of Toronto Press.

Ball, Ian. 1972. Screening of *I Don't Think It's Meant for Us* at the 20th Annual Conference on Housing in Windsor, Ontario. NFB Memorandum to Sandy Burnett, 20 October. NFB Archives, Montreal.

Ballantyne Tree, Tanya. 1966. The Bailey family: Eleven going on twelve. Film proposal, n.d. NFB Archives, Montreal.

– 1989. Formative evaluation of a documentary film on the effects of poverty on a Montreal family. MA thesis, Concordia University.

Barney, Darin. 2005. *Communication technology*. Vancouver: University of British Columbia Press.

Barnouw, Erik. 1974. *Documentary: A history of the non-fiction film*. New York: Oxford University Press.

– 1993. *Documentary: A history of the non-fiction film*. Rev. ed. New York: Oxford University Press.

Barthes, Roland. 1973. The world of wrestling. In *Mythologies*, 15–25. London: Paladin.

Bauman, Richard. 1975. Verbal art as performance. *American Anthropologist* 77:290–311.

Baxter, David. 1971. The utilization of video-tape in the community development process: An exploratory study. MA thesis, University of Calgary.

Beaty, Bart. 2006. The film industry in Canada. In *Mediascapes: New patterns in Canadian communication*, 2nd ed., ed. Paul Attallah and Leslie Regan Shade, 148–62. Toronto: Nelson.

Bégin, Jean-Yves. n.d. Léonard Forest: Un engagement social qui ne renonce pas à l'expression artistique. Service de l'information et de la publicité, Programme de Société Nouvelle. NFB Archives, Montreal.

– 1996. The Vidéographe challenge: Great, good, cheap ... electronic film. In *Video re/View: The (best) source book for critical writings on Canadian artists' video*, ed. Peggy Gale and Lisa Steele, 100–1. Toronto: Art Metropole/V-Tape.

Benson, Eugene, and L.W. Conolly. 1987. *English Canadian theatre*. Oxford, U.K.: Oxford University Press.

Bergman, Teresa. 2004. Personal narrative, dialogism, and the performance of "truth" in *Complaints of a Dutiful Daughter*. *Text and Performance Quarterly* 24:20–37.

Berko, Lili. 1989. Video in search of a discourse. *Quarterly Review of Film Studies* 10:289–307.

Bernard, Murray. 1967. For Negroes in Halifax, black power v. ping pong. *Maclean's*, 1 November.

Berrigan, Frances. 1977. *Access: Some western models of community media*. Paris: UNESCO.

– 1979. *Community communications: The role of community media in development*. Paris: UNESCO.

Berthiaume, Christiane. 1973. Luce Guilbault: Le métier d'acteur, c'est très féminin. *La Presse*, 29 September.

Bhabha, Homi K. 1994. *The location of culture*. London: Routledge.

Blain, Gilles. 1989. *Sonatine*: Un film à la recherche d'un public. In *Le cinéma québécois des années 80*, ed. Claude Chabot, Michel Larouche, Denise Pérusse, and Pierre Véronneau, 134–51. Montreal: Cinémathèque québécoise.

Blondin, Michel. 1971. Animation sociale. In *Citizen participation: Canada – a book of readings*, ed. James A Draper, 159–70. Toronto: New Press.

Blue, James. 1965. One man's truth: An interview with Richard Leacock. *Film Comment* 3.2 (Spring): 16–22.

Bolt, Barbara. 2004. *Art beyond representation: The performative power of the image*. London: I.B. Tauris.

Borris, Rose, with Paulette Jiles. 1989. At a loss for words. In *Best Canadian essays 1989*, ed. Douglas Fetherling, Saskatoon: Fifth House Publishers.

Bourdieu, Pierre. 1998a. *Acts of resistance against the tyranny of the market*. New York: New Press and Polity Press.

– 1998b. Utopia of endless exploitation: The essence of neoliberalism. Trans. J. Shapiro. *Le monde diplomatique*, December.

Boyle, Deirdre. 1992. From Portapack to camcorder: A brief history of guerrilla television. *Journal of Film and Video* 44:67–79.

– 1997. *Subject to change: Guerrilla television revisited*. New York: Oxford University Press.

– 1999. O, Canada! George Stoney's challenge. *Wide Angle* 21.2: 48–59.

Brodsky, Joyce. 2002. How to "see" with the whole body. *Visual Studies* 17:99–112.

Brown, Michael. 1999. *Race, money and the American welfare state*. Ithaca: Cornell University Press.

Brunette, Paul. 1973. Rapport d'évaluation sur la distribution intensive au Nouveau-Brunswick, Challenge for Change. *Cinémathèque Québécoise*, n.d.

Bruzzi, Stella. 2006. *New documentary: A critical introduction*, 2nd ed. New York: Routledge.

Bulbulian, Maurice. 1993. When I talk with people I talk as a Québécois. In *Brink of reality: New Canadian documentary film and video*, ed. Peter Steven, 97–111. Toronto: Between the Lines.

– 2006. Propos recueillis par Diane Cantin et Isabelle Lavoie. *Nouvelles vues sur le cinéma québécois* 5 (Spring). www.cinema-quebecois.net/numero5/pdf/entrevue_bulbulian.pdf.

Burnett, Ron. 1991. Video/Film: From communication to community. In *Video in the changing world*, ed. Nancy Thede and Alain Ambrosi, 54–60. Montreal: Black Rose Books.

– 1995a. *Cultures of vision: Images, media, and the imaginary*. Bloomington: Indiana University Press.

– 1995b. Video space/video time: the electronic image and portable video. In *Mirror machine: video and identity*, ed. Janine Marchessault, 142–83. Toronto: YYZ Books.

– 1996. Video: The politics of culture and community. In *Resolutions: Contemporary video practices*, ed. Michael Renov and Erika Suderburg, 283–301. Minneapolis: University of Minnesota Press.

– 2002. Video space/video time: The electronic image and portable video. http://www.eciad.ca/~rburnett/home.html (accessed 19 April 2009).

– 2009. Lowcast media: Lowcast communication and the public sphere. http://www.ecuad.ca/~rburnett/Weblog/lowcast_media/lowcast_media.html (accessed 3 August 2009).

Burris, Jon. 1996. Did the Portapak cause video art? Notes on the formation of a new medium. *Millenium Film Journal* 29:3–28.

Butler, Judith. 1993. Gender is burning: Questions of appropriation and subversion. In *Bodies that matter: On the discursive limits of sex*, 121–40. London: Routledge.

Canada. 1971. *Report of activities for the first year of the experimental programme Challenge for Change/Société nouvelle: 1970–1971*. April.

Canadian Film and Television Production Association. 2007. Profile 2007: An economic report on the Canadian film and television production industry. Ottawa: CFTPA.

Card, B.Y. 1968. *Trends and change in Canadian society: Their challenge to Canadian youth*. Toronto: Macmillan.

Cardinal, Harold. 1969. *The unjust society: The tragedy of Canada's Indians*. Edmonton: M.G. Hurtig.

Carrière, Louise. 1983. La série de films Société nouvelle dans un Québec en changement (1969–1979). MA thesis, Université du Québec à Montréal.

Castree, Noel. 2004. Differential geographies: Place, indigenous rights and local resources. *Political Geography* 23:133–67.

Chanan, Michael. 2007. *The politics of documentary*. London: British Film Institute.

Chappell, Rosalie. 2006. *Social welfare in Canadian society*. Mississauga: Thomson Nelson.

Charland, Maurice. 1986. Technological nationalism. *Canadian Journal of Political and Social Theory* 10.1–2: 196–220.

Chion, Michel. 1999. *The voice in cinema*. Trans. Claudia Gorbman. New York: Columbia University Press.

Cité Libre. 2007. Wikipedia. http://fr.wikipedia.org/wiki/Cit%C3%A9_Libre (accessed 19 April 2009).

Clandfield, David. 1984. From the picturesque to the familiar: Films of the French unit of the NFB (1958–1964). In *Take two: A tribute to film in Canada*, ed. Seth Feldman, 112–24. Toronto: Irwin.

– 1987. *Canadian film*. Toronto: Oxford University Press.

Clark, Bruce. 1990. *Native liberty, crown sovereignty: The existing aboriginal right of self-government*. Montreal and Kingston: McGill-Queen's University Press.

Clarke, George Eliott. 1992. Interview with Rocky Jones. In *Toward a new Maritimes,* ed. Ian McKay, 25–30. Charlottetown: Ragweed.

Cohan, Henry, and Steven Levy. 1974. VTR in cross-cultural communication. *Access: Challenge for Change/Société nouvelle Newsletter* 11:20–1.

Cohen, Andrew. 1977. An assessment of Challenge for Change/ Société nouvelle and departments and agencies of the government of Canada. A report submitted to Mr Stewart Goodings, Department of the Secretary of State, October. Ottawa.

Cook, Ramsay. 1991. "Au Diable avec le Goupillon et la Tuque": The quiet revolution and the new nationalism. In *An introduction to Canadian history,* 713–29. Toronto: Canadian Scholars Press.

Corneil, Marit Kathryn. 2003. Challenge for Change: An experiment in ethical documentary at the National Film Board of Canada. MA thesis, Trondheim, Norwegian University of Science and Technology.

– 2008. Fra Medieteknologiens kontrarevolusjonær fortid til dokumentarfilmens etiske fremtid: Et intervju med Professor Brian Winston. *Norsk medietidsskrift* 15.3: 237–47.

Couch, David. 2000. Places around us: Embodied lay geographies in leisure and tourism. *Leisure Studies* 19:63–76.

– 2003. Spacing, performing, and becoming: Tangles in the mundane. *Environment and Planning A* 35:1945–60.

Coulombe, Michel, and Marcel Jean. 2006. *Le dictionnaire du cinéma québecois.* Montreal: Boreal.

Crang, Mike. 1997. Picturing practices: Research through the tourist gaze. *Progress in Human Geography* 21:359–73.

Creed, Barbara. 1993. *The monstrous-feminine: Film, feminism, psychoanalysis.* London: Routledge.

Crocker, Stephen. 2003. The Fogo process: Participatory communication in a globalizing world. In *Participatory video: Images that transform and empower,* ed. Shirley A. White, 122–41. Thousand Oaks, Calif.: Sage Publications.

– 2008. Filmmaking and the politics of remoteness: The genesis of the Fogo process on Fogo Island, Newfoundland. *SHIMA: The International Journal of Research into Island Culture* 2:59–75.

Cron, Marie-Michèle. 1995. Circumvolutions: Videographic writings, nomadic speeches. In *Circonvolutions,* ed. Daniel Dion and Marie-Michèle Cron, 35–46. Montreal: Opera.

Cuddon, J.A. 1991. *The Penguin dictionary of literary terms and literary theory.* London: Penguin Books.

Czarnecki, Mark. 1985. The regional theatre system. In *Contemporary Canadian theatre: New world visions,* ed. Anton Wagner, 35–48. Toronto: Simon and Pierre.

Dansereau, Fernand. 1968. *Saint-Jérôme*: The experience of a filmmaker as social animator. *Challenge for Change/Société nouvelle Newsletter* 2:10.

Day, Richard J.F. 2005. *Gramsci is dead: Anarchist currents in the newest social movements*. Toronto: Between the Lines.

Dean, Mitchell, 1999. *Governmentality: Power and rule in modern society*. London: Sage.

Déléas, Josette. 1998. *Léonard Forest ou le regard pionnier*. Moncton: Centre d'études acadiennes.

Denault, Jocelyne. 1982. Écriture cinématographique féminine au Québec. MA thesis, Université de Montréal.

Denzin, Norman. 2003. *Performance ethnography*. Thousand Oaks, Calif.: Sage Publications.

Desrosiers, Pierre R. n.d. Son travail. Radio-Canada, Moncton. NFB Archives, Montreal.

Detchberry, Damien. 2006. Sonatine. In *The cinema of Canada*, ed. Jerry White, 121–7. London: Wallflower Press.

Deutchman, Ira. 2005. The 30th annual grosses gloss: Capt. Spaulding RIP. *Film Comment* 41.2 (March/April): 59.

Dexter, Susan. 1965. The black ghetto that fears integration. *Maclean's*, 24 July.

Dick, Ronald. 1986. Regionalization of a federal cultural institution: The experience of the National Film Board of Canada, 1965–1979. In *Flashback: People and institutions in Canadian film history*, ed. Gene Walz, 107–33. Montreal: Mediatexte.

Doane, Mary Ann. 1990. Information, crisis, catastrophe. In *The logics of television*, ed. Patricia Mellencamp, 251–63. Bloomington: Indiana University Press.

Douglas, Mary. 1966. *Purity and danger: An analysis of the concepts of pollution and taboo*. London: Routledge and Kegan Paul.

Druick, Zöe. 2007. *Projecting Canada: Government policy and documentary film at the National Film Board*. Montreal and Kingston: McGill-Queen's University Press.

D'Souza, Gladys, and Gabriel Gonsalves. 1977. *Education to reality*. Mumbai: Almati Printers.

Duchaine, Andrée. 1982. *Vidéo du Québec*. Montreal: Musée d'art contemporain.

Dyck, Noel, ed. 1985. *Indigenous peoples and the nation-state: "Fourth world" politics in Canada, Australia and Norway*. St John's, Nfld: Institute of Social and Economic Research.

Economic Council of Canada. 1968. *The challenge of growth and change*. Ottawa: Queen's Printer.

Engelman, Ralph. 1990. Origins of public access cable television 1966–72. *Journalism Monographs* 123:1–47.

– 1996. *Public radio and television in America: A political history*. Thousand Oaks, Calif.: Sage Publications.

En tant que femmes: L'ONF n'est plus une affaire d'hommes. 1973. *Le nouvelliste,*
  14 February.

Enzensberger, Hans Magnus. 1970. Constituents of a theory of the media. *New
  Left Review* 64:14–23.

Erin Research Group. 2005. *Breaking new ground: A framework for measuring the
  social impact of Canadian documentaries.* American University, Centre for Social
  Media. http://www.centerforsocialmedia.org/resources/articles/breaking_new
  _ground_a_framework_for_measuring_the_social_impact_of_canadian (accessed
  19 April 2009).

Evans, Gary. 1991. *In the national interest: A chronicle of the National Film Board
  of Canada from 1949–1989.* Toronto: University of Toronto Press.

Eyerman, Ron, and Andrew Jamison. 1998. *Music and social movements: Mobilizing traditions in the twentieth century.* New York: Cambridge University Press.

Faucher, Carol. *La noce est pas finie,* un film acadien politique. *Québec-Presse,* 21
  March.

Ferry, David. 2005. The development of professional theatre in St. John's 1967–
  1982: A personal perspective. *Theatre Research in Canada* 26:142–55.

Fillion, M. 1971. Un film c'est une question: Entrevue de Léonard Forest. Radio-
  Canada, Moncton. NFB Archives, Montreal.

Film Reference Library. n.d. Canadian Film Encyclopaedia: Challenge for
  Change/Société nouvelle (program), 1967–1980. http://www.filmreferencelibrary.
  ca/index.asp?layid=62andcsid1=2andnavid=46 (accessed 19 April 2009).

Finkel, Alvin, and Margaret Conrad. 2002. *History of the Canadian peoples: 1987
  to the present,* 3rd ed. Toronto: Pearson.

Finnegan, Cara. 2003. *Picturing poverty.* Washington: Smithsonian Books.

Fleming, W.G. 1971. *Ontario's educational society.* Vol. 2: *Schools, pupils and
  teachers.* Toronto: University of Toronto Press.

– 1972. *Education: Ontario's preoccupation.* Toronto: University of Toronto Press.

Forest, Léonard. 1969a. Fruits sauvage: Rapport de recherches (1ère étape) (May),
  1–6. NFB Archives, Montreal.

– 1969b. Fruits Sauvage: Un projet de Léonard Forest (June), 1–13. NFB Archives,
  Montreal.

– 1971–72. Fiction film as social animator. *Challenge for Change/Société nouvelle
  Newsletter* 7:18–22.

– 1972. Extrait d'une lettre ouverte à Monsieur Pierre Perrault, cinéaste (13 April).
  NFB Archives, Montreal.

– 1973. *Un soleil pas comme ailleurs:* commentaire de Léonard Forest sur la distribution intensive au Nouveau-Brunswick de son film (May), 1–4. NFB Archives,
  Montreal.

Forget, Robert. 1996. Program committee members' memo re: Vidéographe. In

*Video re/View: The (best) source book for critical writings on Canadian artists'
video*, ed. Peggy Gale and Lisa Steele, 99. Toronto: Art Metropole/V-Tape.

Fortier, D.H., B, Petry, and T. Ford. 1969. To know and to be known: The report
of the Task Force on Government Information. A report submitted to Pierre
Elliott Trudeau, prime minister of Canada, 29 August.

Foucault, Michel. 1978. *The history of sexuality: An introduction.* Vol. 1. Trans.
Robert Hurley. New York: Vintage Books.

– 1979 (1991). Governmentality. In *The Foucault effect: Studies in governmentality*, ed. Graham Burchell, Colin Gordon, and Peter Miller, 87–104. Chicago: University of Chicago Press.

– 1980. *Two lectures. Power/knowledge: Selected interviews and other writings.*
New York: Pantheon Books.

Fox, William S., and James D. Williams. 1974. Political orientation and music
preferences among college students. *Public Opinion Quarterly* 38.3: 352–71.

Fraser, Nancy. 1990. Rethinking the public sphere: A contribution to the critique
of actually existing democracy. *Social Text* 25.26: 56–80.

– 1992. Rethinking the public sphere: A contribution to the critique of actually
existing democracy. In *Habermas and the public sphere*, ed. Craig Calhoun, 109–
42. London: Cambridge University Press.

Fraser, Sylvia. 1966. Africville. *Star Weekly*, 1 January.

Frow, John. 1992. The concept of the popular. *New Formations* 18 (Winter): 30.

Fuchs, Richard P. 1987. "Half a loaf is better than none": The Newfoundland rural
development movement's adaptation to the crisis of seasonal employment. In *The
Canadian welfare state: Evolution and transition*, ed. Jacqueline S. Ismael, 192–
211. Edmonton: University of Alberta Press.

Gagné, Marie-Anik. 1994. *A nation within a nation: Dependency and the Cree.*
Montreal: Black Rose Books.

Gaines, Jane M. 1999. Political mimesis. In *Collecting visible evidence*, ed. Jane M.
Gaines and Michael Renov, 84–102. Minneapolis: University of Minnesota Press.

Galbraith, John Kenneth. 1958. *The affluent society.* Boston: Houghton Mifflin.

Gauthier, Guy. 1973. La femme dans le cinéma québécois. *Image et son* 267
(janvier): 12–17.

Ginsburg, F. 1999. The after-life of documentary: The impact of *You Are on Indian
Land. Wide Angle* 21.2: 60–7.

Gittings, Christopher E. 2002. *Canadian national cinema.* London: Routledge.

Glassman, Marc. 1999. Filmmaker of vision: Interview with Colin Low, part II.
Take One, December, 22–4, 29–33.

Goldberg, Kim. 1990. *The barefoot channel: Community television as a tool for
social change.* Vancouver: New Star Books.

Goldsmith, David A. 2003. *The documentary makers: Interviews with 15 of the
best in the business.* East Sussex: RotoVision.

Gray, Herman. 1995. *Watching race: Television and the struggle for "blackness."* Minneapolis: University of Minnesota Press.

– 2005. The politics of network television. In *Channeling blackness: Studies on television and race in America,* 155–74, ed. Darnell M. Hunt. New York: Oxford University Press.

Grierson, John. 1937 (1971). The Course of Realism. In *Grierson on documentary,* ed. Forsyth Hardy, 199–211. New York: Praeger Publishers.

– 1972 (1977). Memo to Michelle about decentralizing the means of production. In *The Canadian film reader,* ed. Seth Feldman and Joyce Nelson, 132–6. Montreal: Peter Martin Associates.

Gripton, James, and Allan Irving. 1996. Social work and social welfare research in Canada in the post-war years, 1945–1960. *Canadian Social Work Review* 13.2: 205–20.

Gross, Larry, John Stuart Katz, and Jay Ruby, eds. 1988. *Image ethics: The moral rights of subjects in photographs, film and television.* New York: Oxford University Press.

Guant, Marilyn. 2008. From eight man crew to one woman band: My life in television documentary. In *Rethinking documentary: New perspectives, new practices,* ed. Thomas Austin and Wilma de Jong, 157–61. Berkshire, U.K.: Open University Press.

Gwyn, Sandra. 1972. Film, videotape and social change: A report on the seminar organized by the Extension Service. 13–14 March. St John's, Nfld: MUN Extension Service.

Habermas, Jürgen. 1991. *The structural transformation of the public sphere: An inquiry into a category of bourgeois society.* Cambridge: MIT Press.

Haldrup, David, and Jonas Larsen. 2006a. Following flows: Geographies of tourism performances. Paper presented to the Mobilities, Technologies, and Travel Research Seminar, Roskilde University, 20 April.

– 2006b. Material cultures of tourism. *Leisure Studies* 25:275–89.

Hall, Doug, and Sally Jo Fifer, eds. 1990. *Illuminating video.* New York: Aperture Foundation.

Hansen, Miriam. 1991. *Babel and Babylon: Spectatorship in American silent film.* Cambridge, Mass.: Harvard University Press.

Harcourt, Peter. 1999. Two plus two: Contesting the boundaries of identity in two films by Micheline Lanctôt. In *Gendering the nation: Canadian women's cinema,* ed. Kay Armatage, Kass Banning, Brenda Longfellow, and Janine Marchessault, 244–52. University of Toronto Press.

Hardy, Forsyth, ed. 1979. *Grierson on documentary.* New York: Praeger Publishers.

Harrington, Michael. 1963. *The other America: Poverty in the United States.* New York: Macmillan Press.

Hartley, John. 1992. *The politics of pictures.* New York: Routledge.

Harvey, Alec, and Donald Wilson. 2008. The 33rd annual grosses gloss: Not-so-glittering prizes: What went right and what didn't at the U.S. box office in 2007. *Film Comment* 44.2 (March/April): 52–7.

Harvey, David. 1973. *Social justice and the city*. London: Arnold.

Hays, Matthew. 2002. On ethics and aesthetics: *The Things I Cannot Change*. *Take One* 11.38 (July/August): 32–3.

Hénaut, Dorothy Todd. 1968. Film as an instrument of social change. *artscanada*, September, 51.

– 1969a. Editorial. *Challenge for Change/Société nouvelle Newsletter* 1.2: 3.

– 1969b. Implicating people in the process of change: Canada's new kind of film-making. *Film Library Quarterly* 2.4: 44–7.

– 1970. A report from Canada: Television as town meeting. *Radical Software* 1.2: 17.

– 1971–72. Powerful catalyst. *Challenge for Change/Société nouvelle Newsletter* 7:3–7.

– 1972. Challenge for Change. *Radical Software* 1.5: 4–5.

– 1975. Asking the right questions: Video in the hands of citizens – the Challenge for Change experience. Paper presented at an international conference in Austria (10 November). NFB Archives, Montreal.

– 1991a. The Challenge for Change/Société nouvelle experience. In *Video the changing world*, ed. N. Thede and A. Ambrosi, 48–53. Montreal: Black Rose Books.

– 1991b. Video stories from the dawn of time. *Visual Anthropology Review* 7.2: 85–101.

Hénaut, Dorothy Todd, and Bonnie Klein. 1969. In the hands of citizens: A video report. *Challenge for Change/Société nouvelle Newsletter* 4:2–5.

Heritage Canada. 1996. L'Office national du film du Canada. http://www.pch.gc.ca/pgm/flm-vid/publctn/2006-01/104-fra.cfm (accessed 19 April 2009).

Hill, Annette. 2007. *Restyling factual TV: Audiences and news, documentary and reality genres*. Oxon, U.K.: Routledge.

– 2008. Documentary modes of engagement. In *Rethinking documentary: New perspectives, new practices*, ed. Thomas Austin and Wilma de Jong, 217–31. Berkshire, U.K.: Open University Press.

Hill, Chris. 2002. *Attention! production! audience! performing video in the first decade, 1968–1980*. Newark Valley, N.Y.: Video History Project.

Hillyard Little, Margaret. 2007. Militant mothers fight poverty: The Just Society Movement, 1968–1971. *Labour/Le travail*, March, 179–97.

Hopkins, J., C. Evans, S. Herman, and J. Kirk, eds. 1972. *Video in community development*. London: Ovum.

Hulchanski, David J. 2005. Rethinking Canada's housing affordability challenge.

Discussion paper prepared for the Government of Canada's Canadian Housing Framework Initiative, Centre for Urban and Community Studies, University of Toronto, Ontario.

Ismael, Shereen. 2006. *Child poverty and the Canadian welfare state: From entitlement to charity*. Edmonton: University of Alberta Press.

Jaeger-Rydall, Tom. 2006. *Jaeger Report 1*: http://www.youtube.com/watch?v=NsjF-lsSMs8 (accessed 19 April 2009).

Johnston, Claire. 1976. Women's cinema as counter-cinema. In *Movies and methods*, vol. 1, ed. Bill Nichols, 208–17. Berkeley: University of California Press.

Jones, David Barker. 1977. *The National Film Board of Canada: The development of its achievement*. PhD diss., Stanford University. Ann Arbor, Mich.: University Microfilms.

– 1981. *Movies and memoranda: An interpretative history of the National Film Board of Canada*. Ottawa: Canadian Film Institute.

– 1988. The Canadian Film Board Unit B. In *New challenges for documentary*, ed. Alan Rosenthal, 133–47. Berkeley: University of California Press.

Jones, Rocky. 1969. Letter to the editor: "Do you want to make a movie?" *Challenge for Change/Société nouvelle Newsletter* 4:10.

Kant, Immanuel. 1784 (1959). What is Enlightenment. In *Foundations of the metaphysics of morals*, 86–7. Indianapolis: Bobbs-Merrill.

Karch, Anton V. 1971–72. VTR in Drumheller, Alberta. *Challenge for Change/Société nouvelle Newsletter* 7:8–10.

Kellner, Douglas. 1992. Public access television and the struggle for democracy. In *Democratic communications in the information age*, ed. Janet Wasko and Vincent Mosco, 100–13. Toronto: Garamond Press.

Kemeny, John. 1968. Preliminary report on initial distribution of materials for Challenge for Change programme. NFB Archives, Montreal.

Kennedy, Timothy. 1984. *Beyond advocacy*. PhD diss., Cornell University.

Kent, Anthony. 1970. Memorandum: Challenge for Change distribution budget. NFB Archives, Montreal.

Kermoyan, Mireille. 1971. Avant-première du film de Léonard Forest: *La noce est pas finie*. Communiqué (5 March). NFB Archives, Montreal.

Khouri, Malek. 2007. *Filming politics: Communism and the portrayal of the working class at the National Film Board of Canada, 1939–46*. Calgary: University of Calgary Press.

Khouri, Malek, and Darrell Varga, eds. 2006. *Working on screening: Representations of the working class in Canadian cinema*. Toronto: University of Toronto Press.

Kidd, J. Roby. 1971. Adult education, the community, and the animateur. In *Citizen participation: Canada*, ed. James A Draper, 137–58. Toronto: New Press.

Kinik, Anthony. 2007. From chants populaires to chansons contemporaines: Pop, politics, and film, *Nouvelles "vues" sur le cinema quebecois* 7 (Spring/Summer): http://www.cinema-quebecois/net (accessed 31 July 2008).

Klein, Bonnie, and Dorothy Todd Hénaut. 1969. VTR in community organization: An interim report, VTR *St-Jacques* production file. NFB Archives, Montreal.

Kristeva, Julia. 1982. *Powers of horror: An essay on abjection*. New York: Columbia University Press.

Kroker, Arthur, and David Cook. 1991. Theory in ruins: Habermas's compromise. In *The postmodern scene: Excremental culture and hyper-aesthetics*, 235–61. Montreal: New World Perspectives.

Kurchak, Marie. 1972 (1977). What challenge? What change? In *The Canadian film reader*, ed. Seth Feldman and Joyce Nelson, 120–8. Montreal: Peter Martin Associates.

La France, Mireille. 1995. *Pierre Falardeau persiste et filme! Entretiens*. Montreal: l'Hexagone.

Lambert, Phyllis. 2004. Preface. In *In the 1960s: Montreal thinks big*, ed. André Lortie. Montreal: Canadian Centre for Architecture.

Lareau, Danielle. 1974. *Souris, tu m'inquiètes* synthèse du compte-rendu des commentaires et réactions recueillies par téléphone à la suite de la présentation du film à la télévision. NFB Archives, Montreal.

LaRochelle, Réal. 2006. Maurice Bulbulian. In *Le dictionnaire du cinéma québécois*, ed. Michel Coulombe, 100–1. Montreal: Boréal.

Larsen, Jonas. 2005. Families seen sightseeing: Performativity of tourist photography. *Space and Culture* 8:416–34.

Leach, Jim. 2006. *Film in Canada*. Toronto: Oxford University Press.

Leach, Jim, and Jeannette Sloniowski, eds. 2003. *Candid eyes: Essays on Canadian documentaries*. Toronto: University of Toronto Press.

Lee, Benjamin. 1993. Going public. *Public Culture* 5.2: 165–78.

Levin, G. Roy. 1971. *Documentary explorations: 15 interviews with filmmakers*. Garden City, N.Y.: Doubleday and Co.

Leys, Colin. 2001. *Market-driven politics: Neoliberal democracy and the public interest*. London: Verso.

Library and Archives Canada. n.d. Celebrating Women's Achievement. Florence Bird. Changing Women, Changing History: Canadian Women Activists. http://www.collectionscanada.gc.ca/women/002026-297-e.html (accessed 19 April 2009).

– n.d. Celebrating Women's Achievement. Kathleen Shannon. Canadian Women in Film. http://www.collectionscanada.gc.ca/women/002026-714-e.html (accessed 19 April 2009).

Lippard, Lucy. 1997. *The lure of the local: Sense of place in a multicentered society*. New York: New Press.

Litwin, Harold. 1977. Videotape and urban community development in Israel. *Community Development Journal* 12.2: 127–33.

Lopate, Phillip. 1974. Aesthetics of the Portapak. *Radical Software* 2.6: 18–21.

Lorimer, Hayden. 2005. Cultural geography: The busyness of being "more-than-representational." *Progress in Human Geography* 29:83–94.

Low, Colin. 1968–69. Some notes on the Farmersville project. *Challenge for Change/Société nouvelle Newsletter* 1.3: 9.

– 1973. Unpublished article for *Challenge for Change/Société nouvelle Newsletter*. NFB Archives, Montreal.

Lubka, Nancy. 1969. Ferment in Nova Scotia. *Queen's Quarterly* 76.2: 213–28.

Lyons, Nick. 1976. *The Sony vision.* New York: Crown.

MacBride Commission. 1980. *Many voices, one world (International Commission for the Study of Communication Problems).* London: Kogan Page.

McCay, Bruce. 1966. The Nova Scotia project (18 October). NFB Archives, Montreal.

MacDougall, David. 1994. Whose story is it? In *Visualizing theory: Selected essays from V.A.R., 1990–1994,* ed. Lucien Taylor, 27–36. New York: Routledge.

McFarland, M. Carter. 1962. The challenge of urban renewal. *Institute Technical Bulletin* 34. Washington: Urban Land.

MacKenzie, Scott. 1996. Société nouvelle: The Challenge for Change in the alternative public sphere. *Canadian Journal of Film Studies* 5.2: 67–84.

– 2004. *Screening Québec: Québécois moving images, national identity and the public sphere.* Manchester: Manchester University Press.

McNeil, Daniel. 2005. Afro (Americo)centricity in Black (American) Nova Scotia. *Canadian Review of American Studies* 35.1: 57–85.

Macpherson, C.B. 1965. *The real world of democracy.* Toronto: CBC.

McPherson, Hugo. 1968. Challenge for NFB. *Challenge for Change/Société nouvelle Newsletter* 1.1: 2.

Maheu, Pierre. 1972. *Le Bonhomme,* film transcript. NFB Archives, Montreal.

Mann, W.E., ed. 1970. *Poverty and social policy in Canada.* Vancouver: Copp Clark Publishing Co.

Marchessault, Janine. 1995a. Amateur video and the Challenge for Change. In *Mirror machine: Video and identity,* ed. Janine Marchessault, 13–25. Toronto: YYZ Press.

– 1995b. Reflections on the dispossessed: Video and the "Challenge for Change" experiment. *Screen* 36.2 (Summer): 131–46.

Marcorelles, Louis. 1970. *Éléments pour un nouveau cinema.* Paris: UNESCO.

Margulies, Ivone. 1996. *Nothing happens: Chantal Akerman's hyperrealist everyday.* Durham, N.C.: Duke University Press.

Marshall, Bill. 2001. *Quebec national cinema.* Montreal and Kingston: McGill-Queen's University Press.

Marshall, Stuart. 1985. Video: From art to independence. *Screen* 26.2: 66.

Martell, George. 1974. The schools, the state and the corporations. In *The politics of the Canadian public school,* ed. George Martell. Toronto: James Lewis & Samuel.

Massey, Doreen. 1999. *Power-geometries and the politics of space-time.* Heidelberg: University of Heidelberg.

– 2005. Negotiating nonhuman/human place. *Antipode* 37.2: 353–7.

Mellencamp, Patricia. 1990. TV time and catastrophe, or beyond the pleasure principle of television. In *Logics of television,* ed. Patricia Mellencamp, 240–66. Bloomington: Indiana Press.

Melnyk, George, ed. 2007. *Great Canadian film directors.* Edmonton: University of Alberta Press.

Memorial University. 1972. *Fogo process in communications: A reflection on the use of film and videotape in community development.*

Mercer, Kobena. 1994. Welcome to the jungle: New positions in black cultural studies. New York: Routledge.

Miller, Toby, and Robert Stam. 2004. *A companion to film theory.* Chicago: Blackwell Publishing.

Mintzberg, Henry, and Alexandra McHugh. 1985. Strategy formation in an adhocracy. *Administrative Science Quarterly* 30.2: 160–97.

Mitchell, W.J.T. 2005. There are no visual media. *Journal of Visual Culture* 4:257–66.

Monk, Katherine. 2001. *Weird sex & snowshoes and other Canadian film phenomena.* Vancouver: Raincoast Books.

Moore, Rick Clifton. 1987. Canada's Challenge for Change: Documentary film and video as an exercise of power through the production of cultural reality. PHD diss., University of Oregon.

Moreno, J.L. 1985. *The autobiography of J.L. Moreno* (abridged). Boston: Harvard University.

Morris, Leslie Tom. 1964. *Challenge of the sixties: 3-point program for Canada.* Toronto: Communist Party of Canada.

Morris, Peter. 1984. *The film companion: A comprehensive guide to more than 650 Canadian films and filmmakers.* Toronto: Irwin Publishing.

Mouffe, Chantal. 1993. The limits of liberalism. Paper presented at the Institute for Social Research, Essex University, March.

– 2000. *The democratic paradox.* London: Verso Books.

Mowlana, Hamid, and Laurie J. Wilson. 1990. *The passing of modernity: Communication and the transformation of society.* New York: Longman.

Mulvey, Laura. 1989. Visual pleasure and narrative cinema. In *Visual and other pleasures,* 14–26. Bloomington: Indiana University Press. Originally published in *Screen* 16.3 (1975).

MUN (Memorial University of Newfoundland) Extension Service. 1972. *Fogo process in communication: A reflection on the use of film as an inter-community communication.* St John's: Robinson Blackmore Printers.

Muñoz, José. 1995. The autoethnographic performance: Reading Richard Fung's queer hybridity. *Screen* 36: 83–99.

Murphy, Rae. 1967. *Canada's trade union movement: Change and challenge.* Toronto: Central Executive Committee of the Communist Party of Canada.

Nantel, Linda. 1974. *Souris, tu m'inquiètes. Secrets des artistes,* 9 February.

Nash, Catherine. 2000. Performativity in practice: Some recent work in cultural geography. *Progress in Human Geography* 24:653–64.

Negt, Oskar, and Alexander Kluge. 1993. Public sphere and experience: Toward an Analysis of the bourgeois and proletarian public sphere. Minneapolis: University of Minnesota Press.

Negt, Oskar, Alexander Kluge, and Peter Labanyi. 1988. The public sphere and experience, selections. *October* 46 (Autumn): 60–82.

Nelson, Jennifer. 2008. *Razing Africville: A geography of racism.* Toronto: University of Toronto Press.

Nelson, Joyce. 1988. *The colonized eye: Rethinking the Grierson legend.* Toronto: Between the Lines.

Nemtin, Bill. 1967. Proposal for a programme of film activities in the area of poverty and change (16 February). Fogo Island production file. NFB Archives, Montreal.

– 1968a. Report on Fogo Process (3 October). Fogo Island production file. NFB Archives, Montreal.

– 1968b. Fogo Island Films. Fogo Island production file. NFB Archives, Montreal.

New York Times. 1964. Nova Scotia hides a racial problem. *New York Times,* 14 June.

NFB (National Film Board). 1966. Distribution plans for proposed film on poverty (2 September). NFB Archives, Montreal.

– 1967a. Challenge for Change programme: A report prepared by the National Film Board of Canada. Challenge for Change CD-ROM. 18 April 2007.

– 1967b. Proposal for an action-programme of film activities in the area of poverty. Challenge for Change CD-ROM. 18 April 2007.

– 1967c. *The Things I Cannot Change,* discussion guide. NFB Archives, Montreal.

– 1967d. *The Things I Cannot Change,* distribution file. NFB Archives, Montreal.

– 1967e. *The Things I Cannot Change,* "one sheet." NFB Archives, Montreal.

– 1968a. Fogo Island Film and community development project: A report. NFB Archives, Montreal.

– 1968b. *Halifax Neighbourhood Center Project,* NFB notice of test print approval and completion of film (30 September). NFB Archives, Montreal.

– 1968c. Halifax Project, NFB request for funds (22 October). NFB Archives, Montreal.

– 1973. Films completed as of 31 July 1973. NFB Archives, Montreal.

– 1974a. Booking – inventory report: Fiscal year to end December 1973, distribution – Challenge for Change bookings. NFB Archives, Montreal.

– 1974b. Television broadcasts of Challenge for Change films, April 1974, distribution – Challenge for Change bookings. NFB Archives, Montreal.

– 1974c. *I Don't Think It's Meant for Us*, Cumulative information form, NFB Challenge for Change, 1970–71 (corrected 29 January). NFB Archives, Montreal.

– 1974d. *I Don't Think It's Meant for Us*, Cumulative information form (s.d.). NFB Archives.

– 1974e. Report on test screenings of *I Don't Think It's Meant for Us*, Appendix to cumulative information form (s.d.). NFB Archives, Montreal.

– 1974f. *Souris tu m'inquiètes:* Réflexion sur le contenu du film. NFB Archives, Montreal.

– 1975. A summary of recent distribution activity, distribution – Challenge for Change bookings. NFB Archives, Montreal.

– 1977. Distribution workshop – studio meeting: March 1977, distribution – Challenge for Change bookings. NFB Archives, Montreal.

– 1980. Report on the current status of the Challenge for Change/Société nouvelle programme, 31 March. NFB Archives, Montreal.

– n.d. Notes from a conversation with the filmmakers Boyce Richardson and Tony Ianzelo. NFB Archives, Montreal.

– n.d. Production file A80-67, *Wilf*. NFB Archives, Montreal.

– n.d. Single parent family, or film as a research instrument. NFB Archives, Montreal.

– NFB Portraits, *Maurice Bulbulian*. http://www3.onf.ca/portraits/maurice_bulbulian/fr/ (accessed 19 April 2009).

– NFB Portraits, *Bruno Carrière*. http://www3.onf.ca/portraits/bruno_carriere/fr/ (accessed 19 April 2009).

– NFB Portraits, *Fernand Dansereau*. http://www3.onf.ca/portraits/fernand_dansereau/fr/ (accessed 19 April 2009).

– NFB Portraits, *Yves Dion*. http://www3.onf.ca/portraits/yves_dion/fr/ (accessed 19 April 2009).

– NFB Portraits, *Martin Duckworth*. http://www3.nfb.ca/portraits/martin_duckworth/en/ (accessed 19 April 2009).

– NFB Portraits, *Léonard Forest*. http://www3.onf.ca/portraits/l%C3%A9onard_forest/fr/ (accessed 19 April 2009).

– NFB Portraits, *Pierre Lasry*. http://www3.nfb.ca/portraits/pierre_lasry/en/ (accessed 19 April 2009).

– NFB Portraits, *Colin Low*. http://www3.nfb.ca/portraits/colin_low/en/ (accessed 19 April 2009).

– NFB Portraits, *Marilu Mallet*. http://www3.nfb.ca/portraits/marile%E2%84%A2_mallet/en/ (accessed 19 April 2009).

– NFB Portraits, *André Melançon*. http://www3.onf.ca/portraits/andre_melancon/fr/ (accessed 19 April 2009).

– NFB Portraits, *Anne Claire Poirier*. http://www3.onf.ca/portraits/anne_claire_poirier/fr/ (accessed 19 April 2009).

– NFB Portraits, *Michel Régnier*. http://www.nfb.ca/portraits/michel_regnier/en/ (accessed 19 April 2009).

– NFB Portraits, *Kathleen Shannon*. http://www3.nfb.ca/portraits/kathleen_shannon/en/ (accessed 19 April 2009).

– NFB Portraits, *Adam Symansky*. http://www3.nfb.ca/portraits/adam_symansky/en/ (accessed 19 April 2009).

– NFB Portraits, *Mark Zannis*. http://www3.nfb.ca/portraits/mark_zannis/en/ (accessed 19 April 2009).

Nicholas, Garnham. 1993. The mass media, cultural identity, and the public sphere in the modern world. *Public Culture* 5.2: 264.

Nichols, Bill. 1981. *Ideology and the image*. Bloomington: Indiana University Press.

– 1988. The voice of documentary. In *New Challenges for Documentary*, ed. Alan Rosenthal, 48–63. Berkeley: University of California Press.

– 1991. *Representing reality*. Bloomington: Indiana University Press.

– 1993. "Getting to know you …": Knowledge, power and the body. In *Theorizing documentary*, ed. M. Renov, 174–91. London: Routledge.

– 1994. Performing documentary. In *Blurred boundaries: Questions of meaning in contemporary culture*, ed. B. Nichols, 92–106. Bloomington: Indiana University Press.

– 2001. *Introduction to documentary*. Bloomington: Indiana University Press.

– 2006. What to do about documentary distortion? Toward a code of ethics. *Documentary: Magazine of the International Documentary Association*, March-April, 28–34.

Nicks, Joan. 1999. Fragmenting the feminine: Aesthetic memory in Anne Claire Poirier's cinema. In *Gendering the nation: Canadian women's cinema*, ed. Kay Armatage, Kass Banning, Brenda Longfellow, and Janine Marchessault, 225–43. Toronto: University of Toronto Press.

Nouvelliste, Le. 1974. *En tant que femmes*, première d'une série de quatre films ce soir à la TV, 9 January.

Odie, Alan. 1974. Media as mediator: Community-building with films. *Media and Methods* 10.6 (February): 62–5.

O'Donnell, Leo. 1973. Modifications to VTR equipment to provide an improved method of editing half-inch videotape recording. *Radical Software* 2.5 (Winter): 60–1.

Oepen, Manfred. 1990. Communicating with the grass roots: A practice-oriented seminar series. *Group Media Journal* 9.3: 3–5.

O'Neill, Jack. 1969. Neighbourhood Center Project, NFB memorandum to George Stoney (14 July). NFB Archives, Montreal.

Ormond, John. 1967. Some observations in Nova Scotia (31 January). NFB Archives, Montreal.

Ouvrard, Hélène. 1974a. Communiqué: Luce Guilbault, Aimée Danis, Micheline Lanctôt (10 January). NFB Archives, Montreal.

– 1974b. Le mal sans nom des femmes d'aujourd'hui selon la cinéaste Aimée Danis. *Le nouvelliste*, 17 January.

Pachner, Joanna. 2008. Almost famous. *Globe and Mail*. Report on Business supplement, 29 August.

Pal, Leslie A. 1987. Tools for the job: Canada's evolution from public works to mandated employment. In *The Canadian welfare state: Evolution and transition,* ed. Jacqueline S. Ismael, 33–62. Edmonton: University of Alberta Press.

– 1993. *Interests of state: The politics of language, multiculturalism and feminism in Canada.* Montreal and Kingston: McGill-Queen's University Press.

Palmer, Daniel. 2004. Participatory media: Visual culture in real time. PhD diss., University of Melborne.

Paré, Claude. 1994. *Répertoire des archives de Vidéographe.* Montreal: Vidéographe.

Pearce, Pat. 1967. What it's like to be really poor. *Montreal Star,* 4 May.

Peet, Richard. 2002. Ideology, discourse and the geography of hegemony: From socialist to neoliberal development in post-apartheid South Africa. *Antipode* 34.1: 54–84

Penn, Frank. 1967. The two sides of affluence. *Ottawa Citizen,* 4 May.

Perreault, Luc. 1972. Les dix jours qui ébranlèrent l'Acadie. *La Presse,* 29 December.

Petit courrier, Le. 1974a. En tant que femmes. Pourquoi Comment. 17 January.

– 1974b. Histoire de femmes. 17 January.

– 1974c. Souris, tu m'inquiètes. 17 January.

– 1974d. Quatre films faits par les femmes, avec les femmes et pour les femmes. 17 January.

Petro, Patrice. 1999. Film feminism and nostalgia for the seventies. *Canadian Journal of Film Studies* 8.2: 3–20

Phelan, Peggy. 1993. *Unmarked: The politics of performance.* London: Routledge.

Plantinga, Carl. 1997. *Rhetoric and representation in nonfiction film.* Cambridge, U.K.: Cambridge University Press.

Porter, John. 1965. *The vertical mosaic: An analysis of social class and power in Canada.* Toronto: University of Toronto Press.

Poulantzas, Nicos. 1978. *State, power, socialism.* London: New Left Books.

Prinn, Elizabeth. 1971. Challenge for Change: Interview with Léonard Forest and Dorothy Hénault. *Challenge for Change/Société nouvelle Newsletter* 7:17–22.

– 1972a. Société Nouvelle goes back to Acadia: Interview of Léonard Forest and Olivier Fougères. *Access: Challenge for Change/Société nouvelle Newsletter* 10:13–17.

– 1972b. Vive le Vidéographe! *Access: Challenge for Change/Société nouvelle Newsletter* 8:18–22.

– 1974. How goes it, Vidéographe? *Access: Challenge for Change/Société nouvelle Newsletter* 11: 9.

Pryluck, Calvin. 1976 (2005). Ultimately we are all outsiders. In *New challenges for documentary,* 2nd ed., ed. Alan Rosenthal and John Corner, 194–208. Manchester: University of Manchester Press.

Quarry, Wendy. 2006. Excerpt from The Fogo process: An interview with Donald Snowden. In *Communication for social change anthology: Historical and con-*

temporary readings, ed. A. Dragon and T. Tufte, 488–91. South Orange, N.J.: CFSC Consortium.

Quotidien, Le. 1974. Un deuxième film mercredi soir à CKRS: *Souris, tu m'inquiètes.* 15 January.

Rabinowitz, Paula. 1993. Wreckage upon wreckage: History, documentary and the ruins of memory. *History and Theory* 32.2: 119–37.

Raboy, Marc. 1990. *Missed opportunities: The story of Canada's broadcasting policy.* Montreal and Kingston: McGill-Queen's University Press.

Régnier, Michel. 2000. *L'oeil et le coeur: Une passion de cinéma documentaire.* Montreal: Éditions Hurtubise HMH.

Rein, Martin. 1970. Social work in search of a radical profession. *Social Work* 15.2 (April): 13–28.

Relations. 1973. Entre le desengagement et l'utopie: *Le Bonhomme* un film de Pierre Maheu (juin): 186–7. http://www.cam.org/~lever/Articles/bonhomme.html (accessed 26 July 2008).

Rennie, Ellie. 2006. *Community media: A global introduction.* New York: Rowman and Littlefield.

Richardson, Boyce. 1993. The education of a white man. *Canadian Forum*, December, 18–20.

– 2004. *Memoirs of a media maverick.* Toronto: Between the Lines.

Rist, Peter Harry, ed. 2001. *Guide to the cinema(s) of Canada.* Westport, Conn.: Greenwood Press.

Roach, Joe. 1996. *Cities of the dead: Circum-Atlantic performance.* New York: Columbia University Press.

Roberts, John. 1999. Dogme '95. *New Left Review* 238 (November-December): 141–9.

Roberts, L.R. 1974. Distribution in Challenge for Change. Challenge for Change distribution folder. NFB Archives, Montreal.

Rodriguez, Clemencia. 2001. *Fissures in the mediascape: An international study of citizens' media.* Creskill, N.J.: Hampton Press.

Rosenthal, Alan. 1980. *The documentary conscience.* Berkeley: University of California Press.

Roth, Lorna. 1975. Eastern Arctic film distribution, Challenge for Change distribution folder. NFB Archives, Montreal.

Rothman, William. 1998. The filmmaker as hunter. In *Documenting the documentary: Close readings of documentary film and video*, ed. B. Grant and J. Sloniowski. Detroit: Wayne State University Press.

Rousselle, Delphis. 1971. *La noce est pas finie* ou la peinture d'une société du nord. *Le Progrès l'évangéline*, 15 March.

Roy, Sylvia, and Nancy Thede. 1992. An interview with Luiz Fernando Santoro. *Clips*, May, 3.

Ruby, Jay. 2000. *Picturing culture: Explorations of film and anthropology.* Chicago: University of Chicago Press.

Ryan, Paul. 1988. A genealogy of video. *Leonardo* 21.1: 39–44.

Saint-Jean, Armande. 1971. A letter sent to Monsieur André Lamy (16 April). NFB Archives, Montreal.

Santow, Mark. 2007. Running in place: Saul Alinsky, race, and community organizing. In *Transforming the city: Community organizing and the challenge of political change*, ed. Marion Orr, 28–55. Lawrence: University Press of Kansas.

Sarda, Denise. 1974. En tant que femmes. *L'écho de malartic*, 21 February.

Saunders, C. 1999. *Black and bluenose: The contemporary history of a black community.* Halifax: Pottersfield-Nimbus.

Saunders, Marion K. 1970. *The professional radical: Conversations with Saul Alinsky.* New York: Harper and Row.

Scheibler, Susan. 1993. Constantly performing the documentary: The seductive promise of *Lightning over Water*. In *Theorizing documentary*, ed. M. Renov, 135–50. London: Routledge.

Schugurensky, Daniel. 2005. Challenge for Change launched, a participatory media approach to citizenship education. OISE. http://fcis.oise.utoronto.ca/~daniel_sc/ assignment1/1966cfc.html (accessed 19 April 2009).

Sexton, Jamie. 2002. Grierson's machines: *Drifters*, the documentary film movement and the negotiation of modernity. *Canadian Journal of Film Studies* 11.2 (Spring): 40–59.

Shamberg, Michael. 1971. *Guerrilla television.* New York: Holt, Rinehart and Winston.

Shanks, Michael. 2004. Three rooms: Archaeology and performance. *Journal of Social Archaeology* 4:147–80.

Shannon, Kathleen. 1969. Screenings of Cornwall rushes, January 10–12. *You Are on Indian Land* folder. NFB Archives, Montreal.

Shannon, Kathleen, Elizabeth Prinn, Doris Mae Oulton, and Irene Angelico. 1975. Working with film: Experiences with a group of films about working mothers (special issue). *Access: Challenge for Change/Société nouvelle Newsletter* 14.

Sherman, Tom. 2002. *Before and after the I-bomb: An artist in the information environment.* Banff, Alta: Banff Centre Press.

– 2007. *The premature birth of video art.* Experimental Television Centre Video History Project. http://www.experimentaltvcenter.org/history/pdf/Sherman ThePrematureBirthofVideoArt_2561.pdf (accessed 19 April 2009).

Shields, Rob. 1967. *Toronto Daily Star*, 4 May, A26.

Sinclair, Lister. 1967. *Change comes to Canada: Challenge of the changing times, a personal glance.* Canadian Government Pavilion, Expo '67.

Smith, J.B. 1997. An international history of the Black Panther Party. PhD diss., State University of New York, Buffalo.

Snowden, Don. 1984. *Eyes see; ears hear*. St John's, Nfld: Memorial University of Newfoundland.

Sobchack, Vivian. 1999. Toward a phenomenology of nonfictional film experience. In *Collecting visible evidence*, ed. Jane M. Gaines and Michael Renov, 241–54. Minneapolis: University of Minnesota Press.

– 2004. *Carnal thoughts: Embodiment and moving image culture*. Berkeley: University of California Press.

Soleil, Le. 1974a. Films sur les femmes. 9 January.

– 1974b. Vision d'une grande justesse avec *Souris, tu m'inquiètes*. January 18.

Sony Corporation. Sony CV 2200A operating manual. Experimental Television Centre Video History Project. http://www.experimentaltvcenter.org/history/tools/tools_list.php3 (accessed 19 April 2009).

Sørenssen, Bjørn. 2001. *Å fange virkeligheten*. Oslo: Universitetsforlaget.

Sparks, Bob. 1972. Test Screening of *I Don't Think It's Meant for Us*. NFB Theatre, Halifax, 19 September 1972 – 2 PM. NFB memorandum to Sandy Burnett (21 September). NFB Archives, Montreal.

Sparks, Robert S. 1968. The impact of Kwacha House. *Challenge for Change/ Société nouvelle Newsletter* 1.2 (Fall): 5.

Spaulding, Jeffrey. 2004. The 29th annual grosses gloss: The tail wagging the dog. *Film Comment* 40.2 (March/April): 50–3, 78.

Sport, Kathy. 2003. Save our homes: Activist documentaries in 1970–1985. *Metro* 136:139–47.

Staecy, Vera. 1969. Memorandum: Attached letter from Mr Poirier. *You Are on Indian Land* production file. NFB Archives, Montreal.

Starblanket, Noel. 1968. A voice for Canadian Indians: An Indian Film Crew. *Challenge for Change/Société nouvelle Newsletter* 1.2: 11.

– 1969a. Memorandum: n.d. *You Are on Indian Land* production file. NFB Archives, Montreal.

– 1969b. Memorandum: 17 January 1969. *You Are on Indian Land* production file. NFB Archives, Montreal.

– 1969c. Screenings: 17th, 18th, 20th, 21st – Hogansburg (2) and Toronto (2). *You Are on Indian Land* production file. NFB Archives, Montreal.

Starblanket, Noel, and Mike Mitchell. 1969. Proposed shooting for international bridge Saturday, 9 February. *You Are on Indian Land* production file. NFB Archives, Montreal.

Steele, Lisa. 1987. Committed to memory. In *Work in progress: Building feminist culture*, ed. Rhea Tregebov, 39–64. Toronto: Women's Press.

Steven, Peter. 1993. *Brink of reality: New Canadian documentary film and video*. Toronto: Between the Lines.

Stevenson, Nick. 1997. Globalization, national cultures and cultural citizenship. *Sociological Quarterly* 38.1: 41–66.

Stewart, Michelle. 2007. The Indian Film Crews of Challenge for Change: Representation and the state. *Canadian Journal of Film Studies* 16.2: 49–81.

Stikeman, Ginny. 1969. Memorandum: Cornwall Court Cases. *You Are on Indian Land* production file. NFB Archives, Montreal.

Stikeman, Virginia. 1970. *Challenge for Change: Film as catalyst.* NFB Archives, Montreal.

Stoney, George. 1969. A non-rocking boat is a sunken ship. *Challenge for Change Newsletter* 3 (Winter 1968–69): 2–3.

– 1971–72. The mirror machine. *Sight and Sound* 41.1: 9–11.

Strain, Frank, and Derek Hum. 1987. Canadian federalism and the welfare state: Shifting responsibilities and sharing costs. In *The Canadian welfare state: Evolution and transition,* ed. Jacqueline S. Ismael, 349–71. Edmonton: University of Alberta Press.

Street, John. 2003. Fight the power: The politics of music and the music of politics. *Government and Opposition* 38.1: 113–30.

Stuart, Sara. 1989. Access to media: Placing video in the hands of the people. *Media Development* 36.4: 42–5.

Sturken, Marita. 1984. An interview with George Stoney. *Afterimage* 11:7–11.

Sujir, Leila. 1974. Report to Challenge for Change on the promotion of *I Don't Think It's Meant for Us,* January. NFB Archives, Montreal.

Sullivan, J.M. 2004. Nelson Squires 1928–2003: Newfoundland's first filmmaker. *Globe and Mail* (Obituaries), 12 February, R7.

Surman, Mark. 1994. From VTR to cyberspace: Jefferson, Gramsci and electronic commons. Paper presented at the Canadian Community Networks Conference. http://commons.ca/aa_upload/3e0b210495d0e773966747ff6179e499/vtrtocyberspace.pdf (accessed 19 April 2009).

Svenstedt, Carl Henrik. 1970. *Arbetarna lamner fabriken.* Stockholm: Pan/Norstedts.

Tasker, Rex. 1967a. Halifax Projects. NFB document, 16 May. NFB Archives, Montreal.

– 1967b. Poverty – Attitudes. NFB document, n.d. NFB Archives, Montreal.

– 1969. Letter to the editor, response to Rocky Jones. *Challenge for Change/Société nouvelle Newsletter* 4:10.

Taylor, James R., and Elizabeth Van Every Taylor. 1973. *Using video technology for social change: A framework for the generation, selection, operationalization, and evaluation of CC/SN video projects.* Montreal: Université de Montréal.

Thrift, Nigel. 2004. Performance and performativity: A geography of unknown lands. In *A companion to cultural geography,* ed. J. Duncan, N. Johnson, and R. Schein, 121–36. London: Blackwell.

– 2006. Space. *Theory, Culture and Society* 23:139–55.

– 2008. *Non-representational theory: Space politics affect.* London: Routledge.

Thrift, N., and J. Dewsbury. 2000. Dead geographies and how to make them live. *Environment and Planning D: Society and Space* 18:411–32.

Timmerman, Darquise. 1974. *En tant que femmes* ou recherche et expression de l'identité de la femme. *Le Droit*, 8 February.

Torfing, Jacob. 1999. *New theories of discourse: Laclau, Mouffe and Zizek*. Blackwell.

Torres, S. 2005. "In a crisis we must have a sense of drama": Civil rights and tele-visual information. In *Channeling blackness: Studies on television and race in America*, ed. Darnell M. Hunt, 243–66. New York: Oxford University Press.

Tregebov, Rhea, ed. 1987. *Work in progress: Building feminist culture*. Toronto: Women's Press.

Trinh, T. Minh-ha. 1990. Documentary is/not a name. *October* 52:76–98.

United Church of Canada. 1965. *The challenge of change to the rural church*. Toronto: Board of Evangelism and Social Service.

Usmiani, Renate. 1983. *Second stage: The alternative theatre movement in Canada*. Vancouver: University of British Columbia Press.

– 1985. The alternate theatre movement. In *Contemporary Canadian theatre: New world visions*, ed. Anton Wagner, 45–59. Toronto: Simon and Pierre.

Vanstone, Gail. 2007. *D is for daring: The women behind the films of Studio D*. Toronto: Sumach Press.

Véronneau, Pierre. 2002. La régionalisation de la production à l'Office national du film du Canada. *Revue d'histoire de l'Amérique française* 55.4: 507–37.

Verral, K. 2006. Representability: The radical practices of sixties conceptual art and civil rights movements in Halifax. PhD diss., Ontario Institute for Studies in Education, University of Toronto.

Vinebohm, Lisa. 1993. The power of voice. *Interadio* 5.2: 2.

Voix de l'est, La. 1974. Une lutte de libération réfléchie et vécue. 10 January.

Wagner, David. 1989. Radical movements in the social services: A theoretical framework. *Social Service Review* 63.2: 264–84.

Waldman, Diane, and Janet Walker. 1999. *Feminism and documentary*. Minneapolis: University of Minnesota Press.

Walter, Margaret. 2005. *Feminism: A very short introduction*. New York: Oxford University Press.

Walz, Gene. 1997. The NFB is a state of mind: An interview with Ches Yetman. *Film History* 9.2: 132–48.

Wasko, Janet. 2003. *How Hollywood works*. Thousand Oaks, Calif.: Sage Publications.

Watson, Patrick. 1970 (1977). Challenge for Change. In *Canadian film reader*, ed. S. Feldman and J. Nelson, 112–19. Toronto: Peter Martin Associates. Originally published in *artscanada*, April 1970, 14–20.

Waugh, Thomas. 1984. Why documentary filmmakers keep trying to change the world, or why people changing the world keep making documentaries. In *Show us life: Toward a history and aesthetics of committed documentary*, ed. Thomas Waugh, xi–xxvii. Metuchen, N.J.: Scarecrow Press.

– 1988. Lesbian and gay documentary: Minority self-imaging, oppositional film practice, and the question of image ethics. In *Image ethics: The moral rights of subjects in photographs, films and television,* ed. Larry Gross, John Katz, and Jay Ruby, 248–72. New York: Oxford University Press.

– 1989. Introduction: Vidéographe. In *Vidéographe: Sélections vidéo/video selections,* 5–6. Montreal: Vidéographe.

– 2002a. Petting to climax: Direct cinema, direct sex, 1956–1970. *Take One* 11.38 (July/August): 46–50.

– 2010. Sufficient virtue, necessary artistry: The shifting challenges of revolutionary documentary [history]." In *The right to play oneself: Historical essays on documentary film by Thomas Waugh,* ed. Thomas Waugh. Minneapolis: University of Minnesota Press.

White, Jerry. 2006. The Winds of Fogo. In *24 Frames: The cinema of Canada,* ed. Jerry White, 73–9. London: Wallflower Press.

–, ed. 2006. *The cinema of Canada.* London: Wallflower.

White, Jerry, and William Beard, eds. 2002. *North of everything: English Canadian cinema since 1980.* Edmonton: University of Alberta Press.

Whiteman, David. 2002. The impact of the uprising of '34: A coalition model of production and distribution. *Jump Cut* 45 (Fall): http://www.ejumpcut.org/archive/jc45.2002/whiteman/index.html (accessed 19 April 2009).

Wiesner, Peter K. 1992. Media for the people: The Canadian experiments with film and video in community development. *American Review of Canadian Studies,* Spring, 65–99.

Willener, A., G. Milliard, and A. Ganty. 1976. *Videology and utopia: Explorations in a new medium.* Trans. Diana Burfield. London: Routledge.

Williams, Raymond. 1977. Structures of feeling. *Marxism and literature.* New York: Oxford University Press.

Williams, Yohuru R. 1997. American exported Black nationalism: The student nonviolent coordinating committee, the Black Panther Party, and the worldwide freedom struggle, 1967–1972. *Negro History Bulletin* 60.3: 13–21.

Williamson, Tony. 1988a. *The Fogo process.* St John's, Nfld: Snowden Centre for Development Support Communications, Memorial University.

– 1988b. Origin of the Fogo process. Adapted from *Cinema as Catalyst,* a report by Sandra Gwyn, 1972. St John's, Nfld: Snowden Centre for Development Support Communications, Memorial University.

Wilson, Alexander. 1991. *The culture of nature: North American landscape from Disney to the Exxon Valdez.* Toronto: Between the Lines.

Winnipeg Free Press. 1967. Poverty study in NFB film, 29 April–6 May.

Winston, Brian. 1988. The tradition of the victim in Griersonian documentary. In *Image ethics: The moral rights of subjects in photographs, films and television,* ed. Larry Gross, John Katz, and Jay Ruby, 34–57. New York: Oxford University Press.

– 1995. *Claiming the real*. London: British Film Institute.

– 2000. *Lies, damn lies, and documentaries*. London: British Film Institute.

– 2007. The nadir of human achievement. Paper presented at Visible Evidence XIV, Bochum, Germany, 18–21 December.

Wintonick, Peter. 2005. Reality check: On the rebirth of documentary. Unpublished essay.

Wise, Wyndham, ed. 2001. *Take One's essential guide to Canadian film*. Toronto: University of Toronto Press.

Wright, Ronald. 2004. *A short history of progress*, Massey Broadcast lectures. Canadian Broadcasting Corporation CD series.

Young, Colin. 1969. Film and social change. *Journal of aesthetic education* 3.3: 21–7.

Young, Iris Marion. 1990. The ideal of community and the politics of difference. In *Feminism/Postmodernism*, ed. Linda J. Nicholson, 300–20. New York: Routledge.

Youngblood, Gene. 1970. *Expanded Cinema*. Boston: E.P. Dutton.

Zannis, Mark. 1974. Distribution report: *Cree Hunters of Mistassini* (September). NFB Archives, Montreal.

Zimmerman, William. 1967. *Canada welfare* 32 (May-June): 32–3.

Contributors

■

IRENE ANGELICO began her career in filmmaking with the Working Mothers film *"... and They Lived Happily Ever After"* (co-directed with Kathleen Shannon and Anne Henderson, 1975) and went on to become a participant in Studio D. Her three-part documentary *The Cola Conquest* (1999) won the Best Documentary Series by an Independent prize at the Hot Docs Festival (Toronto), and she was the winner of the 1999 Gemini Award for Best Writing in a Documentary or Series.

MICHAEL BRENDAN BAKER is a PhD candidate in the Department of Art History and Communication Studies at McGill University and part-time faculty member at Concordia University's Mel Hoppenheim School of Cinema. A past recipient of the Gerald Pratley Award for his research on Canadian film history, his recent publications include essays in the *Canadian Journal of Film Studies* and *24 Frames: The Cinema of Canada* (ed. Jerry White, Wallflower Press).

KASS BANNING, co-editor of *Gendering the Nation: Canadian Women's Cinema* (Toronto University Press, 1999), has authored many papers and publications on Canadian cinema, specializing in African-Canadian cinema and representations of racial diversity, and teaches cinema studies at the University of Toronto.

DEIRDRE BOYLE is associate professor in the Department of Media Studies and Film at the New School in New York City. She is the author of *Subject to Change: Guerrilla Television Revisited* (Oxford University Press, 1997) and *Video Classics: A Guide to Video Art and Documentary Tapes* (Oryx Press, 1986), among other books. She is currently writing about the films of Errol Morris. She has new essays forthcoming in *Documentary Testimonies: Global Archives of Suffering,* edited by Bhaskar Sarkar and Janet Walker (Routledge, 2009); *The Tin Drum Trilogy: Paul Chan* (Video Data Bank); and *50 Years of Bay Area Experimental Film and Video,* edited by Steve Seid (Pacific Film Archive).

RON BURNETT, president of the Emily Carr Institute of Art and Design since 1996, has published three books, including the recent *How Images Think* (MIT Press), and over 150 book chapters and journal articles. His second book, *Cultures of Vision*, was recently published in China. Burnett has been an educator and administrator for nearly forty years, a strong advocate for post-secondary education in Canada, a former professor and administrator at McGill University, and the founder and editor of one of Canada's first cultural studies and film journals.

GERDA CAMMAER is an assistant professor at the School of Image Arts of Ryerson University (Toronto). Both as scholar and as filmmaker she specializes in experimental and documentary film. Her PhD thesis includes a major film/video project that builds upon her passion for film history, documentary, and found footage. She is also a freelance programmer of Canadian experimental film and video. Her publications include *Collages and Bricolages: Artistic Audits and Creative Revisions of Mainstream Media in Recent Canadian Shorts* (Halifax: MSVU Art Gallery, 2005) and *Lipsett's Legacy: Recollecting Collage Films from the NFB and CFMDC* (Halifax: Afcoop, 2007).

STEPHEN MICHAEL CHARBONNEAU is an assistant professor in the School of Communication and Multimedia Studies at Florida Atlantic University, where he teaches courses in film history, theory, and aesthetics. His research interests include documentary film and video, youth culture, community media, and cultural policy. His work has been published in *Spectator*, *Mediascape*, and *Encyclopedia of Documentary Film*. Currently he is collaborating with filmmaker Marina Goldovskaya on a documentary film, oral history project and is researching the history of the Community Film Workshop Council in the United States.

KATERINA CIZEK's films have helped instigate criminal investigations, have changed United Nations policies, and have been screened as evidence at an International Criminal Tribunal. Since 2006, Cizik has been the National Film Board of Canada's Filmmaker-in-Residence at St Michael's Hospital, Toronto, partnering media with medicine in order to fuel social and political action. She co-directed the prizewinning documentary *Seeing Is Believing* (with Peter Wintonick), about new technologies and human rights; the film showed on television in over fifteen countries, and played at more than seventy international film festivals. Earlier, she wrote, edited, and narrated the prizewinning *Dead Are Alive: Eyewitness in Rwanda* (1996), which was translated into twelve languages.

MARIT KATHRYN CORNEIL is a research fellow teaching at the University of Trondheim and North Trondelag University College. She is currently finishing her doctoral dissertation on the Digital Eye Project 2004–2008 (Norwegian Research Council), led by Professor Bjørn Sørenssen. In 2003 she published her master's thesis, *Challenge for Change: An Experiment in Ethical Documentary at the National Film Board of Canada*. In 2007/08 she was "researcher in residence" at the Concordia Documentary Centre in Montreal. Her recent publications include a chapter on *cinéma direct* in *Beyond the Visual* (Intervention Press, 2009) and an interview with Brian Winston in *Norsk Medietidskrift* 15.3 (2008).

LIZ CZACH is an assistant professor in the Department of English and Film Studies at the University of Alberta. She has worked as a film programmer with the Toronto International Film Festival (1995–2005), the experimental film exhibition group Pleasure Dome (1990–95), and the Toronto Lesbian and Gay Film and Video Festival (1991–93). She has published work on film festivals and home movies. She is the organizer of Edmonton's Home Movie Day.

FERNAND DANSEREAU, one of Quebec's most distinguished filmmakers since 1956, headed with Robert Forget the Groupe de recherches sociales, the forerunner of Société nouvelle. He received the Prix Albert-Tessier in 2005, and his many films include *Saint-Jérôme* (1968) and *La brunante* (2007).

JEANNE DESLANDES, a freelance writer and researcher based in the Cantons de l'est, has taught at the National Taiwan University of the Arts. Her research has focused mainly on sound technology, music in cinema, and current Canadian film policy, as well as Taiwanese cinema.

DAN DRISCOLL worked in the distribution offices of NFB Toronto, Montreal, and Charlottetown from 1968 to 1984, during which time he wrote the editorial included in this collection. He currently resides in Goa, India, and is actively involved in the Xavier Centre for Historical Research.

ZOË DRUICK is an associate professor in the School of Communication at Simon Fraser University. Her books include *Projecting Canada: Documentary Film and Government Policy at the National Film Board* (2007), *Programming Reality: Perspectives on English-Canadian Television* (with Aspa Kotsopoulos, 2008), and a study of Allan King's film *A Married Couple* (1969) for University of Toronto Press (forthcoming). In addition, she has published articles in journals such as *Screen, Television and New Media,*

Canadian Journal of Communication, Canadian Journal of Film Studies, and *Studies in Documentary,* as well as in various anthologies. She is currently vice-president of the Film Studies Association of Canada and sits on the organizing committee of Cinephemera, Symposium of Canadian Orphan Cinema.

LÉONARD FOREST, Acadian director, editor, producer, scriptwriter, and poet, began his career at the National Film Board in 1953 and retired in 1983. His many films include *Mémoire en fête* (1964) and *Les Acadiens de la dispersion* (1967), as well as his films for Société nouvelle, *La noce est pas finie* (1971) and *Un soleil pas comme ailleurs* (1972). He received an honorary doctorate from the Université de Moncton in 1992.

MARIE-ÈVE FORTIN, a doctoral candidate at the Université de Montréal, completed her bachelor's and master's degrees in film studies at Concordia University. She has worked for the Concordia Documentary Centre under the supervision of Thomas Waugh, is collaborator in the documentary film project entitled *Possible Movements* (Marielle Nitoslawska), participated in the Locarno Summer Film School in Switzerland, and completed a film internship at the Walker Art Center, Minneapolis. Her publications include interviews with filmmakers such as Abderrahmane Sissako and Anja Salomonowitz. Her research interests are documentary film ethics, film aesthetics, autobiographical and interdisciplinary cinema, spirituality, and African film.

RINA FRATICELLI, founder and executive producer of Wild Zone Films, has written, directed, and produced documentaries for over twenty years, both in the independent sector and as executive producer of the NFB's Studio D from 1987 to 1990. Most recently, she was executive producer at the Pacific & Yukon Studio in Vancouver, from 2002 to 2006. Her writing credits include the internationally acclaimed six-hour documentary series *Women: A True Story,* as well as a number of shorts for BravoFact. She brings to her film work extensive experience in the arts, particularly in theatre dramaturgy and as editor of the feminist literary journal *Fireweed.* She was the author of an influential study on the status of women in Canadian theatre for the Applebaum-Hebert Commission.

JASON GARRISON is a culture hobo.

JOHN GRIERSON, 1898–1972, the Scots pioneer of the British documentary movement, founded the National Film Board of Canada in 1939, where he was government film commissioner until 1945.

DOROTHY TODD HÉNAUT, director, producer, scriptwriter, was a pioneer in the video wing of Challenge for Change beginning in 1968 and the program's most visible international advocate. In 1977 she joined Studio D, where her most famous production was *Not a Love Story: A Film about Pornography* (Bonnie Sherr Klein, 1981). *Firewords* (1986) is among the films she directed. She left the Board in 1996 and remains a documentary activist on the Quebec film scene.

NAOMI KLEIN, Vancouver-based documentarist and author, was the writer for the 2004 documentary *The Take* (Avi Lewis, 2004) and authored the influential anti-globalization bible *No Logo* (2000) and the best-selling *The Shock Doctrine: The Rise of Disaster Capitalism* (2007), slated to be translated into seventeen languages to date. The six-minute companion film to *The Shock Doctrine*, created by Alfonso Cuaron, was an Official Selection of the 2007 Venice and Toronto International Film Festivals and a viral phenomenon as well, downloaded over one million times. A collection of her work, *Fences and Windows: Dispatches from the Front Lines of the Globalization Debate*, was published in 2002. Klein's regular column for the *Nation* and the *Guardian* is syndicated internationally. In 2004 her reporting from Iraq for *Harper's Magazine* won the James Aronson Award for Social Justice Journalism.

BONNIE SHERR KLEIN is a filmmaker, author, and disability rights activist. Her work at the NFB began in 1967 and she was a key figure in the Challenge for Change program (the five-part Organizing for Power series; VTR St-Jacques, 1969). In 1975 she joined Studio D and left her mark with *Not a Love Story: A Film about Pornography* (1981). After suffering a stroke in 1987, Klein became an advocate for disability rights and shifted the focus of her work to the issues and obstacles she confronts in her own life. *Finding My Place: A Journey into the World of Disability* (CBC Radio, 1992) won the Gold Medal at the 1993 International Radio Festival of New York, while the NFB production *SHAMELESS: The ART of Disability* (2006) returned her to her roots of assisting others in making their own images. She was honoured with the Governor General's Award in Commemoration of the Persons Case (2004) for her outstanding contributions to the quality of life for women in Canada.

JASON LINDOP is currently working towards a master's degree in film studies at Concordia University. His thesis explores the relations between narrative and rhetoric, the latter term signalling both a specific genre and a function within fiction. Among his case studies are the occasionally otherworldly NFB docudramas of the late 1950s. His other writings on cinema have appeared at Offscreen.com, and most recently he has been writing short stories, illustrating them with woodcut prints and binding the results into smallish books.

MICHAEL ANDREW LITHGOW is a PhD student at Carleton University, School of Communications (Ottawa). His dissertation research focuses on cultural citizenship and dialogical frameworks for cultural production. He has worked as a community media advocate and journalist in radio, print, and television. He is currently a research associate with the Campaign for Democratic Media and a contributing editor at *Art Threat Magazine*.

BRENDA LONGFELLOW is an award-winning filmmaker whose work has been screened at festivals around the world. Her most recent film, *Weather Report,* was broadcast on *The Nature of Things,* CBC. *Tina in Mexico,* a portrait of photographer Tina Modotti (2002), won the Golden Rose at the Montreux Film and Television Festival and Best Cultural Documentary at the Havana Film Festival, among other prizes. Awarded the Canadian Genie for Best Documentary Short in 1998 for *Shadow Maker,* a portrait of poet Gwendolyn MacEwen, Longfellow has also written extensively on Canadian and feminist cinema. She teaches in the Department of Film and Video at York University, where she is currently the chair.

COLIN LOW joined the National Film Board of Canada in 1945 through a summer training program set up by Norman McLaren in an effort to create a Canadian animation facility. Throughout his career as a leading documentarist at the Board, Low brought innovations to many genres of documentary – from hand-held direct cinema (*Corral,* 1954), to still-photo compilation (*City of Gold,* 1957), to visual ethnography (*Circle of the Sun,* 1960), to large- and multiple-screen new formats (*In the Labyrinth,* 1979). Low was a founding producer of Challenge for Change and developed the Newfoundland Project, renowned around the globe for the "Fogo process." Recipient of the Prix Albert-Tessier in 1997, Low retired from the Board after making his autobiographical film, *Moving Pictures* (2000).

SCOTT MACKENZIE is cross-appointed to the Cinema Studies Institute and the Department of French at the University of Toronto. He is co-editor of *Cinema and Nation* (Routledge, 2000) and *Purity and Provocation: Dogma '95* (British Film Institute, 2003) and author of *Screening Québec: Québécois Moving Images, National Identity and the Public Sphere* (Manchester University Press, 2004). He has published in numerous journals, including *Cineaction, Public, Canadian Journal of Film Studies,* and *Screen.* He is currently completing *Films into Uniform: Film Manifestos and Cinema Culture* and a short monograph on the films of Guy Debord.

JANINE MARCHESSAULT holds a Canada Research Chair in Art, Digital Media, and Globalization at York University. She is the author of *Marshall McLuhan: Cosmic Media* (Sage, 2005) and is the (co)editor of several collections, including *Fluid Screens, Expanded Cinema* (University of Toronto Press, 2007); *Wild Science: Reading Feminism, Medicine and the Media* (Routledge, 2000); *Gendering the Nation: Canadian Women's Cinema* (University of Toronto Press, 1999); and *Mirror Machine: Video and Identity* (YYZ Books + CRCCI, 1994). She is a founding member of the Public Access Curatorial Collective and the journal *Public: Art/Culture/Ideas*.

CHRISTOPHER MEIR is lecturer in film at the University of the West Indies, St Augustine, in Trinidad and Tobago. He completed a PhD project at the University of Warwick on film policy and Scottish cinema. He has published research on Scottish cinema, documentary filmmaking, and Canadian cinema. He is currently preparing a manuscript based on his doctoral thesis and working on a comparative study of the film industries of the nations of the Commonwealth.

LIZ MILLER is a documentary filmmaker, community media artist, and professor in communication studies at Concordia University. For the last fifteen years, she has developed community media projects and documentaries, including *Novela, Novela* and *The Water Front*. Miller has exhibited her work around the world and won numerous awards. Having lived in Central America for half a decade, Liz is committed to cross-cultural collaborations and conducts media workshops for international organizations like Witness. She is a board member of the International Association of Women in Radio and Television and is committed to using video for social change.

VIJAYA MULAY has taught at Patna University and has held important portfolios in ministries of education and information and broadcasting in India. Concern for social justice led her to use media in innovative ways in the education and development of marginalized populations. She has received several national and international film awards and has twice been honoured with national lifetime achievement awards for her work in documentaries and educational communications. Her research on the portrayal of India in films made by non-Indians from four continents over the entire twentieth century is due to be published by Seagull Books of Kolkata, India.

DORIS MAE OULTON was involved in the first phase of distributing the Working Mothers films and went on to a career in social justice and advocacy work. She was head of Manitoba's Women's Directorate, held the position of chief executive officer for the Children and Youth Secretariat, and worked on the first national statement on violence against women issued by the ministers for the status of women in 1990.

KALLI PAAKSPUU's dissertation at the University of Toronto examines cross-cultural storytelling in early photography as mediations in international relations. Her recent publications include chapters in *Media Literacy: A Reader* (2007) and *Canadian Cinema and the Film Director* (2007) and journal articles in *Textual Studies of Canada* (2008) and *Bulletin of Science, Technology and Society* (2007). A Genie-winning filmmaker, Paakspuu created "World without Water," an interactive new media experience, with Suzette Araujo and Tahir Mahmood during a 2007 residency at the Canadian Film Centre. The work premiered at the Lennox Gallery during the Nuit Blanche Festival and is planned for an exhibition in Mexico at UNAM (Universidad Nacional Autónoma de México) in 2009. Paakspuu was the chair of the jury at the Estdocs Film Festival in 2008, and she teaches culture and expression at York University and politics and public administration at Ryerson University.

ELIZABETH PRINN was the editor of the *Access/Médium-Média* newsletter from 1972 to 1974. Her background in media and workshop design paved the way for her work as a social animator in the screenings of the Working Mothers films.

BRIAN RUSTED is an associate professor in the University of Calgary's Faculty of Communication and Culture. He teaches courses in visual culture, folklore, documentary, and performance studies. He is the past chair of the Visual Communication Division of the National Communication Association and is on the editorial boards of *Visual Studies* and *Visual Communication Quarterly*. He has been a board member of Calgary's artist-run video production centre, EM/Media, and had media works exhibited at the Museum of Modern Art, the National Gallery of Canada, the Southern Alberta Art Gallery, and the Banff Centre's Walter Phillips Gallery.

KATHLEEN SHANNON, 1935–1998, joined the NFB in 1956 and worked as an editor, sound editor, director, and producer. In 1973 Shannon launched the Working Mothers series – a collection of eleven films co-directed and produced by Shannon – under the Challenge for Change banner. In 1974 she established Studio D, the first permanent, state-funded women's film unit in the world. She won the 1979 Academy Award for Best Documentary Short for *I'll Find a Way* (1978), the portrait of a young schoolgirl overcoming the challenges of spina bifida. Before she retired in 1992, Shannon was appointed to the Order of Canada.

NOEL STARBLANKET was a member of the National Film Board's original Indian Film Crew within Challenge for Change. In 1971, at the age of twenty-four, he was elected chief of the Starblanket Cree Nation in Saskatchewan. He served as chief of the National Indian Brotherhood from 1976 to 1980. From 1971 to 2004 he was actively involved in treaty land entitlement research, negotiations, and development. *Starblanket: A Spirit Journey* (2006), an autobiographical video work, won the Best Documentary Short Award at the 31st American Indian Film Festival.

MICHELLE STEWART is coordinator and associate professor of cinema studies at SUNY-Purchase. With Pam Wilson (Reinhardt College), she recently co-edited *Global Indigenous Media: Cultures, Poetics, and Politics* (Duke University Press, 2008). The collection brings together the work of well-respected scholars and producers of indigenous media from around the world, addressing shifting national and international policy and law, as well as reviewing international scholarship on indigenous media and the question of sovereignty. Her current research concerns film policy, the European state, and minor cinema, with an emphasis on the cinematic production of North and West Africans in France.

GEORGE STONEY, born in 1916, is a pioneer in the field of documentary film and public access television and is still teaching film at New York University. Known for the groundbreaking portrait of an African-American midwifery program, *All My Babies* (1953), Stoney was brought to the NFB as executive producer for a two-year term in 1968, where he consolidated its methods and activities. Stoney went on to co-found the Alternate Media Center in 1972, applying CFC/SN methods to the development of public access television in the United States.

THOMAS WAUGH, programmer, lecturer, and critic, has since 1976 taught film studies at Concordia University, Montreal, where he has also developed curriculum on queer studies and HIV/AIDS. His books are *"Show Us Life": Towards a History and Aesthetics of the Committed Documentary* (ed., 1984); *Hard to Imagine: Gay Male Eroticism in Photography and Film from Their Beginnings to Stonewall* (1996); *The Fruit Machine: Twenty Years of Writings on Queer Cinema* (2000); *Out/Lines: Gay Underground Graphics from before Stonewall* (2000); *Lust Unearthed: Vintage Gay Graphics from the Dubek Collection* (2004); *The Romance of Transgression in Canada: Queering Sexualities, Nations, Cinemas* (2006); *Gay Art: A Historic Collection* (with Felix Lance Falkon, 2006); *Comin' at Ya! The Homoerotic 3-D Photographs of Denny Denfield* (with David Chapman, 2007); *The Right to Play Oneself: Essays on Documentary by Thomas Waugh 1976–2001*

(2009); and the forthcoming *Joris Ivens: Essays on the Career of a Radical Documentarist.*

JERRY WHITE is an associate professor of film studies at the University of Alberta and a member of the education staff of the Telluride Film Festival. He is the author of *The Radio Eye: Cinema in the North Atlantic, 1958–1988* and *Of This Place and Elsewhere: The Films and Photographs of Peter Mettler;* co-editor of *North of Everything: English-Canadian Cinema Since 1980;* and editor of *The Cinema of Canada.* He publishes in academic journals, writes for film magazines such as *Cinema Scope* (Toronto), *Vertigo* (London), and DOX (Copenhagen), and has contributed reports and reviews to the *Edmonton Journal* and Radio-Canada.

PETER K. WIESNER wrote his chapter in this book in 1992, when he was working in the Educational Activities Department of the Institute of Electrical and Electronic Engineers.

EZRA WINTON is interested in the unprovable but entirely plausible power of cinema to move mountains (of people into action). He is currently pursuing a PhD in communication studies at Carleton University, where he is focused on fallacies of the scholarly framing of audiences, political documentary cinema, pedagogy, and representations of terrorism. He has made documentaries, starred in them, programmed, judged, and theorized them, and hopes one day to teach them. Winton created Cinema Politica in 2001, a pan-Canadian network of political documentary screening sites that has over forty locals in Canada and more in Europe, Latin America, Asia, and the United States. His recent publications include articles in POV *Magazine* and a chapter in the second edition of *Mediascapes,* an undergraduate textbook for communications student.

Index